Sport Management: The Business of Sport

Third Edition

Dr. William F. Stier, Jr.

Distinguish Service Professor
Director of Sport Management & Athletic Administration
State University of New York at Brockport—College at Brockport
Brockport, New York

american press
60 State Street #700
Boston, MA 02109
www.americanpresspublishers.com

[cover photo courtesy Robert Morris]

The first edition of this book was previously published by Pearson Education, Inc., under the title of *Managing Sport, Fitness, and Recreation Programs: Concepts and Practices.*

Copyright © 2008, 2014 by American Press
ISBN 978-0-89641-528-7

Printed in the United States of America.

DEDICATION

Sport Management—The Business of Sport is dedicated to my wife, Veronica—for her loving encouragement and unselfish support—without which this book would not have been written and revised three times. I also wish to dedicate this book to our five children, Mark, Missy, Michael, Patrick and Will III; and, our ten grandchildren, Samantha, Joshua, Katie, Mike, Jessica, Jackson, Dalton, Daphne, Alicia and Dahlia.

A special dedication to Colonel Mark T. Martin, one of the founding editors of the United States Army's *Stars and Stripes* during the second world war and a highly decorated army officer, successful businessman and entrepreneur, who was responsible for establishing, upgrading and managing many businesses, programs, and organizations during his 45-year career in the armed services and in the world of business.

ACKNOWLEDGEMENTS

I wish to acknowledge and thank the numerous sport, recreation, and fitness administrators and staff members, vendors and spectators with whom it has been my pleasure to work during the past 30 years. I have gained a great deal through my 48 years of experience within a wide range of sport, fitness, and recreation organizations and I owe much to my coworkers, associates, spectators, and clients. I wish to thank and acknowledge the numerous institutions, organizations and individuals who provided me with numerous photographs, figures and diagrams that are included within this book. Without their unselfish and meaningful assistance this book would not have been written.

In addition, I need to acknowledge the significant contributions of my graduate and undergraduate students at the State University of New York, College at Brockport, with whom I field-tested portions of both the first two editions and this, the third edition. I have indeed been blessed with exceptional students in pursuit of their own careers within the world of sport, fitness and recreation management. From my association with these outstanding individuals, I have learned much as a result of their inquiring minds, challenging questions and insightful suggestions.

Finally, I wish to express a sincere appreciation to Ms. Rebecca Fox, who served as the supervising editor for this book on behalf of the publisher, American Press, and who provided meaningful suggestions and input in terms of the final version of this third edition.

CONTENTS

SECTION ONE
SPORT MANAGEMENT—FOUNDATIONS OF A PROFESSION

3 THEORIES AND PHILOSOPHIES ASSOCIATED
WITH SPORT MANAGEMENT 67

Section Two
Developing Competencies—
The Processes of Sport Management

6 EFFECTIVE COMMUNICATION, PERSUASIVENESS AND CONFLICT RESOLUTION

SECTION THREE
PRAGMATIC ASPECTS OF THE MANAGEMENT OF SPORT

15 PROBLEM SOLVING IN THE WORLD OF SPORT AND SPORT MANAGEMENT 497

Appendix

A SOURCES OF INFORMATION PERTAINING TO FACILITIES AND EQUIPMENT 517

PREFACE

This book, *Sport Management—The Business of Sport*, has been written and revised specifically for students in introductory collegiate courses in sport management programs. Readers are given a realistic glimpse into the challenges and opportunities that exist now as well as in the future within the exciting world of sport and sport management. This third edition has updated information and data, including an increase in the number of *concepts* [see *unique features of this book, below*] presented throughout the book. An additional chapter has been added to provide more in-depth material in the areas of facilities and the law. This edition also includes a number of Discussion Topics at the end of each chapter as well as space for the student to insert the answers to these questions.

The purpose of third edition of this book is to provide the reader with a comprehensive introduction to the body of knowledge that serves as the foundation for the study of management within sport and sport-related organizations. Specific objectives include assisting the future sport management professional to be capable of:

1. Developing a beginning philosophy of sport and a philosophy of management (in sport, fitness, and recreation organizations);
2. Understanding the relationship(s) between sport, the business of sport, and the management of sport;
3. Understanding basic managerial theories and principles as well as concepts of management that form the foundation of sport management;
4. Understanding the types of positions, jobs, and career opportunities available in sport management and how one becomes more marketable in the world of sport business;
5. Developing essential managerial competencies, survival skills, and leadership attributes appropriate for today's complicated and complex sport, fitness, and recreation organizations;
6. Instilling within the reader the ability to continue to learn, to remain at the cutting edge of knowledge in the wonderful and exciting—and ever changing—world of the *business of sport.*

How the Book Is Organized

The book is divided into three sections. The first (Chapters 1-3) deals with the foundation of sport management and provides an overview of the profession of sport management, including a historical glimpse of sport and sport management. The current status of sport management and professional preparation programs in sport management in this country is examined. A general discussion of career and employment opportunities in the management of sport is provided along with a review of essential skills needed by sport managers in the twenty-first Century. Additionally, the reader is introduced to the process of building a philosophy of sport management and exposed to some of the pertinent theories of management as they relate to sport organizations.

The second section (Chapters 4-6) introduces the reader to the processes and skills involved in successful sport management as an administrator or manager. The reader is then introduced to the areas of leadership, motivation, and decision-making within various types of sport management businesses and organizations. This section also includes treatment of the essential competency of communication in the management of sport as well as conflict management and resolution.

The third and final section (Chapters 7-15) deals with practical and pragmatic issues that exist today and will exist in the future in the world of sport and sport management. The reader is introduced to various strategies and tactics for dealing with the challenges and problems associated with the management of all aspects of sport and sport-related organizations and programs. These nine chapters should prove especially helpful for the modern day sport manager in terms of decision-making and taking specific courses of action.

Unique Features of This Book

A unique feature of this book is the existence of 453 concepts relating to sport management that are strategically located throughout the 14 chapters. These managerial concepts can help the reader appreciate and understand the body of knowledge that serves as the foundation for successful sport management.

The concepts also suggest possible alternatives in terms of decision-making. That is, concepts may serve as "food for thought" for the reader in considering a problem, an obstacle, or a challenge and arriving at one or more acceptable conclusions involving one or more courses of action.

The concepts presented herein are applicable to almost any managerial situation one might face within the areas of sport and fitness/wellness, as well as leisure/recreation programs. These concepts are based on both sound administrative theories as well as practical experiences in the world. Finally, throughout the book are suggestions for handling various situations that the modem-day sport manager might confront.

Each chapter also has, at the beginning, a list of *Chapter Highlights* which should enable the reader to more fully understand the major contents of the specific chapter. In addition, at the end of each chapter is a list of *Discussion Topics* which should prove helpful in group discussions or as individual questions or topics the reader might ask oneself as a review of the chapter.

Dr. Stier has over 50 years of sport management experience in various sport, recreation, and fitness organizations and businesses as well as within colleges and universities. He has been President and CEO of the consulting firm, *Education and Sport Management Consultants (ESMC)* since 1985. Additionally, he has served as the director of Sport Management/Athletic Administration at the State University of New York, Brockport, since 1990 and as Graduate Director since 1994 through 2008.

His most recent national award was the **Luther Halsey Gulick Medal** which he received at the 2013 National American Alliance Convention April 25, 2013. The **Luther Halsey Gulick Medal** *is awarded as the highest honor the American Alliance can bestow in recognition of long and distinguished service to one or more of the professions represented in the Alliance.*

Dr. Stier was honored with the **Sport Management Scholar Lifetime Achievement Award** by the Southern Sport Management Conference and Troy University. April 15, 2010 and received the **1st Annual Sport Management Achievement Award** in "honor of extensive contributions to the field of Sport Management" by the *Sport Management Council (SMC)/National Association for Physical Education and Sport*, April 22, 1999.

This is Dr. Stier's twenty-seventh book.

SPORT MANAGEMENT— FOUNDATIONS OF A PROFESSION

Chapter

1 The Profession of Sport Management

Promotions are an essential element of sport today.
[photo courtesy of Washington State University Sports Information]

CHAPTER HIGHLIGHTS

This chapter will help the reader to:

- Cite the number of professional preparation programs offering sport management in the U.S. as a curricular offering and offer implications for this number;
- Define the terms administration and sport management;
- Understand some general principles of management; and be able to relate such principles to the real world of managing sport;

- Indicate reasons/rationale for the study of sport management at the college/university level;
- Explain why the management of sport goes by many names; and supply a sampling of such names;
- Understand basic terminology in sport management;
- Explain why the management of sport is a business;
- Discuss the advantages and disadvantages of high schools as well as community or junior colleges offering a major in sport management;
- Differentiate between the "art" and "science" of management;
- Justify the need for the formal study of sport management;
- Appreciate the importance, from a historical perspective, of managerial achievements in different societies;
- Reveal why the study of sport management is a recent phenomenon and its relative importance to our society;
- Explain the advantages and limitations of college instructors in sport management possessing practical experience in the real world of managing sport and recreation programs; and provide possible solutions for securing instructors with real life sport management experience;
- Describe the growth and current status of sport management professional preparation programs; and explain the rational for such growth;
- Cite areas of controversy surrounding sport management programs in colleges and universities; and provide possible solutions to such controversies and potential problems;
- Acknowledge the importance of securing appropriate educational experience within the area of sport management; and cite examples of such appropriate experiences.

SPORT MANAGEMENT—SPORT ADMINISTRATION: WHAT IS IN A NAME?

The field of study that the author refers to as *sport management* has been and continues to be referred to by a variety of different names. In fact, the name of the discipline has been the subject of close scrutiny and many debates in its brief history. And the discussion, debate, and disagreement continue today. In reality, there are many terms used interchangeably to describe the profession or the field of study.

CONCEPT #1:   *The management of sport goes by many names.*

Such terms as *sport(s)* or *athletic management, sport(s) business* or *administration,* as well as *athletic administration* (among others) have all been in vogue at one time or another or are even currently being used. Although there is no consensus in terms of the name of the discipline or profession, the purpose of all the college and university professional preparation programs in sport management remains essentially the same. That is, to prepare future sport professionals-other than teachers and coaches-for managerial careers in the world of sport and sport-related endeavors (Bridges & Roquemore, 1996; Parkhouse, 1996).

Traditionally, the general public has viewed sport management as being associated only with the administration and management (general operation) of competitive sport programs in secondary schools, in colleges and universities, or, perhaps, at the professional level. Yes, sport management is intimately involved with such programs, and much, much more. Today, sport management is in reality a multifaceted domain offering a multitude of opportunities for employment and self-fulfillment in a wide range of sport and sport related activities, both in the public and the private sectors, as well as in the profit and not for-profit arenas.

Thus, this book is for those men and women who desire to secure and succeed in responsible managerial and administrative positions within private or public organizations devoted to (1) athletic competitive sports programs—at all levels, (2) health, fitness, and wellness programs, as well as (3) leisure and recreation programs. In reality, the scope of sport management is rather extensive. Chapter 2 presents a detailed look into what comprises the world of sport management in contemporary society.

> **CONCEPT #2: *Administration is the management of human behavior and the manipulation of resources.***

UNDERSTANDING THE TERMINOLOGY:
ADMINISTRATION, MANAGEMENT, AND SPORT MANAGEMENT

"Administration is the management of human behavior through good leadership skills and the manipulation of resources toward recognized and agreed upon objectives or goals" (Stier, 2003). One manages, leads, motivates, and guides other human beings. One does not manipulate them. The term *manipulation* carries with it some negative connotations when applied to individuals. However, one does manipulate and control tangible objects, such as resources, equipment, supplies, and facilities.

For the purpose of this book the terms *administration* and *management* are generally used interchangeably. Similarly, terms such as *administrators, managers, sport leaders, supervisors,* and *sport personnel* refer to individuals who assume leadership roles and responsibilities within the sport, fitness, or recreation entity *and* who are involved in one or more essential activities related to or associated with managerial responsibilities.

DEFINITION OF THE TERM SPORT MANAGEMENT

Therefore, for purposes of discussion, one may define successful *sport management* as being the process of striving toward clearly established objectives and goals as a result of working with others and exercising prudent and judicious use of resources and assets—all within the context of a sport or sport-related organization. Being a successful sport manager requires the possession of certain competencies and the use of specific skills in working with human beings, individually, in small and large groups, and as part of informal and formal organizations.

> **CONCEPT #3:** *Sport management is an all-encompassing term associated with the management of sport, fitness/wellness as well as leisure/ recreation programs.*

Sport management is currently used as an umbrella phrase or term encompassing a large number and variety of sport, fitness/wellness, and leisure/recreation programs and activities. Provided below is a partial list of these specific programs and activities frequently thought of as falling within the purview of sport management (Sawyer, 1993; Stier, 1996; Ross, Jamieson, & Young, 1997, Kluka & Schilling, 2001).

1. Amateur competitive athletics
2. Professional sports
3. Sport agencies and league or conference operations
4. Municipal recreation and sports
5. Manufacturing of sporting equipment and supplies
6. Sport merchandising and service organizations
7. Sports news media
8. Health, wellness, and fitness activities
9. General recreational resort and hotel operations
10. Specialized sport resorts and instructional programs

> **CONCEPT #4:** *There are general principles of management that may be applicable in a variety of organizational structures under various settings, circumstances, and situations.*

SPECIFIC PRINCIPLES OF MANAGEMENT

There are numerous general principles of management that may be applicable in a variety of organizational situations and circumstances. Being able to apply these principles of management and administration can prove to be a significant advantage when faced with the innumerable daily problems and challenges that exist in the world of sport management.

> **CONCEPT # 5:** *Management is management and administration is administration: Regardless of the setting, the principles and concepts remain essentially the same.*

Thus, the reader should strive to develop an understanding and appreciation of these general principles (guidelines). With a thorough grasp of these fundamental managerial principles individuals having responsibility for (1) personnel, (2) programs, and (3) resources will have a realistic and meaningful body of knowledge they can use to make effective and efficient decisions within any sport-related organization (see Figure 1.1).

Whether one has administrative or managerial responsibilities within a high school or college, a fitness club, a YWCA/YMCA, a corporate health club, a resort, or a professional team, the principles and concepts underlying sound administrative practices, decision-making, and actions remain the same. Administration is administration, management is management, period.

The same principles of administration are also applicable whether one is involved in (1) the *business* of manufacturing widgets or sport products, (2) the *business* of providing participatory opportunities or services

FIGURE 1.1
Areas of Responsibility for Managers

in sport, fitness, recreational, or leisure activities, or (3) the *business* of providing opportunities or services for spectators at various sport, recreational, or leisure programs or activities.

> **CONCEPT #6:** *The management of sport is a business.*

Although the concept that administration is administration and that management is management is certainly valid, there still exists the need to possess specific understandings and to develop specific job skills and knowledge relating to the particular organization in which one finds oneself employed. In this respect, there is specific and sometimes unique knowledge that is pertinent and absolutely necessary for a particular sport organization or entity. For example, knowledge of NCAA eligibility rules is a must for an athletic administrator having responsibility for student athlete eligibility within any NCAA institution. However, this knowledge has no relevance whatsoever within a private health club or a public resort facility.

CONCEPT #7:   *There are very distinct understandings, skills, and knowledge that must be mastered by the sport manager, that are specific to the organization in which one is employed.*

Management is both *a science and an art.* It is a science because there are fundamental, scientific principles and a body of knowledge underlying and supporting the tasks involved in managing and administering sport. These foundational tenets hold true and are applicable in a variety of settings, at different levels, and under varying circumstances. However, management can also be considered an art, because the actual delivery and implementation of the administrative techniques and managerial strategies and tactics can be significantly affected and, in fact, enhanced, through the creative and innovative utilization of these principles and applications of the knowledge pertaining to management.

CONCEPT #8:   *Management is both a science and an art.*

The art of management involves the creative application of managerial principles and the creative resourcefulness of those involved in sport management situations. Ingenious adaptations and utilization of these management principles, strategies, tactics, and knowledge is necessary if one is to be a successful sport leader, manager, or administrator. However, these adaptations should be made in light of the individual's strengths and limitations as well as the setting and circumstances in which one finds oneself (Stier, 1994).

CONCEPT #9:   *Understanding the principles of management can facilitate appropriate and timely decision-making.*

One of the objectives of this book is to provide you, the reader, with appropriate knowledge and understanding of the administrative-managerial processes. Such knowledge and understanding will enable you to develop and refine the necessary skills, abilities, and competencies that will facilitate making wise, fair, appropriate, and timely decisions, and then taking expedient action. It is indeed imperative that decisions be made in light of the existing circumstances, that is, resources and limitations, which currently exist or will manifest themselves in the future (see Figure 1.2).

FIGURE 1.2 The Basics of Effective Decision-Making

Why Study Sport Management?

Unfortunately, "historically over 98 percent of all first time managers in all types of organizations are placed in their first supervisory jobs without being trained to manage first" (Bridges & Roquemore, 1992, p. 4). This is truly an unfortunate and deplorable situation. It is unfair to the person to be placed in such a situation. And, all too frequently, it is unfortunate for the organization, its programs, and others associated with the organization. This horrific practice often hinders progress of the organization rather than facilitates its growth and advancement. However, it reinforces the tremendous need for formal training for those men and women who desire to move into positions of authority involving administrative-managerial responsibilities under the sport umbrella (Stier, 1995; Berg, 1996).

Increased Need for Trained Professionals

It is highly advantageous for those who wish to become actively involved in a sport or sport-related organization to study the management of sport formally for three specific reasons. First, there is an increasing need for professionals trained in the managerial and business aspects of sport (Stier, 1993b; Lefton, 1999). Through a sport management curriculum you will be able to develop essential skills and refine broader and more sophisticated managerial competencies needed in the world of sport. Such skills and competencies will put you in good stead if and when you are in a position to assume managerial responsibilities within the sport organization, either with or without an official title or designation.

> *CONCEPT #10: The sophisticated and complicated world of sport requires managers and administrators to be appropriately prepared through formal training and education.*

The job demands, both today and in the future, necessitate that you, the sport management professional, possess a depth of knowledge and a broad range of specific competencies. These competencies include, but are not limited to, administrative theory, business practices, communications, computer applications, and law in order to be capable of dealing successfully with changing challenges and problems associated with the business of sport. This includes any number of certifications that can be earned by specialists working within the sport industry (Cioletti, 1999). The mastery of pertinent knowledge and proper utilization of managerial skills can prove most beneficial for your daily survival and your future advancement within any organization.

Non-managers Work with Managers— Administrators and Other Non-managers

The second reason to study the management of sport is that, if you do not hold the official title of *manager* in your particular position within a sport organization, you nevertheless will work for and with administrators and managers. Knowledge of managerial principles and concepts will facilitate the building of positive relationships with administrators and managers. In working with managers (bosses), it is especially important that you have an understanding and knowledge of the role(s) of managers.

You need to develop a global perspective of the organization and see the situation from the viewpoint of the administration or management. You need to understand why they act as they do. It is most helpful to have an understanding and appreciation of where (your own) managers or administrators are "coming from." Such knowledge will put you in good stead in your efforts to do your own job within the organization.

> *CONCEPT #11: The essential skills and competencies for successful managers and administrators are also very effective for the non-management employee or associate.*

Also, as a non-manager you must be capable of working successfully with your peers and the general public. Understanding principles and concepts of good management and demonstrating specific organizational skills and managerial competencies are most helpful to non-managers. You will use such skills, knowledge, and understanding in your everyday tasks—working by yourself as well as with non-managerial personnel.

One Needs to Utilize Managerial Skills to "Manage" Oneself

> **CONCEPT #12:** *Individuals assume managerial and administrative duties and responsibilities at almost every level within an organization—even in entry-level positions.*

The third reason to study sport management is that, in fulfilling your specific job responsibilities, regardless of what they may be or at what level you find yourself in the organization, you must "manage" yourself. You must manage your time, prioritize goals, and complete the tasks for which you are responsible. And, of course, you exercise good judgment in terms of your daily professional relationships with others, both inside and outside of the organization. To accomplish these objectives, it helps to be professionally trained in the managerial, administrative, and business aspects of sport.

MANAGEMENT AND ADMINISTRATIVE ACHIEVEMENTS IN ANCIENT TIMES

> **CONCEPT # 13:** *There have been many outstanding examples of managerial and administrative skills since ancient times.*

Managerial skills and administrative competencies have been demonstrated for eons throughout recorded history. The origins of many so-called modern concepts and practices of management and administration can be traced from ancient civilizations. Whenever formal organizations existed there has been the need for managerial, organizational, and planning skills. In fact, all great leaders throughout history were outstanding managers and organizers. These leaders managed and carried out wars, they managed to construct impressive physical structures and buildings, they planned and managed vast explorations, they developed complex political systems, and they managed and controlled the lives of vast populaces. In three specific areas, (1) architecture, (2) warfare, and (3) political conquest, one can see examples of complex management systems from the earliest time of recorded history.

King Solomon: Manager, Organizer, and Leader

The famed biblical ruler, Solomon, directed the establishment of elaborate trade agreements, managed vast construction projects, and negotiated peace agreements in the

10th century B.C. Even before Solomon's time, other ancient rulers utilized wise managerial practices (delegation) by having their servants act as their official representatives, with appropriate authority and power, on behalf of the ruler.

Architecture: The Managerial Challenges of Constructing the Pyramids

The creation of the Pyramids took thousands of individuals decades to build. Such feats took extraordinary skills in terms of logistics, organization, and management. The Egyptian pyramids are living monuments to the extraordinary managerial ability and organizational ingenuity of the Egyptians. To understand what was then involved in constructing a pyramid, consider that one pyramid covers 13 acres of land, contains some 2,300,000 stone blocks, each weighing an average of 2.5 tons. In terms of manpower alone, it is estimated that over 100,000 workers toiled for over 20 years in the most difficult of living conditions.

In addition to architecture, there are many examples available in Egyptian literature of the early (2160 B.C. to 1788 B.C.) understanding of management principles and concepts. For example, in the Old Kingdom, Middle Kingdom, and the New Empire, the leaders exercised effective control of an extended physical domain through a highly decentralized, and later, centralized governmental structure.

Military Management and Political Organization: Alexander the Great

Military examples of management, administration, and organization can be seen from the earliest times of structured armed conflict. The organizations of armies throughout recorded history are examples of the necessity of great organizational, motivational, and managerial skills. The staff principle was very important in military success as was the involvement of staff planning, coordinating subordinates in delegated tasks. Perhaps the greatest example of successful use of the staff system took place during the reign of Alexander the Great (336 B.C. to 328 B.C.). Alexander the Great conquered the known world through extraordinary administrative skill, exceptional competency, and exquisite timing.

Empire Building: the Romans

Another outstanding example of effective and efficient management was the creation and maintenance of the empire of Rome. At one point, through superior managerial, organizational talents and ruthless use of power, the Romans held control over 50 million people. The empire extended from Great Britain in the West to Syria in the East, and included Europe and all of the north of Africa. Mismanagement, or non-management, led to the eventual breakdown of the Roman Empire and the dissolution of its sophisticated (for the time) way of life.

Sport Activities and Competitions from a Historical Perspective

The planning and the management of sport and sport-related activities is certainly not a new phenomenon (Parks & Zanger, 1990). From a very real and practical perspective, sport management has been in existence from the earliest times of human existence. For literally centuries, throughout written history, individuals and groups have gathered together for informal and/or formal competition in physical activities. And, there have been individuals involved in the planning, organizing, and supervising of such activities.

CONCEPT #14:   *The management of sport is not a new phenomenon.*

The first written accounts of sport competition and organized athletics are found in the *Iliad* and the *Odyssey.* These epic poems depict athletics, games, sport, and dance that became an integral part of Greek life. The descriptions of these games by Homer "are the first literary account of athletics" (Swanson & Spears, 1995, p. 343). In fact, contemporary sport concepts and managerial principles are evident when these games and competitions are clearly described in the poems.

THE ANCIENT GREEKS AND THE MANAGEMENT OF SPORT

The ancient Greeks excelled in conducting competitive athletic events for their citizens during the 1200 years of the athletic festivals, beginning around 776 B.C. and ending with the banning of the games by Emperor Theodosius I in A.D. 393. Of course, whenever such athletic competitions and sporting festivals were held, there had to be individuals involved in their planning, organization, management, and implementation.

In reality, there were four major athletic festivals, games, or competitions that became an extremely important part of Greek life. These festivals, or competitions, involved athletes from throughout Greece. So much so that wars were stopped, temporarily at least, to allow free passage to the sites of the competition and for the competitions themselves. The four major games were the Olympic (beginning in 776 B.C. in Olympia), the Pythian (beginning in 582 B.C. in Delphi), the Isthmian (beginning in 582 B.C. near Corinth), and the Nemean games (beginning 573 B.C. in Nemea) (Swanson & Spears, 1995).

As a result, extensive and relatively sophisticated stadia and supporting structures (for the time) were constructed for the competitors and spectators. In addition to the sites where actual competitions took place, there were facilities constructed for the training, feeding, and housing of athletes and those who accompanied the athletes. There were also facilities to treat and rehabilitate injured competitors. Finally, there were statues and columns bearing inscriptions about specific athletic contests and individual successful competitors. Such examples of highly organized sport facilities have been discovered at Olympia, Delphi, and at Epidaurus (Yalouris & Yalouris, 1989).

The types of athletic competitions held during the 1200 years of the ancient Greek games included footraces, jumping contests, throwing of the discus and the javelin, wrestling, and boxing. There were also exciting chariot and horse races. Additionally, there was also athletic competition that involved a combination of several of these activities in a competitive event. Two such examples are the pentathlon (involving a footrace, jumping, a discus throw, a javelin throw, and wrestling) and the pentathlon (a semi free-for-all combination of boxing and wrestling).

HISTORY OF THE FORMAL STUDY OF SPORT MANAGEMENT

> *CONCEPT #15:*   *The formal study of sport management is a recent phenomenon.*

Prior to 1966 there was no formal study per se of *sport management*, as we know it today, at the collegiate or university level. Although there had been many instances of colleges and universities offering courses in physical education administration, some as early

**Dr. James Mason,
Father of Sport Management,
Being Honored at Ohio University**

as the latter part of the 19th century. There had even been doctoral programs dealing with administration in physical education in the 1920's (Columbia Teachers College and New York University). There had not been a degree program specially geared to prepare people to work in the business of sport outside of schools (Earle Zeigler, personal communication, March 1, 2001).

However, in 1966 all that changed. It was in that year, at Ohio University (Athens), that the first formal educational degree program (at the master's level) in the world was initiated in sport management, under the direction of Dr. James G. Mason, who is recognized by many as the *father of sport management*. What was really different or new about this program at Ohio University was the fact that this new program involved "the introduction of a commercialized sport management emphasis outside of Educational Institutions at all levels with an accompanying downplaying of the physical education administration element" (letter from Dr. Earle Zeigler, March 19, 2001).

Ohio University was once referred to as the "Harvard of sport management" by then Oakland A's executive vice president Andy Dolich (J. G. Mason, Personal Communication, January 6, 1997). This program at Ohio University was the first example of sport management being offered as part of a college curriculum leading to an actual degree in *sport management*, a program designed to prepare professionals to manage and administer sports programs in the world of business (Stier, 2005).

However, the impetus for this initial educational program started much earlier, 1957 to be exact. It was in that year that Walter O'Malley, then the president of the Brooklyn Dodgers, shared his concern with Dr. James G. Mason, then a professor of Physical Education at the University of Miami, about the lack of formal educational programs for those individuals seeking employment within professional baseball. It took Dr. Mason, who subsequently moved to Ohio University, almost a decade (1966) to establish the first sport management course of study in Athens, Ohio, at Ohio University (J. G. Mason, Personal Communication, May 6, 1997). The second graduate program was implemented at the University of Massachusetts in 1971 by Dr. Harold J. VanderZwaag, while the third graduate program in sport management was developed in 1972 at Western Illinois University (Macomb, Illinois) under the leadership of Dr. Loren Dittus.

Only six years later, in 1978, there were a total of 20 sport management graduate programs in the United States (Parkhouse, 1978). Additionally, the first 3 undergraduate programs were established at Biscayne College (now St. Thomas University), at the State University of New York, College at Brockport, and at St. John's University (Stier, 1993a). In 1982, Lewis indicated that there were a total of 44 graduate and undergraduate professional preparation programs in existence. And, in 1988, the number of undergraduate sport management programs had ballooned to 75, while graduate programs almost tripled to 58 professional preparation programs in the United States (Sports Inc., 1988).

By 1993 there had been literally an explosion of both undergraduate and graduate programs with a total of 193 United States colleges and universities and 14 Canadian institutions of higher education offering undergraduate and/or graduate programs in sport management or athletic administration (NASSM/NASPE, Sport Management, 1993). By 1997, eight doctoral level programs were in existence in the United States, including programs at (1) University of Northern Colorado, (2) The Ohio State University, (3) University of Massachusetts, (4) Florida State, (5) University of New Mexico, (6) University of Connecticut, (7) University of Iowa, and (8) the United States Sports Academy (Daphne, Alabama).

At the turn of the century, it was reported in a study involving a comprehensive survey effort, that in the United States alone there were 137 undergraduate sport management programs, 99 programs at the master's degree level and 22 doctoral programs (Stier, 2001). Outside the U.S., this same study found 29 undergraduate programs existing, 20 at the master's level and 14 doctoral programs. In total, worldwide, the 2001 survey revealed the existence of 166 undergraduate, 119 programs at the master's degree level and 36 doctoral programs.

NASSM's November 2006 listing (web site) of sport management programs in the United States listed 169 undergraduate programs, 120 master's programs and 19 doctoral programs. By 2015, it is estimated that there will be more than 200 undergraduate and 175 graduate programs in existence within the US, including 25 doctoral programs (Stier, 2005). If this prediction is accurate, that is, nearly 400 professional preparation programs being in existence within this country alone by 2015, producing numerous graduates each and every year, the profession faces tremendous challenges in terms of where these sport management graduates will find gainful employment at suitable salary levels. And, yet, the number of institutions offering such professional preparation programs in sport management (including recreation management) continues to grow—with no end in sight.

CONCEPT #16:   *Formal education and training is the future for professionals involved in the challenging environment of sport management.*

Rochester Red Wings Manager Marv Foley Congratulates Team Members after Another Victory.
[photo courtesy of Rochester Red Wings, Barbara Jean Germano, photographer]

The trend is clear. Formal education and training is the future for professionals involved in the challenging environment of sport management. The job demands required, now and in the future, of the sport professional in managerial positions "necessitate that individuals possess a depth of knowledge and a broad range of specific competencies in business and in sport to be able to deal successfully with ever changing challenges and problems associated with the business of sport" (Stier, 1993a, p. 1).

This is best achieved through formal and informal education combined with meaningful, practical experience in sport management. Numerous professional organizations have recognized the need for formal training and education of their members in the area of management. Three such organizations that have provided opportunities for their members to experience in-service education are: (1) The National Association of Collegiate Directors of Athletics (NACDA), (2) the College Athletic Business Managers Association (CABMA), and (3) the National Collegiate Athletic Association (NCAA). In fact, the NACDA has had a long history of conducting multiday managerial workshops as part of its *Management Institute*, which is held in conjunction with the organization's annual membership meeting. Similarly, the NCAA has held two management workshops each year in addition to its annual convention, for several years.

REASONS BEHIND THE EXTRAORDINARY GROWTH OF SPORT MANAGEMENT PROGRAMS

Although the initial sport management program at Ohio University was created in response to a very specific and real need, the same cannot be said of the seemingly extraordinary growth spurt of both undergraduate and graduate programs during the past decade.

Parkhouse (1991, p. 6) revealed that "by 1988 only 10% of the programs had been in existence for more than 5 years." By 1990 there had been a 200% increase in the number of sport management programs over the previous five years (NASPE/NASSM, 1993, p. 1).

Most of the early sport management professional preparation programs evolved out of Physical Education departments. Even today the majority of such curricular programs, both at the undergraduate and graduate levels, are administratively housed in Physical Education/Kinesiology/Sports Studies departments (Sawyer, 1993; Ross, Jamieson, & Young, 1997). However, other academic departments also house some sport management programs, most notably departments of business as well as recreation and leisure studies.

There are several reasons behind both the accelerated and sustained growth in the number of sport management professional preparation programs and their positioning within departments of physical education.

Sports—An American Tradition
[photo courtesy of University of Montana, Todd Goodrich, photographer]

1. There has been an effort, on behalf of some institutions, to meet a real and recognizable need for professionally trained administrators and managers within the broad context of sport and sport-related organizations.

2. There has been a recognition and an acceptance of the viewpoint in some academic quarters, resulting from a natural outgrowth of the study of sport, that physical education is a broad-based academic discipline and therefore should encompass sport management as an integral part of its academic curriculum (that is, not be limited to teacher education).

3. There has been a reduction in the number of college students seeking to become physical education teachers. This situation itself places in potential jeopardy the job security of those college/university physical education faculties within the teacher preparation programs (Stier, 2005).

CONCEPT #17:   *Not All Sport Management Programs Have Been Established for the Right Reasons.*

This lack of students pursuing education as a career may be a result of the fact that there exists an overabundance of would-be physical education teachers already seeking positions when there are none. And one of the reasons for the job shortage is that there has been a reduction in requirements for daily physical education classes in many school systems, with the result that fewer physical education teachers are needed.

4. There have been conscious and concerted efforts by professionals within higher education to save the jobs of college physical educators (that might have been in jeopardy due to the lack of students pursuing traditional teacher preparation programs in physical education) by providing an alternative academic career path or option, sport management. This type of situation may very well call into question the accountability of some sport management programs (Arbogast and Griffin, 1989).

5. There have been additional colleges and universities that have joined the sport management bandwagon once they realized that such programs could attract significant numbers of college students. The creation of sport management programs therefore provided a justification for retaining college level physical education faculty who might otherwise have had their positions threatened as a result of a reduction of the number of students pursuing courses within the physical education teacher education tracts or programs.

CONSEQUENCES OF THE EXPANSION OF SPORT MANAGEMENT PROGRAMS

CONCEPT # 18:   *Not all growth of sport management professional preparation programs has been warranted or welcomed.*

Unemployment and Underemployment

The extraordinary growth experienced by the sport management profession, both in terms of the number of professional preparation programs and the number of individuals who are products of such programs, has not been without controversies, challenges, and problems. One of the challenges facing the profession is the matter of the significant excess of sport management graduates seeking employment. The dangers of saturating the job market with highly trained and experienced professionals competing for a limited number of vacancies, many with low wages, are obvious. The reality is that there are more applicants for jobs than there are jobs available (especially well-paying positions).

CONCEPT #19: *There is an overabundance of sport management graduates seeking professional positions today.*

The consequences have been predictable. First, a high rate of unemployment or underemployment for many of these would-be sport management professionals. Second, a low rate of pay combined, in many instances, with menial or mundane job tasks with few meaningful responsibilities. Third, a high turnover rate among those employed within the sport management arena due to the low pay, menial tasks, limited advancement opportunities, and overabundance of unemployed or underemployed sport management hopefuls.

ADDITIONAL AREAS OF CONTROVERSY, CHALLENGES AND PROBLEMS: DAUNTING QUESTIONS

1. *Should sport management be an undergraduate or graduate offering?*

A problem that continues to haunt the sport management field of study at the professional preparation level is the lack of consistency in the curricular offerings available at the various institutions. That is, at what level should professional preparation programs be offered to the student?

Not a few within the field feel that the subject matter of sport management should be solely a graduate curriculum. These individuals argue that the body of knowledge in sport management is such that it is best broached at the master's and doctoral level following, and based on, an undergraduate degree in the liberal arts. Others strongly argue that sport management must be an undergraduate level field of study. Some within the field would even argue that junior and community colleges should offer terminal degree programs in sport management.

Compounding the confusion is the fact that some undergraduate programs call their sport management programs a "major," while others provide a concentration, others a minor, some a specialization, and still other institutions call their curricular offerings an emphasis in sport management. This lack of consistency in the curricular aspect of sport management programs continues to be controversial and, sometimes, destructive.

2. *Are junior/community colleges usurping the curriculum of four-year institutions?*

There has been some evidence that, in some institutions, most notably at the junior and community college level, the study of sport management has been reduced to the freshman and sophomore levels. In these institutions, students barely out of secondary school are enrolled in courses usually made available at the four-year institutions exclusively for juniors and seniors.

CONCEPT #20: **Some sport management courses are being offered too early within the college experience.**

Again, the need for students to enroll (and thus to justify and save faculty members' jobs) within a college or a specific department—even at the two-year college level—seemingly is the driving force to establish a sport management curriculum that might attract much-needed students. There is a great deal of controversy regarding the appropriateness of having sport management as a "major" at the community college or junior college level (Stier, 2000). Many in the profession feel that two-year institutions should concentrate on general education type courses (offering the first two years of a four year college curriculum) (Case & Dollar, 2002). However, there are others within the profession who see such offerings as less offensive (Judd, Sawyer, Hatten, Grabel & Klein).

CONCEPT #21: *Junior and community college sport management offerings sometimes cause problems for the four-year institutions with undergraduate sport management programs.*

Junior and community college programs in sport management create two problems for four-year institutions. The first problem is caused by the graduates of the two-year institutions, those who leave with a terminal degree in sport management and have no desire to continue their education at the four-year institution. They enter the job market with a two-year degree and compete (with lower pay expectations) with graduates from four-year institutions and with students from graduate programs. This further complicates and saturates an already glutted job market.

The second difficulty concerns those graduates of two-year colleges who do pursue their baccalaureate degree in the area of sport management. These students enter the four-year institutions with numerous sport management courses taken during their freshman and sophomore years at the junior college/community college and often expect full transfer credit, even for junior and senior level courses at the four-year institution. Such articulation and transfer problems will only get worse with the continued proliferation of the number of junior college professional preparation programs in sport management.

3. *What department should house the sport management program or curriculum?*

A growing controversy revolves around the question of where in the college/university setting to house the discipline of sport management. Should it be administered by the physical education department? Should it be included within the business department? What about the recreation and leisure department? Or, should sport management be a separate academic field of study, a separate entity altogether?

Some professionals argue that sport management should no longer be housed within the traditional physical education department. "The umbrella of physical education is no longer, and never was, broad-based enough to cover the

The Ultimate Objective of Student-athletes is the Securing of a Quality Education
[photo courtesy of University of Tennessee, Sports Information office]

ever-expanding field of sport management" (Sawyer, 1993, pp. 4-5). Sawyer recommends that sport management curricula be folded into the existing departments of "recreation management or recreation and leisure studies, forming a new, expanded department of recreation and sport management" (p. 5).

Others within the field have made equally convincing arguments for the movement of the sport management curriculum to the department of business or business administration. The discussion goes on within the profession and will undoubtedly continue for some time in the future.

> *CONCEPT #22: Where sport management professional preparation programs are housed is less important than the quality of the curricular offerings and the competency of the faculty who teach in the program.*

4. *Is curricular rigor a myth or reality?*

One of the challenges facing the field of sport management involves academic sophistication and integrity (Brassie, 1989). Sport management should be more than a bunch of physical education courses clumped together with other courses from other departments in a so-called "package" and, thereby, creating a "sport management" program. A sport management professional preparation program, whether it is called a major, a concentration, an emphasis, or a minor, should be more than merely a collection of physical education courses combined with courses selected from business, communications, sociology, philosophy, computer science, and mathematics (among others).

What are needed are actual courses and classes that are devoted to appropriate and specific content areas within the sport management discipline or field of study. The majority of these courses should be taught by professors with terminal degrees (or, at least, at the master's level) who have had meaningful experiences in the realm of sport management.

CONCEPT #23: *Increased rigor in curricular offerings tends to increase the quality of entering students as well as increase the competency and skill levels of those who graduate.*

The American Alliance for Health, Physical Education, Recreation and Dance (AAHPERD) published an article in the *Journal of Physical Education, Recreation and Dance* (JOPERD) (1989, November/December) titled "A Student Buyer's Guide to Sport Management Programs," written by Stan Brassie. This article provided much-needed insight into the quality of sport management programs from the perspective of would-be students. It also provided guidance in terms of curricular offerings and program structure to administrators and teachers alike at colleges and universities with sport management programs.

5. *Is there a lack of professionally trained educated faculty and an overabundance of self-taught faculty?*

Related to academic integrity is the question of the qualifications of the faculty involved in administering the program and teaching the courses. Are the faculty members professionally trained as sport managers? Are their degrees in sport management, administration, or management? Do they have successful, meaningful, recent, and relevant experience in some aspect of sport management? Do they possess an adequate knowledge base for the classes that they teach? Are they able and willing to be true scholars within the discipline? Finally, are there sufficient full-time faculty available to teach as well as advise and counsel? Or, is there a sizable number of a program's faculty who are part-timers?

The faculty teaching the college sport management courses and the administrators managing such programs should be professionally trained and educated in the fields of management and sport management. *And, ideally, they should possess practical, relevant, and recent experience within the field* (Schneider & Stier, 2006). However, far too many sport management faculty members are merely self-taught. That is, they have no formal training in sport management at the master's or doctoral levels and/or have neither extensive nor meaningful experiences in the field. On the other hand, there are also too many faculty whose own real experience in the business world of sport management is severely limited, all too frequently restricted to classroom theory and instruction.

CONCEPT #24:   *Qualified faculty should be professionally trained in management (of sport) and possess meaningful, relevant, and recent sport management experience.*

The assigning of faculty who have not been professionally trained and who lack substantial administrative and managerial experience in the field of sport continues to plague our profession, although not as badly as in past years due to the tremendous growth in graduates of master's level and doctoral level sport management programs. The presence of self-taught faculty is also less of a problem on many campuses today than in years past. This is because of the fact that there are so many more graduates with advanced sport management degrees today than ever before, both at the doctoral and master degree levels. However, while many college faculty have been able to retrain in the sport management field, there continue to be significant numbers of supposedly self-taught, inexperienced teachers involved in the sport management courses and programs.

CONCLUSIONS

Whether one experiences success or failure as a professional employed in a sport management position is dependent on many factors, some within the individual's control and many that are not. Nevertheless, in order to have an opportunity to achieve success it is necessary that you, the future sport manager, understand sport as well as the management processes involved in administering a program and working with individuals, groups, and organizations. The time when a potential sport professional could gain access to the world of sport management and thrive professionally without formal training and education, coupled with a willingness to remain at the cutting edge of knowledge and skill, is long gone, if it ever existed.

Today, the consummate professional engaged in some aspect of sport as a manager or administrator needs a wide range of skills, competencies, and experiences, plus the intrinsic motivation necessary to take advantage of those skills, competencies, and experiences. Finally, the sport professional needs to be able to make adjustments, to make changes in light of the circumstances and situations in which one finds oneself. For, the one thing that is certain in the future is that change is inevitable. Nowhere is this more true than in the world of sport and sport management.

REFERENCES

Arbogast, G.W. and Griffin, L. (1989). Accountability-Is it within reach of our profession? *Journal of Physical Education, Recreation and Dance, 60*(6), 72-75.

Berg, R. (1996, November). Head hunting. Athletic Business, 20(11), 9.

Brassie, P.S. (1989). A student buyer's guide to sport management programs. Journal of Physical Education, Recreation and Dance, 60(9), 25-28.

Bridges, EL. and Roquemore, L.L. (1992). Management for athletic/sport administration: *Theory and practice.* Decatur, GA: ESM Books.

Bridges, EL. and Roquemore, L.L. (1996). *Management for athletic/sport administration: Theory and practice* (2nd ed.). Decatur, GA: ESM Books.

Case R. and Dollar, John. (2002). Sport management education: The case against two-year colleges. *International Journal of Sport Management, 3*(3), 171-179.

Cioletti, J. (1999, August). The paper chase. *Club Industry,* pp. 15-19.

Judd M.R., Sawyer, T., Hatten, T., Grabels, D., and Klein, D. (2002). Sport management education: The case for two-year colleges. *International Journal of Sport Management, 3*(3), 161-170.

Kluka, D., & Schilling, G. (eds.). (2001). *The business of sport—Perspectives. Volume 3.* International Council of Sport Science and Physical Education (ICSSPE/CIEPSS)— Berlin, Germany. Oxford, UK: Meyer & Meyer Sport.

Lefton, T. (1999, May). Wanna buy a team? *Sport.*

Lewis, G. (1982). *Degree programs in athletic and sport administration.* Unpublished report, University of Massachusetts.

NASPE/NASSM. (1993, May). *Sport management program standards and review protocol.* National Association for Sport and Physical Education (NASPE)/North American Society for Sport Management (NASSM). Reston, VA: National Association for Sport and Physical Education.

NASSM/NASPE. (1993, March). *Sport management-Directory of professional programs.* North American Society for Sport Management (NASSM)/National Association for

Sport and Physical Education (NASPE) Sport Management Task Force. Reston, VA: National Association for Sport and Physical Education.

Parkhouse, B.L. (1978). Professional preparation in athletic administration and sport management. *Journal of Physical Education, Recreation and Dance, 49*(5), 22-27.

Parkhouse, B.L., Ed. (1991). *The management of sport: Its foundation and application.* St. Louis, MO: Mosby.

Parkhouse, B.L., Ed. (1996). *The management of sport: Its foundation and application* (2nd ed.). St. Louis, MO: Mosby.

Parks, J.B. and Zanger, B.R., Eds. (1990). *Sport & fitness management: Career strategies and professional content.* Champaign, IL: Human Kinetics Books.

Ross, C.M., Jamieson, L.M., and Young, S.J. (1997). *Professional preparation in sports management.* Bloomington, IN: Indiana University Press.

Sawyer, T. H. (1993). Sport management: Where should it be housed? *Journal of Physical Education, Recreation and Dance, 64*(9), 4-5.

Sports Inc. (1988, May 23). A class compendium, p. 3.

Schneider, R.C. and Stier, W.F., Jr. (2006) Sport Management Field Experiences as Experimental Learning: Insuring Beneficial Outcomes and Preventing Exploitation. *The Sport Management and Related Topics Journal* (SMART Journal, 2(2), 36-43. http://spectrum.troy.edu/~smart/fieldexperience.pdf

Stier, W.F, Jr. (1986). Challenges facing physical education. Alternative career options. *Journal of Physical Education, Recreation and Dance, 57*(8), 26-27.

Stier, W.F, Jr. (1993a, August). *Alternative career paths in physical education: Sport management.* Washington, DC: ERIC Digest-Clearinghouse on Teaching and Teacher Education.

Stier, W.F, Jr. (1993b, July 9). Meeting the challenges of managing sport through marketing, fundraising and promotions. Paper presented at the International Meeting of the World University Games, Buffalo, NY.

Stier, W.F, Jr. (1994). *Successful sport fund-raising.* Dubuque, IA: Wm. C. Brown & Benchmark.

Stier, W. F, Jr. (1995, June 19). The future of fundraising and promotions in international sport competition. Paper presented at the annual convention of the Ontario Hockey Association. London, Ontario, Canada.

Stier, W.F, Jr. (1996). *Sport management handbook-State University of New York. Brockport, NY:* SUNY-Brockport Press.

Stier, W.F, Jr. (2000). The Past, Present and Future of Sport Management. PROCEED-INGS—Current Situations and New Directions for Sports Management: From the

Perspectives of Cultural Differences. International Sport Management Congress, Korean National University of Physical Education, and the Korean National Physical Education Association, Seoul, Korea.

Stier, W.F., Jr. (2001). The current status of sport management and athletic (sport) administration programs in the 21st century at the undergraduate and graduate levels. (2001). *International Journal of Sport Management, 2*(1), 60-97.

Stier, W.F., Jr. (2003, April 2). Hints on job hunting strategies and how to become more marketable (employable) within HPERD and athletics. Presentation made at the National Conference of the American Alliance for Health, Physical Education, Recreation and Dance, Philadelphia, Pennsylvania.

Stier, W.F., Jr. (2005, November 11). Introduction to the future of sport management and professional preparation programs in sport management. Presentation at the 46th World Congress of the International Council of Health, Physical Education, Recreation—Sport and Dance (ICHPER-SD).

Swanson, R.A. and Spears, B. (1995). *History of sport and physical education in the United States.* Dubuque, IA: Wm. C. Brown & Benchmark.

Yalouris, A. and Yalouris, N. (1989). Olympia: Guide to the museum and the sanctuary. Athens, Greece: Ekdotike Athenon S.a.

DISCUSSION TOPICS

1. Explain the concept of management in general and in terms of sport in particular.

2. Cite examples of sport management being both an art and a science in today's society.

3. Why should those individuals involved in various leadership roles within sport organizations be educated and professionally trained as sport managers?

4. Provide a brief sketch of how managerial skills have been used in various forms and in different societies from the earliest times of recorded history.

5. Summarize several examples of early management of sport.

6. Trace the development of formal professional preparation programs in sport management from their inception to the present time.

7. Differentiate between and explain several of the current controversies within the sport management field.

8. What are the advantages for professors of sport management to possess both a terminal degree as well as real, practical and successful experience in the world of managing sport and/or recreation programs?

9. Explain the difficulties or problems that might be experienced for the profession if junior and community colleges offer a so-called major in sport management or recreation management for graduates of such schools.

10. What are the advantages as seen by the junior and community colleges that desire or actually offer sport management programs/majors on the two-year level?

Chapter

2 Preparing for a Career within the World of Sport

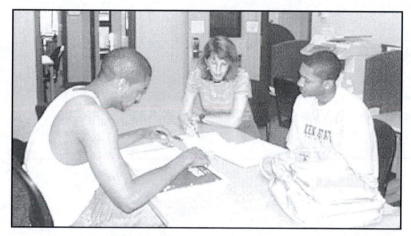

Advising Students for Careers in the World of Sport.
Kent State University Learning Specialist Deborah Keith Advises Student-athletes
[photo courtesy of Kent Photographic Services]

CHAPTER HIGHLIGHTS

After reading this chapter you will be able to:

- Illustrate the negative consequences of the Internship Model of Staffing and provide possible alternate methods of staffing;
- Explain under what conditions, according to the Labor Department, may interns be used by businesses without being in violation of the law; and explore the extent to which this law is violated and the consequences of such violations;
- Understand possible opportunities for employment within the field of sport management and be specific of the different areas of the world of sport;
- List numerous specific sport organizations that hire individuals who are professionally trained in the management of sport;
- Explain the interdisciplinary, multi-disciplinary or integrated basis of educating future sport managers;

- Differentiate between the three general components or elements of a professional preparation education program in sport management;
- Justify the importance of field experiences, especially at the undergraduate level, in preparing future professionals in managing sport programs and organizations;
- Provide examples of the positive attributes as well as negative characteristics associated with various types of internships;
- Explain why the internship is viewed as the quintessential culminating experience for sport management students; and outline the negative consequences of inappropriate or poor internships;
- Indicate steps to follow in securing an appropriate internship;
- Understand the importance of networking; and cite how networking actually works in the real world;
- Cite examples of current curricular standards being utilized in sport management programs;
- List professional journals important for the modern manager of sport programs.

SOURCES OF EMPLOYMENT

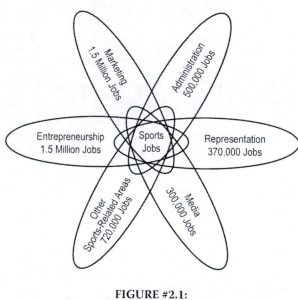

FIGURE #2.1:
Types of Job and Career Opportunities in Sports

More than a decade ago, in 1991 to be exact, a sports executive career recruiter, Mark Tudi, estimated that there existed approximately 4.5 million sport related jobs at all levels, in this country alone. He broke these employment opportunities into six broad categories: (1) marketing, (2) entrepreneurship, (3) administration, (4) representation, (5) media and (6) other sports related areas. The number of job opportunities in each of these areas are presented in figure #2.1 (Markiewicz, 1991). By the year 2010 the estimated number of total job and career opportunities should be 20% to 30% greater.

Witness the tremendous growth just in the minor league baseball segment of the world of sport. Between 1985 and 1999 there have been 87 brand new minor-league ballparks either opened up or ground breaking construction has been initiated. And there is BIG MONEY involved even at the minor-league level. For example, in 1991 a Class-A team cost around 2.5 million, with some going for as much a $3.8 million (Everett, Washington, AquaSox, Single-A) to $10 million (Triple-A Ottawa [Ontario, Canada] Lynx). It was estimated that if the Buffalo Bisons Triple-A club (which are perennial leaders in attendance) was sold the price would be in excess of $15 million (Lefton, 1999, Stier, 2000, August 26).

> **CONCEPT #25:** *There are currently more than five million sport related jobs in the United States—and the number is growing.*

SPECIFIC JOB AND CAREER OPPORTUNITIES WITH APPROPRIATE SPECIALIZED TRAINING

There are numerous job opportunities in the world of sport (Gleason, 1986). The following is a partial list of general career opportunities for graduates of sport management programs, assuming candidates have successfully completed appropriate general education and specialized training at the undergraduate and/or graduate level (Stier, 1996a).

> **CONCEPT #26:** *There is a great diversity of job and career opportunities available in the world of sport and sport related organizations.*

---

1. Amateur, competitive sports—youth, junior and senior high school, collegiate/ university levels
2. Amateur, competitive sports/leagues and conference offices
3. Amateur sport agencies—NCAA, NAIA, AAU, etc.
4. Armed services recreation and competitive sports
5. Athletic representation firms
6. City and state sport commissions
7. Corporate and industrial fitness and wellness programs
8. Corporate sport marketing departments (Kodak, Pepsi, etc.)
9. Entrepreneurship opportunities
10. Facility and stadia management—recreation, intramural and sport activities
11. Federal recreation/parks—tourism and travel
12. Fitness, health and wellness clubs
13. Football bowl organizations—Rose Bowl, Sugar Bowl, Cotton Bowl, and Fiesta Bowl, etc.
14. International sport management
15. Law—representation, agency relationships
16. Municipal sports authorities

17. Non–profit youth agencies involving recreation and/or sport (such as the YMCAs/ YWCAs; Boys Clubs; Girl Clubs; and, Catholic Youth Organizations).
18. Municipal recreation organizations
19. Professional sports—individual teams
20. Professional sports—league offices
21. Proprietary recreation businesses, i.e., "Discovery Zones"
22. Public and private racquet, golf, aquatic clubs
23. Recreation youth camps
24. Resort and hotel recreation and leisure organizations
25. Special event firms
26. Specialized sport clubs and racquet clubs
27. Sports announcing/broadcasting—radio, television
28. Sport governing bodies
29. Sports information and media relations—college, university and professional level
30. Sport manufacturing
31. Sport merchandising—wholesale and retail sales
32. Sports statistics—collegiate, professional, media
33. Sports writing/journalism—newspaper, magazine and book publishers
34. Sport tourism, travel—cruise opportunities
35. Sport marketing agencies
36. Sport promotion, marketing and event management entities
37. State recreation/parks—tourism and travel
38. Summer sport camps

VARIOUS CAREER PATHS IN SPORT AND SPORT MANAGEMENT

Individuals seeking managerial positions should recognize that there are various paths leading to a variety of different positions in the world of sport, fitness and recreation. In short, there is no one single method or avenue to managerial posts of positions or authority within a sport or sport related business or organization.

Fitness Organizations

There are many fitness type employment opportunities available within the fitness, health and wellness industry for the motivated and competent sport management graduate. Whether it is with a national chain, a locally owned single site facility, a recreation department or college/university fitness facility, the opportunities for sales jobs, managerial positions, fitness instructors, personal trainers, financial and accounting personnel as well as a host of other job titles are plentiful. Specific types of skills needed by employees of such fitness entities can be seen from the top ten most popular offerings or programs provided by fitness, health and wellness organizations that were revealed in a recent survey (1) personal training, (2) group strength training, (3) stretching/flexibility, (4) step aerobics, (5) abdominal classes, (6) circuit training, (7) boxing-related classes, (8) low-impact classes, (9) interval training, and (10) yoga (Top 10 Fitness Programs, 1999).

Horse Racing is another Attractive Sport for Sport Managers in which to Pursue a Career.
[photo courtesy of Batavia Downs, Batavia, New York. Photo by Paul Write]

School Based Sport Organizations

Up until recent years, athletic directors within school based sport programs such as colleges and universities came from the ranks of coaches, successful coaches. Usually, however, these individuals had little if any formal training in the management of an athletic department.

Today, however, more and more collegiate athletic directors have had formal training in administration as well as post baccalaureate educational experiences. While a few ADs hold the doctorate degree, most hold the master's degree with a few possessing the baccalaureate degree. There is even a movement, especially at the NCAA division I level, towards hiring individuals from the business world who have had successful experiences in the so-called real world of business and management. Advancing up the career ladder today at the college level typically involves assuming an entry level position and then working one's way up the organizational ladder, gaining valuable experience holding a variety of jobs and assuming different responsibilities, as well as perhaps an advanced degree (or two).

There is a significant difference in terms of educational requirements (expectations) of those individuals who hold the position of athletic director at the NCAA division I and II levels and those who are athletic directors at division III institutions. In the latter case, the athletic directors usually are required to hold at least one advanced degree. And, not infrequently, such institutions advertise that they prefer candidates to hold the doctoral degree.

At the secondary level, the typical athletic administrator is one who possesses the master's degree as well as extensive experience in teaching and coaching. However, even at this level it is increasingly important for the individual to have had some type of formal education and training in management to be seriously considered for the top (sport) administrative position of athletic director.

Holders of advance degrees continue to earn the notice and respect of superiors and employers. This is because possession of such a degree is indicative of not only additional education but of increased skills and competencies as well as a high degree of persistence and dedication. More and more, the advance degree in today's world of sport business (depending upon the situation) could be a master's degree, a master's of business administration (MBA), a law degree, as well as a doctoral degree.

Movement within the Sport Industry

The avenue to an upper level administrative post within the ranks of professional sports varies somewhat depending upon the sport. Having played the sport at the professional level still is important in some circles—again, depending upon the specific job and responsibilities accompanying the position. However, demonstrating successful work experience within professional sports, at the entry and middle management levels, is also becoming a very important factor in being able to work one's way up the proverbial ladder to a position of greater authority. Being able to demonstrate prior successful experience in related or identical positions (even at a lower level) is advantageous for the upward bound sport management employee.

There is even a trend for greater movement of highly trained and experienced personnel between and among different professional sports (football, basketball, baseball, ice hockey, soccer, lacrosse, etc.). Being a successful employee in one sport can facilitate one's marketability for a similar post in an entirely different sport.

Expected Pay at Various Levels of Employment in Professional Sports

Pay and other forms of compensation for sport personnel working at the upper echelon of sport organizations and businesses can be very lucrative indeed. However, one does not start at the top. Hence, it is important to realize that in many sports, recreation and fitness related positions, salary can be minimal—at least at the entry level. And the time spent at the entry level or near entry level can seem to be extremely long in some cases.

Entry-Level Positions in Professional Sports

Entry-level positions in the world of sport often provide relatively low salaries when compared with comparable professional positions in other career avenues, such as teaching. This is especially true in the so-called minor leagues. Many positions in minor league sports involve a combination of salary plus incentives or commission. This is true also of many positions in the fitness and wellness arena as well. Many entry-level positions in professional sports as well as in the fitness industry involve some type of selling. And, when there is selling to be done part of the compensation is usually based upon commission. Another factor regarding entry-level positions is the matter of job security. There is precious little job protection at the entry and middle management levels within many sport and sport related businesses. In fact, many organizations do not even have an employment contract for their personnel at the lower levels of the organization. Instead, these personnel work at the will of the employer.

CONCEPT #27: *There exists fierce competition for employment within the world of sport management.*

Yet, there remains fierce competition for almost all positions within many sport businesses whether the job involves professional sports, fitness and wellness businesses, school based sport programs or any of the other numerous career avenues cited earlier in this chapter. This is because of the nature of the "beast." There are many individuals who have a strong desire to become involved in the business of sport (in some type of managerial role). They are highly motivated to do so. And many are willing to make whatever sacrifices that are necessary in order to secure such positions. The law of supply and demand continues to affect the job market at all levels and in every avenue of sport businesses and sport organizations.

For those who have the determination, the motivation, the dedication and the persistence and the willingness to make sacrifices—increased financial rewards and adequate compensation are often available when the professional employees advance up and within the organization. Greater responsibility generates increased compensation, financial and otherwise.

In evaluating one's career opportunities, it would be safe to say that one needs to acquire an appropriate education, secure meaningful experiences, and be willing to pay one's dues in a variety of tasks if one is to experience success within the world of sport management, regardless of the specific venue that one has chosen for one's life work. One must also be patient and be willing to assume meager or less glamorous tasks when first starting out in one's career. Proving one's worth, one's level of competency in the performance of the tasks assumed is critical in experiencing success within the business world, the business of sport.

SPORT MANAGEMENT PROFESSIONAL PREPARATION IN THE 21ST CENTURY

Today, in the United States, sport management professional preparation programs are based upon an interdisciplinary, multi-disciplinary or integrated approach (DeSensi, Kelley, Blanton, and Beitel, 1990). Examples of such fields of study as physical education, sport, business, computers, psychology, sociology, and communications are all intricately intertwined in the academic preparation of future sport administrators and managers. Sutton (1989) indicates that sport management is a hybrid field of study that encompasses many other disciplines.

Wise Athletic Administrators and Coaches Take Advantage of Well-spoken Athletes to Represent the Team/Athletic Program
[courtesy of University of Tennessee, Sports Information Office]

Brassie (1989a, p. 27) indicates that "sport management is a broad field serving many different types of work settings. Each type of setting requires a somewhat different preparation: the curriculum should provide flexibility for various options." Institutions of higher education are not in a position in today's society to prepare the student for every single eventuality of the individual's career (Uhlir, 1990, p. 6). What college and university professional preparation programs can do is to provide a firm foundation of general knowledge and specific skills upon which graduates—once they are working in the field—can build upon and expand in light of the different and ever changing challenges facing them (Murray & Mann, 1993; Stier, 1996b).

> **CONCEPT #28: *Collegiate professional preparation programs are based upon an interdisciplinary, multi-disciplinary or integrated approach.***

Graduates of undergraduate sport management programs at colleges and universities are usually thought of more as generalists rather than specialists. The graduate level (masters and doctoral) is reserved for those individuals desiring to specialize in one or more specific areas of sport management. However, this does not mean that undergraduate students do not receive specialty training or do not possess a high level of competency in one or more areas. Quite the contrary.

UNDERGRADUATE CURRICULAR OFFERINGS WITHIN SPORT MANAGEMENT PROFESSIONAL PREPARATION PROGRAMS

Generally speaking, undergraduate sport management professional preparation programs involve four basic components. First, a variety of general liberal arts core courses that are required of all undergraduate students. Second, cognate or foundation courses related to or supporting sport management. Third, specialty or major courses dealing with specific aspects of the management of sport, fitness/wellness and leisure/recreation programs. And, fourth, some type of field experiences, consisting usually of a practicum and/or an internship (Stier, 2002).

CONCEPT #29: *A strong, exemplary professional preparation curriculum is based upon offerings involving the liberal arts, cognate courses, theory of management courses, and field experiences.*

THE FOUNDATIONS OF A LIBERAL ARTS EDUCATION INVOLVES GENERAL EDUCATION CORE COURSES

Most undergraduate institutions require a selection of core courses that every student must complete regardless of the major that student is pursuing. This is the basis of the so-called liberal arts degree that is so highly prized in our culture. These so-called core liberal art classes might be taken from the areas of humanities, social sciences, natural sciences (with and without laboratory experiences), fine arts (with and without a performance component), contemporary issues, computer literacy, etc.

Specific courses taken by a sport management student can include, but not be limited to, history, political science, foreign language, English, communication, geography, art, philosophy, anthropology, chemistry, physics, African & Afro-American studies, economics, health, psychology, sociology, theater, etc. The goal of the general education courses is to provide the student with a broad based, liberal arts education. Such an educational experience would help the person to be a well-educated, well-rounded individual, and one who would be willing and capable of continuing one's learning and intellectual development following graduation.

> **CONCEPT #30:** *A mark of an educated individual is the ability to continue to learn throughout one's life—both for the sake of learning as well as to keep abreast of one's field or profession.*

COGNATE OR SPORT MANAGEMENT FOUNDATION COURSES

These are classes within a variety of other academic departments which are related to the field of study called sport management and which form the foundation of further, more specialized courses, for the sport management student. Examples of such courses include, but are not limited to, communications, management and organizational behavior; interpersonal relations; business law; general accounting; ethics; finance; economics; business law; statistics; and the historical, sociological, psychological, kinesiological, and philosophical perspectives of sport (Widdon, 1990; Stier, 1993).

MAJOR OR SPECIALTY COURSES

The major or specialty courses are frequently referred to as the core classes within the sport management curriculum. They are applied courses geared specifically to the discipline of sport management (Brassie, 1989b; Ross, Jamieson & Young, 1997). Ideally, professors of sport management teach these courses within the department where the discipline of sport management is housed within the institution.

> **CONCEPT #31:** *The sport management core courses should be taught by doctoral faculty who possess real world experience in the field.*

Examples of such courses include introduction to sport management; sport marketing; sport fundraising; sport sponsorship; sport management theory; public relations in sport; research methods; recreational sports programming; risk management in sport; problems and issues in sport management; facility planning; facility and event management; computer applications to sport; ethics in sport and sport management; sport finance; sport budgeting; sport economics; legal aspects of sport; administration of sport; among numerous others. These courses are of such a nature that the instructors should possess the terminal degree as well as have had meaningful and successful real life sport experience.

FIELD EXPERIENCES

Almost all undergraduate sport management programs offer some type of field experiences (Sutton, 1989; Verner, 1993; Marston, 1993; Ross, Jamieson & Young, 1997). Generally speaking, there are two types of field experiences commonly associated with sport management, a practicum and an internship. Both are very important for the modern sport management student in providing the individual with a glimpse into how sport and sport related organizations and programs operate. Additionally, depending upon the student and the student's skills, such field experiences can enable the individual to demonstrate specific skills and competencies while upgrading and expanding one's knowledge base.

Typically, a practicum is a pre-internship, part-time field experience in which the student is physically at a sport management site. The practicum could involve any site including professional sports, fitness clubs, wellness programs at large corporations, collegiate athletic programs, etc. The practicum provides students the opportunity to experience, on a limited basis, what it is like to work in the real world within some type of sport management setting, under the direct (on-site) supervision of a professional in the field.

Excitement, Excitement and More Excitement!
[courtesy of University of Montana, Todd Goodrich, photographer]

The practicum is normally taken while the student is actively taking cognate and/or specialty courses within the sport management curriculum. Usually, the practicum experience or practica experiences (if more than one such experience is provided) are part of a regular course. However, on some campuses the practicum experience is offered as a stand-alone class.

> **CONCEPT #32:** *Both practica and internship experiences provide the sport management intern with meaningful real life experiences and skills.*

The culminating field experience for sport management students usually involves a full-time commitment, either for an entire semester or a quarter (Campbell and Kovar, 1994). Some internship experiences are for two semesters or three quarters and a limited number of internships involve a 12-month commitment on behalf of the student intern (Cunnen & Sidwell, 1993).

The number of credits given to students involved in the internship experience typically range from 3 to 15 semester hours. During the internship the student is usually enrolled in no other course work and has no other major commitments. The student intern is expected to demonstrate a competency level of a beginning, first year professional and provide meaningful assistance to the organization and staff where the individual is interning.

EVALUATION OF THE STUDENT INTERN

The intern is evaluated both by an on-site supervisor and a college or university faculty member (Bell & Countiss, 1993). In some instances, the college supervisor/faculty member periodically travels to the site of the internship to personally supervise and oversee the intern. However, in many programs, a campus faculty or supervisor does not personally visit the student intern at the site unless there is a definite problem. Rather, the student intern is evaluated on site only by the on-site supervisor (for whom the intern works). In this situation, the college supervisor oversees the intern from a distance, via phone, e-mail, and regular mail.

Another common practice is to require interns to maintain a diary or journal of their involvement and accomplishments that they periodically share with the campus faculty member assigned to them (Campbell and Kovar, 1994). Even when the intern is not visited by a representative of the college or university there is usually periodic communication by phone and/or between the intern and the college as well as between the on site supervisor and the college representative.

THE FINAL EXIT INTERVIEW FOR INTERN CANDIDATES

Another practice which has been utilized quite successfully on some campuses is to require an exit interview for would-be interns. This individual interview is held prior to the semester in which a student will begin the field (internship) experience. The exit interview consists of the future intern being interviewed by a group of 4-6 practicing professionals within the world of sport management (Schneider & Stier, 2006).

The interview questions are geared to determine the level of competency of the student and whether or not the student should be given permission to undertake the internship in a subsequent semester. If the responses to the questions reveal that the student is not ready to undertake the internship then remedial courses as well as independent work is required prior to beginning the internship. On some campuses this exit or pre-internship interview helps the student become familiar with the interview process, a factor that is critical in successful job hunting following the internship.

PROBLEMS WITH THE INTERNSHIP OR FINAL FIELD EXPERIENCE(S)

> *CONCEPT #33: Not all internship experiences are created equal.*

Not all is well with the internship concept. In fact, the internship experience has been involved in a number of controversies in recent years. The suitable location of internship sites is absolutely essential for the sport management programs and for the students who are nearing the completion of their formal sport management education and training. This fact coupled with the large number of students seeking internships, both undergraduate and graduate, creates potential problems or challenges, for the colleges preparing interns, for the interns themselves and even the organizations accepting interns.

THE AVAILABILITY OF SUITABLE INTERNSHIP SITES

There is always the question of whether or not there are sufficient numbers of suitable internship sites available, sites that will provide an adequate culminating, on-the-job training, for interns (Ruder, 1993). With the significant number of students seeking quality, high visibility internship sites, it is sometimes difficult to adequately match interns with the available sites that are the students' first choices, or even second and third choices. The quality of the learning experience associated with any internship site is the major challenge facing both the potential intern and the college or university sport management program that is preparing the student for a career in the management of sport.

> *CONCEPT #34: Sport management internships have three possible consequences and two of them are negative.*

Woody Hayes, former football coach at The Ohio State University, was credited with saying that there were three things that could happen when a team attempted a forward pass, and two of them were negative. Well, sport management is a lot like football in that regard. There are three possible consequences associated with an individual's internship experience, and two of them are negative.

First, the host site can take advantage of the intern and abuse the individual by making the intern work "25 hours" a day in performing all types of tasks and duties. Whether these tasks are menial, mundane or, on the other hand, rather sophisticated, the point is that the intern is taken advantage of as a form of cheap labor.

A second possible negative scenario involves the host site (supervisor) literally ignoring the intern by giving the individual almost nothing to do as part of the internship experience. And, what is assigned to the intern is mundane and meaningless. Both of these scenarios are negative and defeat the purpose of the culminating internship or field experience.

> **CONCEPT #35: *The intern should be given meaningful responsibilities***
> ***and tasks commensurate with the individual's skills, abilities,***
> ***capabilities and training.***

The third consequence (and the one positive outcome) of an internship involves the intern being assigned appropriate, meaningful and adequate work responsibilities and tasks, commensurate with the intern's capability, willingness and training, so as to provide the intern with a meaningful learning experience. This type of learning experience will also provide to the intern's supervisors ample opportunities to evaluate the abilities and accomplishments of the student intern.

The meaningful sport management internship experience also helps the intern to master new skills or refine and broaden existing competencies while demonstrating to the supervisors how effective and efficient the intern can be on "the firing line"—in the real world. Finally, such a superb internship experience will expedite the person's chance for a full time sport management position, in some appropriate organization or company following the conclusion of the internship or field experience.

> **CONCEPT #36: *A secondary, but nevertheless significant, objective***
> ***of the internship experience is to help the student intern secure***
> ***full time employment following the internship—somewhere.***

The ideal concept behind the internship is that such an experience not only will help the student intern develop, enhance and refine skills and competencies but will also aid in the intern securing full time employment at the conclusion of the internship, in some suitable and appropriate organization. Sometimes the site where the student completes the internship might do the hiring since the competency level of the student intern would be well known to that organization. Other times the student cannot be hired at the internship site because of a lack of a vacancy there. Nevertheless, a strong recommendation on the intern's behalf to other organizations (especially those in the same business, association or league) might provide the job seeker with a leg up on other applicants not possessing such a strong, recent and relevant recommendation.

THE STUDENT INTERN MUST NEVER BE VIEWED AS CHEAP LABOR

In recent times it seems that some organizations are only too happy to accept interns—but not for the right reasons. In reality, most interns are usually highly motivated and relatively competent, possessing appropriate skills and experience. Plus, the interns are also, simply put, cheap or free labor. This is because the vast majority of internship experiences are non-paying. In fact, in some instances, selected organizations that accept interns do so in lieu of hiring someone to fill that particular role and assume those responsibilities.

> CONCEPT #37: *Relatively few internship sites offer meaningful pay to the intern—usually the experience is for no pay at all.*

Even though there are some organizations that do pay or provide a meager stipend for their interns, these are relatively few and far between. Nevertheless, some organizations, such as the NCAA, that do provide stipends reserved them exclusively for women and minorities. White males need not apply for these paid internships. Other organizations provide unrestricted stipends, some more financially beneficial than others.

SOME INTERNS ARE USED BY ORGANIZATIONS AS REPLACEMENTS OR SUBSTITUTIONS FOR FULL-TIME EMPLOYEES

However, a disturbing and insidious trend that is being seen more and more among some segments of the sport industry is the advertisement for so-called "internships" that include stipends involving cash payments or some combination of cash and free room and/or food for individuals willing to assume specific duties. The problem is that a full time employee really should assume these duties and responsibilities. In this situation the organization is replacing, or not hiring, a full time employee because of the availability of a temporary intern. The organization can accomplish this at a fraction of the cost and with absolutely no long-term obligation for employment towards the intern. Granted that meaningful experiences may be gained by the intern, however, actual paying job opportunities on a full time basis may never become available. This is an example of intern exploitation as well as exploitation against potential employees since would-be employees are not hired because they are not needed—their positions having been assumed by unpaid or underpaid interns.

Whenever an intern accepts an internship (with or without pay) and the administrators or organizers of that site expects the intern to realistically perform *as an employee*, there is a problem. The problem is that the intern is, in reality, taking the place of a would-be paid employee (and preventing a person from becoming a paid, full time employee). The term coined to reflect this type of questionable employment or staffing strategy is called the "*Internship Model of Staffing*" (Stier, 1990a).

Stier (2001a, p. 5) conceptualized the phrase "*internship model of staffing*" to denote the situation in which: "sport organizations are more than willing to take advantage of interns, most of whom are unpaid volunteers, by using these individuals in lieu of hiring entry-level professionals to work within their organizations." This technique or tactic whereby staff is secured via means of unpaid or underpaid interns is suspect at best and unethical, and possibly even illegal, at worse. For example, there is a little known law called the *1938 Fair Labor Standards Act.*

This ACT stipulates that there are six criteria that determine whether a company or organization may or may not pay any student-intern the current prevailing minimum wage. These factors are: (a) the employer does not immediately and materially benefit from the presence, work and contributions of the intern, (b) the intern does not replace a regular, paid employee, (c) the internship experience is similar to what would be offered in a vocational school, (d) the intern is fully cognizant that no pay is forthcoming, (e) the intern is not guaranteed employment following the field experience, and (f) the field experience is strictly for the benefit of the student intern and not primarily for the sport entity or business (Schneider & Stier, 2006).

When businesses and organizations want to utilize interns in an acceptable, and legal, manner, they should look at the major criterion that the Labor Department utilizes. This criterion is referred to as: *Who Benefits Most?* In answering this question, if the intern's contributions and involvements clearly outweigh the advantages or benefits accruing to the intern, there is a need for adequate and full financial payment to the student. If no pay is forthcoming, the student intern may be considered to be exploited and the entity "using" (abusing) the intern might be engaged in an illegal act. On the other hand, if the intern is the recipient of the greatest benefit(s) as a result of the internship, instead of the entity providing the internship, there is no legal requirement that the student intern need be paid (Unpaid Interns, 1996).

CONCEPT #38: *Interns must not be placed (or left) in a situation where they will be misused, abused or neglected.*

At the conclusion of an internship such an organization merely replaces (recycles) one intern with another at a low salary (stipend) or with no compensation and the cycle is repeated again and again. In this scenario the intern has little chance of securing a position with the organization when the internship is over simply because the organization is going to secure the services of another eager beaver intern, with little and or obligation.

And, in some instances, the type and caliber of work assigned to the intern is not advantageous for the intern in any stretch of the imagination. In fact, it may even be counterproductive for the intern because the intern has, at the conclusion of the internship, no meaningful experiences, no significant accomplishments to point to as the individual seeks a full time position.

CONCEPT #39: *An internship can be viewed as a two–way sword.*

So, the internship experience is a two-way sword. On the one hand the colleges and universities are totally dependent upon sport and sport related organizations to provide their students with meaningful internship experiences. On the other hand, however, some of these same internship sites, these same organizations, companies and corporations have little incentive to hire the interns once the field experience is concluded.

This is because there is always another skilled and highly motivated student intern lurking just around the corner "begging" for the opportunity to work for nothing, 14 hours a day, seven days a week, for an entire semester, or even longer. The large number of professional preparation programs in sport management, especially at the undergraduate level, exacerbates this situation.

CONCEPT #40: *Each internship has the potential for being a positive and a negative experience for the intern.*

All internships have the potential for success and failure, for good and for bad, for the student. It is imperative that those involved in the professional preparation of future sport managers be alert to potential situations that might misuse and abuse interns. In the final analysis, the following question needs to be answered. Does the internship experience provide meaningful learning experiences for the intern, opportunities for the student to demonstrate one's competencies and range of skills to others, and aid the individual in the search for an appropriate full time position? (Stier, 2001a).

In other words, are the assignments given by the organization to the intern made because they are helpful to and are in the best interest of the intern? Or, are the assignments made merely because the organization needs cheap work completed? It is indeed a thin line which colleges that prepare interns as well as organizations that accept interns must walk.

CHARACTERISTICS OF AN IDEAL INTERNSHIP

CONCEPT #41: An appropriate internship experience can benefit the intern the host site/organization and the college/university.

When the internship experience is such that the student intern is able to learn, to expand one's capabilities, as well as to contribute meaningfully to the host organization—the best of all worlds exists. The student intern benefits because of this opportunity to learn, to increase skills, to mature, and to demonstrate a high level of competency. The host site benefits because the organization is able to take advantage of a highly motivated intern who is able and willing to provide significant contributions to the organization—at a most reasonable cost. And, the college or university which has prepared the student for the internship benefits by developing and reinforcing its reputation as an institution with a quality sport management program. Every institution that offers such a curricular program desires for its graduates to be successful. Such success tends to breed success by attracting and retaining quality faculty and students to the program.

CONCEPT #42: The internship experience is deemed to be the quintessential culminating experience for sport management students.

In reality, the internship is important, very, very important. In fact, it is deemed to be the quintessential culminating learning experience for the sport management student (NASPE, 1987). It is probably not an exaggeration to say that no other single learning experience is as important or has more significant impact upon the student in terms of knowledge and mastery of subject matter as well as upon potential job placement than the final field experience or internship (Ebersole, 1996).

HOW TO GO ABOUT SECURING AN APPROPRIATE INTERNSHIP

CONCEPT #43: There are many factors that must be considered when evaluating a potential internship site.

What should an appropriate internship experience consist of? First, it should be a place where the intern is able to further enhance one's knowledge base. The student should be able to learn on the job. The ability to refine and further develop competencies and master skills is critical to the success of the intern, both at the internship site and later when employed by a sport organization.

Second, the student should have appropriate support as well as critical feedback and guidance from the staff at the internship site as well as the college or university faculty. Third, it is also essential for the intern to have opportunities to visibly demonstrate, in the real world of the internship site, one's dedication and commitment, one's knowledge, one's abilities and aptitudes, and one's competencies in getting jobs and tasks completed in an effective, efficient, and acceptable fashion. Being judged by others to have performed in an exemplary fashion as an intern by the on-site and college based staff is critical. This is because exceptional performance as an intern generally generates most positive recommendations from one's supervisors, recommendations that are absolutely critical in successfully entering the job market.

> **CONCEPT #44:** *Would-be interns should select a site which is similar to the type of organization where they would like to secure full time employment.*

Naturally, the internship should be in, or closely related to, the area or segment of the sport management profession in which the student wishes to gain employment. To do otherwise is simply a waste of one's time if not actually counter-productive. It would indeed be foolish for a student to complete an internship at a locally owned health club or a race track if that same individual wished to secure full time employment within a professional football organization in the area of marketing.

It is absolutely essential that the student secure the very best internship opportunity possible. Good internship sites don't just happen. They don't normally fall into the lap of the student. It takes great effort, dedication, old fashioned work, some networking and a little bit of luck on behalf of the student to be able to successfully nail down a meaningful internship site.

One word of warning to those students contemplating accepting any offer for an internship. Would-be interns need to take time to carefully evaluate every facet of the potential internship experience. Don't make the mistake of falling in love with the potential site or organization because of its name, its size or the caliber or reputation of the organization. Carefully scrutinize every aspect of the would-be site, looking at the people who are involved, the type of tasks one would be involved in, the range of responsibilities one would be given, the opportunities for further professional growth, and, finally, the full time job prospects there and elsewhere following the successful conclusion of the internship.

Only when these assessments have been completed should the prospective intern make a decision.

Students should begin to look at potential internship sites as early as their sophomore and certainly by the beginning of the junior year. This involves examining different aspects of the sport management profession, assessing the advantages and disadvantages of taking various types of jobs and possibly making a career in a specific segment of the business of sport.

The Search of the Available Literature for Information on Sport and Sport Related Organizations

Once a student has decided in what segment or area of sport the individual would possibly like to work in it is necessary to initiate some research into specific groups, individuals, organizations and associations. Such publications as *Sports Market Place* (Gottlieb, 2006) and *The Sports Business Directory* (Attanqsio, 2002) are just two examples of directories which provide a great deal of information about a wide range of sport organizations, including the names of individuals holding specific jobs within each organization.

If one is to begin an internship in the fall semester, letters of inquiry should be sent out some 12 months earlier. To whom should the letter be sent? It is best to have a name to address the letter. To secure the name try calling the organization and request the name of the individual who is in charge of interns. There may be more than one depending upon the skill specialty of the intern. Or, one person may handle all intern requests.

CONCEPT #45: *One must be assertive, professionally assertive, if one is to be successful in the world of sport and sport management.*

Don't be put off by being informed that there is no person with responsibility for interns. Try and find the name of the person who has responsibility for the general area in which you wish to intern. For example, if you are interested in marketing, then obtain the name of the marketing director. Also, don't be discouraged if you are told that the organization or company has never taken interns. Secure the name of the person(s) you want to write to and attempt to create your own internship. Just because an organization has never had an intern doesn't mean that you cannot be the first intern. Don't be bashful, be assertive, but be professionally assertive.

The Introductory Letter Seeking an Internship

The introductory inquiry letter (one page) should include pertinent information about the student and why the student seeks an internship with this particular organization. If you know that a paid internship is not available, indicate that you are seeking an unpaid internship. Come right out and indicate you are not seeking a paid internship. To do otherwise might cause some recipients to think you are looking for a paying position and may dismiss your letter out of hand.

CONCEPT #46: *Résumés should be personalized, informative, and be no more than two pages in length.*

Along with the letter provide an updated, personalized, one-page, résumé. Usually, résumés should be one page in length. However, in unusual instances, the résumé may be two pages. This occurs when the individual's experience warrants more than one page. Don't leave off important and informative data just because the résumé would be two pages.

However, be careful lest you merely pad your résumé with unnecessary information. Personalize the résumé, so that the recipient knows that you are definitely seeking a specific position in that specific organization. The letter accompanying the résumé may request general information about a possible internship opportunity. Or, it may request an official application for an advertised internship. Or, it may be a request for a personal interview.

The Use of the 3-D Résumé

In recent years the use of a 3-D résumé has become more common. The 3-D résumé includes one or more physical objects or devices such items as a video tape, a CD ROM, a film, an audio tape, copies of news releases and/or printed programs created by the candidate, etc. These tangible objects can provide great insight into the candidate's experiences, skills and potential professional growth. Just as an artist might show paintings or a singer might provide an audiotape to reveal one's skills, so too might a sport management candidate submit three-dimensional objects as part of the résumé package.

Subsequent Follow-Up Phone Calls

Following personal letters of inquiry the future intern should follow-up with personal phone calls to determine whether one's application has been received and whether any other information might be needed. Also, a request for an interview might be made.

Again, if you desire an interview, indicate that you are willing (if you are) to cover all travel expenses associated with the interview.

Maintaining Contact with the Potential Internship Sites

After the student has initially contacted those organizations where one might want to intern it is important to remain in contact with the various organizations' intern coordinators or some other appropriate individuals. It is important that one or more people at the potential site be aware of and periodically reminded of your sincere interest. However, don't be a pest, be professionally assertive. Personal letters and phone calls can be most effective, both from the would-be intern as well as from professors and other people of influence.

Expenses Involved in Seeking the Internship and During the Internship

In today's marketplace, if there are travel expenses involved in traveling to the organization for an internship interview, the costs are almost always paid by the candidate. There are just too many applicants willing to pay such costs for organizations to have to foot the bill.

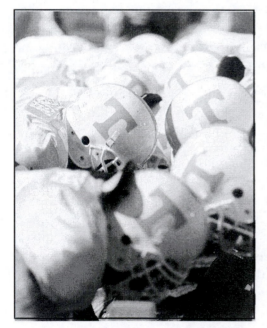

Teamwork and Cooperation—Two Essential Elements for a Successful Athletic Program
[courtesy of University of Tennessee, Sports Information Office]

If the candidate is some distance from the location of the internship site, provide information that transportation and housing would not be a problem. For example, indicate that you have funds for renting an apartment or a room close to the site if selected as an intern. Or, if you have a relative living in the area and you could live there while serving as an intern, mention this fact. Or, if you are attending a college or university a great distance from the organization where you desire to intern but your family lives near the internship site, share this fact.

The reason is simple. Many organizations don't want to be hassled with any potential problems involving living accommodations of their interns. In reality, there are just too many colleges and universities in close proximity to ideal internship sites. These organizations, without too much work, can accept quality interns who can live at home and commute to the intern site. As a result, make it easy for the organization to accept you without having to jump through hoops. Most of them just won't do it because of the multitude of quality internship candidates seeking sites.

Visiting the Potential Internship Site Prior to Accepting the Position

If at all possible, and you have the necessary finances and time available, attempt to visit the internship site prior to accepting the position, if it is offered. Plan on visiting with those individuals with whom you will be working. Such personal contact is often very revealing and can also help you get a jump start on your activities once you do report read for duty—with "bells on."

NETWORKING—DROPPING NAMES OF HEAVY HITTERS OR CENTERS OF INFLUENCE

Don't hesitate to network. Networking involves keeping in touch with individuals and keeping them abreast of where you are at, what you are doing and what your goals are for the future. The more important these individuals are, the more influential they are—the better. That is why the terms "Heavy Hitters" and "Centers of Influence" are used to denote those individuals who are viewed with respect and admiration by others within the community.

> **CONCEPT #47: *Networking is an important key in securing internships as well as full-time employment.***

These are the individuals who have influence over others and are able to get things done due to their contacts, prestige, reputation, image, position and/or charisma. Timely and effective communication is at the heart of networking. People need to have your name in the back (or front) of their brain. They need to know what you are all about and what you have done and what you are currently engaged in. They need to have developed a positive, a favorable, image of you, your abilities, your competencies.

Network with your professors. Network with your former and current employers. Network with people you know (and who know you) in and out of the sport's world. If you (or your parents, relatives, friends or their acquaintances) know of individuals within sport organizations, use them to open doors for you. Drop their names (with their permission, naturally) in your initial communications with the potential internship sites. Ask your contacts to communicate, on your behalf, directly with their friends or acquaintances within the sport organization.

Networking is vital in finding out about potential internship sites as well as in securing an internship. Networking is also indispensable in securing full time employment. Now is not the time to be timid, to be bashful or fainthearted. Be bold, be assertive, but professionally so.

Identifying One's Network of Contacts, Colleagues and Associates

To assist you in identifying your current networking contacts please refer to table 2.1 (Stier, 1995). In the left column, under the category "People I Know In Sports," place the names of those individuals you personally know who are either involved in some fashion with the world of sport or who have contacts with sports people or sport organizations, even though they themselves might not be associated with the sport world.

In the middle column, under the heading "People in Sports Who Know Me or Know of Me" place the names of individuals associated with the sports arena (or who know people who are) and who readily know you, know something about you, your competencies and your activities. Under the right column, "People in Sports Who Would Give Me a Professional Recommendation," write the names of individuals in sport (or who have contacts with people in sport) who would feel conformable in providing you with a positive professional recommendation.

TABLE 2.1: *Identification of One's Networking Contacts in Sports*

People I Know In the Sports Profession	People in Sports Who Know Me or Know of Me	People in Sports Who Would Give Me a Professional Recommendation
1.	1.	1.
2.	2.	2.
3.	3.	3.
4.	4.	4.
5.	5.	5.
6.	6.	6.
7.	7.	7.
8.	8.	8.
9.	9.	9.
10.	10.	10.
11.	11.	11.
12.	12.	12.
13.	13.	13.
14.	14.	14.
15.	15.	15.

Naturally, you will have the largest number of names in the left column and the least number of names in the right column. The objective is to begin now, as a student, to fill up all three columns so that you begin to have a significant network of contacts that you know, that acknowledge knowing you, and who feel comfortable in providing both written and verbal recommendations on your behalf.

Increasing One's Contacts, Expanding One's Network

You need to make sure other people are aware of you, your qualities and your potential. There are many ways to accomplish this. One is to become professionally involved in a variety of volunteer activities, even as a student. Another is to attend workshops and clinics and interact with other professionals in the field. Don't hesitate to introduce yourself to others. Yet a third is to actively seek out current professionals and communicate with them.

And, if you work your way through college, take jobs that are related to your future career activities. Secure part-time positions in the sports field or in a sports related business. While a job at Arby's or McDonald's is acceptable, a job working for a specific sport organization will carry more weight in terms of being applicable to one's career aspirations.

CONCEPT #48: It is never too early or too late to begin to network.

It is never too early (or too late) to start developing one's contacts, one's network of professional associates and colleagues. Now is the time to begin to deliberately and consistently work on expanding one's network of contacts. Networking is essential not only for one's internship search but also for all subsequent job searches. As the saying goes, "today is the first day of the rest of your life."

CURRENT CURRICULAR STANDARDS FOR SPORT MANAGEMENT PROGRAMS

In the last decade, there has been a growing concern among some quarters of the profession about the lack of consistency and the quality existing within the sport management curricular offerings among the large number (200±) of colleges and universities in the United States offering sport management as a field of study. There is a need for accountability in every profession (Arbogast and Griffin, 1989). As a consequence, there have been several attempts to provide guidance in curricular matters for those colleges and universities preparing future professionals in fitness and sport management positions.

The North American Society of Sport Management (NASSM) has established two sets of curricular standards, one for undergraduate and one for graduate programs in sport management (Schneider & Stier, 2000). These standards (one for undergraduate level and another for graduate level) have been established to serve as a guide for the establishment of curricular programs at the undergraduate and the graduate levels (Stier & Schneider, 2000).

Accreditation Activities within the World of Higher Education

Accreditation is nothing new for colleges and universities in this country. In fact, as early as 1913 the North Central Association of Colleges and Secondary Schools initiated the general process of accrediting colleges and universities. This effort was made possible by the institutions voluntarily joining together to meet agreed upon standards and criteria in an effort "to demonstrate that institutional quality was commensurate with the standards for membership" within that association (Uhlir, 1990, p. 6).

Specialized accreditation for specific curricular offerings or programs had existed even prior to that point in time. For example, there were very specific standards identified and utilized by the American Medical Association in approving and accrediting specific medical educational institutions and their graduates or practitioners (Uhlir, 1990).

CONCEPT #49: *There has been concern in early years about the lack of consistency in sport management professional preparation programs.*

In the area of fitness and wellness, the document Standards for Programs Preparing Undergraduates for Careers in Fitness, was published in 1988 by the National Association for Sport and Physical Education (NASPE, 1988). This publication sought to specify the standards that colleges and universities should operate by in the preparation of professionals for jobs and careers in the fitness arena.

Two years earlier, 1986, a sport management task force was created by the National Association for Sport and Physical Education (NASPE) for the purpose of developing curricular guidelines for both undergraduate and graduate sport management programs. The guidelines were promulgated in written form the following year in the document Guidelines for Undergraduate and Graduate Programs in Sport Management: Membership Report (NASPE, 1987, February). And, in 1989 this task force evolved into a joint committee made up of NASPE members and individuals representing the North American Society for Sport Management (NASSM). Over the next four years input was solicited from professionals throughout the nation actively involved in the field of sport management via surveys and meetings held at national conferences.

EARLY EFFORTS AT APPROVAL OF PROFESSIONAL PREPARATION PROGRAMS IN SPORT MANAGEMENT

Four years later, in May of 1993, a milestone was reached when the National Association for Sport and Physical Education (NASPE) and the North American Society for sport management (NASSM) cooperatively published the approved standards and protocol for the approval of both undergraduate and graduate sport management curricula. This 41-page publication included information (standards) needed for institutions to prepare for sport management program review at the undergraduate, master's and doctoral levels.

CONCEPT #50: *Approval efforts of sport management professional preparation programs is a rather recent phenomenon.*

The publication also provided a general overview of the approval review and the timelines for the program review. It also established a comprehensive list of minimum competency areas for the baccalaureate level, for the master's level and for the doctoral level. The competency areas for the undergraduate sport management professional preparation programs included: (NASPE/NASSM, 1993, May, pp. 3-6).

1. Behavioral dimensions in sport
2. Management and organizational skills in sport
3. Ethics in sport management
4. Marketing in sport
5. Communication in sport
6. Finance in sport
7. Economics in sport
8. Legal aspects of sport
9. Governance in sport
10. Field experience in sport management

CONCEPT #51: *The creation of approval procedures and criteria indicates strengthening of the sport management profession.*

Two years later seven institutions in this country had received approval for their sport management programs. In the spring of 1995 the National Association of Sport and Physical Education (NASPE) announced the names of these seven programs which had been approved by the sport management program review council (SMPRC) (The Freshman Class, 1995). At that point there was one institution at the doctoral level, three at the master's levels and three at the undergraduate level. Only Temple University (Philadelphia) had received approval at all three levels (subsequently, Temple University ceased offering its doctoral degree in sport management). Georgia Southern University received approval at the undergraduate and the master's levels. Other programs that received early approval included the University of Louisville's master' program and the undergraduate program at the University of New Haven (Stier, 2000, March 24).

THERE IS A SIGNIFICANT DISTINCTION BETWEEN AN APPROVAL PROCESS AND THE ACCREDITATION OF CURRICULA AND PROGRAMS N HIGHER EDUCATION

However, the evaluation process of NASSM is not an actual *accreditation* per se of a curricular offering or program but, rather, is a so-called *approval* process. That is, NASSM would give its approval of those colleges' and universities' sport management professional preparation programs that met NASSM's standards and criteria. However, NASSM itself did not meet the standards/criteria which would authorize it to grant what is commonly referred to in education circles as actual *accreditation*. Thus, for a time, NASSM is left with the far less impressive and significant *approval* process.

In recent years there has been an increase in the number of schools seeking and obtaining NASSM approval. To illustrate the increase in the number of programs approved by NASSM, the NASSM web site [http://www.nassm.com/] was accessed on November 7, 2006 and it revealed 40 colleges and universities in the United States with approval status at the undergraduate level. This is out of a total of 169 schools that NASSM had identified as having undergraduate sport management program (23.6%). At the master's degree level, the web site showed that of the 120 schools offering such programs, 28 (23.3%) have successfully obtained approval. And, at the doctoral level, there were a total of 19 such programs, and 5 (26.3%) have obtained approval status.

> **CONCEPT #52:** *There is a major difference between a so-called approval process and an actual accreditation process of a higher education curriculum or program.*

During the early years of the NASSM approval process the vast majority of the institutions offering sport management curricula simply did not see an advantage or a real need to seek the so-called approval process. This decision really hinged upon three factors. First, there were so many students seeking to enroll in college level sport management programs that schools did not need to possess (and advertise) an approved curriculum by NASSM.

Second, many schools had had a sound and well respected (and successful) sport management curriculum for years and had earned a well-deserved reputation of quality. These institutions and programs did not feel a need to be approved by an organization such as NASSM since they were able to attract superior students in great numbers on the basis of their reputation in the field. Third, campuses did not eagerly accept NASSM's so-called approval process as being important or, on some campuses, even meaningful, because this process of assessing and evaluating sport management programs and curricula was not an actual *accreditation* process but was merely an *approval* process.

In higher education there is a world of difference between an approval process and an official accreditation process. In point of fact, the *approval* process by NASSM was a poor second on college campuses which were more accustomed to having superior programs *accredited* by national or regional organizations or entities which, in turn, were accredited (given the power and authority to grant sport management accreditation) by a national accrediting organization.

NASSM AND THE POSSIBLE MOVE TO AN ACCREDITATION PROCESS

Discussion has continued into the 21st century relative to the merits of discontinuing the NASSM approval process and replacing it with an actual accreditation process. In 2006, NASSM officials begin to look more seriously at the possibility of NASSM becoming an accredited entity authorized to grant **accreditation** to sport management curricula and programs within higher education (Personal communication, Christine Bolger, November 6, 2006).

In the fall of 2006, the approval process was put on hold. Subsequently, NASSM and NASPE, in cooperation with the International Assembly Collegiate Business Education (IACBE), "have agreed to establish an accreditation process that will be submitted for Council on Higher Education Association (CHEA) recognition" (Commission, 2007, p. 17). The process will launch fall of 2007.

PROFESSIONAL ORGANIZATIONS DEALING WITH ASPECTS OF SPORT MANAGEMENT

CONCEPT #53: There are several professional organizations in different parts of the world that deal with sport management.

Since the start of the sport management profession there have been numerous organizations that have either been established or which have adopted sport management as an important element of their existence. In addition to the North American Society of Sport Management (NASSM) previously mentioned, there is the European organization called the European Association for Sport Management (EASM) [http://www.easm.net/]. In Australia and New Zealand, sport management professionals organized the Sport Management Association of Australia and New Zealand (SMAANZ) [http://www.griffith. edu.au/school/gbs/tlhs/smaanz/ home.html].

And, there is still another professional organization, established in 1991, that deals with recreation management in Australia and New Zealand, it is called the Australia and New Zealand Association for leisure Studies (ANZALS) [http://www.staff.vu.edu. au/anzals/]. And, a more recent professional organization came onto the scene in 2005. It is the *Sport Marketing Association (SMA)* and deals (as the name implies) with the whole area of marketing, promotions, fundraising, publicity and public relations. This entity held its first national convention in 2003 and continues to hold an annual convention for its membership (Personal Communication, Dallas Branch, November 6, 2006).

PROFESSIONAL JOURNALS DEALING WITH ASPECTS OF SPORT MANAGEMENT

One measure of the importance and impact that the management of sport holds in our society can be determined by the number and type of professional and trade publications which deal with various aspects of the management of sport, fitness/wellness and leisure/recreation arenas. In this respect, the growth of sport management as a distinct body of knowledge took a giant step when in January of 1987 *The Journal of Sport Management* became a reality (Stier, 1990b).

> **CONCEPT #54:** *The first scholarly blind-review journal for the sport management field was the* **Journal of Sport Management (JSM).**

The Sport Management Association of Australia and New Zealand (SMAANZ) publishes the peer-review journal *Sport Management Review*. The Australia and New Zealand Association for Leisure Studies (ANZALS) started publishing the Annals of Leisure Research in 1998 as a fully refereed journal, published quarterly.

In January of 2000, the *International Journal of Sport Management* (IJSM) began publishing scholarly (blind review) articles in the area of sport management, athletic administration and recreation management—on an international as well as a national level. This journal, published quarately by American Press (Boston, MA) was the first international, scholarly, refereed journal, dedicated to the exclusive study of sport administration or management by including within the contents *only scholarly articles* (no so-called public-cation fillers, such as book reviews, advertisements, etc.). In 2006, it expanded the number of pages in each issue by 50% to make it the largest scholarly (international) journal devoted exclusively to publishing scholarly articles in the area of sport management.

The European Association for Sport Management (EASM) has a scholarly, peer-reviewed journal that it publishes and it is called the *European Sport Management Quarterly*. And, the *Sport Marketing Association (SMA)* became associated with the *Sport Marketing Quarterly* which has been the organization's official journal since 2003.

A national professional organization in the United States that deals exclusively with marketing in the world of sports at the collegiate/university level is the National Association of Collegiate Marketing Administrators (NACMA). This organization began in 1990 and by late 2006 had over 900 members (Personal Communication, Dan DeVos, November 17, 2006). This organization also publishes a professional journal, *Athletics Administration,* and hosts an annual convention for its members (www.nacma.com).

In late 2006 NASSM and NASPE announced a new blind-review journal to be published under the auspices of both organizations. The journal, *Sport Management Education Journal* (SMEJ), was scheduled to have its inaugural issue published in the spring of 2007.

There have been and continue to be other journals and periodicals that address specific issues associated with the management and organization of sport. However, many of these publications are either not exclusively devoted to sport management [the contents include advertisements, book reviews, and other non-scholarly contents) or they are not refereed (Stier & Stier, 1992). A refereed publication is one that utilizes a blind review as part of the evaluation/selection process of the articles that appear within the publication. That is, each manuscript submitted for publication is reviewed/evaluated by a number of experts in the field who do not know of the identity(ies) of the writer(s) of the manuscript and the authors of the manuscripts do not know who the reviewers are as well.

CONCEPT #55: *There are numerous scholarly, blind-reviewed journals that deal, at least in some respect, with the management and organization of sport.*

Examples of publications that are refereed and which periodically carry articles devoted to some aspects of sport management include, but are not limited to, the following:

1. *Academic Athletic Journal*
2. *Academy of Management Journal*
3. *Academy of Management Review*
4. *Aethlon: The Journal of Sport Literature*

5. *Annual of Applied Research in Coaching and Athletics*
6. *Annals of Tourism Research*
7. *Applied recreation research annual: practical ideas and concepts*
8. *Applied Research in Coaching and Athletics Annual*
9. *Athletic business*
10. *Athletic management*
11. *CAHPER Journal, Canadian Association for Health, Physical Education and Recreation*
12. *Case Studies in Sport Management,*
13. *Contemporary Athletics*
14. *Enterprise Risk Management (for Sport Professionals)*
15. *Entertainment and Sports Lawyer*
16. *European Journal of Sport Management*
17. *European Sport Management Quarterly (ESMQ)*
18. *Florida Entertainment, Art & Sport Law Journal*
19. *Hospitality & Tourism Management*
20. *International Journal of Coaching Science*
21. *International Journal of Motorsport Management (IJMM)*
22. *International journal of Physical Education*
23. *International Journal of Revenue Management (IJRM)*
24. *International Journal of Sport Communication (IJSC).*
25. *International Journal of Sport Finance (IJSF)*
26. *International Journal of Sport Management*
27. *International Journal of Sport Management, Recreation & Tourism (ijsmart)*
28. *International Journal of Sport Marketing & Sponsorship*
29. *International Journal of Sport Psychology*
30. *International Journal of Sports Science & Coaching*
31. *International Review for the Sociology of Sport*
32. *International Sports Journal*
33. *International Journal of Sports Marketing and Sponsorship (IJSMS)*
34. *International Sports Studies Journal*
35. *Interscholastic Athletic Administration*
36. *Journal for the Study of Sports & Athletes in Education*
37. *Journal of American Fitness Association*
38. *Journal of Applied Sport Management*
39. *Journal of Applied Sports Science Research*
40. *Journal of Business Research*
41. *Journal of Case Studies*
42. *Journal of Coaching Education JCE*
43. *Journal of Consumer Research*
44. *Journal of Contemporary Athletics*

45. *Journal of facility planning and design*
46. *Journal of International Business Studies*
47. *Journal of Issues in Intercollegiate Athletics (JIIA)*
48. *Journal of Leisure Research*
49. *Journal of Management*
50. *Journal of Management and Organization*
51. *Journal of Management Studies*
52. *Journal of Marketing*
53. *Journal of Marketing Research*
54. *Journal of the National Intramural Recreation Sports Association (NIRSA)*
55. *Journal of Park and Recreation Administration (JPRA)*
56. *Journal of Philosophy of Sport*
57. *Journal of Physical Education, Recreation and Dance (JOPERD)*
58. *Journal of Physical Education and Sport Management (JPESM)*
59. *Journal of Research—ICHPER-SD (International Council for Health, Physical Education, Recreation, Sports and Dance)*
60. *Journal of Revenue & Pricing Management*
61. *Journal of Quantitative Analysis in Sports (JQAS)*
62. *Journal of Sponsorship*
63. *Journal of Sport Administration & Supervision (JSAS)*
64. *Journal of Sport and Tourism (JS&T)*
65. *Journal of Sport and Social Issues*
66. *Journal of Sport Behavior*
67. *Journal of Sport and Exercise Psychology*
68. *Journal of Sport and Social Issues*
69. *Journal of Sport Behavior*
70. *Journal of Sport Business*
71. *Journal of Sport History*
72. *Journal of Sport Management (JSM)*
73. *Journal of Sport Sciences*
74. *Journal of Sport and Social Issues*
75. *Journal of Sport Tourism*
76. *Journal of Sports Economics*
77. *Journal of Sports Marketing & Sponsorship*
78. *Journal of Sports Media,*
79. *Journal of Sports Psychology*
80. *Journal of Sport Tourism*
81. *Journal of Teaching in Physical Education*
82. *Journal of the International Council for Health, Physical Education, Recreation, Sports and Dance (ICHPER-SD)*
83. *Journal of the Legal Aspects of Sport*

84. *Journal of the Quantitative Analysis of Sports*
85. *Journal of Tourism Marketing*
86. *Journal of Venue and Event Management*
87. *Kinesiology Review*
88. *Legal Issues in College Athletics*
89. *Leisure Science*
90. *Leisure Studies*
91. *Management Decision*
92. *Management Science*
93. *Mid-Atlantic Journal of Business*
94. *Marquette Sports Law Review*
95. *Moving Mountains: Journal of Sport for Development and Peace*
96. *Organizational Behavior and Human Decision Process*
97. *Palaestra: The Forum of Sport, Physical Education & Recreation for the Disabled*
98. *Parks and Recreation*
99. *Physical Education Review*
100. *Play and Culture*
101. *Quest*
102. *Recreational Sports Journal*
103. *Performance Measurement and Leisure Management),*
104. *Research in Organizational Behaviror*
105. *Research Quarterly for Exercise and Sport*
106. *Schole, A Journal of Leisure Studies & Recreation Education*
107. *Seton Hall Journal of Sport Law*
108. *Sloan Management Review*
109. *Sociology of Sport Journal*
110. *Sport Business Journal*
111. *Sport Business and Management (SBM)*
112. *Sport in Society: Cultures, Commerce, Media, Politics (sportsoc)*
113. *Sport Management Education Journal (SMEJ)*
114. *Sport Management and Related Topics (Smart)*
115. *Sport Management Education Journal (SMEJ)*
116. *Sport Management International Journal "Choregia"*
117. *Sport Management Review*
118. *Sociology of Sport Journal*
119. *Sport Marketing Quarterly*
120. *The Sport Psychologist*
121. *Sport Science Review*
122. *Strategic Management Journal*
123. *Strategies*
124. *The Journal of Sports Law & Contemporary Problems*

125. *The Journal of the Legal Aspects of Sport*
126. *The Physical Educator*
127. *The Applied Research in Coaching and Athletics Annual (ARCAA)*
128. *The Journal for the Study of Sports and Athletes in Education*
129. *The Journal of Sport*
130. *The Journal of Sports Law & Contemporary Problems*
131. *The Journal of the Legal Aspects of Sport*
132. *The Sports Law Forum at Fordham University School of Law*
133. *The Sports Lawyers Journal*
134. *The Texas Review of Entertainment & Sports Law*
135. *The Villanova Sports and Entertainment Law Journal*
136. *Tourism Management*
137. *Tourism Recreation Research*
138. *University of Miami Entertainment & Sports Law Journal*
139. *Virginia Sports and Entertainment Law Journal*
140. *Women in Sport and Physical Activity Journal (WSPAJ),*
141. *Omen's Sports And Fitness*
142. *Sport Management Review*
143. *Sociology of Sport Journal*
144. *Sport Marketing Quarterly*
145. *The Sport Psychologist*
146. *Sport Science Review*
147. *Strategic Management Journal*
148. *Strategies*
149. *The International Journal of Sport Communication (IJSC)*
150. *The Journal of Sports Law & Contemporary Problems*
151. *The Journal of Intercollegiate Sport (JIS)*
152. *The Journal of the Legal Aspects of Sport*
153. *The Physical Educator*
154. *The Journal of Sport*
155. *The Journal of Sports Law & Contemporary Problems*
156. *The Journal of the Legal Aspects of Sport*
157. *The Sports Law Forum at Fordham University School of Law*
158. *The Sports Lawyers Journal*
159. *The Texas Review of Entertainment & Sports Law*
160. *The Villanova Sports and Entertainment Law Journal*
161. *Tourism Management*
162. *Tourism Recreation Research*
163. *University off Miami Entertainment & Sports Law Journal*
164. *Virginia Sports and Entertain*
165. *Woman in sport and Physical Activity Journal (WSP AJ)*

> **CONCEPT #56:** *There are also numerous professional journals that deal, at least in some respect, with the management and organization of sport.*

A partial list of non-refereed magazines and publications that either are exclusively devoted to administrative and managerial areas of sport or that periodically carry such articles include:

1. *American Fitness*
2. *American School & University—Facilities, Purchasing and Business Administration*
3. *Athletic Administration*
4. *Athletic Business*
5. *Athletic Management*
6. *The Chronicle of Higher Education*
7. *Club Industry*
8. *Corporate Fitness and Recreation*
9. *CoSida Digest*
10. *Educational Resources Information Center (ERIC)*
11. *Fitness Management*
12. *Health Values: Achieving High Level Wellness*
13. *Interscholastic Athletic Administration*
14. *JUCO Review*
15. *Lawn & Landscape*
16. *NCAA News*
17. *Runners World*
18. *Scholastic Coach*
19. *Sport Marketing Letter*
20. *Street & Smith's Sport Business Journal*
21. *Texas Coach*
22. *Team Marketing Report*

In addition, there have been the introduction of BLOGS that sport management students and professionals might find interesting as well as informative. Some examples of sport management and sport marketing BLOGS include:

1. Business of Sport Management Blog:

   http://businessofsportmanagement.blogspot.com/

2. The Sport Business Education Network to join smnstaff@yahoo.com
   to view blog:

   http://blog.myspace.com/index.cfm?fuseaction=blog.ListAll&friendID=30757100&
   MyToken=7d11d9ed-6f9d-4f74-8d64-aa156afc7959ML

3. Sport Marketing Special Interest Group Blog:
   http://sportmarketingsig.blogspot.com/

4. Sport Management List-Serv
   SPORTMGT@LISTSERV.UNB.CA to submit
   SPORTMGT@UNb.CA to subscribe

CONCEPT #57: *Sport managers must remain at the cutting edge of their profession by being well-read and up-to-date in their field(s) of specialization.*

The number of professional journals and trade publications, as well as web sites, that devote at least some of their pages to some area of sport management speaks well to the growing professionalism of the discipline. It reveals that increased emphasis is being placed upon the study and evaluation of the numerous areas or components that go to make up the field commonly referred to sport management. It also indicates that there is a significant need on behalf of practitioners as well as scholars to read such journals, thus remaining current in the field.

CONCLUSIONS

There are a multitude of job opportunities for the would-be sport manager. To be competitive in the sport job market today and in the future it is necessary for one to possess formal training and education including meaningful field experiences. The internship experience is a critical part of the formal education of any future sport manager. Many of the strategies and tactics that are utilized to secure meaningful internships can also be used in the pursuit of paid positions upon graduation.

REFERENCES

Arbogast, G.W. and Griffin, L. (1989). Accountability—Is it within reach of our profession? *Journal of Physical Education, Recreation and Dance, 60*(6), 72-75.

Attanqsio, J.A. Editor. (2002). *The sports business directory.* Maryland: Bethesda, Maryland: E. J. Krause & Associates.

Bell, J. and Countiss, J. (1993). Professional service through sport management internships. *Journal of Physical Education, Recreation and Dance, 61*(1), 45-47, 52.

Brassie, P.S. (1989). A student buyer's guide to sport management programs. *Journal of Physical Education, Recreation and Dance, 60*(9), 25-28.

Brassie, P.S. (1989b). Guidelines for programs preparing undergraduate and graduate students for careers in sport management. *Journal of Sport Management, 3*(2), 158-164.

Campbell, K. and Kovar, S.K. (1994). Fitness/exercise science internships: How to ensure success. *Journal of Physical Education, Recreation and Dance, 65*(2), 69-72.

Commission on Sport Management Accreditation. (2007, Spring). NASPE News, p. 17.

Cunnen J. & Sidwell, M. (1993). Sport management interns—Selection qualifications. *Journal of Physical Education, Recreation and Dance, 64*(7), 91-95.

DeSensi, J., Kelley, D., Blanton, M., and Beitel, P. (1990). Sport management curricular evaluation and needs assessment: A multifaceted approach. *Journal of Sport Management, 4*(1), 31-58.

Ebersole, P. (October 7, 1996). What's a liberal arts degree worth? *Democrat & Chronicle*, Rochester, New York, pp. 1, 2.

The freshman class of approved sport management programs. (1995, Spring/Summer). *NASPE News*. Reston, VA: National Association for Sport and Physical Education, page 11.

Gleason, T. (1986, February). Sport administration degrees: Growing to fill a need/supply overwhelms demand. *Athletic Administration*, pp. 9-10.

Gottlieb, R. Editor. (2006). *Sports market place*. Greyhouse Publishing. Millerton, NY.

Lefton, T. (1999, May). Wanna buy a team? *Sport,* p. 26.

Markiewicz, D. A. (1991, July 30). More fans line up for careers in sports. *USA Today*, 7-B.

Marston, R. (1993). Developing professionalism at the undergraduate level. *Journal of Physical Education, Recreation and Dance, 64*(7), 36, 37, 40.

Murray, M. & Mann, B. (1993). Is our professionalism showing or slipping? *Journal of Physical Education, Recreation and Dance, 64*(7), 30, 31. 35.

NASPE. (1987, February). *Guidelines for undergraduate and graduate programs in sport management: Membership report*. National Association for Sport and physical Education (NASPE). Reston, VA: National Association for Sport and Physical Education.

NASPE. (1988). *Standards for programs preparing undergraduates for careers in fitness*. National Association for Sport and Physical Education (NASPE).

Reston, VA: National Association for Sport and Physical Education. NASPE/NASSM. (1993, May). *Sport management program standards and review protocol*. American Alliance for Health, physical Education, Recreation and Dance. Virginia: Reston.

Ross, C.M., Jamieson, L.M. & Young, S.J. (1997). *Professional preparation in sports management*. Bloomington, Indiana: Indiana University Press.

Ruder, K. (1993). Being professional now. *Journal of Physical Education, Recreation and Dance, 64*(7), 29, 35.

Schneider, R.C., & Stier, W.F., Jr. (2000). Sport management curricular standards 2000 study—graduate level. *International Journal of Sport Management, 1*(2), 137-149.

Schneider, R. C. and Stier, W. F., Jr. (2006) Sport management field experiences as experimental learning: Insuring beneficial outcomes and preventing exploitation. *The Sport Management and Related Topics Journal (SMART Journal), 2*(2), 36-43. *http://spectrum.troy.edu/~smart/fieldexperience.pdf*

Stier, W.F., Jr. (1990a, March 3). *Securing volunteers for sports programs.* Presentation made at the Escuela Nacional de Depotivos, México City.

Stier, W.F. Jr., (1990b) Wanted: Athletic Directors as Renaissance Leaders, (1990). *Athletic Director, 7*(3), pp. 8.

Stier, Jr., W.F. and Stier, M.M. (1992). Alternative considerations for the would-be writer. *Journal of Physical Education, Recreation and Dance, 63*(9), 68-72.

Stier, W.F., Jr. (1993, August). Alternative career paths in physical education: Sport management. Washington, D.C.: *ERIC Digest*—Clearinghouse on Teaching and Teacher Education.

Stier, W.F. Jr., (1994). *Successful sport fund-raising.* Dubuque, Iowa: Wm. C. Brown & Benchmark Publisher.

Stier, W.F., Jr. (1995). *Successful coaching—Strategies and tactics.* Boston, MA.: American Press.

Stier, W.F., Jr. (1996a). *Sport management internship handbook—State University of New York. Brockport*, New York: SUNY Brockport Press.

Stier, W.F., Jr. (1996b, April 16). *Becoming marketable within the HPERD and A profession.* Paper presented at the National Conference of the American Alliance for Health, Physical Education, Recreation and Dance (AAHPERD), Atlanta, Georgia.

Stier, W.F., Jr. & Schneider, R. C. (2000). Sport management curricular standards 2000 study—Undergraduate level. International Journal of Sport Management, 1(1), 56-69.

Stier, W.F., Jr. (2000, March 24). Perceptions of sport management standards: views from professionals and academicians—Undergraduate standards. Presentation made at the National Conference of the American Alliance for Health, Physical Education, Recreation and Dance, Orlando, Florida.

Stier, W.F., Jr. (2000a, August 26). The past, present and future of sport management. Presentation made at the 2000 International Sport Management Congress: "Current Situations and New Directions for Sport Management: From the Perspectives of Cultural Differences," Seoul, Korea.

Stier, W.F., Jr. (2001a, spring). Sport management internships—A double-edged sword. *The Clipboard, 2*(3), 5.

Stier, W.F., Jr. (2001b). The current status of sport management and athletic (sport) administration programs in the 21ˢᵗ century. *International Journal of Sport Management, 2*(1), 66-79.

Stier, W.F., Jr. (2002). Sport management internships—From theory to practice. *Strategies, 15*(4), 7-9.

Sutton, W.A. (1989). The role of internships in sport management curricula A model for development. *Journal of Physical Education, Recreation and Dance, 60*(7), 20-24.

Top 10 Fitness Programs. (1999). *Club Industry, 15,*(12), 12.

Uhlir, G.A. (1990). Professionalism—The role of the college and university. *Journal of Physical Education, Recreation and Dance, 61*(8), 6.

Unpaid interns: Cheap, effective and often illegal. (1996, August 26). *The Dominion Post,* p. 4-D.

Verner, E. (1993). Developing professionalism through experiential learning. *Journal of Physical Education, Recreation and Dance, 64*(7), 41-44.

Widdon, S. (1990). Graduate dual preparation programs in business and sport management. *Journal of Physical Education, Recreation and Dance, 61*(3), 96-98.

DISCUSSION TOPICS

1. Describe the various types of jobs and career opportunities available under the sport management umbrella.

2. Outline the essential elements of sound undergraduate professional preparation sport management programs.

3. Speculate as to how you might prepare yourself for a suitable internship experience.

4. Cite the three possible outcomes of sport management internships and how you might go about insuring that your internship experience is a successful one.

5. What are the characteristics of an ideal internship?

6. Illustrate (and provide examples) how networking can be an effective technique for both securing an internship and actual employment.

7. Outline the current efforts in approval and accreditation of sport management professional preparation programs in the United States.

8. Review various professional journals and cite five such publications that hold particular interest for you (and why) in terms of your current career plans in the area of sport management.

9. What is the name and web site for the sport management List Serv? And what are the purposes of this List Serve?

10. Explore the World Wide Web (WWW) and cite the links to at least three sites that have content related to some aspect of sport management.

Chapter

3 Theories and Philosophies Associated with Sport Management

Even the Very Young Love Sports
[courtesy of Clemson University Sports Information, Bob Waldrop, photographer]

CHAPTER HIGHLIGHTS

This chapter will help the reader to:

- Understand the value of possessing an adequate philosophy of management, a philosophy of life and a philosophy of a profession;
- Understand how one's philosophy is a reflection of one's experiences, beliefs, values and attitudes;
- Articulate your current philosophy of life;
- List various administrative styles and explain the potential benefits and deficiencies of each;
- Be willing to take reasonable risks in the conduct of one's professional endeavors (opportunities and challenges);
- Explain the Machiavellian Style of Management;
- Describe democratic management in light of other types of management;

67

- Express your ethical beliefs in light of your professional responsibilities;
- Differentiate between various views of management thought and management theories;
- Outline the essential elements of the scientific method of investigation and how its origins emanated from Greek civilization;
- Outline the essential elements of Maslow's Heirarchy of Needs;
- Trace management thought from ancient times to the present;
- Define what a theory is and articulate various theories as they relate to management and leadership styles;
- Explain the essential elements of Total Quality Management (TQM) and how this concept or method can have implications for sport management.

DEVELOPING APPROPRIATE PHILOSOPHIES

> *CONCEPT #58:   Managers need to develop appropriate philosophies.*

Every professional in every field of endeavor or professional discipline needs to develop and refine one's philosophy or philosophies. "Each administrator has a philosophy, whether or not he or she realizes it" (Tillman, Voltmer, Esslinger, and McCue, 1996, p. 16).

> *CONCEPT 59:   A philosophy is a reflection of one's experiences, beliefs, values and attitudes.*

What exactly is a philosophy? Webster's New Collegiate Dictionary (1973, p. 861) indicates that a philosophy is "an analysis of the grounds of and concepts expressing fundamental beliefs" and "most general beliefs, concepts, and attitudes of an individual or group." Thus, an individual's philosophy may be thought of as how that person views any given situation. A philosophy is a reflection of a person's personality, beliefs, attitudes and values. And, most importantly, one's philosophy has a tremendous effect upon what decisions are made and actions taken by an individual.

A philosophy is a result of and can be impacted upon by one's formal and informal education, training, environment, skills, knowledge as well as by life's experiences. In short, a person's philosophy is affected "by the sum total of all that affects and touches the individual" (Stier, 1995, p. 40).

> **CONCEPT #60:**   *One's philosophies are not stagnant—they evolve in time as a result of experience, education and training.*

RESULT OF EXPERIENCES, EDUCATION AND TRAINING

A person's philosophy is not stagnant. Rather, it is flexible. It can change. It can change imperceptibly or significantly. It can shift in an abrupt fashion or it may change through an evolutionary process. This flexibility is necessary in order for an individual to be able to grow as a professional and to remain current, competent and up-to-date in this modern world, a world of full of change.

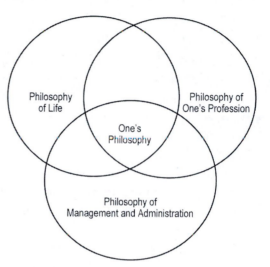

FIGURE 3.1: Multiple Philosophies

A Single Philosophy or Multiple Philosophies?

A sport manager needs to be concerned with more than a single philosophy. In reality, there are three distinct, but related, areas that form the foundation of a philosophical perspective for the modern-day sport manager. These three philosophical dimensions are: (1) *a philosophy of life itself,* (2) *a philosophy of one's profession,* and (3) *a philosophy of management or administration.*

> **CONCEPT # 61:**   *Administrators need to develop a philosophy of life, of one's profession as well as a philosophy of management.*

A Philosophy of Life

In the most simplistic view a philosophy of life is one's personal philosophy. One's philosophy of life may be thought of as how an individual views one's own life as well as the lives of others on this planet—within the society of humankind. A person's philosophy of life helps define who and what that individual is and reflects one's value system as a member of the greater society of all human beings.

A well thought out, sound philosophy of life helps one serve as a meaningful member of and contributor to society, as a citizen of the world. It deals with the purpose(s) of life, the value of life, and how one deals with and relates to others. In short, it serves as the foundation for how one lives during one's brief stay on this earth.

A Philosophy Relating to One's Profession

As a professional one needs to also develop and refine a philosophy of one's own profession. In some cases the profession might be that of education in which case it is imperative that a sound, defensible *philosophy of education* be conceived. For some people the profession might be that of fitness and wellness. Thus, these individuals would need to forge a reasonable and thoughtful *philosophy of fitness/wellness*. And, for still others the profession could be amateur/professional sports or recreation and leisure, etc. In these scenarios professionals would need to develop either a *philosophy of sports* or a *philosophy of recreation and leisure*.

When developing or expressing a professional philosophy, one should be able to answer the question of "what do I think concerning—" about any number of things or situations within the particular professional domain. For example, what do you think about the value of education? What is the purpose of public or private education? What do you think about amateur or professional sports? What should be the priorities in a school based sports program? What are the values of recreational activities? What do you think about the financial base of education or sports? What is the value of exercise? What role should government play in fitness and wellness programs? How should specific programs be financed and promoted? What do you think about different types of exercise? What about the ethics of specific strategies and tactics associated with selling and marketing? The answers to these and innumerable other questions would be indicative of the sport manager's professional philosophy.

A Philosophy of Management

The third philosophical dimension is that of management itself. The administrator needs to develop a philosophy of management (administration)—within the confines of the specific professional arena or organization in which the person is involved. This philosophy of sport management is rooted in the formal historical study of management, in modern theories of management as well as the individual's own professional and personal experiences.

The professional sport manager needs to come to grips, philosophically speaking, with such areas as motivation, leadership, communication, decision making, evaluating, budgeting, directing, staffing, planning, organizing, problem solving, prioritizing, coordinating, reporting, recording, facilitating, etc. The sport manager needs to be conscious of how one's philosophy, how one's philosophical perspective, can play an important, significant and ongoing role in the individual's efforts to manage the behavior of other people and to manipulate resources towards appropriate objectives and goals.

CONCEPT #62: *Successful managers are able to effectively articulate one's philosophy of life, of one's profession and of management.*

It is very important that the sport manager not only possesses a philosophy of life, of the profession and of management but also be able to consistently, effectively and effi-ciently communicate these philosophies to oth-ers. This is because other individuals, groups, and in some instances the general public, need to understand from "whence the manager is com-ing." Others need to understand the philosophy and thinking of the sport manager. They need to understand the decisions and actions of the manager. Without such sharing of one's philoso-phies (and rationale for actions) there are tre-mendous opportunities for miscommunication, partial communication or even failed commu-nication between individuals, both inside and outside of the sport organization itself.

A person's philosophies should be consistent in terms of value systems, priorities, goals and relationships with others, etc. Since one's deci-sions and actions are the direct result of one's philosophies it is important that consistency be the watchword when it comes to making deci-sions and taking action in real life situations.

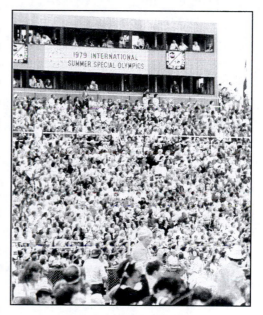

Sports are for Everyone—
Special Olympics Stadium, SUNY Brockport
[courtesy of State University of New York, Brockport.
James Dusen, photographer]

STYLES OF MANAGEMENT

Depending upon one's philosophies, one's experiences, one's training, one's percep-tions, it is possible for a sport manger to exhibit one or more different styles of manage-ment. Typically a sport manager can exhibit a variety of managerial styles during one's tenure in an organization.

CONCEPT #63: *A person's style of management may shift from one paradigm to another depending upon the situation and the circumstances.*

In fact, the manager can exhibit different management and leadership styles at different times and in different situations. Such a shift can even be within the same week or during the same day. It depends upon the specific situation and the existing circumstances (including historical implications) in which the individual is involved.

Some situations may call for a dictator on the part of the sport manager. Others may require that the manager assume the role or style of a benevolent dictator. And still other circumstances might find that the laissez-faire (or permissive) style would be most productive. The important point is this—different managerial styles may be more appropriate at different times depending upon the talents and experiences of the sport manager, the current situation or circumstances, the type of organization itself, and in light of what has taken place previously.

The President of the United States as a Manager (with a MBA)

President George W. Bush, with a MBA from Harvard, is an example of a manager whose management style has been described as right out of the organizational behavioral texts read by many future MBAs in graduate schools. President Bush has been described as (1) managing by MBWA (Managing By Walking Around, or Administering by Walking Around, ABWA), (2) utilizing "creative tension" among subordinates (encouraging staff to take/defend opposing positions while the manager listens, guides and encourages), (3) delegating expertly, and (4) installing accountability for personnel. Such managerial efforts enables the manager to concentrate on strategic thinking and planning—the major responsibility of any manager or administrator (Jones, 2001).

The Machiavellian Style of Management

There has been some discussion within the business world relative to just how ruthless successful managers need to be in modern times in order to be successful and to climb the proverbial ladder of success in the business world. A book written a few years ago by Stanley Bing, a pseudonym for Gill Schwartz (then aged 48 and a senior vice president for CBS), titled: *What Would Machiavelli Do?* deals with the topic of just how ruthless successful managers and administrators need to be. The book presents the opinion that one needs to be very ruthless in dealing with others in order to be successful. The author subscribes to the Machiavelli [1469-1527] philosophy that the "ends justify the means" and cites such highly successful (financially) people as Martha Stewart, Bill Gates, Michael Eisner and Donald Trump as Machiavellian role models for those wishing true success in the world of business. The acronym WWMD—What Would Machiavelli Do—is presented in the book as the criteria for judgments and actions by the truly ruthless manager of the 21st century (Miller, 2000).

The Authoritarian or Autocratic Administrator

The autocratic administrator is one who controls and manipulates almost every aspect of a situation. The individual is a dictator in the truest sense of the word. Subordinates are viewed as inferior. They are dominated and restricted in their actions and communication by the controlling and repressive actions of the autocratic manager. Subordinates are to listen, obey and to follow directions.

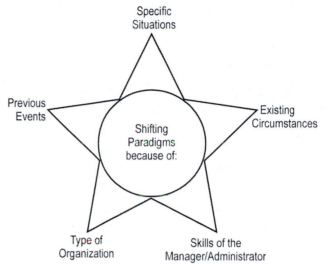

FIGURE 3.2: Factors Affecting Administrative Styles

The autocrat or dictator controls situations by imposing one's will upon others. Intimidation and manipulation are two watchwords that describe the atmosphere existing within the organization controlled and dominated by an authoritarian or autocratic administrator. Fear and apprehension are quite prevalent within the organization since any action or voice not in tune with the dictator type administrator is subject to discouragement, if not actual outright censure.

The Benevolent Dictator

While there is still the element of control by the benevolent dictator, this type of administrative style has the manager doing the controlling, the leading, the subjugation due to the fact that the manager feels that he or she knows what is best for others. As a result, this manager acts in a benevolent or parental fashion in determining what is the most appropriate course of action and how it will be accomplished. There is no sense of malevolence in the intent or motivation of such an administrator. Rather, the benevolent dictator acts much as a kindly patriarch or matriarch for one's "children" so that the youngsters' needs are met. Nevertheless, this manager makes the major decisions, sets the tone and controls the climate for the organization (Stier, 1995).

The Pragmatic Administrator

The pragmatic manager is one who is driven by "doing what it takes to get the job done." Expediency is the watchword of this style of administrator. Politically astute, this individual is willing to take risks in trusting others. There is willingness to give responsibilities to others, and to delegate tasks to others if such action will result in objectives realized and goals reached. The emphasis in this type of management style is directly related to the objectives and goals associated with the organization.

The Democratic Administrator

The democratic administrator is one who insures that input is consistently secured from a wide range of subordinates. Although the final decision rightly rests with the administrator or manager in charge, this does not discourage the individual from seeking counsel, opinions, ideas and suggestions from others. The atmosphere established by a democratic manager is such that individuals feel comfortable in having opportunities to play a part in the bigger picture of the organization. Relationships between managers and non-managers are noted for their openness and the free exchange of ideas.

CONCEPT #64: *Democratic administration does not mean management by committee or management by popular vote.*

However, one would be mistaken to assume that the democratic style of management removes the need for the administrator or manager to make decisions. Quite the opposite. There can be a democratic style of governance within the organization but the final decision in terms of the major decisions certainly must rest with the person in charge. In this case, the manager or administrator. Although democratic administrators frequently utilize a participatory approach to management, this does not preclude the administrators from making final decisions. Democratic administration is not management by committee or management by popular vote.

The Humanistic Administrator

This type of manager possesses true empathy and sympathy with others, both in and out of the organization. The humanistic manager interacts with others as true individuals, as human beings, with sincere dignity. Such relationships involve demonstration of compassion and understanding of the needs of others. This type of manager deliberately attempts to get to know others as important individuals. The corner stone of the treatment of others is the *Golden Rule*—treat others like one would like to be treated by others. The humanistic manager acknowledges one's own strengths and weaknesses as well as the strengths and weaknesses of others. In this light, this type of manager recognizes that people are human, that they are fallible, capable of making mistakes and errors as well as appropriate decisions and performing in a suitable fashion.

The Laissez–Faire or Permissive Administrator

This type of administrator can be recognized for the freewheeling atmosphere where there is very little structure or organization. This type of administrator often fails to assume an active role in many of the important aspects of the organization. Often criticized as the lazy person's method of managing (if this style is the predominate approach to management), the permissive style is identified by the presence of few parameters in terms of how things should be planned, accomplished or implemented.

The manager allows others to perform many of the tasks and to assume many of the responsibilities that might rightfully be within the purview of the administrator. The "head person assumes a very low profile and allows the organization to operate on its own" (Horne, 1991, p. 9). Rather, the laissez-faire manager allows others to do as they see fit without a great many checks and balances in place. Symptoms of this type of managerial approach include an overabundance of delegating and infrequent, if any, follow-up and supervision.

The Empowering Administrator

The administrator who seeks to empower others within the organization in effect facilitates others in the performance of their specific tasks. This type of administrator attempts to provide to others ample opportunities to express their own individuality and to demonstrate their own competency. The empowering administrator is trusting in allowing others to assume responsibilities, to assume important roles and to carry out significant tasks. One is not afraid to delegate suitable tasks or to entrust responsibilities to others. Quite the opposite. The empowering manager will deliberately seek ways to facilitate the professional growth and expansion of subordinates by allowing freedom within limits in the performance of their duties.

ETHICAL BEHAVIOR AND SOCIAL RESPONSIBILITIES IN THE MANAGEMENT OF SPORT

Closely aligned with one's philosophy of life, of the profession and of management, are the areas of morality and ethical behavior. Managers are consistently faced with making decisions. Many of these decisions revolve around moral or ethical issues. Appropriate, just and right decisions are the responsibility of the manager, the leader. One leads through example.

The world, which we live in, can be a challenging one in terms of ethical or right (just) behavior. Similarly, the sport or sport related organization in which we work can also provide significant challenges in terms of what is right and just, what is improper and aberrant, in the areas of ethics, integrity, decency, and morality.

Administrators must have the highest of morals. They must be guided by the highest principles of good conduct and right choices. Their integrity must be beyond reproach. The responsibilities, temptations and challenges facing managers in the 21st century are such that individuals with great integrity are needed, individuals who are able to make appropriate and right decisions in the face of extreme pressure, coercion and urgency.

In many, many situations, the right decision may not be the easy decision. On the contrary. Being able to withstand the onslaught of outside and inside pressures, the ability to resist the "easy way out", and the willingness to take risks for the sake of justice, fairness, and legitimacy, equitableness and righteousness—is solely needed.

CONCEPT #65:   *Managers must be able to assume great risks in terms of making right decisions—or "get out of the kitchen." (Harry Truman)*

Sport managers are in a position to play a major role in social responsibility. Every citizen has such an obligation. However, the sport manager is in a unique position in terms of making decisions, taking actions and implementing programs that can have an impact upon society. This responsibility should not be taken lightly. The impact of many decisions by managers is far reaching, extending beyond the artificial boundaries of the sport organization itself.

In many instances, managers "need to take a stand" in terms of doing what is right, what is just. Not everything in this world is right. In reality, "things may not be just, they may not be right, they may not be fair—but they happen anyway." That is unfortunate indeed. Courageous administrators will be willing to assume risks to insure that appropriate, just and fair decisions are the norm rather than the exception to the rule in terms of their areas of responsibilities.

Mascots Provide a Rallying Point for Fans, Students, Athletes and School Officials
[courtesy of University of Tennessee, Sports Information Office]

> **CONCEPT #66:** *It may not be just, It may not be right, it may not be fair— but it happens.*

A GLIMPSE OF THE HISTORY OF MANAGEMENT THOUGHT AND THEORIES

There are several advantages of viewing the history of management thought as well as the history of earlier managerial efforts. Such a review not only provides a glimpse into past practices and how we got to where we are today, but it also helps us in our current and future efforts to successfully serve as sport managers. It also aids in one's efforts to more effectively and efficiently develop a working philosophy and understanding of sport management. Finally, it helps to identify various strategies and tactics that might be appropriate and applicable in a variety of settings if one is to experience success as an administrator or manager.

> **CONCEPT #67:** *Good theory results in good practice.*

It is also advisable to review the applicable and more common managerial theories as they relate to the management of "sport" and all that that term encompasses. Doing so enables the practitioner to more successfully integrate both practice and theory in the day-to-day operations of the sport organization in which the individual is involved. An aphorism in management states that good theory results in good practice. Today's sport manager needs to be a student of history and of management if one is to keep theory and practice in proper perspective as one attempts to prevent, react and solve problems and challenges faced today.

Management Thought in Ancient Times

Management is certainly not a twentieth century concept. To the contrary. The current status of management thought and the level of managerial practice have obtained their present status and position in our society through the efforts of a large number of individuals, groups and cultures throughout the centuries.

> **CONCEPT #68:** *Management is not a twentieth century concept.*

Management as a separate process was initially verbalized during the time of Socrates (400 BC) and Plato (350 BC). However, even then, the principles and concepts of management were not united into any type of scheme or grand design. This was not accomplished until many centuries later. Nevertheless, major contributions to what has become modern management thought, ideas, practices and theories can be traced to the contributions of the early Greeks who played a major role in providing the basic foundations for western civilization. For example, the origin of the scientific method of investigation had its origins from Greek civilization.

Similarly, numerous individuals, cultures and societies in ancient times have played significant roles, as was previously pointed out in Chapter One, in the development of rather sophisticated and significant management practices, strategies, tactics and techniques. These achievements were in the areas of (1) architecture, (2) warfare, and (3) political organization. Examples of superior managerial achievements included King Solomon (trade agreements, large construction projects); the Egyptians (the pyramids); Alexander the Great (military management and political organization); as well as the Roman society (empire building). Numerous other contributions have been consistently made throughout history.

Significant Changes in the Eighteenth Century—and their Impact Upon Individuals, Management Thought and the Structure of Organizations

Beginning in the early 1700s a number of separate developments took place in Europe that had significant impact upon managerial practices and thought at the time and for centuries to come. The first of these important developments was the growth of cities. It was this tremendous expansion of humanity within a limited geographical area that so drastically altered the so-called rural makeup of society at the time.

The second development involved the application of the principle of specialization—in terms of individual skills and competencies. The extended use of the printing press was the third significant development that proved to have a significant impact upon the common citizenry. And, the fourth development that rocked civilization to its basic foundation and would have a profound impact upon all society was the beginning of the Industrial Revolution in England.

As a result of these and other occurrences or developments there gradually emerged a whole new generation of managers, administrators, organizers, planners, and leaders. These individuals, within a variety of organizations, began to look at the then present challenges from the perspective of how to get things accomplished, effectively and efficiently.

English Industrial Revolution—1700-1785

Between 1700 and 1785 the English Industrial Revolution saw England dramatically evolve from a rural setting to the so-called workshop of the world. In fact, England was the first European nation to successful make the adjustment from a rural agrarian society to a society based upon industrial commerce. This transition was not without hardships and challenges and sacrifices—for both individuals and the country. It should be emphasized again that many of the management strategies employed in the 1700s in reaction to these sweeping changes of society were not totally new. In fact, many of the managerial ideas, strategies and tactics used in the 18th century can be traced to much earlier times.

> **CONCEPT #69:**   *The interpretation and utilization of management strategies and tactics evolved during the English industrial revolution.*

Nevertheless, this fact does not detract from the significance of the managerial efforts at the time. Although a large number of the management strategies, techniques and tactics utilized in the 1700s were not totally new, their interpretation, application and utilization in meeting the new challenges and problems of society during the English Industrial Revolution (1700–1785) was unique. And, indeed, there were new concepts, strategies, techniques and tactics employed as well to meet new obstacles and challenging problems.

Society in the 18th century had rather quickly become an ever changing and more complicated world to live in. There was a need to rethink how members of the society would meet the challenges that were quickly and consistently emerging during these rapidly changing times. As a result, there was a shift in the management process itself that involved how people viewed themselves as members of the society, how they viewed others, and their perception of the work process itself and the organizations that evolved.

Scientific Management Efforts in the United States

Up to this point in time development and application of scientific management production techniques had taken place for the most part in England. Soon there were similarly significant advances across the sea—in America. For example, in the latter part of the 1700s Eli Whitney initiated the system for the milling machine that was used to smooth and shape both wood and metal. This development became the foundation of modern factories. Eli contributed greatly to the foundation upon which the early pioneers of the scientific management built their discipline.

CONCEPT #70:   *Eli Whitney had a major influence upon the thinking of early pioneers of the scientific management.*

Eli was also involved in interchangeable parts manufacture for making muskets for the government at a considerable profit. Similarly, he also developed an extensive cost accounting system, in which every component and every process carried it's own dollar value. Finally, he used a form of quality control in his Mill Rock factory. In fact, Whitney invented a score of modern machines (including cotton gin) which made large-scale enterprises possible—and profitable.

Management Thought in the United States during the 19ᵗʰ Century

The 1800s brought about a wealth of literature on management and management processes in America. Economists at this time thought and wrote about (1) managerial concepts, (2) functions of management and (3) application of management theory. Early writers dealt principally with fundamentals. No unified management theory was developed at that time. The important point is that individuals were at this point of time at least attempting to make an effort, a beginning, to think critically about management, about managers and the process of management.

With the advent of the American Civil War (1860) a new industrial era began in the United States. This was caused by the (1) expansion mechanical industries and by the (2) abolition of slave labor. Financiers such as J. Gould, J.P. Morgan and Cornelius Vanderbilt built up large business organizations (FIRMS) and these organizations had a tremendous influence on the development of the American economy throughout the 19ᵗʰ century. During this time period America's most dramatic enterprise, the railroads, grew in importance and stature.

BEGINNINGS OF "SCIENTIFIC MANAGEMENT"—1880-1898

It is generally acknowledged that modern management movement began around 1880. In fact, the term "scientific management" was first used during this time frame. Between that time period and the early or mid–1920s management thought exploded with different ideas, theories, systems and strategies and techniques all related to ways of looking at management and the management process.

CONCEPT #71:   *Management thought exploded between 1880 and the mid–1920s.*

During the latter part of the 19th century American business was undergoing significant changes in the United States. The west was being settled and "civilized." Large businesses and organizations were creating a schism between the management and the workers (labor). And, finally, there emerged a new and important group of people in the society, the managerial class.

These managers became involved with solving problems associated with bigness and consequently moved from the area of the "big business" concept to the area of "things within the business or firm." For example, they became concerned with processes, the location of equipment and plant layout, production techniques, incentive systems, etc. Management was also becoming *"THINGS"* oriented instead of *"FIRM"* oriented as it had been in the past. And finally, management began to evolve away from the brush fire mentality (crisis management) to more of an anticipatory style (planning) of management.

CONCEPT #72: *Insightful thinkers examined management from the scientific perspective—1880-1898.*

The result was that a manager was recognized with greater respect and esteem. And, the subject matter of management was beginning to be recognized as a significant field of study by both academics and those involved in the business of management. In reality, management as a separate discipline or area was coming into its own, at least in a small but nevertheless significant way.

In addition, people became interested in exchanging ideas and information about the processes of problems of management. This resulted in numerous publications dealing with management being created. Numerous meetings and conferences were also held to discuss the challenges and problems facing organizations, workers and management. As a result the ground swell to consider management as a separate entity or field of study grew in momentum. In fact, during this time management was recognized as a teaching curriculum at a leading university for the first time.

At this time there also emerged a group of far–reaching thinkers studying the concept of management and the organization from a scientific perspective. These individuals provided significant and far-reaching contributions to management thought not only for their time but also for the present. In fact, in examining the development of today's managerial concepts, principles, theories and strategies—it becomes necessary to look at the specific contributions and thoughts of a number of outstanding leaders in the modern management thought, table 3.1.

TABLE 3.1: *Major Pioneers in Early Scientific Management Thought*

Contributors (approximate times)		Contributions
Henry Towne and Henry C. Metcalfe (1886)	1.	Unified system of management rather than the usual hit-or-miss practices employed in earlier times;
	2.	Called for managers to form professional organizations;
	3.	Encouraged the publication of journals devoted to management;
	4.	Exchanged findings and views with others.
Frederick W. Taylor (1900)	1.	Developed the idea of scientific management, "Father of Scientific Management";
	2.	Establishment of uniform job procedures;
	3.	Job selection by qualification;
	4.	New roles for supervisors;
	5.	Time-motion studies.
Frank B. Gilbreth (1900)	1.	Science of motion study;
	2.	"Father of Work Simplification";
	3.	Process charts and flow diagrams.
Lillian Gilbreth (1900)	1.	Science of motion study;
	2.	Psychology of the workplace; bridge the gap between people and things;
	3.	Motion studies.
Henry L. Gantt (1901)	1.	Gantt Chart (daily balance chart) of output time;
	2.	Humanitarianism in employee treatment and pay;
	3.	Teaching and training employees;
	4.	Service as an objective.
Hugo Munsterberg (1910)	1.	Created field of industrial psychology;
	2.	Initiated system of tests and measurements of psychological differences between employees.
Harrington Emerson (1910)	1.	Broader focus on the organization structure and its importance;
	2.	Emphasis on the objectives of a firm and their relation to its organization;
	3.	Emphasis on use of experts, staff, consultants, and the like;
	4.	Twelve principles of efficiency.
Harlow S. Person (1911)	1.	Gave academic recognition to scientific management;
	2.	Emphasized total scope of management, lifting it from a movement dedicated to the stopwatch and speedup.
Henri Fayol (1916)	1	Concept of universality of management;
	2.	First comprehensive theory of management;
	3.	Need for teaching management in schools and colleges;
	4.	Need for better leadership in management.
Oliver Sheldon (1923)	1.	Emphasis on social aspects of management;
	2.	Social responsibilities of managers;
	3.	Conceptualization of (philosophy of) management, bringing it to a higher theoretical level;
	4.	Management as a separate, distinct function in industry that revolved around a given set of principles that could be analyzed and studied.

Contributors (approximate times)	Contributions
Elton Mayo (1927-47)	1. Hawthorne studies: attitudes and reactions of groups under varying conditions (Western Electric's Hawthorne Works); 2. Importance of psychological and social factors on productivity; 3. Effect of "morale" on productivity; 4. Experimental rather than theoretical research.
Mary P. Follett (1930)	1. Contributed to the study of leadership; 2. Individuals can be trained to be leaders; 3. Importance of education for managers/leaders; 4. Examined motivating desires of individuals and groups; 5. Importance of group dynamics and human behavior.
James D. Mooney (1931)	1. Scaler principle (1926): superior and subordinate relationships arranged in an heir apparent fashion; 2. Classic treatise on the nature of and creation of the organization. *Onward Industry*, 1928; 3. A tight engineering approach to management; excluded human side or social aspects of management.
Chester Barnard (1938)	1. A behaviorist; 2. Great influence on understanding organizations; 3. Logical analysis of organization's structure; 4. Theory of cooperation and organization; 5. Description of the executive process; importance of the competent executive.

School of Scientific Management

> **CONCEPT #73:** *Frederick W. Taylor is credited as the "father of scientific management".*

Because of the far-reaching efforts by Frederick W. Taylor, the so-called "school of scientific management" became a reality. His accomplishments are many and varied. For example, managers were encouraged to utilize the processes of planning, organizing and controlling. Stop-watch studies of workers' performances were conducted. The work site was organized so that the working conditions were standardized in an effort to make standards of worker performance possible and meaningful. Feasible standards were established on the basis of per person or per machine hour. Accountability was a key element in Taylor's view of management.

Frederick Taylor also emphasized the importance of good supervision of an employee and the working conditions. The supervisor was relieved of the so-called "whip persuasion role" and provided with incentives to offer workers instead in an effort to increase individual productivity. Supervisors became specialists to facilitate productivity and accountability. And, finally, Taylor attempted to devise ways in which workers would be identified for specific jobs in light of the individual worker's skill and potential for performing the task(s).

Early practitioners of scientific management were indeed pragmatists. They had no reluctance in tackling problems on the basis of urgency or need. As a result the most urgent problems or challenges naturally received the greatest attention. Consequently, some of the initial problems that were dealt with initially centered upon such production questions as:

1. What is a fair day's work?
2. How long should a worker take to do a given job?
3. What is the best location for a plant?
4. How should workers be supervised?
5. What is the best way to select a worker for a job?

Taylor served as both a flashpoint and a foundation for those who followed him and adhered to his concepts relating to scientific management. There were a large number of individuals—associates, contemporaries and followers—who subscribed to his general scientific management philosophy. Many of them went on to refine the then current thinking relating to organizations and management. Others developed their own versions of the science of management. And still others make significant contributions to the overall scientific study of management. Some of these individuals include, but are not limited to, the following: Harlow S. Person, Hugo Munsterberg, Henry L. Gantt, Harrington Emerson, Henri Fayol. All played a part in extending the knowledge we now have of "management" as a distinct field or body of knowledge.

Impact of Early Leaders in Managerial Thought

These and other leaders, within a matter of a few decades, played a very real and important role in elevating the management process as well as the study of management to a recognized profession based upon scientific knowledge. Their contributions serve as a firm foundation for the further study and expansion of knowledge relating to management by current and future professional managers and scholars.

Managers in the olden days made decisions and initiated actions because they were reacting to what worked before in attempting to solve today's problem. However, the modern day manager utilizes the analytical scientific approach to preventing and solving problems. Thus, the proponents of scientific management followed the practice of investigating the facts and making decisions in light of these facts. When faced with challenges, these individuals would seek the best way to approach the problem, today.

Since sound management is based upon facts, upon data, and upon scientific reasoning, what has worked before in other situations and under different circumstances might not be either applicable or appropriate in today's organization, in today's setting and under today's circumstances.

Management Thought Following World War II

Management thought just before, during and immediately following the Second World War was somewhat in disarray. As a result, there was a great effort by a large number of practitioners and scholars after the war to bring some resemblance of order to the mass of theories that had grown up since the initiation of Taylor's scientific management.

BEGINNINGS OF A PHILOSOPHICAL APPROACH TO MANAGERIAL THOUGHT

One of the factors that distanced modern day management from earlier management efforts is the philosophical approach to managerial thought. This philosophical perspective evolved gradually and represents a significant distancing from the earlier mechanistic thinking associated with management. Today, the realm of values and value judgments play an important role in management and management thought. Today, there is a great deal of emphasis placed on group dynamics, the social dimension of groups.

CONCEPT #74: *A philosophical approach to management thought is a modern phenomenon.*

Schools of Management Thought That Evolved in the 20th Century

During the course of the 20th century there evolved, under the leadership of various researchers and students of management and organizations, several schools of management thought. The major schools of management thought include: (from *The history of management thought—A study guide for administrative core—Unit 1. (1974).*

1. *The Traditional or Scientific School of Management Thought*

Sometimes referred to as the Classical School, this perspective of management thought resulted from systematic observations of how things are produced. The emphasis was on specific techniques such as time studies, the layout of plant equipment, "time and motion" studies, division of labor, organizational structure, effect of various wage incentives, and production planning and control. There were efforts to truly research and analyze various elements of the so-called operation of the "shop" or the plant in an effort to determine their impact, effectiveness and efficiency. Frederick Taylor was the single most important and influential individual within the Traditional School.

2. *The Behavioral School*

This school of thought was based upon the interpersonal relationships which exist within the workplace or organization. The centrality of the individual became the focus of this school of management thought. It was recognized that organizational goals and objectives could be achieved through the efforts of individuals. Consequently, the behaviorists concentrated early on upon the motivational factors of individuals and groups. The area of group dynamics became an important field for study with close examinations of individual drives, group interactions and relations. Eclectic in their approach, proponents of the Behavioral School incorporate most of the social sciences including psychology, sociology, social psychology and anthropology in their efforts to examine management and the organizational process.

3. *The Management Process School*

As the title suggests, this theory or management thought is based upon the processes involved in managing or administering. Management is viewed as management—regardless of the type of organization. Management is universal in its perspective. Proponents of this theory of management examine and study the functions of a manager; the processes of management (refer to chapter four, **PPOSDCoRRFEB**).

4. *The Quantitative School*

Emerging since 1940, the Quantitative School represents a scientific effort to take advantage of knowledge from a wide range of different disciplines in studying and examining organizations and in solving problems associated within organizations. Supporters of the Quantitative School would rely upon experts, operating in closely integrated research teams, from various academic disciplines (utilizing their scientific tools and resources) in attempting to come to a conclusion or to solve a particular problem existing under the umbrella of management or within an organization.

THEORIES, PRINCIPLES, AND CONCEPTS OF MANAGEMENT AND LEADERSHIP

"A theory is accepted principles devised to analyze, predict, or explain the nature of behavior of a specified set of phenomena. Theories are tested by research" (Parkhouse,

1991, p. 32). A more thorough definition is provided by Jensen (1992, pp. 11, 12) who states:

> "A Theory is one step beyond an assumption or hypothesis. It is a guide, which has some evidence in its support, but is still not validated. Theories are useful in education in the formulation of administrative practices. Sometimes, a theory gradually evolves into a standard procedure, a policy, or a principle after sufficient evidence has been accumulated to support it. In other cases, theories become discarded because attempts to prove their validity and usefulness are unsuccessful. Theory can be viewed as a starting point for the development of facts, policies, principles, and laws. Administrative theory precedes administrative practice and nurtures it."

McGregor's Theory X and Y Motivational Leadership Styles

Douglas McGregor, while a professor at MIT, wrote the book, *The Human Side of Enterprise* (1960). He investigated ways in which workers were viewed by their managers and superiors. He expressed the belief that there are two styles of motivational leadership in light of the needs and capabilities of workers. He referred to one style as Theory X and the second style as Theory Y.

In Theory X, workers are thought to be lazy, lacking in ability and motivation and with significant amount of distaste for work. They need to and want to be told what to do, when to do it and how to do it. Workers do not desire responsibility, instead preferring security, sanctuary and safety. As a result workers need to be controlled. They are to be coerced and threatened if they are to perform at an acceptable level in terms of effectiveness and efficiency (Tillman, Voltmer, Esslinger, McCue, 1996, pp. 42, 43).

Horine (1995, p. 21) states that the manager who subscribes to the Theory X line of management thinking "requires a tight authoritative structure to supervise employees directly (called the "scalar principle"), and the staff needs to be consistently pressured to maintain adequate performance." See below for additional information relating to the "scalar principle".

However, the opposite side of the proverbial coin is expressed in Theory Y. Those who subscribe to Theory Y believe that workers not only truly enjoy their worth but that they desire responsibility and independence. Additionally, employees are viewed as self-motivated and are self-directed. They need less supervision and direction and can operate successfully and continually at a high performance level with a less rigid and less threatening organizational structure. In short, workers can be productive, efficient and effective with less direct control, less supervision and with a less restrictive environment.

Theory Z

William Ouchi coined the term "Theory Z" in his book, *Theory Z: How American Business Can Meet the Japanese Challenge* (1981). This treatise dealt with a close examination of various cultures within organizations. This theory has elements of highly successful

Japanese business management tactics and strategies adapted to the American scene with its own particular organizational climate and culture (Tillman, Voltlmer, Esslinger, McCue, 1996). Key concepts of this theory revolves around the need for trust, loyalty, openness and positive relationships between management and workers; the benefits of having educated workers; the need for workers to have the best interest of their organization at heart; as well as the need for inspirational and visible leadership on the part of management (Plunkett and Attner, 1994).

Theory Z stipulates that not only management but workers should be in a position to have an understanding and knowledge of the resources available to the organization as well as the problems and challenges facing the organization (Horine, 1995). Problem solving should be a cooperative venture with both workers and administration working together for the common good (the organization) in solving the problem(s). Towards this end it is necessary that workers play an integral role in the establishment of the objectives and goals of the organization or program. Workers who have a say in the establishment of objectives/goals tend to work harder to realize these same objectives/goals.

Quality Circles

The essence of Quality Circles is that productive, effective and efficient performance of the work force (as well as change) is best when it comes from within rather than being imposed from the outside. Towards this end, the tactic of utilizing so-called Quality Circles involves small groups of individuals, all working on similar tasks and toward common objectives, meeting on a regular basis. The periodic meetings are held to address common problems and challenges within the organization and to suggest ways to address these hurdles.

Frequently, in an effort to facilitate the group interaction, increase two-way communication and foster trust, an outside leader is often utilized. The objective is to prevent and solve problems, problems that face these individuals who face similar tasks and have similar responsibilities. The process is through frank and democratic discussion. The method involves "give and take", a willingness to accept ideas of others as well as being able to be open (risk taker) in one's dealings with others. This participatory style of management can be traced to the Japanese industry that has utilized this strategy successfully for many years.

Total Quality Management

The "customer is always right" concept is an important facet of Total Quality Management or TQM. TQM as a management style or principle involves educated, motivated and caring employees/workers whose primarily goal is quality in all that they do. Customer satisfaction is critical in the TQM concept. Developed by an American businessman, W. Edwards Deming (1900-1993). TQM was popularized in Japan following the Second World War. In that country, businesses that implemented this stratagem experienced tremendous financial success (Mawson, 1993).

CONCEPT #75:   *"The customer is always right" is a central tenant of TQM*

In recent years, TQM has received equal acclaim here in the United States in a wide range of businesses, both service and product oriented. Even in the realm of education TQM has its strong proponents as many of the principles or concepts are applicable in the not-for-profit sector. At the crux of this to doing business are fourteen essential principles or concepts (U.S. Office of Personnel Management, 1991). These principles are presented in Box 3.1.

BOX 3.1
Fourteen Principles of Total Quality Management (TQM)

1. Establish a constant organizational purpose or role in satisfying customers.
2. Commit to the new quality control philosophy.
3. Cease inspection of the final product or service, but seek improvement in the process instead.
4. Disregard the cost in securing the best quality in organizational resources.
5. Continually improve the process of providing goods and services through statistical analysis of performance data.
6. Institute training and development programs for employees.
7. Select leaders who enable people to excel rather than directing or punishing worker behavior.
8. Drive out employees' fears about asking questions, seeking assistance, or making mistakes, or they will continue to do things wrong or not at all.
9. Eliminate barriers between organization work units to eliminate conflicting competition, or one unit may cause performance problems for another.
10. Eliminate organization slogans and targets for workers, and let them create their own.
11. Eliminate numerical quotas, because they do not account for quality or methods.
12. Encourage pride of workmanship by acknowledgment of intrinsic excellence and elimination of management's standards of performance.
13. Encourage retraining and self-improvement through education in new methods, teamwork and statistical techniques.
14. Take action so the organization's management and all employees can create the new quality system.

Similar in some ways to Quality Circles, TQM involves employees working together for the common good of the organization, i.e., maintaining quality in all that the organization and the workers are involved *and* meeting the needs of the customers. Teamwork and quality control are key concepts in TQM. Care and respect for the organization coupled with an undying desire for quality service and quality products for the customer remain essential elements within TQM. However, the greatest challenge with TQM is attempting to change human behavior. TQM is not about mastering technical skills. Rather, it is the change in how one perceives one's own role within the organization and how one perceives others, including the all-important "customer" (Hillkirk, 1993).

Employment empowerment is a key concept with TQM. Employees are encouraged to seek out problems and difficulties and then to solve or eliminate them. Deming is quoted as saying that "People are entitled to joy in their work and a sense of ownership," (Hillkirk, 1993, p. 1-B). TQM involves attempting to always improve in one's efforts, using hard data for important decision making, attempting to satisfy one's customers, all the while working together in a wholesome team-like atmosphere and involving everyone in the effort to achieve such goals. If TQM is to be implemented, it is important that both management and employees fully understand the concept of TQM if they are to "buy into" the concepts or principles underlying this management strategy. TQM is not a "quick fix" for an ailing organization or business.

Management by Objectives

Management by Objectives, or MBO as it has become known, is a popular method of viewing the planning process. In order to experience success managers and employees working in a collegial fashion need to establish agreed upon objectives. One then manages, administers and works in light of these objectives. Peter Drucker (1964) became famous through the release of his best selling book *The Practice of Management* in which he introduced his theory of Management by Objectives.

> **CONCEPT #76:**   *Peter Drucker, the guru of modern management,*
> *introduced the theory of management by objectives.*

Managerial objectives, in order to be meaningful, must be realistic and obtainable. If they are not then the objectives can prove to be a hindrance to motivation of those working within the organization. However, an important element in the practice of Management by Objectives is the cooperative interaction among those individuals (managers and employees) who are affected by the objectives, criteria or expectations. MBO aids in the analysis of objectives and goals. Although the process can indeed be time consuming, the outcomes are frequently worth the extra efforts (Clegg and Chambliss, 1982).

Maslow's Hierarchy of Needs Theory

This theory attempted to identify and differentiate between various types of needs of individuals on a hierarchical basis, figure 3.3, (Davis, 1994). These five different needs, in the order of their importance, are: (1) basic safety and physiological needs (hunger, shelter, warmth, rest and sex), (2) security or safety needs (protection against danger, illness, property and income loss, and uncertainty), (3) social needs (belonging, acceptance, friendship, and understanding), (4) self-esteem needs (pride, achievement, self-respect, and status needs), and (5) self-actualization needs (self-fulfillment, self-satisfaction, and self-realization).

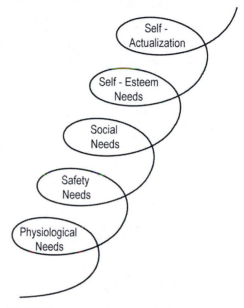

According to this theory individuals are naturally concerned first with the needs on the low end of the hierarchy before being concerned with those needs at the top. In other words, human beings are first and foremost concerned with insuring that their physiological needs are being met before being able to be too concerned with other needs such as those associated with self-actualization or self-esteem. Once those needs at the lower end of the spectrum or hierarchy then individuals can concentrate on those needs higher up the hierarchy.

FIGURE #3.3: Maslow's Hierarchy of Needs

McClelland Motivation Theory

This theory supports the position that there are three essential "motivators" for workers. The first of these is the need for high achievement by individuals. The second is the need for affiliation. And the third is power, power over individuals, processes and things. Davis (1994, p. 103) indicates that "McClelland's research points out that the best managers rate high in their need for power and low in their need for affiliation."

Preference-Expectancy Theory

Victor Vroom published this theory in the book, *Work and Motivation* (1964). In this publication Vroom theorizes that motivation is connected to what he refers to as "preference" and "expectancy". In this concept, rewards are intricately interwoven with specific, identifiable behavior and particular work performance. "Preference" relates to what an individual would like to occur while "expectancy" "is the subjective probability of what will happen if certain behavior patterns are followed" (Bridges and Roquemore, 1992).

Motivational Reinforcement Theory

This theory of motivation in management deals with the connection between positive reinforcement and desired behavior (Skinner, 1976). The reinforcement can take the form of various types of rewards including verbal appreciation, recognition, encouragement and the bestowing of honors and accolades as well as tangible prizes and compensation such as salary, promotion, and increased responsibilities. Positive reinforcement when associated with specific types of behavior tends to motivate and encourage that specific behavior. Negative reinforcement when associated with behavior, on the other hand, tends to discourage those types of actions.

CONCLUSIONS

Successful and Exciting Athletic Programs Attract Paying Fans
[courtesy of University of Tennessee, Sports Information Office]

Competent sport managers need to be well grounded in terms of philosophies of life, of one's profession and of management. Having a well grounded personal and professional philosophy aids in making timely and appropriate decisions. It is also important for the sport manager to understand how different administrative styles can affect the working relationships with others as well as the workplace climate. Finally, understanding the historical perspective of management thought as well as the various managerial theories can aid the inexperienced as well as the experienced manager in the real world of sport business.

REFERENCES

Blake, R.R. and Mouton, J.S. (1978). *The new managerial grid.* Houston: Gulf Publishing.

Bridges, F.L. & Roquemore, L.L. (1992). *Management for athletic/sport administration: Theory and practice.* Decatur, GA: ESM Books.

Clegg, C.C. and Chambliss, G. (1982). Management by objectives: A case study. *Journal of Physical Education, Recreation and Dance, 53*(4), 45-46.

Davis, K.A. (1994). *Sport management: Successful private sector business strategies.* Madison, Wisconsin: Wm. C. Brown and Benchmark.

Drucker, P. (1954). *The practice of management.* New York: Harper & Row.

Hillkirk, J. (1993, July 26). Manufacturers take quality lead. *USA Today*, p. 2-B.

Hillkirk, J. (1993, December 21). World-famous quality expert dead at 93. *USA Today*, pp. 1-B, 2-B.

The history of management thought—A study guide for administrative core - Unit 1. (1974). Brockport, New York: State University of New York Press.

Horine, L. (1991). *Administration of physical education and sport programs* (2ⁿᵈ ed.). Dubuque, Iowa: Wm. C. Brown Publishers.

Jensen, C.R. (1992). *Administrative management of physical education and athletic programs.* Philadelphia, PA: Lea & Febiger.

Jones, D. (2001, January 19). How MBAs might reshape the White House. *USA Today*, pp. 1-A, 2-A.

McGregor, D. (1960). The human side of enterprise. New York: McGraw-Hill.

Mawson, L. Marlene. (1993). Total quality management: Perspectives for sport management. *Journal of Sport Management, 7*(5), 101-106.

Miller, Martin. (2000, March 23). The ruthless approach. *Democrat & Chronicle*, p. 3-C.

Mooney, J.D. (1931). *Onward industry*. New York: Harper & Brothers.

Ouchi, Wm. (1981). *Theory Z: How American business can meet the Japanese challenge.* Reading, MA: Addison-Wesley.

Parkhouse, B.L. (1991). Editor. *The management of sport—Its foundation and application.* St. Louis: Mosby YearBook.

Plunkett, W.R. and Attner, R. (1994). *Introduction to management* (5ᵗʰ ed.). Belmont, California: Wadsworth Publishing Company.

Skinner, B.F. (1976). *About behaviorism*. New York, Random House.

Stier, W.F. Jr., (1995). *Successful coaching—Strategies and tactics.* Boston, MA: American Press.

Tillman, K.G., Voltmer, E.F., Esslinger, A.A. and McCue, B.F. (1996). *The Administration of physical education, sport, and leisure programs.* Boston: Allyn and Bacon.

U.S. Office of Personnel Management. (1991). Federal Quality Institute. Federal total quality management handbook: *Introduction to total quality management in the federal government.* DC: U.S. Government Printing Office.

Vroom, V. H. (1964). *Work and motivation.* New York: John Wiley and Sons.

Webster's new collegiate dictionary. (1973). Springfield, Massachusetts: G. & C. Merriam Company.

DISCUSSION TOPICS

1. Describe your philosophy of life.

2. How would you describe yourself, at the present time, in terms of operating under a particular style? Why?

3. Why should you, as a sport manager, vary your administrative style at different times and in different situations? Provide examples.

4. Cite some significant occurrences that have taken place in earlier times which have had a profound influence on modern day managerial thought and practice.

5. Explain how McGregor's theory X and Y might have an effect upon a sport manager's administrative style.

6. If you as a sport manager wanted to follow the tenets of Total Quality Management, provide examples of decisions you might make and actions that you might take that would be consistent with TQM.

7. What is the Machiavellian Style of Management?

8. Outline various styles of management.

9. Explain the role that Eli Whitney had as a major influence upon the thinking of early pioneers of the scientific management.

10. Describe the Motivational Reinforcement Theory and its importance in today's world of sport.

DEVELOPING COMPETENCIES—
THE PROCESS OF SPORT MANAGEMENT

Chapter

The Competencies, Roles and Processes
of Competent Sport Managers

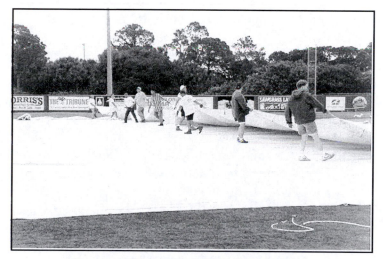

**Everyone "Pitching In" after a Rainy Delay—
Teamwork is an Essential Ingredient in Sport Management**
[photo courtesy of St. Lucie METS, Port Lucie, Florida]

CHAPTER HIGHLIGHTS

This chapter will help the reader to:

• Acknowledge the importance of being a Renaissance person as a sport manager; and provide examples of such individuals working within the sport "arena;"

- Illustrate the importance of timing and time management in the world of sport and sharing appropriate examples;
- Describe the difference in working with paid staff and volunteers and cite the advantages and disadvantages of working with each group;
- Describe the basic processes of management [PPOSDCoRRFEB];
- Explain the different types of jobs and positions available within a variety of sport and sport related organizations;
- Specify ten responsibilities typically assumed by sport managers;
- Be familiar with specific computer software applicable to sport businesses;
- Understand the importance that perceptions plays in dealing with people and in businesses and provide examples in the world of sport;;
- Provide examples of administering in light of the "worse case scenario" concept;
- Outline the concept of remaining in the "help mode";
- Outline what sport managers do in their various jobs;
- Cite the rationale behind the importance of sales in the world of sport;
- Define the Diamond Concept of Management;
- Appreciate that graduating from a college in sport management is only the first step in a long process of developing competency in the management of sport.

THE ESSENTIAL PROCESSES OF MANAGEMENT

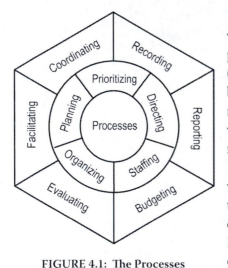

FIGURE 4.1: The Processes
of Management

Seven essential processes for managers (leaders) were identified by Gulick and Urwick in 1937. These processes are (1) planning, (2) organizing, (3) staffing, (4) directing, (5) coordinating, (6) reporting, and (7) budgeting. These processes became known by the acronym POSDCoRB. Later, three additional processes were identified. These included the processes of (1) recording, (2) facilitating, and (3) evaluating (Stier, 1994). And, in 1995, yet another essential process with which every manager must be involved was identified, that of prioritizing. Thus, today, the acronym for eleven essential managerial processes has evolved into PPOSDCoRRFEB, figure 4.1 (Stier, 1995, p. 158). Each of these processes is described briefly below and is dealt with in greater detail in subsequent chapters.

Planning

Everyone with management responsibility should be involved in the process of planning. Planning prevents the manager from "flying by the seat of one's pants" (Stier, 1995, p. 158). Planning can involve personnel, goals and objectives, tactics and strategies as well as resources. Planning also involves establishing goals and assessing where one is currently at and where one wants to be.

Planning may be thought of as both "every day planning" as well as "strategic planning". "Every day planning, as the name implies, deals with anticipating what needs to be done on a day-to-day basis. Strategic planning implies a more complex type of planning associated with a longer time frame, a more structured approach as well as a larger perspective of the objectives and goals being sought. Lumpkin (1997, p. 38) defines strategic planning as: "... a formal, continuous process of making decisions based on internal and external assessments." A ten step approach to strategic planning was proposed by Bryson (1995, p. 23) which included the following:

1. Initiate and agree upon a strategic planning process
2. Identify various organizational mandates
3. Clarify the organizational mission, priorities and values
4. Asses the external and internal environments of the entity in an effort to identify strengths, weaknesses, opportunities, challenges and limitations
5. Identify the essential strategic issues which the entity faces in the pursuit of its mission
6. Formulate strategies to manage these issues (# 5 above)
7. Review and adopt the strategic plan(s)
8. Establish an effective and efficient organizational vision
9. Develop an effective and efficient implementation plan and process
10. Continually review, assess and reevaluate the strategies implemented as well as the actual strategic planning process itself.

While much has been written and talked about in terms of planning, in terms of reality there is less real planning that previously thought, especially in terms of small businesses. A survey in the *Wall Street Journal Interactive Edition* was cited in pointing out that only 13% of small businesses actually possess an annual budget in print (writing) while only 14% have an annual business plan in writing. And, even less (12%) possess a long-range plan in writing. The survey went on to reveal that almost 60% of the small businesses surveyed possessed no type of plans "on paper" (hard copy), period (Not thinking ahead, 1999).

CONCEPT #77: *Always plan for the worse case scenario—in an effort to prevent problems from happening.*

In order to prevent the "crisis by management" syndrome, sport managers must be concerned not only with the present but with the future as well. Adequate planning frequently prevents many problems from occurring and often reduces the negative consequences of those problems that do become reality. Managers, as part of their planning process, should anticipate the worse case scenario and then plan to prevent it from happening or plan to mitigate the negative consequences that occur.

CONCEPT #78: *Learn from the mistakes and successes of others— and plan accordingly.*

When planning, be sure and learn from others, both their successes and their failures. Managers do not have sufficient time in their lifetime to learn only from their own mistakes. They must avoid pitfalls associated with their managerial responsibilities and one way this can be achieved is to learn from the experiences of others—both through personal observation and from professional reading and study.

Prioritizing

It is very important that sport managers be skilled in prioritizing those tasks and responsibilities that face them. Simply put, prioritizing means recognizing that there are some tasks that are more important than others and that some tasks must be completed before others. Prioritizing can be associated with tasks, objectives, goals, individuals and resources.

The key to prioritizing is time management. Being able to effectively plan how one utilizes time will enable the manager to take time for vision, to take time to be a leader, to take time to be an effective manager (Hoch, 2002). Mundane tasks, especially those that take valuable time from the administrator's already activity filled day, should be either delegated to others or quickly disposed of so that valuable time can be devoted to more pressing and more important tasks and challenges, those that cannot be easily or adequately done or accomplished by others (Stier, 2005).

CONCEPT #79: *Time is one of the most important resources available to the manager—it must never be wasted.*

Prioritizing is closely associated with time management. Since time is one of the most important resources available to the manager, it is imperative that it not be wasted. To waste time, or any other important resource or asset, is a cardinal sin for the administrator or manager. Time is one thing that is not replaceable, when it is gone, it is gone forever. Prioritizing one's time is an essential element of skilled management.

A Gallup survey some years ago revealed that the average worker received some 190 messages (phone, e-mail, etc.) each and every work day. And, if most of these messages require a reply, well—one can imagine the time one must be spending each day in an effort to handle this information overload. One answer to this ever increasing challenge in terms of time commitment is that people are starting work earlier and leaving work later in an effort to handle this tremendous increase in communication. Another aspect related to this increase in communication, at least in respect to the Internet, is what to believe and what not to believe (Goldsborough, 1999).

The first key to handling this amount of information revolves around deciding what to read and what not to read as well as what communication efforts must be responded to. The second key is to understand that not everything one receives in terms of communication is going to be accurate or true and, as a result, due diligent efforts must be taken to insure that information received is indeed accurate. There are several web sites that are helpful in enabling one to find out whether information on the WWW is accurate or not. Three such sites are: (1) www.clearinghouse.net (2) www.miningco.com and (3) www.looksmart.com (Goldsborough, 1999).

Organizing

Every manager must be personally and professionally organized as an individual, as a professional, and as a leader of others. In addition, successful managers are capable of organizing others, as individuals and as members of small and large groups. Being organized means taking advantage of the modern tools available at the current time. Being at the cutting edge in terms of being organized and proper use of time means utilizing tools such as a computer, a personal information management (PIM) software program (Microsoft Outlook), the WWW, a cell phone, and a personal digital assistant (PDA).

CONCEPT #80: *Highly skilled sport managers must be personally and professionally organized as well as capable of organizing others.*

And finally, one's organization must be thoroughly structured so that all components within the entity are operating at peak efficiency in an effort to reach agreed upon objectives and goals. Being a skilled organizer means that the individual is aware of available resources and is capable of using these resources or assets where they will be best utilized.

Staffing

Since management involves working with human beings, with people, it is essential that the sport manager be highly competent in staffing the organization with highly qualified staff, both paid employees and volunteers. Staffing involves the assignment of qualified individuals to specific tasks or responsibilities. It also involves the total area of personnel management which includes all actions from the initial solicitation of potential employees, the interview process, eventual hiring, training, assigning, assessment, promotion, pay raises and eventual outplacement from the organization.

**CONCEPT #81: *Staffing involves working with both paid employees
as well as volunteers (and interns).***

Staffing is a very important and essential process, one which the competent manager will pay the closest attention to at all times. Staffing can have tremendous impact upon the organization and its ability to adequately function and realize its mission(s). A significant number of the problems found within organizations can be traced to difficulties with individuals working within that entity. And, most of these problems could have been prevented if proper steps had been taken within the staffing (personnel) process. This is especially true when hiring staff members. That is, if proper steps are taken in the hiring process and if qualified, motivated and appropriate personnel are indeed hired (and trained), the likelihood of fewer problems being faced by the administration is greatly increased.

Directing

Directing involves making others aware of what needs to be done, what needs to be accomplished. Sport managers must be capable of directing the energies and efforts of others towards activities that will result in positive results. Directing also includes advising others in a variety of different areas as well as overseeing the activities of people as they perform their responsibilities. Managers can provide direction for both individuals as well as small and large groups and for the overall organization.

Coordinating

Tasks, people and inanimate objects need to be coordinated if the sport manager is to be successful and the organization's goals are to be realized. Like the proverbial juggler who must keep 3, 4 or 5 different bowling pins or balls in the air, the skilled sport manager must be willing and capable of juggling many things at the same time. The sport manager must coordinating the activities of many people, numerous activities, and innumerable objects—all the while keeping in sight the eventual goal of the organization.

> **CONCEPT #82:** *In today's complex sport world and complicated society the process of coordination is absolutely essential.*

The administrative process of coordination in today's complicated society and complex world of sport is so important it is doubtful that effective and efficient sport management is possible without it. Sport and sport related activities have become too big, too complex, not to require an exceptional level of coordination in their implementation. From the seemingly simple tasks associated with the conduct of a high school conference track championship meet to the more complicated tasks involved in the New York City Marathon, there are innumer-

Always Take Advantage of Opportunities to Work With and Inform the Media
[courtesy of Buffalo Bills]

able tasks, "things," and people to be coordinated. If proper coordination is lacking the result is often a catastrophe.

Reporting

An important and ongoing process within any organization is that of reporting. This means keeping others informed of what is taking place. This involves keeping abreast a wide range of individuals, not the least of whom is one's immediate superior(s).

> **CONCEPT #83:** *In sport management one must always keep one's superiors informed of what is taking place—don't surprise one's superiors.*

Not all reporting involves keeping your boss(s) abreast of important developments and information. There are numerous other instances where a sport manager must be able to report facts, information, intentions and opinions to others (individuals and groups). However, the most important person or persons to whom the sport manager must keep up-to-date is one's immediate superior(s). Surprising one's boss(es) is not the way to make friends and influence people.

Recording

Keeping timely and appropriate records is closely associated with adequate reporting. Without accurate records it is more difficult, if not impossible sometimes, to be able to make appropriate reports to others. The types of records that should be kept will vary with the type of organization and the specific responsibility that of the sport manager. However, financial records, records of accidents, contracts, names of donors, names of ticket holders, are only a few that might be appropriate in any given organization.

CONCEPT #84: *Appropriate and accurate records provide a historical snapshot into what has taken place—and can guide future decision-making and actions.*

One of the reasons why keeping accurate and timely records are so important is that such data enables managers and leaders to make correct assumptions and appropriate decisions for the future. Without such data the sport manger is indeed "flying by the seat of one's pants" and is often forced to rely on anecdotal information rather than hard data.

Facilitating

Sport managers are facilitators in the sense that they frequently operate in the help or assist mode. One role of any sport manager, regarding of the type of sport entity one is involved with, is to help others do their tasks, to help others accomplish their jobs, to enable others to achieve their objectives.

CONCEPT #85: *Managers must remain in the help mode as facilitators of others within their organization.*

Toward this end, managers need to assume an unselfish attitude when working with others, especially those for whom they are responsible. This ability to help one's staff, whether they are paid or volunteers, is part of the leadership function. This process of facilitation can involve, but not be limited to, the removal of specific obstacles, allocation of additional resources as well as opportunities for additional education and training.

ks that individual employees actually perform within each of these types of or-
.

ge athletics (Institutions within NCAA; NAIA; NCCAA; NJCAA)—event
agement, compliance/eligibility, facility management, budgeting and finance,
tions, promotion, corporate and group sales and sponsorships, publicity, pub-
lations, marketing, fundraising, tickets, transportation, sports information and
a relations, academic counselor, concessions operations, game operations, etc.

ssional sports (NFL; NBA; WNBA; NHL; MLB; CFL; Arena Ball; World Bas-
ll League; U.S. Basketball League; Major League Lacrosse League; etc.)—
ations, security, sales, tickets and box office, personnel, marketing, promotion,
c relations, publicity, media relations, corporate and group sales and sponsor-
, event management, camp operations, game operations, concessions, souvenir/
handise sales, transportation, budgeting, finance and business operations, etc.

t agencies and governing bodies (Olympics; USOC; NCAA; NAIA; NCCAA;
AA; National High School Federation, various state High school state athletic
ciations; various officials organizations; AAU; National Sporting Goods Asso-
on; etc.)—budgeting and finance, scheduling, personnel, promotions, media re-
ns, marketing, public relations, operations, tickets and box office, etc.

icipal and state recreation entities and federal parks (City Recreation Depart-
ts; County Recreation Departments; State Recreation Departments; Federal
s)—promotion, publicity, personnel, sports and activity programming, grounds
facility management, budgeting, operations, scheduling, etc.

ufacturers of sporting equipment and supplies (Nike; Adidas; New Balance;
tilus; Adidas; Etonic; Rawlings; L.A. Gear; Voit Sports; Reebok; Champion;
—sales, marketing, promotions, camps, budgeting, operations, inventory, super-
n, personnel, etc.

handising and sales of sporting equipment and supplies (Locker Room Sports;
Sport Locker; Champs Sports; etc.)—sales, sales and marketing and sales train-
promotions, advertising, marketing, inventory, budgeting, personnel, inventory,
management, operations, etc.

s media (Daily and Weekly Newspapers; National Publications; Television Sta-
; Radio Stations; etc.)—announcer, broadcaster, research and statistics, sales,
ng, interviewing, marketing and promotions, operations, personnel, reporting,
nical operations, etc.

th, wellness and fitness clubs (Gold's Gym; Bally's; Jewish Community Centers;
—sales, operations, budgeting and finance, front desk operations, facilities, fit-
assessment, fitness programming, sports coordinator, merchandising, personal
ing; membership orientation, etc.

Evaluating

Evaluating encompassing three dimensions. First, assessing one's own capabilities, abilities and accomplishments. Second, evaluating the efforts, effectiveness, efficiency and results of others, both in and outside of the organization. And, third, evaluating the progress of the organization or entity itself, as well as its programs and activities.

> **CONCEPT #86: *The process of evaluation is on-going.***

The process of evaluation should not usually be a one-shot deal. Rather, evaluation is an on-going process in which periodic and consistent measurement is taken in terms of how either an individual is performing or how well an organization itself is operating. Both subjective and objective criteria may be used in the evaluation process, although most personnel evaluations now include at least some element of objective measurement.

Budgeting

Planning for income and expenses is only part of the budgeting process. Accounting of how the money is collected and how it is expended are also two important elements of budgeting. Two key words associated with the budgeting process are (1) accountability and (2) security. Managers in charge of budgets are held accountable for the handling of the monies as well as for the security of the funds. Finally, in some situations the general process of the budgeting umbrella might also include the responsibility of generating sources of additional revenue (such as fundraising).

> **CONCEPT #87: *Problems with the budgetary process can have disastrous consequences for the sport manager.***

So important is the budgetary process that any problem, any weakness discerned with any area of the budget is reason to suspect the competency of the manager whose responsibility it is to oversee the budget itself. The budget is a powerful tool. Having responsibility for a sizeable budget is a major responsibility and gives to the individual with this responsibility significant power. However, to make critical errors with any aspect of one's budgetary responsibilities is often the "kiss of death" in the world of management.

ESSENTIAL RESPONSIBILITIES OF SPORT MANAGERS

Managers today face many and varied responsibilities in their roles as administrators and leaders. Many of these responsibilities are generic to and are assumed by the "manager" regardless of the type of organization one is employed in or the level of management the individual is at within the entity.

> **CONCEPT #88:** *There are essential responsibilities that sport management professionals assume regardless of their position or the type of organization.*

Some of these essential responsibilities associated with being an effective and efficient manager include being a:

1. Leader
2. Problem solver
3. Motivator
4. Communicator
5. Disciplinarian
6. Risk taker
7. Decision maker
8. Teacher/educator
9. Counselor/confidant
10. Delegator

WHAT SPORT MANAGERS DO

Preseason Training Camps Can Being Great Advanced Publicity and Income to the Team
[courtesy of Buffalo Bills]

"Making things happen, getting things done and achieving results is what effective management is all about" (Sattler & Doniek, 1995, p. 52). However, it sounds much easier than in reality it is, especially in modern day organizations. Being an administrator can all too often be an all consuming job. Because of the very nature of the sport manager's job, responsibilities and time involvement it is all the more important to take time to "stop and smell the roses" (Hoch, 2004).

The Value of Delegating to Talented Lieutenant

> **CONCEPT #89:** *Securing the services of talented, motivated subordinates is a key or business.*

In terms of the corporate world (the world of busin cess in corporate business is much more likely to resu exists a *number of highly qualified, experienced and t weaker chief executive officer (CEO)* than in a case whe rior CEP who is surrounded by a "bunch" of average or v implications of such findings are significant in terms o and motivated subordinates and being able and com tasks to them. In addition, relying upon subordinates a nates is paramount for the competent administrators, n of all types of organizations.

Perhaps one of the most important realizations tha that it is imperative to make time to enjoy life and to enj as well as what you do in terms of rest and relaxation. Th makes Jack or Jackie a dull person" is pertinent when c tions of a sport manager. Thus, it is important to take tir family just as it is important to make time to do one's job

Those employed in sport do a lot of different thing situation, they can be involved in a wide range of diffe their jobs. Naturally, the type of things that people do w upon the organization and their job descriptions (Stier, 1

> **CONCEPT #90:** *Sport managers can be involved i of different job related tasks.*

Listed below is a comprehensive list of the types of j are available within various categories of sport and spor nesses, both non-profit and profit entities. The categorie nesses have been defined broadly and arbitrarily and the l

Nevertheless, the list should provide the reader with positions (jobs) available under the umbrella of sport m

types of ta ganization

1. Coll
   man
   ope
   lic r
   med
2. Pro
   ketb
   ope
   pub
   ship
   mer
3. Spo
   NJC
   asso
   ciat
   latic
4. Mu
   mer
   Par
   and
5. Ma
   Nat
   etc.
   visi
6. Me
   Lad
   ing.
   stor
7. Ne
   tior
   wri
   tecl
8. He
   etc.
   nes
   trai

Evaluating

Evaluating encompassing three dimensions. First, assessing one's own capabilities, abilities and accomplishments. Second, evaluating the efforts, effectiveness, efficiency and results of others, both in and outside of the organization. And, third, evaluating the progress of the organization or entity itself, as well as its programs and activities.

CONCEPT #86: *The process of evaluation is on-going.*

The process of evaluation should not usually be a one-shot deal. Rather, evaluation is an on-going process in which periodic and consistent measurement is taken in terms of how either an individual is performing or how well an organization itself is operating. Both subjective and objective criteria may be used in the evaluation process, although most personnel evaluations now include at least some element of objective measurement.

Budgeting

Planning for income and expenses is only part of the budgeting process. Accounting of how the money is collected and how it is expended are also two important elements of budgeting. Two key words associated with the budgeting process are (1) accountability and (2) security. Managers in charge of budgets are held accountable for the handling of the monies as well as for the security of the funds. Finally, in some situations the general process of the budgeting umbrella might also include the responsibility of generating sources of additional revenue (such as fundraising).

CONCEPT #87: *Problems with the budgetary process can have disastrous consequences for the sport manager.*

So important is the budgetary process that any problem, any weakness discerned with any area of the budget is reason to suspect the competency of the manager whose responsibility it is to oversee the budget itself. The budget is a powerful tool. Having responsibility for a sizeable budget is a major responsibility and gives to the individual with this responsibility significant power. However, to make critical errors with any aspect of one's budgetary responsibilities is often the "kiss of death" in the world of management.

ESSENTIAL RESPONSIBILITIES OF SPORT MANAGERS

Managers today face many and varied responsibilities in their roles as administrators and leaders. Many of these responsibilities are generic to and are assumed by the "manager" regardless of the type of organization one is employed in or the level of management the individual is at within the entity.

---

*CONCEPT #88: **There are essential responsibilities that sport management professionals assume regardless of their position or the type of organization.***

Some of these essential responsibilities associated with being an effective and efficient manager include being a:

1. Leader
2. Problem solver
3. Motivator
4. Communicator
5. Disciplinarian

6. Risk taker
7. Decision maker
8. Teacher/educator
9. Counselor/confidant
10. Delegator

WHAT SPORT MANAGERS DO

Preseason Training Camps Can Being Great Advanced Publicity and Income to the Team
[courtesy of Buffalo Bills]

"Making things happen, getting things done and achieving results is what effective management is all about" (Sattler & Doniek, 1995, p. 52). However, it sounds much easier than in reality it is, especially in modern day organizations. Being an administrator can all too often be an all consuming job. Because of the very nature of the sport manager's job, responsibilities and time involvement it is all the more important to take time to "stop and smell the roses" (Hoch, 2004).

The Value of Delegating to Talented Lieutenants/Subordinates

> **CONCEPT #89:** *Securing the services of talented, motivated, dedicated and motivated subordinates is a key to success in any organization or business.*

In terms of the corporate world (the world of businesses), research indicates that success in corporate business is much more likely to result from a situation in which there exists a *number of highly qualified, experienced and talented (supportive) officers with a weaker chief executive officer (CEO)* than in a case where there is a true genius and superior CEP who is surrounded by a "bunch" of average or weak lieutenants (Jones, 2001). The implications of such findings are significant in terms of securing the services of talented and motivated subordinates and being able and comfortable in delegating meaningful tasks to them. In addition, relying upon subordinates and having confidence in subordinates is paramount for the competent administrators, managers and directors at all levels of all types of organizations.

Perhaps one of the most important realizations that any sport manager can make is that it is imperative to make time to enjoy life and to enjoy what you do as a sport manager as well as what you do in terms of rest and relaxation. The adage that "all work and no play makes Jack or Jackie a dull person" is pertinent when one examines the role and obligations of a sport manager. Thus, it is important to take time for one's personal life, for one's family just as it is important to make time to do one's job within the sport entity.

Those employed in sport do a lot of different things. Depending upon their specific situation, they can be involved in a wide range of different tasks in the performance of their jobs. Naturally, the type of things that people do within an organization will depend upon the organization and their job descriptions (Stier, 1988).

> **CONCEPT #90:** *Sport managers can be involved in a wide range of different job related tasks.*

Listed below is a comprehensive list of the types of jobs and job related activities that are available within various categories of sport and sport related organizations and businesses, both non-profit and profit entities. The categories of sport organizations and businesses have been defined broadly and arbitrarily and the list is not meant to be definitive.

Nevertheless, the list should provide the reader with an understanding of the types of positions (jobs) available under the umbrella of sport management as well as the general types of tasks that individual employees actually perform within each of these types of organizations.

1. College athletics (Institutions within NCAA; NAIA; NCCAA; NJCAA)—event management, compliance/eligibility, facility management, budgeting and finance, operations, promotion, corporate and group sales and sponsorships, publicity, public relations, marketing, fundraising, tickets, transportation, sports information and media relations, academic counselor, concessions operations, game operations, etc.

2. Professional sports (NFL; NBA; WNBA; NHL; MLB; CFL; Arena Ball; World Basketball League; U.S. Basketball League; Major League Lacrosse League; etc.)—operations, security, sales, tickets and box office, personnel, marketing, promotion, public relations, publicity, media relations, corporate and group sales and sponsorships, event management, camp operations, game operations, concessions, souvenir/merchandise sales, transportation, budgeting, finance and business operations, etc.

3. Sport agencies and governing bodies (Olympics; USOC; NCAA; NAIA; NCCAA; NJCAA; National High School Federation, various state High school state athletic associations; various officials organizations; AAU; National Sporting Goods Association; etc.)—budgeting and finance, scheduling, personnel, promotions, media relations, marketing, public relations, operations, tickets and box office, etc.

4. Municipal and state recreation entities and federal parks (City Recreation Departments; County Recreation Departments; State Recreation Departments; Federal Parks)—promotion, publicity, personnel, sports and activity programming, grounds and facility management, budgeting, operations, scheduling, etc.

5. Manufacturers of sporting equipment and supplies (Nike; Adidas; New Balance; Nautilus; Adidas; Etonic; Rawlings; L.A. Gear; Voit Sports; Reebok; Champion; etc.)—sales, marketing, promotions, camps, budgeting, operations, inventory, supervision, personnel, etc.

6. Merchandising and sales of sporting equipment and supplies (Locker Room Sports; Lady Sport Locker; Champs Sports; etc.)—sales, sales and marketing and sales training, promotions, advertising, marketing, inventory, budgeting, personnel, inventory, store management, operations, etc.

7. News media (Daily and Weekly Newspapers; National Publications; Television Stations; Radio Stations; etc.)—announcer, broadcaster, research and statistics, sales, writing, interviewing, marketing and promotions, operations, personnel, reporting, technical operations, etc.

8. Health, wellness and fitness clubs (Gold's Gym; Bally's; Jewish Community Centers; etc.)—sales, operations, budgeting and finance, front desk operations, facilities, fitness assessment, fitness programming, sports coordinator, merchandising, personal training; membership orientation, etc.

9. Resort and hotel facilities (Hilton Head; Hilton Hotels; Westin Hotels; Circus Circus; Radisson Hotels; Disney World and Disney Land; Ritz Carlton Hotels; etc., — sales, operations, scheduling and programming, personal training, sports coordinator, activity instruction; private lessons; promotions, inventory, publicity, media relations, customer relations, etc.

10. Specialized resorts and facilities (Vail; Steamboat Run; Sun Valley; etc.)—sales, marketing operations, instruction, personal training programming, promotions, publicity, individual and group sport instruction, media relations, facilities, customer relations, etc.

11. Facility/Arena/Dome Management (Municipal Arenas; Institutional Facilities; Educational Arenas—such as the Rochester (New York) War Memorial; Buffalo's Marine Midland Arena; Cleveland's Quicken Loans Arena; the University of South Dakota's Dakota Dome; and Pittsburgh's Civic Center) advertising, sales, operations, scheduling, publicity, concessions, media relations, facilities, customer relations, etc.

THE IMPORTANCE OF SALES

Many of the job opportunities within the world of sport management involve some type of skills or competencies in the art and science of sales. A survey conducted some years ago of North American colleges and universities with sport management programs by Steve Shaad of Events Unlimited, a promotions management company, revealed that 53% of the schools viewed teaching sales skills to be extremely important; that 42% of the schools had received feedback from employers that sales skills are important in the jobs of sport management employees, but that 56% of the schools did not offer specific courses in sales.

FACTORS THAT DETERMINE SUCCESS OR FAILURE OF THE SPORT MANAGER

Generally speaking, there are four general factors that can have a significant effect upon an individual's effectiveness within any sport or sport-related organization, figure #4.2. It is advantageous to have an understanding of how these factors can have an affect upon one's ability to successfully serve as a sport manager. This is because such knowledge can be an aid to those who must successfully maneuver the organizational maze and climb the corporate ladder of sports and sport related entities today.

FIGURE 4.2: The Diamond Concept of Management

The first of these factors is the individual's own skill. It is important that the professional bring a wide range of personal and professional skills and competencies to the workplace. The second factor involves prior experience. What type of experiences has the manager been involved in and in what type of organizations? What has been the scope of the experience? Were the experiences meaningful, relevant and significant? Was there substance to the experience? What part or role in the experience did the individual play? Were the experiences successful or were they failures? Did the individual learn from the experiences?

CONCEPT #91: With a wide range of experiences the sport manager frequently does not have to reinvent the wheel when facing new challenges.

One of the advantages for a person with a wide range of meaningful experiences is that one is able to learn from such experiences. One is able to grow professionally and personally from experiences, from both good and bad experiences. Thus, experience—both successful as well as unsuccessful can help the sport manager in future situations and circumstances by applying general principles and concepts to new circumstances and making appropriate and timely decisions (Stier, 2006).

The third factor that can have a significant impact upon a person's success or failure in any organization is the type of the current job the individual has. What type of position or job is it? What skills and competencies are required to do the job, to accomplish the tasks, and to complete the mission? What is the level of the position? What type of organization is it? Is it a health club, a high school, a big-time university, a professional sport setting, a Fortune 500 corporate health facility, etc.? The type of job as well as the level of the position can have immeasurable impact upon the effectiveness and efficiency as well as ultimate success of the manager.

The fourth and final factor that can affect the effectiveness of any manager is the situation or circumstance surrounding the job or position. Is the situation such that what is needed is a manager to maintain status quo? Or, is the job or organization in desperate need of a turn-around artist? Or, are the circumstances such that drastic expansion and growth (change) is on the horizon and a true visionary is needed. Is there a financial crisis looming ahead? Is there a political morass lurking in the wings?

Being successful as a sport manager in any job or position, in any type of organization, requires that the professional employee have an understanding of all four of these factors. Not only must the person possess specific skills and competencies but also should have had meaningful experiences. In addition, the individual must discern the requirements of the job or position itself and determine whether there are any special circumstances or situations that may affect the likelihood of success in that position.

Another very important attribute that every successful sport management should demonstrate is referred to by the acronym MBBS, **Management by Being Seen**. This administrative philosophy implies "an attitude of active involvement as well as a conscious desire to be seen by others doing what any knowledgeable, caring, and competent sport manager should be doing" (Stier, 1999, p. 20). It is important to be seen by others as a competent, dedicated and motivated professional sport management administrator.

In addition to the "hard" skills or competencies enumerated above there are additional important skills now referred to as "soft" skills, i.e., managing emotions in the workplace and how one manages oneself in the workplace (in respect to others) and how we hand professional and personal relationships with others. Some of these so-called "soft" skills include (1) self-awareness (knowing one's internal states, preferences, intuitions, etc., (2) managing one's internal impulses, (3) empathy and awareness of others' feelings, needs and concerns, and (4) social skills (Koen, 2000).

Recipe for Success

The famous entrepreneur, salesperson and motivational speaker, Harvey Mackay, espouses four basic principles for success in the business world. These include: (1) mentoring or learning from the *best*, (2) networking, cultivating and maintaining a network of friends, colleagues and contacts, (3) surrounding oneself with people who will help you (the administrator) look smarter/better than you are—finding individuals whom you can trust and rely upon for good advice, knowledge and assistance, and (4) subscribing to the philosophy of "The Godfather's Michael Corleone" ("keep you friends close, but your enemies closer")—that is, use your network to keep informed of what your competitors are doing (Pappas, 1999).

SKILLS AND COMPETENCIES OF SPORT MANAGERS

CONCEPT #92: Managerial success in sport management is dependent upon possession of skills and competencies.

Success as a manager or administrator is dependent upon efficiently utilizing specific techniques and employment of special tactics that have proven to be effective in management and organizational situations. An aphorism in the world of management is that there are three distinct types of managers—those who make things happen, those who watch things happen, and those who are left wondering what happened (Stattler & Doniek, 1995).

As a would-be effective, efficient and successful manager, one needs to be able, capable and willing to develop specific managerial skills, including the skill of self evaluation (Corran, 1999). There are a number of general skills and competencies that all successful managers and administrators seem to demonstrate, to one degree or another. These skills need to be demonstrated by almost all sport management professionals. In fact, these fundamental managerial skills are highly prized regardless of the specific type of organization in which one is employed or the type of position one holds.

CONCEPT #93: **Regardless of the specific management job one holds or the type of sport organization one is associated with—the general skills and competencies needed are very similar.**

If you become a sport manager or administrator there are at least ten very specific competencies and skills which are very important for continual success within the sport entity. Being an effective and efficient manager is a difficult assignment. Not everyone can be successful. It takes dedication, skills, competencies and commitment. Studying the management of sport can help one develop these necessary skills, competencies and attributes.

THE TEN ESSENTIAL ADMINISTRATIVE SKILLS

Katz (1955) identified three essential attributes or skills of administrators. These were technical, interpersonal and conceptual skills. Basic skill, dedication/commitment skills and image skills are three additional categories of managerial skills identified by Stier (1994) as being necessary for sport managers. A year later Stier (1995, p. 165) added "the essential skills of adaptability, leadership, professionalism and vision (see figure 4.3) if the sport manager is to be a well rounded, talented, able, competent and conscientious professional."

FIGURE 4.3: Ten General Administrative Skills for Sport Managers

Basic Skills

Basic skills are those competencies that any well-educated member of this society would possess in the modern world. Men and women involved in sport management should be able (1) to think logically, (2) to write skillfully and creatively, (3) to speak clearly and convincingly, (4) to listen attentively, (5) to be well read in terms of both professional and general literature, (6) to be knowledgeable as well as appreciative of the arts, and (7) to be generally proficient as a contributing member of both today's and tomorrow's society. Those individuals who possess basic competencies "are able to be able to comprehend, analyze, synthesize and interpret accurately and in a timely fashion what they hear, observe, and experience" (Stier, 1995, p. 166).

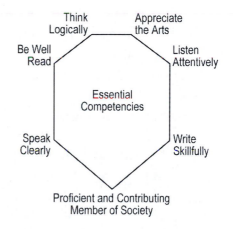

FIGURE 4.4: The Need for Essential Skills

> **CONCEPT #94:** *The sport manager should not be distinguishable from other professionals within our society by one's lack of basic skills, by the lack of basic competencies that would be expected of any reasonably intelligent and educated professional.*

Sport managers usually interact with a wide range of individuals within our society in the conduct of their business. Thus, it is imperative that they possess an adequate repertoire of basic skills enabling them to deal with and relate to others in an acceptable, appropriate, and all too often, sophisticated fashion, see figure 4.4.

Technical Skills

There are numerous technical type skills that must be mastered by the modern sport manager. With society and business so intertwined with the technological age it is obvious that computer competency is an absolute must for anyone desiring to make a career in the business of sport.

Specific Computer Competencies

Although the type of computer skills needed by sport managers today depends upon their responsibilities, there is general agreement that to be deemed computer literate in the 21st century one needs to be competent in the following areas:

1. Word processing, utilizing software such as Microsoft Word or WordPerfect
2. Database, utilizing software such as Microsoft Access
3. Spreadsheet, utilizing software such as Microsoft Excel, Lotus 1-2-3, Corel Quartro Pro
4. Presentation, utilizing software such as Microsoft PowerPoint
5. Desktop publishing, utilizing software such as Adobe PageMaker, Microsoft Publisher, Broderbund Print Shop
6. Photo editing, utilizing software such as Adobe Photoshop
7. Graphics and drawing, utilizing software such as CorelFlow, *CorelDraw*, Adobe Pagemaker
8. Illustration and design Illustration and design, utilizing Adobe Illustrator
9. Professional image editor, utilizing Adobe Photoshop, MetaCreations' Painter or Paint Shop Pro
10. Communications, utilizing e-mail, fax, internet, social media and the World Wide Web (WWW) [with a browser such as the, Netscape Navigator, Microsoft's Explorer]
11. Metasearch Engines (one-stop shopping), utilizing Dogpile, MetaCrawler, or Google
12. Search engines, utilizing Google, MSN, HotBot, Infoseek, Yahoo or Excite
13. Web browser, utilizing software such as Netscape Navigator or Microsoft's Explorer
14. Business accounting, utilizing software such as Intuit QuickBooks Pro, Peachtree Complete Accounting

15. Illustration and image editing such as Adobe Systems Photoshop for Windows, Adobe Systems Illustrator

16. Personal finance, utilizing Qucken Deluxe, Microsoft Money or Turbo Tax Delux

17. Project manager, utilizing Microsoft Project

18. Personal Information Manager, utilizing Lotus Organizer GS, or Microsoft Outlook

19. Personal image editor, utilizing Microsoft Picture It, Adobe Photo Deluxe

20. System utilities, utilizing Symnantec Norton Utilities, Helix Nuts & Bolts or Cyber-Media Oil Change

21. Antivirus software, utilizing Symantec Norton AntiVirus, McAfee VirusScan or PC-cillin

22. Web page publisher, utilizing Microsoft FrontPage or Adobe Dreamweaver

23. Directories are collections of websites that are grouped into subject categories. For example, E-Blast is the *Encyclopedia Brittanica's* guide to the Internet and includes more than 150,000 websites that have been reviewed and summarized.

24. Librarian's Guide to the Internet includes many sites on education, exercise, nutrition and sports—sunsite.berkeley.edu/InternetIndex

25. Sites of interest:
    Yahoo! www.yahoo.com
    Google www.google.com
    Infoseek www.infoseek.com
    HotBot www.hotbot.com
    Alta Vista www.altavistasssss.com
    Excite www.excite.com
    Dogpile www.dogpile.com
    MetaCrtawler www.metacrawler.com
    Inference Find www.infind.com
    Profusion www.profusion.com
    Magellan Magellan.excite.com
    E-Blast www.ebig.com

Additionally, there are special software packages that are integrated which provide the user with several software applications that are bundled together. For example, applications for word processing, database, spreadsheet, presentation and communication are bundled together into one package with all of the software applications integrated so as to be used together.

Today there are several popular bundled packages called software suites offered by various computer software firms. These suites typically include numerous integrated software applications including, among others, word processing, database, spreadsheet, presentations and others. Three of the more popular integrated packages are:

1. Microsoft Office Professional, containing (among other applications) Microsoft Word, Access, PowerPoint, Excel and Schedule.

2. Lotus SmartSuite, containing (among other applications) Lotus 1-2-3, Lotus Word Pro, Freelance, Approach, and Organizer.

3. Coral Office Professional, containing (among other applications) WordPerfect, Quartro Pro, Presentations, Flow Chart, and World Net.

There are also graphics suites which "are to designers what office suites are to businesspeople" (Graphics suites, 1997, January). Graphics suites typically include draw and paint programs, graphics utilities and a great deal of clip art. Three outstanding graphics suites include:

1. Micrografx's ABC Graphics Suite

2. Corel Graphics Pack

3. CorelDraw

And finally, there are several software packages created specifically for sport management applications. One of the first examples of such a software package was the Paciolan system created by Paciolan Systems, Inc. This software package includes applications for a variety of tasks facing the modern sport manager such as ticket office operations, accounting and budgeting, fundraising, etc. In fact, 85 of the 107 Division I-A intercollegiate athletic programs in this country utilize the Paciolan software system.

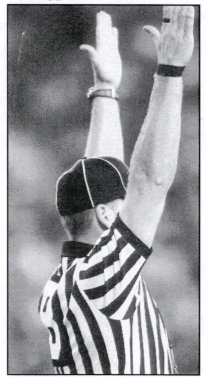

Officials are an Essential Element of All Competitive Sports
[courtesy of University of Tennessee, Sports Information Office]

The University of West Virginia's graduate program in sport management, under the leadership of Dr. Dallas Branch, was the first (1992) institution in the United States to utilize the complete Pociolan software system as part of its professional preparation program for future sport administrators at the master's level. In 1996 Ohio University's master's program, under the direction of Dr. Keith Ernce and Dr. Andy Kreutzer, became the second institution to incorporate this software system in the preparation of future sport managers (Werfelmann, 1996).

There are numerous other technical skills that one might need to develop competency—depending upon the person's specific responsibilities and duties. These include, but are not limited to, the following areas: ticket operations (box office), legal aspects (contracts), telecommunications (phone systems), audio-visual equipment, risk management, fitness assessment, teaching/training, statistics, scoreboard operations, facilities and grounds, security, sales, broadcasting, budgeting and finance, scheduling, personnel, marketing, promotions, fundraising, transportation, concessions operations, inventory, repair of specialized equipment, etc.

> **CONCEPT #95:** *The type of technical skills to be mastered is dependent upon the type of job one has and one's duties and responsibilities.*

Interpersonal Skills

Sport managers deal with people, both inside and outside of the sport organization. And in dealing with people one must be highly skilled in working with and relating to a wide range of individuals as well as small and large groups of people. Doing so requires expertise and experience in interpersonal skills. More professional employees in sport fail because of their inability to demonstrate competency in interpersonal skills than any other single reason (Stier, 1986).

> **CONCEPT #96:** *Sport managers should strive to develop positive working relationships with everyone—both in and outside the sport entity.*

Possessing interpersonal skills enables one to work productively (efficiently and effectively) with others; to gain their confidence, trust, respect and loyalty; to motivate others; as well as to lead others. Since sport managers must work with and through people, those who demonstrate greater skill in doing so will typically experience more sustained success than those who do not.

Managers who are successful are those who comprehend the importance of motivation (relative to their staff, employees, volunteers and interns) and the role that motivation can play in leading staff members to goals and objectives. The basic concept underpinning motivation is the realization that each and every staff member is important. With this realization serving as the foundation of a manager's working relationship with the staff, it is important to realize that inspiration (as a motivating tool) works far better with more positive consequences that intimidation (the motivation of the old "guard"). Employees work better, harder and with more enthusiasm when they are aware of the overall mission of the organization and especially when they have had a role in creating, adjusting or sustaining that mission. Using the three "A"s (awareness, appreciation and acknowledgement) is an excellent method of involving and motivating their staff to do their very best in the performance of their jobs (O'Brien & Sattler, 2000).

Conceptual Skills

Conceptual skills refer to the ability to understand the global picture of any situation. The opposite of conceptual skill is for an individual to operate as if one possesses tunnel vision. Many managers need to be detail persons, some more so than others. However, they simultaneously must be capable of viewing any given situation in light of a more global (total) perspective.

Professionals must not have blinders on and be concerned only with their own world or "fiefdom." They need to be cognizant of the whole "kingdom" if they are to be truly team players with the good of the organization as their major concern.

CONCEPT #97: *Don't lose sight of the ultimate objective or mission of your organization because of your involvement with your own specific job or task(s).*

Too frequently young or inexperienced employees within a sport organization fail to demonstrate conceptual competency. They fail to take the so-called big picture into consideration but get hung up and concerned only with their own immediate area of responsibility or sphere of influence.

Rather, they are concerned only with their immediate tasks, their present challenge. Less frequently, this type of poor judgment is even displayed by experienced personnel.

Adaptability Skills

Administrators and managers need to be adaptable. This is important because of the nature of the beast, the nature of people, the nature of sport, the nature of organizations. The ability to adapt, the ability to remain flexible, is a very important competency for any sport manager.

CONCEPT #98: *Things, organizations and people change— anticipate such changes and be adaptable, be flexible.*

Seemingly everything changes as time goes on. Progress is made. Problems are solved, Rules change. Expectations are altered. Resources shift. Innovations (technological) are made. Society evolves. Needs fluctuate. Goals are refined or replaced. Managers must be capable of changing with the times and adapting to the existing situation, whatever it might be. No one would attempt to manage or administer sport organizations today exactly like they were administered just a generation ago. That is because of the differences today in any number of factors that can have a significant impact upon the sport organization, its employees, and its customers.

Leadership Skills

Sport managers must be leaders. They must be capable of managing the behavior of other individuals. They must be able to guide others in their actions. They must be able to motivate others to action.

Alden (2004) classifies the managing and leading into two different categories with "the management side of directing a program being similar to observing one's responsibilities through a microscope, while the leadership side is more like looking through a wide-angle lens" (p. 41). Management, according to Alden, is micro, short-term while leadership is more macro, long-term. And, of course, as a director of a program or entity or activity, one must be engaged in both, successfully.

CONCEPT #99: *Leadership competency must be earned—it is not the result of merely holding the title of manager or boss.*

Leadership is a skill developed and earned. One demonstrates the ability to lead, one does not lead merely because one holds the title of "manager." The mark of a good leader is the ability to have people to do things and to get things accomplished. Competent managers lead through example as well as by giving directions or orders.

Dedication/Commitment Skills

It is not easy, in any stretch of the imagination, to be a successful sport manager or administrator. One must be personally and professionally committed to being a sport manager. One must be dedicated to the tasks at hand. Dedication simply means being willing and able to do what it takes to get the job(s) completed in terms of effort, time and sacrifices. It also means that one's spouse (and children, if any) also shares a willingness to share this commitment and dedication.

All too frequently one must make sacrifices if one is to fulfill one's responsibilities and successfully complete one's duty. This is where one's family comes into the picture. Sport managers need to have an understanding with their spouses and children in terms of the amount of time, effort and sacrifice their jobs might entail. Being dedicated and committed to one's job or profession does not mean that one must sacrifice one's family or one's family life.

However, being dedicated does mean that one is committed to seeing one's tasks completed on time and at an acceptable level of quality. Being dedicated doesn't mean just working long hours or working "hard." It does imply putting in sufficient hours and enough work that one's responsibilities are fully met and in a timely fashion. It does imply that one must work "smart"—one must expend quality effort and spend quality time on task.

CONCEPT #100:   *Effort alone doesn't count—rather, results count.*

Portable Display Stands Offer Flexibility and Effectiveness in Bringing One's Message to a Wide Audience
[courtesy of ESMC Consultants]

It is not merely a matter of how hard one works. It is never a matter of merely putting in many hours each day. Rather, success as a sport manager is dependent upon actually doing the job, completing the tasks in an acceptable fashion while meeting the deadlines. One shouldn't equate effort with results or competency.

Professionalism Skills

Sport managers need to be professional. They need to demonstrate those skills and competencies that mark or define professionals in our society. One such criterion is being current in one's field. Since there is so much change taking place in our society and in the world of sport and the world of business, sport employees must remain at the cutting edge in terms of knowledge and skills.

> ### CONCEPT #101:   *Sport managers need to remain at the cutting edge of their discipline.*

Managers cannot remain competent for long without making a conscious effort to remain up-to-date in their professional reading and by their attendance at workshops, conferences, clinics and lectures. It is absolutely necessary that today's sport managers remain at the cutting edge in the world of sport, in the world of business, in terms of the latest techniques, strategies and knowledge applicable to their area(s) of responsibility.

Toward this end, manages need to consistently read the latest professional journals and books in the areas of business, sport, and sport management. Just as a physician, a dentist or an accountant needs to remain at the forefront of the knowledge of their profession, so too does a sport manager need to keep up-to-date in terms of knowledge, techniques and strategies needed in the world of sport business.

Image Skills

Sport managers need not only to be professional and competent but they also need to look the part. They need to be viewed by others as competent, qualified and knowledgeable professionals. They need to possess the image of a professional in our society.

> ### CONCEPT #102:   *Perceptions are as important as reality when being viewed by others.*

Image has to do with how one is perceived or viewed by others. This is closely associated with how one dresses, how one presents oneself, and how one acts. An important concept related to image is that of perception. How one is perceived by others is most important. If a sport manager is perceived by another as being unprofessional or acting in a less than professional manner, then that sport manager is indeed unprofessional in the eyes of the person holding that opinion. Even if the perception is faulty, for the person holding that opinion, the perception is very real indeed.

A series of witticisms that dealt with "tongue in cheek" series of administrative definitions was provided by David Peltier, dean of Arts and Sciences at Ohio Northern University (author unknown, mimeograph copy, 1983), table 4.1. These statements have to do with the "tongue in cheek" interpretations or perceptions of statements commonly utilized by managers within a variety of different organizations.

CONCEPT # 103:   *Sport managers need to be competent, caring, experienced, knowledgeable and trained professionals—and give that impression to others.*

TABLE # 4.1: *Administrative Definitions (unknown author)*

It is in progress: So wrapped up in red tape that the situation is almost hopeless

We will look into it: By the time the wheel makes a full turn, we assume that you will have forgotten about it too

A program: Any assignment that can't be completed by one telephone call

Expedite: To confound confusion with commotion

Channels: The trail left by inter-office memos

Coordinator: The guy who has a desk between two expediters

Consultant: Any ordinary guy with a briefcase who is more than 50 miles from home

To activate: To make copies and add more names to the memo

To implement a program: Hire more people and expand the office

Under construction: Never heard of it

Under active consideration: We're looking in the files for it

A meeting: A mass mulling by master-minds

A conference: A place where conversation is substituted for the dreariness of labor and the loneliness of thought

To negotiate: To seek a meeting of minds without the knocking together of heads

Reliable source: The guy you just met

Informed source: The guy who told the guy you just met.

Unimpeachable source: The guy who started the rumor originally

A clarification: To fill in the background with so many details that the foreground goes underground

We are making a survey: We need more time to think of an answer

Note and initial: Let's spread the responsibility for this

See me, let's discuss: Come down to my office, I'm lonely

Re-orientation: Getting used to working again

Give us the benefit of your thinking: We'll listen to what you have to say as long as it doesn't interfere with what we have already decided to do

We will advise you in due course: If we figure it out, we'll let you know

To give someone the picture: A long confused and inaccurate statement to a newcomer

Forward for your consideration: You hold the bag for awhile

Approved, subject to comments: Re-do the thing

Spearhead the issue: You be the goat

Point up the issue: To expand one page to fifteen pages

The issue is closed: I'm tired of the whole affair

Let's plan our strategy: I want to tell you what to do

A coffee break: When and where, all the decisions are make

> **Open-door policy**: A platitude meant to pacify the multitudes
> **A raise**: Increase in pay to help you keep up with the Federal minimum wage law
> **We want you to utilize staff and resources fully**: Everyone is going to have to work harder
> **I'm glad you raised that qu**estion: What are you trying to do? Embarrass me?
> **After every factor was explored in depth**: That's the only reason we're going to give

Thus, sport mangers need to be concerned with the image that they project, with the perception of themselves that others have of them. Such professionals live within a fish bowl in terms of being visible to others, both inside and outside of the sport organization. Sport managers need to project an image that will reinforce the perception that one is a competent, caring, experienced, knowledgeable and trained professional—because one needs, in fact, to be competent, caring, experienced, knowledgeable and trained professional.

Vision Skills

Competent sport managers need to possess vision. They need to be able to look to the future and anticipate how individuals, programs, organizations and technologies might be changed or altered. Because so much in our society is changing it is most helpful if the manager can anticipate and even facilitate such change in a positive fashion in terms of one's own organization or program.

> *CONCEPT #104: Visions skill is needed in the sport management profession lest we blindly go where no one wishes to end up.*

Anticipating change and how such change might affect—both positively and negatively—one's program and one's organization is a highly prized ability. There are numerous examples of individuals, groups and organizations attempting to glimpse into the future so as to be able to successfully meet the challenges and needs of the future.

EXAMPLES OF EFFORTS AT LOOKING INTO THE FUTURE

Two such efforts in the area of curricular planning for sport management occurred in the fall of 1994 and again in the fall of 1995 at the State University of New York, Brockport. In the fall of 1994 a national conference was held in Brockport, New York, dealing with **The Future of the Physical Education Profession—Survival or Extinction**. At this four-day conference leaders throughout the United States and Canada met to discuss and examine the current status in physical education as well as sport management and other allied academic areas in an effort to determine what the future of these academic entities might become.

These leaders, both practitioners and educators, sought to gain insight in terms of the future for physical education, sport management and other related disciplines and what might be done to insure their survival in the 21st century. Strategies were also examined that might insure the survival and healthy growth and development of physical education, sport management, etc., (Stier, Kleinman & Milchrist, 1995, October)

> *CONCEPT #105:   Visionaries not only attempt to anticipate the future but facilitate the change process as well.*

The following year another four-day national conference was also held in New York on the Brockport campus. The purpose of this second conference was different as evidenced by its name, **The Future of the Profession—Developing a Vision**. At this gathering leaders from the two countries sought to arrive at a vision or visions of what physical education, sport management and other academic areas might be well into the next century. The visionaries at this conference sought ways to facilitate the changes affecting our profession and our programs that will inevitably take place in the future. They also examined how to guide the curricular offerings within sport management, physical education and other related areas into possible new configurations, relationships and alliances.

All good leaders and managers are visionaries in some sense of the word. They anticipate the future. But they do more. They also plan for the future, they prepare for the future. In fact, true visionaries help shape the future (Massengale, 1995).

MASTERING THE SKILLS AND COMPETENCIES NEEDED IN SPORT MANAGEMENT

Can the managerial skills and competencies needed by sport managers be taught? Can they be learned? Or, are successful sport managers born with the skills and competencies necessary for success in the world of sport.

> *CONCEPT #106:   Managerial skills and competencies can be taught/learned.*

The answer is simple. Managerial skills and competencies may indeed be taught (Staffo, 1990). Through formal and informal educational efforts as well as through meaningful and pertinent managerial and organizational experiences individuals can significantly enhance their managerial abilities. Would-be managers can indeed become more efficient, more effective, more successful, in a variety of leadership roles through deliberate efforts to learn, to broaden their knowledge base and to develop both general and specific skills.

That is why numerous colleges and universities offer curricular options (preservice educational opportunities) in management as well as sport management. That is why literally thousands of businesses, including sport and sport related businesses, provide in-service educational opportunities to their managers and would-be managers. That is why there are thousands of management consultants who conduct workshops and clinics and deliver speeches and lecturers on numerous aspects of management.

BEING A RENAISSANCE PERSON

The Renaissance Sport Management Professional

Sport managers should strive to be renaissance people (Stier, 1986, Spring). In reality, there are two essential aspects to being a true renaissance individual. First, there is the matter of sport management competencies. The sport management professional needs to be very knowledgeable in a whole range of areas and possess a variety of skills and competencies associated with the management of sport and sport related organizations. Additionally, this person should also become an expert or near expert in one (preferably two) areas within the sport management umbrella.

> *CONCEPT #107:* ***Sport management professionals should strive to be RENAISSANCE PERSONS—highly competent in most areas and an expert or near expert in at least one area, preferably two.***

An example will suffice. An employee in a minor league (AA) baseball operation might be placed in charge of the concession and souvenir operations. This responsibility requires the individual to possess and very specific skills, aptitude and expertise. However, this same individual must understand, at least in a general way, the overall operation of the organization.

> *CONCEPT #108:* ***A bane of sport management professionals is to possess limited skills, experience and expertise.***

Additionally, this person must also be somewhat knowledgeable in a wide range of other areas (tickets, grounds, public and media relations, promotions, etc.) within that specific baseball organization. And, this person needs to be generally knowledgeable in terms of professional baseball and professional sports. The competent sport management employee must not be limited in one's perspective or possess skills that are so specific or limited that the individual is incapable of successfully assuming other responsibilities within that organization or even another entity (Stier, 1990).

The Renaissance Citizen of Our Society, of the World

The second aspect of a sport manager being a renaissance person involves a more global concept and centers around being well read and knowledgeable in a wide range of areas outside the very specific sport management domain. For example, a truly educated individual in our society must be knowledgeable in politics, literature, history, political science, sociology, psychology, music, dance, science, etc.

In other words, the sport management professional, if the person is to be truly educated in our society, today as well as the future, must possess a wide range of knowledge and demonstrate a high degree of specific skills and competencies, not only in the limited domain of sport management but also in the larger, more global perspective of being a citizen of our society, a citizen of the world.

One reason for this that sport management professionals, now more than ever, must possess more global skills, understandings and knowledge as they progress up the proverbial career ladder is that they will deal with a wide range of individuals, groups and organizations in the conduct of their sport management business. These sport management professionals will find themselves personally and professionally involved with doctors, lawyers, salespeople, farmers, civil servants, teachers, business persons as well as "bakers" and "candle stick makers." The sport manager needs to be able to work with and relate to a wide range of individuals, groups, cliques and organizations in the performance of their own jobs.

As a consequence, today's and tomorrow's sport management professional must be a well educated individual, both in terms of general education and knowledge of our society as well as the specialized knowledge, skills and competencies associated with the world of sport management. Sport management professionals needs "to exist within the real world, within our society, and must be able to represent themselves as well-rounded individuals who are bright, articulate, intelligent, educated, and refined" (Stier, 1995, p. 163).

Willingness to Learn

Another very important component of being competent as a professional within the world of sport management is being able and willing to learn. The new graduate of a college sport management program has only begun to master the skills and obtain the knowledge needed during that person's professional life. In fact, it is this ability to learn that is so highly prized today by all businesses and organizations in our fast paced society. And, it will continue to be so in the future.

CONCEPT #109: *Graduating from any sport management program is only a beginning of a lifelong learning process.*

Yes, of course the sport management graduate will possess specific skills. But this same graduate will have to continue to learn and master additional skills on the job, throughout that person's entire professional career. If not, the career will become stagnant and others will pass that individual on the career ladder.

For example, although any sport management graduate will be expected to be computer literate, this does not mean that the individual will possess the skills and be competent in the specific software application used by one's new employer. Many organizations and companies use very specific computer applications. Perhaps the graduate is unfamiliar with that specific software package. However, this same graduate also possesses basic computer competencies and is able to learn and master the new or different software package, within a reasonable amount of time.

CONCEPT #110: *Sport managers must continue to learn, to master and to refine managerial skills and competencies.*

This ability to learn is most highly prized for two simple reasons. First, no undergraduate curricular program can begin to prepare the student to be competent in every single dimension, every aspect of the sport management arena. There is simply too much to learn in too short a time. Besides, the undergraduate professional preparation program, by definition, is supposed to prepare generalists. More specialized knowledge may be mastered at the graduate level or through on-the-job (in-service) training.

CONCEPT #111: *Change is inevitable, change is the watchword for sport management professionals.*

The second reason why the ability to learn is so highly valued by employers is that seemingly "everything" is changing at a very rapid pace in our society. And it will continue to do so, perhaps at an even accelerated pace in the future. New ideas are being explored. New knowledge is being discovered. New products are being developed all the time. New applications, new techniques, new strategies are being studied, evaluated and frequently implemented. Change is the watchword of tomorrow. If one is not able to keep up with the changes in our profession, in our society, one is simply left behind or "out in the cold."

An obvious change (growth) in a tool or asset used by so many of our world citizens (and obviously our sport management compatriots) can be seen in the computer. The year 2004 marked the 30th anniversary of the personal computer, the Altair, a 2 MHz device that contained 256 bytes of RAM, was the computer's primary workspace. What is commonly recognized as the first (1946) electronic computer, ENIAC (Electronic Numeral Integrator and Computer) weighed over 30 tons and filled a room the size of a tennis court (The PC turns 25). Compare both devices with the typical home or office computer and one cannot help but be duly impressed.

Witness also the growth of the internet and the use of web sites by colleges and universities. In 1997 it was reported that a survey revealed that 98% of the NCAA division I schools used computers in their marketing efforts while only 43% of these same schools had a departmental web page (Farrell & Daniel, 1997). Contrast that to what exists today. It is estimated that it would be hard to find a single college athletic department (at any NCAA division) that does not have a web site (Stier, 2006, September 13).

FUTURE DIRECTIONS OF SPORT MANAGEMENT

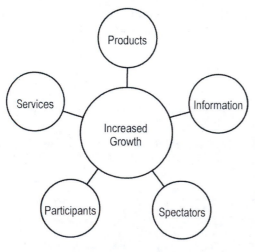

The future of sport, of sport business and sport management will be closely associated with advances in technology and a continued expansion of knowledge. Some of the areas in which tremendous growth will continue to occur will be in computerization and technology; facility and arena management; health, fitness and wellness sport services; private lessons and instruction; recreational activities; competitive sports; sport merchandising; and, sales. There will also be continued growth in the number of sports and sport related activities, both in terms of actual participation and in terms of spectators.

FIGURE 4.5: Potential Growth in Sport and Sport Management

Finally, there will be an ever-increasing growth in terms of sport consumers in terms of services, products and knowledge/information, figure 4.5.

CONCLUSIONS

Managerial employees in sport, recreation and fitness programs should be effective in implementing the eleven processes (PPOSDCoRRFEB) of management in a variety of situations. In addition, there are specific skills that competent manages, regardless of their positions or the type of organization in which they work, should demonstrate in the course of their day-to-day activities. Most managers within the sport world assume a variety of different responsibilities at various times. Truly exceptional managers are considered to be Renaissance persons in that they are experts in one or more specific areas while retaining general knowledge in many areas. It is especially important that modern managers be at the cutting edge in terms of technology.

REFERENCES

Alden, E. (2004). Taking time out. *Athletic Management, XVI*(5), 41-44.

Bryson, J.M. (1995). *Strategic planning for public and nonprofit organizations.* San Francisco: Jossey-Bass.

Farrell, P.V. and McCann, D.J. (1997). Computers, the Internet, and Marketing College Athletics, *Sports Marketing Quarterly,* 6(3), 12-13.

Goldsborough, R. (1999). Information overload. *Athletic Management, XI,* (4), 31-34.

Graphics suites have it all. (1997, January). *PC World,* p. 162.

Corran, R. (1999). Self study. *Athletic Management, XI,* (6) 49, 50, 52, 53.

Gulick, L. & Urwick, L. (Eds.). (1937). *Papers on the science of administration.* New York: Institute of Public Administration.

Hoch, D. (2002, August). Visions of time. *Athletic Management, XIV*(5), *39, 40,42, 43.*

Hoch, D. (2004). Life is too short. *Athletic Management, XVI*(6), 26, 2, 29.

Jones, D. (2001, January 19). How MBAs might reshape the White House. *USA Today,* pp. 1-A, 2-A.

Katz, R. (1955). Skills of an effective administrator. *Harvard Business Review, 33*(1), 34-35.

Koen, D. (2000). Self-control counts more than high IQ. *Democrat & Chronicle,* p. G-1.

Lumpkin, A. (1997). Strategic planning in health, physical education, recreation and dance. *Journal of Physical Education, Recreation, and Dance, 68*(5), 38-40, 46.

Massengale, J.D. (1995). Visionary leadership and the physical educator. *The Physical Educator, 52*(4), 219-221.

Not thinking ahead. (1999, September 20). *Democrat & Chronicle*, p. 3-F.

O'Brien, T. and Sattler, T.P. (2000). Taking management personality. *Fitness Management, 16, (8),* 59, 61, 62.

Pappas, C. (1999). Harvey Mackay. *Success, 46*(2). 50-55.

The PC turns 25. (1999, June 1). *Democrat & Chronicle,* p. 1-E.

Sattler, R.P. and Doniek, C. A. (1995, October). Quantitative analysis for a better bottom line. *Fitness Management, 11*(11), 52.

Staffo, D.F. (1990). Should administrators be specifically trained for positions in HPER-Athletics? *Journal of Physical Education, Recreation and Dance, 68*(2), 62, 63, 78, 79.

Stier, W.F., Jr. (1986, Spring). Athletic administration: Athletic administrators expect qualities, competencies in coaches. *Interscholastic Athletic Administration*, pp. 7-10.

Stier, W.F., Jr. (1988, January). Competencies of athletic administrators. *The Athletic Director, 16*(2), 3.

Stier, W.F., Jr. (1990, July). Wanted: Renaissance athletic directors. *Athletic Director, 7*(3), 34-35, 42

Stier, W.F. Jr., (1994). *Successful sport fund-raising.* Dubuque, Iowa: Wm. C. Brown & Benchmark.

Stier, W.F. Jr., (1995). *Successful coaching: Strategies and tactics.* Boston, MA. American Press Publishers.

Stier, W.F., Jr., Kleinan, S., & Milchrist, P. A. (1995, October). The future of physical education—Survival or extinction. *ERIC—Resources in Education*. ED383644. pp.10.

Stier, W. F., Jr. (1999). Look at Me! *Athletic Management, XI*(6), 20, 21.

Stier, W.F., Jr. (2005, August 19). Everything You Always Wanted to Know about Writing, Reviewing and Editing for Professional/Scholarly Journals—But Were Afraid to Ask. *Proceedings: 1ˢᵗ International Council of Health, Physical Education, Recreation, Sport and Dance [ICHPER-SD] Leadership Conference and Workshop for Asia,* Taipei, Taiwan, pp. 74-77.

Stier, W.F., Jr. (2006). Understanding sport management—From a global perspective. *Proceedings: 4ᵗʰ Congreso Regional Latinoamericano de la ICHPER•SD,* [4ᵗʰ Regional Congress in Latin America of the International Council for Health, Physical Education, Recreation-Sport and Dance], Venezuela: San Carlos.

Stier, W.F., Jr. (2006, September 13). The so-called "secrets" of writing for research and scholarly journals. Paper presented at the *Jamaica Physical Education Association and the Pre-Inaugural International Council of Health, Physical Education, Recreation, Sport and Dance Caribbean Meeting.* Kingston, Jamaica,

Werfelmann, J. (1996, July). *Interface, 8*(4), pp. 2.

DISCUSSION TOPICS

1. Explain the roles that the processes of management play in the management of sport entities.

2. Which of the processes of management (PPOSDCoRRFEB) seem to be the most important for you as a future sport manager? Why?

3. Select one of the ten essential responsibilities of a sport manager and illustrate how this particular responsibility can play an important role in your efforts to serve as a sport manager in a hypothetical business situation.

4. Identify a general employment situation and specify several specific job opportunities that you might wish to pursue as a career. Why?

5. What are the four factors that affect a sport manager's effectiveness in any sport-related entity?

6. Specify computer applications (software) that might be of significant use in a sport management employment situation in which you might find yourself in the future. Be specific.

7. What, in your opinion, is the most important skill or competency of sport managers? Justify your position.

8. Explain how a sport manager should be a Renaissance person, both personally and professionally.

9. Provide examples of why being willing (and able) to learn is an invaluable asset.

10. Outline the significance of being a visionary in the world of sport management.

Chapter

5

Decision Making, Problem Solving, and Risk Taking—Essential Skills for Effective Management

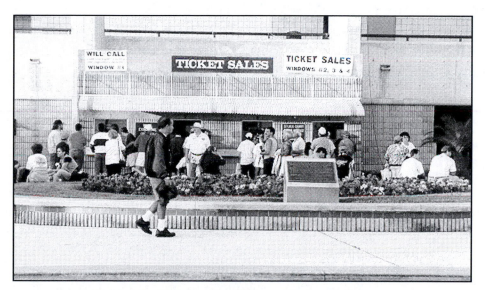

Ticket Sales Form the Foundation of Professional Sports
[photo courtesy of St. Lucie METS, Port St. Lucie, Florida]

CHAPTER HIGHLIGHTS

This chapter will help the reader to:

- Understand the concept of **Road Warriors** insofar as productivity of employees is concerned;
- Understand the concept of leadership as it relates to business organizations;
- List the traits of effective leadership;
- Explain why all managers are not leaders;

131

- Differentiate between formal authority and acknowledged leadership by providing examples of each;
- Cite the challenges of being a leader in a variety of sport environments;
- Illustrate the strategies and tactics of responsible leaders;
- Identify three leadership styles;
- Define motivation as it pertains to managing sport within a complex society;
- Differentiate the roles of the board of directors versus the executive or leader insofar as micromanagement is concerned;
- Specify the differences between intrinsic and extrinsic motivation;
- Describe negative and positive motivational strategies;
- Be familiar with the terms feedback and criticism in terms of motivation;
- List motivational techniques, strategies and tactics;
- Comprehend effective and efficient decision making within a sport organization;
- Understand the basis of effective and efficient decision making;
- Appreciate the role of decision making in problem solving;
- Explain the importance of making exceptions;
- Justify the delegation of some decision making to subordinates.

LEADERSHIP WITHIN SPORT ORGANIZATIONS

Jack Welch, former chairman/CEO of General Electric Co., and one of the most highly recognized and honored leaders among Fortune 500 companies, was selected as "manager of the year" in 1991. He retired in 2001 after 21 years at the helm, at a time when General Electric Co. had 313,000 employees (McGinn, 2005). However, in an interview he indicated that he is not so sure that he wants to be referred to as a so-called "manager." This is because people sometimes mistakenly think of a manager as one who merely "controls rather than facilitates, complicates rather than simplifies, acts more like a governor than an accelerator" ('Manager of year', 1991, p. 2-B).

As the highly effective and revered leader of General Electric Co., Mr. Welch wanted to make sure that his activities as leader of the corporation reflected the positive elements associated with the more modern view of leadership within organizations and businesses. The goal of a modern day manager, a true business or organizational leader, is to be able to increase the effectiveness and efficiency of the organization or business.

The First Organizational Man

Alfred P. Sloan, also a leader within the business world and considered by most to be "one of the most celebrated CEOs of his era" (Byrne, 2005, p. 99), is credited with being ". . . the first Organizational Man, a visionary devoted to bringing discipline to the impulsive, informal, often chaotic capitalist enterprise of the early 20th century (Welch, 2004, p. 24).

As head of General Motors Corporation in the early 20s through the 30s and 40s, he brought to the forefront key ideas, concepts and principles that, today, form the foundation of almost every large corporation in today's society. Some of these principles, presented in his famous *The Organizational Study* (the first management book), include the belief that the business of business could be rationalized, the output of businesses and organizations could be measured, checks and balances within organizations were essential, and managers should be rewarded (motivated) in a way that pushed them to reach for excellence (p. 24). He also was a big proponent of marketing efforts (research), advertising are well as public relations on behalf of the corporation/business/organization.

CONCEPT #112:   To be an effective sport manager one must be a leader.

Sport managers "need to assume a dynamic leadership role" in advancing their organization (Ross & Young, 1997, p. 22). Managers, by the very nature of their role, must be able to work with people, including paid staff, volunteers as well as members of various constituencies and the general public. Being successful in business, sport or otherwise, requires the same essential skills, qualities and characteristics (Success is the same, 1988, September).

The ability to be an effective and efficient leader is an essential ingredient for the modern sport manager or administrator. In today's and tomorrow's complex sport business (profit or non-profit) it is essential the modern style manager be a skilled leader, motivator and decision-maker (Judd, 1995).

Henry Kissinger is reportedly to have said that the task of management (managers) is to take *people* from where they are to where they have not been. To accomplish this it is necessary to lead (direct), motivate (influence) and make effective and efficient decisions (to act) in critical situations.

Leadership Defined

Leadership is a universal phenomenon among human beings (Smither, 1988; Lewis, 1993). Being a leader (a manager) is similar to being an orchestra conductor. Leadership comes in many shapes and sizes. If you look at some of the great leaders in different environments one would see different paths to leadership and different styles of leadership. For example, if one would look at Herb Kelleher (CEO of Southwest Airlines for 30 years) and Bill Gates (Microsoft) in the business world; Churchill and Gandhi in the political world; and Lombardi and Belichick in the world of sport; it is easy to recognize different styles and methods of leadership, each suited to a particular situation and a particular point in time (Welch and Welch, 2005). John Hennessy, the newly appointed president of

Stanford University in 2000, was quoted as saying that: "I think of leaders as servants of their constituents" (Stanford names, 2000).

Although there are many different definitions of leadership, they all have several things in common. First, effective leaders are very good in working with and dealing with people. Second, competent leaders are able to establish appropriate goals for the organization and programs. Third, capable leaders successfully influence, guide and direct the actions of others. Fourth, skilled leaders are successful in having goals realized. In short, most people view a person as a leader who is able to get other people to do things that will lead to a realization of some important and significant objectives or objectives. And, fifth, good leaders are also good followers (or have been good followers somewhere in their careers).

Leaders, according to Jack Welch must be on the lookout for micromanagement from organizations' board of directors (McGinn, 2005). Micromanagement refers to when the board attempts to usurp the day-to-day duties and decisions normally reserved for the executive. In other words, micromanagement involves having a governing board (a global policy making entity) becoming engaged in the day-to-day operation of the organization, a task and responsibility reserved for the executive who has been given that responsibility. This is a common fault among boards and leaders must be given sufficient freedom to carry out the boards approved agenda. Otherwise, leaders (administrators/managers) are hamstrung in terms of their ability to carry out their myriad duties and responsibilities.

Part of being a good (effective and efficient) leader means that one must be able to accomplish four major tasks. First, to hire and retain the best people for the job(s). Second, to confront the actual (and sometimes brutal) facts of any given situation (true reality). Third, to consistently and relentlessly seek to become (and remain) the best. And, fourth, to remain focused on incremental and continuous change within the workplace and competitive marketplace (Collins, 2001, cited in Lumpkin 2004).

An example of a leader attempting to remain at the cutting edge within the so-called marketplace is Vanderbilt University's Chancellor Gordon Gee who, in 2003, disbanded the athletic department as it was then organized/structured within the university (Hill, 2004). Vanderbilt University is the only private university in the highly competitive athletic Southeastern conference.

In his leadership position as Chancellor, Dr. Gee reorganized the athletic program by eliminating the athletic department, as it traditionally exists within Division I universities, and in its place, he moved athletics under the direction of the Vice Chancellor for Student Affairs (Rozin, 2003). There is no longer an autonomous entity called the athletic department at the university.

CONCEPT #113:   An effective leader gets the job done through people.

Leaders must have a constituency. This implies that leaders are involved with people (within an organization, group or loose affiliation) who view or recognize the person as the leader. Leaders have commanding influence upon others and the ability to (1) coordinate people, (2) influence and persuade people, (3) delegate responsibility, (4) guide (show) others in action and direction, (5) motivate (guide) others to action, and (6) having others do things they want done (Krause, 1981; Stier, 2005, November 1; Vick, 1989; & Woyach, 1993).

Dr. David Berg, a Psychiatry professor and leadership expert at Yale University and a frequent speaker at a well-known leadership conference that charges $27,000 per person for training in leadership, cites the belief that "it may not matter who becomes CEO at their company. Success relies less on who leads than on the chemistry between leaders and followers" (Jones, 2003, p. 2-B).

Goal Setting

Leaders (sport managers) need to be concerned with three types of goals. First, there are personal goals of the individual assuming the role of the leader. Second, there are professional goals of the leader. And, third, there are the business goals of the organization within which the leader works. It is the ability to recognize and officially identify a wide variety of appropriate objectives and goals and to work towards these goals (with and through people) that distinguishes the true leader within any organization. For true leaders guide and point the way, they get things done, they get people to work together toward a common objective(s) or goal(s).

Tactics for Effective Leadership

Michael Hammer, author of the 1992 best selling book *Reengineering the Corporation* and the re-release of the book, *The Reengineering Revolution*, stated (only slightly in jest) that leaders should be one part visionary, one part motivator and one part leg breaker (Balog, 1995, p. 1-B). A more useful list of tactics for effective leadership was presented by Dressler (1977, pp. 270-271) and included the following seven suggestions:

1. Know and train yourself, study techniques of good leadership and develop your own personality to be more effective in light of the person's experience, training, and job.
2. Know and control your styles of leadership.
3. Know and support your people (their strengths/weaknesses) and respect differences.
4. Adapt to the characteristics and demands of each situation.
5. Act like a leader, be energetic—dress like a leader, look like a leader, think like a leader.
6. Delegate but don't abdicate, train subordinates but keep important decision making jobs to self.

7. Build a strong team and encourage teamwork—use participatory techniques and develop cohesion, respect, and comradely among team members.

The following are eight suggestions for leaders within the world of business as espoused by Jack Welch (Welch and Welch, 2005, pp. 46-48; Welch, 2005).

1. Leaders must consistently and relentlessly upgrade their team. They must utilize every chance they get to evaluate, coach and establish self-confidence in others.

2. Leaders make sure that others live and breathe the organization's vision (not merely see the so-called vision).

3. Leaders always and consistently emanate positive energy and optimism.

4. Leaders create a bond of trust with others through candor, transparency and the granting of credit where credit is due.

5. Leaders must have demonstrative courage, courage to make tough and sometimes unpopular decisions as well as "gut" calls.

6. Leaders push and probe people with a curiosity that teeters on skepticism, thus insuring that questions receive appropriate, timely and accurate answers, answers that can be converted into meaningful actions.

7. Leaders inspire through example—they encourage risk taking and ever increasing learning/improvement in others through their own examples.

8. Leaders take time and seize the opportunity to celebrate success and achievement since celebration establishes the atmosphere of recognition, reward and appreciation for achievement and accomplishment (individual and collective).

ABSENCE OF LEADERSHIP

What happens when there is no leadership? Or, when there is inadequate leadership? The lack of leadership means a lack of direction, a lack of motivation, a lack of decision making, and a lack of cohesion among those individuals working within the organization. The end result can be confusion, difficulties, problems and chaos. And, of course, the failure to realize objectives and goals (Imundo, 1991).

FORMAL AUTHORITY VERSUS ACKNOWLEDGED LEADERSHIP

There is a difference between what is referred to as *formal authority* and *acknowledged leadership* within the workplace. Authority can emanate from outside the individual and may be bestowed upon a person by another, like a title. Leadership comes from within the individual who is perceived as the leader.

A person may be given power and authority to do something. Acknowledged leadership is when someone is perceived as a leader not necessarily because of having been given a mere title or a specific responsibility but because of who and what that person is and what that person can accomplish.

CONCEPT #114:   *Not all managers are leaders—All leaders are "managers" of people.*

In this light managers can be viewed as different than leaders. *Not all managers are leaders. However, all leaders are "managers" in the sense that leaders get things accomplished through (managing) people.* Managers are appointed and although they have a legitimate right to have the title of "manager" they must still earn the respect of those with whom they work and interact (subordinates, peers and others) in order to be considered as leaders.

LEADERS AND THE EXERCISE OF POWER

Leaders are authority figures and as such can potentially wield significant power. Managers have formal power and authority due to the position they hold. Leaders have power because subordinates and others willingly comply with the superior's or leader's direction (Smither, 1988, p. 359). There are several sources of power (influence) that form the basis for effective leadership and frequently outstanding leaders exhibit power from any combination of the following sources:

1. Reputation power—being influential because of impressions created by one's image/reputation
2. Knowledge (skill) power—abilities enable one to exert influence and get things accomplished
3. Experience power—based upon one's previous experiences
4. Referent or charismatic power—power emanating from one's personality
5. Coercive power—being able to reward and punish
6. Legitimate power—conferred by higher authority

DEVELOPING SKILLS AS A LEADER

People are not born as leaders (Imundo, 1991). Rather, individuals can be trained, can be educated in terms of being leaders and managers. In fact, Staffo (1991) recommends that would-be administrators should be specifically trained for responsible administrative positions in sport.

CONCEPT #115:   *Leaders are made—not born.*

An individual can become a better leader, a more competent manager by working toward that goal. One needs to experience appropriate training in the areas of leadership and management. Formal education can facilitate this learning process. Also, practical experience in leadership and managerial roles are essential if one is to enhance one's skill level. Thus, practice being a leader, practice being a manager of people in everyday situations. Become involved in volunteer activities that involve leadership roles.

Desirable Traits of Competent Sport Managers and Leaders

What makes a good leader? What makes for an effective leader? What are the traits (distinguishing characteristics or qualities) that are usually present in outstanding leaders in any organization? While many leaders exhibit one or more common traits or characteristics, there is no single trait, characteristic or quality that automatically identifies a leader or qualifies one to be a leader.

CONCEPT #116:   *There is no Single distinguishing trait that automatically makes one an effective leader.*

Numerous authors and authorities have voiced opinions regarding skills and characteristics that leaders should possess or demonstrate from time to time in the conduct of their business. Some of the more important skills for an effective leader, according to Flamholtz & Randle (1987), are decision-making, recruiting employees and volunteers, day-to-day leadership and supervision, personnel development, time management, delegation and planning. Other skills are enthusiasm, self-confidence, patience, strength, ability to inspire, to motivate and to generate faith, loyalty, trust and confidence among subordinates as important elements of leadership (Vick, 1989; Staffo, 1991). And, another trait is the ability to work hard and long at important tasks. As Ron Guenther, the University of Illinois athletic director, puts it: "I'm always working because there's always a lot to do" (Martyka, 2001, p. 27).

Of course, effective leaders also need to be capable and willing to solve problems, to resolve conflict, to compromise, to mediate, to mentor, to negotiate, to build teamwork (coalition-building) among subordinates and peers, to be excellent communicators (and listeners) and to display a high achievement drive. In short, leaders need to be competent and caring persons, willing to be responsible for others (Lewis, 1993; Stier, 1998b, Hatcher, 2005).

Various experts suggest that leaders possess the following characteristics, tendencies, skills and aptitudes (Lumpkin, 2004, p. 45).

1. Able and willing to take reasonable risks

2. Being honest, trustworthy and responsible

3. Able to create a shared vision with others and able to have others buy into this shared vision

4. Being energetic, enthusiastic, honest, trustworthy and responsible

5. Able to demonstrate and model excellent and effective human relations and inter-personal skills within a collaborative environment

6. Capable of nurturing open and effective communication

7. Able to make appropriate, timely, efficient and effective decisions

8. Capable of developing a culture within the organization of mutual trust and respect.

THE MATTER OF TRUST

Trust is a major factor in terms of effective leadership within all organizations. In fact, it is crucial (Jones, 2001, March 13). And, of course, leaders have power to get things done. Gene Keady, former basketball coach at Purdue, is quoted as saying: "When I say something, it happens, and if I promise I'm going to do something, I do it" (p. 14-B). Technical strengths and skills associated with the tasks at hand are likewise very important.

The former CEO of Pitney-Bowes, Michael Critelli, reveals that trust in leadership is absolutely required if the entity is to be successful. And, this trust is created (won) by the boss through "basic integrity, honesty and action consistent with words" (Jones, 2001, March 13, p. 14-B). Finally, Tom Peters, well-known author and management guru, states: "I trust a leader who shows up, makes the tough calls, sleeps well amidst the furor, and then aggressively chomps into the next task in the morning with visible vitality" (p. 14-B).

Visionary Leaders

Leaders are frequently visionaries (Hoyle, 1995). Being a visionary implies being able to work in a future timeline, to be able to anticipate things that others might not be so capable of discerning. Being a visionary implies skills and willingness to establish appropriate long-range goals, in which goals are in actuality dreams with deadlines. Being a visionary also involves motivating others to follow, accept or share the dream of the leader. For example, Ray Kroc's vision for McDonald's restaurants included the visionary commitment to quality, service, cleanliness and value. These words might very well be attributed to sport organizations in terms of their goals for their customers, patrons or constituencies (Competitive edge, 1990, p. 20).

Leaders Are Risk Takers

Frequently, leadership involves being intuitive in terms of taking into account changes that are taking place or have taken place in society, in institutions, in organizations, and among workers (Renesch, 1992). Being a leader almost always involves making difficult and challenging decisions. Being an effective leader means that one is willing to take risks and to be viewed in an unpopular or negative light. Lets face it, being a leader is not easy. Far from it. Being a leader is difficult, challenging, frequently frustrating and often involves risk, both personal and professional. Leadership demands courage and grit by the individual attempting to lead, direct, influence, motivate and make decisions. It should be noted that being a leader makes it almost impossible to please everyone all of the time. Table 5.1 illustrates in a humorous fashion this challenge.

TABLE 5.1: *The Challenges of Being a Leader*

THE LEADER

1. If he begins on time	he is a tyrant
2. If he waits for late-comers	he is too tolerant
3. If he requires constant attention	he is a despot
4. If he does not care	he makes himself foolish
5. If he assumes the spokesman's role	he becomes a bore
6. If he yields	he becomes unnecessary
7. If he calls for silence	it is an abuse of power
8. If he permits disorder	he fails in authority
9. If he is firm	he takes himself too seriously
10. If he is good natured	he does not maintain his rank
11. If he expounds his own ideas	people are perforce against him
12. If he asks for a choice	he is irresolute
13. If he is dynamic	he is worked up
14. If he remains cautious	he is inefficient
15. If he does everything on his own	he is conceited
16. If he delegates	he is lazy
17. If he is attentive to the ladies	he is obsequious
18. If he is not	he is a snob

Adapted from "The Club President"—*The Rotarian*—July 1982, by J.P. Guillon, Rotary Club of Marmande, France. Translation by Wallace Flint, Rotary Club of Hilton Head Island, South Carolina, USA.

BEING A RESPONSIBLE LEADER—STRATEGIES AND TACTICS

There are numerous techniques, strategies, and tactics that have proven, in some situations and under certain conditions, to be helpful to managers who are in a leadership role. Some of these strategies include:

Projecting an Image of a Leader

Leaders look and act the part. It is very important that managers project the professional appearance (image and actions) that is usually associated with leaders. Leaders are as leaders do (and look). If one is to be perceived as leaders then one must act and look the part.

ABWA

Wise and experienced managers practice leadership by *Administering by Walking Around.* This means that one leads by being involved. One leads by being seen as being involved. One leads by being an integral part of the organization and its programs. One cannot hide in one's office or be aloof and be an effective leader, at least not for long. Many managers practice ABWA by physically walking around and among the "troops" as they work. This is done in an effort to find our first-hand what is going on within the organization.

Being Able to Do the Job

Being able to be viewed as competent, as capable and worthy of the trust of subordinates, peers, and others is an important goal. Part of being viewed in this manner involves being able to do one's job as a manager in an acceptable manner and at an acceptable fashion. Being able to actually produce, to be successful, as a manager will instill trust and confidence in others—essential elements in terms of being a successful leader.

Lead by Example

Quality managers who are leaders tend to lead by example. This pertains to every facet of life within the organization. Leaders demonstrate their competency by being able to do that which they expect of others in terms of professionalism, competency, dedication and image.

Enable (Empower) Each Person to Reach His or Her Potential

Competent leaders (managers) are able to facilitate others to accomplish their specific objectives and goals within the umbrella of the organization. Part of the leader's responsibility and obligation toward subordinates is to see that they reach their potential or near potential insofar as their job responsibilities within the sport organization or business.

Being Reasonable—Not a "Stress Inducer"

Good managers are able to influence others in a positive manner without undue pressure or stress upon these individuals. Good leaders are reasonable in their expectations of others and in their judgment of what can be accomplished and what cannot be accomplished within a specified time frame. The so-called manager who gives others (and oneself) ulcers is what is termed a "stress inducer." Such a manager actually impedes progress within the organization with such behavior. Stress can significantly degrade the organizational climate and can impair the workers' capacity for quality performance.

CONCEPT #117:   *Crisis management is no management at all and reflects an absence of planning and organization.*

Quality managers exhibiting good leadership skills practice stress management so that they and their subordinates (as well as peers) do not have to operate under severe adverse stressful situations or circumstances. Part of this effort involves keeping emergency projects or tasks to a minimum. Also, don't give employees too many tasks to perform or projects to complete in too short a time period. As stated elsewhere in this book "crisis management" is not quality management but is the absence of management and depicts a lack of planning and organization.

Strategic Planning

Good leaders and managers are excellent planners. However, there is a difference between having a plan (such as a strategic plan) and actually implementing the plan in the real world of day-to-day sport and recreation activities. It is much easier creating a plan than it is in carrying out the plan. The implementation of the plan is the true test of leadership. In fact, a strategic plan must be a living, breathing document (including both short-term and long-term goals/objectives) that is adaptable to ever changing conditions and situations that sport personnel often find themselves in. The strategic plan and the implementation of the plan strengthens and builds teamwork among the personnel of the organization, both paid and volunteer staff. (Alden and Hughes, 2005).

And, practically speaking, the strategic plan can be used as a basis for future (and tough) decision making situations by the leader/manager since the administrator can point to the existence of the strategic plan and the point out that the plan was created previously after careful and thoughtful deliberation and is the source of today's decision. The strategic plan used in combination with the contents of the organization's handbook—Policies, Procedures, Practices, Priorities and Philosophy [the 5 PPPPPs] will go a long way to protect and insulate the manager/leader from being criticized as one who operates "by the seat of one's pants" or through crisis management (Stier, 2003).

"SATISFYING" BOTH THE BOSS AND ONE'S SUBORDINATES

> *CONCEPT #118: Most leaders (managers) walk a tightrope between their subordinates and their superiors.*

When one is engaged in a leadership role it is often necessary to walk the proverbial tightrope between one's superior(s) and one's subordinate(s). In many sport organizations the manager (especially at the middle management level) is responsible FOR the actions of subordinates while simultaneously being responsible TO one or more superiors. It is important that the leader be perceived to be competent and working in the best interest of the organization, the program, by both subordinates and superiors. Thus, being able to represent oneself in such a fashion is an important skill or ability for the individual who is in this type of situation.

> *CONCEPT #119:   There are no universal traits of leaders.*

Just as there are no distinguishing traits that automatically makes a person an effective leader there are no universal traits that all leaders possess. Leadership is truly an individual matter when it comes to attempting to describe what a leader is and what a leader does and how a leader performs. Many traits, characteristics, qualities and skills are possessed by acknowledged leaders. But these vary among individuals to such an extent that one is not able, with certainty, to say that possessing any of these will automatically make one a leader or that all leaders possess any single skill or quality.

THE LEADERSHIP PROCESS—DIFFERENT FOR ALL SITUATIONS AND CIRCUMSTANCES

The way or manner in which a person leads, that is, exhibits skills (acts, conduct oneself, performs) as a leader is termed a leadership style. Leadership styles vary among people just as there are many different skills that different leaders possess. *There is no one single best style or process of leadership.* No particular leadership process or style is right for all employees, in every situation and all circumstances (Chung, 1984; Woyach, 1993). Different people use different techniques, strategies and tactics in their efforts in being leaders—and success depends upon the individual leader, others involved as well as the situation and circumstances which exist at the time.

CONCEPT #120: *Leadership styles vary depending upon the situation and circumstances.*

Leadership styles "are prismatic in that they may change from situation to situation, or be described completely differently by various individuals with whom they interact"

Major Sport Programs Must Have Top Flight Facilities
[courtesy of Indiana University, Sports Information]

(Lewis, 1993, p. 2). Leaders can have many styles, many backgrounds, many abilities but almost all leaders relate to and work well with people (Chelladrai, 1990). A leader's style will reflect that person's personality, experiences, education, training as well as the type of sport organization and the specific circumstances one finds oneself. Also, effective leaders do not act in the same particular behavioral style all the time. Different situations and circumstances call for different styles and wise leaders know when to adjust their style, strategies, and tactics.

Three Identifiable Leadership Styles

In 1939 three different leadership styles were identified (Lewin, Lippitt, & White). These were (1) authoritarian, (2) democratic, and (3) laissez-fair. Democratic is viewed as being supportive while authoritarian is more directive. Laissez-fair has been traditionally viewed as the least effective of these three global descriptive terms. Again, leadership style can change in light of the circumstances and situation as well as the type of people involved. When the task at hand involves mere routine directions perhaps an authoritative style of leadership might be effective. However, in a more creative and challenging situation leaders might choose a more participatory technique.

MOTIVATION OF PERSONNEL WITHIN SPORT ORGANIZATIONS

Managing Sport within a Complex Society

Today's sport managers are often faced with working within ever increasingly complex organizations. One of the reasons why managing in the 21st century is different than in decades past is that the "diversity of today's workforce presents managers with a problem of considerable magnitude" (Green, 1992, p. 1). The employees and volunteers associated with sport businesses and organizations are different than in years past. Personnel, paid and otherwise, have different needs. They have different "hot buttons" in terms of motivation. They need to be treated as individuals within the workplace in order to take advantage of their skills and capabilities and maximize their effectiveness and efficiency. Managers must be capable of adjusting and adapting to these and other changes if they are to be effective.

CONCEPT #121: *Managing (leading) within a complex society can be a daunting process.*

There have been many changes within the 20th century in terms of management thought and how motivation is viewed within businesses and organizations. The typical employee and volunteer today is a much more complex individual than in the past. Society itself is more complex. There are more pressures on managers, subordinates and on the organizations themselves. And, subordinates have greater stressors (problems, aspirations and needs) affecting their personal and professional lives and the lives of their family members. As a result of all of these changes personnel are more demanding, more mobile and less loyal, resulting in significant turnover.

CONCEPT #122: *The one certainty in the future will be continued change.*

Perhaps the only thing that is certain in the future is that the future will continue to bring about change. Back in 1919 Fred Taylor, as part of his machine theory or economic man theory, postulated that money equals motivation. Today, we recognize that money is not the best motivational tool for all situations. Quite the contrary, the organizational climate or atmosphere plays a much more important role in the motivation of professionals engaged within an organization.

MOTIVATION DEFINED

Many practicing professionals view a motivated individual as one who looks and acts motivated. People who are motivated are excited about the job, the challenge, the opportunities that their job, their involvement, their program presents. A motivated person thinks about and fantasizes about the tasks at hand. Such a person is frequently goal oriented, directed and driven to go beyond what is normally expected of someone in that position. In short, a motivated individual is excited about and really cares about the job and responsibilities associated with the position.

Motivation is the force that moves people to act, to perform their jobs (Smither, 1988; Petri, 1996). Motivation can involve the changing of a person's behavior and/or the reinforcement of that person's behavior. Organizational motivation involves any external stimulus that influences, persuades or directs behavior of human beings. Such stimuli can include actions of individuals, policies of businesses as well as working conditions or environments within the business or organization (Chung, 1984). A "motivational system" within an organization includes everything that is done (consciously or unconsciously) and everything that exists within an organization that influences, direct or affects behavior within that entity (Gellerman, 1992, p. 21). Thus, motivation can be conceptualized around three factors, (1) the person initiating the motivating action, (2) the person being motivated and (3) the situation or circumstances affecting the organization and individual being stimulated or affected.

CONCEPT #123:   *Motivated personnel don't necessarily perform well.*

Although motivation is an important facet of any sport organization, it would be a mistake to think that motivated employees and volunteers always perform better. This is just not true. There are numerous antidotal stores as well as documented cases in which highly motivated personnel failed to perform up to satisfaction. There is simply a difference between being motivated and being competent. If the individual is already competent and then is also highly motivated the likelihood of superior performance in enhanced. However, it is not always a foregone conclusion that motivated employees always necessarily perform well (Green, 1992, p. 5).

Intrinsic and Extrinsic Motivation

Motivation can come from within as well as from the outside (Lawler, 1994). When a person is motivated from within it is said that the person is self-motivated or is intrinsically motivated. When an individual does things because that person wants to do them, because that person likes to do them, these motives are intrinsic or from within. Motivation emanating from outside the individual, from others or from the work environment or climate, is referred to as extrinsic motivation. Thus, when a subordinate does something because the boss tells the person to do it we have external motivation. The reason for doing something originates from outside of the individual.

> **CONCEPT #124:**   *Managers can choose from positive or negative motivational techniques.*

Positive and Negative Motivation

Motivation can also be thought of as either positive or negative in nature (Boyett, 1991; Mumford, 1999). Positive motivation includes some type of reward or pleasurable consequence, i.e., the "carrot" approach. Negative motivation involves just the opposite, some type of unpleasant consequence or punishment, i.e., the "stick" approach. Motivation can also be physical as well as psychological in nature.

Examples of positive motivation include being praised, receiving positive feedback or criticism, an increase in salary, greater fringe benefits, a larger office, more job security, additional training or education, etc. Negative motivation can be negative criticism, being ignored, having excessive demands made of oneself, fear of being fired, demoted, not re-hired, being embarrassed, losing perks, receiving negative performance reviews, etc.

Fear can have an especially debilitating effect upon subordinates. Although fear can be somewhat effective in the short term, in the long run the use of fear to motivate is counter-productive, both in terms of the employee and the organization. Although employees may accept (take) such abuse from superiors their production levels frequently drop in direct proportion to the amount of fear (abuse) heaped upon them by others. People simply dislike being placed in a position of being fearful. If possible, such abused employees simply leave the organization.

MOTIVATION FOR THE MANAGER AND SUBORDINATES

> **CONCEPT #125:**   *Fear is a poor motivator of people in the long run.*

Motivation should be examined from two perspectives, i.e., from the vantage point of the manager and the subordinate. Not only do sport managers need to be motivated as leaders and doers but they need to be concerned with the degree to which their subordinates, paid and volunteers, are motivated in their roles and with their responsibilities within the business or organization.

Peter Druker—A True Leader in Management

Peter Druker is considered by many to have been the world's pre-eminent management expert (Rosenstein, 1999). A true guru and legend of management, many believe him and his thinking to be the fountain head of how today's approach to organizations and management are viewed in the 21st century. He died on November 11, 2005. "What John Maynard Keynes is to economics or W. Edwards Deming to quality, Drucker is to management" (Byrne, 2005, p. 98). In fact, Tom Peters, a prolific writer in the area of management himself, was quoted as saying: "He was the creator and inventor of modern management" (p. 98) and Jack Welch echoed the acclaim laid at Drucker's feet by saying: "The world knows he was the greatest management thinker of the last century" (p. 99).

Druker, as a leader in the field of management, championed the following concepts relating to leading people and institutions, businesses and organizations in this complex world that we live and work in (Byrne, 2005).

1. The job of leading is a complex and difficult one, requiring training, experience and dedication.

2. Picking the best (correct, appropriate) people is one of the keys to any organization's success.

3. The need to focus on opportunities and not problems is crucial for the success of any entity (look upon challenges as opportunities, not problems).

> **CONCEPT #126:   *Leaders look upon challenges as opportunities rather than problems.***

Achievements of this leader (Drucker) in management are summarized below (Byrne, 2005).

1. He introduced, in the 1940s, the idea of decentralization which eventually became the underlying principal or basis for almost every large organization or business on this planet.

2. He was the very first expert (in the 1950's) to extol the fact that workers must be viewed not as liabilities to be gotten rid of but, rather, as assets who can help the organization or business become and remain successful.

3. He encouraged managers to view the corporation as a human community – again built on respect, trust and cooperation with employees/workers – that exists not just to create profits.

4. Again, in the 1950s, he emphasized the importance of customers, without which there would be no successful businesses.

5. A decade later, he led the moment toward recognition of substance over style as well as institutional practices and procedures over mere cult or magical (charismatic) leaders.

6. And another decade later, Drucker again emphasized the importance of employees as knowledgeable workers who contributed greatly to the business or organization and its objectives and goals.

Peter Druker "put the study of people first: how they think, their personal values, what motivates them and how to communicate with them" (Rosenstein, 1999, p. 12-B). Peter characterized motivation as the following equation presented in figure 5.1. In this equation **M** stands for **motivation** (stimulation to action), **P** stands for **probability** (what is the perceived probability that the person can actually do the task or the job?), and **V** represents **Value** (what benefits can be derived from the action for the person?) (Young, 1991).

$$M = P \text{ times } V$$

FIGURE 5.1: Peter Drucker's Formula for Motivation

Mary Parker Follett, a Woman Leader in Management

Of course, men were not alone in being early leaders in the world of management. One should not forget Mary Parker Follett, who many considered the woman who invented management" (Shapiro, 2005, p. 16). Born in 1868 and passing away in 1933, Mary Parker rose to prominence in her role as a management consultant in the 1920s. She stressed such management concepts or principles that management should be "based on human relationships, teamwork, win-win situations, leadership through shared purpose, and so-called knowledge work" (p. 16).

Can People Really be Effectively Motivated?

There are many professionals who feel that it is not really possible to motivate people. They believe that all people are already motivated, at least to some extent. People are already predisposed to do some things and not do other things. Thus, the reasoning goes, managers need to redirect and focus this already existing motivation towards an appropriate end for the good of the organization.

Other experts and experienced practitioners are of the opinion that individuals can indeed be motivated, directed, and influenced to act in a predetermined fashion. These professionals hold to the belief that persons can be encouraged and induced to act in a specific manner, to perform at a certain level, and to achieve identifiable objectives and goals through a variety of motivational strategies and techniques, allowing for individual differences and a variety of circumstances.

MOTIVATION—DETERMINING THE MOTIVES OF OTHERS

One cannot study motivation without seeking to determine the motivation of others. Weiner (1992) suggests that almost everyone functions as motivational psychologists because human beings continually seek to find out why other people think and act as they do. Motives of others are important as they shed light on the reasons why people act in a specific manner. If people are already motivated or inclined to act, it is easier for the manager to lead them in a specific direction. Since people within organizations often have complex and competing forces tugging at them and their time it is important for modern sport managers to have an insight into what stimulates others to act or not to act in any number of ways in a variety of situations and circumstances (Lawler, 1994).

CONCEPT #127:   Sport managers should be cognizant of motivational "ghosts."

When sport managers become involved with personnel it is wise that they become aware of the past history of the organization insofar as how people were previously treated (and reacted) within the organization. There may have been a variety of motivational tactics and strategies used as well as other factors in existence that might have caused lasting (negative and/or positive) impressions upon the personnel. Current management must be aware of such lingering effects, referred to as motivational "ghosts." These past motivational "ghosts" can have long lasting and significant effects upon individuals, sometimes much stronger than current motivators (Gellerman, 1992, p. 281).

IMPORTANCE OF MOTIVATION WITHIN THE WORKPLACE

The concept of motivation is very important in terms of the overall health of the sport organization as well as the ability of the organization to reach its goals. When contemplating the hiring of new personnel, managers need to consider how motivated the potential employee is as well as the person's abilities (skills and competencies). In many instances motivation can serve as a predictor for potential success as an employee or subordinate.

A national management study (based on a Gallup survey) was conducted by Dr. Donald Gibson, a professor at Yale University, revealed that the American worker was "generally somewhat angry at work" (Knowlton, 1999, p. 3). The cause of such so-called workplace anger (or resentment) comes from the actions or inactions of their supervisors, managers, superiors and bosses. In addition, the lack of appreciation coupled with the reality or perception of being overworked can easily lead to anger in the workplace among employees.

Lack of Motivation

Lack of motivation can result in poor performance, indifference, absenteeism, confrontation, personal use of business facilities and equipment (copy/fax machines, computers, telephone, and office machines) turnover, and eventual failure. When there is insufficient motivation among personnel, the entire interpersonal relationship climate suffers and with it the capability of the entity to function properly.

> *CONCEPT #128:* **Managers should be situationally sensitive when motivating others.**

Managers need to be sensitive to the situation and circumstances in which personnel work (Hoyle, 1995). Toward this end managers should exhibit flexibility in terms of motivational style to suit different situations and circumstances. Motivation can also be enhanced if leaders are able to change, adapt or alter the circumstances and situation in which subordinates perform and work. Cardone (2005) emphasized the importance of motivating individuals by involving them as true stakeholders in the organization, in the program, in the activity.

STAFFING THE SPORT ORGANIZATION—THE USE OF MOTIVATION

> *CONCEPT #129:* **The use of honey is more effective than vinegar in dealing with personnel (McGarvey, 1991, p. 132).**

Ultimate organizational success is dependent upon the individuals who make up the organization. Thus, staffing is a matter of great concern for any organization. If competent and motivated personnel are hired by the sport business the likelihood of success for the business is much greater than if lesser skilled persons were selected. Thus, success in staffing is dependent upon four factors. First, selecting appropriate people. Second, getting these individuals aboard the organization. Third, nurturing, developing, training and motivating these employees so that they are truly competent as staff (preventing the "warm body syndrome" Hanley, 1996). And fourth, retaining quality personnel as members of the organization's team (Loyle, 1997; Peaummer, 1997).

Playing the Turnover Game

> **CONCEPT #130:   Success equals motivation, persuasiveness, and communication.**

The key to attracting *and* retaining quality personnel is motivation. And to motivate one must be extremely skilled in communicating (see chapter 6). One of the big challenges facing management in the world of sport is that of attrition of quality staff. This so-called turnover game with personnel is a contest that competent managers must win.

Why People Leave their Positions

Not all employees are happy or satisfied in their jobs or with their role within the company, business or organization. In fact, a national poll that enjoyed wide national exposure and was taken by Gallup found that 55% of employees had no enthusiasm for their work. The study found that 19% (one in five) employees "are so uninterested or negative about their jobs that they poison the workplace to the point that employers might be better off if they called in sick" (Jones, 2001, May 10, p. 2-D). Such unproductive and useless employees have been given a nickname, **ROAD Warriors**, standing for *Retired On Active Duty.*

An earlier study/survey conducted in 1994, in New York City by the national outplacement firm, Challenger, Gray & Christmas Inc. (involving some 1000 individuals), revealed that the leading reason that employees sought to leave their current positions and seek a different (new) jobs was due to the fact that they disliked their current boss. In other words, these employees were willing to relocate simply because they perceived their boss or supervisor or superior to be incompetent as a supervisor/manager/leader/motivator (Most look, 1995).

> **CONCEPT #131:** *Happy and satisfied (motivated) employees tend to be better and more efficient workers.*

The second reason, as revealed by this same study for employees seeking a job change, was that they felt underutilized in their job. In other words, their managers (leaders) failed to take advantage of the employees' skills, motivation and competencies. As a result these employees were unmotivated, dissatisfied and ungratified to the extent that they wanted a change. The lack of sufficient money was a far distant third in terms of reasons why these employees wanted a change in jobs to a different company.

Enjoying Quality Personnel while They Are on Staff

Over the long run it is far better to have excellent personnel on staff and then to lose them to another organization (hopefully, a bigger, better entity with greater responsibility and authority) than not to have had them at all. *The alternative is to have less competent people within the organization who are not attractive to other businesses or organizations.* If subordinates are treated with the respect that they deserve, provided with support and assistance (education and training) they need; and, motivated appropriately and in a timely fashion, managers may not have to replace them as frequently.

> **CONCEPT #132:** *It is better to have high quality staff and lose them to other organizations than to have mediocre staff whom no other organizations would want to hire.*

Besides, what better motivational ploy (to use with potential employees) than to say that previous personnel, who were loyal, hard working and extremely competent, are now employed in even better positions in larger businesses with greater responsibilities and authorities. For many potential and current staff members the possibility or likelihood for further professional growth can be a truly motivating prospect.

> **CONCEPT #133:** *Many personnel are motivated with the prospect of a better position, more responsibility, and greater authority— in the future.*

JOB SATISFACTION "MOTIVATORS"

Any number of factors within a sport organization can motivate individuals. One of the more important motivating factors or "motivators" revolves around their job satisfac-

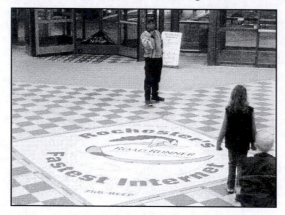

Ads Can Even be Found on the Floor at Airports (Rochester, New York)
[courtesy of ESMC Consultants]

tion. There are seven specific job satisfaction "motivators" including having opportunities for: (1) important areas of responsibilities, (2) increased recognition in the performance of one's tasks, (3) potential professional growth, (4) significant achievement(s), (5) professional advancement, (6) the continued enjoyment and satisfaction of the work itself, and (7) the challenge posed by the job, the tasks, and the responsibilities.

Managers should consider allowing their personnel to cross-train in different areas of responsibility within the organization. This can be a very effective motivational ploy in that such involvement can prevent boredom from setting in among these individuals. Another advantage is that such a broad range of experiences helps make the individual employee a more highly prized and skilled employee for the employing sport organization. And cross-training, changing jobs or redesigning responsibilities for a subordinate also makes the individual more marketable as a potential employee for other businesses. As such, being allowed to increase one's marketability can be a significant motivational factor for some personnel.

> **CONCEPT #134:** *Cross-train subordinates to give them diversity in experience, increase their marketability and to keep them from being bored.*

WORKING WITH VOLUNTEERS

> **CONCEPT #135:** *Volunteers need to be motivated through means other than money.*

Volunteers are dedicated and interested individuals who donate their time, services, skills and talents to the sport organization—for no monetary compensation. Of course these persons receive rewards or "payment" in other ways. There are almost as many different reasons why people volunteer their time to help a sport organization as there are people. Some of the reasons (potential motivational **hot buttons**) include, but are not limited to, the following:

1. A desire to be close to the sport organization
2. A desire to be associated with the people who are involved in the organization, i.e., athletes, coaches, administrators, etc.
3. A desire to give something back to the sport or a sport organization
4. The experience becomes an "ego trip" for some individuals
5. Abundance of free time and the desire to spend it in a worthwhile fashion
6. The experience is simply enjoyable (it is fun) to help out in some way with a worthwhile organization
7. A desire to make a difference and the individual has a specific skill or experience that will prove beneficial to the sport organization

Motivating Volunteers

> **CONCEPT #136:   *Volunteers need to be trained and motivated.***

Volunteers need to be motivated just as much as any paid staff member needs to be motivated. However, volunteers need to be motivated in different ways than the traditional full or part-time staff member. This is because of their unique situation—they are not paid for their services or contributions. Money, never a good motivator of personnel, is not even a factor for the volunteer, for the obvious reason (Plummer, 1997).

Although volunteers might receive, from time to time, some kind of token reward for their efforts, contributions or accomplishments on behalf of the sport organization, they essentially receive no significant monetary compensation for their allegiance, assistance or contributions to the organization. Therefore, motivation of these individuals hinges upon making the volunteers feel worthwhile, making the persons feel that they are making a contribution, enabling the individuals to enjoy themselves, to take pride in one's activities, and making them aware that the organization and other people associated with the sport entity appreciate all of the efforts and assistance provided by the volunteers.

WORKING WITH AND MOTIVATING EMPLOYEES

When working with subordinates it is important to consciously stimulate and motivate their behavior in those areas that will result in better performance (Perlson, 1990, p. 10). Towards this end it is important to (1) be clear in asking for specific performance levels, (2) use positive reinforcement (feedback) for those behaviors that are acceptable and desirable, (3) build positive professional relationships with others, (4) try and understand the point of view of others (walk in their shoes), (5) model the behavior that you desire in others, (6) expect a high level of performance; and, (7) appropriately reward competency.

The Use of Feedback and Criticism

A technique that can be very effective in motivating subordinates is the use of constructive, positive feedback. Not to be confused with negative criticism, constructive feedback is making the recipient aware of how well the person is performing (Wakin, 1991). The emphasis here is on making improvement in those areas needing improvement and/or providing positive reinforcement for those areas of performance that are already at a high level. An important facet of providing meaningful feedback (and positive criticism) is selecting the right situation and environment to communicate one's feelings to the person.

CONCEPT #137:   Don't embarrass or humiliate others when providing feedback.

Criticism, when used judiciously, can be positive in nature by pointing out how an individual could improve or elevate one's performance level. Criticism, to be effective, should be objective in nature and not personal. When used in a negative vein, criticism can be threatening, stifling, humiliating and destructive. Thus, the emphasis should be on remaining in the so-called help mode so that the subordinate can improve and become a more effective contributor to the overall mission of the sport entity.

A study reported by the Associated Press found that delivering bad news via e-mail is often preferable to either sharing the information face-to-face or though the phone (Have some bad news? 1999). The basis for this conclusion is that deliverer(s) of bad news—when provided in person or via phone—tend(s) to sugar-coat negative news to make the negative news softer and less threatening ("dumming down the message) in an apparent effort to make it easier for the recipient(s) to receive and internalize the information/message (p. 3-A).

CONCEPT #138:   Praise given publicly can be doubly effective.

An essential part of feedback is providing praise rather than criticism. Criticism for criticism sake is counter-productive when faced with the opportunity to consider the following factors (Blanchard, 1989, p. 48). First, inform the person that you intend to compliment him or her. Second, do so as soon as feasible after the person's outstanding performance. Third, tell the person specifically what act or performance warranted the praise or compliment. Fourth, let the person know how proud or how good you feel because of what the person accomplished or did. Fifth, allow the comments of praise to sink in, to register with the person. Sixth, encourage the individual to continue to perform at this level. And, seventh, by vocal or physical means demonstrate that you are sincere and honest in your comments.

MOTIVATIONAL TECHNIQUES

People are motivated for any number of reasons. The challenge facing sport managers is to discern the needs of each subordinate and then to coordinate or synchronize the motivational wants and needs with the needs, goals and mission(s) of the organization or business. Just as there are different leadership styles, there are also different motivational styles. Thus, it is important for the modern sport manager to be flexible in one's motivation style depending upon the situation as well as a whole host of other factors.

CONCEPT #139: *To motivate another find out what that person's hot buttons are—and push them.*

Managers need to find out what makes Mark or Martha "run"—what motivates subordinates and peers. What are the other person's **hot buttons** insofar as motivating "triggers" that will induce or stimulate the individual to action? Remember, not all people are motivated in the same way. And, of course, managers should never assume that others are motivated in the same way that they had been in the past. To do so would be foolish and self-defeating. And, contrary to popular thinking, there is no proof that (motivational) speeches are significant and effective motivational or inspirational tools. This is in spite of the fact that the motivational speech industry has grown into a multi-billion industry/business in recent years (Jones 2001, May 10).

One way to go about finding out the person's **hot buttons** or "triggers" is to ask the person, talk with the individual, carefully listen to what the person says and how it is said; and, finally, observe closely how a subordinate behaves, acts and reacts in a variety of different situations and circumstances.

There are any number of specific motivational strategies and tactics espoused by various practitioners and scholars. Young (1991, p. 36) provides 6 such strategies for motivating employees:

1. Communicate candidly and show others that you care about them and that they are both needed and appreciated—through positive motivation.

2. Empower employees by getting them involved in the business and the process of planning and decision-making.

3. Develop staff and volunteers professionally through in-service education thus providing opportunities for others to develop skills and experiences (professional growth).

4. Show appreciation through approval, praise, public recognition and other forms of positive reinforcement.

5. Manage ethically, honestly and impartially—don't have favorites—create a trusting environment.

6. Promote workplace wellness in an effort to help alleviate stress—sponsor wellness and health programs (smoking cessation, fitness, stress reduction, etc.) for employees (Sattler & Doniek, 1995).

Motivating and Rewarding Employees within the Fitness and Wellness Industry

Eleven free or low-cost employee rewards for the fitness and wellness industry were highlighted in an article in *Club Industry* (Staff management, 1997).

1. Make the reward or praise of the subordinate public.

2. Offer perks, gift certificates (local merchants' trade outs), free items to the employee.

3. Give the "token money bonus"—usually a brand new, in pristine condition, 2-dollar bill (or whatever the market will bear).

4. Prepare a memo and provide praise in writing to make it personalized—hand write it or sign in color ink.

5. Award time off some afternoon or morning off or allow the person to leave early.

6. Implement an in-house reward and recognition system whereby employees get points for good deeds, for going beyond the call of duty.

7. Award blue ribbons, simple blue ribbons, to a staffer to signify a job well done.

8. Provide a variety of benefits to deserving employees, perhaps involving a payroll deduction plan.

9. Make special phone calls to outstanding personnel, after hours, to congratulate them and to show your sincere appreciation.

10. Utilize an "employee of the month" reward system with a plaque displayed for all to see.

11. Take outstanding personnel, along with other peers, out to lunch to show respect for the prized employee and to acknowledge superior performance.

> **CONCEPT #140:** *Motivational techniques need not be overly complicated or expensive—sometimes the simplest tactic can be very effective.*

Money is no longer a great motivator in most situations, if in fact; it ever was a major factor, motivation-wise. In reality, money may not have been a significant motivator for some time in the workplace in our economy. That is, money is not a universal motivator of people. Of course it depends upon the person and situation, but money ceases to be a major motivator of personnel once employees are recipients of a decent living wage.

In fact, Armour (1998) indicates that employees are so desperate for guidance in today's complicated workplace that they desire, seek and *prefer* meaningful input from their supervisors and managers (bosses) over a pay hike. Although pay raises or cash bonuses are always certainly welcome by employees, such a motivational strategy is hardly sufficient in today's complicated and high stress workplace (Armour, 1998).

Professional workers today demand more than a mere paycheck in compensation for their contributions to the business, the organization or the entity. Workers today want to feel wanted and appreciated (Armour, 1998). In fact, a recent study conducted on behalf of American Express sought to determine what employees wanted most. The number one objective sought was personal feedback, revealed by 46% of the respondents. Money or financial reward was revealed as the number one objective sought from employers by only 32% of those answering the survey. (Carey, 1999).

> **CONCEPT #141:** *Money is not the cure-all motivator in business.*

Stated another way, money is not what makes a person happy on the job but the absence of a fair and just compensation system can make the individual have a level of dissatisfaction. Money can be a significant or major factor when the job is menial or routine, when it is boring, and when the salary is minimal. Money is of a concern when the compensation is insufficient to provide a decent living wage. In this sense, the person's basic survival needs might not be met by such a minimal wage scale.

THE ORGANIZATIONAL CULTURE, CLIMATE AND WORKING ENVIRONMENT

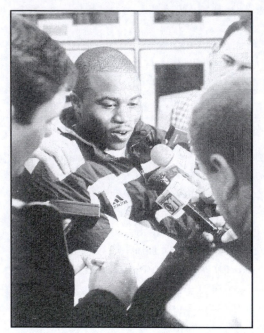

A Quality Interview Can Bring Many Benefits to the Athletic Program and the School
[courtesy of University of Tennessee, Sports Information Office]

An organization's culture is described by Whetten (1984) as a set of beliefs, assumptions, values and norms that are shared by the members in terms of how things are (or should be) done within a group. The culture, climate or environment within the organization can go a long way to facilitate or hinder employee performance. And employee morale can be significantly impacted by motivation. Morale decreases when the needs of the individual(s) are not being met. And the climate and environment of the workplace can affect motivation. Moral, in turn, has a direct relationship upon performance, absenteeism and turnover.

Manages must remember that it is to their advantage to create an environment in which workers feel motivated and even empowered. The successful business environment today is one that attracts and retains quality personnel who enjoy the challenges posed by a positive and rewarding work environment, one that fosters creativity development (Young, 1991).

CONCEPT #142: *Employees seek recognition, appreciation, positive assessments as well as effective feedback and mentoring.*

Today, employees desire more responsibility and authority associated with their jobs within the workplace. Employees desire autonomy as they fulfill their job responsibilities on a day-to-day basis. And, employees need to know that they are appreciated and recognized for their good work and contributions to the organization or business. This recognition can take several forms, from very positive reviews/evaluations to receiving a series of promotions. Such so-called rewards can have greater positive impact over the long run for the employer and employee than the granting of mere money in the form of a paycheck and/or bonus. And, a large part of this recognition and positive assessments involves securing feedback from one's boss(es) and the higher administrators within the entity (Armour, 1998).

> **CONCEPT #143:** *A positive work environment or climate facilitates employee performance and motivation.*

The importance of a positive work environment, one in which individuals developed and worked together in teamwork was highlight in the General Electric studies during the 1930s. In fact, the term "Hawthorne Effect" describes how workers were motivated not by outside, extrinsic elements but by a psychological environment in which teamwork and self-esteem played a major role. The workers in this study continued to improve their performance because of the social dimensions and interactions of the individuals. The group dynamics were such that positive reinforcement, mutual encouragement and self-esteem became significant "motivators"—and the result was increased performance. Losoncy (1995) reinforces the importance of managers using encouragement and a pleasant work environment (physically and psychologically) to motivate personnel.

These results are supportive of numerous other studies that show that it is the work environment that is so important insofar as the satisfaction level of personnel and in terms of their overall level of competency, efficiency and effectiveness (Stier, 1987). Management must provide a healthy work atmosphere or environment. People need an environment in which they have good relations with their superiors and their peers. *They need to have an environment in which they are appreciated, supported and nurtured, both by their peers and by management.* They need to be helped, guided, directed and counseled.

Additionally, individuals are more productive and satisfied within an environment in which they are challenged and can experience a sense of accomplishment, a sense of importance, a sense of being an important and integral member of "the team." They need to be adequately utilized and to feel that they are properly valued in terms of their abilities and skills. They need to be involved in the important processes within the sport firm and feel that they have an important part in the overall success of the organization. They need to be given opportunities to spread their wings and to soar, to take risks, to be at the cutting edge. And they need to take pride in themselves, their work, their contributions, their organization, the programs and activities associated with the firm, and in their potential to be even better contributors to the organization and the team in the future.

TEAM BUILDING

It is essential that management strive to build a team concept among all personnel (paid and volunteer) within the sport organization (Beck & Yeager, 1994). Administration involves getting things done through people. And motivation enables people to get things accomplished. Henry Ford is credited with the saying that while coming together is a beginning, keeping it together is progress, and working together is deemed to be success.

Thus *teamwork* is essential for the smooth running of any organization, business or program.

Ken Blanchard, author of *The One Minute Manager* reveals that leaders or managers need to be and to be seen as motivators, motivators of teams comprised of personnel ready to compete. He emphasizes the competition is not among and between one's own workers or staff. Rather, there is teamwork among the organization's personnel and competition in the marketplace against other organizations and personnel (Balog, 1995, p. 2-B). Thus, it is important to develop the best team approach to management that one can if one is to not only survive but prosper in the competitive sport marketplace in the 21ˢᵗ century.

Individuals working within an organization (employees and volunteers) should be treated as team members, not as hired hands (Jones, 2003). It is important to train the team members in order that they become highly effective. If personnel within the sport organization work as a team, things will happen. There is strength in numbers. Membership on the team should be voluntary, not mandatory. Invited individuals should be those people with whom other members of the team can work with effectively and efficiently. For those members of the team it is important to be sure and create clear goals and establish reasonable responsibilities for each team members, and for the group as a whole. And, finally, be sure and reward both individuals and the team as a whole when performance warrants it (Eng, 1997, 5-E).

Employers will work harder, work better and, in the end, be more productive if they are *empowered with a meaningful role* within the entity. This feeling of empowerment coupled with being a true team player within the organization creates an atmosphere where the employee is more productive and whose work is highly valued.

DECISION MAKING WITHIN SPORT ORGANIZATIONS

Effective and Efficient Decision Making

A maxim in management states that effectiveness is doing the right things and that efficiency is doing things right. Success is the result of doing the right things for the right reasons (Moore, 1990). *In terms of decision making, arriving at a correct or acceptable decision involves doing what is right for the correct reasons, based upon one's fair assessment and interpretation of available information in light of one's philosophy, experience and training.*

CONCEPT #144:   *Sport managers are judged on their decisions.*

Leadership and decision-making are intertwined in that good leaders make good decisions and good decisions are the result of good leadership (Heller, 1992). And, for sport managers/leaders, there are literally hundreds, if not thousands, of decisions that sport managers and leaders must make on a daily basis. In many instances, these decisions are the result of one's philosophy of life, education, work as well as prior experiences (Docheff, 2005; Schneider & Stier, 2003).

Many of these decisions are of a mundane nature. However, others are of a far greater magnitude. For example, Jack Welch (General Electric) has become famous for his well publicized decision that the unmotivated and unproductive employee can no longer be tolerated and, subsequently, he decided that the lower 10% of employees in his organization shall be removed (as dead wood) and replaced by highly qualified and motivated new employees (Stier, 2005, November 11).

Sport managers, supervisors and leaders must have the ability to make good and wise decisions relative to the sport organization itself, the programs and activities sponsored by the entity, and the personnel associated with the business. Managers must exercise sound judgment and mature thinking in making correct, timely and appropriate decisions, decisions that facilitate the work of others, coaches, athletes, support staff, volunteers, members of the public, etc.

> **CONCEPT #145:** *The ability to make appropriate and timely decisions is a mark of a superior decision maker (manager).*

TYPES OF DECISION MAKING

Decision-making involves a sequence of events including (1) use of good judgment, diagnosis and evaluation, (2) determination of action, and (3) implementation (Beach, 1997, p. 14). Arriving at a decision means making a bundle of interconnected activities revolving around getting information, weighing various options, alternatives and choice, receiving input from others, and then arriving at a determination of some type of action or no action at all (Guzzo, 1995, p. 4). Decision-making can be an individual matter or it can revolve around a team approach to determination (Hirokawa & Poole, 1996).

Individual Versus Group Decision Making

Team or group decision-making is significantly different than individual decision making. In *individual decision making* the "buck" stops on the desk of the person making the decision. This is true even if input or consultation took place prior to arriving at a decision. In this instance, accountability and responsibility is quite evident—it rests with the manager or leader who made the final decision. One of the worse things a manager can do is to blame decisions that are the purview of the administrator on others, such as subordinates or (worse yet) on committees, even if there were interactive participation with subordinates.

CONCEPT #146: *Competent manages are capable of making hard decisions (the buck stops at their desks).*

In terms of group decision-making (such as with committees) there is the matter of the unique chemistry involving the group and the individuals comprising the group. The potential for social interactions within a group helps make decision making different and, in some instances, more challenging than individual decision-making. Nevertheless, those involved in the team approach to (group) decision making often become highly motivated since they really feel part of the process. Additionally, the combined thinking, assessments and contributions of the group members can prove to be instrumental in arriving at superior decisions. One of the problems in group decision-making is that consensus is often difficult to achieve. Additionally, accountability, in terms of responsibility for the decision, is often more difficult to determine with group decisions.

THE BASIS (CRITERIA) OF EFFECTIVE DECISION-MAKING

Decisions can be arrived at on the basis of objective criteria and/or subjective criteria. Objective criteria include tangible facts, documentation and authenticated evidence. Subjective decisions are arrived at on the basis of the person's prior experiences, education, philosophy, feelings, and intuition. Yet, these so-called judgment calls are just as defensible as decisions based upon cold, hard facts (Stier, 1998a).

Decision Making and Problem Solving

The majority of a sport manager's decisions are made in order to either prevent a potential problem, solve a problem or to resolve a present or potential problematic situation. Both objective criteria and subjective criteria should be taken into account in arriving at a timely and appropriate decision. Timely and accurate facts as well as one's prior experience coupled with adequate knowledge make for better decisions.

The challenges that confront sport managers when faced with difficult decisions are many. Some of these difficulties include the fact that frequently *time is of the essence.* Also, all too often inadequate or imperfect information, facts or data are not available (Baird, 1989). There is outside pressure as well as internal pressure put upon the decision maker to act, to act now and/or to act in a specific manner. Uncertainty is another big concern.

There is uncertainty in terms of the consequences of various decisions. The uncertainty of the whole situation in which the decision(s) must be made can complicate the entire process (Heifetz, 1994). The complexity of the situation is another factor that can cloud the issue (Bacharach and Hurby, 1991). And, finally, the people who are involved and the power that they wield are additional factors that can complicate matters for the sport manager.

CONCEPT #147:   *Making decisions is like playing in a chess match.*

When contemplating various solutions to any problem it is essential for the sport manager to look at alternatives in terms of possible consequences. In this sense, making decisions and solving problems can be likened to playing chess. Just as chess players think two, three, four or more moves in advance—anticipating the consequences of each of their potential moves on the board, the sport decision maker must likewise think of possible consequences of various decisions and actions. There are always choices and alternatives for the decision maker. It is a matter of closely examining and evaluating these alternatives in light of consequences down the road that distinguishes the competent decision maker from the incompetent.

GOOD DECISION MAKERS ARE MADE AND NOT BORN

Just as leaders are made and not born, effective decision makers are made (Guzzo, Salas & Associates, 1995). This simply means that one can learn to make good decisions as a sport manager. Formal training or education coupled with experience in making decisions will help the sport manager become more proficient in exercising the skills involved in decision making.

DECISION-MAKING INVOLVES A REAL ELEMENT OF RISK

CONCEPT #148:   *It takes courage to make THE BIG DECISIONS in critical situations—but that is why you were made a sport manager/administrator.*

Decision-making is not for the faint of heart. It takes courage, it takes guts, to make many decisions. This is especially true when the decisions are not popular or when they adversely affect people. It is always true in *critical situations* when much is at stake and the consequences (positive or negative) can be significant (Stier, 1990). It is this ability to make sound and defensible decisions, decisions that are fair, just and equitable, that makes the sport administrator so valuable for the organization or business.

Risk taking is part of every sport manager's job. However, a key element for the sport administrator is knowing what are acceptable risks and what risks are unacceptable. This is especially true in the area of decision-making.

Making Exceptions

Many of the decisions of sport administrators will fall under the category of "making exceptions", exceptions to policy, exceptions to procedures, exceptions to practices. Yet, these decisions can all be valid and justified. As stated earlier in this book one of the reasons why there is a need for trained, educated and skilled sport administrators is because organizations cannot always be "run by the book."

CONCEPT #149:   *In some instances sport administrators must decide to make exceptions to the standard operating procedures.*

There are times (many times) when individual administrators must make decisions, make exceptions, in order to expedite the process, to move forward, to make progress, and to do the right thing. The decision to make an exception also falls under the category of risk taking by the very nature of the act. But, extenuating situations call for deviation from the normal, standard methods of operating within the organization.

DELEGATING DECISION MAKING

The ability to delegate is an important skill in a good sport manager (Imundo, 1991, Tegper, 1995). Today, no person can do it all by oneself. Today, the emphasis is on the team approach. Collegiality, cooperation and collaboration are current buzzwords in the management of sport business and in business in general. Thus, it is important to decide which areas of responsibilities can be successfully delegated to subordinates so that others can make decisions under your general supervision.

CONCEPT #150:   *Managers should not attempt to kill a flea with a howitzer.*

There are several advantages of delegating tasks to others. First, this frees up time for managers and administrators to devote to more important and critical areas for the health and well being of the organization or program (Horine, 1996). Second, delegating tasks to subordinates enables these individuals to upgrade their skills and to demonstrate their increasing level of competency. Third, delegating tasks can facilitate the creation of a team atmosphere among those subordinates involved.

It is important that sport managers not squander their time, efforts or skills doing tasks than could be done successfully by subordinates. The key concept is simple. Organizations should expend *the appropriate amount* of resources to get any job done or task accomplished—*and no more*. Organizations that waste personnel resources while accomplishing tasks, when it is possible to complete the tasks with less, are ineffectual at best and incompetent at worse. Managers who fall into the trap of "killing fleas with a howitzer" are wasting valuable resources, resources that could well be allocated to other important areas and tasks.

CONCEPT #151:   *Administrators have the responsibility to decide what tasks should be delegated to subordinates.*

There are two very important things for sport managers to remember when delegating tasks to subordinates. First, although administrators may well delegate tasks to others—it is impossible to totally delegate away one's own responsibility for these same tasks. And, second, one should never delegate responsibility without also providing that person with the authority and power necessary to carry out the delegated tasks.

Delegating Some Tasks While Retaining Ultimate Decision Making Responsibilities

Some areas of responsibility within an organization can be more easily delegated than others. For example, in the area of budgets or financial affairs, some delegation of tasks is appropriate and even mandatory. However, this does not mean that the administrator in charge of this area abdicates the ultimate decision making responsibility.

CONCEPT #152:   *Some decisions may be delegated while others should not.*

In the case of a university athletic director, the day-to-day responsibility for financial affairs, insofar as record keeping, data collection and reports, etc., might very well (and probably should) be delegated to a budget clerk or an accountant. However, when it comes time to make important decisions relative to the budget (allocation of funds, priority changes, significant expenditures, etc.), it should be the responsibility of the administrator in charge to make these major, critical decisions.

DIFFERENT TYPES OF DELEGATION

Good Planning Can Result in Appropriate Fan Support
[courtesy of University of Montana, Todd Goodrich, photographer]

There are different degrees of delegation in terms of the amount of freedom the person has who has been delegated specific tasks. For example, an athletic director at a major university delegates the task of coaching the football team to the head football coach. In this situation, the AD leaves it up to the discretion of the head coach to do the (coaching) job without undue influence. Although the head coach is responsible to the athletic director, the athletic director will not (usually) be telling the head coach how to conduct his business of coaching the team. A second kind of delegation can be seen when a health club manager or owner delegates to the sales manager the task of selling memberships for the health and fitness club. In this situation, the GM or owner says to the sales manager "do the job and check with me periodically in an effort to keep me informed of your continued progress."

A third type of delegation takes place when the president of a professional football team assigns the care of the field to the head grounds keeper and instructs this individual to perform the tasks normally associated with keeping the field in tip-top shape. In this situation there will probably be no need for any direct communication unless there are problems or questions.

And, the last type of delegation involves a sport administrator who is in charge of media relations and who delegates to a new college graduate the task of designing the front cover of the media book for the athletic team. In this case, the administrator doing the delegating might well indicate to the inexperienced staffer that "you decide how you would do it and run your ideas past me before any final decisions are made."

SURVIVAL TIPS FOR DECISION MAKERS

Maureen Dowd, former White House correspondent, wrote about survival tips involving decision making in business (1991). These suggestions are appropriate for sport managers just as they are appropriate for politicians and for business people. This is because, in a very real sense, managers, supervisors and administrators in sport organizations are politicians and also business people. It is just the nature of the beast. The thirteen survival tips include:

1. Don't make enemies you don't have to.
2. Don't start believing you are indispensable.
3. Don't confuse what is good for you with what is good for the boss (or organization).
4. Don't forget that you are not the boss.
5. Don't start blaming the boss if you get in to trouble.
6. Don't unilaterally announce you are going to run things, rather than letting the boss announce who will run things.
7. Some must pay the price when the status and the reputation of the organization (or of the boss) begin to plummet, and anyone who has maintained a high profile will be a prime target.

Decision making is a learned skill, an acquired competency. Managers become better in making decisions through experience, their own and the experiences of others. Decision making is not without perils and risks. However, on the other hand, decision making can be extremely rewarding, both personally and professionally. This is because individuals who are adept at making appropriate decisions, who are not afraid of biting the bullet, who get the job done in critical situations—are in high demand. As a result, those sport managers and administrators who can show a track record of effective and efficient decision making have a leg up on those would be professionals who fail to demonstrate a proficiency in this all important area within the world of sport business.

CONCLUSIONS

Sound sport management is dependent upon leadership, proper motivation and timely and appropriate decision making. Part of being an effective leader is being able to assume reasonable risks and to solicit loyalty from one's staff and one's constituencies. Being able to use a variety of motivational techniques (both intrinsic and extrinsic) in light of differing circumstances enhances the effectiveness of the leader, the sport manager. And, of course, sport managers need to be willing and able to make decisions, decisions of all kinds. Decision making ability and a willingness to delegate appropriate tasks to others are two key elements that are trademarks of the successful sport manager. Leadership skills, motivation skills and decision making skills can all be learned and improved upon by the sport manager who is willing to work to enhance one's professional competency level.

REFERENCES

Alden, E. & Hughes, J. (2005, April/May). A working document. *Athletic management, XVII, (3)*, 39-42.

Armour, S. (December 16, 1998). Cash or critiques: Which is best? *USA Today,* pp. 6-B,

Bacharach, M. & Hurby, S. (eds.). (1991). *Foundations of decision theory: Issues and advances.* Oxford, England: Basil Blackwell Ltd.

Baird, B.F. (1989). *Managerial decision under uncertainty: An introduction to the analysis of decision making.* New York: John Wiley & Sons, Inc.

Balog, K. (1995 May 17). Coaches find fans in management. *USA Today.* P. 1-B, 2-B.

Beach, L.R. (1997). *The psychology of decision making: People in organizations.* London, England: SAGE Publications, Inc.

Beck, J.D.W. & Yeager, N.M. (1994). *The leader's window.* New York: John Wiley & Sons, Inc.

Blanchard, K. (1989, March). It pays to praise. *Today's Business*, p. 48.

Boyett, J. H. (1991, February). Iron hand or kid gloves? *Entrepreneur, 19*(2), 20-21.

Byrne, H. (2005, November 28). The man who invented management: Why Peter Druker's ideas still matter. *BusinessWeek*, pp. 97-106.

Cardone, D. (2005). Restoring Luster, *Athletic Management, XVII* (2), 41-49.

Carey, A.(1999). 9-to-5 not for everyone, *USA Today*, p. B-1.

Chelladurai, P. (1990). Leadership in sports: A review. *International Journal of Sports Psychology, 21*, 328-354.

Chung, K. H. (1984). *Motivational theories and practices.* Columbus, Ohio: Grid, Inc.

Collins, J. (2001). *Good to great: Why some companies make the leap . . . and others don't.* New York: HarperBusiness [as cited p. 47 in Lumpkin, A. (2004). Enhancing the effectiveness of department chairs. *Journal of Physical Education, Recreation and Dance, 75*(9), 44-48.]

Competitive edge—Winning strategies from a pro. (1990, September). *Entrepreneur, 18*(9), 20.

Docheff, D. (2005). A little philosophy. *Athletic Management, XVII*(3), 21-22.

Dowd, M. (1991, December 8). Survival tips within the political world of business. *Democrat & Chronicle*, p. A-3.

Dressler, G. (1977). *Management fundamentals.* Reston, Virginia: Reston Publishing Company.

Eng, S. (1997, August 25). How to build a better team. *Democrat and Chronicle*, 5-E.

Flamholtz, E.G., & Randle, Y. (1987). *The inner game of management: How to make the transition to a managerial role.* American Management Association.

Gellerman, S.W. (1992). *Motivation in the real world.* New York: Penguin Books USA, Inc.

Green, T.B. (1992). *Performance and motivation strategies for today's workforce.* Westport, Connecticut: Quorum Books.

Guzzo, R.A., Salas, E. & Associates. (1995). *Team effectiveness and decision making in organizations.* San Francisco: Jossey-Bass Publishers.

Hanley, M. (1996, February). Develop employees. *Fitness Management, 12*(2), 32, 34.

Hannon, K. (2005, April 14). Welch show the "winning" side of business for all. *USA Today*, p. 5B.

Hatcher, K. (2005). Show 'em the books. *Athletic Management, XVII*(3), 19-20.

Have some bad news? Send it by e-mail. (June 26, 1999). *USA Today*, p. 3-A.

Heifetz, F.A. (1994). *Leadership without easy answers.* Cambridge, MA: The Belknap Press of Harvard University Press.

Heller, F. (ed.). (1992). *Decision-making and leadership.* Great Britain: Cambridge University Press.

Hill. D. (2004). Reform and restructuring. *Directing Athletics, XVI*(2), 6-10.

Hirokawa, R. Y. & Poole, M. S. (Eds.). (1996). *Communication and group decision makers* (2nd.). Thousand Oaks, California: SAGE Publication.

Horine, L. (1996). Deciding to delegate. *Athletic Management, VIII*(4), 13.

Hoyle, J.R. (1995). *Leadership and* futuring: Making visions happen. Thousand Oaks, California: Corwin Press, Inc.

Imundo, L.V. (1991). *The effective supervisor's handbook.* New York: American Management Association [AMACOM].

Jones, D. (2001, March 13). Top coaches earn trust . . . so do CEO's. *USA Today*, p. 14-B.

Jones, D. (2001, May 10). Firms spend billions to fire up workers—with little luck. *USA Today*, pp. 1-D, 2-D.

Jones, D. (2003, December 10). What do these three photos have in common? *USA Today*, pp.1-B, 2-B.

Judd, M.R. (1995). A gender comparison of competencies (traits) important for success in college athletic administrator. *The Physical Educator, 52*(1), 1995.

Knowlton, (1999, August 12). Nearly one-fourth of adult. *The Americas.* P. 3.

Krause, R. (1981). *Recreation leadership and supervision: Guidelines for professional development.* New York: Saunders College Publishing.

Lawler, III, E. E. (1994). *Motivation in work organizations.* San Francisco, California: Jossey-Bass, Inc.

Lewin, K., Lippitt, R., & White, R. K. (1939). Patterns of aggressive behavior in experimentally created 'social climates,'" *Journal of Social Psychology, 10,* 271-299.

Lewis, A. (1993). *Leadership styles.* American Association of School Administrators.

Losoncy, L. E. (1995). *The motivating team leader.* Delray Beach, Florida: St. Lucie Press.

Loyle, D. (1997, March). Nobody's perfect. *Club Industry, 13*(4), 27-28, 30, 32, 34.

Lumpkin, A. (2004). Enhancing the effectiveness of department chairs. *Journal of Physical Education, Recreation and Dance, 75*(9), 44-48.

Manager of year' shuns 'managing'. (1991, July 16). *USA Today,* p. 2-B.

Martyka, J. (2001, June 11-17, 2001). Workaholic gives it al l to job of his dreams. *Street & Smith's SPORTBUSINESS JOURNAL,* p. 27.

McGarvey, R. (1991). Positive criticism. *Entrepreneur,* pp. 130-132, 134-135, 137.

McGinn, D. (2005, April 4). Jack on Jack: His Next Chapter, *Newsweek.* pp. 41-44.

Moore, R.B. (1990). Why take fifteen years to become an overnight success? *Learning 2001,* pp. 6-7.

Most look for new job to escape boss, survey says. (1995, January 2). *Democrat & Chronicle,* p. 3-A.

Mumford, V. (1999); Fun at work. *Athletic Management, XI*(3), 13-14.

Peaummer, T. (1997). Staffing for success. *Fitness Management, 13*(10), 31, 33-36, 39-40.

Perlson, M.R. (1990, May). The game of management. Rochester Business Magazine, pp. 10-13.

Petri, H.L. (1996). *Motivation theory, research, and applications.* (4th ed.). Pacific Grove. California: Brooks/Cole Publishing Company.

Plummer, T. (1997, October). Staffing for success. *Fitness Management, 13*(10), 31, 33-36, 39-40.

Renesch, J. (ed.). (1992). *New traditions in business: Spirit and leadership in the 21st century.* San Francisco, California: Berrett-Koehler Publishers.

Rosenstein, B. (1999). How the guru came to be. *USA Today,* p. 12-B.

Ross, C.M. & Young, S. J. (1997). Research: The key to the future of recreational sport management. *Parks & Recreation, 32*(8), 22-29.

Rozin, R. (2003, October 20). A whole new ball game, *BusinessWeek.* pp. 100-105.

Sattler, T.P. & Doniek, C.A. (1995, December). Worksite wellness for the health of it. *Fitness Management, 11*(13), 18, 20, 22.

Schneider, R. & Stier, W.F., Jr. (2003, November 21). Necessary Skills for the Successful High School Athletic Director. Presentation made at the State Convention in New York State, the New York State Association for Health, Physical Education, Recreation and Dance, Buffalo, New York.

Shapiro, M. (2005, December 19). ReadersReport, *BusinessWeek*, p.16.

Smither, R.D. (1988). *The psychology of work and human performance*. New York: Harper & Row, Publishers.

Staff management. (1997, February). *Club Industry, 13*(2), 35-36.

Staffo, D.F. (1991). Should administrators be specifically trained for positions in HPER-Athletics? *Journal of Physical Education, Recreation and Sport, 62(2), 62-79.*

Stanford names next president (2000, April 4). *USA Today*, p. 3-A.

Stier, Jr., W.F. (1987). Competencies of athletic administrators. *The Bulletin, the Connecticut Association for Health and Physical Education, Recreation and Dance Journal, 33*(2), 4-6; Reprinted in *The Athletic Director* (AAHPERD) January 1988, p. 3.

Stier, Jr., W.F. (1990). Wanted: Renaissance athletic directors. *Athletic Director. 7*(3), 34, 35, 42

Stier, Jr., W.F. (1998). *Successful coaching: Strategies and tactics* (2nd ed.). Boston, MA: American Press.

Stier, Jr., W.F. (1998, April 8). *Marketability in the 21st century*. Presentation at the national convention of the 1998 American Alliance of Health, Physical Education, Recreation and Dance, Reno, Nevada.

Stier, W.F., Jr. (2003, April 2). *Hints On Job Hunting Strategies and How To Become More Marketable (Employable) within HPERD and Athletics*. Presentation made at the National Conference of the American Alliance for Health, Physical Education, Recreation and Dance, Philadelphia, Pennsylvania.

Stier, W.F., Jr. (2005, November 1). Physical Education and Sport in North, Central and South America—Trends, Problems and Solutions. Presentation made at the UNITED NATIONS' International Conference for Sport and Education in Bangkok, Thailand.

Stier, W.F., Jr. (2005, November 11). Introduction to the future of sport management and professional preparation programs in sport management. Presentation made at the 46th World Congress of the International Council of Health, Physical Education, Recreation•Sport and Dance (ICHPER-SD), Istanbul, Turkey.

Success is the same in business or sports. (1988, September). *Athletic Business, 12*(9), 30-32, 34, 36.

Tegper (1995). *Effective delegation skills*. West Des Moines, IA: American Media Publishing.

Vick, C G. (1989). *You can be a leader: A guided for developing leadership skills*. Champaign, Illinois: Sagamore Publishing.

Wakin, E. (1991, August). Give employees feedback, not criticism. Make sure feedback will have a positive effect, will do some good. *Today's Office*, pp. 22, 23.

Weiner, B. (1992). *Human motivation: Metaphors, theories and research.* Newburg Park, California: SAGE Publications.

Welch, D. (2004, March 22). Reinventing the company. *Business Week,* p. 24.

Welch, J. & Welch, S. (2005, April 4). How to be a good leader. *Newsweek,* pp. 45-48.

Whetten, R. W. (1984). Effective administration: Good management on the college campus. *Change, 16,* 38-45.

Woyach, R. B. (1993). *Preparing for leadership.* Westport, Connecticut: Greenwood Press.

Young, B. B. (1991). Motivating your employees. *Athletic Business, 15*(1), 35-38.

DISCUSSION TOPICS

1. Why do sport managers need to be leaders?
2. Elaborate on tactics that a sport manager can utilize to be an effective leader.
3. Provide examples of the use of formal authority (or power) and acknowledged leadership within a sport entity.
4. Explain why there are or are not universal traits of leaders.
5. Is money a good motivation for employees? Explain.
6. Cite examples of intrinsic and extrinsic motivation as used by sport managers for their employees.
7. What are job satisfaction motivators? Provide examples in the sport workplace.
8. Outline a strategy for motivating both paid employees and volunteers.
9. Illustrate with an example why some decision making and problem solving is like playing a game of chess.
10. Outline some effective survival tips for sport managers, leaders and decision makers.

Chapter

6   Effective Communication, Persuasiveness and Conflict Resolution

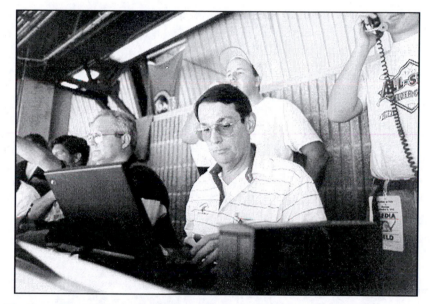

The Press Box is Where the Action Off the Proverbial Playing Field Takes Place.
[photo courtesy of Washington State University Sports Information]

CHAPTER HIGHLIGHTS

This chapter will help the reader to:

- Explain the importance of persuasiveness in communicating with others;
- Appreciate of the importance of communication in sport business;
- List the seven components of communications;
- Describe the hindrances to effective communication and provide examples;
- Illustrate how feedback can led to efficient communication;
- Value the importance of listening in the communication process;

- Recite the Ten Essential Elements of Communicating;
- Differentiate between horizontal and vertical organizations;
- Cite examples of proper use of the chain of command;
- Reveal sources and signs of conflict within an organization;
- Outline some of the hindrances to effective communication;
- Describe techniques and strategies for preventing or managing conflict;
- Understand the role of stress and stress management in the overall health of a sport organization;
- Realize the values and shortcomings of the committee process.

In chapter four it was pointed out that possessing interpersonal relationship skills is very important for the sport manager. An integral element of interpersonal skills is the ability to communicate. And, closely associated with communication competencies is the ability to deal with conflicts—preventing conflicts, managing conflicts, as well as resolving them. Put another way, the lack of adequate communication skills prevents one from adequately leading and managing the organization (personnel) resulting in ever reappearing and repeating problems and difficulties within the organization or business.

In 1999, Personnel Decisions International, a management and human resources consulting company, conducted a survey of 1,000 workers that revealed that more that a third of the respondents (in a cross section of businesses) felt that communication is the most important attribute of a good boss. The second and third most important attributes were understanding employees' needs and helping employees develop needed skills (both important elements in conflict resolution (Bosses must communicate, 1999).

CONCEPT #153:   *The ability to communicate is an essential element of interpersonal relationships.*

ESSENTIALS OF COMMUNICATION

Communication is more than merely talking to someone or telling a person something. Communication can be thought of as a process in which information, facts or concepts are passed from one person to another by means of some medium or instrumentality (Stier, 1998). Communication can also involve persuading others to action or to accept or change an action or an opinion or position. And communication can often be an essential element in selling a product or service (Hadden, 2004). "Any time you work with people, good communication is the key to success—without it, you won't achieve the goals you seek" (Wilson, 2003).

Communication involves one or more of the following: writing, speaking, reading, observing, and listening (Helitzer, 1995). Many of the problems associated with communication (or lack thereof) stem from an overemphasis on the attempt at delivery and insufficient attention on the message itself, its reception and its understanding by others.

In order for communication to take place there must be four essential elements present. First, there must be a *sender,* someone who sends or attempts to send a message. Second, there must be an *actual message* that is conveyed to another. Third, there is the matter of the *medium* used by the sender to transmit the information. And fourth, there must be a *potential receiver,* someone who is the intended or unintended recipient of the communication effort.

CONCEPT #154:   *It takes two to successfully communicate.*

The Sender

Communication is not possible without someone initiating the attempt (Bridges & Roquemore, 1996). The sender of communication (the <u>message</u>) can be a single individual, several individuals, a group or an organization or business (Bucher & Krotee, 1993). However, this does not mean that all communication is necessarily deliberate. In fact, messages emanating from individuals or organizations can be classified as deliberate, accidental or incidental.

Deliberate communication, as the term implies, denotes intentional conveyance of a message to another or others. This type of communication allows the sender adequate time to consider all aspects of the message, the medium and the potential effects the message and messenger might have upon the intended receiver(s). Thus, intentional communication should be the most effective and efficient because the sender has time to consider all aspects or ramifications of the communication. However, this is not always the case, obviously. Just because one has time to consider and plan what and how to communicate does not necessarily mean that the communication will be successful.

Accidental communication is that which takes places without pre-planning. It is communication without anticipation. It happens without conscious effort on behalf of the sender. Nevertheless, there is a message that is sent and received, whether planned or not.

Incidental communication takes place when the message received is incidental or collateral to the main message included within the communication. Incidental communication is contingent in nature, but can potentially be very important—for both the sender and receiver.

Both accidental and incidental communication messages can have far reaching consequences for the sport manager and the sport organization. The fact that these messages are not necessarily planned in advance has nothing to do with whether they are received or how others receive them.

The Essence (Content) of the Message

> **CONCEPT #155:**   *The purpose of the communication determines the medium and timing of the effort.*

This concept refers to the type of message and the purpose for which it to be conveyed. Why is a particular message being conveyed? What is in the message or the communication attempt? What exactly is the purpose? Is the message one of general information? Is it inquisitive in nature? Is it essentially a persuasive communication? Is the purpose educational? Does the communication attempt to solicit or provide information of some type? Or, is the communication an effort to motivate others, to a particular course of action perhaps?

The purpose of the message can significantly affect other elements of communication. Specifically, how the communication is to be conveyed to others, when and where it is to be conveyed, and the actual form the communication takes.

Efforts at communication can range from the simplistic to the complicated and anywhere in-between. Frequently, the content of the message will dictate the sophistication level of the effort, although not always. Simplistic communication efforts are sometimes the most effective, both in terms of effort expended and the likelihood of the message being received and understood.

> **CONCEPT #156:**   *Some of the most effective communication efforts are also the simplest.*

The Medium

How the communication is conveyed or transmitted can sometimes be as influential as the message itself. In this respect the medium (the method) can be as much of a message as the actual content of the communication effort. There are numerous communication formats or mediums. It is important that the appropriate medium be utilized in light of one's situation or circumstances. In today's technological society sport managers are not limited exclusively to pen and paper and the printed word but may take advantage of radio, television, telephones, the world-wide web, e-mail, etc.

> **CONCEPT #157:**   *The medium can sometimes be the message— the format can be as important as the message.*

The significant advances in the area of printed materials developed and produced by high tech computers (and various software packages) and printers have raised the level of the so-called "playing field" of communication to a very, very high (sophisticated) level. It is imperative that the modern sport manager be knowledgeable and experienced in these modern forms of communication. However, this does not mean that one can neglect the old fashion way of communicating, i.e., by speaking to others.

Not all communication attempts need to be verbal (Davis, 1994). Non-verbal communication can be equally effective. Examples of such communication efforts include the printed word, computer messages, one's physical actions and body language. Body language and the physical image that one presents to others are examples of communication that can convey a variety of messages. Often, but not always, these messages (especially with body language) are without the conscious thought or deliberate intention of the individual sending the communication. Nevertheless, body language is still a viable means of sending messages—deliberately, accidentally or incidentally.

CONCEPT #158: *The absence of communication can be a form of communication.*

Even the absence of formal communication efforts can be, in itself, a form of communicating. In fact, failure or refusal to communicate can send important messages to others. That is why sport managers must be careful not to be incommunicative, especially when faced with problems or in times of crisis. Such a posture is seen as a sign of weakness and even incompetence.

The Recipient(s) of the Message

All the communication efforts in the world are for naught if a receiver is not able and willing to receive same. Thus, it is very important to consider the abilities, experiences and characteristics of the person(s) to whom the message is conveyed. What are the distinctive characteristics of the recipient(s)? Are the persons adults? Young adults? Children? What are their backgrounds in terms of sports? How knowledgeable are they in the area of sports and/or your sport organization, etc.?

CONCEPT #159: *Know your audience before communicating a message.*

One of the common problems that sport managers or administrators experience in the area of communication is that they fail to take into consideration who their intended audience might be. The message must be compatible with the recipients in terms of appropriateness, timeliness, and level of knowledge required to understand the communication.

No one would attempt to deliver a formal speech to a large group of individuals without first ascertaining the make-up of one's potential audience in terms of the individuals' background, experience, and general knowledge of the speech's subject matter. The same care should be taken in terms of one's communication efforts with others, both individuals and groups. The concept is simple, think before you speak, think before you write, think before you act. Everything a person does or fails to do, everything about an individual has the potential of sending various messages to others and these messages can leave lasting impressions, either positive or negative.

> **CONCEPT #160:** *Think before you speak, before you write, before you act.*

HINDRANCES TO COMMUNICATION ATTEMPTS

The ability of the recipient of any message to correctly interpret what the sender had intended to communicate is paramount to any successful communication (Stier, 1994, p. 61). Failure to successfully translate and understand what the sender intends can be traced to any number of factors, figure 6.1. For example, many words are subject to different interpretations or misinterpretations. The various interpretations may be traced to any number of factors including different social/economic backgrounds (and cultures) of the

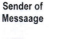

Sender of Messaage	Barriers to Communication	Potential Receiver

Different social/economic backgrounds
Different cultures of the people
Various prior experiences
Various educational experiences,
Some words have double meanings
Words taken out of context
Lack of interest, daydreaming
Personality conflicts
Varying circumstances
Excessive note taking
Timing of the commun ication
Limited vocabulary
Age differences
Sex differences
Political differences biases and prejudices,
Religious beliefs
Superstitions
Distractions

FIGURE 6.1: Factors That Play a Part in Hindering Communication

people involved, their personal and professional experiences and their formal education. Also, some words are just less definitive in terms of their meanings than others. Thus, careful choice of words, phrases and sentences is a first step to clear and understandable communication.

Other factors that can play a role in making it difficult to decipher and understand a message include words that are taken out of context, varying circumstances surrounding the communication effort, the timing of the communication, the age, sex or political differences between the sender and the receiver, lack of interest by the recipient, biases and prejudices, religious beliefs, superstitions, as well as distractions such as noise, etc. (Zeigler & Bowie, 1983; Horine, 1991).

THE COMPONENTS OF SUCCESSFUL COMMUNICATION

Jensen (1988) identified several components that make for successful communication. These components include (1) content, (2) clarity, (3) credibility, (4) context, (5) continuity, (6) consistency, and (7) channels of communication. Stier (1998) added an additional component, that of continuance (timing), to form the Eight "Cs" of communication include:

Content

CONCEPT #161:   *"Fluff" can significantly impede communication.*

Sports People Must Cultivate a Positive Relationship with the Media
[courtesy of Buffalo Bills, Tom Wolf, photographer]

The content of the communication effort must be accurate. If the communication involves inaccuracies or fluff there is great potential for confusion in the interpretation of the message. Thus, unnecessary elaboration, enhancement or embellishment of the facts—while seemingly defensible or even necessary to the sender—can sometimes have severe negative consequences in terms of the acceptance of the communication. Any communication that is based on inaccuracies (or exaggerations) tends to undermine the credibility of the sender and the actual message.

Clarity

> **CONCEPT #162:**   *Keep messages brief and to the point—briefness facilitates clarity in communication.*

The communication must be absolutely clear lest misunderstandings develop. Keeping the communication effort brief and simplistic frequently helps in this regard. Keeping sentences brief frequently aids in making messages clear and to the point. Whereas, unnecessary verbiage tends to over-complicate matters for the recipient of the communication. Sport managers should strive to be crystal clear and to the point in their attempts to convey a message to others.

Credibility of the Messenger

The credibility of the sender of the communication has a significant role to play in the acceptance of the message. People tend to accept facts, information and opinions from those whom they have confidence in, from those whom they trust. Thus, the individual initiating the communication attempt must be believable. And, to possess such credibility means that the person must have a track record, a reputation, for truthfulness, for honesty, for frankness, and for sincerity.

> **CONCEPT #163:**   *To be viewed as credible one must have a track record of truthfulness, of candor, of frankness.*

This points out the advisability, if not the necessity, for the sport manager to develop trusting relationships with others if one's communication efforts are to be fully effective. Part of this building of trust or credibility involves being a good communicator, speaking with authority, clarity and credibility. One builds trust and credibility by being honest and forthright with others and being viewed as such.

Context of the Message

In order for a communication attempt to be effective it is essential that the context or environment in which the message takes place be conducive to be received and accurately interpreted. This refers to the situation in which the communication is attempted. It also refers to the timeliness or the circumstances that might have an adverse effect upon the sending or the receipt of a particular message. Finally, there is the matter of the appropriateness of the message in light of the intended audience. Is the intended recipient capable of understanding the true meaning of the message under the circumstances in which the message is conveyed?

**Working with the News Media
Is an Essential Element of Sport.**
[courtesy of University of Houston]

Continuity

In any communication effort(s) the ideas portrayed must be presented in a coherent fashion in order to be understood. Messages that contain disjointed concepts, disorganized facts or irrelevant information only tend to confuse the communication effort. When communicating one should attempt to have the essential elements of the message flow smoothly together so as to be easily understood and less prone to misinterpretation. In other words, there should be organization or structure associated with verbal and written interaction.

Consistency

Consistency also refers to proper organization and structure of the communication effort but specifically addresses whether the words, information and ideas are consistent. Lack of consistency can easily create confusion on behalf of the audience. Thus, it is important that words and concepts be chosen carefully and utilized in a consistent and compatible fashion so as to present an intelligible and comprehensible message.

Channels

Without adequate means of transmitting a message all efforts to convey ideas or information are for naught. Thus, choosing an appropriate method of channeling the message is most important. Whether the communication effort is to be made verbally (in a one-on-one situation), in written form (letter, pamphlet, signs, posters, newspapers, magazines) or electronically (phone, computer, etc.), the concept is the same. The method of disseminating the message must be appropriate for the audience and the situation or circumstances that exist at the time.

Continuance of Communication Efforts

Continuance of communication refers to the time factor of such efforts. In the area of timeliness, the following factors should be considered. First, when is the most appropriate time (timeliness) for a particular message to be disseminated? Second, how long should each message be? Third, what should be the duration of the total communication effort (all messages combined)? And, fourth, what should be the interval between communication efforts?

> **CONCEPT #164:   *Timing is an essential component of effective communication.***

Sport managers, in this modern era, need to pay particular attention to the matter of timeliness in their communication efforts. The total effectiveness and efficiency of communication attempts can be significantly enhanced or hindered by the time factor. And knowing one's audience is a necessary prerequisite for evaluating the timeliness of the communication effort. Experience coupled with common sense and an awareness of the essential principles of communication will put the individual sport administrator in an excellent position to engage in meaningful dialogue with others, both individuals and groups.

ONE-WAY VERSUS TWO-WAY COMMUNICATION

All communication efforts involve either a one-way attempt at conveying a message or a two-way interaction or dialogue. The type of communication (one-way versus two-way) to be attempted will determine, for the most part, the method (the medium) of conveying the message, the timing of the attempt as well as the actual format. For example, in one-way communication the sender of the message is doing just that, sending a message without anticipating any response from the audience (an individual or many individuals). It can involve a person-to-person situation in which an individual tells something to someone. It can also be more of a long-distance effort (involving a written or electronic message). Typically, one-way, deliberate communication is suitable for disseminating factual information to large numbers of persons, information that does not need a direct or immediate response. For example, advertisements, promotional flyers, signs, etc., are all examples of one-way communication efforts (Graham, 1994).

> **CONCEPT #165:** *Being able to think on one's feet is a mark of an effective communicator in two-way communication settings.*

In contrast, two-way communication involves interaction between the sender and another person, persons or groups of individuals. In this situation communication flows both ways, back and forth, between two or more parties. Such communication is fluid. It is dynamic. It can be evolving in nature. It is frequently immediate. It can also be simplistic in nature or very complicated, elaborated and involved. Typically, but not always, two-way communication involves verbal (voice or electronic) interaction. Less frequently, but yet common, it also involves the written or printed word or 3-mail communication.

Two-way communication places a great degree of responsibility on the participants to think on their feet and to react appropriately in response to what is being communicated to them. It is this ability to react to and respond or counter with an appropriate message or exchange of ideas that marks the successful sport manager. Taking time and expending the effort to understand what the other person is attempting to convey is an important element in developing competency in two-way communication. Part of this process involves being aware of the background and motivation of the person with whom one is communicating or conversing with. Similarly, being able to be flexible in one's thinking and beliefs as well as communication strategies can facilitate one's communication efforts.

IMPORTANCE OF FEEDBACK IN COMMUNICATION

> **CONCEPT #166:** *Without adequate feedback meaningful communication efforts are in peril.*

Feedback is vital to good communication. Feedback involves obtaining some type of reaction to one's efforts at communicating, at sending a message. Without feedback one is unable to discern whether the message is being or has been received and correctly deciphered or interpreted. Good communication is just more difficult without some type of feedback. On the other hand, feedback, if utilized correctly, can greatly enhance communication.

The importance of feedback within a sport management setting can be seen when a manager delegates a task to a subordinate. It is important to seek some type of feedback in terms of verbal or physical cues from the person to whom the responsibility has been given. Does the person indicate understanding of the assigned task(s) in some fashion? If feedback is not forthcoming from the subordinate, how does the sport manager know that the person truly understands what needs to be accomplished? If the supervisor doesn't obtain adequate feedback there is always a risk of miscommunication or misunderstanding with disastrous consequences.

Verbal and Non-Verbal Feedback

Feedback is important both in verbal or written communication. Feedback is necessary, or at least helpful, in being able to judge the effectiveness and efficiency of one's communication efforts. Feedback can take the form of verbal acknowledgement (cues) that a message was received and understood—or that it was not. Feedback can also involve physical or body language that can convey as much, if not more, than verbal or written communication.

> **CONCEPT #167:   Feedback is important in both one-way and two-way communication efforts.**

Feedback is essential if one is to make suitable and often times necessary adjustments, corrections or improvements in communicating with others. Without meaningful feedback one is almost working in the dark or being blindfolded. Without feedback one cannot know with certainty how one's message is being interpreted, or if it is being received at all. Without adequate feedback, the sender of the message is at a decided disadvantage. With such feedback, however, the sender is in a much better position to structure, adjust and time subsequent messages specifically to the intended audience. The end result is better communication, communication that adequately and appropriately conveys a message that is clearly understood by the recipient(s).

Even in one-way communication, such as in the dissemination of advertisements or distribution of written materials to various constituencies or the general public, it is important to gauge the reactions of the individual(s) to whom the message(s) was(were) sent. For example, sport managers involved in promotion and public relations need to ascertain the effectiveness of their communication efforts relative to a specific promotional or publicity campaign. This type of feedback is very important in order to adequately gauge the effectiveness of prior communication (promotional and publicity) attempts.

LISTENING—AN ESSENTIAL INGREDIENT FOR MEANINGFUL COMMUNICATION

Typically, when one considers the concept of communication, the emphasis is on the person doing the communicating, the speaking, the writing, etc. However, it is important not to forget about the art of listening. It does take two to complete the communication process. All communication efforts are wasted if there is no one listening, no one hearing, no one understanding or comprehending the message that is being sent. "Of all the communication skills necessary for our business and social activities, listening is usually neglected, although it can be considered the most important" (Jenkins, 1999, p. 59). Although listening can be learned and developed into a finely tuned skill, Donald Caudill, University of North Alabama, revealed that different studies indicate that most people are poor listeners. For example, 75% of what people hear is typically heard incorrectly or misunderstood. And of the remaining 25%, we forget around three-fourths of what we do hear correctly, within weeks. In terms of retention, our efforts are hardly better with one study pointing to the fact that the average person forgets or fails to retain 50% of what one hears *immediately* and loses 75% within a day or two (Jenkins, 1999, p. 59).

Jenkins (1999) has suggested the following steps to enhanced listening, i.e., establishing effective and efficient listening habits.

1. Have a sincere attitude of wanting to improve one's listening skills
2. Prepare to listen (to a speech) by reading and thinking about the topic
3. Listen for key words and concepts and don't get bogged down in details
4. If appropriate, ask pertinent questions—be involved as an active listener
5. Don't allow your mind to wander
6. Focus your attention on the big message
7. Keep an open mind while minimizing or eliminating one's bias
8. Focus on the speaker's message rather than the person's appearance, style or clothing (or lack thereof)
9. Take limited notes (key words, phrases, ideas)—too many notes and one can miss important points
10. Pay no attention to distractions, concentrate on the message
11. Remain humble and non-judgmental
12. Don't allow yourself to be bored, find something of interest or value in the experience
13. Be on the lookout for nonverbal cues (facial expression, body language)

CONCEPT #168:   It takes work and effort, to be an effective, proactive listener.

Thus, effective communicators insure that they have a receptive audience prior to initiating communication. It is like talking over the phone. No one would speak into a phone unless they knew that someone was at the other end listening or that an answering machine was connected and ready to record any message that is left. Similarly, in real life situations, sport managers must insure that there is a person who is a receptive listener, ready, willing and capable of understanding what is to be communicated.

Similarly, competent sport managers need to practice the art and science of being good listeners (Harris, 1994; Armstrong, 1997-1998). Just because one is a manager or administrator doesn't mean that one need not be a careful and diligent listener. To the contrary, being an excellent listener (and being perceived as such by others) can facilitate communication in two ways. First, if one really works at being a careful listener and an insightful interpreter of what another person is sharing—one is more likely to better understand and comprehend what the message is and why the sender is transmitting it. The result is that the listener is in a far better position to subsequently respond or act on the basis of the message(s) received than if the original message had been somehow garbled, misinterpreted or misunderstood.

**CONCEPT #169:   *Careful listening reduces misunderstandings
and misinterpretations.***

Second, when an individual is perceived by another (or others) to be an *active listener*, this person is viewed with great respect and as having credibility. Thus, the resultant level of communication can often be significantly enhanced in such situations.

The so-called Ten Essential Elements of Communicating is a list of helpful suggestions that can assist the sport manager and administrator be a better and more effective communicator by paying attention to the essential element called listening (Touhey,1999; Stier, 2005). The list of suggestions is provided below.

1. Take time to stop talking and make time to listen to what other(s) are saying. It is difficult to speak and listen simultaneously.

2. Place the other person(s) at ease. Allow the other individual(s) to speak and contribute to the conversation at his/her/their own pace. Don't hurry the person(s).

3. Relax yourself and encourage the person(s) to also relax. This can be done by one's posture, voice intonation, expression, etc.

4. Demonstrate from your reaction that you desire to hear what the other person has to say. Nod your head in agreement or ask for clarification or further information when you are not. Ask meaningful questions.

5. Remove distractions that would hinder or negate understanding what is being said, shared and communicated.

6. Don't engage in multi-tasking when communicating; stop everything else you are doing and pay *complete attention* to the other person(s).

7. Use objects to facilitate communication such as tools, samples, books, photos, etc.

8. Use audio-visual tools when appropriate such as video tape machine, audio tape machine, computers, etc.

9. Empathize with the other person(s) by trying to picture yourself in the other person(s)' shoes.

10. Restate in your own words the other person(s) position or comments—to indicate that you clearly understand what the individual(s) is(are) attempting to convey.

POTENTIAL COMMUNICATION CONSTITUENCIES

There are any number of differing individuals and organizations with whom the sport manager might be involved in terms of communicating, i.e., sending and/or receiving messages. Figure 6.2 depicts some of these potential communication "partnerships", depend-

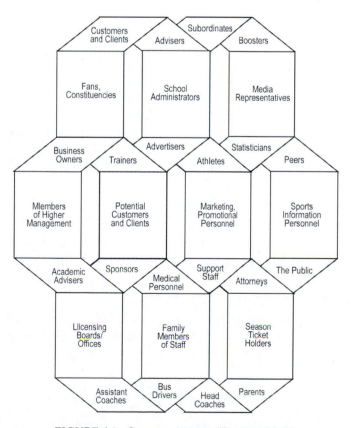

FIGURE 6.2: Communication "Partnerships"

ing upon the type of sport organization or business in which the professional is engaged. In reality, there are innumerable potential communication partners (individuals, groups and organizations) with whom sport personnel must be capable of working and communicating as part of their job responsibilities. Similarly, there are countless situations and incalculable circumstances that can affect communication efforts.

COMMUNICATING WITH HIGHER ADMINISTRATION

Sport managers, at almost every level, have to report to and be responsible to a higher level (superiors) on the administrative chain of command. Sport managers need to walk the proverbial tightrope in terms of communicating, informing and sharing ideas, facts, opinions and plans with their superiors for programs and activities for which they, as sport managers, are held responsible.

One of the major responsibilities of a sport (middle) manager in terms of communicating with one's superiors is to keep one's boss(es) constantly and accurately in the loop in terms of what is happening within one/s own area(s) of responsibility. It is imperative that one keeps superiors (those to whom one reports) consistently updated as to the happenings and future activities and plans of one's own little world within the total organization. No boss likes to be surprised or embarrassed by being shown to be ignorant of what is happening in the organization or business. No boss appreciates being kept in the dark.

CONCEPT #170:   *Superiors and bosses do not like to be surprised or embarrassed by a lack of knowledge in their organization.*

It is important to take advantage of as many avenues as possible to communicate with one's bosses (Alden, 2001). Take advantage of both formal and informal meetings. Take advantage of private as well as public gatherings to convey and reinforce a message, goal or concept. Utilize phone, e-mail and the written word to reach the ear of the superior. But, most important, don't fail to communicate. Don't be incognito. Don't hide in your office. Don't be noticeable by your failure to communicate.

Instead, be visible in the eyes of our boss. Be seen doing a good job. Be judged as a competent and dedicated professional who communicates well and keeps in touch in meaningful and effective ways.

MAKING FORMAL PRESENTATIONS

There will come a day in every sport manager's or administrator's life—and for some it will come much sooner than others—when the opportunity presents itself to make a formal presentation to a group. This opportunity to speak or present may involve a large or small audience. It may involve friends and acquaintances and/or total strangers. It may be an ordinary, run of the mill topic or may involve a very important assignment. There may be a lot riding on the outcome of the presentation/speech in terms of the effectiveness and persuasiveness of the speaker.

> **CONCEPT #171:** *Formal presentations should always be looked upon as an opportunity to make an impression as well as to convey an idea, concept or position to the audience.*

Presentations and speeches can take many forms. Some may be made at various service clubs (Rotary, Kiwanis, Lions, etc.) involving lunch or dinner speeches. Others may be made at professional conferences and symposiums. Presentations can be spontaneous, off-the-cuff type affairs. Or, they can formal and serious events. Some presentations include extensive use of audio-visual aids while others may not.

Regardless of the type of presentation in which the sport management professional finds himself or herself, there are always some constants that one must be cognizant of. First, one must practice (in private and in public) if one is to become a better speaker/presenter. Practice, under all sorts of circumstances and settings, does make one better at the skill of speaking and presenting before others.

> **CONCEPT #172:** *One becomes a master speaker/presenter through practice, practice and more practice—both in private and in the public eye.*

Second, competent speakers look the part. That is, they dress appropriately and professionally. They make a good first, second and third impression. Third, competent speakers are believable because they speak on topics on which they are expert. These expert speakers posses and demonstrate mastery of what is referred to as **product knowledge** (Stier, 2003). In other words, they speak on topics that they know and are familiar with. And, fourth, quality speakers show respect for their audience by speaking at the level of the audience—never above their heads or below their level of comprehension.

Jeary (1999) proposes SEVEN basic steps that every successful speaker or presenter should follow. These include:

1. Understand your audience and direct your presentation to that audience
2. Know exactly what you are trying to accomplish in your presentation
3. Make a great first impression
4. Ask questions of the audience, get them involved
5. Double check the details of your presentation, including how the room is set-up
6. As the speaker, you must have credibility with the audience
7. Plan for a great closing, one that is effective and leaves a positive impression with the audience

THE IMPORTANCE OF IDEAS—SOLICITING IDEAS FROM STAFF (PAID AND VOLUNTEERS)

Businesses and organizations are in constant need to stay abreast of (or ahead of) the competition and current developments within their sphere of influence. An integral part of this keeping up with or ahead of the "Jones" is the use of innovative strategies, techniques, strategies, services and/or product.

The Television of Sport—Expanding One's Audience.
[courtesy of Washington State University Sports Information]

And, what better way to obtain the ideas and suggestions that form the foundation of innovative strategies, services and product than to encourage one's own staff to share or communicate quality ideas and suggestions with management and/or administrators. Managers have often claimed that front line staff members are ideal candidates to provide such innovative ideas, concepts and suggestions because the staff members (workers) are most likely to encounter, evaluate and solve complex issues, problems and challenges on a day-to-day basis.

"Managers who communicate interest in ideas generated by their workers are indirectly telling their employees that they value their opinions" (Jones, 2005, p. 37). The end result of such communication is that the organization or business benefits by the new ideas generated/shared by the employees who are, in turn, recognized for their contributions, and thus are motivated to continue to do exemplary work to generate additional ideas,

ideas that can continue to benefit the organization. Middle and upper management (superiors, bosses and administrators/managers) who actually listen to workers create a much more productive work atmosphere involving a trusting relationship. It is this positive work atmosphere and excellent relationship between worker and employer that is conducive to more productivity and innovation in the workplace and the sharing of additional suggestions and creative solutions to issues, challenges and problems.

> **CONCEPT #173:   *Good ideas from the workforce form the foundation of innovative and creative approach to business practice.***

INFORMAL COMMUNICATION—THE GRAPEVINE

Sport managers should pay special attention to what is commonly referred to as the "grapevine" within the organization. This refers to information and communication channels that exist within any organization. Some would categorize the grapevine as the rumor mill within an organization or business. Members of management should strive to remain in the mainstream of the grapevine so as to be conscious of communication via this method and to be capable of using the grapevine to disseminate appropriate messages or information. Sport administrators should not ignore this form of internal, informal communication. Such a posture would be a severe mistake because such communication channels will exist and will be utilized by members of the organization whether management approves or not. It is better to recognize such channels and to be aware of the communication attempts utilizing same.

LINE AND STAFF—ORGANIZATIONAL CHARTS

Every sport organization has a formal structure, a structure made up of its personnel (Mason & Paul, 1988). Personnel comprise both line and staff positions. An organizational chart, figure 6.3, can illustrate the duties and responsibilities of and the relationships between the various members of the organization. An organizational chart can illustrate the relationships between different employees, in both line and staff positions as well as indicate their general areas of responsibility. The structure of an organization, revealed by such a chart, can either facilitate or hinder communication between various employees and departments.

Those employees who are in line positions have direct responsibility for making decisions and assuming tasks that are directly related to the organization's primary mission(s) (Tillman, Voltmer, Esslinger & McCue, 1996, p. 25). In a professional sports organization

FIGURE 6.3: Organizational Chart of a Professional Football Organization

the coaches and general manager are examples of line personnel. Those individuals assuming a staff position have responsibilities primarily for providing support, advice and counsel to those individuals who are line personnel. Again, in a professional sport organization the equipment personnel, the public relations office, the legal department, as well as the business or financial office represents staff employees. When examining an organizational chart one can differentiate between a staff and a line position in that the former is represented by being placed on a horizontal position and connected to a staff position by a dotted line (see figure 6.3).

The concept of line and staff personnel can be easily seen by examining the organizational structure of the armed services in which the major of infantry is a line officer and a major of transportation is a staff officer. In a professional sports organization the coaches would be considered line personnel because they are involved in the primary mission of the organization, i.e., preparing the team for competition. The employees who are involved in arranging for transportation, communication, accounting, medical, and the like, are all working in staff positions. Those who hold staff positions work in support of (and provide advice to) the personnel involved in line positions, in the primary activities of the sport entity.

Chain of Command

The concept of *chain of command* refers to the reporting structure within any organization. Viewing an organizational chart one is able to see that each subordinate "box" (representing one or more staff members) reports directly to an individual (represented by a "box" on the chart). This reporting to the next higher individual within the hierarchy of the organization is referred to as the chain of command.

CONCEPT #174: One should not jump the chain of command.

Within any organization is it deemed inappropriate, except in extremely unusual situations or circumstances, for individual personnel to "jump the chain of command" and by-pass one's superior in an effort to communicate with an individual at a higher level within the organization. An example can clarify the situation. A grounds keeper for a professional baseball team would not normally by-pass an immediate superior and go directly to the general manager to complain about one's immediate superior. This jumping of the chain of command would be deemed highly inappropriate unless there are very unusual and extenuating circumstances

This does not mean that communication of a social nature or of a non-technical or business nature cannot be consummated by a subordinate with an individual to whom the subordinate does not normally report or work with. It does mean, however, that there are

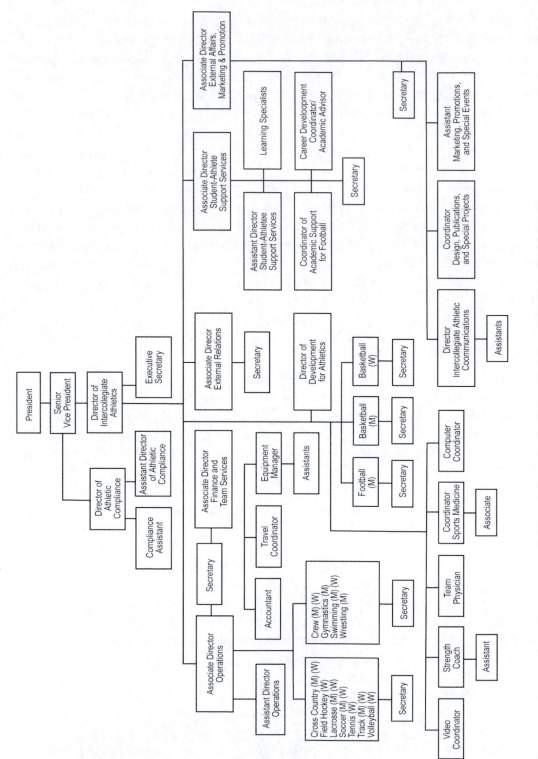

FIGURE 6.4: Organizational Chart of Vertical (Tall) Organization

specific lines or avenues of communication within any organization that employees are expected to utilized in the normal course of business. These normal reporting and communication channels comprise the chain of command.

Horizontal versus Vertical Organizational Structures

Organizational structures can also be conceptualized or described as being either horizontal or vertical. Horizontal (or tall) organizations are characterized by having many layers between the top of the organization and the bottom. Figure 6.4 is an example of a sport organization with a horizontal or tall organizational structure in that there are numerous levels between the lower echelon and top management. The organization or business represented by this chart has very definite reporting channels for its employees but the chain of command involves numerous levels through which official communication must travel before it reaches members of the higher administration or senior management.

Figure 6.5 illustrates a horizontal (flat) organizational structure. As can be seen there are relatively few levels between the top and bottom personnel positions within this organization. The absence of a multitude of layers of personnel facilitates communication between and among the employees, especially between those personnel located at the bottom of the organizational structure (the so-called rank and file) and those within the upper tiers.

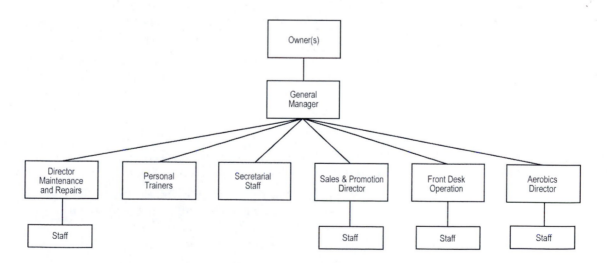

FIGURE 6.5: Organizational Chart of a Horizontal (Flat) Organization

SPAN OF CONTROL

Span of control refers to the number of divisions or departments any single administrator is responsible for within the organization. If an administrator is saddled with too many responsibilities, as represented by being accountable for an inordinate number of different divisions, departments or areas (not to mention personnel), that administrator is susceptible to becoming ineffectual in one or more areas of responsibility. In short, an administrator in such a position can become spread so thin as to be unable to effectively perform all the duties and responsibilities that accompany such a wide span of control, over so many different and diverse areas (and personnel).

Generally speaking, it is recommended that individual managers or administrators not have more than 7-9 major departments, offices or areas reporting directly to them. Of course, the ideal number could be less. What is appropriate for a specific sport organization or business depends upon a number of factors, including but not limited to: (1) the complexity or elaborateness of the subordinate departments or offices, (2) the number of employees involved in the subordinate divisions, and (3) the sophistication of the tasks or responsibilities assumed by these divisions, departments or offices.

ORGANIZATIONAL CONFLICT AND TENSION

Sport managers are naturally concerned with the organizational climate of their business or entity. An important element of organizational atmosphere or ambience is the absence or presence of destructive conflict. Conflict, in general, can be either positive or negative. Conflict within organizations happen (Sattler & Doniek, 1997). Conflict within organizations is natural since organizations involve people. When there are people involved, working together, there is always the potential for conflict. "Conflict should not be feared or avoided. It should be used as an opportunity to improve morale, employee relations and productivity" (O'Brien and Sattler, 2000a, p. 67).

The presence of conflict between or among individuals as well as groups can serve as a motivational factor for the organization and/or result in professional growth for the individuals involved. Conflict can also facilitate growth within the organization itself. On the other hand, some types of conflict within an organization, if not addressed in time, can become so unsettling, so unnerving as to have the sport organization, or its divisions or its personnel, become dysfunctional to such an extent that the day-to-day operation is impeded.

> *CONCEPT #175:   The absence of conflict does not necessarily mean that the organization is healthy.*

On the other hand, the absence of conflict within the entity is not necessarily a positive sign. Some conflict can be healthy. In fact, some conflict is probably necessary for the general health and professional growth of the employees as well as the organization.

Sources of Conflict

That can be many sources or causes of conflict among personnel, among employees and among volunteers (Sattler & King, 1998). Some of the causes of conflict stem from human beings, as stated above. People can be the source of conflict because of (1) inadequate communication, (2) clashes of personality and because of (3) how they treat others. Other sources of conflict include (4) programs, (5) priorities, (6) procedures, (7) standards, (8) practices, (9) administrative or managerial decisions, (10) scarce resources, (11) ambiguous jurisdictions or overlapping areas of responsibilities, (12) organizational size and structure; and, (13) the use, misuse or abuse of power.

> **CONCEPT #176: Personality clashes or friction can be a source of organizational conflict.**

Conflict is often a Power Issue

Conflict is often a power issue between different individuals or factions within an organization. Such conflict frequently arises when there is inadequate or ineffectual leadership within the organization, regardless of the level. It can also occur when there is a lack of specificity in terms of areas of responsibility, authority and jurisdiction. These types of conflict can be avoided or the negative fallout can be greatly diminished by the presence of appropriate policies, practices, procedures and priorities within the sport entity. Again, leadership is the key to both conflict prevention and conflict resolution.

CONFLICT PREVENTION/MANAGEMENT/RESOLUTION

The Proactive Approach in Dealing with Conflict

The best way to deal with destructive conflict within any organization is to prevent it from occurring in the first place. This is the *proactive approach*. Naturally, this is much easier said than done. It is simply impossible to totally prevent conflict. It happens in spite of the best efforts of management and employees. However, the negative consequences of conflict situations can be greatly diminished, mitigated or at least satisfactorily managed in many instances. The essential elements in preventing conflict situations include excellent communication efforts, excellent planning coupled with the ability and willingness to work with and to understand (the motivation of) others.

An example of a proactive approach is the creation of an Interscholastic Athletic Advisory Committee (IAAC) as evidence by the efforts of the administrators at the Milwaukee Public Schools (MPS). At Milwaukee, the administrators formed the IAAC in an effort to better administer the 14 public high schools and their extensive interscholastic athletic activities and offerings. The committee, comprising six constituent groups (principals, assistant principals, athletic directors, coaches, parents and student-athletes), meet once a month to go over all areas of interest and concern relative to the athletic programs within the entire school district (Diverse Committee, 2001).

CONCEPT #177: *Negative consequences of conflict can be mitigated with preplanning and attention to the needs of others.*

The Reactive Approach in Dealing with Conflict

Dealing with the problem situation that has developed as a result of a conflict is the *reactive approach.* Although frequently necessary, dealing with a problem created because of some type of conflict is troublesome from two perspectives. First, one must deal with the source of the conflict itself. And, second, it is necessary to deal with the consequences of the conflict whether they be hurt feelings, damaged communication channels, distrust, anger, loss of motivation, jealousy, or any other such negative attribute or characteristic. The worse thing that management can do in a conflict situation is to do nothing. This approach usually exacerbates an already bad situation.

Recognizing Signs of Conflict

Of course one has to recognize that a conflict situation exists before it is possible to deal with it. If one is unaware that a conflict situation is or could be a significant problem one can hardly take steps to adequately address the situation. Once management is aware of conflict existing in the workplace both managers and employees must be ready, willing and capable of dealing with the conflict situation in order to prevent further discord, friction and hostility.

Conflict is like a disease, a disease that is both contagious and ravenous. Left untreated, organizational conflict has the potential for seriously disrupting the day-to-day operations as well as to severely impede progress at all levels. Negative attitudes, distrust, jealousy, resentment are just some of the negative results of conflict left untreated and should be avoided or prevented if at all possible (Yukelson, 1993). The consequences if the situation (involving causes, consequences and peoples' feelings) is not dealt with in a forthright, timely and decisive manner can be severe, including disruption of day-to-day operations and the eventual failure of the ultimate mission of the sport entity.

TECHNIQUES FOR PREVENTING AND/OR MANAGING CONFLICT

> **CONCEPT # 178:   *In dealing with a conflict situation keep it professional, not personal.***

One of the most important things for sport managers to remember is that they must keep their conduct, their communications efforts, at the highest professional level possible. They should never be judgmental in their actions or in their communication efforts, verbal or non-verbal. Their comments should be descriptive and not judgmental. Administrators do not help a conflict or hostile situation by becoming personally involved, by taking things personally, by reacting as if the difficulties are a personal affront to their professional abilities.

> **CONCEPT #179:   *Communication efforts should be descriptive rather than judgmental.***

Cooperation and Understanding

In all situations involving dissension and discord there is a need for understanding and cooperation. People act the way that they do because they have a reason or reasons. "Perception is everything" (O'Brien and Stattler, 2000b, p. 54). People act or react the way they do and say things they say because of what they perceive to be the truth or to be the accurate situation.

These reasons may be sound, may be logical, and justifiable. Or, they may not be any of the above. Nevertheless, it is important for the supervisor to attempt to understand the rationale behind the action or inaction of those involved in the conflict. Thus, it helps to be able to walk in the other person's shoes, to look at things through the eyes of those intimately involved in the conflict or stressful situation. By doing this one is in a better to diffuse the situation based on an understanding of the root causes of the problem, the conflict.

Involvement of Personnel in the Management Process

Involving personnel in many aspects of the management process, especially in planning and decision-making, can pay big dividends in preventing and managing personal and organizational conflicts. Staff members who have actively participated in the setting of goals, individually or as members of groups, become part of the process within an organization. They have something at stake because they were part of the process (Zander, 1982).

The establishment of clear expectations on behalf of employees can pay big dividends in conflict prevention and management. Clearly defined roles and responsibilities of staff also play a very important role in management especially in terms of group cohesiveness (Copeland & Wida, 1996). Cohesiveness among personnel is an important goal of management. In fact, cohesive groups are more likely to resist disruptive behavior. They are also more likely to work together and to share responsibility for the consequences (Brawley, Carron & Widmeyer, 1988).

CONCEPT #180:   *Organizations must insist upon civility among all personnel—without civility there is anarchy.*

The presence of conflict doesn't necessarily imply a lack of civility among an organization's personnel. To the contrary. Management must insist that all employees and volunteers, at all levels throughout the business organization, be professional and civil in their interactions with one another—even in light of professional disagreement or conflict. Lack of civility, in combination with a negative organizational climate, can result in chaos and mob rule. Yes, there is such a thing as civilized or professional conflict.

General Techniques of Conflict Management and Resolution

Bridges & Roquemore (1996) provided insight into four tactics commonly used in resolving conflicts within organizations. The first is *conciliation* involving a third person working with two dissenting groups or individuals. The conciliator's role is one of defusing the situation while attempting to establish goodwill between all of the parties. "If conciliators are selected from each of the conflicting groups, they may be called *linking pins* because they can present the views of their group and hear the views of the other group or groups" (p. 346).

CONCEPT #181:   *Competent managers must take a proactive approach in dealing with potentially destructive organizational climate.*

**GM Dan Mason at News Conference
for Appreciation Day following
the Rochester Red Wings'
Winning of the Governors' Cup.**
*[courtesy of Rochester Red Wings,
Barbara Jean Germano, photographer]*

The second method of resolving conflict is to attempt to *mediate* the disagreement. This involves a third, impartial individual whose job it is to bring the two warring groups together to deal with their conflict. The third method is to *arbitrate* the problem situation. This is when both groups agree to have an outside, independent and impartial person listen to the pertinent evidence and facts and then to render a decision binding on both parties. The fourth and last method delineated is the *negotiation* tact. In this situation an individual in authority, a manager or supervisor for example, seeks to arrive at a fair, just and acceptable decision (perhaps a compromise) regarding the dispute. The goal is to render a decision that will resolve the disagreement or conflict among the personnel without losing productivity of these same employees.

Negotiation is a skill that sport managers should be familiar with since they will be working with people almost on a daily basis. In fact, Patterson (1996) indicates that we are negotiating all the time, every day, in most of their interactions with others. Additionally, there are predictable responses that one can anticipate when involved in the negotiation process. In negotiating with others, especially in attempting to create a win-win situation for all parties, attitude and temperament are most important. Finally, two essential elements that are the linchpins of negotiation are information/data and the factor of time. One must be in possession of adequate and accurate information. Information is the foundation of wise decision-making. And, time is important because successful negotiation takes time. There is also the matter of timeliness of sharing information, asking questions, listening, etc.

Specific Strategies and Tactics of Conflict Management

Other specific strategies for dealing with conflict management, both in terms of preventing conflict and resolving or managing conflict within an organization include (1) staff meetings and open forum type gatherings, (2) use of committees, (3) open forums, (4) cracker-barrel sessions, (5) open telephone lines, (6) suggestion boxes, (7) periodic operational reviews, (8) in-service educational opportunities, and (9) maintaining an open door policy.

CONCEPT #182:   *The use of committees can be a two-edged sword.*

One word of caution should be mentioned in terms of committees. The use of committees can be a two-edge sword. On the one hand, if used correctly and judiciously, committees can facilitate communication and foster group cohesion while contributing to effective decision making. On the other hand, ineffectual committees can prove to be devastating in terms of creating conflicts and ill will among the employees as well as between the employees and management. Management should use committees judiciously lest they be viewed as a substitute for managerial decision making.

It is also important that management judiciously utilize the periodic operational reviews. These reviews have managers or supervisors going to various work sites or areas and enter into a dialogue with employees in these levels in an effort to learn first hand about the everyday challenges, problems and potential conflict or friction within the entity. However, just as the use of committees can be viewed as a negative, these operational reviews can similarly be viewed as unnecessary prying, snooping and interfering efforts by distrusting and suspicious employees and subordinates.

STRESS AND STRESS MANAGEMENT

Stress can play an important role in organizational conflict both for members of management and for the rank and file. Being able to manage stress on a personal basis is very important for the health of the organization as well as for the health of the individual employee. Thus, it behooves management to provide the means (time, opportunity, education, tools, etc.) to all employees for adequate stress management.

CONCEPT #183:   *Management must take assertive steps to alleviate inappropriate stress experienced by employees and administrators.*

Working in a business is a very competitive and stressful experience. Working in a sport related business can be very, very stressful. Managers and non-managers alike need to be knowledgeable in terms of managing their stress and need to have the time and tools with which to activily combat the effects of negative stress. Thus, stress management strategies and tactics can play a significant role in dealing with organizational and personal conflict, both in terms of preventing conflict and in managing conflict when it does occur.

It is a responsibly of members of management to provide a healthy and positive physical and psychological work environment for employees and volunteers. Doing so will facilitate interpersonal relationships and positive communication among and between employees and will go a long way towards preventing unacceptable and debilitating conflict within the organization.

Conducting effective and efficient (time wise) meetings can go a long way to reducing stress, saving time and increasing productivity of staff as well as administrators and managers. Alberto Paz, president of Robert A. Becker, Inc., a New York marketing firm, cites the Four P's formula for conducting successful meetings. The first of the Four P's refers to **purpose**, meetings must have a clear purpose. The second P stands for **participants**, having the proper people (and only the proper people) at the meeting is absolutely essential. The third P refers to **preparation**, preparing for the meeting, in advance for the meeting, will prevent many problems from arising when the actual meeting takes place. The final P stands for **participate**, the people in attendance must actually participate in the essential discussion and decision making dealing with the topic(s) at hand (Sounding smart, 2002).

COMMUNICATING WITH UNHAPPY, DISSATISFIED OR IRATE CUSTOMERS

An important facet of communication, as well as stress management, is successfully dealing with the sport organization's customers or constituencies (Hart, Heskett & Sasser, 1991). This is especially important when dealing with unhappy or irate customers, patrons or fans. Unhappy customers all too often influence other customers and would-be customers to cease patronizing your service, product or business/organization (Lowndes, 2000).

> *CONCEPT #184: Don't let your emotions gain control when facing an angry, abusive and unhappy customer.*

It is estimated that for each dissatisfied customer there are least ten other individuals with whom the unhappy camper has shared the real or perceived problem concerning the sport entity. And, of course, when there is a problem or difficulty between the sport organization and the so-called customer it is "always" the fault of the sport organization, in the eyes of the customer (and the customer's relatives, friends, and business associates. This is why it is so important to be able to deal with customers, patrons, fans, etc., in a most effective and expedient fashion.

> *CONCEPT #185: Unhappy customers not only go away disgruntled but often try to get even as well.*

An important part of the process of handling complaints (real or perceived) from constituencies is to deal with the problem immediately and to convey to the individual(s) that you are there to help resolve the problem or conflict. Also, allow the dissatisfied patron to express oneself as long as it does not involve abuse of staff. However, this does not mean that the sport manager becomes a "whipping post" for the abusive customer. The content and form of the conversation (communication) must be kept at a professional level. When it descends to abuse or misuse then the customer has stepped out of bounds and needs to be so informed. No one should be treated with disrespect, by customers, patrons, fans or any other category of people.

It is important to find out why the customer is displeased and what the facts of the matter are in order to fully understand the situation. One cannot solve the problem or diffuse the situation unless one fully comprehends the situation, including any extenuating circumstances or factors. When the manager, administrator or supervisor is aware of all of the facts, is calm, cool and collected (3Cs), the solution (decisions and appropriate actions) is far easier to be found. Sympathize and emphasize with the complaining, unhappy customer(s) to show that you really care. This can be done by asking questions, actively listening and staying calm, cool and collected (3Cs).

CONCEPT #186:   *Put yourself in the complaining person's position (shoes) when confronted by the unhappy customer.*

Newell-Legner (2005) provided 11 so-called service points or steps to follow in addressing unhappy or dissatisfied customers and solving their problems. The objective is to make these customers satisfied and happy once again *and* willing to continue to patronize one's business or organization, now and in the future. These service points include:

1. Go to a private area to discuss the situation with the customer
2. Listen and make sure the customer knows you are listening
3. Never interrupt the customer, let the person speak and "get it all out"
4. Follow the 2-second rule, i.e., wait for 2 seconds to respond after the customer has shared the tale of woe
5. Remember the customer's name and use it frequently
6. Be respectful both in words and actions
7. Be careful in one's choice of words such as *policy, I can't, I don't know*
8. Use the "we" word rather than the "I" word, you represent your organization or business rather than yourself
9. If there has been an error always say that your are sorry (apologize to the customer)
10. Move to a quick resolution and appease the customer
11. Always thank the customer for bringing the problem or issue to your attention

---

CONCEPT #187:   *Good customer servicing skills can be learned and effectively put into everyday practice.*

It is important to remember that the dissatisfied, unhappy, complaining or irate customer is actually doing the organization or business a favor by bringing the problem to the attention of the manager or administrator. The reason is obvious. Such action provides management an opportunity to address or solve/resolve the prickly situation before it gets out-of-hand and affects many other customers (thus bringing many, many more complaints).

CONCEPT #188:   *Use a minimum response time to address the problem or controversial issue brought by an unhappy, dissatisfied or irate customer*

In essence, it is imperative to take a proactive professional approach in dealing with the confrontational situation, all the while maintaining eye contact and exhibiting confidence in one's job. It is also most important to understand all of the extenuating factors that are involved in the situation. This may involve taking detailed notes. Managers who create the image that they really do care about the customer's problem or conflict, and that they are trying to do all in their power to address and resolve the situation, lay the foundation for a suitable resolution to the otherwise ticklish situation. If managers are not able to resolve the situation to the customer's satisfaction, it is necessary that this fact be explained including why it cannot be resolved to the customer's satisfaction (8 Steps, 1993).

THE NECESSITY OF BEING AN EFFECTIVE COMMUNICATOR

Communication is an essential competency for sport managers because it is one competency that every employee will need to deal in day-to-day operations regardless of the type of business or organization one finds oneself (Parkhouse, 1991). Communication skills are so essential because so many other skills are dependent upon being able to communicate clearly to a wide range of individuals, groups and organizations. Failure to develop sophisticated communication skills (verbal and non-verbal) places the would-be sport manager at a severe disadvantage in the 21st century. As has been pointed out the lack of adequate communication is one cause of conflict within the organization. Thus, those individuals who are highly skilled in communication are in a position to prevent many problems related to conflict prevention, management and conflict resolution.

CONCEPT #189: *Competency in communication forms the basis for other essential skills of sport managers and leaders.*

Human beings are social animals. As such the ability to clearly communicate is indispensable if they are to not only survive within the organizational structure but also grow and prosper. Being able to relate to, communicate with, and work within a group setting is an absolute requirement for the modern-day sport manager or administrator. Without adequate grounding in communication skills (sending/receiving/deciphering) the prospect of success as a member of management within a sport organization is severely limited.

CONCLUSIONS

Successful sport management is dependent upon sound communication practices. The organizational structure of the organization has a definite impact upon communication channels within the entity. Understanding the communication process and the strategies and tactics that are supportive of good communication will put the sport manager, at every level, in good stead. However, mere awareness of communication techniques is not enough; sport managers need to put such knowledge to actual use in the real world. The importance of feedback cannot be overstated in terms of becoming an effective communicator. And, of course, communication, both verbal and non-verbal, is an essential ingredient in conflict resolution. Although conflict resolution is an important and sometimes imposing challenge facing the sport manager, the ability to prevent conflict from taking place or reduce its negative impact is a quality than cannot be over emphasized.

REFERENCES

Aldon, E. (2001). Presidential politics. *Athletic Management, XIII*(3), 36, 37, 39, 40, 42.

Armstrong, W.H. (1997-1998, Winter). Learning to listen. *American Educator, 21*(4), 24-25, 47.

Bosses must communicate. (1999). *Democrat and Chronicle*, p. 5-F.

Brawley, L.R., Carron, A.V., & Widmeyer, W.N. (1988). Exploring the relationship between cohesion and group resistance to disruption. *Journal of Sport and Exercise Psychology, 10*, 199-213.

Bridges, F.J. & Roquemore, L.L. (1996). *Management for athletic/sport administration: Theory and practice* (2nd ed.). Decatur, Georgia: ESM Books.

Bucher, C.A. & Krotee, M.L. (1993). *Management of physical education and sport*. St. Louis, Missouri: Mosby Year Book.

Copeland, B.W. & Wida, K. (1996). Resolving team conflict: Coaching strategies to prevent negative behavior. *Journal of Physical Education, Recreation and Dance, 67*(4), 52-54.

Davis, K.A. (1994). *Sport management: Successful private sector business strategies.* Madison, Wisconsin: Wm. C. Brown & Benchmark.

Diverse committee provides advice. (2001). *Athletic Management, XXIII* (4), 6, 8.

8 steps for handling complaints. (1993, October). *Club Industry, 9*(8), 43.

Graham, P. J. (1994). *Sport business: Operational and theoretical aspects.* Madison, Wisconsin: Wm. C. Brown & Benchmark.

Hadden, C. (2004). The art of persuasion. *Fitness Management, 20*(7), 26.

Harris, R. M. (1994, May). Articulate listening. p. 116.

Hart, W. L., Heskett, J. L., & Sasser, W. E. (1991, April). Surviving a customer's rage. *Successful Meetings,* pp. 68-70, 72, 75, 76, 79.

Helitzer, M. (1995). *The dream job – $port$ – Publicity, promotion and marketing* (2nd ed.). Athens, Ohio: University Sports Press.

Horine, l. (1995). *Administration of physical education and sport programs* (3rd ed.). Dubuque, Iowa: Wm. C. Brown Publishing.

Jeary, T. (1900, November). Making (not losing) points. *Successful Meetings,* pp. 76-77.

Jenkins, T. (1999, November). Prick up your ears. *Successful Meetings,* pp. 59-62.

Jensen, C.R. (1992). *Administrative management of physical education and athletic programs* (3rd ed.). Philadelphia: Lea & Febiger.

Jones, A. (2005, March). The power of ideas. *Coach and Athletic Director, pp. 36-438, 40.*

Lowndes, L. (2000). Defuse to win. *Athletic Business, 24*(6), 52, 55.

Mason, J.G. & Paul, J. (1988). *Modern sports administration.* Englewood Cliffs, New Jersey: Prentice-Hall.

Newell-Legner, R. (2005). Service points. *Athletic Business, 29*(10), 46, 48.

O'Brien, T. & Sattler, T . (2000a). Steps for cooperative conflict resolution. *Fitness Management, 16*(6), 67.

O'Brien, T. & Sattler, T . (2000b). The benefits of conflict. *Fitness Management, 16*(6), 54.

Parkhouse, B.L. (Ed.) (1991). *The management of sport: Its foundation and application.* St. Louis, Missouri: Mosby Year Book.

Patterson, J.G. (1996). *How to become a better negotiator.* New York: American Management Association.

Sattler, T.P. & King, J.M. (1998). Understanding organizational and personal conflict. *Fitness Management, 14*(1), 20, 22.

Sattler, T.P. & Doniek, C.A. (1997, March). The art of negotiating: Attitude is everything. *Fitness Management, 13*(4), 37.

Sounding smart. (2002, February 27). *Democrat and Chronicle*, p. 1-E.

Stier, W.F., Jr. (1994). *Successful sport fund-raising.* Madison, Wisconsin: Wm. C. Brown & Benchmark.

Stier, W.F., Jr. (1998, April 8). *Marketability in the 21ˢᵗ century.* Presentation at the national convention of the American Alliance of Health, Physical Education, Recreation and Dance, Reno, Nevada.

Stier, Jr., W.F. (2003), *Marketing, Fundraising and Promotions for Sport, Recreation and Fitness Programs.* Boston, MA: American Press.

Stier, W.F., Jr. (2005, November 1). *Physical Education and Sport in North, Central and South America—Trends, Problems and Solutions.* Presentation made at the United Nations' International Conference for Sport and Education in Bangkok, Thailand.

Tillman, K.G., Voltmer, E.F., Esslinger, A.A., & McCue, B.F. (1996). *The administration of physical education, sport, and leisure programs.* Boston, MA: Allyn and Bacon.

Touhey, K. (1999). A new-world mentoring program for athletic administrators. *Coach and Athletic Director, 69*(2), 60-62.

Wilson, S. (2003). Tips for talking. *Training & Conditioning, XIII*(8), 35-44.

Yukelson, D. (1993). Communicating effectively. In Williams, J. (Ed.), *Applied Sport Psychology* (pp. 122-136). Mountain View, CA: Mayfield.

Zander, A.Z. (1982). *Making groups effective.* San Francisco: Jossey-Bass.

Zeigler, E.F. & Bowie, W. (1983). *Management competency development in sport and physical education.* Philadelphia: Lea & Febiger.

Discussion Topics

1. Describe the essential elements for effective communication to take place.

2. Differentiate between deliberate, accidental and incidental communication and provide examples within a sport entity.

3. Elaborate on the various types of hindrances that a typical sport manager might encounter when dealing with employees, with volunteers, and with constituencies or the general public.

4. What can employees working within a horizontal organization do to enhance communication efforts across departments as well as within the chain of command?

5. How can a sport manager go about soliciting feedback in terms of communication so that the individual is aware as to the effectiveness of the communication effort?

6. Why is conflict a power issue? Explain how conflict among personnel within a sport entity might be prevented or resolved? Provide examples.

7. Set the stage for role-playing by creating a situation in which you, as a sport manager, must deal with a subordinate and you wish to initiate communication which is descriptive rather than judgmental.

8. Cite examples where the use of committees would be justified. Also, cite examples where the use of committees might not be warranted.

9. What are the implications that some unhappy customers not only go away disgruntled but also, frequently, attempt to get even? Provide specific examples of what sport managers might do in light of this tendency.

10. Provide examples of *good customer service* and *servicing skills.*

PRAGMATIC ASPECTS
OF THE MANAGEMENT OF SPORT

Chapter

7   Fiscal Management
and Budgetary Accountability

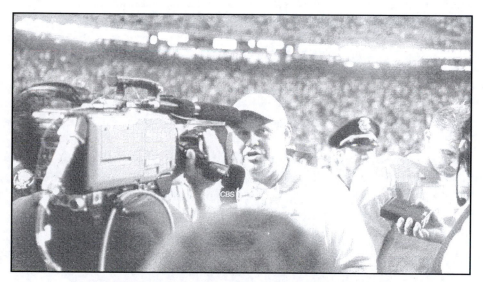

Successful Teams and Coaches Attract National Media Coverage
[photo courtesy of University of Tennessee, Sports Information Office]

CHAPTER HIGHLIGHTS

This chapter will help the reader to:

• Cite recent examples of the tremendous expansion/growth in budgets in sport entities;

- Appreciate the importance of the budgeting process for the success of the sport management organization;
- Understand how proper budgetary planning and implementation can prevent many problems from surfacing;
- Understand that both profit and non-profit sport entities must pay attention to the so-called bottom line;
- Characterize the essential elements of a sound budget;
- Describe the total budgetary process from planning through implementation;
- Differentiate between a fiscal year and a calendar year budget;
- Explain the purposes of an audit of the budget and the budgetary process;
- Outline the various methods of budgeting;
- Define various terms such as formula budgeting, zero based budgeting, bids and quotes;
- Provide examples of different methods of accounting;
- Outline the purchasing process;
- Comprehend how the inventory process can impact sport entities and programs;
- Read and understand a sample budget used within a sport organization;
- Understand the importance of accountability in sound fiscal management.

THE IMPORTANCE OF MONEY IN SPORTS

"From financing the construction or renovation of sports facilities to funding new uniforms for a youth-league team, money has a way of entering every discussion and informing each decision" (Cohen, 1999, p. 9.). Today, it has been estimated that the sport industry will attract some $250-billion to be spent in the United States alone.

On the college level, there has been significant financial growth, an increase of some 34% from 1999 to 2003 among all NCAA division I institutions, with an average yearly income of $29.4 million. In fact, in terms of expenses for the academic year 2004-2005 among the largest division I athletic programs, Ohio State leads the pack with $80.6 million followed by Texas ($74.4), the University of Florida ($73.5), Tennessee ($71.5) Oklahoma ($62.9), Michigan ($61.4), USC ($60;7), Penn State ($60.2), Wisconsin ($59.5) and Texas A & M ($57.4) (Spending that would make, 2006).

While it is important to remain concerned with the amount of revenue any sport entity is capable of securing on a consistent basis, it is equally, if not more important, how the money one has secured is spent. The actual spending plan, that is, what you do with the money that you have, is of paramount importance. Walter Wright, the commissioner of the Sun Belt Conference, said it succinctly when he said, "More money doesn't make you better, what you do with the money makes you better" (Spending that would make, 2006).

The most profitable division I athletic program (largest surplus) in 2005 was the University of Georgia with $23.9 million. This was based on an income of $68.8 million and expenses of $44.9 million leaving $23.9 million. Even this amount had to be reduced further as depreciation and debt service further whittled down the profit to a still respectable $18+ million. Other profitable Division I programs (not considering depreciation and debt service) are listed in Table 7.1 (University of Georgia, 2006; U of L Budget Soars, 2006). And Ohio State? Along with income of $89,700,979 the school had expenditures of $89,580,306 for a net profit (exclusive of debt service and depreciation) of $120,673 in 2005 (Revenues and Costs, 2006).

TABLE 7.1: *Selected NCAA Division I Schools' Athletic Income and Expenses*

Division I Institution	Income	Expenses	Profit (not counting Depreciation/debt service)
Michigan	$78.4	$61.3	$17.1
Wisconsin	$75.3	$59.5	$15.8
Texas	$89.7	$74.4	$15.3
Alabama	$62.3	$49.8	$12.5

THE IMPORTANCE OF EFFECTIVE BUDGETING FOR SPORT ORGANIZATIONS

The process of budgeting, with all of its various components, is an all-important element in the arsenal of the modern day sport manager. Indeed, many sport managers, at different levels and in a variety of sport organizations, do indeed have significant roles to play in the overall budgetary process. The purpose of the budgetary process is to facilitate the realization of the organization's goals and objectives through fiscal responsibility, sound business practices, effective decision making and prudent financial management.

Every business (whether for profit or non-profit) has a bottom line that must be closely watched (Cohen, 1999). And, this includes those sport entities residing within or sponsored by educational institutions. Typically, financial resources are scarce and the sport manager who is able to secure funds and/or adequately manage those monies that are available is in great demand. A solvent sports program is the ideal and any individual who can help make this a reality is worth his or her salt in the world of sport business (and highly employable).

> *CONCEPT #190: One's sphere of influence is greatly enhanced to the degree in which one has financial authority and responsibility.*

Some individuals have more direct responsibility in financial aspects than others. Nevertheless, regardless of the degree of responsibility, the fact remains that all would-be sport managers must be knowledgeable in the overall budgetary picture as well as competent in the basic day-to-day financial operations of the sport entity.

CONCEPT #191:   *The person who controls the budget possesses the power.*

Since the financial aspect of any sport or sport related organization is so important, managers must recognize how important it is to consistently demonstrate sound financial management in the conduct of their duties and responsibilities. Individuals who have a degree of control over finances and financial decision making also wield great power, exert influence and command authority. Thus, it is imperative that sport leaders possess financial acumen and retain financial decision making powers if they are to be effective and efficient managers.

CONCEPT #192:   *Leaders in sport organizations should usually not relinquish total budgetary decision making to others—effective leaders retain control over their budget and financial decisions.*

One usually never relinquishes the budgetary decision making power within one's financial domain. Yes, it is perfectly permissible and even expected that managers will delegate to subordinates specific tasks and responsibilities relating to the budget; however, the ultimate decision making within the budget arena remains with the manager or leader of that unit or area.

There are numerous individuals involved in the budgetary process and financial arena within any sport organization. Various staff and line personnel, coaches, directors, coordinators, bookkeepers, assistants, etc., could all involved, in some way or another, in the financial arena of the organization. Some provide information. Others collect data. Still others provide recommendations. But it is the manager or leader who makes the final decisions based upon the financial data and recommendations provided by the support personnel, assistants and others. It is this decision making power that is the distinguishing factor between a high level administrator and a person filling a support or advising role.

> **CONCEPT #193:**   *One's Expertise in Budgeting and Fiscal Management Provides Insight into the Sport Manager's Level of Competency in the Eyes of Others.*

Since the budgetary process is so important to the general health and welfare (and to the very survivability) of the organization, the financial skills of the sport leader will have a decided impact in terms of how this sport manager is viewed by others, both in and outside of the sport organization (Olson, 1986, April). Ineptitude in things financial or relating to the budget or the budget process can spell disaster in terms of the manager's image—up and down the organizational chart as well as well as in and out of the organization.

> **CONCEPT #194:**   *Budget competency and sound fiscal management are equally important for profit as well as for not-for-profit organizations.*

Every sport organization needs to be concerned with fiscal responsibility and sound business practices, policies and procedures. This is true for both profit and not-for-profit businesses and organizations. The need to develop and follow a sound budget and to make effective and efficient fiscal decisions is essential for every business and organization.

> **CONCEPT #195:**   *Many problems and challenges facing sport organizations can be significantly reduced or prevented entirely with astute financial decision-making coupled with sound budgetary practices.*

Many of the problems facing sport organizations, now and in the foreseeable future, revolve around financial challenges or are fiscally based. However, many of the problems evolving from the financial aspects of any given sport business can be better addressed and the negative impact lessened if not alienated by wise fiscal management and decision making in advance of, or in anticipation of, such financial crises. One of the goals of sound financial management is to prevent fiscal problems or at least minimize the negative consequences or fallout that results from such problems. This can be accomplished by wise decision making, by insightful anticipation, and by judicious accurate prediction of the future—based upon available information and data and coupled with meaningful and relevant experience.

> **CONCEPT #196:**   *Sound financial decision-making and budget construction depends upon accurate data and information.*

Sound fiscal responsibility involves more than merely having a well thought out and accurate budget, although that is very important. Fiscal responsibility implies timely decision making in all matters financial. However, decision making must not be made in a vacuum. Financial decisions are made in light of existing circumstances and situations as well as best projections of what the foreseeable future might be. This requires a great deal of information, data and recommendations to be made available to the ultimate decision-maker and those who serve as advisers and counsel to the decision-maker. Without appropriate and accurate budget information and financial data, sound fiscal decision making is often not possible.

> **CONCEPT #197:**   *The budget can present an accurate snapshot of the current financial situation of the organization as well as a glimpse into the future of the entity.*

THE BUDGET—DEFINITION, PURPOSE AND FUNCTIONS

A budget is a written statement of anticipated income and expenses over a period of time, usually a 12-month period. The use of the budget instrument is important in planning for the future, in implementing in the present and in reviewing of past activities.

> **CONCEPT #198:**   *Budgets consist of statements of anticipated income and expenses over a specified period of time.*

The budget document should be viewed as a means to an end—a tool. In light of the definition of administration provided in Chapter One, the budget is a tool which enables sport leaders to better manage individuals and manipulate resources toward previously agreed upon goals and objectives, within a specified time frame.

> **CONCEPT #199:**   *The budget is a tool—A means to an end.*

Budgets serve as a guide for current as well as future decisions and action on behalf of the sport leaders. Budgets facilitate the planning necessary for the organization itself as well as for the individuals and the programs within the organization. Budgets help individuals make appropriate and timely decisions based on financial climate and current circumstances which affect the organization. And, of course, budgets enable individuals to keep track of the current financial health and well-being of the organization and all of its components. Wise use of budgets enable managers to take a pro-active stance in viewing the financial health of the entity by predicting possible future occurrences in terms of income and expenses all the while providing for various scenarios in the event differing futures come to pass.

ESSENTIAL ELEMENTS OR COMPONENTS OF A BUDGET

The essential elements of any budget consist of (1) anticipated income, (2) anticipated expenses, and (3) cash reserve, if any. Other components that customize or make budgets different from one another include the time factor (calendar or fiscal year) as well as whether the budget is a reflection of the entire organization or merely depicts the financial picture of a component or part of the entire entity.

The Calendar Year Versus the Fiscal Year

Budgets reflect the financial picture of a program or an organization over a specific period of time, usually 12 months. These 12 months can either be on a calendar year or an arbitrarily determined fiscal year. In unusual instances the budget cycle or term might be 24 months or even longer. In the case of the budget based on the calendar year, the financial year starts on January 1st of any given year and concludes on December 31st of that same year. However, using the calendar year as the time frame for the budget cycle is not required. Many organizations, for any number of reasons, choose not to operate on a calendar year. Instead, a specific fiscal year is chosen based on a starting date at any time of the year. For example, a fiscal year might be chosen to being June 1st and end 12 months later on May 31st.

Departmental Budgets Versus the Budget for the Entire Organization

A budget can take many forms. Budgets can also be simplistic in nature or they can be more very complicated. The type and size of the organization, as well as whether the budget reflects the financial situation of the entire entity or merely one subcomponent of the organization, will determine the degree of sophistication of the budget document as well as the process by which the budget document is developed and finalized.

Overall Organizational Budget

This is a budget that illustrates how the entire organization will attempt to spend the dollars available to it as well as how the entity will secure the necessary financial resources with which to support its planned expenditures. Such a budget reflecting the anticipated financial income and expenses (plus any case reserve) for the entire organization will naturally be more encompassing and complicated and detailed than a budget constructed for a small department or component within the organization.

Departmental Budgets

At the college scene, as an example, there is an overall budget for the entire college or university. This overall budget is in turn made up of numerous departmental budgets. For example, there would be a separate budget for Public Relations and Development, another for the department of Political Science, another for Biology, another for History, and one for intercollegiate athletics, etc.

The intercollegiate budget, in turn, may be made up of numerous other sub-budgets. These so-called sub-budgets within the athletic department budget could include a budget for the football team, one for the field hockey team, another the softball team, the cross country team, and so on.

TYPES OF BUDGETS

Classic Car and Truck Shows Can Be Big Money Makers.
[courtesy of ESMC Consultants]

There are different types of budgets which organizations may utilize to help facilitate financial planning and implementation. For example, there is the operational budget which deals with the expenses (costs of doing business) associated with the daily operation of the entity throughout the budget year. The personnel budget deals with the costs of employees within the organization. Some organizations break down their expenses into a capital expenditure budget which forecasts how much is anticipated to be spent on large ticket items such as constructing a building or making major rehabilitation efforts to an existing facility. If there is going to be major (and expensive) equipment purchases in the next budget cycle some organizations will have a separate equipment budget for the entire entity.

Differentiating Equipment from Supplies

Supplies refer to those consumable items that have a very short useful life. Typically, supplies are thought of as wearing out or existing for less than a year or so. *Equipment,* on the other hand, are those items that have a longer usefulness in terms of time. Three to 5 years or even longer may comprise the life of equipment. *Capital expenditures* are those which involve a significant amount of monies coupled with a very long life span (15-20 years and more) in terms of usefulness. For example, the addition of facilities, modification or alterations to existing facilities, and the purchase of certain kinds of major equipment can all be thought of as capital expenditures.

CREATING A BUDGET—THE BUDGET DEVELOPMENT PROCESS

Creating a budget for a sport organization does not have to be a complicated, tedious and time-consuming process. In fact, the so-called budget development process or cycle can be streamlined and facilitated by being aware of some basic concepts and following time tested suggestions which are presented below.

1. *The budget document should be prepared well in advance of the start of the upcoming fiscal or calendar year.*

Planning for future purchases through the creation of a budget frequently places sport managers in a position of anticipating expenses and income many, many months in advance. If the sport organization is on a fiscal year running from September 1st through August 31st it will be necessary to begin work on the budget document well before the September 1st date. For school based athletic departments the budget process can begin as early as October or November for the fiscal year beginning September 1st. This means that the budget document being prepared is being worked on some 12-16 months in advance of when parts of the budget will actually be implemented.

This time factor can have significant repercussions in terms of the type of decisions that must be made by various staff members. For example, the anticipation of actual income and expenditures this far in advance is sometimes rather challenging (Olson, 1986).

> **CONCEPT #200:** *Being able to predict expenses is very important when constructing a budget.*

It is very important to obtain accurate estimates of future expenditures so that when you actually order the items the real costs will be within the range you had expected and planned for. However, it may be difficult to project many expenses due to the advance lead time at which the budget document is actually constructed. For a budget constructed to cover the period of August 1, 2009 through July 31, 2010 it will be necessary to begin building the budget document as early as October or November 2008. This necessitates that actual expenditures which will be made in June or July of 2010 will have to have been anticipated as early as December 2008—some 18 months in advance.

2. *The budget process is initiated by examining the organization's and/or program's objectives, goals and mission.*

It is important to remember that the budget is a reflection of the mission, goals and priorities of the organization or the program. One must not lose sight of the established objectives, goals and mission(s) of the entity for which the budget is being prepared. The budget is a tool that makes it possible for the organization to realize its mission(s) by meeting its objectives and goals.

3. *Information and data must be obtained relative to the needs, strengths and resources of the organization and/or program.*

The type of information and data sought can be include, but not be limited to, input from vendors, previous budgets, inventory of equipment and supplies, future commitments of the program, cost estimates, etc. There is a definite need for accurate financial data before intelligent decisions can be made for the upcoming budget (Lederman, 1993). Today, with the presence of computers and appropriate software, data collection and analysis is available to a greater extent than ever before.

CONCEPT #201:   *Take advantage of technology such as computers in obtaining, evaluating and comparing information and data.*

Essential to this collection of data is to examine what resources are already at hand, what needs to be replaced, and what needs to be secured for the first time. This necessitates adequate inventory records.

4. *Solicit the input, knowledge and expertise of others in the collection and evaluation of information and data as well as in the construction of the budget document itself.*

Seeking input, ideas and suggestions from others is only prudent for the sport leader developing a budget. No person would want to play the role of the Lone Ranger when it comes to the development of a sophisticated budget. Take advantage of the knowledge and experience of others, both inside and outside of the organization. Learn from others with specialized knowledge and skills.

> **CONCEPT #202:**   *An intelligent individual doesn't know all of the answers,*
> *only where to find out the answers.*

5. *Review the data collected and analyze the pertinent available information in terms of what was done previously, what is required now and in the foreseeable future.*

This may necessitate looking at previous years' budgets as well as past expenditures and current costs of items. It will be necessary to make projections in terms of anticipated income and anticipated costs and expenditures. Making good financial decisions and recommendations for the future is only possible with good, appropriate and accurate information and data. It is the analysis of this information and the decision making that follows such an examination that will determine the quality of the budget itself, as well as future financial decisions based upon the budget document.

6. *In the preparation of the budget document follow the stipulations and requirements set forth by the organization or one's superiors.*

Follow directions (standard operating procedures—SOPs) of your boss/organization in the construction, development and presentation of the budget. Use the appropriate forms in the construction, preparation and presentation of the formal budget document. Utilize appropriate formulas and other financial limitations (mileage and other travel costs, for example) when developing the budget.

> **CONCEPT #203:**   *Padding one's budget in anticipation of one's request being cut*
> *is poor financial management and diminishes one's credibility.*

To pad one's budget request is to deliberately overstate the amount that you are requesting in anticipation of your request being reduced or cut. The thinking is that if one asks for more than one needs, and if the so-called inevitable cut comes, then one might end up with what one really needs. This assumes that one's budget request will always be cut.

> **CONCEPT #204:**   *Program and departmental administrators are hired*
> *to make the decisions in terms of budgeting—don't force*
> *superiors to assume budgetary decisions at the program*
> *or department level.*

On the other hand, the superior who is in charge of the budget looks at the individual submitting the budget request suspiciously and anticipates that the budget request has a lot of "fat" in it and is severely padded. Knowing that the budget request is padded with a great deal of "fat," the "powers to be" cut the request. This places the superior (college president, for example, in a school based sports program) in the position of determining how much is needed for the sports program and that is why the college hired the AD in the first place, to make those decisions.

7. *The budget document must be accurate, feasible and realistic.*

Always double and triple check the budget document to make sure that it is accurate and free of errors or omissions, however slight. The image and reputation of the administrator presenting the budget is at stake in the eyes of the board and/or superiors within the sport organization who will examine the document. It should be error free.

**CONCEPT # 205:   *The budget should correctly reveal the financial situation
of the organization at a particular point in time.***

Since important and far reaching decisions, some having significant implications, will be made as a result of looking at the budget, it is imperative that the document be a workable document. This means the budget must be feasible, reasonable and realistic while revealing the current financial situation of the organization.

8. *Submit the completed budget documents to a select few for critical analysis prior to making the formal presentation to the board or one's superior(s).*

Allowing select individuals to review the completed budget document prior to the actual formal presentation to the board or one's superiors provides opportunities to make last minute corrections. It is far better to catch errors or oversights at this point in time than to be embarrassed in a formal presentation session by having a mistake pointed out or by being faced with a question that one can't answer.

There is a very decided advantage in allowing one of the individuals who happens to be on the board which will receive and review the budget document to view an advance copy of the budget. The advantage is that this individual, having reviewed and "passed" on the document, can become a so-called "ringer" (inside supporter) in the meeting(s) where the document is being discussed. Naturally, the person to whom the advance copy is given should be a stout supporter of one's program as well as an influential and well-respected colleague of the other members of the board.

CONCEPT #206: *The budget document must be easily understood and interpreted.*

If the first cardinal sin of budget preparation is having one or more errors in the document, the second cardinal sin is creating a budget document that is confusing and difficult to understand. First and foremost, use a simple format and concise language. Don't hesitate to include detailed footnotes in the appendix of the document to answer any questions that might crop up or to clarify any potentially confusing situation. Footnotes in a budget document are an extremely helpful tool to explain, clarify and interpret potentially confusing, unusual or unexpected elements of the document—to the layperson as well as to the sport business expert.

The ideal goal of the budget presenter is that there should be no unanticipated questions created by the budget document itself. The document should be almost self-explanatory. It must be remembered that many of the individuals who will sit in judgment of the budget document may not be professional accountants or even knowledgeable business people. They may not be familiar with sport, with the business of sport or with financial documents, including budgets. The document itself must be comprehensible for those non-sport oriented individuals.

9. *When making the formal budget presentation anticipate questions and be ready with accurate and timely responses.*

Be prepared to confidently and accurately answer questions during the budget presentation session in a pleasant, helpful and professional manner. Never become irritated or provoked at unreasonable or stupid questions put to you by members of the review board, even if the person(s) should have known the answers. It may be advisable at one specific meeting to distribute the budget document to those in attendance and then to make a short formal presentation related to the document itself. Then, at a second meeting scheduled for just such a purpose, allow general discussion on the document as well as questions from the group.

CONCEPT #207: *Don't take it personally when questioned about the budget recommendations and requests.*

When presenting the budget document to superiors or to a review board the purpose of such a meeting is two-fold. First, to inform and educate the individuals to whom the budget is being shared. And second, and most importantly, to gain approval from these individuals for the implementation of the budget. These two objectives can rarely be accomplished without a great deal of discussion involving a multitude of questions and answers and the sharing of ideas, opinions and suggestions. Don't cut off your nose to spite your face by becoming antagonistic towards those individuals asking the questions or expressing concerns or reservations.

10. *The final step in the budget approval process after the formal approval of the document, with any changes by the appropriate individual or board, is the actual implementation of the budget itself.*

Since the budget is a tool designed to facilitate the work of the sport leader or manager it only remains for the sport manager to implement the budget during the upcoming fiscal or calendar year.

> *CONCEPT #208:   Budgets are not written in stone—flexibility is still the watchword as time progresses and events take place.*

Inevitably there will be changes, some small and some not so small, in the anticipated income and planned expenses within the sport organization. One simply can't anticipate everything regardless of how hard one tries or how much experience one has. The only thing that is certain is that nothing is certain. Consequently, one should anticipate that the working budget document may have to be adjusted at different times during the budget year to take into consideration events and occurrences that were not and could not have been foreseen. Being able to make suitable and timely adjustments or changes is the responsibility of the person in charge of the budget. Such is life in sport and in business.

11. *An audit of the budget is conducted following the conclusion of the budget year.*

The budget cycle is complete when the fiscal or calendar year comes to a close and an audit of the past year's fiscal activities is conducted. This culminating fiscal activity brings to a close the budget cycle that began, in some cases, some 18 months previously. The audit, as stated elsewhere in this chapter, serves two purposes. First, to insure that generally accepted accounted procedures and practices were followed by those responsible for the budget. And, second, to assist the sport manager in becoming an even more proficient and competent fiscal manager and leader.

METHODS OF BUDGETING

Line Item Budgeting

Budgets that utilize the line item method of categorizing income and expenses are very common in the sport business world. Elements of most budgets utilize some aspect of the line item concept in differentiating the various types of income and expense accounts on the budget document. In such a budget each class or type of expense and income is categorized or classified upon a different line identified as a specific item of expense or income. Tables 7.2, 7.3 and 7.4 illustrate the line item concept in budgeting.

In Table 7.2 the expenses are broken down into different categories, including a line item called *team expense.* These figures in turn in broken down (Table 7.3) into 23 different team expenses plus transportation contingency and equipment contingency account.

TABLE 7.2: *Planning Budget for Intercollegiate Athletics—2013-2014*

(in comparison with Prior Planning Budgets for 2005-06, 2006-07, 2007-08)

Revenue/Expense Summary

Anticipated Revenue	2010-11	2011-12	2012-13	2013-14	
Mandatory Athletic Fee	___	___	___	___	(a)
Brockport Student Govt.	___	___	___	___	(b)
*State Funds	___	___	___	___	
Temp. Ser. Officials	___	___	___	___	
Brockport College Fund	___	___	___	___	(c)
Roll-over (estimated)	___	___	___	___	(d)
Gate Receipts	___	___	___	___	(e)
All-Events Tickets	___	___	___	___	(f)
FOBA	___	___	___	___	(g)
**Maurauders	___	___	___	___	
Entry Fees	___	___	___	___	
***Bus Subsidy	___	___	___	___	

Anticipated Expenses	2010-11	2011-12	2012-13	2013-14	
Teams (Table 7.3)	___	___	___	___	(h)
Post Season	___	___	___	___	(i)
Admin. & Selected Team Expenses (Table 7.4)	___	___	___	___	(j)
Training Supplies	___	___	___	___	
Contingency/Miscellaneous	___	___	___	___	(k)
***Outside Bus Expenses	___	___	___	___	

Reserve Account					
Reserve	___	___	___	___	(l)
Anticipated Expenses & Reserve			___	___	

*Exclusive of personnel (team physician/PA/athletic staff) and plant management costs (salaries, utilities, supplies, etc.)   **IFR account with Recreation   *** "Wash"

TABLE 7.3: *Planning Budget for Intercollegiate Athletics—2013-2014*

(in comparison with Prior Planning Budgets for 2005-06, 2006-07, 2007-08)

Team Budgets (BSG, STATE, and SOFT FUNDS)

	2010-11	*2011-12*	*2012-13*	*2013-14*	
Baseball					(m)
Men's Varsity BB					
JV Basketball					(n)
Women's Varsity BB					(o)
Cross Country					(p)
Football Varsity					(q)
"B" Football					
Gymnastics					(r)
Field Hockey					(s)
Ice Hockey					
Men's Varsity Soccer					(t)
Women's Varsity Soccer					
Softball					
Tennis					
Swimming—Men					(u)
Swimming—Women					(u)
Track—Indoor					(v)
Track—Outdoor					(w)
Volleyball					(x)
Wrestling					
"B" Wrestling					(y)
Football Cheerleading					
Basketball Cheerleading					
Trans Contingency					
Equipment Contingency					
					(z)
	Increase	Increase	Increase	Increase	

TABLE 7.4: *Planning Budget for Intercollegiate Athletics—2013-2014*

State Funds	2010-11	2011-12	2012-13	2013-14	
Temp Service	_____	_____	_____	_____	(aa)
Supply & Expense (S&E)	_____	_____	_____	_____	
Dues	_____	_____	_____	_____	(bb)
Supplies	_____	_____	_____	_____	(cc)
Copier Expense	_____	_____	_____	_____	(dd)
Storehouse	_____	_____	_____	_____	
Phone	_____	_____	_____	_____	
Postage	_____	_____	_____	_____	
Central Duplicating	_____	_____	_____	_____	(ee)
State Auto Recharge	_____	_____	_____	_____	
Team Programs	_____	_____	_____	_____	(ff)
Sub-total:	_____	_____	_____	_____	

Soft Funds	2010-11	2011-12	2012-13	2013-14	
Insurance	_____	_____	_____	_____	
Team Programs/Schedule Cards	_____	_____	_____	_____	
Printing, frames, photos, film	_____	_____	_____	_____	(gg)
Books/Publications	_____	_____	_____	_____	
FOSA	_____	_____	_____	_____	
Travel					
MACDA, ECAC, NCAA, SUNYAC	_____	_____	_____	_____	(hh)
State (NYSWCAA) & local	_____	_____	_____	_____	
Equipment	_____	_____	_____	_____	
Generic uniforms/wk-st & teams	_____	_____	_____	_____	(ii)
Supply & Expense (S&E)	_____	_____	_____	_____	
Computer, printer	_____	_____	_____	_____	
Sub-total:	_____	_____	_____	_____	
Total:	_____	_____	_____	_____	

Each of these team expense categories are in turn differentiated, in a line item format, in Table 7.5. In Table 7.5 the expenses of individual teams can be seen to be classified according to the categories of (1) *meals and lodging*; (2) *fees*; (3) *transportation*; (4) *equipment and supplies*; (5) *officials*; and (6) *other.*

Incremental Budgeting

Incremental budgeting involves adding or taking away a specific increment, a certain percentage, 2% or 4% for example, to the previously year's budget. In some instances the incremental budgeting approach gives a specific percentage, an increment, to the total sport program within the overall budget. For instance, in a school based sports program, all of the sport teams within the athletic program might be given a 2.5% rate of increase over the previous year's allocation. The problem with this budgeting approach is that it fails to take into account real needs or special needs of individual sports or sub-programs within the overall athletic program.

Zero Base Budgeting (ZBB)

Peter A. Pyhrr and a team of financial visionaries within Texas instruments, Inc, conceived zero base budgeting in 1969. Some years later, in 1973, Jimmy Carter, then governor of Georgia, became a proponent to this system and with the help of Peter Pyhrr, implemented the ZBB as the official budgeting tool for the state government. "The most important difference is that ZBB avoids the practice of considering last year's budget as the base; and therefore avoids the question of how much is required next year to continue with a particular function" (Jensen, 1992, p. 129).

Zero base budgeting is based upon the requirement that organizations and their programs must justify their *total need* for budgeted resources, not merely their request for an increase (Dirmith and Jablonsky, 1979). Jimmy Carter was a big proponent of zero base budgeting both as President and as governor of Georgia because this process required managers to justify the cost-effectiveness of their operations (Carter, 1977).

Formula Budgeting

Another technique or method utilized in constructing a budget is the use of formulas. A simplistic example of formula budgeting in sports can be seen when the amount to be expended for a specific line item (away game travel) is determined by using a formula, a formula that automatically determines the dollar amount for that expense item.

For example, seasonal expenses for each teams' away contests can be determined by following a very simple formula involving (1) the cost per miles drive (47 cents per mile for the team bus, for example), (2) the number of individuals (players and coaches) comprising the travel team, (3) the number of meals to be consumed by each person, (4) the dollar allocation for each meal, including breakfast, lunch, dinner and after game snack; and, (5) the dollar allocation for hotel accommodations (if needed) for the traveling squad.

> **CONCEPT #209:** *Formula budgeting is effective if prior decisions have been made relative to establishing guidelines or parameters which predetermines maximum costs in specific instances or for specific purchases.*

In the above example it is necessary that advance decisions are made or polices decisions established regarding (1) what opposing teams will make up the away schedule, (2) the cost per mile traveled, (3) the number of individuals comprising a travel squad, (4) the maximum number of people to stay in each hotel room, (5) the number and types of meals to be consumed, and (6) the maximum amount of money to be spent for each type of meal to be consumed. Once these decisions and policies are known, all that is needed is for someone (a budget clerk or a secretary) to follow the policies and to plug in the correct numbers or figures into the formula.

That is, once the staff member has determined the number of miles to be driven to each away site (from a master list of miles to each opponents' city), the number of individuals comprising the travel party for each game (from the policy handbook of the department), the number of meals to be consumed and the number of rooms needed for each away contest (also determined by reviewing the policy handbook of the department)—it is a simple matter to merely plug in the appropriate figures in the so-called formula. The result is the total dollar expenditure for each away contest as well as for all away contests for the entire season for that particular sport.

> **CONCEPT #210:** *In most school based athletic budgets the only discretionary expenses fall under the category of equipment and supplies.*

In many sport budgets the planning of expenditures is actually determined by following decisions and policies that have been made well in advance. In fact, in some sport budgets, especially school-based programs, the major discretionary expense category is that of "equipment and supplies." The reason for this is that the other major expense categories are all predetermined by advance policy decisions or advance scheduling decisions. Once a home and away schedule has been determined the major expenses of any individual team is likewise predetermined by merely filling in the formula categories as cited above. The result is that the amount of (significant) discretionary money to be spent for any individual sport is in equipment and supplies.

> ### CONCEPT #211:   *Maintaining accurate inventory records of current equipment and supplies is quintessential for accurate budgeting and financial decision making.*

And, even in this category the amount needed to be expended is greatly affected by what the inventory of equipment and supplies reveal. Thus, it is very important that accurate records be kept regarding the items of equipment and supplies as well as their current condition and expected useful life-span.

PPBES—Planning, Programming, Budgeting, Evaluating System

Originally known as PPBS (Program Planning Budgeting System) in 1949, this system of budgeting was devised to be based on three factors: (1) function, (2) activities, and (3) objectives. Some five years later (1954), the Rand Corporation devised a performance based budget for use by the Military Industrial Complex. Early proponents of this type of budgeting were the Ford Motor Company and the DuPont Corporation. Later, Robert McNamara, a former Ford Motor Company high Executive, brought the PPBS system to the Defense Department. The results were impressive both in fiscal expediency and in elimination of financial waste. By late 1965, all departments and agencies of the United States federal government were utilizing the budgeting system upon presidential decree. When the process of evaluation entered this budgeting concept the acronym evolved to the current day PPBES (Butcher and Krotee, 1993).

As the name indicates, PPBES budgeting involves establishing programs and activities to coincide with objectives and goals previously planned; and, then budgeting and allocating resources to meet the needs of these programs. Finally, an assessment is necessary to determine the degree, if any, that the budget allocations allow the programming aspects of the organization to facilitate the realization of the established objectives and goals (Haggerty & Patton, 1984; Apostolou & Crumbley, 1988; Horine, 1995).

METHODS OF ACCOUNTING

There must be an understandable and orderly system of keeping track of all monies—both expenses and income. Financial accounting enables the sport leader to ascertain, based upon hard data, a snapshot of the financial status of the organization as well as any program or sub-set within the entity itself. Proper accounting makes it possible to track and to determine whether purchases were made for the purpose they were intended and authorized as well as to determine whether expected income was indeed received and deposited to the correct account(s).

> **CONCEPT #212:** *One goal of accounting is to determine whether or not funds of the organization have been misused, stolen, lost, misplaced, or otherwise unaccounted for.*

Cash System of Accounting

"The cash accounting system tracks income as cash is received and expenses as payment is make. The tracking of transactions is related to the disbursement or receipt of cash regardless of the time period in which the commitments are made" (Railey & Tschauner, 1993, p. 206).

This system of accounting treats expenditures as actual expenditures only when the money is materially spent, that is, when the money is physically sent (by check, etc.) to the person or organization owed the debt. On the other hand, anticipated income is not recorded on the books (income ledger) until the money is actually "in hand."

Accrual Accounting

In accrual accounting, expenses and income are recorded in the organization's financial records or "books" when they are incurred or earned on behalf of the organization or program, regardless of when the money is actually forwarded to the person or entity. Accrual accounting presents a far more accurate picture of the financial state of any organization or program than the cash accounting procedures (Parkhouse, 1996).

Some sport organizations choose to utilize a very conservative approach to accounting by utilizing a combination of both the cash and accrual accounting methods. In this hybrid accounting strategy all income is treated on a so-called cash basis while all expenditures are dealt with on an accrual basis. In this scenario, any income expected or owed to the sport organization would not be recorded as actual income in the financial records (income ledger) until the money was actually in hand, physically in possession of the organization or program.

However, in terms of expenditures, when an expense is committed to be made, the appropriate funds are *encumbered* on the books, that is they are earmarked as future expenditures (for a very specific purpose) even though the money may not physically leave the company's coffers for many months to come. Nevertheless, these same funds, on the books of the sport organization, are treated as if they have indeed already been spent and are not available for use by any other program or segment of the sport entity. In reality, such monies have been earmarked (encumbered) for expenditure and are merely temporarily residing in the organization's asset account until the "check is put in the mail."

PURCHASING AND RECEIVING EQUIPMENT AND SUPPLIES

When initiating purchases it is imperative that steps be taken to insure that the items ordered are the items that one needs and that the items that are ordered are actually received from the vendor. It is a given that accurate records are retained in all aspects of the ordering and purchasing processes.

> **CONCEPT #213:** *Insure that all equipment and supplies are delivered to a central receiving location and check the invoice against the original order form.*

It is very important that all items of equipment and supplies are properly protected once they have been received by the sport organization. This can be accomplished by safe and secure storage combined with accurate inventory control. However, it is also important to provide security for items ordered as these items are delivered. Towards this end it is advisable that all equipment and supplies be delivered to a central receiving location and checked to insure that the items shipped or delivered are indeed what had been ordered and that the individual items are in good condition.

Ethical Decisions Regarding the Purchase of Equipment and Supplies

Well-managed sport organizations have well established and publicized policies guiding the ordering and purchasing process to prevent unnecessary items from being ordered, to prevent misappropriation of equipment and supplies as well as to deter the acceptance of "kick-backs" from vendors.

> **CONCEPT #214:** *Accepting kickbacks or gifts from prospective vendors is wrong, is unethical and dishonest.*

Some vendors advertise that orders totaling at least a specific amount of dollars qualify the person submitting the request for any number of prizes or premiums depending upon the exact amount of the order. Proper ethical behavior would dictate that involvement in such kick-back schemes are not acceptable under any conditions. Purchase requests or recommendations should be made on the basis of real needs without any consideration of any reward or compensation being given to the person initiating the request.

PETTY CASH

Petty cash accounts are a necessary element of the purchasing efforts of most organizations. However, at the same time, such petty cash accounts can also create many problems if they are not managed and supervised properly.

Petty cash accounts are kept for small purchases when it is neither appropriate nor possible to go through the normal purchasing process to secure the item or items. Typically, departments keep a petty cash fund of $100 to $250 dollars on hand. Out of this money, purchases may be made on an emergency or urgent basis when there is insufficient time to go through the more formal and time consuming ordering procedures established by the organization. Once any of the petty cash is expended, the receipt for the item(s) secured is processed through the normal accounting procedures in an effort to replenish the petty cash account.

> **CONCEPT #215:** *A petty cash account should be utilized to handle small purchases in an emergency type situation when it is not possible or advisable to utilize the normal budgetary process.*

It must be strongly emphasized that the petty cash account is not to be consistently utilized as a means of paying for goods and services. Rather, it is to take care of the unusual situation or challenge that presents itself. However, overuse of the petty cash account is a sign of a lack of planning, a lack of managerial competency.

BIDS AND QUOTES

The purpose of bids and quotes are to encourage competition and to reduce the costs of the organization employing the bid/quote process. Those organizations that are state entities utilize the use of bids and quotes to help ensure that the public's money is utilized in the most cost-efficient manner possible (Bidding at all costs, 1995). Ideally, the use of bids should provide the administrator of a public sport or recreation organization to secure goods and services at the lowest possible price. The use of bids and quotes are not limited to public organizations. Private, for-profit entities can also benefit from the use of bids and quotes in securing services and goods for their programs.

Definition of the Bidding Process

The bidding process involves a written solicitation from potential vendors for a specific service or item (good[s]) for a specific price (a bid) based upon a very exacting set of specifications. For example, if a sport administrator was seeking a certain type of paper, the individual would provide specifications outlining the type and quality of paper desired, that is, the dimensions, color, weight, material, etc. The bid specs might also include a date by which the paper would be made available as well as specific delivery requirements.

The potential or would-be suppliers must be able to provide the item or service (or in some cases, the "equivalent") and therefore submits a "bid" for the right to provide said item or service to the organization at a specific dollar amount. Usually, the lowest bidder wins the right to provide the item or service to the organization or entity seeking the bid. However, in many instances, organizations may not be required to accept the lowest bidder. In this situation, the individual purchasers may have to make an argument to a higher authority as to why they are recommending acceptance of a higher priced bid.

The bidding process typically requires that the specifications provided by the organization be in written form and that the solicitation of potential bidders be written. And, the submission of bids by potential or would-be vendors must also be in writing.

Items "On Contract"

Some states have some items and services "on contract." This means that the state has already gone out and secured the lowest bids on specific items and services from numerous vendors. Subsequently, when public organizations and state employees at their jobs seek items which are on contract, the state already has identified specific vendors from whom the item(s) must be purchased by the various state entities (schools, colleges, parks, hospitals, prisons, police agencies, etc.).

In New York State the Bureau of the Budget organizes a periodic meeting of experts from various state agencies. At this meeting the various items which are usually purchased and used by different state entities are examined to determine which specifications would be necessary for different agencies or organizations. For example, many different agencies or organizations might want to purchase basketballs (colleges, parks, prisons, hospitals, etc.) but there might indeed be different needs by each agency in terms of quality and costs. Basketballs purchased for colleges might be of higher quality and cost more than those purchased for use in prisons.

> **CONCEPT #216:   Not all "equivalents" are equal—**
> **beware of the would-be "same as" claim.**

Not everything that is labeled "equal to" or "equivalent to" is truly the same as the item which is being sought. There are numerous (horror) stories about companies or organizations which sought a specific item or its equivalent only to find, when the lowest bidder delivered the item that the item in question was not in the least equal to or equivalent to what was actually sought.

One such story dealt with a state that "let a bid" for "Liquid Paper" or its equivalent. In this case the state let out a contract on behalf of all state organizations and agencies (schools, colleges, hospitals, prisons, recreational entities, etc.) for "Liquid Paper" to use to correct mistakes make by typists. Evidently, the specifications stated that the product could be the item called "Liquid paper" or its equivalent.

The winning vendor submitted the lowest bid that was thousands of dollars less than the next lowest bidder—for a product that was supposedly equal to the product with the trade name "Liquid Paper." However, when the state agencies and organizations ordered and received their equivalent bottle of liquid it was soon discovered that the product was not exactly of the same qualify as "Liquid Paper."

In reality, the substitute "liquid" took almost three minutes to dry whenever it was applied to paper by state employees. This was in contrast to the 10-20 seconds it took for the real "Liquid Paper" to dry when applied.

When one compared the dollar value of the lost time (not to mention the frustration) on behalf of all of the state employees over the next two or three years (the supposed length of the bid contract) who had to wait the 3 or so minutes every time one of them had to use the substitute "liquid"—it was clearly evident that the thousands of dollars initially saved by the state by awarding this contract to the lowest bidder was not really any savings at all. To the contrary, over the long haul, the length of the bid contract, the state probably lost a far greater sum in lost time and productivity by the state employees.

Writing Specifications

This highlights the necessity of carefully writing out the specifications of the item or service that one is requesting bids on. One cannot overemphasize the importance of meticulously writing exacting specifications for the product or service one is requesting. Vendors will be submitting bids based on the minimum requirements specified in the bid document.

> *CONCEPT #217:*   *Write the specifications for the item to be let to bid very,*
> *very, very carefully—then double and triple check*
> *for accuracy and appropriateness.*

It is necessary that someone write specifications detailing exactly what type of product is needed. This is perhaps the most important aspect of the bidding process because if the specifications are not correctly or adequately or stringently written the result could be obtaining inferior or unwanted or unacceptable product(s).

Specifying a Distinct Brand Name

In some instances the person seeking bids from vendors on behalf of the organization may wish (and are allowed) to specify a specific brand name as the only type that is acceptable. In that eventuality, vendors wishing to secure the order for that organization must offer to supply that actual brand of item.

CONCEPT #218:   *Specifying a distinct brand name insure a minimum quality level.*

This frequently happens in the interscholastic or intercollegiate sport scene in which a school's conference dictates that only a specific brand of basketball can be used in conference games. Thus, if Spalding basketballs are required by the conference, the athletic director will specify a specific type. Spalding basketballs as the only brand acceptable in the bidding process. Successful vendors must submit an offer of that specific type of Spalding basketballs for a specific amount of dollars.

Accepting an "Equivalent" Product

In other situations, it is not permissible to specify an actual brand name. in that case, the organization seeking a item or service must write exacting specifications which describes the minimum qualities that are acceptable in the item or service. Thus, a vendor submitting the lowest bid on an "equivalent basis"—providing the item or service which at least matches the minimum requirements of the specifications as written—is given the order.

Definition of a "Quote"

A quote is really nothing more than an informal bid. A quote can be merely a verbal sharing of a price by a vendor with a potential purchaser. Typically, organizations utilize a "quote" when the dollar amount for the item or service is less than that which necessitates the more formal and structured bidding process. Some states or organizations require an informal quote for any item or service that would cost more than $5,000 but less than $10,000. And, for those items costing $10,000 and above, the formal, written bidding process kicks in.

To obtain a quote, one would typically call three or four vendors (whatever the policy stipulates in your organization) and request a price quote for a specific type of item, usually referring to a specific brand name (no exceptions or equivalent accepted).

> **CONCEPT #219:**   *The bidding process is used both by private and public organizations.*

Bids may be sought by private businesses as well as by state agencies or state entities, including public schools and colleges, hospitals, prisons, etc. In most states it is mandated that public organizations utilize the bidding process when the amount of money to be spent exceeds a certain dollar amount. For example, the states of New York, Pennsylvania and Vermont require that expenditures of $10,000 and up made on behalf of schools necessitates written or "sealed" bids (Bidding at all costs, 1995, p. 47).

> **CONCEPT #220:**   *The bid process differs among companies and organizations— as it does among states for state agencies and organizations.*

For public organizations the bidding process can be especially complicated and time consuming. Even in private entities and organizations the bid process can be cumbersome. Nevertheless, the potential good, i.e., reduced costs for quality goods and services, makes the bid process an all-important one in terms of fiscal responsibility and sound monetary management.

PURCHASING FROM LOCAL VENDORS VERSUS DISTANT VENDORS

A common challenge facing many sport organizations is whether to purchase from local companies or to utilize firms that may be a great distance away. In some instances, mail order firms may well be able to provide items at less expense. But there may be other factors to consider when making purchases other than price. Many organizations subscribe to the belief that they will buy locally if the quality of the item is comparable, the time of delivery is similar, and if the price is no too expensive.

> **CONCEPT #221:**   *Generally speaking, it is wise to purchase from local vendors over mail order vendors unless the cost is greater than 10% over the mail order company.*

There are some definite advantages to consider in making purchasers closer to home. One benefit is that it is frequently easier to select the item(s) to be ordered when the vendor is local. This is because the merchandise may be able to be physically seen and physically handled due to the fact that the company selling the item is nearby. It is also often easier to secure service on what is purchased, especially in situations in which an item must be returned or exchanged. Another factor to consider is being a good neighbor by helping to contribute to local vendors. This is important as long as the sport entity is not ripped off by the local vendor charging exorbitant prices for its goods and/or services. Support for local businesses can only go so far.

EXAMPLE OF AN INTERCOLLEGIATE ATHLETIC BUDGET

Table 7.2 (page 245) illustrates a template of the first page of an athletic department's budget from the State University of New York, Brockport, when the author served as athletic director. This budget template illustrates many of the fundamental principles in budgeting and in presenting a budget to staff, high level administrators and board members. Note that the budget contains a summary of anticipated income as well as expenses and anticipated reserve, all on the cover page (Stier, 1989). Also, please note that personnel costs in the form of salaries for professional and support staff (coaches and athletic administrators) is not represented in this budget.

> *CONCEPT #222:* **It is sometimes difficult to compare budgets between two similar sport organizations because some entities do not include all expenditures within the sport budget—some items are included under the entity's general budget expenses.**

Personnel costs were covered by the college's general instructional budget. Thus, although this athletic budget provides a fairly representative example of general income and expense categories for a college athletic department (NCAA Division III), it nevertheless does not reflect the total expenditures made on behalf of the athletic program simply because no coaching or administrative personnel costs are included. That is why it is so difficult comparing athletic budgets even between two similar institutions or programs—because some organizations include some expenses within the sport budget while others do not.

Use of the Contingency or Miscellaneous Account

> *CONCEPT #223:* **A contingency line item account should be carefully utilized, never abused.**

Under Anticipated Expenses on this first page of the budget document there is a line item titled Contingency/Miscellaneous. It is important that this type of category be carefully utilized and not abused. The contingency line item is not a slush fund. Rather the contingency line item refers to emergencies or special situations that the budget planners cannot foresee but nevertheless wish to prepare for by setting aside a particular amount of dollars in the eventuality that such an emergency should occur. In this example of an actual budget, the contingency amounted to $10,000 out of a total budget of $276,935 (exclusive of salaries), which represents less than 4% of the total budget (exclusive of salaries).

MAINTAINING A HISTORICAL PERSPECTIVE— REVIEWING PAST YEAR'S FISCAL BUDGET CATEGORIES

It is important to note that the budget sheet for the current fiscal year in Table 7.2 also includes reference to three fiscal years prior to the current year in addition to the current (2008-2009) fiscal year. This enables the planners (as well as others working with and/or approving the budget document) to have access to a historical picture or insight into the income and expense picture of the entity, in this case, the athletic program.

Being able to look at previous years' budgets, line item by line item, can be helpful in a number of ways. First, one is able to see if there is a pattern or trend in either the income or expenses for the program. Second, one can compare the actual increases or decreases (if any), as well as percentages of such increases or decreases, in individual line item accounts for income and/or expenses. However, one must be careful in merely assigning a specific percentage of increase (or decrease) to a budget (the entire athletic budget, for example) or to sub-areas within the budget (all sports, for example).

Use of Explanatory Footnotes

Adjacent and to the right of some of the income and expense budget figures for the current year are a series of small cap letters. Each letter refers to a footnote contained in the reference section of the budget. This reference section is located at the end of the budget document. These footnotes attempt to explain or further clarify the figures on the budget sheet for those individuals who must review and understand the budget document. Since it is imperative that the budget document be fully understood by those who review or read it, it is important that any unusual or potentially confusing figures be clarified and explained in detail in the footnotes (at the end of the document). In this way there should be not major questions as to what the figures relate to or why or how the specific figures were arrived at.

The goal is to present a concise and clear picture of the financial situation of the sport organization, department or program, not to confuse befuddle, befuddle or mystify those who would attempt to read and understand the document. Many times those who must read, understand and eventually make a recommendation as to the acceptance, rejection or modification of the budget document are not certified public accountants, or even very knowledgeable in terms of financial matters. Thus, it behooves the sport administrator to make the budget document as clear as possible to lessen any difficulty that might arise from misunderstanding the document or misinterpreting the content.

Individual Team Budget Allocations

The second page of the SUNY Brockport's athletic budget template included the proposed (anticipated) expenses for each of the athletic teams and is depicted in Table 7.3 (page 246). Again, just as on the first page of the budget document (illustrating general income, expenses and reserve), the reader is able to gain a multi-year perspective (in this case, three years in addition to the current [2008-2009] year figures) of the total amount of expenses for each of the individual athletic teams.

Detailed Breakdown of Administrative and Selected Team Expenses

The third page of the athletic department's budget (template) consisted of a further breakdown of expenses, that is, administrative and selected team expenses, Table 7.4 (page 247). This page provides still further detail in terms of the types of expenses and the actual dollar cost of specific items required of the athletic department.

Note that these expenses were further broken down into *State Funds* and *Soft Funds*. State funds were those monies given directly by the state to the institution (athletic department). In this particular situation there were specific expenditures which had to be made (either by institutional rules or state mandates) with state allocated monies *(state funds)*. Other expenditures could be made with what was referred to as soft funds, that is, monies generated by the athletic department independent of the State of New York. Rather, these soft funds (money) represented income from such sources as student government fees, concessions, tickets, and fundraising.

As stated above, the individual athletic budget was broken down into the amounts (Table 7.3) to be spent for each of the individual teams sponsored by the college's athletic department. However, as informative as Table 7.3 is, the data provided only shows the gross expenditures for each team. Nothing on this sheet provides any insight into how these gross figures for each team were arrived at, that is, how the money allocated to each team is to be spent in detail.

TABLE 7.5: *Multisport Budget Summary, Year by Year, Athletics*
(in comparison with Prior Planning Budget 2006-2014)

	2006-2007	2007-2008	2008-2009	2009-2010	2010-2011	2011-2012	2012-2013	2013-2014
Baseball								
Meal & Lodging	___	___	___	___	___	___	___	___
Fee	___	___	___	___	___	___	___	___
Trans.	___	___	___	___	___	___	___	___
Equip.	___	___	___	___	___	___	___	___
Official	___	___	___	___	___	___	___	___
Other	___	___	___	___	___	___	___	___
M. Basketball								
Meal & Lodging	___	___	___	___	___	___	___	___
Fee	___	___	___	___	___	___	___	___
Trans.	___	___	___	___	___	___	___	___
Equip.	___	___	___	___	___	___	___	___
Official	___	___	___	___	___	___	___	___
Other	___	___	___	___	___	___	___	___
JV Basketball								
Meal & Lodging	___	___	___	___	___	___	___	___
Fee	___	___	___	___	___	___	___	___
Trans.	___	___	___	___	___	___	___	___
Equip.	___	___	___	___	___	___	___	___
Official	___	___	___	___	___	___	___	___
Other	___	___	___	___	___	___	___	___
W. Basketball								
Meal & Lodging	___	___	___	___	___	___	___	___
Fee	___	___	___	___	___	___	___	___
Trans.	___	___	___	___	___	___	___	___
Equip.	___	___	___	___	___	___	___	___
Official	___	___	___	___	___	___	___	___
Other	___	___	___	___	___	___	___	___

continued

Table 7.5 continued

	2006-2007	2007-2008	2008-2009	2009-2010	2010-2011	2011-2012	2012-2013	2013-2014
Cross Country								
Meal & Lodging								
Fee								
Trans.								
Equip.								
Official								
Other								
Football								
Meal & Lodging								
Fee								
Trans.								
Equip.								
Official								
Other								
B. Football								
Meal & Lodging								
Fee								
Trans.								
Equip.								
Official								
Other								
Gymnastics								
Meal & Lodging								
Fee								
Trans.								
Equip.								
Official								
Other								

Continued

Table 7.5 continued

	2006-2007	2007-2008	2008-2009	2009-2010	2010-2011	2011-2012	2012-2013	2013-2014
Field Hockey								
Meal & Lodging								
Fee								
Trans.								
Equip.								
Official								
Other								
Ice Hockey								
Meal & Lodging								
Fee								
Trans.								
Equip.								
Official								
Other								
M. Soccer								
Meal & Lodging								
Fee								
Trans.								
Equip.								
Official								
Other								
JV Soccer								
Meal & Lodging								
Fee								
Trans.								
Equip.								
Official								
Other								

continued

Table 7.5 continued

	2006-2007	2007-2008	2008-2009	2009-2010	2010-2011	2011-2012	2012-2013	2013-2014
W. Soccer								
Meal & Lodging	___	___	___	___	___	___	___	___
Fee	___	___	___	___	___	___	___	___
Trans.	___	___	___	___	___	___	___	___
Equip.	___	___	___	___	___	___	___	___
Official	___	___	___	___	___	___	___	___
Other	___	___	___	___	___	___	___	___
Softball								
Meal & Lodging	___	___	___	___	___	___	___	___
Fee	___	___	___	___	___	___	___	___
Trans.	___	___	___	___	___	___	___	___
Equip.	___	___	___	___	___	___	___	___
Official	___	___	___	___	___	___	___	___
Other	___	___	___	___	___	___	___	___
Tennis								
Meal & Lodging	___	___	___	___	___	___	___	___
Fee	___	___	___	___	___	___	___	___
Trans.	___	___	___	___	___	___	___	___
Equip.	___	___	___	___	___	___	___	___
Official	___	___	___	___	___	___	___	___
Other	___	___	___	___	___	___	___	___
Men Swimming								
Meal & Lodging	___	___	___	___	___	___	___	___
Fee	___	___	___	___	___	___	___	___
Trans.	___	___	___	___	___	___	___	___
Equip.	___	___	___	___	___	___	___	___
Official	___	___	___	___	___	___	___	___
Other	___	___	___	___	___	___	___	___

continued

Table 7.5 continued

	2006-2007	2007-2008	2008-2009	2009-2010	2010-2011	2011-2012	2012-2013	2013-2014
Women Swimming								
Meal & Lodging	——	——	——	——	——	——	——	——
Fee	——	——	——	——	——	——	——	——
Trans.	——	——	——	——	——	——	——	——
Equip.	——	——	——	——	——	——	——	——
Official	——	——	——	——	——	——	——	——
Other	——	——	——	——	——	——	——	——
Track (combined) Indoor Total								
Meal & Lodging	——	——	——	——	——	——	——	——
Fee	——	——	——	——	——	——	——	——
Trans.	——	——	——	——	——	——	——	——
Equip.	——	——	——	——	——	——	——	——
Official	——	——	——	——	——	——	——	——
Other	——	——	——	——	——	——	——	——
Track—Outdoor								
Meal & Lodging	——	——	——	——	——	——	——	——
Fee	——	——	——	——	——	——	——	——
Trans.	——	——	——	——	——	——	——	——
Equip.	——	——	——	——	——	——	——	——
Official	——	——	——	——	——	——	——	——
Other	——	——	——	——	——	——	——	——
Volleyball								
Meal & Lodging	——	——	——	——	——	——	——	——
Fee	——	——	——	——	——	——	——	——
Trans.	——	——	——	——	——	——	——	——
Equip.	——	——	——	——	——	——	——	——
Official	——	——	——	——	——	——	——	——
Other	——	——	——	——	——	——	——	——

continued

Table 7.5 continued

	2006-2007	2007-2008	2008-2009	2009-2010	2010-2011	2011-2012	2012-2013	2013-2014
Wrestling								
Meal & Lodging	____	____	____	____	____	____	____	____
Fee	____	____	____	____	____	____	____	____
Trans.	____	____	____	____	____	____	____	____
Equip.	____	____	____	____	____	____	____	____
Official	____	____	____	____	____	____	____	____
Other	____	____	____	____	____	____	____	____
B. Wrestling								
Meal & Lodging	____	____	____	____	____	____	____	____
Fee	____	____	____	____	____	____	____	____
Trans.	____	____	____	____	____	____	____	____
Equip.	____	____	____	____	____	____	____	____
Official	____	____	____	____	____	____	____	____
Other	____	____	____	____	____	____	____	____
Football Cheerleading								
Meal	____	____	____	____	____	____	____	____
Trans.	____	____	____	____	____	____	____	____
Equip.	____	____	____	____	____	____	____	____
Basketball Cheerleading								
Meal	____	____	____	____	____	____	____	____
Trans.	____	____	____	____	____	____	____	____
Equip.	____	____	____	____	____	____	____	____
Equipment Contingency								

*These figures do not include postseason.

Detailed Breakdown of Individual Team Expenses

Thus, there is a need for a further breakdown of the anticipated data for each team in terms of (1) meals & lodging, (2) fees, (3) transportation, (4) equipment and supplies, (5) officials, and (6) other (miscellaneous). These data are provided in a different template, represented in Table 7.5 (pages 261-266). These detailed and informative figures show in great detail exactly how each individual team's budget is to be expended. And, there is a eight-year history of prior (to current year 2008-2009) expenditures for each of the teams that were in existence for that length of time.

GENERAL SOURCES OF INCOME FOR SPORT ORGANIZATIONS

What are the actual categories of income for a sport organization? While there are some similarities, there are also different types of income for some sport entities than for others depending whether one is talking about fitness clubs, health clubs, professional sports teams, recreation departments, college or high school athletic teams, or corporate fitness sites.

For health and fitness clubs catering to the general public, a significant percentage of income will be derived from membership fees. Additional income can be realized from sale of apparel and equipment/supplies as well as food and drink. The corporate fitness site might not have membership fees at all since the employees are automatically members by virtue of their working for the organization. In this eventuality, the greatest income might be a specific allotment of monies directly from the company itself to subsidize the operation of the corporate or company fitness or wellness center.

> **CONCEPT #224:** *One key element to a balanced budget is to be able to successfully anticipate the amount of income which will be forthcoming in the foreseeable future.*

In the case of recreation programs sponsored by municipal entities the major source of income might also be in the form of an allocation from the city or county governmental agency to cover the cost of operating the recreation program for the various constituencies or publics. On the other hand, the professional sports team as well as for the school based athletic programs might well enjoy a wide range of income sources.

For example, income at collegiate and professional sport programs typically is derived from various types of profit centers. Profit centers are income producing activities or operations that although related to the sporting event, activity or organization, stand alone in its ability to generate income. Examples of typical profit centers include ticket sales, con-

**Nothing Beats the Excitement that can Occur
On and Off the Proverbial Playing Field**
*[courtesy of University of Tennessee,
Sports Information Office]*

cessions, program sales, merchandise or product sales (souvenir and apparel items), parking fees, user fees for facilities, vending machines, luxury box seating and parking condos (Stier, 1994b, pp. 175, 176). Other sources of income include reserved or special seating, sponsors, direct solicitation of potential donors, radio and television advertising, fence or building advertising, guarantees, gifts and donations, program advertising and sales, as well as other forms of fundraising (Mason and Paul, 1988, Stier, 1994a).

And, of course in the case of big time NCAA Division I sports and professional sports there is the matter of sizeable income via television contracts. Another sizeable source of income for collegiate teams is general student fees, fees accessed all students and earmarked for the intercollegiate athletic programs/teams.

SOURCES OF INCOME FOR MAJOR COLLEGE SPORT PROGRAMS

Even big-time Division I collegiate athletic powers are continuing to experience severe financial challenges (if not downright crises) in their endeavors to remain in the black. In 1994 it was reported that the average major college (Division I-A) athletic department obtained its income from the following sources: football ($6,226,415 or 42.8%); from donations, gifts and investments ($2,452,830 or 16.2%); men's basketball ($2,207,547 or 15.4%); Student fees, state and institutional aid ($1,905,660 or 15.3%; fundraising efforts (such as concessions, program sales, sponsorships, facility rental and sports camps) of $1,396,226 or 9.1%; other men's sports ($132,076 or 0.8%; and women's sports ($56,604 or 0.4%) (Wieberg, 1994, August 25).

In 2006 the athletic budget for Kansas State was $34 million. The revenue side of the budget of the Wildcats' included $11.5 million from ticket sales, $7.1 million from the Big 12 Conference and the NCAA, $5 million from fundraising, $1.5 million from State governmental subsidy and $8 million from advertising, sponsorships, suite leases, as well as other related miscellaneous sources. On the expenditure side of the ledger, there were the following categories: $13.7 million for employees, coaches, and administrators (including $3.9 million in base salaries for 39 coaches), $10 million for team support (business office, sports information, items not tied to a particular team) which includes debt service of $1.5

million, $5.2 million for athletic scholarships, and $5.1 million for team operations (travel, equipment, etc.) (Adams, 2006).

> **CONCEPT #225: *All income must go through (deposited in) the organization's income account—never co-mingle funds.***

A generally accepted principle of accounting and budgeting is that all income generated for the organization should go directly into an appropriate income account. Never co-mingle monies that belong to the sport entity with one's own funds. To insure that all income is properly accounted for it is imperative that all money generated by the organization is deposited into a suitable income account before it is spent.

Only after the income is safely deposited and accounted for it may then be expended through the normal process stipulated in the organization's or department's standard operating procedures. However, to do otherwise, that is, to spend monies generated by the sport entity before it is accounted for by being deposited into the general coffers of the entity is an invitation to disaster. Even the best of intentions will not compensate or protect the transgressor from disastrous consequences ranging from official reprimand to outright dismissal from employment of the organization.

GENERAL EXPENDITURES FOR SPORT ENTITIES

Just as there are similarities in income among different types of sport organizations there are similarities in the type of expenses incurred by various types of sport entities, whether they be professional teams, fitness clubs, corporate wellness and health organizations, recreation departments or school based athletic programs.

> **CONCEPT #226: *The major share of expenditures in collegiate athletic programs rests in personnel (labor) and related costs (benefits).***

For most sport organizations a significant portion of expenses falls under personnel (labor). Labor costs include the direct costs of salaries, wages and benefits, and the indirect cost of staff training. For professional teams this includes players' salaries as well as the salaries for staff—both professional and support personnel. For fitness, health and wellness organizations, personnel is also a sizeable portion of their expenses. And, recreation programs as well as athletic departments also are faced with significant expenditures for professional and support staff. "Labor costs constitute nearly 60 percent of the typical short-term operating budget for an athletic department" (Graham, 1994, p. 176).

Big time NCAA Division I athletic programs have other personnel expenses to be concerned about, specifically, scholarships for their elite athletes. And, with the ever increasing cost of doing business at the Division I level of competition, more and more athletic programs are operating in the red. By some estimates NCAA institutions competing at the elite Division I level (the nation's so-called major athletic programs) are operating at an annual financial deficit run as high as 70% (Wieberg, 1994, August 25). Lederman (1993) claimed that of the biggest college sports programs (Division I) in the NCAA fewer than 50 are believed to turn a profit and the latest statistics revealed in 1989 that the average Division I-A profit was a mere $39,000. This is in spite of the millions of dollars in revenue such programs are taking in through big-time football and men's basketball.

Personnel Expenses at the Professional Sports Level

The average salary of professional athletes in the major sports (Major League Baseball [MLB], National Football League [NFL], National Basketball Association [NBA], and the National Hockey League [NHL]) has grown dramatically in recent decades. In professional football, the average player salary during 1960-1961 was $15,000. In 1993 this figure topped $645,000 and the figures continue to rise each and every year. Other professional sports have likewise enjoyed the tremendous growth in individual salaries with the average player's salary in MLB being $1,076,000; $540,000 in NHL and $1,390,000 in the NBA (Salary escalation continues, 1993; The NFL's Television Contract History, 1994). In 2005 the average MLB player's salary was $2.49 million; in the NHL it was $1.26 million; and in the NBA it was $4.9 million (Players' Salary, 2006).

"Of course, part of the reason why there has been such an escalation in professional athletes' salaries rests in the ever increasing television revenue pouring into the coffers of the teams themselves. In 1960-61 the NFL took in a total of $600,000 in television monies for an average TV income per team of $45,000. Contrast that to the time period 1990-1993 when the TV package involved $3.65 billion dollars for a $32.6 million dollar paycheck to each NFL team" (The NFL's Television Contract History, 1994, p. 19). One wonders what would be the case today without television in the money equation in professional sports.

Other Categories of Sport Expenditure

Other categories of expense that might be appropriate to some sport organizations include, but not limited to the following: recruiting costs, travel, insurance, food, non-game equipment and supplies, capital improvements, capital equipment, capital expenses for structures, facilities maintenance, rental of services, game equipment/supplies/services including uniforms, laundry, security, police, medical, phone, postage, printing, utilities, programs, souvenirs and premiums, paint, brochures, pocket schedule cards, dues, memberships, guarantees, freight, lease or rental costs, photographs, subscriptions and general office supplies (Douple, 1990).

THE QUESTION OF KEEPING EXPENSES IN LINE WITH INCOME

> **CONCEPT #227:** *Another key element to a balanced budget is to keep expenses in line with anticipated income.*

Every administrator is faced with the prospect of making sure that all monies spent under that person's watch are appropriate expenditures. That is, that all monies spent are spent wisely and appropriately and that such expenses facilitates the organization to realize its objectives, goals and mission(s). An important part of this wise spending is being able to keep expenses in line with anticipated income. If sport managers and administrators had all the money and resources they wanted, it would be relatively easy to accomplish most objectives and goals. Needless to say, this is not the case in most instances.

CASH FLOW

Cash flow refers to one's ability to have sufficient cash on hand to pay current bills (debt). It is this ability to pay current expenses with current cash on hand that results in positive cash flow. Unfortunately, some organizations find themselves in a cash flow crisis by having current debt that is greater than available cash, a situation referred to as negative cash flow. This situation can result when the company organization is owed cash from any number of sources but the actual cash is not yet on hand (in the bank) in sufficient amount to pay the bills that are current.

> **CONCEPT #228:** *Profit is important to any sport organization—managers should not neglect positive cash flow if the organization is to survive and prosper.*

Foresighted sport managers need to be constantly vigilant in terms of their organization's cash flow situation. Facing a cash flow crises forces fiscal managers to consider borrowing against receivables or postponing the payment of their own bills. Preventing cash flow problems can be a three-pronged effort. First, one can attempt to accelerate monies owed to one's own organization. Second, efforts can be made to collect late payments or past due accounts as well as bad debts. And, third, one may endeavor to postpone entering into debt until sufficient cash is on hand or seeking more generous payment schedules from those to whom money is owed.

COST EFFECTIVENESS AND SOUND FISCAL MANAGEMENT

> *CONCEPT #229:   The goal of financial managers is to keep costs in line with expenses.*

In today's business of sport the challenge of most administrators is to be able to work within the budget restrictions and limitations created by a lack of income and the presence of a multitude of expenses. Again, the key is to keep the expenses in line with income so that there is a balanced budget at the end of the calendar or fiscal year. Fiscal responsibility is the watchword of the professional sport administrator in the 21st Century.

The budget process is a balancing of two factors, income and expenses (Sattler & Mullens, 1993, February). Simultaneously, today's and tomorrow's sports leader must attempt to increase income while also keeping expenditures in line with the income generated. Part of this challenge can be resolved by prudent and frugal use (management) of financial resources at one's disposal. For in the final analysis, one of the cardinal sins of any sport administrator is to misspend or waste valuable resources (monies). To do so exemplifies the personification of the inept administrator.

> *CONCEPT #230:   If sport managers had all of the money and resources they needed or wanted it would not be difficult to accomplish most objectives and goals.*

Exponential Growth of Big-Time College Athletics

Harris (1994) cited the exponential growth of big-time college athletics having come to an end in the early 1990s when athletic administrators came to a realization that there had to be an end to the continued ever increasing expenses incurred by athletic departments. The 1980 was a time of boom/bust financial cycle for most athletic departments. During the 1990s however the atmosphere became more grim with the realization that financial restraints would be the order of the day rather than ever increasing expansion and ever increasing expenditures. Revenue was not keeping up with expenses and as any business leader recognizes when that happens, the cure is to reduce expenditures and reduce them significantly and quickly.

*Cost re*ducing efforts became the catch-phrase of the athletic/sport community in the 1990s in an effort to place the total athletic programs on an even keel, one which would be close to self-supporting. However, *today only a small number of institutions are truly self-supporting.* The vast majority of all athletic programs, even the major Division I institutions, rely on financial contributions from the institution in one form or another (Stier, 1994a, April 14).

However, as the 1990s turned to the year 2000 it became clear that athletic spending at the collegiate level was expanding at an ever increasing rate. Witness the situation at the University of Wisconsin in 2001 when its $40-million dollar budget made it the 6th largest athletic budget among all 307 NCAA Division I institutions. In that year (2001) the top Division I schools (those in the Sears Cup Top 25) had a budget of 36 million. The rest of the Division I schools averaged only around $25 million (Person to Person, 2001).

Now, fast forward to the year 2006 and see how the athletic budgets at Division I schools have continued to skyrocket into the stratosphere. In 2006, Kansas State had a $34 million dollar budget (which has tripled from a measly $11.6 million in 1996) and was desperately attempting to catch up with the "Jones" of its fellow conference (Big 12) members. Other universities in the conference had truly astronomical budgets lead by the likes of Texas, Nebraska, Missouri, Kansas and Oklahoma State, with budgets in the $50-60-70 million dollar range (Infante, 2006). Of course, these figures pail in comparison to The Ohio State University's athletic budget of some $90 million dollars to cover the expenses of 34 athletic programs and 900 student-athletes (Porentas, , 2006).

> **CONCEPT #231:**   *To misspend money or to otherwise waste valuable resources is the epitome of the incompetent administrator.*

Maintaining A Balanced Budget—Keeping Expenses in Line With Income

One of the ways to keep within a budget (that is, balancing expenses with income) is to reduce costs without sacrificing quality (Sattler & Doniek, 1996). All items of expenditures within a budget should actually be needed. Budgets with "fat" (unnecessary items or expenditures) in them are poorly constructed budgets. The goal is to eliminate such unnecessary expenditures, fat, within any budget (Olson, 1986).

> **CONCEPT #232:**   *When reducing costs the watchword is to do so without reduction in quality (either in goods or services).*

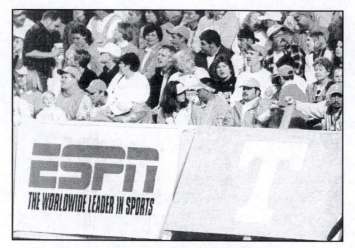

**National Exposure through News Media is a Big Plus
for All Athletic Programs**
[courtesy of University of Tennessee, Sports Information office]

Today, everyone in the business of sports is experiencing financial pains and restraints. As a result, there is a need for ever increasing effective and efficient fundraising and income producing efforts because normal sources of income is insufficient to balance the budget and do what is necessary to be competitive. There is also a great need to cut costs. Ideally, the combination of more income coupled with a reduction in unnecessary costs will produce the desired end result— sufficient funds to operate the

sport program and, in the case with for-profit sport entities, greater net income.

CONCEPT #233:   *Accountability is the buzzword in fiscal management.*

One must be accountable for one's actions and one must hold others accountable. Accountability is important in the securing of new resources, in the care of resources (supplies, equipment and facilities, etc.), in the repair of such resources and in the replacement of items that are of no further use to the sport entity. Competent sport leaders do all they can to be accountable for those resources placed under their responsibility. To do otherwise is not only poor management, but in the final analysis self-defeating.

CONCEPT #234:   *Don't allow equipment or supplies to "walk away."*

With equipment and supplies being so valuable administrators should do all in their power to insure that such items are not misused, misappropriated or lost. Every item that must be replaced takes valuable resources away from the organization, dollars that might have been spent for other important purposes. Being able to reduce, if not eliminate, the expenditures for items stolen, lost or otherwise made unusable, enables the sport manager to put to better use those limited funds available to the sport organization.

BOX 7.1
Checkout and Return Policies
For Intercollegiate Athletics Supplies and Equipment

1. Persons who check out items from the equipment room are required to sign for those items and to provide their social security numbers and other pertinent information.

2. All items checked out become the responsibility of the borrower and must be returned in person to the equipment room. Borrowers will be issued a receipt by the equipment manager upon return of all items.

3. Items must be returned in good condition. Ordinary wear and tear is anticipated.

4. All items must be returned by the deadline (two weeks following the last scheduled intercollegiate contest in the sport for which the items were issued).

5. Borrowers may elect to purchase items they have checked out by paying current replacement cost, as determined by the Department of Intercollegiate Athletics. Payment must be made to the Department by the deadline date.

6. After the two-week deadline date, the Department will proceed to replace unreturned items. Therefore, no items can be accepted for return after the deadline date.

7. After the two-week deadline date, if items have been neither returned nor purchased by the borrower, the Bursar's Office will bill the borrower for all unreturned items.

   (NOTE: Students may not preregister or register for subsequent semesters nor can they obtain grades or transcripts until outstanding bills are paid.)

I have read the above checkout and return policies and agree to return all items listed below (or to pay the current replacement costs associated with each item) within the two-week time period, or upon request by a designee of the Athletic Director).

Items of equipment/supplies borrowed: _____

_____

_____

_____

Items listed above must be returned by: _____

Signature: _____ Date: _____

Name (print): _____ SS #: _____

School Address: _____ Phone: _____

Home Address: _____ Phone: _____

_____
| City/Town | State | Zip Code |

CONCEPT #235: *Every dollar saved is a dollar earned.*

Towards this end, it is imperative that a suitable checkout policy be instituted in those instances in which items of supplies and equipment are checked out by participants or club members. One example of a checkout policy is illustrated in Box # 7.1 (page 276). In this instance, those persons checking out items are held accountable for their safe return, in suitable condition.

If items are not longer useful to the sport organization, and if a decision is made to dispose of some items, it is important that an appropriate disposal process be determined, with the items then being removed from the active inventory list. Sometimes the items are literally destroyed. Other times the decision is consciously made to give the items away. And, in other situations, some organizations dispose of supply and equipment items that they can no longer use by means of a sale or an auction fundraising project. In this fashion, the organization is able to accomplish three objectives simultaneously. Specifically, the items are disposed, there is income produced and there is the possibility of generating favorable publicity on behalf of the sport entity.

ATHLETIC EQUIPMENT MANAGERS ASSOCIATION (AEMA)

A factor that has helped in upgrading the whole operational aspects of securing/ordering, maintaining, safeguarding, issuing and replacing equipment and supplies is the existence of the Athletic Equipment Managers Association (AEMA). This organization, was created in 1974 by a group of equipment managers meeting in Kansas City, Missouri. This national organization is composed of some 1000 professional equipment managers whose skills extend beyond merely issuing and collecting equipment and supplies. There is a professional journal representing the profession, called the AEMA Journal.

In 1991, the organization instituted a certification process leading—through a testing process—to the coveted title of Certified Athletic Equipment Manager. In 2006 there were 818 such professionals certified in the United States and Canada with an anticipated 1000 being certified by the organization's convention in 2007 (Personal conversation with Dorothy Cutting, November 10, 2006). Today's certified athletic equipment manager is expected to possess a high degree of competency and expertise in purchasing, fitting equipment and clothing, maintenance, administration and organization, accountability and management/supervision of equipment and supplies, etc. (AWMA Marks, 1999).

**CONCEPT #236:   *The presence of certified athletic equipment managers
                  within a sports entity facilitates wise use of budgetary expenses***

THE FINANCIAL AUDIT

Financial audits are a necessary element of control in that they provide a check on both the financial procedures of an organization as well as to how well the sport entity treats both financial expenditures and income, that is, whether the entity is in sound financial condition. Not to be viewed as a negative process, rather audits should be thought of in a positive vein, as a helpful tool in the process of fiscal management (Jensen, 1992; Sattler & Mullins, 1993, April). It is normal to double check the financial management of any organization or business that deals with significant amounts of money, both not-for-profit organizations and for-profit entities.

> **CONCEPT #237:** *A financial audit is to be viewed as a helpful tool to determine the adoption of sound financial procedures by the sport organization.*

Generally Accepted Accounting Procedures/Practices (GAAPP)

An audit can point out discrepancies, deviations or irregularities in the management and handling of money within an organization. The management and accounting of monies in businesses and organizations must follow what is referred to in the accounting profession as generally accepted accounting procedures and practices (GAAPP).

Internal and External Audits

There are two types of audits, internal and external. An internal audit is conducted by employees of the organization itself to insure that the organization's own policies, practices and procedures are being followed and implemented in accordance to the organization's own standard operating procedures (SOPs) insofar as the overall fiscal management within the entity is concerned. An internal audit can help prevent fiscal mismanagement. Such an audit can also aid in the increased security of resources and assets of the organization.

Protecting the Resources and Assets of the Organization

In terms of security, sport administrators are constantly on the alert to protect the financial integrity of the organization. This involves three different aspects. First, the security of the resources and assets (supplies, equipment and facilities) of the sport organization must be preserved. Second, there is the matter of the integrity of the organization's own personnel, paid and volunteer. Efforts must be made to reduce absenteeism as well as the misuse or abuse of the organization's supplies, equipment and facilities. And third, there is a matter of protecting the financial well-being of the organization from patrons and/or customers.

CONCEPT # 238:   *The key to dealing with financial audits is to keep detailed written records (paper trail) and to follow both generally accepted accounting procedures as well as the organization's own standard operating procedures, practices and policies.*

External Audits

An *external* (at arms length) *financial audit,* conducted by an outside, unbiased, expert accountant (auditor), seeks to determine whether the accounting procedures and transactions for that specific entity are in line with generally accepted accounting procedure and practices (GAAPP) for that specific type of business or organization.

CONCEPT #239:   *Conduct periodic value audits or analysis of what you do, how you do it and the costs incurred in doing it—is it cost effective?*

An Audit Of the Organization's Value—
A Different Type of Audit or Self-Examination

A value audit looks at everything an organization does and asks the following questions.

1. What is it that we do?
2. What do we do well?
3. Why do we do it?
4. Does it need to be done, this way?
5. Is it essential to our prime mission?
6. Is the cost appropriate to the benefit generated?
7. Is there anything that we do that is unnecessary?
8. Is the cost of what we do necessary?
9. Can we do it more effectively or efficiently?
10. What can we eliminate without diminishing the results of our efforts?
11. How can we do what we do for less cost without sacrificing quality?

EFFECTIVE TACTICS IN BUDGETING

Plan, Plan and Plan—in Advance

An effective strategy used by successful sport managers is that of planning and forecasting revenues and expenses. Whether such a plan is a three-year plan, a five-year plan or even a ten-year plan, the essential point is that sport managers need to anticipate, to forecast what the future might hold for the sport entity. This financial plan is often coordinated with the strategic departmental or organizational plan and is concerned with the so-called financial essentials of the organizational or departmental strategic plan. Alden (2000, p. 35) cites the following five items as essential for any financial plan.

1. The mission, goals, and objectives to be included in the overall departmental plan

2. An analysis of the program's current financial situation of the sport entity

3. An analysis of revenue projections versus expenses projections, including dollars obtained by means of fundraising

4. An analysis of capital projections throughout the time period of the plan, broken down into needs versus ideals

5. Specific information regarding the intended financial state at the end of the time period (of the plan).

Use of a "Wish List" in Budget Planning

Some sport administers have found the use of a so-called "wish list" to be very helpful. This list contains purchase requests for big ticket items (in terms of expense). However, these items are not included within the upcoming budget, but rather requested for a future budget cycle, one within the next 3-7 years. The "wish list" is typically submitted by activity and/or program coordinators along with their regular budget requests for the next year's budget to the department or area administrator.

Following the review of all items from the individual "wish lists," those who had submitted the requested individual big ticket items are told whether specific items have been tentatively approved and when (in what budget year) the items may most likely be placed within the regular budget proposal for that particular sport, program, department or area. For example, an expensive equipment item, such as a specific exercise machine, might be placed on such a list for possible delivery three years hence. However, the organization, through its financial decision makers, might respond with an indication that this exercise machine might be approved not three years in the future, but rather five years hence.

CONCEPT # 240: The use of the "wish list" can facilitate planning
as well as serve as a motivating factor for employees

**Mascots Can Play a Big Role
in Building School Spirit**
*[courtesy of University of Montana,
Todd Goodrich, photographer]*

The major advantages of the formal use of such a "wish list" are twofold. First, when such "wish lists" are used *throughout the sport organization* the immediate and long term planning process, at all levels of the organization, are greatly facilitated. This is because the list provides those administrators who must eventually make final financial recommendations and decisions with greater insight into specific future needs and the accompanying financial commitment to meet these each need. Second, the presence of a "wish list" within a specific sport or program can serve as a motivating factor for the employees who make and support the recommendation. This is because those who support an item on the "wish list" are at least told if the request itself has merit. They are also made aware when (in what year) it might be possible to formally include the item as *part of the regular budgetary process* and, baring some unforeseen difficulty, expect to have the request approved.

Be Open Regarding the Budgetary Process and the Actual Budget

The budget should be open for all to see. If some instances, the state public access laws dictate that financial records, including the budget, of a state entity shall be open for inspection to the general public. Nevertheless, it is a good idea to keep the both the budgetary process and the budget itself open for all to see. The rationale is simple. If there is nothing to hide, then why keep the budget or the budgetary process under a veil of secrecy? Be open in everything that pertains to the budget and the budgetary process.

> **CONCEPT #241:   *Keep no secrets when it comes to the budgetary process
> or the budget itself.***

When the author arrived at the State University of New York (Brockport) as the new Director of Athletics, the student government was demanding to have access to the athletic department's budget for the reason that the student fees constituted a major portion of the income to the sports program.

When the budget for that year (as well as subsequent years) was indeed made available to *everyone* on and off campus (students, coaches, faculty, community members, etc.) it did not take too many years before the student government leaders indicated that they no longer wanted to take the time to review the athletic budget in such great detail. They reasoned that if the athletic administration had anything to hide, the budget would not have been made so accessible so "everyone under the sun." Thus, when the data was truly made available many people lost interest in scrutinizing the document. However, if the budget (or the process) was shrouded in secrecy, there would undoubtedly be demands for more and more people to review the budget and the supporting documents.

Keeping Employees Abreast of the Financial Status of the Organization

An Ernst & Young survey of large companies (Jones, 1995) revealed that 86% of employees/workers would be motivated to help their companies succeed if they were privy to financial data typically seen only by senior managers, such information as balance sheets and cash-flow statements. Also, such information may make it possible for employees to make decisions or devise strategies that will help improve the efficiency of the organization and/or enable the company to save money or find better use of a variety of resources. Some college and university athletics directors subscribe to this principle even to the extent of allowing all coaches on staff to have privy to the team budgets of all other teams at that institution.

CONCEPT #242:   *Employees tend to be more motivated to support and help the organization when kept abreast of its financial health.*

"Open Book Management"

This openness mentality would tend to reinforce the trend in management referred to as "open-book management" which encourages employees to assume a greater role for the end product or service of the organization. No, not everything should be shared with everyone. There are such things as trade secrets which, by their very nature, should be kept within the purview of a small number of individuals who have the necessity to know. For example, there is a very good and valid reason why the recipe for Coca Cola should not become knowledge among the employees or the general public. Those items that should remain a top trade secret should remain so.

CONCLUSIONS

There is perhaps no more important area for a sport manager to be concerned with than the fiscal dimension of the sport business or organization. Whether it pertains to the budgetary planning process, the implementation of the budget or any of the many related activities and processes associated with the budget or monetary elements of the organization, it is essential that sport managers operate from a position of knowledge.

In short, competent sport managers must be familiar with the fiscal dimensions of the sport business in which they find themselves. Failure to be fiscally responsible, at any level within any type of sport organization, is not only professionally inexcusable, but is a frequently a professional "death warrant" for the sport manager. Even non-profit sport entities still must be concerned with the fiscal well-being of the organization. Success for every sport, recreation and fitness business or organization is ddependent, to a great extent, upon adequate planning and sound fiscal management.

REFERENCES

Adams, L. C. (2006, April 28). Money matters. *Kansas State Collegian*, pp.3. 4,

AEMA marks a quarter century. (1999, June/July), *Athletic Management, XI*(4), 8.

Aldlen, E. (2000). Forecasting Finances. *Athletic Management, XII*(4), 33-38.

Apostolou, N.G. & Crumbley, D.L. (1988). *Handbook of governmental accounting and finance.* New York: John Wiley and Sons.

Bidding at all Costs. (1995, August). *Athletic Business, 19*(8), 45-48, 50-51.

Butcher, C.A. and Krotee, M.L. (1993). *Management of physical education and sport.* St. Louis: Mosby Year Book.

Carter, J. (1977, January). Jimmy Carter tells why he will use zero-base budgeting. *Nation's Business,* p. 26.

Cohen, A. (1999). Cold cash. *Athletic Business, 23*(7), 9.

Dirmith, W.W., Jablonsky, S.F. (1979, October). Zero-base budgeting as a management technique and political strategy. *Academy of Management Review, 4*(4), 555-565.

Douple, T. (1990, January). Building a budget. *CAM Magazine,* pp. 54 -58.

Graham, P.J. (ed.). (1994). *Sport business—Operational and theoretical aspects.* Madison, Wisconsin: Wm. C. Brown & Benchmark.

Haggerty, T.R. & Patton, G.A. (1984). *Financial management of sport-related organizations.* Champaign, IL: Stripes Publishing.

Harris, C. (1994, April/May). Back on budget. *Athletic Management, VI*(3), 10-11, 13-17.

Horine, L. (1995). *Administration of physical Education and sport programs.* Madison, Wisconsin: Wm. C. Brown & Benchmark.

- Ask appropriate questions in terms of planning for and evaluating a potential facility for use by sport, recreation or fitness organizations;
- Appreciate the importance of data in facility management;
- Enunciate the potential sources of problems commonly faced by facility planners and sport managers in designing indoor and/or outdoor facilities;
- Be aware of the many problems associated with the management of various types of facilities;
- Acknowledge the importance of Standard Operating Procedures (SOPs) in managing and maintaining facilities;
- Be familiar with costs associated with replacement and annual maintenance of buildings and structures;
- Understand the advantages and disadvantages of utilizing consultants when planning facilities and when maintaining facilities;
- Be able to utilize the formula for determining/calculating maintenance and operating costs.

One of the major challenges that face sport managers deal with the care and managing of indoor and/or outdoor facilities, as well as the myriad of equipment and supplies associated with the various types of facilities (Wallace and Kline, 2005). It was conservatively estimated that $75-million per year was being spent to build and renovate sport facilities in this country in the early 1990s (Pate, Moffitt & Fugett, 1993). By the turn of the century, some experts estimated that the figure was closer to $90-million and the number rapidly approaching $100-million soon thereafter.

Almost every sport organization, by the very nature of the beast, is associated with some type of facilities. And, almost every sport manager, leader or supervisor is involved, in someway or another, with facilities and/or equipment within facilities. The status or state of facilities directly reflects upon the manager(s) in charge and will have a significant impact upon the success or failure of the sport organization, its programs and its activities.

MANAGEMENT AND MAINTENANCE OF FACILITIES

The management of facilities refers to the use, scheduling and operation of the buildings *and* the grounds (turf, fields, and acreage) owned or utilized by the sport organization. Maintenance deals with the upkeep, care and support of these same buildings and grounds. In this sense the grounds associated with the sport entities can be thought of as outdoor facilities while buildings are indoor facilities. Further, indoor facilities can be thought of as possessing both interior and exterior building systems.

Infante, Nick, Editor, *College Athletics Clips.com.* (2006). How can a program be a 'have-not' when its budget is $34 million?

Jensen, C.R. (1992). *Administrative management of physical education and athletic programs* (3rd ed.). Philadelphia: Lea & Febiger.

Jones, D. (1995, December 12). Open-book policy can motivate employees. *USA Today*, p. 1-B.

Lederman, D. (1993, July 21). Draft report by business officers' group says colleges must rein in sports budgets. *The Chronicle of Higher Education, XXXIV*(46), A-27, A-28.

Mason, J. G. and Paul, J. (1988). *Modern sports administration.* Prentice Hall, New Jersey: Englewood Cliffs.

Olson, J. R. (1986, April). Athletic budgeting without headaches. *Athletic Business, 19*(4). 94-96, 98.

Parkhouse, B.L. (Ed.). (1996). *The management of sport—Its foundation and application* (2nd ed.). St. Louis: Mosby.

Person to person. (2001, November). *Athletic Business, 25*(11), 12.

Players' Salary. http://www.usatoday.com/sports/football/nfl/2006-07-07-salary-report_x.htm Retrieved November 9, 2006.

Porentas, J. Ninety Million is not enough—Part one of a two-part series. http://www.the-ozone.net/misc/2006/06finances.htm retrieved July 10, 2006.

Railey, J.H. & Tschauner, P.R. (1993). *Managing physical education, fitness, and sports programs* (2nd ed.). Mountain View, California: Mayfield Publishing Company.

Revenues and Costs for D1-A Schools. College Athletic Clips. Retrieved 6/8/2006. http//www.collegeathleticsclips.com/s/375/index.aspx?sid=375&gid=1&pgid=15&cid=292

Salary escalation continues. (1993, December 27). *USA Today*, p. 2-C.

Sattler, T.P. & Mullens, J. E. (1993, February). How to budget simply, effectively. *Fitness Management, 9*(2), p. 25.

Sattler, T.P. & Doniek, C.A. (1996, April). Trim the extra fat from your facility. *Fitness Management, 12*(5), 38-40.

Sattler, T.P. & Mullins, J.E. (1993, April). How to limit the aggravation of audits. *Fitness Management, 9*(5), 12.

Spending That Would Make George Steinbrenner proud. College Athletic Clips. Retrieved 9/2/06. http://www.cfo.com/printable /article.cf,./7239613?=opotions

Stier, Jr., W.F. (1989, December 7). SUNY Brockport *Intercollegiate Athletic Budget Template.* Brockport, New York: State University of New York Press, pp. 33.

Stier, Jr., W.F. (1994a, April 14). *Fundraising for the 90s.* Presentation made at the national convention of the American Alliance for Health, Physical Education, Recreation and Dance (AAHPERD), Colorado, Denver.

Stier, Jr., W.F. (1994b). *Successful sport fund-raising.* Dubuque, Iowa: Wm. C. Brown & Benchmark.

The NFL's television contract history. (1994, January 3). *Sports Illustrated, 79*(26), 19.

University of Georgia Athletic Program #1 in Profitability. College Athletic Clips. Retrieved 4/27/2006. *College Athletic Clips.Com.*

U of L Budget Soars North of Forty Mill. College Athletic Clips. Retrieved August 22, 2006. *College Athletic Clips.Com.*

Wieberg, S. (1994, August 25). Sport feels effects of the financial crisis. *USA Today*, p. 9-C.

DISCUSSION TOPICS

1. Explain the importance of sound fiscal planning in the successful operation of a sport, recreation or fitness organization.

2. Describe the fundamental elements in the budgetary planning and preparation process.

3. What are the advantages and disadvantages of line item budgeting, incremental budgeting and Zero Base Budgeting for the sport organization?

4. Differentiate between requests for submission of bids and quotes and cite some precautions that sport managers should take to help insure that submissions of bids or quotes are appropriate and realistic in terms of the sport entity.

5. Select a hypothetical sport organization and indicate various categories of both income and expenditures that you feel would be appropriate for that entity.

6. Indicate specific ways (strategies and tactics) that a sport manager might attempt to implement in an effort to reduce costs and demonstrate fiscal responsibility within the hypothetical entity selected in question # 5 above.

7. Outline the advantages and disadvantages of using the so-called "wish list" in terms of fiscal (budgetary) planning for a sport organization.

8. Cite reasons why you as a sport manager might be willing to share budgetary knowledge with others, under what circumstances and conditions would you feel comfortable as a manager in disclosing fiscal information and data to others (specify the exact type of information and the people to whom you would share the data with).

9. Explain what is meant by forecasting revenues and expenses and how this is meaningful for the sport manager.

10. What are the advantages of so-called Open Book Management?

Chapter

8 Indoor and Outdoor Facility Management—Operational Aspects

Adequate Physical Conditioning is the Foundation of Competitive Sport.
[courtesy of Clemson University Sports Information.
Photo of Jervey Center Weight Room by Bob Waldrop]

CHAPTER HIGHLIGHTS

This chapter will help the reader to:

• Cite the advantages of dealing promptly with graffitis;
• Appreciate the importance of proper management and maintenance of both indoor and outdoor sport, recreation and fitness facilities;
• Locate and research professional literature pertaining to management and maintenance of facilities;
• Understand the essence and reason for periodic audits of facilities;
• Cite the essentials of good facilities for sport, recreation and fitness programs;

Infante, Nick, Editor, *College Athletics Clips.com.* (2006). How can a program be a 'have-not' when its budget is $34 million?

Jensen, C.R. (1992). *Administrative management of physical education and athletic programs* (3rd ed.). Philadelphia: Lea & Febiger.

Jones, D. (1995, December 12). Open-book policy can motivate employees. *USA Today*, p. 1-B.

Lederman, D. (1993, July 21). Draft report by business officers' group says colleges must rein in sports budgets. *The Chronicle of Higher Education, XXXIV*(46), A-27, A-28.

Mason, J. G. and Paul, J. (1988). *Modern sports administration.* Prentice Hall, New Jersey: Englewood Cliffs.

Olson, J. R. (1986, April). Athletic budgeting without headaches. *Athletic Business, 19*(4). 94-96, 98.

Parkhouse, B.L. (Ed.). (1996). *The management of sport—Its foundation and application* (2nd ed.). St. Louis: Mosby.

Person to person. (2001, November). *Athletic Business, 25*(11), 12.

Players' Salary. http://www.usatoday.com/sports/football/nfl/2006-07-07-salary-report_x.htm Retrieved November 9, 2006.

Porentas, J. Ninety Million is not enough—Part one of a two-part series. http://www.the-ozone.net/misc/2006/06finances.htm retrieved July 10, 2006.

Railey, J.H. & Tschauner, P.R. (1993). *Managing physical education, fitness, and sports programs* (2nd ed.). Mountain View, California: Mayfield Publishing Company.

Revenues and Costs for D1-A Schools. College Athletic Clips. Retrieved 6/8/2006. http//www.collegeathleticsclips.com/s/375/index.aspx?sid=375&gid=1&pgid=15&cid=292

Salary escalation continues. (1993, December 27). *USA Today*, p. 2-C.

Sattler, T.P. & Mullens, J. E. (1993, February). How to budget simply, effectively. *Fitness Management, 9*(2), p. 25.

Sattler, T.P. & Doniek, C.A. (1996, April). Trim the extra fat from your facility. *Fitness Management, 12*(5), 38-40.

Sattler, T.P. & Mullins, J.E. (1993, April). How to limit the aggravation of audits. *Fitness Management, 9*(5), 12.

Spending That Would Make George Steinbrenner proud. College Athletic Clips. Retrieved 9/2/06. http://www.cfo.com/printable /article.cf,./7239613?=opotions

Stier, Jr., W.F. (1989, December 7). SUNY Brockport *Intercollegiate Athletic Budget Template.* Brockport, New York: State University of New York Press, pp. 33.

Stier, Jr., W.F. (1994a, April 14). *Fundraising for the 90s.* Presentation made at the national convention of the American Alliance for Health, Physical Education, Recreation and Dance (AAHPERD), Colorado, Denver.

Stier, Jr., W.F. (1994b). *Successful sport fund-raising.* Dubuque, Iowa: Wm. C. Brown & Benchmark.

The NFL's television contract history. (1994, January 3). *Sports Illustrated, 79*(26), 19.

University of Georgia Athletic Program #1 in Profitability. College Athletic Clips. Retrieved 4/27/2006. *College Athletic Clips.Com.*

U of L Budget Soars North of Forty Mill. College Athletic Clips. Retrieved August 22, 2006. *College Athletic Clips.Com.*

Wieberg, S. (1994, August 25). Sport feels effects of the financial crisis. *USA Today,* p. 9-C.

DISCUSSION TOPICS

1. Explain the importance of sound fiscal planning in the successful operation of a sport, recreation or fitness organization.

2. Describe the fundamental elements in the budgetary planning and preparation process.

3. What are the advantages and disadvantages of line item budgeting, incremental budgeting and Zero Base Budgeting for the sport organization?

4. Differentiate between requests for submission of bids and quotes and cite some precautions that sport managers should take to help insure that submissions of bids or quotes are appropriate and realistic in terms of the sport entity.

5. Select a hypothetical sport organization and indicate various categories of both income and expenditures that you feel would be appropriate for that entity.

6. Indicate specific ways (strategies and tactics) that a sport manager might attempt to implement in an effort to reduce costs and demonstrate fiscal responsibility within the hypothetical entity selected in question # 5 above.

7. Outline the advantages and disadvantages of using the so-called "wish list" in terms of fiscal (budgetary) planning for a sport organization.

8. Cite reasons why you as a sport manager might be willing to share budgetary knowledge with others, under what circumstances and conditions would you feel comfortable as a manager in disclosing fiscal information and data to others (specify the exact type of information and the people to whom you would share the data with).

9. Explain what is meant by forecasting revenues and expenses and how this is meaningful for the sport manager.

10. What are the advantages of so-called Open Book Management?

Chapter

8 Indoor and Outdoor Facility Management—Operational Aspects

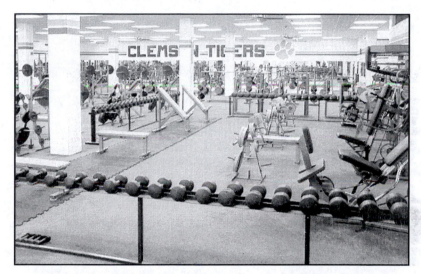

Adequate Physical Conditioning is the Foundation of Competitive Sport.
[courtesy of Clemson University Sports Information.
Photo of Jervey Center Weight Room by Bob Waldrop]

CHAPTER HIGHLIGHTS

This chapter will help the reader to:

- Cite the advantages of dealing promptly with graffitis;
- Appreciate the importance of proper management and maintenance of both indoor and outdoor sport, recreation and fitness facilities;
- Locate and research professional literature pertaining to management and maintenance of facilities;
- Understand the essence and reason for periodic audits of facilities;
- Cite the essentials of good facilities for sport, recreation and fitness programs;

- Ask appropriate questions in terms of planning for and evaluating a potential facility for use by sport, recreation or fitness organizations;
- Appreciate the importance of data in facility management;
- Enunciate the potential sources of problems commonly faced by facility planners and sport managers in designing indoor and/or outdoor facilities;
- Be aware of the many problems associated with the management of various types of facilities;
- Acknowledge the importance of Standard Operating Procedures (SOPs) in managing and maintaining facilities;
- Be familiar with costs associated with replacement and annual maintenance of buildings and structures;
- Understand the advantages and disadvantages of utilizing consultants when planning facilities and when maintaining facilities;
- Be able to utilize the formula for determining/calculating maintenance and operating costs.

One of the major challenges that face sport managers deal with the care and managing of indoor and/or outdoor facilities, as well as the myriad of equipment and supplies associated with the various types of facilities (Wallace and Kline, 2005). It was conservatively estimated that $75-million per year was being spent to build and renovate sport facilities in this country in the early 1990s (Pate, Moffitt & Fugett, 1993). By the turn of the century, some experts estimated that the figure was closer to $90-million and the number rapidly approaching $100-million soon thereafter.

Almost every sport organization, by the very nature of the beast, is associated with some type of facilities. And, almost every sport manager, leader or supervisor is involved, in someway or another, with facilities and/or equipment within facilities. The status or state of facilities directly reflects upon the manager(s) in charge and will have a significant impact upon the success or failure of the sport organization, its programs and its activities.

MANAGEMENT AND MAINTENANCE OF FACILITIES

The management of facilities refers to the use, scheduling and operation of the buildings *and* the grounds (turf, fields, and acreage) owned or utilized by the sport organization. Maintenance deals with the upkeep, care and support of these same buildings and grounds. In this sense the grounds associated with the sport entities can be thought of as outdoor facilities while buildings are indoor facilities. Further, indoor facilities can be thought of as possessing both interior and exterior building systems.

> **CONCEPT 243:** *Sport managers need to hire knowledgeable, skilled and experienced professionals to plan, construct, manage and maintain indoor and outdoor facilities.*

In today's sophisticated world of sports it is highly advisable, at almost every level, for management to secure the services of knowledgeable, skilled and experienced professionals to help plan, design, construct, manage and maintain indoor and outdoor facilities. Things have gotten too complicated for so-called amateurs to be entrusted with the responsibility for these tasks. Even the everyday tasks of managing and/or caring (housekeeping and maintenance) for facilities have gotten so sophisticated that more and more sport organizations are assigning personnel dedicated to these specific tasks.

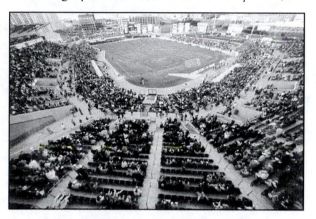

Attractive Facilities Attract Large Crowds
[courtesy of Rochester Raging Rhinos, New York, James D. Lathrop, photographer]

The Importance of Proper Management and Maintenance of Facilities

To put it simply, there is often too much at stake—for the sport organization, for the sport program, for those involved with the organization, including the sport administrators themselves—for anyone other than knowledgeable people to have responsibility for the facilities used by the sport organization. As a consequence, sport employees within the managerial and administrative ranks have a responsibility to develop and maintain a minimum level of knowledge and competency in these areas.

> **CONCEPT #244:** *There is too much at state to assign to rank amateurs the responsibility for the management and maintenance of sport facilities.*

A Variety of Sport Facilities (and Accompanying Equipment and Supplies)

Depending upon the type of sport organization in which the manager or supervisor is working there are a variety of different types of facilities, both indoor and outdoor, to become familiar with, if one is to be successful in the day–to–day operation of the business. Table 8.1 provides a partial list of indoor and outdoor sport facilities that the supervisor or administrator might have overall responsibility for within a sport organization. Some of these facilities might comprise only a single room (a wrestling room, for example) while others might involve a much larger space, one which contains a great deal of internal components or elements that must also be carefully monitored and manipulated (for example, an ice hockey arena).

The sport manager might be required to be somewhat knowledgeable (or become knowledgeable) in terms of any one or more of these facilities. This chapter will provide an introductory glimpse into these facilities. It is the responsibility of the readers to expand upon the foundational information and knowledge presented herein in light of the employment situation which one finds oneself following one's preservice formal education.

TABLE 8.1: *Partial List of Indoor and Outdoor Facilities*

Indoor Facilities	Outdoor Facilities
Badminton Courts	Baseball Fields
Basketball Courts	Field Hockey
Combative Rooms (Wrestling, Judo, etc)	Football Fields
Equipment Rooms	Golf Courses
Fencing Rooms	Lacrosse Fields
Gymnastics Rooms	Rugby Fields
Hockey (Ice and Floor)	Soccer Fields
Hot Tubs	Softball Fields
Locker Rooms	Storage Buildings
Racquetball and Handball Courts	Swimming Pools and Diving Wells
Saunas	Team Handball Fields
Squash Courts	Tennis Courts
Swimming Pools and Diving Wells	Track and Field Sites
Tennis Courts	
Track and Field	
Volleyball Courts	
Weight Rooms	

Being an Expert Versus Being Knowledgeable in Facility Management and Maintenance.

Generally speaking, sport managers need not be experts in each and every type of indoor and outdoor facility that is used by the organization or program. That is why experts are secured in the areas of facility planning, facility maintenance and facility construction. Nevertheless, it is necessary for the typical sport manager or supervisor to be generally knowledgeable in the areas of facility management, maintenance and construction *in order to be able to intelligently converse with such experts in these fields and make appropriate and timely decisions.*

When considering whether to take advantage of outside (facility) consultants it is wise to consider the following factors and weigh the plusses and minuses (White and Karabestos, 1999).

1. Educational background of the potential consultant(s)
2. Similar and demonstrated work experience
3. Appropriate planning experience
4. The consultant's proximity to the projected project(s)
5. Reputation of potential consultant(s)
6. Ability of the potential consultant(s) to work with the project planning committees, architects, engineers, and contractors
7. Ability of the consultant(s) to clearly understand and read blueprints and specification documents
8. Ability to understand the organization's or group's programs and any future needs of such programs

---

CONCEPT #245: *Sport administrators need to be knowledgeable enough and to have sufficient experience in terms of facilities to be able to intelligently work and consult with experts in the area.*

Such knowledge and information will put these administrators in good stead because they will be operating and making decisions from a position of strength, from a position of knowledge. "You can teach the concepts of athletic purchasing, but if you don't understand what you're purchasing, you're just dealing with budgets" (Equipment for success, 1993, p. 30). And competent managers need to know the "why" of things. They need to know why certain things have to be done, why they have to be done at a specific time, why items have to be purchased, why decisions have to be made, and why certain decisions are the most appropriate in light of existing circumstances.

There are numerous opportunities for sport managers and supervisors to make decisions affecting or relating to facilities and such decisions require some degree of knowledge in order to be effective and efficient. For example, the athletic director or an assistant director of a large NCAA division I university doesn't have to be "the expert" in the care of turf grasses. The "director of grounds" is undoubtedly the expert in this area. Nevertheless, the AD or the assistant AD does need to be somewhat knowledgeable in this area so as to be able to successfully interact with the "expert(s)" and to be able to arrive at an appropriate, timely and effective decision based upon facts.

AVAILABILITY OF DATA PERTAINING TO FACILITY CONSTRUCTION, REHABILITATION, MAINTENANCE AND MANAGEMENT

There is a wealth of written materials available to the sport employee in the area of construction, rehabilitation, maintenance and management. It is important for the professional sport administrator to know where to go to secure up–to–date information and data when it comes to these areas of responsibility. For example, there are numerous books and journal articles that address these areas within the world of sport. The following is a sample list of periodicals that cover indoor and/or outdoor facilities and are recommended reading by the potential as well as current sport manager or supervisor.

1. *Buildings*—P.O. Box 1888, Cedar Rapids, IA 52406-1888. (319) 364-6167.

2. *Athletic Business*—1846 Hoffman St., Madison, WI. 53704 (800) 722-8764 or (608) 249-0186

3. *Building Operating Management*—2100 West Florist Ave, Milwaukee, Wis. 53209-3799. 414-228-7701.

4. *Club Industry*—Sportscape, Inc., Framingham Corporate Center, 492 Old Connecticut Path, 3rd Floor, Framingham, MA 0170. (508) 872-2021 [IRSA members receive this publication].

5. *Club Business International*—253 Summer St., Boston 02222 (617) 951-0055

6. *Building Operating Management*—P.O. Box 694, Milwaukee, WI 53201-0694.

7. *National Fitness Trade Journal*—P.O. Box 2378, Corona, CA 92718-2378 (714-371-0606) or 12596 West Bayaud Avenue, 1st Floor, Denver, CO. (303) 753-6422 or (716) 467-4653 [the official publication of the National Health Club Association].

8. *Turf* (Magazine)—P.O. Box 391, 50 Bay Street. St. Johnsbury, Vermont, 05819. (802) 748-8908.

9. *School Planning & Management*—P.O. Box 49699, Dayton, Ohio 45449-0699. (937) 847-5910.

10. *Facilities Manager*—1643 Prince Street, Alexandria, VA 22314-2818. (703) 684-1446 [A publication of the Association of Higher Education Facilities Officers].

CONCEPT #246:   *One doesn't have to have all the answers at one's finger tips— but one does have to know where to get the answers (information, data, and facts).*

Part of being able to get such information has to do with having the ability to keep up in the area of professional reading, attending professional meetings and conferences, and being able to conduct meaningful, productive and fruitful research of the current literature in the area(s) in question. It also involves tapping individuals (experts), organizations and associations in an effort to secure such information, knowledge and advice. It is difficult, if not impossible, even for managers within the sport industry, to remain at the cutting edge in everything within their respective fields or areas of responsibility.

Thus, sport managers must rely upon a variety of sources to retrieve specific data, information and knowledge. A partial listing of professional organizations and publications that are particularly important in terms of being sources of information about facility design and/or specifications of various sport facilities or structures and their components is included in appendix A.

CONCEPT #247:   *Sport administrators need not be embarrassed to admit that they don't now all the answers as long as they are successful in securing the necessary information in a timely fashion.*

Thus, the modern sport administrator should be familiar with general standards as they apply to indoor and outdoor facilities as well as familiar with specification (and maintenance) guides for sporting facilities published by the various sport governing bodies. Additional information relating to the construction, rehabilitation and maintenance of specific sport facilities are written by various experts in the field as well as published by different organizations, associations, governing bodies as well as various manufacturers of products and materials.

It is not the purview of this publication to go into specific detail in terms of facility construction or rehabilitation. Rather, this chapter will delve into the general area of *management and operational aspects of sport facilities*, indoor and outdoor, as well as providing general concepts or principles relative to the planning, designing and constructing of suitable sport facilities. For more detailed reading and investigation into the areas of planning, construction, and rehabilitation of facilities the reader is directed to the "Further Readings" section at the end of this chapter.

PERIODIC AUDIT OF FACILITIES—
AN ESSENTIAL PART OF THE PLANNING PROCESS

It is a wise practice to periodically conduct an audit or a needs assessment of one's facilities both in terms of construction, maintenance and managerial efforts (West, 1998; Hypes, 2006). This systematic examination of the facilities themselves (as well as the pos-

**Athletic Clubs and Fitness Centers
Are Major Players in the Fitness Industry.**
*[courtesy of Midwest Athletic Club, Read Photography,
Cedar Rapids, Iowa]*

sible need for new construction) and the managerial policies, practices and procedures affecting the facilities will provide a baseline of data for wise decision making on behalf of management (Hunsaker, 1992). Without current information, without accurate data, without something to base one's decisions on (other than mere antidotal opinions) management is effectively "flying blind" and resulting decisions will usually be wanting, if not actual impediments to progress.

CONCEPT #248: *Facility audits should be conducted periodically to assess the effectiveness and efficiency of the sport organization.*

Facility audits—called reality checks by some and needs assessments by others—can serve many purposes and may take several different forms. First, some facility audits are conducted to determine whether special maintenance (other than routine repair and upkeep) is necessary. Second, audits are initiated in order to determine whether the organization or business is in compliance with specific regulations, rules or codes (ADA provisions [see chapter 12], zoning, etc.). Third, audits are instituted to see if the facilities themselves and/or use of same conform with federal, state or local laws (Title IX, health and safety factors, etc.) (Steinbach 2000). Fourth, facility audits are established to determine whether the facilities themselves as well as the policies and policies relating to the facilities are safe from a legal liability (risk management) standpoint [see chapter 14]. And, finally, some facility audits are set up to determine if new or refurbished facilities might be warranted.

CONCEPT #249: *Facilities should be periodically evaluated (audited) in terms of safety prior to use.*

Management must be constantly vigilant in terms of the safety factors associated with facilities as well as equipment and supplies. The periodic risk management audit is essential in terms of determining the state of the facility (and contents) as well as policies and procedures of the sport organization as they affect the health and welfare of individuals using the facilities (and equipment and supplies). "Facility operators have a duty to keep playing surfaces reasonably maintained" (Condron and Wong, 2000, p. 24). This "reasonable maintenance" includes safety factors and necessitates that the sport manager pay particular attention to the prevention of accidents and injuries to patrons, employees and others.

Sawyer (2005) indicated that the needs assessment effort typically results in the creation of a comprehensive report, containing statistics, figures, photos, graphs, charts, etc., to upper management and/or the board of directors. Busser (1999) cited five essential elements that make up a comprehensive and easily understood report.

1. Title page
2. Executive summary (really a quick, easily read and understood synopsis)
3. Introduction to the needs assessment study and its purpose(s)
4. Overview of methods and procedures used in the needs assessment effort
5. Results, conclusions and recommendations

CONCEPT #250: *Preventative maintenance is the mark of an effective and efficient manager.*

The cliché "an ounce of prevention is worth a pound of cure" is certainly most appropriate in the world of sport facilities. Preventative maintenance of facilities is an absolute must. Don't be "penny-wise and pound-foolish" when it comes to care and upkeep of sport facilities or equipment/supplies. This is why the periodic audit is so critical in the management of facilities—buildings and grounds. Prudent and timely decisions relative to maintenance will save time, effort and, most importantly, money in the long run. And the opposite is also true; failure to spend money in the upkeep of facilities will cost a sport entity dearly in the long run.

Generally speaking, a building is supposed to be built to last 50 some years. This is only possible if great care is taken to inspect the facility to insure that it is maintained in proper shape—and that any defects or deterioration that takes place is aggressively corrected. One of the greatest dangers to any building is water. Water can come from outside as well as from inside in the form of humidity and condensation, often the result of improper or inadequate insulation, vapor barriers and ventilation. This is especially true where there is a swimming pool within the structure (Keys, 1999).

Graffiti—A Vulgar Expression or an Art Form?

Another example of the need to be proactive with facility management is in the area of graffiti. Seemingly a never-ending problem with both indoor and outdoor facilities, graffiti "grows onto itself." Once vandalism (and that is what graffiti really is) occurs through the medium of graffiti, it is imperative that quick and decisive action be taken by the appropriate authorities. "Vandalism occurs on a scale from minor damage caused by kids or overly enthusiastic fans not in touch with the effect of their actions, all the way to extensive damage perpetrated by persons with criminal intent" (Cohen, 2005, p. 61).

CONCEPT #251:   *To combat graffiti it is important to attack the problem immediately lest it becomes worse.*

First of all, it is necessary that the graffiti be immediately removed. Left unattended, graffiti seemingly replicates itself. Left unattended, graffiti can quickly expand to fill the space that is available. Second, close scrutiny and observation of the offending (or attractive) site is often necessary if repeated instances are to be prevented. This is especially important if the graffiti is especially offensive or vulgar. Third, education can also play a part in the prevention (or reduction) of graffiti attacks.

Demolition of the 66-year old Silver Stadium,
Rochester, New York
[courtesy of Rochester Red Wings]

THE ESSENTIAL OF GOOD FACILITIES

Quality facilities are those that meet the present and changing needs of the organization and patrons. Quality facilities include those that are cost effective to run. And, finally, quality facilities are those that have relatively low maintenance while maintaining their structural integrity for years to come. Form meets functionality in the world or architecture. Thus, the purpose of the indoor or outdoor facil-

New Frontier Field,
Home of AAA Rochester Red Wings Rochester, New York
[courtesy of Rochester Red Wings]

ity dictates what form, shape, arrangement or configuration the structure will take. In short, the ideal facility is one that is patron or fan friendly. It is one that is viewed as being adequate, accessible, clean, safe, convenient, comfortable, visually pleasing and enjoyable by those who are patrons, fans, spectators and sports persons.

Facility Planning and Design

When considering the design of a future facility such as a building there are numerous options and variations possible depending upon the available budget, it's intended use and the creativity of the design team (Shalley & Barzdukas, 1997). And the design team should consist of experts who are experienced in the area of sport architecture, members of the management team of the sport entity,and representatives of the various constituencies for which the structure is being built (Krenson, 1997).

Guidelines of National Organizations

There are guidelines established by what is now known as the Council on Physical Activity and Recreation Venue Design and Management (PARVDM) that will significantly assist the sport manager in planning for a new facility. These guidelines include the following (Hypes, 2006, p. 19):

1. Comply with the Americans with Disabilities Act (ADA)
2. Use a master plan (a comprehensive plan)
3. Use a participatory planning approach
4. Research your funding options
5. Organize a project planning committee
6. Understand when to renovate, retrofit and replace
7. Develop a program statement for the architect
8. Use planning professionals

Another national organization, the United States Consumer Product Safety Commission (CPSC) has issued specific guidelines in 2001 for bleacher safety. Called the *Guidelines for Retrofitting Bleachers* (effective 1/1/2001), these guidelines have become in effect the *standard of care* to be used when attempting to determine liability or negligence in bleacher accidents. With some 20,000 bleacher related injuries annually that require emergency care, it is obvious that this is one area that managers need to pay particular attention to. Typically, 58% of injuries (in 1998) involved falls, 23% involved a fall from the bleachers while 35% were a result of fall onto or on the bleachers (LaRue, 2002).

A list of 12 major areas that managers should examine relative to the safety factors of outdoor playground and recreation facilities. These areas include (Conklin, 1999, p. 65):

1. Improper protective surfacing
2. Inadequate fall zones
3. Protrusion and entanglement hazards
4. Entrapment in openings
5. Insufficient equipment spacing
6. Trip hazards
7. Lack of supervision
8. Age-inappropriate activities
9. Lack of maintenance
10. Pinch, crush, shearing and sharp edge hazards
11. Platforms with no guardrails
12. Equipment not recommended for playgrounds

Advantages of Multi-Purpose Facilities

One of the changes in modern times when it comes to planning and designing sport facilities has been to design multipurpose facilities. An integral part of a multipurpose facility is incorporating a plan in which one space opens to another rather than having compartmentalized areas set aside for individual and formal group physical. The important concept for the future is *flexibility* in planning a building or facility that is expected to last 40, 50 or more years. The ability to design "a major capital project like a field house is better justified when the design includes plans for adapting to future changes" (Krenson, 1997, p. 76). Again, flexibility within the facility is a key concept for the present as well as the future.

Important Considerations in the Planning and Designing Phase of a Building

In the design and planning stage of any building there is always a constant juggling act between available money, space needs and design considerations. Consequently, many planners and architects look to combine those sports and/or activities that have common functional and operational needs in a common space (Johnson, 1991, p. 33).

Venue Management and Security in the post 9/11 World that We Live In

And, in this world today with the threat of terrorists and bomb threats, sport managers must remain cognizant of the need to develop appropriate safety protocols, security measures and training programs in the event of a potential bomb threat and other potential disasters. These include detection methods, evacuation plans for indoor and outdoor facilities as well as shelter management (post Hurricane Katrina).

CONCEPT #252:   *Post 9/11 sport managers must remain vigilant of the potential for man-made and natural disasters affecting facilities*

Such efforts can involve, among others, such tactics as surveillance cameras, additional security personnel, changing of locks for day of game activities, better communications equipment, pat-down searches, real-time day-game audits, photo identification, baggage checkpoints at stadium gates and other strategic locations, on-site bomb detection equipment and dogs, and concrete planters and other devices that can be used to protect and separate the stadium perimeter from access by vehicles. Today, the competent sport manager is insightful in terms of potential problems and challenges that might result from such catastrophes as bomb threats, fan violence, and natural disasters.

Steinbach (2006) revealed that in August of 2004 International Association of Assembly Managers held the inaugural Academy for Venue Safety & Security, in Dallas, Texas. At this conference some 85 managers were trained in the use of a risk-management software program and were introduced to various scenarios as to what to do in term of preventing and reacting to real and potential disasters. The United States Department of Homeland Security, in 2005, developed its own online self-assessment tool for large (seating more than 30,000 [more than 400 exist in this country]) stadiums. Later, a similar version was made available for arenas. In this post 9/11 mentality that pervades out society, managers must be alert to dealing with the unexpected threat to their facilities and to their patrons, fans, boosters and employees.

CONCEPT #253:   *The use and purpose of facilities will depend upon the mission(s) of the sport organization.*

Regardless of the type of facility planned, there are numerous questions that should be asked or areas that should be closely examined by members of the design team. These include:

1. Where should the building be erected, that is, where is the site of the proposed structure?
2. When does the facility have to be in place?
3. What about access to and from the structure?

4. What type of parking is required for this building?

5. What should be the layout and actual design of the structure?

6. Should the facility be multi-purpose in nature or a single purpose building?

7. Who will be using the facility? Will there be outside groups using the site?

8. What type of utilities will be involved? Any special needs in this regard?

9. What are the electrical and mechanical requirements?

10. What role does the weather play in the construction and use of the facility?

11. What type of landscaping should be incorporated?

12. What type of maintenance will be required for the structure itself as well as the components of the building, including the mechanicals?

Aiming for the Well-Deserved Goal.
[courtesy of Rochester Raging Rhinos, NY.
James D. Lathrop, photographer]

There are several steps to be taken during the initial discussion and planning process for any facility (Maegher, 1990; Fawcett, 1997). These include: (1) identification of the real needs of the organization, (2) determination of how much money might be available to spend for the facility, (3) solicitation of input and suggestions from potential user groups, various constituencies and staff, (4) consultation with appropriate governmental and regulatory agencies (fire marshal, building inspectors, etc.) to secure information relative to requirements, stipulations or limitations affecting the proposed facility, (5), anticipation of how various parts of the facility might interact or interfere with one another, and, (6) search for a suitable architect.

PROBLEMS ASSOCIATED WITH FACILITIES

There can be a multitude of problems and challenges facing sport managers relating to indoor and/or outdoor facilities. The causes of these difficulties can be many and varied. Looking at some of the more common sources of problems associated with sport facilities one is able to conclude: (Gimple, 1992; Stier, 1993; Cohen, 1995).

1. There was poor up-front planning for the facility in the first place (a lack of anticipation of the future, of future needs)

2. There was a lack of oversight on someone's part during the planning or construction phase (someone failed to double check to insure that some things actually got done)

3. There was an attempt to cut corners, to cut costs (the resulting compromise failed to meet the need)

4. The planners lacked experience in designing a sport facility (the architect(s) and/or consultant(s) failed to have a broad or extensive knowledge of sport architecture or needs of sport programs)

5. There was failure to recognize the importance of storage space for the facility

6. The planning and building schedule was unduly accelerated (frequently, in the world of professional sports the time between the awarding of a contract and the time when the facility is needed is short , too short, with the result being a "rush job"

7. The building has a new client with different needs (the building was planned, designed and constructed in such a way that does not lend itself to easy modification or adaptation for new or different needs)

8. Legal or code mandated modifications that are not reasonable in light of the purpose of the building or room(s) (the state of Louisiana required sprinkler heads (fire code) to be installed in the ceilings of a club's racquetball courts—1500 gallons of water spilled onto the wooden floor when a racquetball struck and broke a sprinkler head)

9. Too much compromising during the planning phase (different and often conflicting needs of various groups necessitate granting concessions with the result that important elements of the building might be altered or left out with negative consequences)

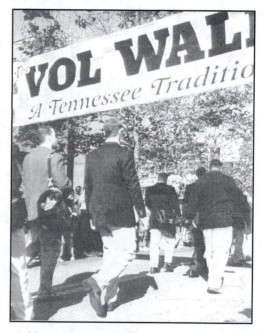

Athletes Participating in Community Service Projects Brings Publicity and Respect to the School and Athletic Program
[courtesy of University of Tennessee, Sports Information Office]

Refurbishing or Replacing a Facility

Management is constantly faced with the question of whether it is more prudent to repair (rehab, retool or refit) a facility or to actually replace it. Of course the answer to this all-important question depends upon a whole host of variables. Consequently, there can be no simple answer to this very important question. Nevertheless, this question is one that will be facing more and more members of management as the sport facilities built 20, 30, 40 and more years ago continue to age and pose ever greater challenges to those sport organizations that continue to use them. In fact, in professional baseball, around 60 new baseball parks have opened up in professional baseball since 1985 (Cohen, 1995, p. 35).

In some cases the answer to this perplexing question is made for the sport enterprise. For example, in professional baseball there is *Rule 40, Facility Standards and Compliance Inspection Procedures*. This rule was included within the 1990 Professional Baseball Agreement, the seven-year working contract that was adopted by the major and minor leagues. The rule's 13 sections cover (as recommendations or minimum requirements) almost everything relating to baseball facilities. For example, the rule affects such things as recommended seating grades, distribution and spacing of seating, minimum seating capacity of parks, size of parking lots, as well as specifications for rest rooms, concession areas, beer gardens, ticket windows, first-aid stations, sound systems, scoreboards, press facilities, and administrative areas, etc. (Cohen, 1994).

CONCEPT #254:   To repair or to replace—that is the $64,000 question.

Ice Hockey is Enjoyed Throughout the Country.
[courtesy of Bemidji State University (BSU) Photography Services]

As a result of this rule, plus the acknowledgement by leaders in the sport, there have been a significant number of upgraded facilities and not a few totally new ballparks among minor league baseball franchises. For example, until recently, the oldest minor league park within triple AAA was the 66 year-old *Silver Stadium* (built in 1928) which was located in Rochester, New York. Home of the International League's Rochester's Red Wings, then an affiliate of the Baltimore Oriole organization, the aging facility did not meet the new standards stipulated by *Rule 40* and was replaced by a brand new ballpark, *Frontier Field*, located in downtown Rochester. On opening day, April 11, 1996, the hometown fans were treated to a truly beautiful facility, one that included picnic areas, volleyball courts as well as extensive grassy areas, see page 299.

IMPORTANCE OF APPROPRIATE FACILITIES

In today's marketplace modern sport facilities play a major role in enabling management to provide the amenities expected by the public. Such amenities can serve to entertain the patrons and fans as well as facilitate the marketing of the sport entity itself among the public and various constituencies. One should not overlook the importance and impact of an appropriately well-kept and properly maintained facility in terms of the overall public relations and publicity surrounding the sport organization and its personnel (see chapter ten).

During the late 1990s and early 2000s there has been, and continues to be, a literal explosion in the construction of sport facilities within the United States. Witness the full blown construction efforts among Big 12 Conference schools where the University of Texas expanded its Darrell K. Royal-Texas Memorial Stadium to seat 90,000. This followed an earlier renovation of sport facilities which was part of a $90 million facility upgrade. In addition, Oklahoma State received a $165 million gift from athletic supporter T. Boone Pickens to build and upgrade the university's athletic facilities.

Not to be outdone, Texas A&M now boasts one of the very best facilities in the conference with the luxurious Bright Football Complex which contains a 15,000-square foot athletic training room, 28 digital coaching booths for film work, meeting rooms with super large (60 inch) plasma screens to view game films, a 6500 foot locker room as well as a very large auditorium for athletic team meetings. Not to be outdone, the University of Nebraska started a $50 million Osborne Athletic Complex as well as a 80,000 square foot indoor facility that also includes a full-length indoor football field. And, the University of Kansas had its $31 million sports complex completed in 2008 which involved offices, meeting rooms, weight room and other sport and coaching related components. Other conferences and schools have joined the so-called arms race for facilities. Witness the University of Michigan which is spending a $226 million renovation to its football facility that will provide for an additional 83 suites and a whopping 3200 club seats (Spending, 2006).

Reacting to accusations that colleges and universities are involved in excessive and even wasteful spending, sports administrators and athletic directors claim that their schools and athletic programs are merely staying competitive (keeping up with the Jones syndrome). To quote Ed Goble, the Texas Associate AD for business: "You got to have great facilities if you are going to remain competitive. If we can pay for it, we'll do it" (Spending that would, 2006). The so-called arms race in terms of athletic facilities is off and running among NCAA Division I schools.

The Importance of Image and Professionalism

Frequently, it is the little things that count for so much, especially in terms of image and perceptions. Appearances are very, very important. Perceptions count for a great deal, both with the public and with members within one's own organization. It is amazing what a fresh coat of paint, clean bleachers, seat padding, colorful banners, an improved sound systems and acoustical panels, as well as dressed up scorer's tables can do for a facility (Cohen, 1995). Proper appearances can help motivate people and facilitate the development of pride and self-esteem, a not insignificant consequence (Garner, 1997).

MAKING EFFECTIVE (BEST) USE OF A FACILITY

As stated above the facility must meet the needs of the various constituencies, groups and individuals who might possibly utilize the building or outside site. One way to see if a facility actually is meeting their needs of the constituencies, as well also the general public, is to examine its usage rate. Is the building being used on a consistent basis? Is the facility occupied a high percentage of time? And, in some instances, are there significant monies being generated from the usage of the facility or site? Many organizations today are looking towards multi-purpose sport facility so as to help insure that the site will be utilized to its maximum (Johnston, 1991).

Use of the Mezzanine Concept in Facility Conversions

More and more sport organizations, especially fitness clubs and recreation type entities, are attempting to make better use of every square foot of their facilities. Towards this end a unique tactic has emerged in respect to getting more out of one's facility, namely, converting an existing structure by constructing a mezzanine level above the existing floor space. The potential for such a move is to almost double the organization's existing usable space. The advantage is obvious, being able to double the working square footage without expanding the structure's "footprint" is very cost effective. This strategy is referred to as "creating more space by looking up" (Jastrow, 1997).

CONCEPT #255: *Scheduling facility usage is a major challenge—*
it is difficult to please everyone all the time

The impact of computers and computer technology (software and hardware) in our society is evident everywhere and anywhere. And the area of sport is no exception. Perhaps nothing has aided the facility manager more in the day-to-day aspects of the job than the advent of the computer and applicable software packages that facilitate the booking and scheduling of facilities. Indeed, the task of facility scheduling and keeping track of scheduled books can be daunting to say the least. If the booking and scheduling system is not computerized then the manager is left to the old fashion method of pen or pencil and the trusty calendar. Needless to say, the manual method of keeping track of a multipurpose facility is neither time efficient nor is it effective (Ross & Wolter, 1997).

The question is not so much whether to utilize the computer and a software package but which software application to choose from. Management would do well to consider the following factors before rushing out to purchase one of the many software applications that might be suitable in booking facilities as well as scheduling overall maintenance of the buildings and grounds: (Ross & Wolter, 1997; Stier, 1997).

1. Knowledge of the *policies* and *priorities* governing facility usage
2. Knowledge of *processes* used in scheduling use of facility
3. *Cost-effectiveness* of both hardware and software
4. Knowledge of specific *hardware requirements* for commercially prepared software programs
5. *Technical difficulty* in terms of mastery of the software package
6. *Capability, willingness and eagerness* of the staff to use computer assisted technology
7. Available *technical support and documentation* (in house or second party)
8. *Cost* of technical support, documentation and maintenance

Ross & Wolter (1997) lists seven software companies that produce software that might be suitable for some sport organizations in terms of facility management and scheduling. These companies, along with their phone numbers, are:

1. A. E. Klawitter & Associates (847) 392-6880
2. CEO Software Inc. (800) 441-2581
3. Escom Software Services (800) 661-1196
4. THE-Programmed For Success (800) 488-PFSI
5. Overtime Software (800) 467-0493
6. R.I.C. Corporation (219) 432-0799
7. Vermont Systems, Inc. (802) 879-6993

Managing the Site for Maximum Potential Net Income

One of the major shifts in the design of new stadiums and arena in the country has to do with the addition of revenue enhancement components or elements (built into the structures themselves). One example is the ever increasing presence of luxury boxes, special VIP seating, VIP lounges, special restaurants for the general public and for VIPs, and even parking condos. These so-called creature comforts and attractions are quickly becoming the norm as more modern facilities are leaping off the drawing boards to become brick and motor (Orlowski, 2000).

CONCEPT #256:   *In many sport organizations the more usage a facility receives the better.*

If the facility is to be used by outside groups the first question that comes to mind is whether or not such groups will be charged for their usage. If the answer is "yes" then policies and procedures need to be established governing such outside groups. For example, outside groups might be required to post a bond for damages. Additionally, such groups might be required to pay a sum, in advance, covering all costs (security, preparation, cleanup, etc.) associated with such usage plus a sum that will be the net profit for the owners of the facility.

CONCEPT #257:   *When allowing outside groups to use facilities be sure to take a proactive approach in terms of potential damage(s).*

It is highly recommended that a representative of the facility and the outside group tour the facility before and after its use by the group. This is done so that detailed, written records can be maintained in terms of the condition of the facility and its contents. These records (including photographs, if appropriate) can go a long way to prove the condition of the facility before and after the outside event. This proactive approach to damage control is most important. It does not take much to cause significant or permanent damage to sport facilities by uncaring or unthinking individuals. And, whether damage is intentional or accidental is not really the ultimate question. Damage is damage. Repairs have to be made. And, in most cases, the facility cannot be tied up for long for needed repairs because other groups have been scheduled to use the same facility.

Security Factors in Allowing Outside Groups to Use the Sport Facility

Also, even though security costs are paid for by the outside group, in many instances it is recommended that the owners of the site hire (provide) the security personnel. This insures that adequately trained security officers are on hand for the outside event or program and that the security personnel represent the owners and not the outside group or association.

One last word regarding security, or the lack of security, due to problems with keys, specifically missing, stolen or misplaced keys. The cost to replace a single key that has been lost is not the issue. What quickly becomes an issue, and an expensive one at that, is when a missing key jeopardizes the security of an entire facility and a decision must be made relative to the feasibility of rekeying the entire building. This type of situation is exacerbated when there is widespread use of the so-called master key. Losing or misplacing a master key is a very, very serious matter. That is why management typically restricts the number of people possessing master keys to the bare minimum.

> **CONCEPT #258:** *Restrict the use of master keys to the minimum number of personnel.*

The issue of unauthorized use of keys can quickly become the bane of facility managers. This is especially true in the aftermath of 9/11 and this country's warranted concern with terrorists and deliberate attacks against the populace. Not only is security compromised but there is always danger of injuries to individuals who have gained unauthorized access to buildings or grounds when keys are floating around. With the loss of security many facilities have to be re-keyed—a process that is time consuming and costly. In many instances managers suggests that buildings simply be re-keyed every five years as a matter of policy because of the concern about lost or missing keys (Ryder, 1994).

Others suggest a more frequent re-keying schedule, as frequently as every year or two. And still others believe that the changing of the locks is going about the seemingly perpetual problem from the wrong direction. These proponents suggest that stricter policies regarding issuing and handling of keys to buildings *coupled* with persistent educational efforts for those personnel who have been issued keys, are more effective in winning the battle against stolen, lost or misplaced keys.

The cost of changing the locks or "re-keying" an entire facility can reach into the thousands of dollars. And yet security of buildings and grounds is a critical issue for management. Preventative (proactive) measures, if effective, can be worth their "weight in gold." Reactive measures, such as re-keying an entire building, will usually cost their "weight in gold" not to speak of the adverse publicity spilling over the administrator in charge of the facility.

MANAGERIAL STRATEGIES AND TACTICS FOR FACILITIES

One of the keys to wise and prudent management of facilities is to establish "standard operating procedures" (SOPs) for the operation of all facilities and the equipment and supplies within or associated with these facilities. These SOPs should be included within what is commonly referred to as a "standard operation procedures/policies handbook." Included within such a handbook will be policies, procedures and practices pertaining to the operation and management of the sport facilities under a wide range of circumstances. Such a handbook facilitates decision making in terms of the operation and maintenance of facilities and their contents.

> *CONCEPT #259:*   **The standard operating procedures handbook serve as a guide for decision making.**

The format or structure of the handbook itself can vary. Some administrators utilize a three-ring booklet with loose-leaf sheets containing various procedures and policies for ease of inserting and removing. Others utilize a more formal bound volume containing pages of policies and procedures permanently inserted.

> *CONCEPT #260:*   **Establishing appropriate policies for use of facilities will help insure facilities are available for safe usage and a longer lifespan.**

These procedures, policies and practices should be thought out well in advance to the time when they are needed. In point of fact, managers don't have time to think up policies and procedures "on the fly"—rather, experienced and successful members of management rely upon time tested and well thought out policies and procedures to deal with the innumerable challenges and decisions that face them day in and day out. This is especially important when it comes to so-called unexpected emergencies or problems that assuredly arise periodically. It is far more effective to think about and consider various possible alternatives when facing emergencies when one is not harried, when one is calm, cool and collected (3Cs).

> *CONCEPT #261:*   **Establish an emergency set of procedures to deal with unexpected problems or difficulties associated with the use of facilities.**

Examples of *selected contents within a Facility Standard Operating Procedures Handbook* include statements as to which group or individuals have priority in terms of usage of parts of the facility (i.e., booking and scheduling priorities), costs of using the facility by outside groups; restrictions on the use of the facility itself; hours of operation; setup and break down procedures; availability of security personnel; emergency procedures; scheduled care relative to housekeeping and maintenance of various segments of the facility; recommended actions to take in event of emergencies; advertising and marketing efforts; signage; ticket and box office operations; concession operations; garbage removal; insurance; issuance of keys; snow plowing (in northern climates); availability of medical personnel; utility usage during events; restrictions on people's behavior (smoking, drugs, use of food/drink; parking, etc.); charges for usage of the facility by inside groups; and, staffing of the facility. Of course the actual contents and organization of material within such a SOP handbook will depend upon the sport organization, its mission(s) as well as the situation and circumstances in which management finds itself.

Decisions Maximizing Financial Savings

Well thought out and prudent facility policies can end up saving the sport organization big time, in terms of money, in terms of use of personnel, in terms of public relations, and in terms of effective and efficient use of the facilities. Prudent practices and procedures in the area of energy costs can result in significant savings for the sport entity. "Energy cost avoidance has always been and will always be one of our key money issues" (Leach, 1997, p. 15).

Staff Members Must Be Quick to Respond when in the Spot Light.
[courtesy of University of Tennessee, Sports Information Office]

Keeping doors closed during the day, turning off lights in unoccupied areas within a building, minimizing the use of exhaust fans, keeping both inlet and outlet air passages clean and free of obstacles, and removing on-site access to thermostats are just some of the steps that management might consider to maximize financial savings associated with facilities. Being energy efficient should be a goal of every member of management.

> **CONCEPT #262:** *Appropriate facility policies and practices can reduce energy costs and save money.*

Decisions Maximizing Staff Effectiveness

Having established appropriate policies and procedures relating to the facilities management places one in a position, generally speaking, of following these same policies and procedures with a minimum of oversight and allocation of staff. It is not that facilities do not warrant consistent attention. It is just that with advance planning (SOP Handbooks) much of the challenge of dealing with and utilizing facilities can be significantly reduced. It should be remembered that sport facilities are tools, are instruments that are used to fulfill an organization's mission(s). *As such, facilities should not consume an inordinate amount of time, effort, attention and money of management.* To be otherwise would indicate a poor choice of priorities, or poor management of facilities, or both.

THE USE OF MULTIPLE SOP HANDBOOKS FOR INDIVIDUAL SPORTING EVENTS

Within a broad based school athletic program involving a large number of different sports and facilities, the concept of such a SOP handbook might actually involve a number of different handbooks, one for each varsity sport team. Thus, there might be a SOP handbook for the football games that would deal with the use of, and setup of, the facilities used during the football games. Similarly, for the softball team there would be a separate SOP handbook that would detail how the softball and related facilities would be set up and utilized before, during and after the actual softball game.

Adaptations of Ideas of Others

In developing a method of operating within one's facilities and in establishing policies for the use and maintenance of facilities it is not necessary or even advisable to attempt to reinvent the wheel. Rather, borrow, beg and steal ideas from others and adjust them to fit your particular situation and circumstances (Glazier, 1997; Schneider and Stier, 2006). Talk with other professionals involved in facility management or supervision. Solicit information and advice. Observe and learn. Borrow those ideas that fit your circumstances and adapt or adjust strategies and tactics of others to accommodate your own situation.

> **CONCEPT #263:** *Borrow, beg and steal ideas and strategies from others—*
> *adapt, adjust and tailor what has worked elsewhere*
> *to one's own situation.*

INDOOR FACILITIES

When one considers indoor facilities the first thought that most often comes to mind is a building, a structure with four outside walls, windows, interior structural elements, interior walls/supports, a roof, and a floor. Once that picture is firmly entrenched in one's mind there comes the additional realization that there is more to a building than its outer shell or the structural component, much more. In addition to a building's overall outer structure (the shell) there are three additional elements that most facilities or buildings possess. These include electrical components (lights, motors, pumps, etc.), mechanical elements (heating, air conditioning, ventilation, etc., and a plumbing system (sewage, water, etc.).

COSTS ASSOCIATED WITH REPLACEMENT AND ANNUAL MAINTENANCE/UPKEEP OF A BUILDING

Replacement Costs

Typically, buildings are constructed to last 50 years. Thus, ideally, management should be placing 2% of the replacement value of the facility aside each year so that eventually when you have to replace the structure there would be funds available to either replace or rehab the facility. Of course, timely and appropriate repairs and rehab efforts on most buildings can extend their usefulness well beyond the normal 50-year life span.

Annual Maintenance and Upkeep Costs for the Operation of a Building

Today most managers estimate the "cost for operation" of a typical building to be in the neighborhood of around 4% or 5% of the replacement value of the structure. One can obtain a rough estimate of the replacement value of an average building by assuming that each square foot is worth at least between $100 to $125. The "cost of operation" includes those expenses incurred to operate the so-called average building each year just for normal expenditures in the areas of repair and general maintenance.

Determining Actual Cost of Doing Business— Formula for Calculating Maintenance and Operating Costs

This is a commonly used formula for determining the maintenance and operating costs of a facility. Morrison (1998) summarizes/describes the formula as the total of *all annual expenses* of the facility's operations and maintenance, exclusive of debt service. Some examples of such expenses include electricity, water, heat, air conditioning, repair/upkeep, custodial staff, equipment, supplies, personnel (including benefits), and even advertising, etc. These expenses are divided by the gross square footage of the facility in *order to determine the operational cost per square foot on an annual basis.* To determine the cost on a daily basis simply divide the total expenses by the number of days in the year.

CONCEPT #264: **It is easier and less expensive to perform periodic maintenance than to make alterations to a facility.**

Wise managers insure that proper and timely maintenance and upkeep is done to facilities. This is one area where procrastination or hesitation will cost big dollars in the future. Routine maintenance, upkeep and preservation are absolutely essential if the facility is to remain capable of fulfilling its mission and meeting the needs of the sport organization and programs. In short, postponing or skimping in these areas is being foolish at best, and negligent at worse.

REFERENCES

Busser, J.A. (1999). Conducting a needs assessment survey. *ESM Magazine, 42*(9), 28-31.

Cohen, A. (1995, August). Rains of error. *Athletic Business, 19*(8), 28-34.

Cohen, A. (2005, April). Damage control. *Athletic Business, 29*(4), 61, 62, 64,66, 68.

Condron, S.C. and Wong, G.M. (2006). Safe at home. *Athletic Business, 24*(7), 24, 26.

Conklin, A.R. (1999). On Unsafe Ground. *Athletic Business, 23*(5), 62-67.

Equipment for success. (1993, August). *Athletic Business, 17*(8) 27-30.

Fawcett, P. (1997, May). Deep trouble. *Athletic Business, 21*(5), 43-44, 49.

Garner, S. (1997, Aug/Sep). Fresh coat of paint. *Athletic Management, IX*(5), 47-50.

Gimple, J. (1992, Sept). Laying the foundation. *Athletic Management, IV*(5), 32, 35, 37-39.

Hunsaker, D.J. (1992, Dec). Under the surface. *Athletic Business, 16*(12), 67-68, 70-72.

Hypes, M.G. (2006). Planning and Designing Facilities. *Journal of Physical Education, Recreation and Dance, 77*(4), 18-22.

Jastrow, S. (1997, Feb). Facility planning. *Club Industry, 13*(2), p. 37.

Johnston, R. J. (1991, May). All in one. *College Athletic Magazine, III*(3), 28-33.

Keys, C. (1999). Dodging the wrecking ball. *Athletic Business, 23*(5), 73-75, 80-83.

Krenson, F. (1997, April). Making it multipurpose. *Athletic Business, 21*(4), 67-68, 70, 72, 74, 76.

LaRue,a R. (2002). Safe in their seats. *Athletic Management, XIV*(5), 61-63.

Leach, K. (1997, March). An energy audit in action. *School Planning & Management, 36*(3), 14-17.

Morrison, T. (1998). Cost Equation. *Athletic Business, 22*(6), 14.

Orlowski, D. (2000). Into the arena. *Athletic Business, 24*(1), 42-50.

Pate, D.W., Moffit, E., Fugett, D. (1993). Current trends in use, design/construction, and funding of sport facilities. *Sport Marketing Quarterly, II*(4), 9-14.

Ross, C. & Wolter, S. (1997, April). On-time facilities. *Athletic business, 21*(4), 55-61.

Ryder, C. (1994, Summer). Unauthorized keys: A risk management headache. *Sport Supplement*, p. 3.

Sawyer, T.H. (Ed.). (2005). *Facility design and management for healthy, physical activity, recreation, and sports facility development* (11th ed.). Champaign, IL: Sagamore.

Schneider, R.C. and Stier, W.F., Jr. (2006) Sport Management Field Experiences as Experimental Learning: Insuring Beneficial Outcomes and Preventing Exploitation. *The Sport Management and Related Topics Journal (SMART Journal)*, 2(2), 36-43. http://spectrum.troy.edu/~smart/fieldexperience.pdf

Shalley, W. & Barzdukas, A. (1997, March). Dive right. *Athletic Business, 21*(3), 41-42, 43, 44, 46, 48, 50, 51.

Spending that would make Steinbrenner proud. (2006). *Athletic Clips.* http://www.cfo.com/printable/article.cfm/7239613?f=options, retrieved October 3, 2006.

Steinbach, P. (2000). Opening doors to equity. *Athletic Business, 24*(12), 111, 112, 114, 115, 116.

Steinback, P. (2006). Enemy at the Gates. *Athletic Business.* http://www.athleticbusiness.com/$spindb.query.readarticle.abview.9.42.1206. Retrieved June 9, 2006.

Stier, Jr., W.F. (1993). The ins and outs of evaluating coaches. *Athletic Management, V*(3), 34-37, 39.

Stier, Jr., W.F. (1997, June 3). *Physical Education and the Use of Technological Strategies and Tactics.* Presentation at the Sixth Annual FACT Conference on Instructional Technologies (CIT)—Learning with Technologies, Brockport, New York.

Wallace, B.J., and Kline, D.E. (2005). Prevent defense. *Athletic Business, 29*(4), 77, 78, 80, 82.

West, B. (1998, January). It's time for an audit. *Lawn & Landscape, 19*(1), 66, 68, 70, 72.

White, H., & Karabestos, J. (1999). Planning and designing facilities. In T.H. Sawyer (Ed.) *Facilities planning for physical activity and sport: Guidelines for development* (9th ed.; pp. 11-28). Dubuque, IA: Kendall Hunt.

Readings and Organizations Regarding Safety and Facilities

U.S. Consumer Product Safety Commission, Washington, DC 20207 (800-638-2772)— *Handbook for Public Playground Safety*

United States Consumer Product Safety Commission (CPSC)—specific guidelines in 2001 for bleacher safety. Called the Guidelines for Retrofitting Bleachers

Council on Physical Activity and Recreation Venue Design and Management (PARVDM)

National Intramural-Recreational Sports Association (NIRSA)—www.nirsa.org—*Planning Principles for Colleges and University Recreation Services*

Society for College and University Planning (SCUP)—www.scup.org

Further Readings—Facilities

A baseball facility: Its construction and care. The United States Baseball Federation. (609) 586-2381.

Farmer, P.J., Mulrooney, A.L., & Ammon, R. (1997). *Sport facility planning and management.* Morgantown, West Virginia: Fitness Information Technology, Inc.

Flynn, R.B. (1993). *Facility planning for physical education, recreation and athletics* (2nd ed.). Reston, Virginia: American Alliance for Health, Physical Education, Recreation and Dance.

Martens, R. (1995). *Event management for sport directors.* Champaign, Ill: Human Kinetics.

Pate, D.W., Moffit, E. & Fugett, D. (1997). Current trends in use, design/construction, and funding of sport facilities. *Sport Marketing Quarterly, 2*(4), 9-14. in references ALSO

Planning facilities for athletics, physical education, and recreation. (1974). Washington, D.C.: American Alliance for Health, Physical Education, and Recreation; Chicago, Illinois: Athletic Institute.

Polk, R. (1983). *Baseball playbook.* Mississippi State, Mississippi 39762: P.O. Drawer 5327. [called the Baseball Bible by many]

Perry, F. (1994). *Pictorial guide to quality groundskeeping: Covering all the bases.* Orlando, Florida 32809: Holland communications, Suite 423. (800) 809-3952.

Perry, F. (1995). Groundskeeping—Floyd Perry's pictorial guide to quality groundskeeping II, "There ain't no rules". [Grounds Maintenance Services] Orlando, Florida 32809: Holland communications, Suite 423. (800) 809-3952.

Sawyer, TlH. (2005). *Facility design and management for health, fitness, physical activity, recreation, and sports facility development.* (11th ed). Champaign, IL: Sagamore Publishing.

USTC & TBA track construction manual, Latest edition. The United States Tennis Court and Track Builders Association, 3525 Ellicott Mills Drive, Suite N., Ellicott City, MD 21043 (410) 418-4875.

DISCUSSION TOPICS

1. Explain the importance of having appropriate management and maintenance of indoor and outdoor facilities.

2. Discuss the following statement: *It is not always necessary for the top-level sport manager to be an expert in facility management and maintenance.* Justify your position.

3. Specify ways in which management can be engaged in preventative maintenance of facilities.

4. Select a specific indoor or outdoor facility commonly utilized by a sport, recreation or fitness organization and outline potential problems that astute managers should be aware of in terms of management and maintenance of the facility.

5. Cite some specific contents within a hypothetical Standard Operating Procedures Handbook for a specific sport organization and explain how this information can play an important role in the maintenance and management of a facility.

6. List some major advantages of utilizing outside consultants in managing and/or maintenance of facilities.

7. What might be some disadvantages of utilizing outside consultants in the management and maintenance of facilities?

8. Explain what facility audits are?

9. What are the end results of a so-called needs assessment report?

10. What is the formula for determining calculating maintenance and operating costs? Explain its use.

Chapter

9 Facility Management—Maintenance of Indoor and Outdoor Facilities

Exciting Athletic Events Attract Paying Customers
[courtesy of Rochester Red Wings]

CHAPTER HIGHLIGHTS

This chapter will help the reader to:

- Possess a fundamental awareness of the proper care of indoor facilities for various sporting venues;
- Appreciate the importance of the proper care of flooring for sporting activities;
- List the ten essential elements of grass and lawn management;
- Enunciate different types of floors and the advantages of each;
- Cite the advantages of dividers placed within sports facilities;

- Explain the essence of maintenance of the major components of facilities that are utilized by sport, recreation and fitness organizations;
- Demonstrate a beginning knowledge of the proper care of outdoor facilities, i.e., grounds and grasses;
- Ask appropriate questions in terms of proper pool maintenance and management as a matter of public health;
- Understand the basics of proper pool maintenance;
- Be aware of roots, root growth and the proper core of roots for normal growth;
- List specific strategies for maintaining a superior strength and conditioning facilities;
- Appreciate the need for proper sanitation in proper pool management.

GENERAL COMMENTS REGARDING MAINTENANCE AND UPKEEP OF FACILITIES

It is very important that sport managers have a sound and comprehensive understanding of their facilities, both indoor and outdoor. This knowledge is not limited to that which pertains to the construction or building of facilities but, equally important, also to the day-to-day operational aspects of facilities. The information in this chapter will provide some important facts and data that can be helpful to the sport administrator in terms of the operational aspects of facilities and their components or essential elements.

Asbestos

Any building over 25 years has asbestos within the structure. If required, removal is costly. However, under certain conditions it is not necessary to remove all asbestos from a building. For example, in years past some ceiling and floor tiles were made with asbestos. If such tiles are currently in buildings they may remain unless the asbestos is disturbed and exposed to the air. For example, if individuals puncture the tiles or scratch the tiles so that the asbestos particles are exposed to the air then these tiles are a health hazard or must be removed.

Placement of Drinking Fountains

Do not have water (drinking) fountains situated in exercise areas where there are wooden floors. It doesn't take much to have water overflow onto the floor with the potential for real (and expensive) damage resulting to the floor.

Painting

Establish a painting schedule for different facilities or buildings. Many facility managers choose to paint on a 7 to 10 year cycle. Additionally, since labor costs accounts for the majority of costs associated with painting it is recommended that quality paints be used so that painting can be done less frequently.

The Source of Monies to Pay for Routine Maintenance

When management first considers constructing a facility or building there should be a plan whereby sufficient money can be set aside and the interest from which will be sufficient to cover the costs of yearly maintenance and upkeep for the future.

Maintenance and Upkeep Efforts Are Sometimes Dictated by Outside Sources

Management must abide by and adhere to the rules, regulations, policies and standards of various associations and governing bodies when it comes to proper maintenance and condition of facilities. For example, in the sport of swimming there are maximum and minimum water temperature ranges established by the NCAA in order for competitive swimming events to be sanctioned in a given pool.

SELECTED INDOOR FACILITIES OR COMPONENTS NECESSITATING SPECIAL CARE

There are some areas within an indoor facility that require special mention. Generally speaking, these facilities or elements of facilities require special care in terms of maintenance as well as the management for their intended use.

Floors

Interior floors, especially those surfaces that participants play or run, must be a matter of concern of the first magnitude for management. Catalano (2003) suggests that managers should ask themselves and others (especially potential users) exactly how and where the floor will be used, the frequency of use and who will be the main users.

Wooden floors (such as basketball courts) are especially susceptible to abuse, misuse and significant damage. Wooden floors can be easily marred, scuffed and scratched. Both temperature and humidity can also affect them.

> ***CONCEPT #265:*** ***"The worst crime against wood floors is neglect,***
> ***since even the smallest amount of care can prolong their life"***
> ***(Cohen, 1992, p. 56).***

The Maple Flooring Manufacturers Association (MFMA—[847] 480-9138) has a booklet describing techniques and strategies for the general care and repair of hardwood sports floors. Prudent managers should familiarize themselves with the contents of this publication. A question that frequently arises is whether in-house custodial staff should attempt periodic maintenance and repairs or should such tasks be farmed out to professionals specializing in such work. "Most sport floor or sport floor finish manufacturers will help train novices with seminars or demonstrations of different products" (Cohen, 1992, p. 54).

Of course there are other floor surfaces besides wood. Today, more and more sport organizations are finding that alternate surfaces work every bit as well, if not better than the traditional wood. For example, practice and competitive surfaces can include vinyl composition (VCT) of multipurpose rooms, interlocking plastic tile (volleyball), various types of textured surfaces (jogging tracks), synthetic surfaces (basketball), ceramic tile in rest rooms and locker rooms, as well as combination of surfaces such as rolled-rubber flooring (weight room and fitness facilities) and concrete concourses (Bynum, 2003).

Floor Coverings

To protect wood floors from abusive foot traffic (street shoes, etc.) it is necessary to utilize appropriate floor coverings. This is part of preventative maintenance. Most floor covers are made of vinyl-coated or laminated polyester, vinyl or vinyl nylon and all must be fire-retardant. These covers must be cared for and cleaned just as carefully as one would clean the floors.

Viklund (1995, p. 46) suggests before selecting a particular surface for a floor in one's facility that the following steps be taken in an effort to become an informed and educated buyer.

1. Select the room or space to be considered
2. Prioritize the sports/activities that will occur within the space
3. Decide whether the preferred floor should be area elastic (more resilient) or point elastic (low absorption levels)
4. Review the performance criteria for the selected floor type
5. Test flooring options by reviewing samples and comparing costs
6. Compare life-cycle costs for flooring options—initial costs plus maintenance costs should be compared over 10 and 20-year period to get a full value picture

7. Play on different surfaces
8. Check the manufacturers' referenced projects
9. Make the final decision

Moveable Dividers or Barriers within a Facility

Dividers are typically utilized in large open spaces such as gymnasiums, field houses and indoor tennis courts for the purpose of quickly and efficiently separating a large open space into one or more smaller areas. Dividers have added advantages in that they can often reduce the noise factor emanating from other sources within the overall facility. Additionally, use of dividers can help significantly reduce distractions from interfering with what is taking place within the newly defined space. And finally, dividing a large space into smaller areas can reduce the likelihood of physical injuries occurring to participants from other individuals running into their "space."

CONCEPT # 266: *Moveable dividers (electric motor driven) can be very, very expensive to repair.*

There are four main types of dividers in use today within gymnasiums. First, there is the traditional type with *accordion-type doors* that are moved across an open space by electric motors. The biggest challenge with these types of dividers is that they are expensive to purchase and expensive to repair. The remaining three styles of dividers are typically constructed of vinyl-coated materials heat-sealed together. The dividers themselves may be constructed entirely from either solid vinyl or mesh, or a combination of both. If a

Construction of a New Big-League Basefall Facility—
Always an Exciting Time
[courtesy of Robert Rogers/Tampa Bay Devil Rays]

combination of both is used, the solid vinyl will comprise the bottom 15 feet while the mesh (net) is used for the top thus providing increased air circulation, resulting in improved ventilation (Catalano, 1995, February/March, p. 49).

The second type of divider is a vinyl-coated sliding curtain that is usually *pulled by hand across* a space on a tracking system located along the ceiling. When not in use separating a space, the curtain is positioned hanging from the ceiling along an end wall. The third type of divider is a *roll-up* type that has the curtain being rolled up to the ceiling or lowered (rolled) down to the floor by means of an electric motor. The fourth type of divider has a *folding* type curtains similar to a venetian blind. An electric motor is used to fold the curtain completely up to the ceiling and to unfold the curtain down from the ceiling to the floor (Catalano, 1995). Both the roll-up type and the folding style of curtain dividers can be expected to last around 15 to 18 years, depending upon usage.

Weight Rooms and Fitness Centers (Strength & Conditioning)

The modern weight room is a far cry from what it was only a few years ago. In the past, the stereotypical weight room was perceived to be a gloomy, dingy, smelly, fluorescent lit, and unglamorous space where males almost exclusively grunted and intimidated their way through workout sessions. No more.

CONCEPT #267:   *Weight rooms must be kept spotless and physically attractive.*

Today, the strength and conditioning facility is a spacious, well illuminated with a combination of indirect and uplighting, adequately ventilated, acoustically proper, properly decorated and visually pleasing area, which is attractive for both males and females. Frequently floors are covered in a combination of carpets, synthetic covering and/or rubber tiles. Wood platforms are provided for free weights lest weights that are dropped might permanently damage the base flooring of the facility. Suitable music is perpetually piped in. And, hardwood floors are provided for aerobic exercises.

CONCEPT #268:   *Daily check the weight room(s) for broken or abused items of equipment.*

Specific strategies for maintaining a superior strength and conditioning facility include: (Sherman, 1997; Glazier, 1997).

1. Insure that the ventilation system distributes clean air throughout the facility. An increase in the number of air changes within the area is necessary in response to the potential for extensive odor buildup.

2. Equipment must be kept in immaculate condition in terms of cleanliness and visually. This includes free weights, exercise machines, padded upholstery, etc.

3. Locker rooms, showers as well as collateral items of equipment such a hot tubs, saunas, etc., must be kept in perfect condition.

4. Mirrors are prominently displayed throughout the exercise areas.

5. The facility should be brightly decorated to attract and retain both male and female clients and patrons.

6. Establish a non-intimidating atmosphere through policies and practice.

7. Seek input from customers or patrons (through surveys and questionnaires) as how to upgrade the facilities and equipment as well as improve the service.

8. Establish suitable hours to meet the needs of one's clientele.

Locker and Dressing Rooms and Shower Facilities

Just as weight room facilities have undergone a significant makeover in recent years so too has the so-called locker room, or changing room or dressing room. Today, image is everything (Strock, 1991). And this is certainly true in the area of locker and dressing facilities. Today's locker room patron tends to stay longer in the dressing facility and view it as more than just a place to change into a different set of clothes. As a result, management is attempting to make this area more pleasant and pleasing (Dillon, 1996). Consequently, dressing facilities (locker rooms) are functional, airy, brightly lit, freshly painted, appropriately decorated, clean and spacious.

CONCEPT # 269: *Locker rooms and dressing areas need to be functional, safe and secure for the client.*

Spaciousness of locker and dressing rooms provide easy movement and access between elements such as locker areas, showers, drying areas, the toilet room and perhaps the steam room or sauna (Viklund & Coons, 1997). Presence of rough surfaces on the floor of the dressing area as well as slip resistant flooring in the showers insures safe use of the facility. Additionally, the facility should be designed so that vandalism can be held to a minimum while cleaning and maintenance efforts are made easy (Heugli, Richards, Graffis, Kroll, & Epley, 1991).

Lockers

An integral part of the locker/dressing facility are the lockers themselves. There is a need for durable, secure, well-ventilated and visually pleasing lockers. The type of lockers to add to the dressing facility will depend upon the type of use the site will have as well as the type of clientele. Permanent metal lockers might be most suitable in a school setting designed with an open face or a closed face with air louvers.

In other settings, solid plastic lockers, solid phenolic lockers, wooden lockers, wood-laminate or plastic-laminate, welded metal lockers, knock-down metal lockers might be more suitable. Welded lockers are welded together in groups of 3 or 6 at the factory and shipped that way to the facility where they are installed. So-called knock-down lockers arrive on site as separate pieces and must be assembled with nuts and bolts (Browser, 1997). Some lockers are constructed so as to be free standing while others are to be built in. Permanently installed benches might be used or moveable benches can be selected (The Right Lockers, 1996).

Swimming Pools, Whirl Pools, Spas and Hot Tubs

The National Spa and Pool Institute (NSPI) in cooperation with the American National Standards Institute (ANSI) has established and disseminated revised guidelines [American National Standard for Public Spas (ANSI/NSPI-2 1992) for the design, installation and use of public spas and hot tubs (Staying out of, 1993).

CONCEPT #270: *Proper pool maintenance and management is a matter of public health.*

Pools are often the focal point in many sport facilities that offer such a facility. Yet, taking care of pools (of all types) can be one of the more challenging tasks facing facility managers and sport. One of the reasons for this is that the public's health is at stake should anything go awry (Schmid, 1997, October).

Managers must realize that the act of draining the swimming pool should be at the top of the maintenance list. Although the closing of a pool results in significant down time and lose of revenue as well as disgruntled patrons, if this is not done on an periodic (annual) basis so that essential on-going maintenance and repairs can be effected, operators will find that the result may be a decline in water clarity, paint peeling, presence of fumes, leaks, scum buildup, poor lighting, plumbing problems, and loose/broken deck tiles, etc. (Fawcett, 2004).

In an effort to combat the challenge of mastering maintenance of public pools the state of New York instituted a requirement that every organization that has a pool open to members of the public designate at least one personnel on staff as the expert pool manager. This certification process places the burden of responsibility directly upon the organization or business operating the pool to see that a properly trained and experienced individual is in charge of the day-to-day operation of the pool. This individual is required by state law to attend specific courses and classes in an effort to master the intricacies of pool management and maintenance.

CONCEPT #271: *Commercial pools are different than home pools in terms of maintenance and care.*

Managers of large commercial pool operations (schools, health clubs, recreation departments, etc.) should be very cautious in accepting so-called expert counsel from the neighborhood pool supply clerk. The reason for this is that the most important factor in the safe and efficient operation of any pool lies in the number of swimmers the pool has on a given day. "The number is the central determinant for the amount of contaminants in the pool, which in turn affects the chemical consumption and the amount of debris to be filtered out by the system" (Schmid, 1997, October, p. 52). Thus, "the greater the number of swimmers or bathers the greater the strain that is placed upon the chemicals and the harder the pool's filtration system has to work (p. 52)." Therefore, pool managers need to be careful to solicit advice and counsel from appropriate sources who are familiar with the type of pool operation for which the sport manager is responsible.

Sanitation—The Essence of All Pool Management

One of the critical factors when dealing with pools of all kinds and types is sanitation. "Sanitation management is really an euphemism for disease prevention" (Vest, 1995, p. 42). One cannot be too careful when dealing with health matters, from the perspective of what is right and proper and from the perspective of legal obligations and potential for being successfully sued.

In this light it is always better to play it safe, to be cautious and to establish rigorous guidelines governing supervision, testing and maintenance of water facilities such as swimming pools, whirl pools, spas and hot tubs. When dealing with the sanitation or such facilities there are three elements that must be dealt with, water, air and surface areas (Vest, 1995, p. 39). Thus, standard operating procedures (SOPs) in terms of facility maintenance and management must include these three elements.

Cleaning Up a Fecal or Vomit Accident

It is frequently difficult enough keeping a pool safe and sanitary for one's clients under normal circumstances. However, there is always the challenge of addressing additional challenges brought about either by accidents on behalf of youngsters or deliberate acts by those who should know better.

CONCEPT #272: *The Health of the Patron Must Take Precedence Over the Convenient Use of Facilities.*

When such an accident occurs, such as a child eliminating in the pool or someone vomiting in the water, immediate and decisive action must be taken. In fact, two actions by management are required immediately. First, everyone must be immediately removed from the water. Second, the fecal matter or vomit must also be removed. The pool should be closed down for a minimum of 24 hours. In a typical commercial swimming pool this allows for four 6-hour cycles of water.

Additionally, Vest (1995) recommends that management must (1) shock the area where the incident occurred with Chlorine to a level 20 to 30 parts per million, (2) super-chlorinate the pool, (3) backwash and clean the filters with a chlorine-based solution, (4) subsequently the pool chlorine should be neutralized with sodium thiosulfate (down to 5 parts per million), and then (5) backwash and clean the filter a second time before the pool is reopened. Even after the pool is opened for public use there must be biological testing repeated for several days to ensure it is safe.

Common Myths of Pool Maintenance

There are many myths in the area of pool maintenance. Many of these myths have been perpetuated by ignorance and lack of formal training on behalf of those individuals who have been given the responsibility for overseeing and managing pools of all types. Some of these myths are harmless while others are indeed not only costly or inefficient to the sponsoring organization, but also have the potential to be dangerous to those individuals utilizing the pools. Schmid (1997, October, pp. 48-54) lists the following 13 top myths of pool operation and maintenance.

1. Pools with high-rate sand filters need to have the filters running 24 hours a day.
2. The best way to maintain clear water and save operational expenses is daily or scheduled backwashing of pool and spa sand filters.
3. An indoor pool doesn't need a cover [to the contrary—commercial operators can save $30,000 in natural gas costs and by conserving a 1/3 of a million gallons of water on an annual basis (p. 50).
4. If total dissolved solids (TDS) accumulate to levels over 2,000 parts per million (or 1,500 parts per million above the water-supply value), it becomes necessary to empty and then refill the pool—and chlorine can lose up to half its effectiveness.
5. Use of bleach (sodium hypochlorite) to sanitize pools necessitates large amounts of acid to maintain an acceptable pH level.
6. Total dissolved solids (TDS) affect the water clarity or give it color.
7. One can superchlorinate a pool with the cover on.
8. Cyanuric acid improves chlorine by making it better, stronger and more effective.
9. High cyanuric acid levels have no significant effect on chlorine's efficacy.
10. Chlorine does not kill cryptosporidium.
11. New algicides are regularly developed for pool use.
12. It is o.k. to store liquid chlorine out in the sun as it does not degrade.
13. If a pool has an underdrain system, it won't hurt the pool to drain it.

OUTDOOR FACILITIES—FIELDS, LAWNS AND ATHLETIC TURF

The goals of management insofar as fields, lawns and athletic turf are concerned center around three major elements. First, to insure that there is healthy turf growing. Second, that there is a full ground cover (no bare spots where grass is suppose to be) over the appropriate areas, thus providing for safe usage. And third, to satisfy the participants who play or compete on the grass surface and those patrons or spectators who view the activity (Stier, 1991).

Turf, Grass and Athletic Field Management—Problem Areas

There are a number of sources of potential problems facing administrators in their quest to maintain healthy turf and grass fields. The number one problem is soil compaction brought about by constant use, overuse or abuse. A second problem revolves around the time that it takes to establish new turf or the time it takes for grass to grow back to where it can be utilized in a sport setting.

CONCEPT #273: *The #1 challenge with athletic turf is soil compaction.*

The weather can be still another source of problems in terms of soil and grass condition either by creating saturated soil conditions or drought–like conditions. Whenever there is inclement weather one must be concerned about the general field conditions, the safety conditions of the field itself and the safety of the participants and spectators.

Two factors related to the weather that can create havoc with the condition of fields, turf and grasses are the poor crowning (raised area extending throughout the middle of a field and slopping to the edges) and/or insufficient or inefficient drainage (Watson, 1998). And, of course, drainage capabilities, compaction rate

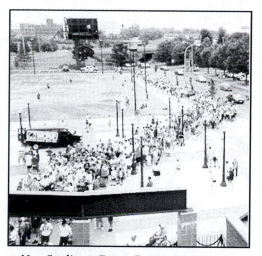

New Stadiums Foster Better Attendance.
[courtesy of Rochester Red Wings]

and growth rate of grasses are directly related to the type of soil (hard clay, for example) that exists. And finally, the presence of pests, specifically, fungi (the cause of most lawn diseases), insects and weeds can prove to be significant challenges for management (Dernoeden, 1997)

TYPES OF GRASSES

It is the responsibility of management to establish a routine turf and field management and maintenance program and then to follow it (Schmid, 1992, May). An essential part of any management or maintenance program is being knowledgeable of various types of grasses, soils and seeds as well as methods and techniques of enhancing the growth and development of athletic fields and lawns. Generally speaking, seed selection is determined on the basis of desired color, density of the grass, its disease resistance, fertility requirements, moisture needs, mowability and germination time.

---

*CONCEPT #274:   **Weather and soil type will determine
the type of grass utilized for Athletic Fields.***

Warm Season Grasses

There are a variety of grasses that may be appropriate for different athletic, competitive and recreational fields depending upon the sport or activity planned for the site, the type of soil and the general weather pattern. Grasses can be classified as *warm season grasses* and *cold season grasses.* With some fourteen different warm weather grasses the two that are best suited for athletic fields because of their growth habit are Bermudagrass and Zoysiagrass. The majority of football and soccer fields are Bermudagrass. Other warm weather grasses include St. Augustine or Bahiagrass (Rogers & Stier, 1995).

Cold Season Grasses

There are three general types of cold season grasses, Kentucky bluegrass, perennial grass, and tall fescue. The more common cold season grass species include bluegrass, tall fescue/bluegrass mixture, and perennial ryegrass/bluegrass mixture. Since Kentucky bluegrass is a slow growing grass and difficult (time wise) to repair, it is not recommended for football or soccer competition due to the high volume of physical activity. Although perennial grass germinates rapidly it fails to recuperate from heavy traffic, and it does not easily spread to fill in open or bare spots. Tall fescue is very tolerant to heavy traffic due to its wide and course blade. It is a very good cold season grass for football as long as there is not a time factor in terms of establishing the grass on the field since this grass requires a good deal of time to firmly establish on a field.

ROOTS

For adequate plant growth one of the essential elements is to have sufficient roots, both in terms of quality and quantity. Without strong and vibrant roots the grasses, the grass blades simply cannot grow and prosper. Roots serve as the anchoring points for plants and grasses. They also facilitate the absorption of nutrients and water.

The root systems in some warm season grasses (Bermudagrass, St. Augustine or Bahiagrass) can be as deep as 5-7 feet since their peak time for growing is during the summer months. On the other hand, cool season grasses grow more in the spring (and somewhat in the fall) and have more abbreviated root systems, usually between 18 and 24 inches (Howell, 1997, p. 56, 59).

Root Replacement

Some grasses retain their roots over a number of different growing seasons and as such are referred to as perennial rooting grasses. An example of such a grass is Kentucky bluegrass. On the other hand, there are grasses that must replace almost all of their roots each and every growing season. Thus, these grasses are called annual rooting grasses. Bentgrass, perennial ryegrasses and rough bluegrass are examples of the annual rooting grasses.

Root Growth

Successful root growth is dependent upon a number of different factors. Weather, geographical location, type and looseness of the soil, sufficient nutrients, adequate drainage, appropriate mowing and sufficient moisture are all essentials for adequate root growth. Roots must be sufficiently deep to be able to serve as a foundation for the grass blades above the ground and to enable the plant to withstand stress, especially during times of drought. Similarly, without strong root growth grasses cannot survive under the almost constant bombardment of foot traffic and activity usually associated with sports and vigorous physical activity. To be better able to assess the current status of a root system it is recommended that soil core samples be periodically taken (Schmid, 1992, May; Indyk, 1997).

PROACTIVE STRATEGIES AND TACTICS TO COMBAT FIELD AND GRASS PROBLEMS

In order to insure that athletic fields and grassy areas are adequately cared for so as to provide for appropriate and safe competition or participation, it is important that a turf or field management program be in place, one that is based upon sound agronomic practices and involves regularly scheduled, proactive maintenance activities. Figure 9.1 depicts ten elements of grass and lawn management for sport management fields. Depending upon the individual situation in which a sport organization finds itself, any of these elements might be critical in the proper management of fields, lawns, and grassy areas used for competitive or recreational activities.

An interesting web site that deals with information on dealing with weed control of fields is www.weedalert.com. This site is maintained by PBI/Gordon Corp. and provides a wealth of information about weeds and weed control. This is an interesting and informative site for any manager or administrator involved with establishing and maintaining turf and controlling weeks.

FIGURE 9.1: Elements of Grass and Lawn Management

1. *Seeding and Overseeding*

Seeding refers to distributing seed, usually by a mechanical spreader, over the (bare) ground area for the purpose of growing grass within the near future. This is done while the ground area is not being used for physical activity, that is, while the ground is not being compacted by foot traffic. Germination time for various types of grasses will vary depending upon the type of seed being used as well as general weather conditions. Overseeding implies the application of additional seed distributed over grassy areas in an attempt to encourage additional growth while the field or grassy area is being used for competitive or recreational purposes.

2. *Watering*

The challenge when dealing with the use of water (H_2O) on fields or grass is being careful to apply the correct amount, that is, not too much and not too little. A guiding principle in water application is that irrigation should be scheduled when needed and supplemental to Mother Nature's rainfall.

CONCEPT #275: *Supplemental irrigation efforts should be planned around natural rainfall.*

Grass requires sufficient water in order to grow. However, too much water and the ground becomes saturated and growth is stunted, if not thwarted altogether. And, if insufficient moisture gets to the roots the grass can be deprived of essential nutrients and the end result will be the same, insufficient growth. Experienced turf managers irrigate when there are signs of initial moisture stress. Such irrigation is usually to a depth of 6 inches. On medium type soils irrigation is typically one inch per week during the peak-growing season.

Naturally, one would not want to water just before the field or grassy area is to be used since the foot traffic would tend to destroy or injure the wet grass. Finally, if when watering the field water runs off it is recommended that one stops watering and allows the moisture to soak into the ground. Overwatering to the extent that water merely drains off the surface of the ground without penetrating into the layers of the soil beneath the grass blades is wasteful and can result in over-saturation of the ground itself.

3. *Aerating*

As stated earlier, compaction can be a major problem for turf and field management. Compaction is when the ground becomes so hard, so compacted from foot traffic (and weather conditions) that moisture and nutrients cannot penetrate beneath the ground to reach the roots. Ground compaction can cause real root damage and can result in the eventual death of the turf.

CONCEPT #276: *Ground Compaction Can Result in Root Damage and Eventual Root Destruction.*

Aerating (also called coring) helps break soil compaction up by pulling plugs of earth (3" or 4" cores) from the ground (depositing them on the ground) thereby leaving holes in the earth. Aerating should be completed before one fertilizes so that nutrients can get to the root zone. Typically, coring is completed twice a year, once before fertilization and again during mid-summer. When aerating a field it is recommended that two passes at a minimum (in a criss-cross or interlocking pattern) be made over the ground area. Aeration should take place when the ground is moist, not wet and not when very dry.

There are a variety of aerators on the market today (Aerators, 1997). Essentially, they all perform the same task, that is, they accomplish the same results of reducing compaction, improving drainage, improving water, air and fertilizer absorption as well as providing for better conditions for seed development or germination. The end result is improvement in the root development of the turf or grass. The plugs or cores pulled from the earth may be left on the ground. It is also possible to drag the field thereby breaking up the plugs/cores and spreading the soil over the ground.

4. *Top Dressing—The Introduction of Soil Modification Materials*

The condition of grasses and turf may be improved by the addition of a soil amendment to the earth. There are various soil modification materials that consist of commercially prepared chemicals as well as sand. These materials may be added straight to the soil, usually not more than an 1/8th of an inch in depth. These modification materials can be especially effective when administered to a field that that has recently been aerated as the materials can be deposited beneath the surface of the ground. Top dressing can be completed after coring in an effort to level and smooth areas of the field that have been damaged due to heavy use.

5. *Fertilizing*

The spreading of fertilizer on a field can pay big dividends if applied at the proper time of the year and in the correct amounts. Most fertilizers are absorbed by the roots. Relatively few fertilizers are actually absorbed by the leafs of the grass. On the individual container of fertilizer is a three number sequence indicating the proportion of three essential chemicals, namely, nitrogen, phosphorous and potassium. The three number combination might read 10-6-4. This signifies that the three chemicals are in the fertilizer in the following combination, 10 parts nitrogen, 6 parts phosphorous and 4 parts potassium.

Exactly what do these chemicals do? Nitrogen helps make the grass green. Phosphorous aids in the photosynthesis process. It also facilitates root growth and is the least important of the three ingredients. Potassium is the key chemical in that it helps roots grow.

6. *Mowing and Thatching*

Proper mowing is essential if the grasses on the sport or recreation fields are to reach their potential. Two important factors relate to mowing grass. The first factor is the quality of the cut, that is, the sharpness of the blade doing the cutting. The cutting effectiveness can be affected by sharpness of the blade(s), therefore the blade(s) must be kept sharp or there will be damage to the grass. Other factors that can have an effect upon the effectiveness of the mowing effort include the speed of blade(s), the cutting unit suspension, wheel base size, grass discharge, and dispersion characteristics as they relate to terrain and grass conditions (Trotter, 1996, p. 61).

The second factor involves the cutting height. The health of the grass is directly determined by the height of the grass. As a result, one must remember the one-third rule, that is, no more than one-third of the leaf or blade should be removed at a single cutting. The greater the percentage of the blade or leaf removed from the grass the less extensive the root system may be. And too shallow a root system is a potential source of trouble for all grasses.

CONCEPT #277: *To create striping or cutting designs on playing fields utilize reel mowers and cut in opposite directions.*

There are two types of mowers with two distinct types of different cutting actions, *impact* and *sheer.* The impact cutting action is what is normally seen from gas powered mowers with the blades moving in a rotary type movement (rotary and flail mowers). On the other hand, sheer cutting is the result of using reel mowers that cut with a scissors-type action. This is the type of mowing machines that can be used to create a striping or creative pattern on the field. Such striping patterns can be seen on professional baseball and professional football fields on game days. The reel mower pushes the blades of the grass down in one direction. When the mower is moved in the opposite direction on the return cut, again pushing the blades in the opposite direction, there is created an appearance of both dark and light shaded grass on the field (Trotter, 1996, pp. 62-63).

CONCEPT #278: *A little bit of thatch is desirable—too much thatch can inhibit growth of roots and grass.*

Similar to watering efforts, cutting of grasses should not be done on a regular schedule but rather only as needed. In fact, excessive mowing can result in an accumulation of too much thatch. What is thatch? Well, it is nothing more than a layer of organic material that is decomposing while sitting between the dirt or soil and the living turf or grass. A little bit of thatch is fine, in fact, it is highly desirable in that it serves as a cushion for the ground should participants hit the dirt.

However, too much thatch can prove to be a negative. Too much thatch can choke the grass by inhibiting or preventing altogether water, fertilizer and other nutrients from penetrating the too-thick organic substance and reaching the all-important root system. An overabundance of thatch can also prove hazardous to athletes with cleats on their shoes as the cleats can get caught in the thatch resulting in potential ankle and knee injuries. Thus, systematic removal (thatching) of this potential impediment, twice a year and more frequently if needed, is suggested to prevent this buildup of a barrier that can prove cataclysmic to the root system. A 1/8th of an inch of thatch is no problem in most cases. Thicker patches might prove to be a potential problem.

7. Pest Control—Weeds, Fungi and Insects

Any comprehensive and effective program of field and grass management must include pest control, which includes weeds, fungi and insects. Weed management is influenced by three factors, (1) the species of grasses and weeds, (2) the type of usage of the field (light, moderate or heavy), and (3) the season of use (Lewis, 1994). The objective is to be able to create a turf or ground cover that is vigorous, strong and competitive with weeds. Weeds not only look bad but they compete for water and fertilizer with grass. Strong grass (leafs) will choke out weeds if the grass is allowed to get a competitive head start. Weeds overtake the ground when grass is in a weakened condition and is unable to stave off the emergence of the weeds. Thus, strong, vibrant and vigorous grass is one of the best determinants in reducing weed problems.

CONCEPT #279: *Healthy grasses and turf help keep weeds in check.*

Insects and diseases can ravage turf. Don't hesitate to seek help from area universities or county extension offices to detect potential problems and identify insects and diseases that are threatening your fields. There are a variety of pest control products that can be safely used to combat potential disasters. The key is to get to the root (no pun intended) of the problem early and to address the challenge with both barrels of the proverbial shotgun. Hesitation and procrastination are not qualities of successful outdoor facility managers.

Delivery of Distribution Systems

Pest control products (such as pre-emergence and post-emergence herbicides) may be spread on the soil when rain is anticipated because most such products need to have moisture to be effective. However, not so in the case of fungicides. When distributing fungicides it is best to have them land on soil that is dry. A variety of distribution techniques can be used to broadcast the numerous pest control material such as spreader, sprayer, aerator, mower, etc.

One caution. Be sure and have the individual who is involved in using pest control products wear protective clothing while spraying or spreading and that this person has the necessary applicator's license that is applicable in your locale.

8. *Providing Relief for Beleaguered Fields through a Rotation System*

Perhaps one of the easiest solutions to giving fields and grassy areas a breather from the heavy usage and activity of recreational or competitive physical activity is to simply take that specific field or area out of circulation for a period of time. That is, utilize other fields for the activity and allow the heavily worn facility to have a rest, a breather. This period of rest will enable the roots and grass to make a much needed comeback on the beleaguered field.

CONCEPT #280:   ***Don't destroy your own field or playing area by overuse or misuse.***

Of course this sounds easier than it is in actual practice. For those sports organizations that do not have extra fields to which to rotate activities this option is not available to them. Nevertheless, supervisors should attempt to explore all possible avenues in which additional fields may be used so as to provide a period of down time for the much worn or damaged field to make a come back.

One should not destroy one's own field through use, misuse or abuse. During the down time major repairs and renovations can be initiated to assist the soil, root system and grasses to recuperate from the wear and tear of heavy use. In many instances, time is a great healer with Mother Nature providing much of the way of assistance to rejuvenate a tired field.

9. *Reconstructing and Recrowning*

Reconstruction of a field involves heavy-duty repairs as well as sizeable sums of money. Some examples of reconstruction include digging up the ground under and around a football field to install new subsurface drainage pipes or tiles or removing the top surface of a baseball field and replacing the soil with an upgraded version. Recrowning involves improving drainage by digging up surface of a field and creating an elevated portion of ground in its middle running from one end to the other with the land gradually slopping to the sides. The result is that water run-off can easily move from the center of the field to the sides where subsurface drainage system can take the excess water to the storm drains.

10. *Draining Water (Drainage)*

Lack of proper drainage is the bane of most outdoor facility managers and coaches of outdoor sports. There are three kinds of permanent drainage systems used to combat the problem of surface water on fields. First is the passive system or surface drainage in which the slope of the field (crowning) allows the water to drain or run off the field. The second system is referred to as the subsurface system. This involves moving water through the

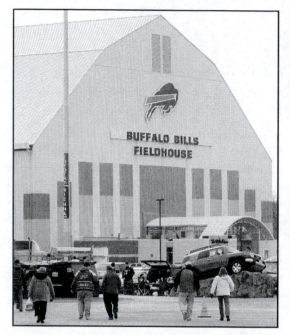

Teams in Northern Climates Face Challenges from the Weather—Special Indoor Practice Facility of the New York Buffalo Bills
[courtesy of Buffalo Bills, Scott Berchtold, photographer]

porous level of soil and sand at the top of the ground to the subsurface where the water is collected at various collection points and guided along an underground perforated tile system to various drainpipes and into the storm sewer or other suitable outlet. The third system of drainage is a combination of the two methods. Additionally, there is yet a fourth technique utilized to remove surface water, especially in an emergency. This involves sucking the water via mechanical means, by electric or gas pumps, and moving it to an area where it can drain away from the affected field.

By some estimates, 80% to 90% of all athletic fields are native soil-fields with heavy clay content that does little for proper drainage. Drainage can be maximized by having turf that relies on a root-zone mixture that is heavy on sand, light on clay, with sufficient amount of peat to provide nutrients for the grass. The presence of sand enables excess water to drain naturally under the surface. (Berg, 1993).

Managers should not overlook the fact that drainage is equally important, if not more so, with outdoor tracks. Inappropriate track drainage is likened to a vehicle without adequate tires. A lack of adequate track drainage significantly reduces the life of the track itself. It is being "penny wise and pound foolish" to the utmost. Two organizations that provide surface design and installation specifications are the American Sports Builders Association as well as the International Association of Athletics (IAAF) (Bynum, 2006).

ARTIFICIAL TURF VERSUS NATURAL TURF

There is no definitive evidence that artificial turf is safer than natural grass (Forbes, 1993; Patterozzi, 1997, p. 41). Artificial turf has been around for a generation. Today, the newest innovation is what is referred to as hybrid fields that use an integrated package of natural and synthetic elements. For example, that the Baltimore Ravens designed and constructed their new hybrid turf field at Memorial Stadium around a combination of natural and synthetic elements, including a sophisticated drainage and a system that heats the field during inclement weather (Schmid 1997, September, p. 42). Because of the multitude of different systems that are available today there is no consensus as to which type is superior. That is a decision that must be made by management (Patterozzi, 1997).

LIGHTING

There are two factors that are used to determine quality lighting for athletic and recreational activities. The first is the brightness of the light as measured in *footcandles.* Average sunshine is considered to be 8,000 footcandles during the summer months. Moonlight is a mere .01 footcandles. The second is the *uniformity ratio.* This is the smoothness or evenness of light throughout the area over which the light is dispersed. Uniformity is commonly conceptualized as a comparison between the darkest location and the brightest location of the total area being lit.

> **CONCEPT #281:** *Proper lighting facilitates safe and appropriate physical activities.*

Outdoor Security Lighting

In selecting the most appropriate outdoor lighting for security purposes one should consider the effectiveness of the lights and their efficiency (cost, etc.). Additionally, management should take into consideration the quality of light given off and how people as well as colors look under various lights. In terms of getting the "most bang for one's buck," high-intensity discharge (HID) bulbs give off the most light for the least amount of electricity. While these bulbs are more expensive to purchase they last up to 20 times as long (20,000 hours compared to 700-1,000 hours) as a standard light bulb (Dulley, 1997).

Three popular types of security HID bulbs include (1) high-pressure sodium, (2) metal halide and (3) mercury vapor. High-pressure sodium lights provide a warm golden glow while enhancing natural colors. Metal halide is a cool white light that is used to emphasize blues and greens. Mercury vapor lights, like metal halide lights, enhances plant and focal points among grounds and gardens. Mercury vapor lights also enhance excellent moonlighting effects outdoors (Dulley, 1997, p. 3-E).

Artificial lights are also calibrated or categorized according to the specific color-rendering index (CRI). This is defined as the ability of the light source to accurately reproduce the color of the object under the artificial light in comparison with sunlight. The resulting value is given as a percent where sunlight is 100%. For example, an incandescent lamp has a CRI of 95% and is recognized as projecting a warm feeling. On the other hand, the high-pressure sodium lamp has a much hotter feel and a CRI of only 22%. And, metal halide lamps, with a cool feeling has a CRI of 70%. Metal halide lamps are the lights of choice for most outdoor playing field due to their high CRI, lamp life, lumens per watt, and the high color temperature (Thieken & Love, 1995).

Comparisons of Lighting Requirements at Different Events

Lighting for sporting events has been around for a long time. The first baseball night game took place in Lynn, MA in 1924. This was some 11 years before the Major League's first official night game at Cincinnati's Crosley Field in 1935. Today major league's baseball games usually have 300-footcandles in the infield and 200 in the outfield. The requirements for AAA and AA teams are 100 footcandles for the infield and 70 in the outfield with a 1.2 to 1 uniformity ratio. Recreational baseball and softball competition typically requires 30 footcandles in the infield and 20 footcandles in the outfield as does Little League baseball (Lindstrom, 1993, pp. 47, 50). On the other hand, high schools stadiums with fewer than 2000 seats require 30 footcandles, with more than 2000 seats 50 footcandles. College and university stadiums (NCAA) will have 50 footcandles while professional teams' stadiums will have lighting at 150 footcandles (Rogers, 1994).

Pool Lighting

Swimming pool facilities need a high intensity discharge lamp such as the metal halide type. High pressure sodium lamps are also appropriate. These tend to be more efficient than the metal halide variety. Their drawback, however, is that they lack the sharpness or crispness as well as the spectrum of color that metal halide seems to project. They also don't last as long. (Johnston, 1996).

Parking Lot Lights

Low-pressure sodium lights, as well as mercury lights, can be used for parking lots as well as for weight rooms. However, low-pressure sodium lights, while being very efficient, has poor color quality (monochromatic yellow) and they are slow to start up (Dulley, 1997). However, neither would be appropriate for areas that require reading or quiet concentration since they cast a blue light and are slightly noisy.

THE IMPORTANCE FOR SPORT MANAGERS TO BE KNOWLEDGEABLE ABOUT FACILITIES

The world of sport management has many challenges. One area in which there are challenges in abundance is facilities. Not only are the management and maintenance of facilities very important but the process of dealing with facilities can be very complicated and time consuming. There is so much to learn about facilities and the various components associated with facilities that the typical sport manager or administrator (other than one who is officially designated as "facility manager") is hard pressed to keep up with the latest trends and innovations.

Nevertheless, it is very important in today's fast paced world of sport and business to at least be generally knowledgeable and aware of the basics associated with the management and maintenance of selected indoor and outdoor facilities. The extent of one's knowledge will be dependent upon the exact job responsibilities one holds within the organization. Nevertheless, sport administrators in the 21st century will find it hard to operate within a sport business environment without coming into contact with some aspect of the facility side of the organization. To that extent, it behooves every future member of management to strive to develop and maintain a minimal level of competency and knowledge in the fast moving and expansive world of sport facilities.

CONCLUSIONS

For many sport organizations the management and maintenance of facilities comprise a major responsibility for the entity. Thus, sport managers who find themselves involved with such businesses or organizations must be familiar with the basic fundamentals and foundational knowledge relating to indoor and/or outdoor facility management and maintenance. Of course, not all sport managers will necessarily have direct oversight responsibility for the day-to-day management and/or maintenance of either indoor or outdoor facilities. Nevertheless, it is important that such sport managers be sufficiently knowledgeable that they can adequately interact with, supervise and successfully delegate to others who do have such day-to-day oversight responsibility.

REFERENCES

Aerators. (1997, November). *Turf,* p. C-3.

Berg, R. (1993). High Tech Turf. *Athletic Business, 17*(5), 47-50.

Browser, III., J. E. (1997, Nov). Move over, metal. *Athletic Business, 21*(1), 16.

Bynum, M. (2003, November). Clean sweep. *Athletic Business, 15*(11), 86,-88, 90, 92.

Bynum M. (2006). No drain, no gain. *Athletic Business, 30*(9), 54-55.

Catalano, J. (1995, Feb. Mar). A gym divided. *Athletic Management, VII*(2), 49-53.

Catalano, J. (2003). 20 Questions underfoot. *Athletic Management, XV*(2), 55-58.

Cohen, A. (1992, March). Easy does it. *Athletic Business, 16*(3), 53-57.

Dernoeden, P. (1997, March). 6 turf diseases and their cures. *Lawn & Landscape, 18*(3), 39, 42, 44-45, 48, 50, 52, 54.

Dillon, J. (1996, August/September). Changes in the changing room. *Athletic Management, VIII(5)*, 45-49.

Dulley, J. (1997). Outdoor security lighting best deterrent to vandals. *Democrat and Chronicle*, p. 3-E.

Fawcett, P. (2004). Annual Checkup. *Athletic Business, 28*(3), 61, 62, 64, 66.

Forbes, G. (1993, Nov. 18). The jury's still out on Astro Turf. *USA Today*, p. 5-c.

Glazier, J. (1997, June/July). From weight room to fitness center. *Athletic Management, IX*(4), 42-46.

Heugli, R., Richards, T., Graffis, K., Kroll, B., & Epley, B. (1991, May). *Weights & Measures.* AD, pp. 18-21.

Howell, C.N. (1997, March). Better root growth. *Lawn & Landscape, 18*(3), 56, 59, 62, 64-65.

Indyk, H.W. (1997, June). The basics of soil management. *Turf,* pp. A6-A11, A15, A16, A18-A19.

Johnston, R. (1996, December). Inside-out pools. *Athletic Business, 20*(12), 81-84, 86-88.

Lindstrom, C. (1993, September). Light up the night. *Athletic Business, 17*(9), 47-48, 50-51.

Lewis, W. (1994, April/May). Weeding out unwanted growth. *Athletic Management, VI*(3), 28-30, 32, 37, 40.

Patterozzi, V. (1997, September). Turf tech. *Athletic Business, 21*(9), 41-43, 46-48.

Rogers, J. (1994, December). Bright prospects. *Athletic Business, 18*(12), 52-56.

54:

Rogers, J.N. & Stier, J. C. (1995, May). Sowing Seeds. *Athletic Business, 19*(5), 49-56.

Schmid, S. (1992, May). Grass – roots maintenance. *Athletic Business, 16*(5), 51-55.

Schmid, S (1997, September). Year-round turf. *Athletic Business, 21*(9), 42.

Schmid, S. (1997, October). Pool maintenance. *Athletic Business, 21*(10), 47-48, 50, 52, 54, 56.

Sherman, R. M. (1997, October). Strengthening weight rooms. *Athletic Business, 21*(10), 23, 74, 76, 78, 80.

Staying out of hot water, part 2. (1993, January). *Athletic Business, 17*(1), 17.

Stier, Jr., W. F. (1991, Fall). A winning combination—Physical education. American School & University—*Facilities, Purchasing and Business Administration, 63*(6), 52f-52h.

Strock, R. E. (1991, April). A dozen locker room dilemmas—solved. *Club Business International, 12*(4), 31-37.

The Right Lockers. (1996, November). *Athletic Business, 20*(11), 52-58.

Thieken, H. & Love, G. (1995, Apr/May). Let there be light. *Athletic Management, VII*(3), 26, 28-30.

Trotter, B. (1996, January). The cutting edge. *Athletic Business, 20*(1), 61-64.

Vest, S. E. (1995, March). Sound sanitation. *Athletic Business, 14*(3), 39-44.

Viklund, R. (1995, July). High-performance floors. *Athletic Business, 19*(7), 41-42, 44-47.

Viklund: , R. & Coons, J. (1997, Sept). Locker rooms. *Athletic Business, 21*(9), 63-66, 68-71.

Watson, J. R. (1998, January). Waterworks. *Athletic Business, 22*(1), 59-61, 64.

Readings and Organizations Regarding Safety and Facilities

1. The U.S. Commission Product Safety Commission's web site is: www.cpsc.gov/cgi-bin/recalldb/key.asp [click on "Guidelines for Retrofitting Bleachers"]
2. American Society for Testing an Materials, 100 Barr Harbor Drive West Conshohocken, PA 19103 610-832-9500—Publishes a set of public playground equipment standards (F 1487-95).
3. American Sports Builders Association—track specification and drainage
4. The International Association of Athletics (IAAF). Guidebook dealing with structing outdoor tracks and drainage.
5. The National Spa and Pool Institute (NSPI) and American National Standards Institute (ANSI)—revised guidelines [American National Standard for Public Spas (ANSI/NSPI)]

DISCUSSION TOPICS

1. Indicate some critical factors when dealing with a swimming pool, both in terms of management and maintenance.
2. Explain some general concepts relative to the maintenance of outdoor fields for recreation and/or competitive use.
3. Arbitrarily select five elements (components) of an indoor sport facility and explain factors relating to the maintenance and upkeep of such components.
4. When planning for a new facility the organizers/administrators should plan well in advance to insure there are sufficient funds for two purposes. What are these two purposes?

5. What is the difference between reconstruction and recrowning of fields?

6. What are the advantages of using dividers within a sports facility such as a school?

7. How should an administrator go about cleaning up a fecal or vomit accident?

8. What are some common myths of pool maintenance?

9. What are two factors related to the weather that can create havoc with the condition of fields, turf and grasses?

10. Why would you use any of the three popular types of security HID bulbs?

Chapter

10 Securing, Assessing, Motivating and Managing Personnel

CHAPTER HIGHLIGHTS

This chapter will help the reader to:

- Understand the importance of providing excellent compensation packages for high quality employees;
- Recognize how important personnel are to the success of any sport organization;
- List five types of personnel within an organization;
- Reveal the advantages and disadvantages of outsourcing;
- Understand the importance of personality and attitude in selecting personnel;
- Appreciate the potential value of diversity within personnel of a sport entity;
- Comprehend the process of attracting, selecting, hiring and keeping quality personnel;
- Indicate potential sources of personnel for various sport, recreation and fitness organizations and programs;
- Outline the 20-70-10 concept of ranking by General Electric;
- Acknowledge the importance of networking within the personnel process;
- Explain the relevance of various federal laws pertaining to the hiring process and the use of interns;
- List various electronic home pages where job announcements may be found;
- Differentiate between various qualification parameters of potential employees;

Coach Mike Krzyzewski, Duke University—
Outstanding Coaches Bring Much Respect
and Positive Exposure to the School
and the Athletic Program
*[courtesy of Duke University
Sports Information Department]*

323

- Cite the purposes of evaluating personnel and various techniques of such evaluation;
- Explain the Peter Principle;
- Outline and explain the six components of the personnel process;
- Describe the advantages of using a departmental or organizational Personnel Handbook.

A GLIMPSE INTO THE HEART OF ANY ORGANIZATION— PERSONNEL MANAGEMENT

At the heart of every sport entity or program, regardless of whether it is a for profit or a not-for-profit organization, are the people who work with and for the organization. Adlai Stevenson is credited with the statement that: "There are only three rules of sound management: pick good people, tell them not to cut corners and back them to the limits. *But remember, picking good people is the most important*" [emphasis added] (Sattler, 1994, p. 40). Another truism is that employers who hire the right person, provide the right training and offers the right support are going to be way ahead of the employment and retention game (Tulenko, 2003).

It is indeed the people who work for the organization, the personnel, who make the organization what it is. It is the people who work within the organization who make the organization the success or failure that it is or will become. This is true whether the so-called "people" are top level administrators, middle managers, supervisors, or entry-level staff.

CONCEPT #282: *When defining the terms "staff" or "personnel" one should include both paid employees as well as volunteer helpers.*

It is imperative that managers and administrators view the terms "staff" or "personnel" in the broadest sense to include those who are paid and those who volunteer. Today, many sport administrators find themselves frequently working (sometimes on a daily basis) with a variety of volunteers. It would be a severe mistake not to consider these volunteers to be anything other than members of one's staff. Granted that there are differences, in light of special circumstances and varying situations, in how volunteers are treated when compared with salaried staff. Nevertheless, both categories of people—paid and volunteer—should be viewed as "personnel."

CONCEPT #283: *The ultimate success of every organization is dependent upon the people who make up that organization.*

Experienced and successful sport managers recognize that the eventual success or failure of their individual organizations is dependent upon the quality of the people comprising the staff—both paid staff and volunteer staff (Stier, 1997a, March 23). Similarly, the success of individual programs or activities is also dependent upon the individuals who have responsibility for implementing the programs and carrying out the activities associated with such programs. Harvey Mackey, president of Mackay Envelope Corp. and author of *Swim With the Sharks Without Being Eaten Alive* and *Beware the Naked Man Who Offers You His Shirt,* states that success in business is not simply a matter of "how and what to buy cheap and sell high," but rather "a better understanding of people" (Success, 1988, p. 32).

PERSONNEL MANAGEMENT— A MAJOR RESPONSIBILITY OF SPORT MANAGERS

Thus, the skill level and scope of competencies possessed and demonstrated by personnel, at all levels, are keys to having an effective and efficient organization, one that achieves its various objectives, goals, and ultimate mission(s). A major responsibility of today's administrator is to be on top of what is referred to as "personnel management", that is, *being capable and willing to attract, train and retain qualified staff and to successfully work with various personnel within the organization.* That is what this chapter is all about, working with individuals who make up, in one way or another, the organization's team.

CONCEPT #284: *Competent sport managers surround themselves with superior staff.*

It is vital that administrators and managers surround themselves with bright, articulate, motivated, competent and dedicated personnel. The reason for this is obvious. No person in the business world of sport, in today's society, can be successful unless that individual is willing to work with others <u>and</u> to delegate appropriate responsibility and commensurate authority to others, i.e., personnel and staff.

Sport managers and administrators can look brilliant if they have capable and skilled personnel working for and with them. On the other hand, these same managers and administrators can look truly incompetent or woefully inadequate if their personnel or staff members fail to perform as expected, and the resultant failure reflects negatively upon the administrators in charge.

> *CONCEPT #285:   **Teamwork and teambuilding are two essential components of personnel management.***

Competent managers must have abilities, must possess competencies—this goes without saying. However, a significant aspect of this competency is the ability to recognize abilities and competencies in other people. Additionally, managers need to demonstrate confidence in their personnel, give them the tools they need to do their jobs, provide adequate support as well as adequate supervision and training. This, of course, implies teamwork and teambuilding, two vital elements of any successful business or organization (Barlow, 1993).

Teamwork is so important because "8 out of 10 US workers are involved in some kind of workplace teamwork " (Balog, 1995, p. 2-B). Teamwork among personnel implies skill in interpersonal relationships, a skill that is highly prized in the sport business world. In fact, it is estimated that as high as 85% of employees who fail at their jobs do so because of a lack of interpersonal skills or what business leaders refer to "personality."

An individual managerial approach toward one's staff is highly advisable since the "one-size-fits all" concept is not very effective or efficient in the modern day workplace. The *golden rule* for effective managers today would seem to say that good managers should "treat each person as he would like to be treated, bearing in mind who he is" (Memmott, 1999, p. 8-D).

FIVE TYPES OR CLASSIFICATIONS OF PERSONNEL OR STAFF

Generally speaking, there are five types or classifications of staff members or personnel working for, with, or on behalf of any sport entity. First, there are those individuals who are employed on a full time basis. Second, there are those who are employed on a part-time basis. The third category of personnel includes those individuals who are volunteers. The fourth category of individuals includes those persons who serve as paid consultants. The fifth and last category includes those individuals who are hired by the sport business on a contracting out basis.

WORKING WITH PAID STAFF, VOLUNTEERS, CONSULTANTS, AND "CONTRACT" COMPANIES

Depending upon the situation, there are varying advantages for the sport entity to utilize different categories of personnel or staff. It is up to the administration to assess their own situation and the varying circumstances in which the organization finds itself before committing the resources of the organization towards the use of paid (full time or part-time), volunteer, consultant or outsourcing staff or personnel (Stier, 1989). There are advantages as well liabilities of using each type of staffing for sport programs. It is up to those individuals who have the power and authority to make such decisions to come up with a rationale for moving in one direction or another in terms of the type of staffing that will be pursued for any given task, activity or program.

> **CONCEPT #286:** *There are different advantages of working with paid staff, volunteers, consultants, and outsourcing companies.*

1. *Working with Full Time Paid Staff*

Full time paid staff include those individuals, as the term implies, who work full time for the sport entity and receive a decent, living wage and, typically, full benefits. These are the persons whose livelihoods depend upon the sport entity that hires them. And, as such, these employees owe their total allegiance and professional time commitment to their employers. Securing full time employees is a major commitment on behalf of the organization and involves a significant financial stake as well. And, when dealing with full time employees the employing business is faced with rather strict legal interpretations relative to how these full time employees are to be treated in respect to terms of employment, expectations, evaluations, benefits and termination.

> **CONCEPT #287:** *Many sport jobs involve both salary and a commission type arrangement—especially at the entry level or with sales positions.*

It should be noted that in many instances the concept of a full time paid position may involve a specified salary plus additional income in the form of commission based upon some previously agreed upon formula. This is frequently found in professional sports where the employee is significantly involved in sales.

For example, in the health, fitness and wellness industry it is common for salespeople in the area of memberships to be paid a salary plus commission based on the number of new members or renewals secured. In some sport businesses salaries for some personnel might be totally based upon the commission concept. In professional sports, commission plus a base salary is common in some specific jobs involving selling and marketing tickets to events.

2. *Working with Part-Time Paid Staff*

Part-timers are those employees who have limited rights as employees (in comparison to full time employees) and, usually, no significant benefits in terms or vacations or life, health or dental insurance, etc. Also, part-time employees, as the term implies, are rarely paid sufficient monies to be able to earn a living wage. Rather, these individuals typically earn minimum sums from the businesses for their part-time work. Unless these individuals have other sources of income such as retirement benefits from prior place of employment (or is independently wealthy), they frequently must supplement the part-time salary from the sport business with income from other employment.

Thus, the loyalty and the time commitment of the typical part-time employee are frequently also limited or "part-time." Yet, for many tasks, securing part-time help or assistance is indeed the best way to proceed. The use of part-time employees usually necessitated when the job is very specific and involves tasks that do not require persons working on task for 40 hours a week. Also, part-time help is frequently necessitated when the rate of pay is going to be very low.

CONCEPT #288: *Administrators should treat full and part-time personnel similarly and yet differently.*

Whether the salaried personnel are full time or part-time, there are times when they should be treated in a similar fashion, if not an identical manner. This is because employers and supervisors need to build a cohesive team consisting of all of the paid staff. Thus, in this light both part-time and full time staff need to be dealt with similarly as both groups of personnel frequently need to work together to accomplish tasks and to reach objectives and goals.

However, on the other hand, these two groups of personnel need to be treated differently because of the very nature of their employment. For example, part-time employees may not be involved in some of the high level, decision-making meetings because they are indeed part-time staff. On the other hand, in some instances these part-timers might be included in some discussions and meetings.

Then there is the matter of confidentiality. In many situations part-time employees have no need for some facts or knowledge nor do they need to be privy to confidential information or future plans. There is no all-encompassing rule or regulation that states when or to what degree part-timers are to be involved in such activities or to be provided with information or knowledge. This is an individual judgment call by the management and individual supervisors depending upon the situation and any extenuating circumstances.

The point that supervisors and administrators need to remember is that just because a person is a part-time employee does not mean that that individual can't have real contributions (in terms of ideas, suggestions, questions, etc.) to make just as any full time employee. Nevertheless, there are times when the part-timer needs to be treated differently than a full timer staffer because of the nature of their employment.

3. *Working with Volunteers*

Whenever volunteers are involved it is imperative that supervisors and administrators recognize that these persons occupy a rather unique position in light of the other personnel associated with the sport organization or business. This uniqueness is that these people can up and quit at any time if they are not satisfied, if they feel that they are not appreciated, if they feel that their efforts have no positive impact, or if they are unhappy in any way. Paid employees can't really do this as readily. Even part-time employees who find themselves in real need of the extra cash often do not have the luxury of just quitting. Not receiving monetary payment for one's services places the volunteer in a slightly different situation than the paid staff member.

Administrators certainly need to recognize the subtle and not so subtle distinctions between their paid and volunteer personnel. However, both categories (paid and volunteer) should be thought of as the organization's personnel for both represent the sport entity to the general public as well as to the organization's constituencies. If these people, paid or volunteer, represent the organization—or are perceived to represent the organization—then it behooves the administrators and supervisors to see to it that volunteers act and behave in as professional a manner as the paid staff.

> **CONCEPT #289:** *Expect volunteers to demonstrate the same professionalism, dedication and image as paid personnel.*

Volunteers represent the sport entity just as much as paid staff does. Often the general public is unable to distinguish between volunteer staff and paid staff. To the public, staff members are staff members, workers are workers. One of the fundamental tenets to effective personnel management is recognizing the importance of seeing that all personnel, whether paid or volunteer, bring credit and distinction to the organization in everything that they do or don't do.

Towards this end it is advisable to employ various strategies that will impart to and impress upon the volunteers the importance of assuming the role or persona of a regular staff member or personnel in terms of the quality of their image and work on behalf of the sport entity. This act of *inclusion* towards the part-timers (in terms of expectations) is imperative if successful teamwork and team building is to take place. And teamwork and team building is essential for true success in the business world of sport.

Just as with part-time paid employees, there is the ever-important matter of confidentiality that must be addressed when dealing with volunteers. Because these individuals are volunteers and not paid staff there are some things that should remain confidential. There are reasons for volunteers not to have access to some information, some data, and some plans—because of the nature of their association with the sport entity. Keeping some information confidential in no way diminishes the importance of the volunteers or of the work that they do for the organization.

4. *Working with Consultants*

The use of outside (paid) consultants enables the sport organization to secure the temporary use of experts, with specialized skills, to address specific needs. Typically, the use of consultants is necessitated or warranted when one of three situations exists. First, when the sport organization does not possess personnel or staff with the necessary skills, competencies or experiences to address a specific task or solve a particular problem, all within a specified period of time. Second, when the organization cannot spare qualified staff or doesn't want to redirect the efforts of their regular personnel to address a specific issue, problem or situation. And third, when there is a need for a fresh perspective, a different vantage point, or an outside expert's opinion(s) (expertise) concerning a particular issue, a problem, or situation.

CONCEPT #290:   *The use of paid consultants can provide a new perspective concerning a particular problem, issue or situation.*

Consultants are often referred to as "hired guns" as they come to an organization from the outside with specific skills, competencies and experiences (and a fresh perspective) to deal with a definitive situation. This is not a negative conceptualization. Their major responsibility is to provide, within a temporary time frame, information, data and advice as well as to make assessments, carry out evaluations and to provide specific recommendations for the organization to consider.

It is not normally the job of the consultant(s) to carry out or implement the recommendations. Rather, it is the job of consultant(s) to provide insight, assessment, input, suggestions and recommendations. It is up to those in authority within the sport entity to weigh the data, the information, the input and the recommendations—and then to decide whether to implement the suggestions fully, partially or not at all. Sport administrators need not abdicate their responsibilities when employing expert, outside consultants. Rather, consultants are used as another tool or another source of information or data. The final decisions must still be made by those administrators and managers who have the power, authority and responsibility to do so.

> **CONCEPT #291:** *Sport administrators must not abdicate their administrative and managerial responsibilities when working with outside consultants.*

There are numerous types of consultant situations. A single person might serve as an individual consultant. Other situations might call for a corporation or group of consultants and involve any number of different individuals, all performing various tasks on behalf of the sport organization. Regardless of the actual form that the consultancy takes, the essential elements include: (1) the consultant(s) is(are) hired from outside the sport organization, (2) the consultants are paid for a specific task assigned by the sport organization, (3) the consultancy is for a designated period of time, (4) the consultants are responsible for how they are to address the task, problem or assignment, (5) payment is for the specific task(s) identified, (6) financial payment is made by the sport entity directly to the consultant (or the consulting firm) for the job(s) or task(s) agreed to, and, (7) the consultants are responsible for making their recommendations or providing their services to the sport administrators in the form that the consultants deem most fitting or suitable.

As with regular paid staff and volunteers, consultants can also be viewed as "personnel" of the sport entity and as such can affect how the public and various constituencies view the organization. Thus, it is imperative that the behavior and actions of such consultants be exemplary in every sense of the word. How the public views consultants working on behalf of the sport entity reflects directly upon the sport organization, its programs and activities, its personnel, and everything that the organization represents. Thus, it is important that sport managers pay strict attention to the actions and image of their paid consultants.

5. *Working with "Contract" Companies or Firms*

Contracting out jobs is a common method in which a sport business is able to secure, on a regular and consistent basis, professional assistance in performing a job or assuming a specific responsibility. Contrary to consulting, contracting is a longer-term prospect and calls for the outside company and its personnel to actually perform (not just advise but to execute or implement) a specific job or series of jobs on behalf of the sport business—for a long period of time. Examples abound and include, but are not limited to, contracting out security for home events, securing secretarial assistance (from temp service firms), contracting out for financial services such as accounting, etc., contracting out food and/or concession operations, contracting out cleaning and/or maintenance of facilities, and contracting out travel arrangements, etc.

There are numerous advantages of contracting out for services and jobs. Some of these benefits include: (1) not having to devote the time, regular staff or energies to these jobs or tasks, (2) taking advantage of the highly technical expertise and extensive experience of firms and their employees who specialize in these types of responsibilities and activities, (3) not having to spend time training staff to perform special or technical jobs, and (4) passing on the legal responsibility and (in many cases) the risk to the firm or company accepting the contract to perform the job(s) or task(s).

Outsourcing—A Form of Contracting Out

A type of contracting out is called *outsourcing*. Outsourcing refers to the management of the sport business or company taking jobs that are currently being filled by regular full or part-time employees and outsourcing these jobs out to firms whose staff will, in the future, do these jobs and perform these tasks. Thus, there will be employees of an outside firm being paid by the outside firm and performing jobs or tasks on behalf of the sport organization. *One possible result of this type of arrangement is that the sport entity's regular staff who had previously performed these jobs or tasks find themselves with no justification for being employed and frequently find themselves seeking employment elsewhere.*

Contracting out makes a lot of sense for sport businesses in respect to those areas of responsibilities that are rather specialized or require very special training, such as in terms of travel, security, food operations, etc. The more specialized and complicated the tasks are the more likely they will be looked at as possible candidates for contracting out. Similarly, the more distant the tasks are from the primary operation of the sport entity the more likely they are to be contracted out.

CONCEPT #292:   *Contracting out can (sometimes) save money while improving service or performance.*

In reality, contracting out and outsourcing is done for one or two basic reasons. First, to save money (and/or time and headaches) on behalf of the sport firm. Second, to assure a high quality service that might not have been possible otherwise without a great deal of effort, time and money. It frequently comes down to the financial bottom line—how can things be accomplished with the least financial exposure or risk?

Risks Associated with Contracting Out

What are the risks to contracting out in all of its different forms or variations? On the downside, there is one fear that every sport manager has in terms of contracting out or outsourcing jobs. This apprehension is well deserved and it relates to the fact that the jobs (that are contracted out) might not be done properly or with as much professionalism as desired or expected. There is always the danger that the management of the sport entity will lose a certain degree of oversight or power over the jobs that are contracted out or outsourced.

This is due to the fact that the company to whom the job was contracted out has direct, day-to-day supervisory responsibility and control over its personnel assigned to these tasks. *Nevertheless, it is still the sport business that will be held responsible, sometimes in the eyes of the law and always in the eyes of the public, if the employees of the firm contracted to do a job for the sport organization fails to do the job satisfactorily.* In this very real sense, these employees of an outside firm that has been contracted to do one or more specific jobs are seen by others (public and various constituencies) as the "personnel" or "staff" of the sport business. This has significant implications for the management of the sport business.

EXPECTATIONS OF STAFF AND PERSONNEL

As stated earlier in this chapter, personnel working for and with the sport organization are all important. The sport manager who understands how to work with one's staff and manage the overall personnel process will be much more successful than the would-be manager who does not. Sport businesses rely upon teamwork and cooperation as much, as if not more so, as the traditional sports team that so many sport businesses are involved with today. The key words are *cooperation* and *teamwork*. It cannot be overestimated how important these attributes are for the eventual success or failure of the organization and its programs.

Coaching Can Be a Demanding and Challenging Profession
[courtesy of Bemidji State University (BSU) Photography Services]

> *CONCEPT #293:*　*Staff and personnel who demonstrate an innate ability and willingness to learn and improve are worth their weight in gold.*

Expectations of Staff

A book (1999) by two of the Gallup organization's researchers, Marcus Buckingham and Curt Coffman, titled *First, Break All the Rules: What the World's Greatest Managers*

Do Differently, outlined and summarized the results of more than 80,000 managers and 1-million workers over the previous 25 years. At the core of the book was a look at the most productive workplaces. The following is a list of questions to which employees at the most productive workplaces answered in the affirmative (Murphy, 1999).

1. Do I know what is expected of me?
2. Do I have the materials and equipment I need to do my work right?
3. Do I have the opportunity to do what I do best every day?
4. In the last seven days, have I received recognition or praise for good work?
5. Does my supervisor, or someone at work, seem to care about me as a person?
6. Is there someone at work who encourages my development?

Desirable Characteristics of Staff

What do managers want from staff? They need and want people who are competent. People who are skilled (capable) in the tasks assigned to them. Individuals who possess cutting-edge proficiencies in areas critical to the organization's success. Individuals who are, for the most part, self-starters and who are self-motivated.

Managers need leaders. They also need followers (one can't be a leader all the time). They need persons who are loyal to their organization, the program and to the management. They need honest, dedicated and committed personnel. People with the proper attitude and personality. And, perhaps above all, individuals who have the ability and willingness to learn, to improve, to expand their horizons, and who don't think they know it all (Stier, 1990, p. 35).

Personality and Attitude—Twin Pillars
Essential Traits for Potential Personnel

Before a sport business or organization begins the process of adding new members to its personnel ranks it is imperative that management decide well in advance exactly what type of individual(s) would be most desirable, in terms of specific qualifications, experiences, skills, capabilities, competencies, personality, attitude and potential for professional growth. Only then should the search process be initiated. Without such soul searching the search process can be an exercise in futility.

Two characteristics that are receiving special attention by today's sport managers are personality and attitude. Although many skills can be learned on the job, some more easily than others, personality and attitude are two attributes that cannot. Both personality and attitude are the result of life's experiences in addition to formal education and interactions with other people (McDermott, 1993). Yet, both personality and attitude are very important for the professional engaged in the business of sport, at every level (Stier, 1994).

An individual who works in the people oriented world of sport and possesses an appropriate personality and a positive attitude has a tremendous advantage over the person who lacks these attributes. Kurt Einstein, a professor and behavioral scientist at the Einstein Institute in North Carolina delivered a speech several years ago in which he indicated that capability only leads to performance while personality leads to behavior. He also indicated that most failures in organizations are the result of people with the wrong personality attempting to perform the wrong job. "Personality must suit the work and vice versa, so 90 percent of what I teach is how to evaluate personality" (Balog, 1995, p. B-2).

The Value of Diversity within a Sport Organization

And, finally, there is the need for diversity within the organization in terms of personnel: Diversity in terms of their life's experiences as well as professional experiences; diversity in terms of skills and skill level; diversity in terms of culture; diversity in terms of gender; diversity in terms of race; diversity in terms of education; and diversity in terms of perspective.

Such diversity brings an important element to any organization specifically different perspectives and different ways to address tasks, challenges and problems. Diversity among the personnel can also bring about new options, new ideas, new approaches, etc. In short, diversity can be good for the organization because such diversity among individuals fosters creativity, ingenuity and productiveness—all desirable attributes for any business or organization.

THE CHALLENGE OF HIRING AND KEEPING QUALITY PERSONNEL

It is obvious that a quality organization, a quality program, and quality activities are dependent upon quality personnel. Although good personnel cannot guarantee a successful program, successful activities or a successful organization, it is almost impossible to have a successful sport organization or program without good personnel/staff. Just as "location, location and location" is a mantra within the world of real estate, "personnel, personnel and personnel" could be considered an equally significant mantra within the world of successful sport business.

> *CONCEPT #294:* **Desirable personnel are those individuals who exhibit superior skills, competencies, attitude, personality and the potential for professional growth.**

One of the recent trends in terms of selecting and hiring personnel is the so-called "raising of the bar." This refers to sport companies raising standards and expectations of its personnel (across the board). Even in tight job markets, in terms of companies and firms, many managers are taking the posture of going that extra step to insure that their new personnel are of the highest quality in terms of skills, competencies, attitude, personality and potential for professional growth (Jones, 1997).

Dealing with "People Problems" Outside of the Sport Organization

Because of the nature of most sport entities, whether they are professional sports teams, amateur sport teams, health and fitness organizations, recreation-related programs, profit or non-profit organizations, public or private firms, most of their problems or challenges will be because of people. It is just as simple as that.

CONCEPT #295:   *The majority of problems faced by a sport organization can be traced to people problems.*

Anytime any organization deals with people, with human beings, and most sport related organizations deal with a great many people, both internally and externally, it will be people who create the most challenges, difficulties and problems. It is sometimes a formidable task indeed dealing with various constituencies, the general public, (and in some cases) athletes, customers or patrons, fans, plus the press to boot.

DEALING WITH "PEOPLE PROBLEMS" INSIDE THE SPORT ORGANIZATION

Just as a majority of the problems facing most managers/administrators in the world of sport are generated from people, most of the internal difficulties within a sport organization itself can be traced to staff and personnel problems. Thus, it is very important, in fact it is critical for modern management to be extremely successful in securing the services of highly qualified, dedicated and professional personnel. Doing so will reduce, although not entirely eliminate, many of the problems that seem to plaque many sport businesses in this country.

CONCEPT #296:   *The majority of internal problems within a sport organization can be traced to staff/personnel problems.*

Having the support of the "right" personnel is the first step to being a successful sport organization. Locating, attracting, securing, retaining and working with competent staff is one of the fundamental challenges facing management today. Mastery of all of the phases in the personnel process are important for the health and well being of the sport entity, its personnel, and its programs or activities.

THE PERSONNEL PROCESS

What exactly is meant by the phrase "personnel process"? Although these words can mean different things to different people in different organizations, generally speaking, the phrase refers to activities, treatments, procedures, policies and practices affecting personnel throughout the time when these individuals are an integral part of the sport organization or being considered as potential personnel.

Thus, the personnel process involves steps or procedures to follow when dealing with staff (paid and volunteer) at every conceivable point along a continuum from the beginning of employment or association to the end or termination of said employment or association. This includes activities and decisions associated with or related to the search for new personnel, the interview process, hiring or selecting new personnel, treatment of personnel within the workplace, as well as those activities associated with termination, resignation or retirement.

> *CONCEPT #297:*   *Members of management must be fully aware of all aspects of the personnel process.*

In reality, the personnel process can be viewed as six distinct but yet related stages, activities or actions. First, the attempt to identify potential personnel or staff members who might be a suitable match for the organization. Second, the activity of officially seeking out and recruiting qualified candidates for a position (Byrnes, 2005). Third, the interviewing stage of potential personnel or staff. Fourth, once hired, the personnel process goes into a proactive stage in which management attempts to insure that the new staff member will experience success. The fifth stage consists of consistent, fair and continual evaluation and assessment of personnel. And, sixth, are actions that management takes in light of (as a consequence of) the perceived performance level of the each personnel.

1. *Identification of Potential Personnel or Staff Members for the Organization*

Almost every sport organization, at one time or another, becomes involved in the process of adding new personnel. One secret to the process of securing quality staff is for members of management to always be in a "search mode" or "watch mode." This simply means that one is always seeking to identify outstanding professionals. Once one becomes aware of highly skilled and competent professionals the business is in a better posture, if and when an opening becomes available sometime in the future, to seek out these persons as potential candidates for a vacancy.

This is sometimes referred to as "networking in reverse" and it refers to keeping an eye out for potential employees so that when one' own organization has an opening there already is a list of quality professionals whom management might wish to consider as new additions within their own organization or business. The best time to identify potential personnel is when the company doesn't presently need to hire anyone. Rather, developing a list, a database, of highly desirable individuals who might be suitable as additional personnel in the future is similar to planning for a rainy day, and can pay big dividends when a vacancy does occur.

> **CONCEPT #298:** *Maintain an active database of highly qualified individuals who might be candidates for potential positions before there is an actual need to fill such vacancies.*

Some sport administrators have voiced an opinion that they would prefer not to hire anyone for an opening within their sport entity who applied only as a result of an advertisement. Rather, these members of management take the position that they want to pursue the very best candidates for vacancies within their sport organizations or businesses by inviting outstanding individuals to apply for their position(s). The rationale being that high quality personnel might not apply on their own. Thus, it becomes the responsibility of management where the vacancy exists to take a proactive approach to seeking out highly qualified individuals, identifying possible candidates, and then pursuing them in an effort to entice them to become interested in the position.

Consequences of Imprudent Hiring

The consequences or risk of ending up with the wrong candidate for a position within a sport organization is too great to treat the selection process in a cavalier fashion. Rather, great care must be spent in terms of identifying the right candidate(s) for the position. This takes work, it takes effort, it takes commitment, and it takes time. But, the ultimate consequence, i.e., a competent professional (paid or volunteer) being a part of the personnel team can have far reaching, positive consequences.

> **CONCEPT #299:** *Poor hiring efforts usually results in poor hires and future problems for the organization as well as for the employee(s).*

A cardinal sin of the hiring process is for managers to rely on their overall or "gut level" impression of candidates. This informal "seat of the pants" approach by administrators is nothing more than relying on the process of intuitive judgment, a process that is suspect at best. Such efforts lack sophistication and substance. It is important that management be capable of correctly evaluating the actual skills and abilities of potential personnel if there is to be appropriate employee selection and eventual success on the job, in the real world of sport business (Hopp & Swedburg, 1996, p. 58). Such decision making should be based upon facts rather than hunches or gut feelings. Poor or inadequate selection of personnel can have devastating consequences for the climate of the organization itself as well as upon other staff. The risks are just too great for management to take unnecessary chances. Thus, the search and selection process of appropriate personnel should take top priority in today's sport business arena.

Consequences of Prudent Hiring

Selecting the right person for the right position or job has obvious benefits for the organization, management, other personnel as well as the new staff member. First of all, the job for which the new person was selected will be able to be accomplished and the objectives and/or goals realized. Second, the interpersonal relationships between individuals working within the organization will be facilitated.

> **CONCEPT #300:** *It is important to match the person to the job if one is to expect success with employees*

Prudent and appropriate hiring of personnel greatly decreases the likelihood of hiring an individual who may be disloyal, who may shirk one's duties and responsibilities, who may adopt a strict 9-to-5 pattern of work (clock watcher), and who is or becomes mismatched to the position or to the current personnel pool already in place. Thus, it is important for employers to determine those qualities, characteristics and traits that are essential for employees to be successful—and then seek candidates who possess those qualities (Alm, 2002).

> *CONCEPT #301:*   **Selecting quality people to work for the sport entity prevents many problems in the future.**

Third, less difficulties and fewer problems will result from the latest addition to the personnel "team." And fourth, prudent and timely selection of personnel may significantly reduce costs associated with employee turnover (e.g., hiring, screening, training, evaluating, etc.) (Miller, Pitts & Fielding, 1993, p. 47). Sport business success in the real world is difficult enough even with all appropriate and necessary resources. Without a resource as vital as skilled personnel such success can easily be out of reach regardless of the effort expended and the time spent working at it.

PUTTING TOGETHER A WINNING COMBINATION OF PERSONNEL

Sport managers at all levels shouldn't hesitate to seek personnel who may be more experienced or more highly skilled than they are. Administrators should not be intimidated by their own personnel just because these individuals possess unique skills or highly advanced skills (Robert, 1993). On the other hand, there is a very real danger of hiring overqualified individuals for specific positions. This is especially true in the health and fitness industry (Pessin, 1997, p. 32).

> *CONCEPT #302:*   **Managers should not feel intimidated in being surrounded by highly skilled, motivated and talented personnel.**

This is because overqualified individuals may feel that they are underutilized and become dissatisfied in their current positions—therefore being less productive than expected or even disruptive within the organization. And, then of course, there is always the possibility, the probability that this overqualified and dissatisfied staff member will end up leaving for another position as soon as a more suitable post becomes available. When that happens the entire search and hire process for the company must begin all over again.

Surrounding oneself with highly skilled and motivated people is one way to insure that the total team possesses sufficient experiences and adequate skills to get the job done. Managers have certain strengths and weaknesses. Wise and confident managers seek to surround themselves with individuals whose own skills, competencies and experiences compliment and add to the skills of the manager. In this instance, the whole is indeed greater than the sum of its parts. In this regard, synergism is an important element in the personnel process (Robert, 1993).

PROVIDING ADEQUATE COMPENSATION— ATTRACTING/RETAINING QUALITY PERSONNEL

An important concept that managers need to remember is that in order to attract and retain high quality personnel it is also necessary to be able to provide these much needed and attractive staff members an appropriate and attractive compensation package (salary and fringe benefits). Compensating quality employees involves two factors. The first is the actual salary itself. The second is the matter of the fringe benefits, both actual cash equivalent benefits (health insurance, dental and vision insurance, retirement contributions, use of vehicle, etc.) and non-cash benefits (office space, work environment, availability of co-workers, promotion opportunities, etc.). It is interesting to note that in a national study (Benefits, 1999) it was found that women (50%) were much more likely to be influenced by so-called "soft" benefits than were men (17%).

> **CONCEPT #303:**   *To attract and retain quality personnel requires meaningful compensation packages.*

SOURCES OF PERSONNEL

Where are potential employees found? What are the various sources of personnel for the ever-increasing number of sport organizations and businesses in the United States? Specifically, where does management go to obtain the necessary skilled workers needed in the modern day sport business? What options are open in terms of soliciting appropriate personnel in sport? The sources of potential employees are many as are the methods of finding out about potential employee candidates. Some of these techniques, tactics and strategies are presented below.

**Preparing for the Big Game—
Involves More than Mere Xs and Os**
[courtesy of University of Tennessee, Sports Information Office]

Retired or Older Workers

One source of ready-made staff is the retired or older individual who may be looking for an association, involving part-time or full time employment, with a sport organization or business. Research as well as antidotal information leads one to believe that there may be significant advantages to having the typical older and/or retired worker as a member of one's organization (Plummer, 1997). Some of these advantages include, but are not limited to, the following:

CONCEPT #304: *Not only is it illegal to discriminate against potential employees on the basis of age, it is also bad business practice.*

---

1. Anticipation of patrons' or customers' needs
2. Punctuality
3. Low absenteeism
4. Positive role model for younger counterparts
5. Possesses life's experiences
6. Maturity facilitates wiser decisions and positive interactions with people
7. Possesses a wide range of skills, competencies and capabilities
8. Has a track record of performance as an employee or worker in the real world
9. Infrequent turnover

"GROWING" ONE'S OWN PERSONNEL

"Growing" one's own personnel refers to looking internally to select individuals for vacancies that occur. Such a practice has the advantage of positive motivation as hiring one's own people encourages others within the organization to hope for and look towards similar happenings with them. On the other hand, hiring one's own people can be likened to inbreeding. This is because there may be fewer opportunities for new ideas as well as less creativity and less ingenuity because of promoting/hiring from within. Nevertheless, use of the so-called "feeder system" in filling vacancies has merits.

Interns from Collegiate Professional Preparation Programs

A variation of the "home grown" method of selecting personnel is the use of sport management interns. These college students serve an internship (typically a semester or, less frequently, a calendar year) within a sport organization. Management is able to take advantage of these interns in two ways. First, to put them to real work doing real jobs in the real world of sport business. In reality, many sport organizations could not run their actual business operations without the use of sport management interns. These interns, usually college seniors and graduate students, are able to provide significant assistance in the day-to-day operation of many sport businesses and organizations.

INTERNSHIP MODEL OF STAFFING

The term coined to reflect questionable employment/staffing strategy through the use of interns to replace paid salaried personnel is called the *Internship Model of Staffing*, reflecting the fact that professional (paid) staffing is replaced with free intern workers. There is a very real danger in the utilization of interns in this manner and it revolves around the exploitation of interns and the violation of the 1938 Fair Labor Standards Act (see chapter two).

The Labor Department uses the criterion: *Who Benefits Most?* That is, if the greatest benefit of the internship (field) experience is realized by the sport business/organization offering the internship, rather than the student intern, there is a need for pay to be given to the student intern. However, if the student intern's work and contributions to the company/organization do not outweigh the benefits gained by the student, financial remuneration for the student is not required. The key is determining whether or not the student is being exploited at the hands of the business or organization.

> *CONCEPT #305:* **Sport managers should carefully select and evaluate their interns as potential future employees.**

The second way management is able to utilize individuals serving as interns is to be able to size them up, to evaluate the interns under pressure and in real life situations, in an effort to determine whether these students have what it takes to be a professional in this exciting business. As a result, those interns who have distinguished themselves in the internship setting frequently find themselves being selected as employees by the organization where they interned, or at another organization as a result of the positive recommendations received from their internship site.

"STEALING" OR ATTRACTING STAFF DIRECTLY FROM OTHER ORGANIZATIONS—SPORT AND NON-SPORT ENTITIES

Outstanding employees are seemingly fair game insofar as being coveted and sought by other employers. Today, many organizations attempt to steal or appropriate other organization's outstanding and talented employees. In fact, this raiding of highly qualified and competent personnel is quite frequent in some aspects of the sport business world, especially in the health, fitness and wellness industry. Part of the reason for this is that sufficient numbers of quality personnel are frequently difficult to find (for the wages paid), and harder yet to keep. One way to prevent having highly qualified, talented and valuable personnel from being "stolen" is for management to provide a healthy work environment, consistent training, adequate professional support and a decent wage (Plummer, 1997, p. 36).

> **CONCEPT #306:** *Management must treat their personnel well lest highly qualified and desirable staff jump ship and go to work for another organization.*

NETWORKING WITHIN THE BUSINESS COMMUNITY

Just as prospective employees are encouraged to network in order to find out about possible jobs, employers are getting into the act in an effort to find out about talented and desirable personnel. Networking in this instance involves a process of communicating, keeping in touch, with other individuals in an attempt to keep abreast of current developments within the personnel arena. In particular, such communication efforts, both formal and informal, can be initiated with both managers as well as non-managers at businesses of all types, descriptions and sizes.

In fact, professional and productive networking is possible with a wide variety of individuals within the community who might have knowledge of and experience with talented personnel. Potential personnel for sport organizations do not necessarily have to have prior experience in the world of sport or sport business. They could come from any type of business or work experience. This is because in many instances specific skills and competencies can be learned on the job. This is especially true when the individual already possesses a propensity for learning and possesses important attributes like a positive attitude, an appropriate personality, drive and is a self-starter who is intrinsically motivated.

> **CONCEPT #307:** *There is a difference between professional networking and the improprieties associated with the "good old boys network."*

One should not confuse proper networking for employee candidates with the unprofessional "Good Old Boys Network" or the "Good Old Girls Network." In the former instance there is no discrimination or exclusion involved at all. Rather, members of management and search committee members seek to find out about possible prospective candidates without reservation or limitation as to who the individuals are or whether they are male or female, or whether they are black, white, blue or purple, etc. The problem with the traditional interpretation of the "Good Old Boys/Old Girls Networks" is that they excluded people from consideration on the basis of factors that (legally and morally) should not enter into the employment equation (see below).

2. *Planning for and Initiating an Official Search for an Actual Vacancy within the Organization*

It is very important when initiating an official search for a position to follow both the letter and intent of the laws of the land as they affect the hiring process (see chapter 12, *Sport Management and the Law*). This is important for two reasons. First, it is the right thing to do to from a professional and ethical standpoint. Second, it is a matter of law. And violations of law can result in severe punishments and embarrassments for the individuals involved, as well as for the sport entity itself.

CONCEPT# 308: *Good hiring practices are a matter of law as well as ethics.*

Two very important Acts or Laws relating to the personnel process include (1) the *Civil Rights Act of 1964 and* (2) the *Age Discrimination in Employment Act of 1967.* The importance of the *Civil Rights Act of 1964* is that this piece of legislation sought to stop unfair *employment practices.* It essentially prohibits and forbids discrimination on the basis *of race, color, sex, religion or national origin* in areas of employer-employee relationships. This includes advertising for employees, discrimination against current employees, termination or retirement practices.

The ADEA, *Age Discrimination in Employment Act of 1967* (as amended), forbids discrimination against employees *or* job applicants because of age. Specifically, when applicants or employees are *age 40 or greater* the provisions of ADEA are applicable (Hiring, 1993). The opportunity to select or invite one or more individuals to join one's organization as staff is so important that the process and activities associated with the selection process must be flawless.

Writing the Job Description

Preparation is the key in the search process. One of the first steps to take when a vacancy becomes available is to be sure that management has a clear concept of what the person is to do and what skills and attributes the person should possess.

CONCEPT #309:   *Advance planning is absolutely essential in the hiring process.*

In order to identify the character traits necessary for any position, management should answer such questions as what needs to be done in this particular job? What responsibilities would be assumed by the new hire? What skills and attributes are needed to do these tasks effectively and efficiency? What qualifications would be necessary for a person to be able to successfully complete these tasks and do the job required (Stattler & Mulloen, 1994)?

Only after one has such information can the search process really begin. Thus, developing a clear job description is one of the first steps in the hiring process (McCutcheon & Robinson, 1997).

An important element of the job description is a list of qualifications. Many employers choose to utilize two categories of qualifications, (1) required and (2) preferred. Similarly, it must be decided what potential candidates must submit as part of their application for the position. Typical requirements include:

1. Letter of application addressing specific requirements of the position
2. Résumé or vita
3. Either list of references [with addresses, phone numbers, e-mail addresses] or actual recommendations from references sent to the search committee

ADVERTISING AND RECRUITING EFFORTS

The ultimate goal of management is to find the best candidate for the vacancy that exists within the sport organization. However potential candidates cannot find out about a vacancy without being made aware of it. Usually this involves publicly announcing the vacancy or anticipated vacancy through the media as well as mass mailings and individual contacts with others via the mail, phone, internet or in person. Networking is very important to insure a sufficiently large applicant pool.

CONCEPT #310:　*Utilize all available means of communication when announcing job vacancies.*

Examples of communication and announcing job vacancies include, but are not limited to, the following:

1. Sending out printed announcements of the vacancy to:
    a. College placement offices
    b. Other sport organizations
    c. Specific college/university departments of sport management
    d. Selected individuals working within the field

2. Submitting advertisements for the vacancy in national, regional and statewide publications such as *The Chronicle of Higher Education, The New York Times, JOPERD, UPDATE*, etc.

3. Submitting the announcement to various electronic home pages or checking out "World Wild Web" sites for candidates, including:
   a. http://www.careermosaic.com
   b. http://www.monster.com
   c. http://www.fentonnet.com/jobs.html
   d. http://www.tiac.net/users/jobs
   e. http://www.recruiting-links.com
   f. http://www.ipa.com
   g. http://www.washingtonpost.com/parachute
   h. http://www.careersite.com/
   i. http://www.cweb.com
   j. http://www.careerpath.com/
   k. http://www.espan.com
   l. http://wwwnapehe.org

4. Searching the World Wide Web for potential candidates who have created and posted their own home page.

5. Attending national, regional and state conventions and conferences (such as winter meetings in the sport of baseball) and posting notices of the vacancy.

Establishing Qualification Parameters

In evaluating potential employees selection committees and management typically look at a number of different factors, depending upon the type of vacancy being filled and the organization itself (Alden, 2001). Some of the factors used to differentiate between various candidates and used to help identify those individuals who are most likely to experience long term success within the organization include:

1. Formal education of applicants
2. Formal and informal training
3. Type of certification(s) held (if applicable), such as:
   a. American College of Sports Medicine,
   b. Various aerobics certifications
   c. American Council on Exercise (ACE),
   d. Certified Public Accountant (CPA)
4. Professional and personal experiences
5. Specific skills and capabilities
6. Proper personalities and attitudes

A recent national study sponsored by the Education Department of some 3000 managers indicated that there were four very important factors or criteria to take into consideration in the hiring of new personnel. These factors and their respective ranking on a 5-point scale were attitude (4.6), communication skill (4.2), work experience (4.0), and previous employers' recommendations. Interestingly enough, the respondents indicated that grades earned in college were deemed to be the least important factor in terms of whether an individual is hired or not (Henry, 1995).

REVIEWING, SCREENING AND ASSESSING APPLICANTS' APPLICATIONS

Once applications have been received by the search committee or by management it is necessary to screen and assess the contents of each application package. At this point in time it is recommended that management double check to insure that the pool of applicants is sufficiently large to warrant further action by the search committee. If the advertisement and dissemination of the vacancy notices were adequate, the pool of aspirants should be fairly large. If the search process up to this point has failed to produce an adequate pool of candidates, a decision must be made whether to continue to the search or to abort and try again.

> **CONCEPT #311:** *There must be a sufficient number of applicants to warrant continuation of the search process.*

Assuming that the pool of candidates is sufficient in terms of numbers and diversity, the next step is to begin to evaluate the application packets or materials submitted by those interested in the position. In many searches the range of applicants in terms of their qualifications can vary greatly. In some searches there are large numbers of people who apply who do not even meet minimum qualifications. However, with an effective search and advertisement (notification) effort there should be a sufficient number of minimally qualified aspirants for the position.

The process of wading through numerous application folders can be daunting to say the least. To facilitate this process, and to be objective in this initial evaluation stage, it is highly advisable to have a written list of criteria or factors with which to evaluate applicants. The list should also include the preferred and minimum (required) qualifications included in the advertisement for the position. With this list management and the search committee can begin to assess and evaluate each of the applicants.

To create order to the screening process of applicants it is suggested that candidates initially be placed in one of three categories. For example, category or group "C" would be for those applicants who failed to meet the minimum advertised requirements for the post. Group "B" would include those individuals who met the minimum requirements but were thought not sufficiently strong to warrant a personal interview. Those candidates who meet the minimum requirements, score high in terms of the preferred qualifications and are possible candidates who might be invited for an interview, are placed in the third group, the A" group.

> **CONCEPT #312:**   *Background checks for finalists for positions are essential if potential or future problems are to be avoided.*

CONTACTING REFERENCES—ANOTHER PHASE OF THE SCREENING PROCESS

At this point in time it is highly advisable to begin to check references and backgrounds of each of the candidates in group "A." This is done in an effort to further cull the number of candidates in this category to a select few, perhaps 2, 3 or 5. Many search committees do not limit their communications with those references whose names were supplied by the candidates but seek to cast a wider net. They do this by contacting individuals who might know of an individual candidate and who had not been identified as a references by the candidate. In this case, the applicant is asked if he committee may contact others.

> **CONCEPT #313: Double check the veracity of résumés and vitas.**

In addition to checking references, conscientious committee members should also verify information supplied by candidates, including the credentials and licenses claimed by potential employees (Cioletti, 1999). These background checks are essential (Kerr, 2005). For example, such items as employment history, certifications, degrees, skill level, and professional accomplishments and honors should be verified. Conducting such checks thoroughly may save management from making a very costly mistake in terms of money, image and staff morale.

There is a need to be very careful and cautious in believing everything that one reads on a person's résumé or vita. Not every résumé or vita is 100% accurate (Stull, 1990). In fact, the increasing creep of inadequacies, exaggerations, fluff, and outright falsehoods found on many of today's résumés and vita places even greater pressure on search committees and management. Double-checking, certainly in the case of the finalists, should be automatic.

INVITING CANDIDATES FOR AN INTERVIEW

Inviting one or more candidates to an interview with the search committee and se-lected administrators is a critical stage in the hiring process. Great care must be taken to identify—from the written application dossier and the follow-up phone calls and personal inquiries of references and others—a small number of highly qualified individuals who might be a good match for the position. When these individuals have been identified from those applications within group "A" the next step is to extend an invitation for a personal interview to these persons.

3. *Interviewing Prospective Candidates*

There is a science and an art to successfully interviewing candidates for sport man-agement positions. There are fundamental things to do such as attempting to make the applicant at ease and asking the "right" questions, for instance. There are also things that should not be done—such as not asking questions that would be discriminatory, offensive or no one's business other than the candidates. Everyone who is in management or who serves on search committees can be made aware of all of these so-called standard issues or standard operating procedures as they relate to the interview process, in a minimum amount of time. During the interview inquiries are made of each candidate in an effort to secure answers to such questions as: (Fritz, 1992)

1. Does the candidate meet all of the job requirements?
2. Does the person have the mental and physical capabilities necessary to perform the tasks associated with the job?
3. Does the person have the knowledge, skills and understandings essential for achiev-ing outstanding performance?
4. Is the individual motivated?
5. Does the person's personality or attitude match the demands of the position and the employment climate of the organization?
6. Will the person live up to the organization's expectations? (Is there evidence or indi-cation that would support this assumption?)
7. What are the long-range career plans of the candidate?
8. Whether the aspirant possesses a basic understanding of the organization, its per-sonnel and its mission(s)?
9. Does the person have the potential for further growth within the profession and within the organization?
10. What type of contributions night this individual make to the sport entity?

> **CONCEPT #314:** *Interviews should delve into the very essence of the person who is seeking the position to determine if there is a suitable match.*

However, the art of interviewing is not so easily taught or learned. This aspect of the interviewing process involves getting into the heart and the soul of the applicant to determine what resides inside the individual. Interviews should serve more of a purpose than merely to confirm what the individual's application had provided. The real essence of an interview experience from the perspective of the employer is being able to get inside the human being to find out what makes Johnny or Jeannie really tick, what makes Johnny or Jeannie "run"? What is the true essence of the individual who wants to join the organization and be part of the team? Will this person be a good partner in terms of the sport organization and in respect to other personnel? Will the person be a good fit or a good match in all aspects of the organization, its programs, its activities and its "people"?

Thus, the kind of atmosphere or climate that is created for each of the candidates during all phases of their interview experience is of paramount importance. This is true both for the formal interview session(s) as well as subsequent informal meetings, gatherings and discussions held with the candidates. The type of environment that evolves is frequently dependent upon the personality and attitude of the candidates themselves as well as members of the search committee.

In reality the interview is a two-way, give-and-take experience in which both the interviewer(s) and the candidate are able to project an image and to learn about the other. It should be a time of mutual evaluation and information sharing. Toward this end, it is strongly advised to have a set of questions that have previously been agreed to by members of the search committee and management that speak directly to the individual candidates' ability to fill the position. These questions should be based on what information is desired. The questions should focus on integral job-related issues. And, the same questions should be asked of each candidate interviewed to insure fairness and consistency (Carpenter, 1997).

> **CONCEPT #315:** *Never hire just to fill a slot—better to abort the search and start again than to take "second best" or worse.*

Not all searches end on a positive note. Sometimes, for whatever reason, the search fails to produce the right individual for the position. Or the perfect candidate is offered the position but turns it down. What does the organization do if at the end of the search process there is not an acceptable match between the sport organization and an individual?

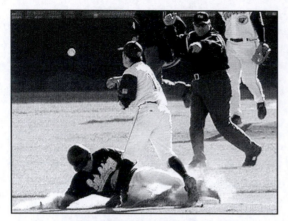

Fans Love Exciting Plays
*[courtesy of Bemidji State University (BSU)
Photography Services]*

Should management offer the permanent, full time position to someone who is not really a good match for the job or for the business? The answer is simple, **NO!** Instead, start the search process again. Don't hire just to be hiring. Generally speaking, it is better to abort the search and start again to locate an acceptable candidate than to be saddled with an inferior or unacceptable staffing choice. An offer of a full time, permanent position is a big decision and commitment on behalf of the organization. Accepting such an offer can be even more of a big decision by the candidate. Of course, if the search process has been carried out with due diligence then the likelihood of finding one or more suitable matches among the finalists is greatly enhanced.

4.   *The Proactive State of the Personnel Process—Helping Personnel Experience Success*

Management has an obligation to help each and every individual working for the organization. After all, it was the organization that hired the individual working for the business. It is important that managers, administrators, supervisors and other employees take this responsibility, this obligation seriously. In fact, these same managers, administrators, supervisors and peers should be shocked if a staff member fails to experience success as a member of the organization's team. If an individual is not successful, as an employee, then not only has this person failed but so too has management, as well as the entire organization. For in reality either the selection/hiring process was flawed or the support process provided that should have been available to the individual as an employee was lacking. Or, perhaps both were deficient.

**CONCEPT #316:   *Failure of an employee is an indictment against management
and the organization.***

Use of Mentors

Management's responsibility for personnel continues of course after the individual is hired. In fact, it intensifies if anything. Now that the person is a member of the personnel team it behooves the organization, management and other personnel to see to it that the person experiences success in the job. Part of this process rests in the day-to-day support given to the staff member. In some organizations a formal mentor system is employed in which an experienced staffer (a mentor) is paired with a new person to watch over the new hire and to advise, guide and otherwise help the person adapt to the new surroundings, the new environment or job climate. Whether this mentoring relationship is a very informal one or a formal mentoring program, the fact is that mentoring of new hires is a wise step in enabling the new employee to become better acclimated to the workplace. "A formal mentoring program, usually includes the assignment of one or more mentors, requires participation in regularly scheduled meetings with the mentor(s), and provides training and compensation for the mentor" (Gaskin, Lumpkin & Tennett, 2003, pp. 49-50).

CONCEPT #317: *Management should provide in-service education opportunities for personnel in order for them to remain at the cutting edge.*

Another important aspect of helping staff members is education and training. Providing opportunity for personnel to engage in formal and informal (in-service) educational programs or training sessions is vital for the health of the individuals involved and for the business (Stier, 1987). Examples of such educational experiences include formal classes (on or off site), workshops, clinics, training sessions, peer tutoring or counseling, travel, access to telecommunication classes, correspondence or internet courses, and the like. Supporting in-service education for personnel involves a mindset that recognizes that the learning never stops among an organization's staff.

Of course both neophyte and experienced personnel within the sport organization should be given appropriate educational opportunities. Generally speaking, the lower the level of employee the more training and supervision that individual may require (Plummer, 1997). Nevertheless, such educational options helps to insure that one's staff remains at the cutting edge, or at least close to it. And, in this fast paced world of sport management, this is very, very important for the health and longevity of the organization.

CONCEPT #318: *Employees must maintain a healthy balance between their work responsibilities/time commitments and their home responsibilities/time commitments.*

Managers need to encourage employees to "work smart" rather than to "work long hours" as many employees, especially those who are young and inexperienced, feel that they must work 24/7 in order to be successful and to be viewed as successful and productive by others, especially by superiors. However, it is frequently just the opposite. The following quote that appeared in the *Baltimore Sun* was cited by Hoch (2005, p. 41) and is most appropriate in this regard: "Job performance depends more on the organized life, rest, and good working conditions than on non-stop toil." Employees should be encouraged to maintain a healthy balance between their work responsibilities, obligations and time commitment and their home/family responsibilities, obligations and commitment.

HIRING PERSONNEL AND LETTING THEM HAVE THE FREEDOM TO DO THEIR JOBS

An important element of managing personnel is allowing them to do the job(s) for which they were selected in the first place. Far too often managers and supervisors interfere and meddle in the affairs of their subordinates to the extent that they actually interfere with or impede the progress of their staff.

CONCEPT #319:   *Managers must resist the temptation to micromanage.*

Being able to delegate responsibilities and then to stand back while subordinates go about their business of doing their job is sometimes difficult for supervisors—but it is an important part of the managing process. Members of management must resist the temptation to micromanage (Stier, 1997b, October 6). There are employees who enjoy being given a great degree of freedom in terms of *how* as well as *when* they, as employees, are expected to do their job. AND, many employees are able to operate with great effectiveness and efficiency with minimal oversight. On the other hand, there are also a large number of employees who need and want greater oversight and supervision in order to be operating at their best.

CONCEPT #320:   *The challenge of managers and supervisors is to determine the type of supervision and oversight each employee needs for optimal performance.*

Fringe Benefit Packages (or Lack Thereof)

Employees today are as concerned about fringe benefits such as health insurance, dental insurance, retirement programs, etc., as they are about their regular salary, if not more so. This is especially true in some segments of the sport industry since many employees, both those working full time and those working part-time, are not recipients of significant fringe benefit packages. In fact, many employees within the sport industry have no meaningful benefits to speak of at all.

In today's marketplace insurance and health packages have become more and more important in terms of attracting and keeping quality employees. For those personnel working for sport organizations who receive the low wages with few, if any, health insurance or retirement benefits, there is little incentive to remain with the sport firm. Rather, these minimally paid personnel are often just marking time in their current place of employment while constantly looking for a better employment environment, one in which they are better compensated for their efforts. This type of situation does little to establish stability and longevity among the personnel. With constant turnover comes low morale and poor performance.

5. Evaluation and Assessment of Staff

There are eight questions that sport managers should answer before engaging in personnel appraisal or job performance evaluation. First, what is the purpose of the appraisal? Second, what exactly should be evaluated or assessed? Third, what specific criteria will be used to assess personnel? Fourth, who should conduct the assessment? Fifth, when should it take place? Sixth, where should it take place? Seventh, what specific techniques or "instruments" shall be used? And, lastly, how will the results be used?

CONCEPT #321: *Performance review (evaluation) is a necessary element of personnel management.*

The evaluation and assessment process of personnel is an essential component of the overall personnel process. Staff evaluation is conducted for numerous reasons (Stier, 1993; Haney, 1995). These include:

1. To let employees know how they are doing
2. To motivate employees
3. To help the individual in terms of efficiency, productivity and competency
4. To enhance communication and employee feedback
5. To improve employee weaknesses in job performance
6. To encourage ownership, accountability and employee involvement
7. To justify specific personnel actions by management, such as:
   a. Promotion
   b. Reassignment
   c. Salary increase, decrease or no increase
   d. Increase or decrease in autonomy

    e. Increase or decrease in authority and responsibility

    f. Granting a sabbatical for study

    g. Provision of additional educational (training) opportunities

    h. Giving a letter of reprimand or letter of warning

    i. Demotion

    j. Firing or termination

The most important justification (purpose) for evaluating one's personnel (both paid and volunteer) is to help them become better employees, to assist them in developing greater skills, etc. In this sense, assessment is done to evaluate, critique and improve the performance of personnel. Thus, management must always remain in the "help" mode when considering the evaluation process.

CONCEPT #322:   *Remain in the help mode when evaluating personnel.*

THE IMPORTANCE OF CONSTRUCTIVE FEEDBACK

When dealing with employees who are performing at an unacceptable level, supervisors should concentrate on providing constructive feedback rather than consistent criticism. Supervisors need to be sensitive. *Correction or criticism should never be made personal.* Critical remarks should be made in private and praise should be given in public. Similarly, if correction is warranted cite the work or the mistakes that are the subject of the correction, not the individual staff member.

In other words, deal with the problem itself, deal with specifics rather than generalities and keep the criticism on the problem and not the person. Of course if the problem is with a person's behavior or attitude then obviously the subject of the correction will be the offending individual (Wakin, 1991). When providing feedback concerning errors or mistakes, supervisors should always point out ways that these problems could be corrected. Also, share a willingness to assist the employee, thus remaining in the help mode.

CONCEPT #323:   *Consistent feedback is an essential component for good performance appraisal.*

Many employees view personnel appraisals in a negative manner because of the factor of negative personnel decisions such as dismissals, demotions or other forms of punishment. Thus, they see staff evaluation as punitive, threatening, intimidating and menacing.

Some even see something sinister about the entire process. Nothing should be further from the truth. This is why it is sometimes recommended that the personnel be involved at the onset when performance appraisals are first being considered within the sport organization (Koch, 1994). If such appraisals are already in place management should endeavor to educate the staff as to the positive purposes for which the process is implemented Thus, in this way management remains in the help mode.

ESSENTIALS OF A PERFORMANCE APPRAISAL/REVIEW SYSTEM OR PROGRAM

Any method of evaluating or assessing an individual must be good enough to distinguish between top performers, average performers and poor performers. Such a system (as well as any instrument or procedure) must also be, and be viewed as, fair, just, objective, consistent and actually capable of measuring what is attempted to be measured.

Stier (1993, p. 39) provides ten commandments of evaluating personnel in sport organizations. These include:

1. Follow the kiss concept, keep it simple and short
2. Make sure that expectations are reasonable, clear and understood and in writing
3. Seek input from many individuals, use subjective and objective criteria
4. Inform the staff of deficiencies as soon as they are detected and don't hesitate to compliment when warranted
5. Provide opportunities for the staff member to improve, remain in the help mode
6. Have high standards and expectations—mediocrity breeds mediocrity
7. Take the evaluation process seriously and your staff will too
8. Be honest, fair and consistent in implementing the system and be sensitive to the needs and concerns of each coach.
9. Don't let personality clashes distort or cloud the evaluation process
10. Don't make mountains out of molehills—concentrate on those areas that can affect the quality of the person's experiences.

OBJECTIVE AND SUBJECTIVE CRITERIA IN PERFORMANCE APPRAISALS

Employees may be evaluated using both objective and subjective criteria. The important point is that employees must know what is expected of them in advance as well as how they are going to be evaluated so that they can plan and act accordingly. Evaluation of staff is really an ongoing process although formal evaluations of personnel are more common at regular intervals such as every 6 or 12 months. The important thing is that if there is to be performance appraisal then it should be done periodically (Fardelmann, 1994).

One of the challenges of personnel appraisal with both paid and volunteer staff is that supervisors often have a difficult time actually implementing the evaluation process. Research reveals that supervisors tend to give higher ratings when they know the subordinate will see it. And yet, it is imperative that this is allowed. Otherwise, how will the employee know what to work on to improve?

Also, most supervisors find it difficult to recognize and discern superior performers as well as incompetent performers. It gets more difficult with average performers. Finally, there is often a lack of consistency among members of management and supervisors as they evaluate different employees. Some are very lenient in their assessment of subordinates while others hold their subordinates to a much higher standard. This lack of consistency threatens the very essence of the appraisal system.

Performance Appraisal Instruments

There are numerous pen and paper instruments currently in use by all types of sport businesses to assess the competency and performance of their personnel. The common elements of the forms include statements that reflect upon the subordinate's job responsibilities and the person's ability to perform at an acceptable level. Next to each statement are spaces for the evaluator to check off indicating at what level the person is currently performing. For example, for each area of performance or job responsibility there might be spaces marked: (1) excellent, (2) above average, (3) average, (4) below average, and (5) unsatisfactory. In addition, some instruments provide for space for the supervisor to provide narrative remarks clarifying the numerical ranking.

> **CONCEPT #324:** *Employees should have a right to see and react to their job performance appraisal.*

Many such forms also provide a place at the bottom of the appraisal instrument for the employees to sign and to add their own comments if they so wish. In reality the employee's signature really only attests that the individual has at least read the document. For example, at the bottom of an typical appraisal form might be a statement: *"The signature of the staff member below does not necessarily indicate agreement with the above performance appraisal statements but merely indicates that the staff member has read it. The staff member may attach a memo explaining any factor concerning this evaluation form or explaining the staff member's disagreement or agreement with any part or phase of the assessment."*

Specific performance indicators (PIs) are helpful in facilitating the supervisor's awareness of just how successful individual employees are and what areas individual employees might be deficient. The performance indicator is a goal or objective that is clearly stated, easily understood and measurable. The PIs allow the manager or supervisor to determine to what extent, if at all, one or more employees are meeting their objectives (Mumford & Fuller, 2002).

6. *Personnel Actions Resulting from Performance Appraisals*

What are the options open to management if an employee's performance is such that it is unsatisfactory? What are the possibilities if the assessment reveals that the person is performing at a satisfactory or superior level? In either instance the employee needs to be informed of how the person is viewed by management. In the case of the exceptional or satisfactory worker it is important that the individual receive positive feedback and knows how much the person is appreciated.

Naturally, even with personnel performing at an acceptable level (or higher) there will always be areas in which improvement can be made or areas or tasks which might necessitate special effort or attention in the future. However, with those personnel who are adequately performing their tasks and fulfilling their responsibilities, it is a matter of showing genuine appreciation, continuing to challenge and motivate them, adequately rewarding them and seeing to it that they remain at or even improve upon their current level of competency.

Options Open to Management when Employees Fail

In respect to those individuals who do not fare well as a result of an employee appraisal the question really boils down to three scenarios. First, the person could be retained as an employee and life could go on within the organization with little if anything happening to or with the employee. Second, the person could be dismissed, i.e., either fired or not rehired. And, third, the person is retained (at least for a time) but is put on notice that performance is sub-par.

In the third scenario, management may alter the person's job responsibilities and duties, i.e., change one's duties (reassignment) and restrict areas of responsibilities (demotion). Additionally, management may provide specific assistance (help mode) to aid the employee in overcoming deficiencies and increasing skills and competencies in the hope that performance will be enhanced in the future. Such assistance may require that the employee participate in some kind of training, clinics, workshops, tutoring, and formal class work.

CONCEPT #325:   *General Electric's famous 20-70-10 concept of ranking employees has significant implications for many other companies.*

General Electric, under then CEO, Jack Welch, implemented its 20-70-10 plan in 1996, a plan which involved a ranking of all managerial and professional employees. Those in the top 20% are richly rewarded so that they won't depart the organization. Those in the bottom 10% are given an opportunity to improve, but if such improvement is not quickly forthcoming these employees are in real danger of being discharged from GE. In fact, Jack Welch wrote the following in his last annual report to company's shareholders shortly before he retired: "Companies should 'love' and nurture's the top 20% of its employees but actively weed out the bottom 10%" (Jones, 2001, February 27).

General Electric is not alone in this effort to identify the top performers and those who are performing at a sub-par level—and getting rid of those who fail to improve their productivity, effectives and efficiency. For example, Ford Motor Company grades all 18,000 managers on an annual basis. In 2000 these employees were placed in groups of 30 to 50 and in each group 10% had to earn a grade of "A", 80% had to earn a grade of "B", and 10% will be given the grade of "C"—which is like being classified as having failed, as in the grade of "F". In 2001 Ford eased its criteria and then only required that 5% had to be identified as "C" (read failure) employees.

Sun Microsystems ranked all 43,000 employees in 2001. In this system, the lowest ranked employees are given 90 days to improve and if they do not they are given the choice of either resigning with severance pay or having one more chance at earning a higher ranking—and if unsuccessful, being discharged without a severance package. Cisco Systems had identified as a goal removing 5% of employees each and every year. Even Microsoft ranks all 45,000 of its employees on a scale of 2.5 to 5 on an annual basis (Jones, 2001, May 30).

The practice of ranking employees, that is, identifying the top producers as well as the apparent slackers or unproductive employees involves the practice of rewarding in very real ways those top employers the company or organization wishes to retain and punishing or failing to reward those less valued employees, in the anticipation that these lower producers will either significantly improve or leave their place of employment.

> **CONCEPT #326:**   *It Is "Easy" to Fire Someone—It Is Far More Difficult to Help the Individual to Improve Performance and Become Competent and More Skilled.*

The Cost of Terminating an Employee

Management should not be so eager to merely discharge or terminate an employee. In many instances firing someone is just too easy a way out, a "cop-out"—for the employer or sport organization. The employing entity usually has a great deal of time, effort and money invested in each of its employees. To remove or get rid of a seemingly unproductive person is an admission that management has failed, failed in fostering professional competency among its employees, failed in the selection/hiring process, failed in the teaching or training efforts and/or failed in spotting earlier potential performance deficiencies among its personnel.

It is also very expensive and time intensive to go through a complete search process to replace a discharged staff member. If the sport entity had hired the right person for the right job, and then had supported that person appropriately and provided the person with suitable resources, the likelihood of that employee being successful would have been greatly increased.

It is very important that management provide to an employee the resources (time, money, assistants/staff, training, equipment, supplies, etc.) necessary for that individual to experience success as a member of the sport organization's team. Since it costs additional monies and time to secure the services of a replacement for a fired staffer, management should ask itself if discharging or firing an employee is appropriate or necessary.

Frequently, in the world of sport business, if the former employee had received the support (financial and otherwise) that the new employee will inevitably be given perhaps there might not have been a need to discharge the previous employee. And, in many cases, the new employee replacing a fired individual will certainly be given "all of the resources requested" since management would not want to see a second failure on their hands.

CONCEPT #327: *Firing an employee should be the last resort.*

Employees typically do not become incompetent overnight. In the case of a nonperforming or underperforming employee there surely must have been early warning signs (cues) along the way pointing to the performance slippage of the person in question. If management and peers failed to pick up on these cues then they too must bear the burden and share the responsibility for the failure by the underperforming or non-performing employee. *Firing someone is the avenue of last resort, it is an act of desperation, and it is an acknowledgement of failure on behalf of management.*

CONCEPT #328: *Firing an employee is an admission of failure by the employing organization.*

Questions to Ask Oneself when an Employee Underperforms

Supervisors and managers need to ask themselves some searching questions whenever a subordinate fails to perform as expected. There could be many reasons why a person is acting a certain way or performing in a specific manner. The task of the supervisor is to find out why and then to take corrective action, if possible.

For example, does the employee understand what the job is and the responsibilities are? Does the person understand specifically what tasks are to be accomplished and the time restraints? Does the person know what and how to give superiors what they want? Does the person want to do the job? Has the person been given adequate resources to do the job? Does the person know how to do the job? Are the job expectations and time restraints reasonable? Or, is it a case of the so-called Pete Principal, proposed over three decades ago by Laurence Peter? Members of management need to remember that even a "superhero" cannot create miracles nor meet unreasonable expectations (Pitts, 1996). There is a shared responsibility between management and the employee for the employee's success.

CONCEPT #329:   *The Peter Principle (Laurence Peter) states*
that an individual may be continuously promoted based on
merit and performance until that person is promoted
to one's level of incompetence—and then stays at that level
or returns to the previous level.

"REWARDING" THE INCOMPETENT AND "PUNISHING" THE COMPETENT

There is always the danger that management will fall into the trap of "rewarding" the incompetent and "punishing" the competent when it comes to assigning tasks to various personnel. What this means is that when personnel fail to perform satisfactorily having been assigned important tasks to complete, they are less frequently to be trusted with significant responsibility in the future. This is especially true when there are other personnel who have demonstrated, by past accomplishments, that they are willing and capable of successfully completing important tasks within specified time restraints.

Supervisors tend to delegate major tasks and significant responsibilities to those individuals to whom they have the greatest confidence. Thus, the competent employees seemingly are "punished" by being given more and more tasks to do and greater and greater responsibilities to assume. And the less competent personnel are not given ("rewarded") tough assignments for fear that they will fail to produce or perform up to expectations. If this scenario plays out to its natural conclusion the consequences are obvious.

The workplace climate suffers, the job performance and overall production can suffer and internal dissention can result.

Thus, management must be careful and not allow personnel to escape responsibilities by performing at an unacceptable level. In fact, supervisors must be constantly on the alert to detect, at the earliest possible time, any significant deficiency among staff members in terms of their job performance. Supervisors must also not engage in "punishing" the competent and "rewarding" the incompetent as in the examples above. Rather, they must insist that all personnel assume their fair share of the total job responsibilities and perform at an acceptable level of competency on behalf of the sport business.

TERMINATION OF EMPLOYEES

Inevitably there will be times when it will be necessary to terminate an employee, as regrettable as that prospect might be—both from the perspective of the sport organization and from the viewpoint of the employee. Management must consider a variety of legal issues and consult with appropriate legal counsel prior to initiating termination proceedings. The whole termination process can be likened to a minefield. Maneuvering through this minefield requires careful thinking and cautious planning.

> **CONCEPT #330:** *Beware of wrongful termination suits—follow the letter of the law, be just and keep exacting records.*

The exact nature of the termination process depends to some extent upon the type of employment contract, if any, the employee has and the type of organization employing the person. Nevertheless, there are some general principles that are applicable in almost every personnel situation. For example, it is essential that supervisors keep excellent written records. Similarly, regular reviews and performance appraisals should be conducted. There are certain expectations of performance reviews that must be present if companies are to avoid successful wrongful termination suits brought by disgruntled current or former employees. There are certain obligations that the sport organization has in respect to employees. For example, members of management should:

1. Provide clear, specific and consistent expectations of performance
2. Include regular reviews and evaluations that should be given to the employee and maintained in personnel records of the sport organization.
3. Tell the employee of deficiencies as soon as they are detected
4. Cite the employee's strengths as well as weaknesses
5. Provide tips and suggestions on how to improve performance

6. Take specific steps to help the employee improve performance and keep records of such actions

7. Encourage and give opportunities for the person to improve

8. Document everything in writing and keep detailed records

9. Officially inform the employee that if improvement does not take place that dismissal will occur

10. Include a witness when meeting with an employee to discuss serious breaches of job responsibilities and non-performance of tasks

Some managers suggest that employees be asked to sign new job contracts that outline their specific duties and exact responsibilities within the organization, at least once a year, even if their jobs have not changed. This provides a paper trail relating to job assignments and performance expectations.

Wong (1997) indicates that when an employer has utilized objective criteria as part of an appropriate personnel evaluation system, has provided verbal and written notice to the individual of inadequate performance, has expressed reasonable expectations of the individual for the future—there is an obligation on the part of said employee to meet these expectations in order for employment to be continued.

Finally, if the overall evaluation process and the specific performance appraisal were proper and effective, the affected employee would have been forewarned. And, as such, the individual certainly should not be totally surprised that one's performance has been viewed as unsatisfactory and that the employment is being terminated—for cause.

WORKING WITH PERSONNEL WITHIN A UNION SETTING

Sport managers need to be cognizant that in some instances there is yet another wild card to be played in terms of personnel management. That wild card is the union shop. Many sport businesses have employees who are unionized. Many sport organizations work with firms whose employees are represented by unions. There are many advantages involving the presence of unions just as there are many challenges when unionized employees are part of the organization's personnel.

One of the major challenges facing administrators and supervisors when dealing with employees represented by a union(s) is that there are specific (and detailed) expectations and obligations placed upon both management and employee, especially in terms of performance expectations, benefits, and working conditions, among others. In this regard sport administrators need to be cognizant of the contents of their own personnel handbook, the union contract and the applicable laws governing employment practices when dealing with personnel matters.

THE PERSONNEL HANDBOOK

A helpful tool for management in the area of personnel management is the personnel handbook. This handbook contains all of the pertinent and relevant policies, practices and procedures concerning personnel (paid and volunteer) for that particular sport business or organization. With such a document to guide future actions management is aided in its efforts to make wise, timely and appropriate decisions. The personnel handbook provides guidance in terms of what actions and decisions are appropriate and what are not appropriate as well as spelling out specifically, and in some instances exactly, what steps should be taken in numerous situations dealing with and affecting personnel within the organization.

> **CONCEPT #331:** *Personnel handbooks provide a blueprint for future action and decisions relating to people working within the organization.*

Such a handbook also serves as an important informational tool for all people within the sport organization including those in management. This is because everyone needs to be fully aware of what is expected of both personnel and management and be able to plan and act accordingly. Finally, such a handbook means that with the establishment of appropriate and timely policies, procedures and practices, there is no need to reinvent the wheel when it comes to making decisions or implementing various procedures, policies or actions which affect people within the business.

Besides, it is always better and more effective to establish procedures, policies and practices relating to staff well in advance of when they are needed. Waiting until a "situation" exists (especially a controversial one) and then attempting to create or establish such procedures and policies as well as make major or significant decisions in "the heat of battle" is not only foolish, but also self-defeating in the long run.

THE IMPORTANCE OF QUALITY PERSONNEL

The key to the success of most businesses rests in the personnel of the organization. It is personnel who work with the public. It is personnel who deal with issues, problems and challenges, both internally and externally. The sport leader who is skilled and experienced in dealing with personnel (paid/unpaid) and knowledgeable about all aspects of personnel management is in an excellent position to be a successful manager. It takes a person who is aware of the general principles of personnel management and who possesses excellent interpersonal skills to successfully serve as a leader and manager within a sport business in today's society. And it will only become more difficult in the future. The challenge is sometimes daunting but the rewards and satisfaction can be significant, both on a personal and professional level.

CONCLUSIONS

The heart of any sport, recreation or fitness organization is the people who work within the entity. Sport managers need to be highly skilled and adept in working with personnel, paid and volunteer. It is especially important that one is competent with the process of attracting, selecting, hiring, evaluating, training, rewarding and retaining qualified and competent personnel. With adequate, talented and motivated personnel the sport manager will have the necessary resources with which to successfully meet the myriad challenges which surely will be present in most profit as well as not-for-profit organizations.

REFERENCES

Alden, E. A. (2001, October/November). Goal: A good hire. *Athletic Management, 13*(6), 41-42, 44, 46, 48.

Alm, R. (2002, November 10). Author: Companies must focus on identifying employee strengths. *The Sun.* p. 2.

Balog, K. (1995, May 17). Coaches find fans in management. *USA Today*, p. 1-B, 2-B.

Benefits influence job candidates. (1999, December 13). *USA Today,* p. B-1.

Barlow, S. (1993). Words of wisdom: Harvey Mackay tells how to out swim the

sharks. *Entrepreneur, 21*(4), 75-79.

Buckingham, M., and Coffman, C. (1999). *First, Break All the Rules: What the World's Greatest Managers Do Differently,* New York: Simon & Schuster.

Byrnes, N. (2005, October 10). Star search. *BusinessWeek,* pp. 68-71.

Carpenter, L.. (1997). Interview questions. *Strategies, 10*(4), 11-12.

Cioletti, J. (1999, August). The paper chase. *Club Industry,* pp. 15-19.

Fardelmann, M.A. (1994). Up-to-date ideas in evaluations. *Athletic Management, VI*(6), 41-44.

Fritz, R. (1992, June). The competitive edge—Managing your entrepreneurial company. *Entrepreneur, 20*(6), 58, 60-61.

Gaskin, L.P., Lumpkin, A., and Tennett, L. K. (2003). Mentoring new faculty in higher education. *Journal of Physical Education, Recreation and Dance, 74*(8), 49-53.

Haney, M.W. (1995). Employee evaluations. *Fitness Management, 11*(12), 38-40.

Henry, T. (1995, February 21). On a five-point scale. *USA Today*, p. D-1

Hiring—No longer a piece of cake. (1993, Fall). *NASPE NEWS*, Issue # 5, p. 5.

Hoch, D. (2005, October/November). Lifesaving Techniques. *Athletic Management, XVII*(6), 41-45.

Hopp, B. & Swedburg, R. (1996). Hiring the wrong candidate. *Journal of Physical Education, Recreation and Dance, 67*(3), 58-59.

Jones, D. (1997, December 11). Employers going for quality hires, not quantity. *USA Today*, p. B-1.

Jones, D. (2001, February 27). Welch: Nurture best workers, pose bottom 10%. *USA Today*, p. 2-B

Jones, D. (2001, May 30). More firms cut workers ranked at bottom to make way for talent. *USA Today*, pp. 1-B, 2-B.

Kerr, K.M. (2005, September). Screen play. *Athletic Business, 29*(9), 44, 46 48.

Koch, W.B. (1994). Common evaluation goals with unique faculty roles in higher education. *The Chronicle of Physical Education in Higher Education, 6*(1), 1, 11.

McCutcheon, B. & Robinson, M.J. (1997). New coach on the block. *Athletic Management, IX*(4), 23-24, 26-29.

McDermott, M. (1993, March). High-stakes headhunting: 15 tips on hiring the best employees. *Club Industry, 9*(8), 24-31.

Memmott, C. (1999, June 1). Employers learn one size doesn't fit all. *USA Today*, p 10-B.

Miller, L.K., Pitts, B.G., & Fielding, L.W. (1993). Legal concerns in writing job recommendations. *The Physical Educator, 50*(1), 47-51.

Mumford, V. and Fuller, V . (2002, August). Creating a new scoreboard. *Athletic Management, IX*(5), 24, 27, 27.

Murphy, D. (1999, May 31). Great bosses break the rule. *San Francisco Examiner*, p. 8-D.

Pessin, F. (1997, March). Hiring by degree. *Fitness Management, 13*(4), 31-33.

Pitts, E. H. (1996, March), Getting the desired job performance. *Fitness Management, 12*(4), p. 6.

Plummer, T. (1997). Staffing for success. *Fitness Management, 13*(10), 31, 33-36, 39-40.

Roberts, W. (1993). *Victory secrets of Attila The Hun*. New York: Doubleday Publishers.

Sattler, T.P. & Mullen, J.E. (1994, December). Hiring for success. *Fitness Management, 10*(13), 40, 42, 44.

Schneider, R.C., and Stier, W.F., Jr. (2006). Sport management field experiences as experiential learning: ensuring beneficial outcomes and preventing exploitation. *SMART Journal, 2*(2), 36-43. http://spectrum.troy.edu/~smart/fieldexperience.pdf

Stier, Jr., W.F. (1987). Competencies of athletic administrators. *The Bulletin: The Connecticut Association for Health and Physical Education, Recreation and Dance Journal, 33(2),* 8; reprinted in *The Athletic Director,* (1988, January). American Alliance for Health, Physical Education, Recreation and Dance, January, p. 3.

Stier, Jr., W.F. (1989). Doing their part—Employment of part-time employees in Sports. *College Athletic Management, 1(3),* 38-39.

Stier, Jr., W.F. (1990) Wanted: Renaissance athletic directors. *Athletic Director, 7(3),* 34, 35, 42

Stier, Jr., W.F. (1993, May). The ins and outs of evaluating coaches. *Athletic Management, V(3),* 34-37, 39.

Stier, Jr., W.F. (1994, April 15). *Job Marketability and Career Planning Within HPERD & A.* Paper presented at the National Conference of the American Alliance for Health, Physical Education, Recreation and Dance (AAHPERD), Denver, Colorado.

Stier, Jr., W.F. (1997, March 23). *How to Secure a Professional Position in the 21st Century.* Paper presented at the National Conference of the American Alliance for Health, Physical Education, Recreation and Dance (AAHPERD), St. Louis, Missouri.

Stier, Jr., W.F. (1997, October 6). *The Essentials of Corporate Sponsorship (Partnership) in Physical Education, Sport and Recreation in the Americas.* Presentation at the International Conference on "Alianza Estratégica Para La Educación Física, El Deporte Y La Recreación". ["Strategic Alliance for Physical Education, Sport and Recreation], México City, México.

Stull, G.A. (1990). The effective vita veracity, integrity, truthfulness, accuracy. *Journal of Physical Education, Recreation and Dance, 61(1),* 28-29.

Success is the same in business or sports. (1988, September). *Athletic Business, 12(9),* 30-32, 34, 36.

Tulenko, P. (2003, March 24). Take the time to hire the right sales staff; train them well. *Herald-Tribune,* p. 21.

Unpaid interns: Cheap, effective and often illegal. (1996, August 26). *The Dominion Post,* p. 4-D.

Wakin, E. (1991, August). Give employees feedback, not criticism. *Today's Office,* pp. 22, 23.

Wong, G.M. (1997, May). The official story. *Athletic Business, 21(5),* 20, 22.

DISCUSSION TOPICS

1. Explain the advantages and disadvantages of working with the five different types of personnel or staff within a sport, recreation or fitness organization.

2. Identify a specific sport, recreation or fitness entity and relate how outsourcing might be most appropriate in terms of use of personnel.

3. Arbitrarily select a hypothetical sport business and identify a specific task(s) facing the entity—then enumerate the specific qualities of personnel whom you would want to be involved with addressing the task(s).

4. Differentiate between various sources of personnel for any typical sport, recreation or fitness organization. Specify the advantages and disadvantages of each source.

5. Write a specific job description for a new employee whose main responsibility will be to market and sell season tickets for a triple-A minor league baseball team located in a metropolitan area with some 500,000 population.

6. Write a specific job advertisement suitable for national distribution for the imaginary job mentioned in # 5 above.

7. Search the WWW and secure 20 listings of openings for positions related to the sport, recreation and fitness industries.

8. Establish appropriate questions to ask of potential interviewees in the imaginary job mentioned in # 5 and # 6 above.

9. Establish ways and means of evaluating and assessing one's own personnel within a hypothetical work situation in the world of sport, recreation or fitness.

10. Explain the concept behind the statement "punish the competent and reward the incompetent."

Chapter

11

Marketing, Fundraising, Promotions, Publicity and Public Relations in the World of Sport

Students Can Play a Major Role in the Excitement Associated with Sport.
[courtesy of Montana Sports Information, David Steele, photographer]

CHAPTER OBJECTIVES

This chapter will help the reader to:

• Appreciate the importance of winning teams upon successful marketing and promotion of sport programs;
• Reveal the implications of the growth in NCAA Division athletic budgets;
• Understand the importance of generating additional resources for sport entities;
• Differentiate between marketing, fundraising and promotional activities;

- Appreciate the need for sport managers to be competent in generating additional resources for their organizations;
- Cite three types of resources or tools commonly sought by sport organizations;
- Understand that fundraising is a means to an end and not an end in itself;
- List three common methods of generating additional financial resources;
- Outline the components of fundraising;
- Cite the implications of the "Flutie Factor;"
- Conceptualize the essential elements of a successful corporate sponsorship or partnership agreement;
- Illustrate the differences between hard and soft data;
- Define the role of marketing within a sport organization;
- Explain the components (5Ps) of the marketing mix;
- Understand techniques used to facilitate donor management;
- Define the term, Lexus Lots;
- Outline the importance of sales of Luxury Suites;
- Provide examples relating to the eleven fundamental standards of fundraising.

THE PROBLEM TODAY—THE LACK OF ADEQUATE FINANCIAL SUPPORT

American sports, at all levels, have undergone more change in recent years than at any other time in the history of our country. And, the world of sports continues to change and evolve at the present time in response to many outside forces in our society.

Accompanying these changes are myriad problems, as well as challenges and opportunities unprecedented in our history (Fox, 1990). Many of these problems and challenges revolve around money, or, more aptly put, the absence of sufficient monies to adequately fund a variety of sport programs at all levels from youth and recreational sports to the professional level (Stier, 1998).

As a result, successful modern sport managers are those individuals who are able to secure sufficient funding for their programs. In the past, this has usually meant being able to secure funding through the normal budgetary process of the organization. Today, and in the foreseeable future, this also involves the securing of resources through outside fundraising and promotions. The purpose of this chapter is to provide a glimpse into an exciting and demanding area of sport in which there have been significant changes in recent years, seeking outside financial support and funding through fundraising, marketing, and promotions.

THE CHALLENGE TODAY—
ADAPTING TO THE CHANGES IN THE SPORT SCENE

One of the major tasks currently facing managers at all levels of sport is to remain current and up-to-date and to continue to learn and to be able to adapt to the changes and innovations that occur in all areas and levels of sport. One area that has seen a great deal of change in recent years is the need for additional financial and moral support for most sport programs. Both school and non-school sports programs are seemingly always in need of more financial resources. Failing to obtain outside support has required some sport organizations and some schools to curtail segments of their activities or eliminate entire programs (Stier, 1987a).

> CONCEPT #332:　*Sport mangers need to be up-to-date and abreast of changes in the profession—and be able to meet current demands and needs.*

Because financial resources are becoming more difficult to obtain through the traditional budgetary request process made within the sponsoring organization, the frugal management of available funds and the securing of additional (outside) financial resources remains a formidable challenge. This remains true whether one is at the youth sport level or in recreation programs, a school based athletic organization, or involved in professional sports. The modern sport professional is expected to be highly skilled in a variety of fundraising strategies as well as educated in the allied activities of promotions, marketing and public relations (Stier, 1993b).

Three recent and very effective means of generating funds to support sporting events and activities are (1) use of endowments by schools to pay for coaches' salaries as well as scholarships for the athletes, (2) selling naming rights for almost anything, buildings, grounds, entrances to stadiums, scoreboards, signs, etc., and (3) use of sponsorships by organizations and entities for individual teams, whole athletic departments, as well as for physical buildings and sites, etc.

IMPORTANCE OF SPORTS TO THE PROMOTION/
FUNDRAISING/MARKETING SCENE AT THE COLLEGE LEVEL

Successful athletic teams at the college/university level can have a tremendous positive impact upon the schools themselves in terms of marketing, branding, alumni relations, school spirit, licensing and even admissions to the institution of higher learning. Dr. Jo Ann Gora, then president of Ball State University, was quoted as saying: "Division I athletics gives you an opportunity to achieve national recognitions that you could work 50 years on the academic side and never achieve. When alums come back, they don't sit in an English class" (College Athletic Clips, 2006, p. 1).

The so-called "Flutie Factor" is alive and continues to exert its considerable influence. The "Flutie Factor" refers to the tremendous positive financial, marketing, and publicity impact upon a school and athletic program when that school has an outstanding (read winning) sports team (Stier, 2003).

Witness, in 2006, the tremendous success of the upstart and very successful Division I basketball team from George Mason University. The winning team's tremendous success (final four appearance) in the post season NCAA tournament had a very definite positive impact upon the school's admissions efforts as well as its fundraising efforts for both the athletic department as well as for the entire university. In fact, Andrew Flagel, the dean of admissions at the school, indicated that there is no way an institution of higher education could responsibly spend the amount of money that it would take to replicate the type of positive exposure that George Mason University enjoyed (Alesia, 2006).

UTILIZING MODERN TOOLS—COMPUTERS AND THE INTERNET

Sport organizations of all types must take advantage of the cutting edge knowledge and tools available to businesses. These include, but are not limited to the various computer tools and the Internet. Some 20± years ago saw 98% of the NCAA Division I athletic (marketing) programs utilizing computers in their marketing efforts but only 42.9% (49 out of 114) utilized the internet and only 37.7% (43 out of 114) had a departmental web page (Farrell & McCann, 1997). Today, those figures seem ludicrous indeed. Today, no sophisticated sport entity would not possess a meaningful, informational and updated web presence on the Internet. Indeed, even high schools now employ the power of the internet and computers and web sites to promote and market their programs and inform/educate their constituencies.

THE NEED TO GENERATE ADDITIONAL RESOURCES

> *CONCEPT # 333: Fundraising and promoting have become essential responsibilities for many sport organizations today— at all levels.*

The reason that the need to generate additional resources for sport programs has never been greater can be traced principally to two factors. First, the increasing cost of supporting quality sport programs require it. This increase in cost is due to both inflation and the desire or the perceived need to do more and more within individual sports programs. Second, money that is being allocated to sports programs through the normal budgetary process is often insufficient to get the job done (Stier, 1992).

Inflation affects all areas of sport. Salaries, insurance, equipment and supplies, and rent as well as transportation are just a few of the areas that are hard hit by annual inflation. Almost everything costs more today than yesterday and there is no end in sight. Almost every category of expenditure in the area of sport will continue to increase the cost of doing business in the future. Even the cost of raising additional resources will continue to rise (Palmisano, 1984).

The result is that youth sport groups, recreational departments, and athletic programs in schools and colleges, as well as professional sport organizations, are more and more frequently experiencing increasing pressure to obtain additional monies if sizable deficits are to be avoided (Wieberg & Witosky, 1991b; Stier, 1994b). Today, the budget allocation of many sport organizations meets less of the programmatic needs of their constituencies, because money via the regular budget is not inexhaustible. Even attempting to increase the efficiency and effectiveness of the day-to-day fiscal operations with an eye to saving money through the wise management of existing resources will free up only a finite amount of funds, which is frequently insufficient.

As a result of these frequent budget shortfalls, coupled with the increased cost of doing business, those involved in the management of sport are forced to increasingly look to outside sources to obtain additional assets (money, goods, and services). Frequently, the only alternative left, in schools as well as outside of the school based sport programs, lies in fundraising and promotional activities (Wieberg & Witosky, 1991a). As a result, sport leaders need to possess an accurate and comprehensive understanding of the total fundraising process and all that that entails. Only by having such an understanding will individual sport organizations be able to meet the financial challenges facing them now and in the years to come.

> **CONCEPT # 334:** *Many financial challenges are not solvable merely by the frugal management of available funds.*

Even frugal money management and parsimonious spending may not be enough to provide a quality athletic experience in the 21st century. Sports people need to face reality and contemplate the possibility of engaging in some type of internal and/or external fundraising activity, in addition to their efforts to secure money through the regular budgetary process and by frugal money management, see figure # 11.1.

FIGURE 11.1 The Funding Model of Sports: Climbing the Steps to Fiscal Solvency

The problem, however, is that most sport managers in the past have had no formal training or education in fundraising, promotions, and marketing. Rather, many have learned the ins and outs of fundraising and promotions through the school of hard knocks, that is, experientially. This has to change if sport administrators are to remain in the forefront of managerial professionals—and indeed this situation is rapidly changing with more sport managers being trained in the fundamentals of fundraising, marketing, promotions, public relations and publicity.

College Athletics Is a Big Time Business

College athletics, at the NCAA Division I level, is truly a big time business. During 2004-2005, over $845 million dollars were donated to NCAA Divison I athletic programs.

Also during 2004-2005, there were 15 NCAA Division I schools with a budget (source: U.S. Department of Education, individual schools' 2004-2005 EADA reports) greater than $60-million. These schools included: (1) The Ohio State University—$89.7, (2) University of Texas—$89.6, (3) University of Michigan—$78.4, (4) University of Florida—$77.3, (5) University of Wisconsin—$75.2, (6) University of Tennessee—$71.5, (7) University of Georgia—$68.7, (8) University of Oklahoma—$63.7, (9) Texas A & M University—$62.8, (10) Virginia University—$62.3, (11) University of Alabama—$62.2,—$60.7 (Revenues and costs for D1-A schools, College Athletic Clips, 5-20-06). Note: the United States government requires that every college and university that accepts federal money must file an annual financial report to the United States Department of Education (US DOE), according to the Equity in Athletics Disclosure Act (EADA).

The Story of One University's Efforts at Balancing the Budget

The Ohio State University, with the largest athletic budget among all NCAA Division I schools in 2006 ($90-million operating budget) is faced with the daunting task of supplementing this seemingly staggering sum. Two-thirds of this $90-million operating fund comes from ticket sales with various fundraising efforts accounting for the remaining $30-milion. Examples of such efforts include, but are not limited to corporate sponsorships, rental of facilities, program sales, parking fees, tailgating, etc. (Porentas, 2006).

TYPES OF RESOURCES AND TOOLS

What resources should the sport administrator or fundraiser seek? What types of resources are there? When one thinks of fundraising one naturally conjures up efforts to raise dollars—cold, hard cash. This is entirely understandable. However, fundraising efforts should not be limited to mere *cash solicitation* but can include attempts to garner needed *services* as well as tangible *goods* and *products.*

CONCEPT #335: *Fundraisers are involved with the solicitation of various types of resources, tools and assets.*

Fundraisers need to think in terms of cash, of course. However, they should not neglect the solicitation of any resource when seeking contributions. In point of fact, anything that can be used for the benefit of the sport organization becomes a legitimate objective of any fundraising effort. Services can include accounting services, graphic arts assistance, secretarial help, legal advice, reconditioning of equipment, laundry services, and so forth. Goods and products encompass a whole range of physical objects donated such as food, specific sport equipment and supplies, actual vehicles, facilities, and office supplies and equipment, among others.

CONCEPT #336: *Fundraising is merely a means to an end—not an end in itself.*

Resources (money, services and goods) should typically be viewed as means to an end and not as an end in themselves. Money raised enables administrators to purchase needed services and/or goods for the benefit of the sport program (Wieberg, 1991). The donation of resources, such as goods, products, or services, frees up money that may have been earmarked for the purchase of such goods or services.

For example, an owner of a print shop who agrees to provide the paper and printing free of charge for an athletic department's football brochure might save the school some $4,000 to $6,000 in production and material costs. The money saved can then be spent to satisfy other needs. Similarly, when an accounting firm agrees that there will be no charge (a donation of services) for conducting this year's annual audit, the money thus saved may be appropriated for other purposes. The donation of services and goods should be viewed in the same way as the receipt of cash, because such donations free up cash to be used elsewhere within the sport program.

Financial resources form the foundation on which most successful sport programs rest. Resources are the tools that enable the program to realize its objective. Without adequate resources the sport administrator sits behind the proverbial eight ball and is left without a full arsenal with which to sustain the sport operation. Thus, the generation of sufficient resources and their effective and efficient management are essential responsibilities of the modern, competent, sport administrator (Stier, 1990b).

MODERN–DAY FUNDRAISING

Modern fundraising efforts are those activities designed to generate, from other than the traditional budgetary process, additional financial resources. These resources can take the form of monies, and goods as well as services.

CONCEPT #337: *All fundraising projects involve promotional activities.*

By definition, all fundraising projects are associated with promotional activities. One cannot have a fundraising project without also involving promotional strategies, tactics, and activities. Planning a fundraising project means having some type of activity or activities, which helps promote the sponsoring organization.

COMPONENTS OF FUNDRAISING

Figure 11.2 illustrates a conceptualization of the fundraising process. At the core of the process is the specific fundraising project or activity itself. The process is dependent on successful relationships among various individuals, both one's own staff (paid and volunteers) and with the various constituencies or segments of the public toward whom the fundraising effort is to be geared or targeted. Additionally, the process may be enhanced through the prudent use of specific marketing, promotions, and public relations tactics that facilitate the successful implementation of the actual fundraising project.

FIGURE 11.2: Conceptualization
of the Fundraisng Process (Stier, 1992)

Permeating the entire process of fundraising and fundamental to its success is the planning of all details within a specified time frame. Planning is also an active component in the strategic marketing or "positioning" of an idea, a service, or a product, in the selection of *effective promotional techniques*, and in the establishment of an *efficient public relations effort.* A successful fundraising experience is contingent on the existence of all of these components (Stier, 1990a).

Because the planning process is the very essence of any fundraising, promotion, and marketing strategy, those professionals involved in the management of sports and sport–related entities should be familiar with the planning process as well as with the fundamental principles or concepts involved in developing and implementing effective and efficient fundraising projects, promotional tactics, and marketing strategies (Stier, 1995).

DEVELOPING A FUNDRAISING AND PROMOTIONAL PLAN

A fundraising or promotional plan should be established through a meaningful, realistic, and accurate assessment or evaluation process that identifies the needs and the limitations or parameters as well as the attributes or resources of the athletic entity and the public(s) that are to be targeted. The goal of such a plan is the creation of a road map to guide the staff's actions toward the ultimate objective, the creation of a more visible entity, a more positive public image, a more viable and attractive athletic, sport, or recreational program, solvent both in terms of financial resources and in terms of human resources (Stier, 1996).

Stier (1994a) has created a template containing essential categories

**An Attractive Store for Selling Sport Merchandise
at Training Camps and Other Strategic Locations
Can Bring Many Benefitrs, Financial and Otherwise.**
[courtesy of Buffalo Bills]

for *planning* that are applicable for each and every type of fundraising and promotional project one might implement, table 11.1. Filling in the appropriate information, in sufficient detail, will greatly aid the potential fundraiser and promoter in planning, organizing, and understanding all aspects of the project and will further aid in the implementation and subsequent evaluation of the total effort.

TABLE 11.1: *Components of a Fundraising Plan*

1. Detailed description of the fundraising plan or scheme
2. Desired objectives
    A. Resources sought (money, goods and/or services)
    B. Desired image
3. Level of difficulty of the project
4. Written summary of the details of the project
5. Support and backing required
    A. The facilities needed
    B. The equipment and supplies necessary
    C. The publicity, promotional and public relations efforts that are required
    D. The time frame—in terms of planning as well as the actual length of the fundraising effort itself
    E. The cash needed
    F. The people and/or organizations necessary (special skills or competencies needed)
6. The initial risks, perils or hazards to be anticipated
7. Permissions and approvals that are necessary
8. Other information that might be helpful to explain the project

IDENTIFYING SPECIFIC MARKETS

> *CONCEPT #338:   The identification of specific markets is essential in fundraising, promotions and public relations.*

One essential element in the strategic market planning process is to identify specific target market(s) (McCarthy, 1960; Parkhouse, 1996, p. 257). Potential fundraisers, promoters, and marketers need to identify those individuals and groups who will most likely respond in a positive manner to the fundraising project or promotional effort. Qualifying prospects by identifying those most likely to contribute (on the basis of a variety of criteria) to the request for financial assistance and then narrowing one's efforts on these high priority "targets" saves time and effort in the long run, and thereby increases the overall effectiveness and efficiency of the fundraising effort (Stotlar, 1989).

GENERATING RESOURCES FOR THE SPORT PROGRAM

> **CONCEPT #339:** *Administrators must be adept at solving the fundraising puzzle—in addition to their other duties and responsibilities.*

Because there is a recognized increase in the need for sport fundraising, it is essential that sport managers develop a sound knowledge base as well as practical skills and experience in the area of fundraising. How does one go about raising resources? Essentially, there are four generally accepted categories of generating additional resources, whether such resources are actual money, goods, or services. Within each of these broad categories are literally thousands of individual fundraising ideas, techniques, strategies, methods, projects, and activities.

> **CONCEPT #340:** *There are 1001+ different fundraising projects.*

Those who would be successful fundraisers need to examine the numerous possibilities that exist within each of the four categories listed below for potential ideas that may be helpful in their own future fundraising programs. The key is to be able to utilize basic fundraising principles, guidelines, or concepts outlined in this chapter while borrowing and adapting ideas from others so that one can create an individualized, personalized fundraising project or activity that will be successful in light of one's own situation or circumstances.

Four General Methods of Generating Resources

The first method of raising resources is to simply ask (solicitation) people and organizations for contributions and donations (of money, time, services, goods). This strategy includes both single–person cultivation and appeals to groups and organizations. Examples include solicitation via phone, the mail as well as person-to-person contacts. The second method may be generated through securing special projects or fundraising tactics such as bingo nights, cow chip bingo, antique car shows, auctions, and raffles. The third method involves establishing various profit centers (concessions, ticket sales, merchandise sales, parking, etc.) within the sport area. Fourth, money as well as other resources may be generated through sponsorships or partnerships with businesses, organizations, and corporations (Stier, 1994b; Stier 1995).

An Example of One Unique Attempt to Generate Funds

Two professional teams have come up with similar and yet unique marketing and fundraising efforts. Two stadiums, the Turner Field in Atlanta, Georgia and the Miami's Office Depot Center, organized, with backing form Lexus dealerships, so-called "Lexus lots." These facilities were reserved parking for drivers of Lexus automobiles. This unique and innovative revenue source proved very successful both in terms of increasing funds as well as creating excellent public relations both for the Lexus brand and for the stadiums (Sawyer, 2006a).

CORPORATE SPONSORSHIPS AND PARTNERSHIPS

Today, a major avenue of securing big money for sport programs is based on financial arrangements with businesses and organizations. It is estimated that $9-million is spent on sponsoring sporting events, venues and teams. These have become known as corporate sponsorships and partnerships (Irwin, 1996). What exactly are corporate sponsorships or business? Today, they are not usually considered philanthropy. "With the price of sponsorship escalating, traditional corporate rationale may no longer suffice. Return on investment has replaced the philanthropic philosophy of the past" (Lough, 1996, p. 11).

Luxury Seating in Sport Facilities

One of the fastest growing means of generating significant funds for big-time sport organizations, especially in the world of professional sports, is the "sale" of luxury seating, i.e., suites. In 2001, the four major professional sport leagues had a total of 11,926 suites with an average annual lease price of over $98,000. Table 11.2 shows the number of suites for each of the four major professional leagues and their annual lease price.

TABLE 11.2: *Luxury Suites in Sport Facilities during 2001* **(Sawyer, 2006b)**

League	# suites	# teams	annual lease price
MLB	2,286	30	$ 85,000.00
NBA	2,533	29	$113,000.00
NFL	4,294	31	$100,000.00
NHL	2,813	30	$ 77,000.00
Total	11,926	120	$98,730.00 average

It is a mutually beneficial business arrangement entered into for very specific purposes from the perspective of the corporation as well as for the sport entity (White and Irwin, 1996). From the corporate side, the objectives include the potential enhancement of the corporate image, the increase of the company's visibility and its awareness among various publics, the reaching of new market segments, the securing of a greater market share, the development of new distribution channels, and the increase in sales (Gray, 1996, p. 33).

CONCEPT #341: *In sport sponsorship agreements, one hand does indeed wash the other.*

Of course, the ultimate objective of the business or corporation is to improve the financial bottom line and to enhance its image. But there has to be significant benefits accruing to the sport entity as well. From the perspective of the sport organization, business partnerships and corporate sponsorships are desirable because of an infusion of additional financial resources, coupled with a sharing of the positive image of the business partner or sponsor. The bottom line for the sport organization is money, much needed additional resources.

"Perhaps at no time in history has there been more competition among sport properties for corporate sponsorship funding" (Morris & Irwin, 1996, p. 7). Where once such sports–related sponsorships or partnerships were thought to be the exclusive domain of the professional sports setting, this is not the case today. In fact, such sponsorships and partnering efforts have not only grown at the collegiate levels but have permeated secondary school sports, as well as the recreation area.

Women's sports have been especially successful in securing significant corporate sponsorships, especially in professional golf and tennis and at the NCAA Division I level. "The projected future growth rate in sponsorships from sport industry leaders has been estimated at 20% per year" (Lough, 1996, p. 11, citing Schlossberg, 1990). Stotlar (1993) estimated that the combined dollars spent for sport marketing and sport sponsorships in the United States totaled $2.4 billion in 1990. Only a year later (1991) this spending figure had increased over 50 percent to some $3.5 billion. And not only has the spending increased, but the number of businesses and corporations becoming sponsors has similarly risen (Stotlar, 1993).

CONCEPT #342: *Hard data is needed by businesses in order to evaluate the effectiveness of any corporate sponsorship.*

In order for any sponsorship agreement to be truly successful there must be an appropriate match between the sport entity and the business partner, with the likelihood of benefits being realized by both parties. In order for any business organization to make an accurate assessment of a proposed sponsorship, and the possible benefits resulting from such an agreement, hard data must be provided to show the likelihood of meaningful benefits accruing to the potential sponsor.

Likewise, there must be accurate records kept in terms of the actual results of any sponsorship or partnership so as to prove to the business entity that such an arrangement is indeed worthwhile. Without such documentation about the impact such an agreement has had on the company's image enhancement, increased visibility, greater awareness among groups or constituencies, new market segments, greater market share, new distribution channels, and/or increase in sales, there might be little optimism for a repeat agreement with the same corporation or business.

In conducting marketing research, Stotlar (1989, p. 47) cites two different ways to conduct marketing research, utilizing primary or secondary sources. Primary research sources are those conducted directly with customers. For example, the use of mail surveys,

**Building Fan Support with Youngsters—
the Paying Fans of the Future.**
*[courtesy of St. Lucie METS, Port St. Lucie, FL,
photo by Erin Rescigno]*

and phone and personal interviews. Secondary research efforts are conducted from other sources, such as an analysis of data that already exists. For example, the examination of the organization's past activities, tickets sold and to whom, gross sales from concessions operations or from the apparel store staffed by sport staff. Other examples of using secondary sources would be searching for information (hard data) from the public library, Chamber of Commerce, and/or subscribing to any number of professionally constructed or researched databases of statistical data.

Some examples of such organizations include *Team Marketing Report, IEG Sponsorship Report,* and the *Sports Report.* Using hard data from any of these sources enhances the sport manager's ability to make (and justify) informed, current, and appropriate decisions. Possession of such information also helps inform others and helps to justify courses of action (Stotlar, 1996).

CONCEPT # 343: *Donor management is essential—use development software to keep track of current and potential fans, ticket buyers, sponsors, etc.*

MARKETING

Marketing is often referred to as the essential component in identifying the needs of others. Marketing activities can be used to motivate people to want your product, service, program, or to accept your ideas and positions. It means satisfying an individual's real or perceived needs. Marketing encompasses all of the efforts used in moving goods and services (and ideas) from the sport administrator (producer) to the general public (consumer) and can involve the acts of selling, promoting, advertising, and packaging. (Guarlnik, 1970; Buell, 1984: Cutlip, Center, & Broom, 1985; Railey & Railey, 1988).

CONCEPT #344: *Consistency is an important concept in marketing and promoting—no one wants to be considered a so-called "flash in the pan."*

Bogh tangible goods as well as intangible concepts and ideas, may be marketed to individuals or groups. Buell (1984) indicated that marketing not only identifies needs and wants of constituencies but also helps marshal the organization's resources to produce the desired products or services. "Marketing is the key to securing and satisfying customers. In a free market economy consumers have a variety of choices as to how they will satisfy their needs. Therefore, those institutions that survive are the ones that are most efficient at identifying the needs and wants of consumers" (Buell, 1984, p. 616).

Marketing can also help create needs in individuals where such needs either did not previously exist or the potential customer was not aware of such needs (Stier, 1987b). Effective marketing can even help persuade potential consumers to partake of products or services because of a perception that it's offerings will satisfy a real or perceived need. The 4Ps of marketing (the marketing mix), coined by E. Jerome McCarthy, refers to the four basic components of marketing (that is, how any product, service, or idea might be acquired or procured by individuals and/or groups) that includes *product, price, place,* and *promotion* (Mullin, 1983; Railey & Railey, 1988; Stotlar, 1993, p. 24; Horine, 1996).

Today, the marketing mix might properly be thought of as the 5Ps with the addition of the category, Publics (Stier, 1990a). Thus, the marketing mix can be viewed as:

1. The **Product,** service, or idea that is to be accessible;
2. The **Place** or niche in which the product, service, or idea will be most readily acceptable, distributed, or shared;
3. The appropriate and acceptable **Price** that the market will bear;
4. The **Promotional** activity or strategy associated with the product, service, or idea;
5. The **Public(s)** or constituencies that will be identified as potential customers, or consumers or recipients.

In marketing, as well as in fundraising, one needs to be concerned with the product (service or idea) that is to be marketed to the intended consumer. Additionally, the price or cost of that which is marketed needs to be established as well as the place or site where the marketing will take place. In addition, one must be concerned with the promotional aspects of those specific techniques designed to garner increased sales and/or acceptance by the targeted population. Finally, those individuals and/or groups (publics) to whom the marketing will be targeted should be identified.

A STRATEGIC FUNDRAISING, PROMOTIONS, AND MARKETING PLAN

It is essential that a global athletic strategic fundraising, promotions, and marketing plan, one compatible with the sport program's multiple missions, be identified, developed, and implemented. Such a plan or strategy needs to be established by means of a realistic and accurate identification and evaluation of the needs, the limitations or parameters, as well as the attributes or resources of the athletic entity.

Thus, the strategic marketing plan serves as a road map to guide staff members' actions toward the ultimate objective, i.e., a sound program, both in terms of financial and human resources. Such a program results in greater visibility, a more positive public image, and ultimately a more viable and attractive athletic program (Buell, 1984).

PROMOTIONAL ACTIVITIES

Sport promotion is associated with the selling of ideas (images, attitudes, and opinions), services, and products to the general public. The goal is to motivate others to accept specific ideas or concepts and/or to purchase or accept specific services and/or products as a result of identifiable promotional and communication efforts (Stier, 1994b). Promotion involves specific activities or techniques used to further or advance the organization by increasing the sales of ideas, services, and/or products to others (Horine, 1996, p. 67). Promotion is thought of as part of the marketing process. Promotional efforts may be implemented to establish, reinforce, or even change opinions and attitudes regarding the sport program. "The promotional tools consist of personal selling, publicity, advertising and sale promotion" (Graham, 1994, p. 9).

**CONCEPT # 345:   *Not all promotional activities are associated
with fundraising efforts.***

The key to promotion is innovation, uniqueness, appropriateness, and attractiveness as viewed by the public or the targeted population. Such activities may motivate specific changes in behavior concerning not only the sports program itself but also those individuals associated with the program. Promotional activities can also be used to increase or create a demand for a product or a service or the acceptance of an idea. Promotional activities do not necessarily have to be related to or associated with fundraising efforts.

**CONCEPT # 346:   *You have to have something of worth, of interest to promote
to emphasize, to highlight.***

A sport program that offers (promotes) a special family night experience to the community, complete with special activities for all family members, is attempting to sell the concept that the sport event itself can be a family affair and enjoyed by youngsters and adults alike. Other reasons for conducting such a specific promotion might be to generate additional paying fans in the future as well as to help create a positive image and wholesome reputation on behalf of the sporting event and the sponsoring organization itself. However, the promotion is more effective if members of the general public find the activity to be of value or of interest. There has to be a motivating factor (a hot button) that entices individuals to action, to take part, to become involved.

PUBLIC RELATIONS AND PUBLICITY

Public relations can involve everything associated or connected with the sport organization. Everything, literally, having to do with the sport program becomes part of or is a component of public relations. Public relations are the aggregate product of all activities and things existing under the umbrella of the sport entity (Stier, 1986). The objective of public relations is to secure support or a positive acceptance from others (Bucher, 1987).

The manner in which any home athletic event is organized and carried out in terms of concessions, treatment of officials, conditions of the bleachers, lighting in the facility, cleanliness of the restrooms, availability of suitable and safe parking, the actions of coaches and athletes—can affect the public relations efforts of the host organization either positively or negatively.

> *CONCEPT #347:   Public relations involve everything that is associated or connected with the sport entity.*

When considering fundraising and promotional activities, it is important to recognize that there is a significant difference between the isolated, fragmented promotional or fundraising type effort and a planned, coordinated system or strategy or athletic promotional activities designed to achieve objectives on a large scale (Ensor, 1988). How many sports–minded people become caught up in the rat race of conducting and promoting multiple, isolated and fragmented fundraising efforts without the benefit of an overall strategic marketing plan? In all probability, too many.

Publicity is a sub-set of public relations, but its goals and purposes are more immediate (Mason and Paul, 1988). Its message is more short–term and is meant to inform (provide very specific information to others) or establish a general (positive) awareness of something, some program, or someone among those to whom the publicity is directed. Publicity may be thought of as targeted or general in nature. As targeted publicity, the message is geared toward a specific targeted population. General publicity is more of a shotgun approach aimed at the general public.

COORDINATING PROMOTIONAL ACTIVITIES, FUNDRAISING TACTICS, MARKETING STRATEGIES AND IMAGE ENHANCING EFFORTS

When a sport program's promotional activities, fundraising tactics, marketing strategies, and image–enhancing efforts are considered, it is absolutely essential that these activities be part of an overall, coordinated, approved institutional or organizational plan. No, this is not suggesting that every single activity (associated with promotions, fundraising, publicity, public relations, etc.) of the sport entity must be scrutinized and approved by others outside of the sport arena or by higher–ups within the sport organization.

What is indicated, however, is that there is a need for all individuals involved in sport management, in the planning and the implementation of sport promotional activities, to cease acting and competing like the "Long Ranger" and to begin to act as members of the overall sport organization's team, a team that views areas of publicity, image enhancement, public relations, fundraising, and promotional activities, from a larger perspective of the total institution or organization. Only through close cooperation with other entities within the overall organization can the sports program survive unscathed, both internally and externally, in its efforts to achieve objectives that can be facilitated by promotional activities.

FUNDRAISING VIEWED AS A CURE-ALL

Fundraising itself is not a guaranteed solution to the financial crunch or other challenges that currently plague so many of our sports programs and organizations, at all levels. Nor is fundraising as easy as it looks or as simplistic as many would have us believe. There is usually more to fundraising than merely gathering a bunch of youngsters together and having a car wash at the local convenience store to raise $300 on a Sunday afternoon.

CONCEPT # 348: *Fundraising is not a cure–all.*

Fundraising should not be merely selling candy bars in the school or around the neighborhood whenever the fancy strikes us. Unfortunately, fundraising is all too frequently viewed as nothing more than nickel-and-dime car washes or the nonchalant selling of candy bars. And, all too often, the results are ill-conceived projects, resulting in wasted or failed efforts, and bruised or negative feelings generated among the general public as well as among supporters of the sport or athletic programs.

CHARACTERISTICS OF FUNDRAISERS AND PROMOTERS

Successful fundraising requires specific knowledge, skills, and experiences. Those involved in fundraising need to understand the concepts and the principles that are applicable to all fundraising efforts and projects. Not everyone can be a successful sport fundraiser. It takes effort and work and an understanding of general fundraising concepts and principles.

CONCEPT # 349: *Successful fundraisers and promoters are producers, not mere talkers.*

An adage in fundraising circles is that "talk is cheap." It is far more challenging to be truly successful (effective and efficient) in fundraising and promotion. There are many wannabes and would-be promoters and fundraisers in the sport world today. However, there are also fewer producers in terms of meaningful, sustained promotions, fundraising —project marketing plans and public relation efforts.

CONCEPT # 350: *Fundraisers are risk takers and quick learners.*

Of course, no self-respecting fundraiser or promoter could exist for long without being capable of taking *calculated risks* tempered with good *judgment* based on *facts* and *data* (as well as just a smidgen of intuition). Successful sport managers are no strangers to risk taking. This trait serves them well in the area of fundraising, promotions, and marketing. Another positive attribute of successful fundraisers is *the* willingness to learn from their own experiences and the experiences (both successful and unsuccessful) of others. This characteristic, the ability to learn from past experiences, involves both the willingness to borrow ideas and the skill to adapt them to suit one's own peculiar circumstances, needs, resources, and objectives.

**Encouraging Youth Support
is an Absolute Necessity.**
*[courtesy of University of Tennessee
Sports Information Office]*

Another factor that can help an individual become more proficient in fundraising and promotions is further education. One must remain at the cutting edge of fundraising, promotion, marketing, and public relations if one is to be competitive. Toward this end, it is recommended that would–be practitioners of the art and science of fundraising, marketing, and promotions attend clinics, workshops, conventions, and forums as well as to be avid readers of the professional literature. Only by doing so can one remain at the cutting edge of a very, very competitive field. There are thousands and thousands of variations of fundraising activities and more adaptations are being developed every day. One must keep up with the latest innovations.

QUESTIONS TO ASK PRIOR TO INITIATING ANY FUNDRAISER

There are many different factors that must be considered and questions that must be answered when making informed decisions regarding the implementation of any specific fundraising project. Ten such questions are listed below to aid the would-be fundraiser– promoter in arriving at an informed decision about whether to implement a fundraising and promotional project (Stier, 1996, May).

Guiding Questions for Potential Fundraisers and Promoters

1. Is there a bonafide, legitimate need for the fundraising effort?
2. What special conditions or unique circumstances exist that might affect the fundraising project?
3. What special skills, competencies, or experiences are needed by the individuals involved in this project to make it a success?
4. What are the realistic time and priorities for the project?
5. Are there any organizational restrictions or philosophical differences that might interfere with or restrict the effort?
6. Will outside staff be utilized in addition to one's own personnel?
7. Will only one project be initiated or will there be multiple fundraising activities?
8. How will the activities be evaluated? What criteria will be used?
9. What can reasonably be expected in terms of net profit (goods, services, and cash)?
10. What are the reasonable and obtainable objectives of the organization insofar as public relations and promotion activities associated with this fundraising project?

ELEVEN FUNDAMENTAL STANDARDS OF FUNDRAISING

There are numerous general principles of fundraising and promotions. In fact, Stier (1994b) provided 127 such principles. Listed below are an additional 11 fundraising guidelines that are applicable for all types of fundraising projects and promotional activities sponsored by a high school, a college, a recreation department or a professional sports team. These guidelines originally appeared in the journal *Athletic Management* (Stier, 1993a).

> 1. *Develop an overall plan for fundraising and promotion within your organization not only for the immediate present but for the future as well.*

Those involved in fundraising must be organized and have thought through both the process and the potential challenges. Each project or event must be carefully thought through from beginning to end. Organizers should undertake a "needs" and a "wants" assessment. The organizers must have a clear idea of why they are going to raise funds and how the money will be put to use.

CONCEPT #351: *Have a clear reason and rationale for one's fundraising efforts—don't raise funds just for the heck of it.*

It is important to remember, when fundraising plans are being made, that decisions must be based on facts rather than emotions, hunches, or mere anecdotal information. Planning well in advance also prevents the sport fundraiser from interfering with the organization's overall development and fundraising efforts. This is especially important in schools and colleges where the central administration might well be involved in more general fundraising efforts.

The kiss of death for athletic fundraisers in schools is to fail to obtain prior permission to initiate a specific project from high-level administrators within the school or college. This is where a supportive central administration is invaluable. Don't be surprised, however, if specific individuals or organizations are declared "off limits" to athletic fundraisers by the central administration.

2. *Evaluate your fundraising efforts continuously—keep meticulous records to facilitate repeat projects.*

Good record keeping is an absolute must. It facilitates the conduct of repeat fundraising projects. Some projects lend themselves to being annual events. Others may not be annual projects but can be repeated at some time in the future. Always look to see how your event or project can be improved if and when you implement it again. The time to evaluate is while you are engaged in the event and immediately afterwards, while the ideas and memories are still fresh in your mind. Even projects that are one-time fundraising events should be critically evaluated because the organizers and promoters can learn things from such an event that might be applicable towards a completely different type of fundraising project.

CONCEPT #352: *Plan repeatable fundraising projects—they are easier to implement the second and third time around.*

There are three types of fundraising projects when one considers the factor of time. First, there is the one-time fundraising event. This activity will only be conducted one time. It will not be repeated. Perhaps the sports building or turf is being replaced. Parts of the old facility might be packaged and sold to the general public and fans. However, once the building is torn down or the turf is pulled up and sold—there will be no similar fundraising project the next year.

Second, fundraisers can become an annual event, much like the annual spring golf outing that patrons eagerly look forward to every year. Third, there are fundraising projects that are thought of as repeatable events. These are activities that can be repeated but are usually not for any number of reasons. Instead, this event might be conducted every two, three or four years, but it is not of such substance that it is considered worthy of being an annual event. This category of fundraising project falls between the one-time event and the annual fundraiser.

There are two reasons why it is much easier to run fundraising projects that have been implemented successfully in the past. First, the organizers can learn through their experiences and therefore can improve their skills and competencies. The workers are able, in later years, to bring off the project with less worry and work because they have done it before. Second, those participating in the fundraising event (athletes, boosters, community people, etc.) also become familiar with the project because they enjoyed attending the activity and being a part of it. In fact, they anticipate the next time that it will take place, and they eagerly agree to participate in the fundraiser when it is implemented once again.

3. *Keep things simple—both in terms of the number of fundraising activities and in their implementation.*

Keep the actual fundraising event simple in its concept and its implementation. Don't overcomplicate matters. Complex projects are prone to becoming bogged down due to myriad details. Also, keep the actual number of fundraising events to a minimum. Generally speaking, planning for three–five projects a year should be all that is necessary for school–based athletic programs. This is especially true if the projects are well planned and are big producers in generating a great deal of money, goods, and/or services (not to mention positive public relations).

CONCEPT #353: *Don't plan 1001 different fundraising projects in a single year— do fewer projects but do them well.*

It is important to be a strong advocate of keeping fundraising events simple in their structure and few in number, but, in initiating fewer projects, it is essential that they are quality projects and that they are well executed. However, fundraising events should be highly visible and they must generate significant revenue, otherwise effort and time is wasted. It is important not to waste time and effort on nickel-and-dime fundraising projects. It is better to have two fundraising projects generating some $20,000 in net profit than 15 smaller projects raising a mere $10,000. Fewer projects that are quality events can generate significant resources for the sport program.

4. *Anticipate and plan for the worse possible consequences so that the prospect of failure is minimized.*

You can't prevent problems if you don't anticipate them. And you can't anticipate problems or roadblocks if you don't plan. It is important to be able to anticipate pitfalls and problems through realistic fundraising planning while at the same time remaining flexible. Unsuccessful promoters find themselves operating in a crisis management mode much of the time. Successful fundraisers are known for their foresightedness and anticipatory skills.

CONCEPT #354:   *All fundraising projects will have problems—that is just the nature of the beast—anticipate them so you can prevent most of them.*

One can sometimes avoid failure or negative consequences by copying or adapting other people's and other organizations' successes. There are few things that are really new or truly unique in the world of fundraising. Usually events and tactics are variations and adaptations of what has been done previously, somewhere else. For example, the *athletes' walk*, an event during which pledges are solicited on behalf of those taking part in a walk over a predetermined distance, has been successfully utilized by a number of schools.

The women's athletic department at the University of Nebraska at Omaha has successfully conducted such an event for some years. The concept has also been implemented at Northern Kentucky University and is called the *NKU Women's Walk*. The event has also been used at Cal State Bakersfield as well as Boise State, where it generated some $28,000 in its first year and over $65,000 four years later. Similarly, the Fabulous Reverse Raffle that is held annually on the evening of the NCAA national basketball championship game (which allows participants to watch the big game on various large screen TVs strategically placed around the room) has been successfully used as a fundraiser for years at Ohio Northern University as well as the State University of New York, Brockport.

5. *Practice preventative measures in terms of risk management and legal liability.*

Reduce legal liability by conducting a risk management study and taking appropriate precautionary action. This is an area in which advance planning and anticipation can pay big dividends. No one wants anyone injured as a result of his or her involvement in the sport organization's fundraising project. Not only would such an occurrence result in poor public relations and negative publicity, but there is always the distinct possibility of a successful lawsuit being brought against the organizers of the fundraising project as well as against the sponsoring organization itself.

CONCEPT #355:   *It is far better to prevent legal exposure than to defend against the charge of negligence.*

Organizers need to be especially conscious of potential hazardous situations. The goal is to provide a safe environment for all of the organizers, workers and participants. Thus, great care must be taken in the training of workers (both paid and volunteer), the provision of appropriate supplies, equipment, and facilities, as well as the actual fundraising activities themselves.

CONCEPT #356: *Sport fundraisers must be knowledgeable about applicable state, county and local laws, rules and regulations.*

---

6. *Adhere to all state, county and local laws, regulations, and rules.*

Fundraising organizers must be aware of all the legal implications surrounding the fundraising event. It is imperative that all state, county, and local rules and regulations are complied with to the fullest extent. Such rules might involve special permits and licenses that authorize the sponsoring group to conduct a specific activity. Additionally, there may be restrictions against a specific type of activity without special permission being granted, for example, peddling items on a door-to-door basis without a peddler's or hawker's permit.

CONCEPT #357: *When dealing with the law, it is always best to secure advance permission than to seek forgiveness after the fact.*

Adhering to appropriate laws and regulations is especially important for those fundraisers who are involved with gambling activities and those who provide or sell liquor as part of a fundraising project. Even food events have the potential for difficulty in terms of meeting specific health standards before being able to secure appropriate licensing and permits.

It is important to secure permission before embarking on a specific course of action rather than having to seek forgiveness if one gets caught in the act of violating a law or regulation. If there are permits that should be secured or licenses that must be obtained, do so. Don't assume that just because you are associated with a sporting organization or that your group is a non-profit entity that you are exempt from meeting the standards set out in various governmental laws and statues or community rules and regulations. One must never run afoul of the law. The negative consequences, both in terms of actual penalties and embarrassment, can be significant for the sponsoring organization as well as for the individuals involved.

7. *Keep the fundraising process in its proper perspective—fundraising is a mechanism to reach an objective or goal.*

Those involved in fundraising should never forget that the purpose of their efforts is to garner additional and much needed resources (money, goods, and services) so that these resources can then be utilized to meet other, larger objectives and goals. *Fundraising is merely a vehicle.* It is not the end or the ultimate objective in and of itself. Obtaining these additional resources enables the administrators to use these resources to satisfy other wants and needs.

CONCEPT #358:   ***Don't lose sight of the ultimate objective—better support for the athletes, the team, and the program.***

Publicizing how the money generated from a fundraising event will benefit athletes or the overall sport program also helps make the event successful. Always promote and publicize how each fundraising project or activity will result in a better sport program. Emphasizing how the amateur athletes will benefit from the additional resources can be a key motivating tactic or strategy in soliciting donations for the program.

8. *Fundraising must be cost-effective, in terms of money, personnel. and time utilized.*

One must never waste resources. One should not spend a dollar to make a dollar, much less to raise only a quarter. Yet, all too frequently this is exactly what happens in some instances when all factors are considered. In some instances, the time, money, and effort spent to generate additional resources turns out not to be worth more than what is actually raised in new or additional resources.

CONCEPT #359:   ***To be truly successful every fundraising project must be cost and time–effective.***

Two of the criteria used to judge the success of any fundraising activity are the *cost* and *time effective*ness of the effort. This involves the weighing of expenditures in terms of personnel, money, time, and other resources against the actual net results gained. If the fundraising effort is neither time nor cost—effective in terms of net advantage(s) accruing to the sponsoring organization, the fundraising project is a failure. The mark of a truly successful fundraising effort is one which is cost and time–effective in terms of generating needed resources for the sport organization while establishing or reinforcing positive rapport with various outside constituencies and with the paid and volunteer staff.

9. *Fundraising projects should be appropriate for the sponsoring organization and for the community.*

CONCEPT #360:   *Before initiating a fundraising project check to see what would be appropriate and acceptable within your community.*

Sport organizers must be sensitive to the mores and the expectations of the community. Don't risk offending the community with inappropriate or unacceptable fundraising projects. Skilled and experienced fundraisers should know or find out what can be accomplished in a given community and what the community will find acceptable in the way of a fundraising project.

In some communities dancing might be frowned on. In others, card playing or other forms of gambling, including bingo might be taboo, while in others, alcohol may be disapproved. Every community has the potential for being different in terms of what might be appropriate and suitable as a fundraising project. Similarly, it is also imperative that the fundraising project doesn't become a burden or nuisance to either your volunteers, boosters, or to the people or businesses in the community who will be asked to donate or otherwise participate in your fundraising effort. In other words, don't wear out your welcome in the community either by too many events or by inappropriate projects.

10. *Work closely with volunteers—educate and motivate them.*

Sport administrators and coaches usually do not do all of the fundraising work themselves. In fact, just the opposite. Volunteers, students, parents, booster club members, community people, and alumni comprise the bulk of the fundraising team led by the sport manager or administrator appointed by the organization.

In school–based sport programs, a booster club or athletic support group (ASG) can be of immense help if the club is properly structured, organized, and supervised. Such booster organizations provide much needed elbow grease, support and numbers that are so necessary for major fundraising projects (Stier, 1987c).

CONCEPT #361:   *Sport managers need to orient, train, and motivate volunteers helping with the fundraising effort.*

Volunteers form the hub or any such booster or support group. It is important that fundraising organizers and leaders take time to orient, train, and motivate the helpers, the boosters who have been recruited or who have volunteered. No one needs well–meaning volunteers standing around, getting in the way, and becoming discouraged. Rather, organizers must work closely with boosters and volunteers to see that they are given meaningful tasks that they can successfully complete. This usually requires some formal training or orientation.

11. *Never fail to express your appreciation and thanks to donors, supporters, and helpers—both within the organization and in the community.*

Not only is it polite to say "thank you" to those who have contributed to your program by donating money, time, effort, and/or services as well as general support, but it is also simply good business. Most fundraising organizers will return to the same constituencies and publics to solicit resources and assistance once again. Having paid the proper respect in the past helps pave the way for subsequent successful fundraising projects.

> **CONCEPT #362:** ***Always, always express publicly your gratitude to those who help you—you may need their assistance again in the future.***

Involve the Family in Supporting the Local Team.
[courtesy of St. Lucie METS, Port St. Lucie, Florida, photo by Jimmy Fertitta]

It is very important that volunteers and donors not be taken for granted. In fact, many success stories in fundraising would not be possible without the support and assistance of highly dedicated, skilled volunteers and boosters. It is important that these individuals not be taken for granted. Quite the contrary. Those who have helped in the past should be made aware of how much they are appreciated and how much their assistance and backing has meant to the overall success of the fundraising process. To accept the help, the assistance, the services, the money from others—and then not to respond in a demonstrative and definitive (and public) fashion—is foolish indeed.

THE FUTURE OF SPORT FUNDRAISING AND PROMOTIONAL ACTIVITIES

Sport fundraising and promotional activities are here to stay. In the past sport people sometimes dabbled in fundraising merely because they liked the idea of being involved in such activities. However, the current situation is such that fundraising is all too frequently becoming a necessary venture. The generation of outside resources is necessary if sport programs—in youth sports, in junior and senior high schools, at the collegiate levels, in recreational departments as well as at the professional sport level—are to survive at an acceptable level in terms of both quality and quantity.

CONCEPT #363: *Fundraising and promotional activities are permanent fixtures in sport.*

It is important for sport personnel to have a realistic understanding of the fundraising process and to be able to make sound decisions with respect to the generation of outside resources. In today's world, keeping fundraising in its proper perspective is essential if the overall goals of the sport organization are to be realized.

As fundraising becomes more of an integral and expected part of the total funding process of sport organizations, it behooves those involved in such programs to develop and refine their understanding and skills in fundraising and promotions. This is especially important if one's peers are likewise engaged in fundraising efforts and are providing competition for the already scarce dollars, goods, and services.

In the end, those who fundraise need to be highly skilled and motivated, unafraid of taking calculated risks, and capable of learning from past experiences. It is these experiences, coupled with the ability to adapt general principles involved in fundraising to their present situation, that enable successful fundraisers to make appropriate and timely decisions in the world of fundraising and promotions.

CONCEPT #364: *Fundraising is either a necessary evil or a golden opportunity for sport personnel to demonstrate their competency.*

The information provided within the earlier sections of this chapter provides a beginning point for sport personnel and booster organizations to begin to build their own, individualized fundraising plan to generate the much needed resources for their own sports teams. One does not need a crystal ball to foretell that in the future more demand and greater stress will be placed on the financial capabilities of sport programs and organizations than ever before. It is up to the sport personnel to be willing and able to meet this challenge through effective and efficient fundraising tactics and methods involving the coordination and management of highly qualified, thoroughly trained and motivated individuals.

CONCLUSIONS

Sport managers must be capable of adapting to the changes that are continually taking place in the world of sport and in our society. Part of this challenge is for sport managers to be capable of securing sufficient resources (money, goods, and services) with which to run their respective programs and promote and market their organization and their various programs. Almost every sport, recreation, or fitness organization is faced, at some time or another, with the necessity and the challenge of becoming actively involved in marketing, promoting, and fundraising. For those sport managers who are prepared to aggressively address this challenge, with both an understanding of and an appreciation for the potential benefits of such involvement, the future is bright. For those who are less prepared, and who do not possess the knowledge and skills relating to fundraising, promotions and marketing, the future is bleak.

REFERENCES

Alesia, M. (2006, March 30). Colleges play, public pays. *Indianapolis Star,* p.21. http://www.indystar.com/apps/pbcs.dll/article?AID=/20060330/SPORTS/603300460/ 1004/SPORTS, retrieved April 1, 2006.

Athletics Moneygoround. (2006, April). *College Athletic Clips,* p. 1.

Bucher, C. (1987). *Management of physical education & athletic programs* (9th ed.). St. Louis: Times Mirror/Mosby College Publishing.

Buell, V.P, (1984). *Marketing management: Strategic planning approach.* New York: McGraw-Hill Book Co.

Cutlip, S.M., Center, A.H., and Broom, G.M. (1985). *Effective public relations* (6th ed.). Englewood Cliffs, N. J.: Prentice-Hall.

Ensor, R. (1988, September). Writing a strategic sports marketing plan. *Athletic Business, 12*(9), 20-23.

Farrell, P. & McCann. (1997). Computers, the Internet, and marketing college athletics, *Sport Marketing Quarterly, 6*(2), 12, 13.

Fox, D. (1990). A time to sow, a time to reap—Marketing and promotions. *Journal of Physical, Education, Recreation and Dance, 61*(3), 65-70.

Graham, P.J. (1994). *Sport business—Operational and theoretical aspects.* Madison, Wisconsin: Wm. C. Brown & Benchmark.

Gray, D.P. (1996). Sponsorship on campus. *Sport Marketing Quarterly, V*(2), 29-34.

Guarlnik, D.B. (Ed.). (1970). *Webster's new world dictionary of the American language* (2nd ed.). New York & Cleveland: The World Publishing Company.

Horine, L. (1996). *Administration of physical education and sport* (3rd ed.). Madison, Wisconsin: Wm. C. Brown & Benchmark.

Irwin, R.L. (1996). The data-driven approach to sponsorship acquisition. *Sport Marketing Quarterly, V*(2), 7-10.

Lough, N.L. (1996). Factors affecting corporate sponsorship of women's sport. *Sport Marketing Quarterly. V*(2), 11-19.

McCarthy, E J. (1960). *Basic marketing: A managerial approach.* Homewood, Illinois: R.D. Irwin Publishers.

Mason, J.G. & Paul, P. (1988). *Modern sports management.* Englewood Cliffs, New Jersey: Prentice-Hall.

Morris, D. & Irwin, R.L. (1996). The data-driven approach to sponsorship acquisition. *Sport Marketing Quarterly, V*(2), 7-10.

Mullin, B.J. (1983). *Sports marketing, promotion, and public relations.* Amherst, MA: National Sport Management cited by Railey, J.J. & Railey, P.A. (1988).

Palmisano, N.J. (1984), May). Fund-raising first rule: Get organized. *Athletic Business, 9*(5), 20-23.

Parkhouse, B.L. (Ed.). (1996). *The management of sport—Its foundation and application* (2nd ed.). St. Louis: Mosby Year Book.

Porentas, J. (2006, June 6). Ninety million is not enough. *www.O-Zone.com.*

Railey, J.J. & Railey, P.A. (1988). *Managing physical education, fitness, and sports programs.* Mountain View, California: Mayfield Publishing Company.

In Sawyer, T.H. (2006). Financing facilities 101. *Journal of physical education, recreation and dance, 77(4), 23-2,* Revenues and costs for D1-A schools, College Athletic Clips, 5-20-06). http://www.collegeathleticsclips.com/s/375/index.aspx?sid=375&gid=1&pgid=15&cid=292&newsid=83

Sawyer, T.H. (2006b). Financing facilities 101. *Journal of physical education, recreation and dance, 77(4), 23-28.* ADAPTED FROM; Howard, D.R. & Crompton, J.L. (2004). *Financing sports. (2nd ed.). Morgantown, WV: Fitness Technology.*

Schlossberg, H. (1990, June). Hispanic market strong but often ignored. *Marketing News,* p. 26.

Stier, Jr., W.F. (1986, June 26). *Fundraising and promotional activities for the successful athletic department.* Presentation at the National Convention of the High School Athletic Coaches Association, Orlando, Florida.

Stier, Jr., W.F., (1987). Managing for survival in higher education: Athletics in academe. *The Journal of Applied Research in Coaching and Athletics, 2*(3), 153-167.

Stier, Jr., W.F., (1987, August 6). *Promotional techniques and ideas for a small budget.* Presentation at the National Convention of the National Collegiate Athletic Association (NCAA)—Professional Development Seminar, Washington, D. C.

Stier, Jr., W.F., (1987c, October). The establishment of an effective athletic support group. *JUCO Review* (Journal of the National Junior College Athletic Association), pp. 4-6.

Stier, Jr., W.F. (1990a, January 3). *Fundraising tactics and promotional practices for intercollegiate athletic programs.* Presentation at the National Convention of the National Collegiate Athletic Association (NCAA)—Professional Development Seminar, Dallas, Texas.

Stier, Jr. W.F. (1990b, August). ADs walk fine line on promotion. *Athletic Administration, 25*(4), 18-19, 21.

Stier, Jr. W.F. (1992). Understanding fundraising in sport: The conceptual approach. *Sport Marketing Quarterly, 1*(1), 41-46.

Stier, Jr. W.F. (1993a, July). Project profit. *Athletic Management, V*(4), 44-46.

Stier, Jr., W.F., (1993b, July 9). *Meeting the challenges of managing sport through marketing, fundraising and promotions.* Paper presented at the International Meeting of the World University Games (and FISU/CESU Conference), Buffalo, New York.

Stier, Jr. W.F. (1994a). *Fundraising for sport and recreation.* Champaign, Illinois: Human Kinetics.

Stier, Jr. W.F. (1994b). *Successful sport fund-raising.* Dubuque, Iowa: Wm. C. Brown & Benchmark.

Stier, Jr. W.F. (1995, June 19). *The future of fundraising and promotions in international sport competition.* Presentation at the annual convention of the Ontario Hockey Association. London, Ontario, Canada.

Stier, Jr. W.F. (1996, May). An overview of administering competitive sport programs through effective marketing, fundraising and promotion. *Applied Research in Coaching and Athletic Annual, 11*(1), 116-128.

Stier, Jr. W.F. (1998, April 8). *Fundraising, promotions, public relations and publicity for the 21st century.* Presentation made at the national convention of the American Alliance for Health, Physical Education, Recreation and Dance, Reno, Nevada.

Stier, Jr., W.F. (2003), *Marketing, Fundraising and Promotions for Sport, Recreation and Fitness Programs.* Boston, MA: American Press.

Stotlar, D.K. (1989). *Successful sport marketing and sponsorship plans.* Dubuque, Iowa: Wm. C. Brown.

Stotlar, D.K. (1993). *Successful sport marketing.* Madison, Wisconsin: Wm. C. Brown & Benchmark.

Stotlar, D.K. (1993). Sponsorship and the Olympic winter games. *Sports Marketing Quarterly, 2(1)*, 35-43.

Stotlar, D.K. (1996). On teaching about sponsorship. *Sport Marketing Quarterly, V*(2), 41-42.

White, A.B. and Irwin, R.L. (1996). Assessing a corporate partner program: A key to success. *Sport Marketing Quarterly, V*(2), 21, 24-28.

Wieberg S. (1991, October 16). Spiked—Sports cut to trim costs. *USA Today*, p. 5-C.

Wieberg, S. and Witosky, T. (1991, October 14). Most college sports lose money. *USA Today*, p. 1-C.

Wieberg, S. and Witosky, T. (1991, October 16). Schools seek solutions to athletic budget woes. *USA Today*, p. 5-C.

DISCUSSION TOPICS

1. Differentiate between fundraising, marketing, promoting, public relations and publicity in terms of sport entities.

2. Provide examples of the type of resources or tools needed by various sport organizations.

3. Why is it frequently necessary for sport managers to go outside to secure needed resources?

4. Create an outline of a specific fundraising project utilizing the components of a fundraising plan presented in this chapter.

5. Enumerate various target markets for a fictional sport management organization and indicate how a sport manager might seek to reach selected target markets.

6. Outline a potential situation in which a sport organization might solicit a corporate sponsorship or partnership with an outside business and describe how such an arrangement might be mutually beneficial to both parties.

7. Cite sources and examples of both hard and soft data and reveal how both forms of data can be used as tools in sport promotion, marketing, and/or fundraising.

8. Indicate some of the very real risks involved in fundraising, marketing and promoting activities and how these risks might be avoided or lessened by mangers in sport, recreation, and fitness programs.

9. What effect or impact does the so-called "Flutie Factor" have for sport managers, promoters and fundraisers?

10. What are the questions to ask prior to initiating any fundraiser?

Chapter

12   The Law and the Management of Sports

Being Prepared Protects the Organization and Staff.
[courtesy of Washington State University Sports Information]

CHAPTER HIGHLIGHTS

This chapter will help the reader to:

- Cite the threshold age for the Age Discrimination in Employment Act (ADEA);
- Explain how race can be used as a factor to achieve diversity and in deciding whether to admit students;
- Appreciate the importance for sport managers to be knowledgeable in the law insofar as their organizations and programs are concerned;
- Understand the two key elements in successfully meeting the legal challenges of managing sport programs;
- Explain how the Fair Labor Standards Act impacts sport organizations;

- Be familiar with the employment laws relating to sport organizations;
- Differentiate between employees and independent contractors;
- Recognize the importance of affirmative action and understand the various forms of discrimination within the employment scene and provide examples of illegal discrimination;
- Describe the four patterns of hiring minorities and women;
- Define and provide examples of sexual harassment in the workplace and how such discrimination might be avoided;
- Provide illustrations appropriate for sport, recreation, and fitness programs regarding the importance of American with Disabilities Act of 1990 (ADA) and Section 504 of the Rehabilitation Act of 1973;
- Cite the relevance of the Family and Medical Leave Act for the modern sport manager;
- Illustrate how the Occupational Safety and Health Administration (OSHA) plays a major role in the management of sport and sport-related organizations and businesses;
- Understand the importance of sport licensing laws;
- Be appreciative of and sensitive to the need to be politically correct in the business of sport, recreation, and fitness.

UNDERSTANDING THE LEGAL ASPECTS OF MANAGING SPORT

Every sport manager, regardless of the type or level of the organization, must pay particular attention to the laws, rules, and regulations that may affect the organization itself as well as the myriad activities associated with it. Because sport management revolves around people, both as individuals and as members of various groups, the ramifications of adherence (or failure to adhere) to legal directives can be significant.

CONCEPT #365:   *Knowledge of the law itself is not sufficient for the sport manager—appropriate and timely action is also required.*

When dealing with the legal aspects of sport and sport management and making appropriate decisions, it is imperative that managers and administrators be knowledgeable about the laws, rules, and regulations that may affect their organizations, personnel, and programs. However, knowledge in and of itself is not enough. Sport managers must also be capable of anticipating how the laws and regulations might affect their organization and their obligations to others, both individuals and groups.

This understanding of the possible impact of laws, regulations, and rules enables sport professionals to make appropriate decisions and take suitable steps (corrective action), if necessary. The objective is to insure that the organization, the program(s), the activity(ies), and the personnel involved are in full compliance with all applicable legal requirements and directives.

> **CONCEPT #366:**   *Anticipation and prevention are two key elements in successfully meeting the legal challenges of managing sport programs.*

Accurate anticipation of possible consequences relating to applicable legal directives is absolutely essential for the sport manager. Such anticipation aids in the ability to prevent negative consequences. It is imperative that everything be done that can be to prevent negative consequences or problems for the people who are involved in or associated with the organization, either as paid/volunteer personnel or as customers and/or consumers. In short, for the ultimate success of the sport organization all legal obligations must be fully met (see Figure 12.1). To do otherwise is not only foolish but self-defeating and capaciously negligent.

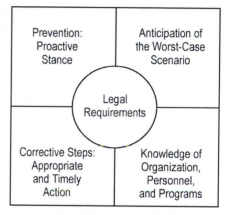

FIGURE 12.1: Dealing with the Legal Challenges of Sport

By meeting the legal requirements and being in full compliance with all applicable rules and appropriate regulations, the sport organization takes a giant step toward protecting the organization itself, its personnel as well as the general public, especially those individuals who are involved as spectators or as consumers of the sport entity.

> **CONCEPT # 367:** *Failure to adhere to legal requirements can have disastrous results, both in terms of finances and public relations.*

The consequences of failing to adhere to the requirements and rules or of violating laws can be severe, both in terms of monetary damages and irreparable damage to the reputation of the organization and those associated with it. Of course, in many instances, one obeys laws and regulations not just because one is fearful of "breaking the law" or getting into trouble, but because "it is the right thing to do."

Usually, laws and regulations are in effect for good reasons, for the health, welfare, and safety of people. Adherence to such regulations and rules may be considered, in effect, self-serving in that these directives enable the organization to better meet the needs of its customers and personnel. Thus, the task of reaching the objectives and goals of the sport entity are facilitated.

> **CONCEPT # 368:** *Naiveté is no excuse when it comes to obeying the law or being in compliance with legal requirements and regulations.*

It should be pointed out here that it is the responsibility of the competent sport manager to be knowledgeable about the authoritative restrictions and legal requirements affecting one's organization and programs. One cannot shirk this obligation. Naiveté is no excuse.

If the sport manager is ignorant of the law, the responsibility remains with that individual. The appropriate response to such ignorance is that the individual should have known the legal requirements and been aware of the consequences of not adhering to the stipulations of the directive. The responsibility is still that of the sport manager. One cannot avoid or delegate away that responsibility.

THE SCOPE OF LAWS AND LEGAL REQUIREMENTS PERTAINING TO SPORT

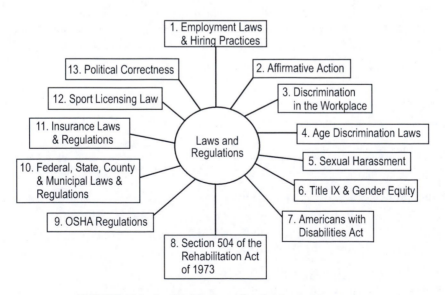

FIGURE 12.2: **Applicable Laws for the Sport Manager**

There are a number of areas in which laws and regulations are especially important for the sport manager in the twenty-first century. Many of these legal decrees are also applicable for any type of business or educational institution. Some of the more important legal directives or categories of laws and regulations that sport managers must be especially attentive to are listed in Figure 12.2.

EMPLOYMENT LAWS AND HIRING PRACTICES

Every business organization, whether it be a for-profit or a not-for-profit entity, must adhere to the appropriate local, state, and federal employment laws. Some of these laws relate to affirmative action, discrimination, harassment, and workers' safety. Other applicable laws, rules, and regulations involve the areas of taxation (income, sales, payroll unemployment, etc.), and insurance. Some laws and regulations are applicable at the federal level, others at the state level, and still others at the local or county level.

DIFFERENTIATING BETWEEN EMPLOYEES AND INDEPENDENT CONTRACTORS

Some sport entities utilize employees to staff their organizations. Others utilize employees and volunteers while still others utilize independent contractors in addition to employees and/or volunteers. Because the organizations that utilize independent contractors pay only a specified salary and it is up to the individual who is classified as an independent contractor to pay withholding tax, it is essential that the person being classified as an independent contractor be so viewed by the IRS.

Today, what determines whether one is an independent contractor or an employer is often in a "gray area" (Perry, 2001). In fact, in many instances it comes down to a judgment call by a representative of the Internal Revenue Service (IRS), because the criteria by which a person might be classified as an employee or an independent contractor has changed as changes have occurred in our society. For example, in the past anyone who worked from home was considered, almost automatically, as an independent contractor. Today, with the shift of more and more employees to working from their homes, this is no longer the case. Similarly, in the past employees used to wear the uniforms of the employing company. Today, more and more independent contractors are wearing the uniforms of the company for which they are serving as independent contractors (Jones, 1996).

It is very important, in terms of complying with federal tax laws, to understand the legal difference between employees and independent contractors (Wong, 1996), because failing to do so can have severe legal and financial repercussions. Organizations need to have a clear-cut standard for determining whether a person providing services is an independent contractor or an employee. According to the current safe-harbor law, employment taxes that might result from an employment relationship are not the responsibility of the employer if the organization or individual receiving the services had: (1) a "reasonable basis" for treating the individual as an independent contractor, (2) filed the required tax returns at the federal level, and (3) had not considered or treated as an employee any other worker doing similar task(s) as the individual being claimed as the independent contractor (Gray, 1995, p. 28).

Some of the other factors (part of the 20-part test utilized by the IRS) that can help prove that the individual was an independent contractor and not an employee include: (1) the person utilizes his or her own tools, (2) the person consistently seeks employment from other companies or individuals, (3) the person is allowed to hire one's own assistants to do the work, (4) the person works on a schedule established by the individual and not by the organization or company, (5) the person cannot just quit or be fired without there being a breach in the contract, and (6) the company or organization does not determine when, where, or how the work is to be carried out (Jones, 1996).

AFFIRMATIVE ACTION

Affirmative action seeks to achieve, at all levels and segments of an organization, prompt and full utilization of women and minorities wherever deficiencies in their representation exists. This is accomplished through a set of very specific guidelines and procedures that guide businesses and organizations in their "good faith" efforts to be fair, just, and lawful. The purpose of affirmative action is to establish criteria and procedures that guide employers to make good faith efforts to provide equal employment opportunity to qualified applicants.

Affirmative action was not designed to be permanent but to address a specific ill in our society. The initial purpose of affirmative action was certainly laudatory; that is, it sought to remove barriers of discrimination and eliminate injustices based on race, gender, religions, and ethnicity. A significant facet of affirmative action is that it is supposed to take a proactive stance against discrimination. As a result, affirmative action policies seek to create a positive environment to insure that individuals are treated fairly and appropriately, now and in the future.

Any employer that has 50 or more employees and has entered into at least one government contract for $50,000 or more in any 12-month period with a federal "executive" agency is considered a "contractor" or "subcontractor" and as such is required to develop a written Affirmative Action Program (AAP). Many other organizations and businesses, while not legally required to have an affirmative action program and policies, nevertheless establish them.

> *CONCEPT #369:*   *The United States has actively sought to encourage adherence to affirmative action practices through significant enticements-including tax breaks and cash incentives.*

Even private organizations, if they receive federal money or have a federal contract, must adhere to affirmative action rules and regulations. In fact, there are entitlement awards, special grants, to organizations that follow affirmative action rules. These include tax breaks (incentives) and actual cash awards. These are very powerful incentives for organizations to adhere to affirmative action rules. Some have called these efforts "social engineering."

> *CONCEPT #370:*   *An important element of affirmative action is the availability of a grievance process—such a process insures the possibility of redressing an injustice.*

Affirmative action involves grievance processes to protect one's rights. Grievance can be prevented with good policies and good faith efforts to do away with discrimination and provide a just and fair environment where people are treated equally.

Components of Grievance Procedures and Policies

Grievance procedures usually include the following:
1. An established policy in terms of to whom should the individual go;
2. Stated procedures involving the dates within which to bring a complaint;
3. An honest effort to treat each complaint seriously and with due diligence;
4. Assurance that the relevant facts will be dealt with;
5. A conscious assumption that either party may be right;
6. If more than one form of harassment/discrimination developments, each is treated separately.

Equal Employment Opportunities

> *CONCEPT #371:*   *One of the goals of affirmative action is to prevent employers from practicing overt as well as covert discrimination on the basis of race, gender, ethnicity, or religion.*

Minor League Baseball Possesses "Big League" Facilities.
*[courtesy of St. Lucie METS, Port St. Lucie, Florida,
photo by Jimmy Fertitta]*

The organizational climate is all-important in the workplace in terms of creating an environment for discrimination or nondiscrimination. The work climate must be free of harassment, free of discrimination, and free of intimidation. The work climate within the sport entity must be conducive to enabling those present to do their jobs and to fulfill their respective responsibilities without undue hindrance, obstruction, or interference.

Equal employment opportunities include effective recruitment and retention of minorities, nondiscrimination policies, practices, and procedures, effective and impartial performance appraisals; successfully communicating and disseminating the nondiscrimination policies, practices, and procedures to appropriate constituencies, and educating and training personnel (including supervisory and administrative personnel) in terms of equal employment opportunities.

CONCEPT #372: *The organizational and work climate is one of the most important factors in terms of establishing and maintaining discrimination or nondiscrimination within the workplace.*

One of the goals of affirmative action is to provide equal employment opportunities for citizenry, by redressing wrongs, protecting minorities and other protected classes, providing for equal employment and protection in the workplace against discrimination as well as charges of reverse discrimination against males and members of the white race.

CONCEPT #373: *Affirmative action seeks to recognize and remove barriers that discriminate against individuals.*

Affirmative action seeks to correct past evils and injustices, prevent current injustices involving discrimination, and prevent future discrimination from taking place. Affirmative action policies and procedures should help those individuals who have been unfairly excluded or held back, who have been denied equal opportunity, who have been passed over unfairly, who have been screened out inappropriately, and who have been underutilized unfairly.

Lack of Women and Minorities Involved in the Business of Sport

Numerous studies (Acosta & Carpenter, 1992b, 1992c; Baize, 1995) have revealed the shortage of women and minorities involved in sport, both as coaches and as administrators and managers. It is imperative that great effort be taken to insure that these individuals are not discriminated against in their efforts to secure appropriate employment commensurate with their education, training, and experience. Roadblocks and hindrances must be removed for women and minorities in order for them to be able and willing to become involved as coaches, leaders, and managers in the world of sport (Acosta & Carpenter, 1992a). Role models are needed as are mentors to potential employees and volunteers in the world of sport.

The move to select women as athletic administrators within the NCAA Division I level has been extremely slow, although some progress has been made. As of October 1996 there were only 17 female athletic directors at 305 NCAA Division I schools. Among those NCAA Division I schools (totaling 111 universities) that play big-time (Division I-A) football, there were only six women serving as athletic directors. The first woman athletic director at an NCAA Division I-A football school was Mary Alice Hill, who served as AD at San Diego State between 1983 and 1985, when she was fired (Blauvelt, 1996, October 2).

Backlash against Affirmative Action by Angry White Males: The California Initiative

> **CONCEPT #374:** *Many critics claim that reverse discrimination is frequently a consequence of affirmative action—critics believe that "white males need not apply" (WMNNA) when affirmative action policies are strictly implemented.*

In 1995 and 1996 affirmative action came under tremendous criticism as being discriminatory against white males. California led the way in challenging the way affirmative action programs were being implemented (Holland, 1996). The California Civil Rights Initiative (CCRI) involved a statewide ballot question that would forbid the use of ethnicity or gender "as a criterion for either discriminating against, or granting preferential treatment to, any individual or group" by the government (Klein, 1995, February 13, p. 105).

Johnson, in a 1995 article in *USA Today,* revealed how affirmative action, its interpretation, and its implementation have been and are being closely scrutinized by the citizens of this country. In more recent times it has also been examined by the United States Supreme Court, which also will continue to examine the effects and implications that affirmative action continues to have on our society.

Critics of affirmative action, such as Northern California Republican state senator Bernie Richter, claim: "Affirmative action has become a vile and corrosive system that threatens to blow us asunder" (Johnson, 1995, p. 2A). Those in favor of affirmative action cite the need to redress and prevent current discrimination. These individuals feel that both minorities and women need, as said by the Reverend Zedar E. Broadous, "time to find themselves on equal footing in the workplace and in the classroom and that time has not come" (Johnson, 1995, p. 2A).

California (1996) Rolls Back the Impact of Affirmative Action with Proposition 209

During 1995 legislation was introduced in 26 states as well as in the United States Congress to repeal or significantly diminish affirmative-action programs. None passed during that year. However, this trend came to an abrupt halt when Proposition 209 passed in the most populous state in the union, California, by a 54 percent to 45 percent majority (Calif. proposition, 1996). In fact, 4,736,189 Californians voted for Proposition 209, which contained the words: "The state shall not discriminate against, or grant preferential treatment to, any individual or group on the basis of race, sex, color, ethnicity or national origin" (Beck, 1997).

Proposition 209 asked the voters: Should the state "not discriminate against, or grant preferential treatment to any person or group in public employment, education or contracting?" With the passage of this first statewide attack against what has become known as affirmative action, the citizens of California authorized the amendment of the constitution to ban race and gender considerations in public hiring, contracting, and college admissions.

One immediate consequence of this was at least three lawsuits designed to block the enforcement of this amendment to the state constitution. On the other hand, gaining encouragement from the victory in California, those individuals leading the anti-affirmative action efforts in other states rallied to submit similar amendments to their state constitutions. Needless to say, the question of affirmative action and its value or worth to the U.S. public remains at the forefront of the nation's consciousness (Prop. 209 still under fire, 1996).

In early April of 1997, the 9th Circuit Court of Appeals decided in favor of California's hotly contested Proposition 209. The ruling (3-0) swept aside an earlier injunction established by United States District Judge, which had prohibited Proposition 209 from being implemented. The ruling indicated that voters can indeed ban affirmative action based on race and gender in government hiring, contracting, and education (Price, 1997).

CONCEPT #375: *Quotas are illegal within affirmative action—but "everyone knows that 'goals and timetables' means 'quotas'" (Leo, 1995, p. 18).*

The impact of the Bakke decision (1978), in which Allan Bakke sued Regents of University of California at Davis, was significant and far-reaching. Bakke claimed "reverse discrimination" based on quotas in admissions practices that the university used in their efforts to remedy what they called past discrimination against minorities. The decision struck down a university program that set aside 16 of the 100 open slots to medical school for minorities.

The Supreme Court of this country states that less formal race-conscious efforts might be acceptable while outlawing such blatant quota systems as that used by the University of California. As a result of the Bakke decision, goals and timetables replaced quotas. However, Leo (1995, p. 18) believes that, although quotas were supposedly done away with, in reality, "Everyone knows that 'goals and timetables' means 'quotas' but nobody is suppose to say so out loud."

Although Title VII, Section 703 (j) clearly prohibits preferences by race, gender, ethnicity, and religion in business and government, interpretation has evolved over the past 30 years. The courts and bureaucrats have adopted, adapted, and otherwise converted and explained away the clear statements in Title VII that prohibit preferences based on race, gender, ethnicity, and religion, all in the interest of a greater good, a higher justice. As a result, the interpretation involving a system or proportional representation by race and gender has evolved (Leo, 1995).

The University of Michigan in 2000 came under criticism for using race as a factor in admissions to that prestigious institution of higher learning. The university was sued over this tactic by the Washington based Center for Individual Rights, the same entity that successfully sued the University of Texas Law School in 1996 and won that case. In 2001, a federal judged agreed that the University of Michigan used unconstitutional criteria and standards in its law school admissions procedures because the school used race as a factor in admitting minorities (Marklein, 2001; Altman, 2001).

In June of 2003, the University of Michigan's undergraduate admissions procedures were also declared unconstitutional as well (Marklein, 2003, October 2). And, at the same time, the University of Maryland also came under attack for giving preferences to minority students.

Today, the current law of the land (per a ruling by the Supreme Court in June 2003) is that it is permissible to use race as a "factor" to achieve diversity and in deciding whether to admit students (Marklein, 2003, December 23). *The challenge is for schools and other entities and organizations to determine how exactly how that can be accomplished* without overstepping the legal standards established by the highest court of the land.

Four Patterns of Hiring Minorities and Women

McWhirter, in his book *Your Rights at Work* (2nd edition, 1993), describes several different versions of hiring plans. Some of these efforts are associated with affirmative action employment plans. Some of these practices have been accepted at some levels while at other levels they have been rejected as inappropriate or illegal. Some of the different versions of hiring plans include:

1. Instances in which employers actively encourage minorities and women to apply for positions. In such cases, the companies actively seek out and recruit such underrepresented individuals for vacancies. Although this is not really affirmative action, according to McWhirter, this practice has gained wide acceptance throughout the nation.

2. When two otherwise qualified candidates (one male or non minority individual and the other a woman and/or minority candidate) are essentially comparable or equal in their qualifications, the company hires the minority or female candidate over the non-minority or male candidate if the applicant is underrepresented within that particular company or entity. The United States Supreme Court has approved this kind of affirmative action plan or policy.

3. Companies hire women or minorities (if they meet the *minimum qualifications for the position)* even though there are clearly more qualified white male candidates. Court decisions differ in accepting this type of affirmative action. Some (typically on the state and local levels) have declared it unacceptable while others (on the federal level) have endorsed the concept and permitted this pattern of hiring to continue.

4. Organizations continue to search for an acceptable woman or minority, regardless of whether or not a qualified male is presently available for employment. McWhirter (1993) indicated that this not only involves a very rigid quota system but is currently illegal. Such a practice is not viewed as part of affirmative action and has not been upheld in the courts.

Recent Actions by the United States Supreme Court Limiting Affirmative Action

The Supreme Court on June 12, 1995 made two decisions that significantly affected affirmative action as well as how affirmative action had been interpreted in this country during the previous 30 years. In fact, the decisions "took a direction far removed from the traditional liberal approach to civil rights" (Mauro, 1995, I-A).

One case, *Adarand Constructors v. Pena*, involved a situation in which Adarand was the losing bidder as a subcontractor on a federal highway project even though that company had submitted the lowest bid. The winning bid went to a minority-owned company because under the affirmative action program of the Federal government the main contractor received a cash bonus having given the work to the Hispanic-owned company. The other case that had far-reaching consequences had the high court siding with the state of Missouri, which sought to end federal supervision of the Kansas City, Missouri school desegregation efforts.

Both decisions "expressed outright exasperation with civil rights remedies that take race into account, give minorities a boost in government contracts and hiring, and involve the courts in running public schools" (Mauro, 1995, p. 2-A). In essence, the Court has moved in a direction that will significantly diminish the role of the courts at the Federal level as well as Federal agencies in remedying racial and gender bias.

Supreme Court Justice Clarence Thomas made a statement that probably represented best this shift of the high court when he said, "These programs stamp minorities with a badge of inferiority and may cause them to develop dependencies or to adopt an attitude that they are 'entitled' to preferences" (Mauro, 1995, p. 2-A).

The *New York Times* reported on March 8, 1996 that President Bill Clinton effectively put affirmative action programs on hold in early 1996 when he elected to suspend, for at least three years, all federal programs that reserve some contracts exclusively for minority and female-owned firms. Many experts believed that this three-year moratorium on set-aside programs would be very difficult to reintroduce at the end of the three years, effectively making this decision more far-reaching (Clinton to put, 1996; Administration to suspend, 1996).

Examples of Arguments against Affirmative Action

Steele (1994) has provided several reasons affirmative action should not be followed: (I) people should be selected on the basis of merit alone, (2) our society should be a color-blind society, (3) affirmative action balkanizes the community, (4) causes reverse discrimination, (5) produces feelings of inferiority in women and people of color, (6) creates negative stereotypes about women and people of color, (7) young people of color expect affirmative action to get them jobs and promotions, and (8) minorities stand to lose more from affirmative action than they gain.

DISCRIMINATION IN THE WORKPLACE

There are several laws that purport to protect employees against discrimination in the workplace. Typically, these laws prohibit discrimination on the basis of sex, sexual preference, race, age, religious beliefs, national origin, and physical limitations.

Section Three — Pragmatic Aspects of the Management of Sport

Unlawful Discrimination in the Form of Unequal Pay for Essentially Equal Work

One such law is the Equal Pay Act. This federal law stipulates the same pay for men and women who do substantially equal work, requiring substantially equal skill, effort, and responsibility under similar working conditions in the same establishment (Wong & Barr, 1994). Yet, studies continue to reveal that women, across the board, typically receive less salary than their male counterparts in the business world. The same is true for faculty members at the college and university levels throughout the country, both private and public.

The Family and Medical Leave Act

Yet another law (Act) that has placed additional pressure on employers is *The Family and Medical Leave Act.* Becoming effective on August 5, 1993, this piece of legislation requires employers with 50 or more workers to provide them with up to 12 weeks a year of unpaid leave to care for a new baby or sick family member. This has proven to be expensive for the companies that have to hire and train temporary replacements while still paying the health benefits of those employees on leave.

Age Discrimination Laws

Since 1967 when Congress passed the Age Discrimination in Employment Act (ADEA), discrimination due to age (the threshold age for the ADEA is 40) has been illegal in the United States (Hill, 2003). The Age Discrimination Act of 1975, as amended, prohibits discrimination on the basis of age in programs or activities receiving federal financial assistance. This act specifies that it is unlawful for an employer to fail or refuse to hire or to discharge any individual or otherwise discriminate against any individual with respect to compensation, terms, conditions, or privileges of employment, because of an individual's age.

CONCEPT # 76: **The Equal Employment Opportunity Commission was created in 1972 as the enforcement agency in cases of discrimination on the basis of race, color, religion, sex, or national origin.**

The Civil Rights Act of 1964 prohibits and provides relief against discrimination in public accommodations, protects constitutional rights in public facilities and public education, and prevents discrimination in federally assisted programs. The Civil Rights Act was amended (Title VII of the Civil Rights Act of 1964 as amended by the Equal Employment Opportunity Act of 1972) in 1972 to include prohibitions against discrimination in employment on the basis of race, color, religion, sex, or national origin. This act created the Equal Employment Opportunity Commission as the enforcement agency in cases of such discrimination"

CONCEPT #377: *Nondiscrimination policies should be prominently displayed in the workplace.*

Nondiscrimination policies and statements are very important in any organization and must be widely disseminated. However, there must be more than merely posting signs. There is also a need to actively train and educate employees and members of management to recognize, react, prevent, and redress discrimination. And, of course, there must be a willingness by management to treat the whole subject of discrimination in a serious vein. This means that the sport leaders and managers must be willing to take positive action to prevent (proaction) any form of discrimination and be prepared to react to such abominable behavior in a decisive manner.

SEXUAL HARASSMENT

The United States Supreme Court has ruled that sexual harassment is illegal discrimination covered by Title VII of the Civil Rights Act (Discrimination because of sex, 1980; Meyer et al., 1981). This Act recognizes that adverse employment conditions subject workers to stresses that have nothing to do with actual job performance. In addition, sexual harassment is frequently accomplished by threats of adverse job actions or promises of raises or promotions or other rewards (Carpenter, 1989). Sexual harassment is also a violation of many state laws as well. In the state of New York it is a violation of NYS Human Rights Laws (Article 15 of Executive Law, Sections 290-301).

Sexual Harassment Defined

There are several key concepts that define sexual harassment: (1) being unwanted, (2) being intentional, (3) frequently being repeated, (4) resulting in intimidation, (5) involving cohesiveness, (6) being demeaning and insulting, and (7) interfering with one's normal performance (work, school, or play). The Equal Employments Opportunity Commission (EEOC) defines sexual harassment as any:

> "Unwelcome sexual advances for sexual favors, and other verbal or physical conduct of a sexual nature (takes place) . . . when 1) submission to such conduct is made either explicitly or implicitly a term or condition of an individual's employment; 2) submission or rejection of such conduct by an individual is used as the basis for employment decisions

affecting such individual; or, 3) such conduct has the purpose or effect of substantially interfering with an individual's work performance or creating an intimidating, hostile, or offensive working environment" (Stier 2005, p. 14).

One of the Finest Basketball Facilities in the Nation, Quicken Loans Arena, Cleveland.
[courtesy of Phyllis Salem, Cleveland Cavaliers/ Quicken Loans Arena, photo by Trepal Photography]

Sexual harassment may be thought of as any *repeated* or *unwarranted* verbal or physical sexual conduct or advances, sexually explicit derogatory statements, or sexually discriminatory remarks made by someone in the workplace that are offensive or objectionable to the recipient, or that cause the recipient discomfort or humiliation, or interfere with the recipient's job, work, recreational, or school performance (MacKinnon, 1979; Sandler et aI., 1981; Somers, 1982; Dziech and Weiner, 1984).

Examples of Sexual Harassment Activities

Specific examples of sexual harassment include, but are not limited to, the following:

1. Sexist remarks about a person's clothing, body, or sexual activities
2. Unnecessary touching, patting, pinching, or cornering
3. Visual harassment-leering at or ogling of a person's body
4. Demanding sexual favors accompanied by implied or overt threats concerning one's job, grades, letters of recommendations, and so on
5. Physical sexual assault
6. Verbal harassment or abuse-propositions, lewd comments, sexual insults
7. Subtle pressure for sexual activity
8. Overt solicitation of sexual favors (in the face of a threat of some type of punishment)
9. Subtle or overt pressure or solicitation of sexual favors in exchange for a promise of a reward ("quid pro quo" harassment)

Employers need to also be aware of and concerned that employees do not practice subtle discrimination through the use of "code words." The 3rd Circuit Court of Appeals ruled in late 1996 that a jury was to decide whether or not a pattern of code words used by white workers and managers at a Maple Shade, New Jersey, furniture rental store constituted discrimination. This decision will have significant repercussions throughout the workplace. One consequence will be that "words spoken at work that aren't literally racist-such as 'you people,' 'poor people,' and 'that one in there'—now can be grounds for employment discrimination lawsuits" (Jones, 1996).

Sport businesses need to educate their employees and volunteers. They also need to police the actions of these individuals in the entire area of discrimination and racism to insure that improper actions and communication do not take place. The key is to make everyone involved, employees and volunteers, managers and nonmanagers, aware of what is expected in terms of actions and attitude and that improper behavior (overt or covert) will not be tolerated, and that all complaints will be thoroughly and impartially investigated.

CONCEPT #378: *Companies and organizations need to take a proactive stance against all forms of (blatant and subtle) racism and discrimination, not only to prevent lawsuits but because it is the right thing to do.*

Many companies expect a great deal of litigation as a result of the action of the 3rd Circuit Court of Appeals. The response from many companies has been to formally communicate with their employees warning them of the law and the need for a nondiscrimination atmosphere in the workplace. Others have begun to offer sensitivity training for their employees, including supervisors and managers (Jones, 1996).

CONCEPT #379: *Women and men may be offenders as well as victims in respect to sexual harassment—although a far greater number of offenders are men and a far greater number of women are usually the victims.*

Although the vast majority of sexual harassers are men, this is not to say that women are not guilty of such sexual misconduct. Sexual harassment may also involve males harassing males as well as females or females harassing females as well as males.

CONCEPT #380: *Sexual harassment can take place anywhere, at anytime.*

Sexual harassment can take place at any time. It can take place anywhere: in the workplace, in the school environment, and in recreational settings. Various studies have indicated a very high rate of sexual harassment in the workplace. Some studies indicate that over 50 percent of women in the total workforce have experienced sexual harassment. It is estimated that 20 to 30 percent of female college students experience some form of sexual harassment during their academic careers. A survey released in the early 1980s by the Merit Systems Protection Board (MSPB) indicated that 42 percent of all women working for the federal government indicated that they experienced sexual harassment. This was the same percentage that an earlier study found in 1981.

There is a growing phenomenon in educational institutions involving students suing the school and school personnel for the sexual harassment that they perceive from other students. A mother (Pat Schofield) charged in 1994 that her daughter (Eve Bruneau) was sexually harassed by her sixth-grade class at an elementary school in New York State's South Kirtright Central School district and that the school officials failed to respond in a timely fashion. Specifically, the suit claims that the young girls in the sixth-grade "were often referred to as lesbian, prostitute, retard, scum, bitch (and) whore" (Henry, 1996). The lawsuit claims that the district violated Title IX's prohibition against gender discrimination in schools receiving federal aid. The suit also claims punitive damages in addition to compensatory damages.

The trend is clear. There are increasingly greater numbers of lawsuits as a result of peer sexual harassment in the school setting. Athletic officials and administrators must be extremely careful lest this type of unacceptable behavior take place within the sport environment.

> *CONCEPT #381:   Sexual harassment typically involves "power" that the offender wields over the victim and can happen to anyone.*

Sexual harassment usually involves "power." Such instances typically take place when one person has power over another. The person in authority, the person with the power over another, can utilize this power to intimidate and coerce or reward another individual in a sexual manner by means of such power.

Sexual harassment can happen to anyone. Employers can sexually harass employees. Coaches can sexually harass athletes. Coaches can be sexually harassed by administrators (Lackey, 1990). Bosses can sexually harass their secretaries. Superiors can sexually harass their assistants. Anyone can sexually harass anyone else (Pike, 1994).

Same-Sex Harassment

The United States Supreme Court decided in a unanimous decision in March of 1998 that federal law provides protection against same-sex harassment in the workplace. The court indicated that the " . . . person's gender or sexual orientation didn't matter. The critical issue under federal civil-rights law, the court said, was whether a person was singled out and discriminated against because of his or her sex" (Same-sex harassment illegal, 1998, p. I-A). As a result of this court decision, the determination of what is and what is not appropriate behavior in the workplace has become even more complex than before (Nasser, 1998). The court made its decision on the basis of Title VII, which prohibits discrimination (in the workplace) on the basis of race, color, sex, or national origin.

CONCEPT #382:   *Employers (individuals and organizations) are responsible and liable for actions of their employees and non-employees.*

Sport entities must be very careful regarding sexual harassment, not only because such actions are inherently wrong and hurtful to the victims but also because the sport organization (and management) can be held liable for the actions and inactions of its employees. The tort law doctrine of *respondent superior* holds that the employer is liable for all acts of an employee committed within the scope of the employee's employment or job responsibilities (Pike, 1994). In fact, the organization and management can be held liable for the actions (sexual harassment) of non-employees, if such individuals engage in such offensive behavior.

The consequences of a business or organization being found guilty of sexual harassment can be significant. Under current federal law (the Civil Rights Act of 1991) plaintiffs can sue companies with less than 100 employees/workers for up to $50,000 in damages (Workplace, 1992). At larger businesses and organizations successful plaintiffs can collect compensatory and punitive damages of up to $300,000. If related claims, such as assault, battery, or intentional infliction of emotional distress, are involved, there is no limit (Loyle, 1995).

CONCEPT #383:   *Employers and managers need to create an environment that is free of sexual harassment.*

Management and/or owners should know of such reprehensible behavior among its employees as well as nonemployees associated with the sport entity, its programs, and its activities. The point to remember is that sexual harassment is not to be tolerated. As a result, concerted steps must be taken to educate individuals in terms of what constitutes sexual harassment, how to deal with such harassment as a victim, and how to prevent such occurrences in the first place (Marchell et aI., 1992).

> **CONCEPT #384:** *The existence of employment policies prohibiting harassment and discrimination does not guarantee that such discrimination, harassment, or intimidation is not present or prevalent.*

An integral part of creating a harassment-free work, play, or educational environment consists of appropriate training and education of those individuals associated with the organization or business. A suitable anti-harassment program involving a written policy statement prohibiting sexual harassment is highly recommended. Additionally, a public acknowledgment that the climate within the organization is such that sexual harassment will not be tolerated is also advisable as part of the overall educational and informational efforts on the part of the company or organization. Of course, the essence of any appropriate environment is that there be swift, fair, and just reactions to instances of sexual harassment.

Sexual Harassment within Schools and Colleges: Violation of Title IX

> **CONCEPT #385:** *Sexual harassment is now a violation of Title IX.*

Sexual harassment of students is a violation of Title IX of the 1972 Educational Amendments. In August of 1981, the United States Department of Education, Office of Civil Rights (OCR), reaffirmed its jurisdiction over sexual harassment complaints under Title IX. The OCR defines sexual harassment as "[consisting] of verbal or physical conduct of a sexual nature, imposed on the basis of sex, by an employee or agent of a recipient (any educational program or activity receiving federal financial assistance) that denies, limits, provides different, or conditions the provision of, aid, benefits, services or treatment protected under Title IX."

AMERICANS WITH DISABILITIES ACT OF 1990 (ADA) PL 101-336, TITLE 42, U.S.C. 12101 ET SEQ: U.S. STATUES AT LARGE, 104-327-378

"Two major pieces of legislation during the disability rights movement were the Americans with Disabilities Act of 1990 *and* the Individuals with Disabilities Education Act (IDEA) of 1990 I(PL 101-476)" (Petersen & Piletic, 2006, p. 39). The ADA sets a legal standard of minimal facility accessibility for individuals with disabilities.

Viewed as the most significant civil rights legislation in 25 years, the Americans with Disabilities Act of 1990 (ADA) was signed into law on July 26, 1990, by then-President George Bush. The final rules were published by the Department of Justice, the entity that has the authority and responsibility to interpret the ADA guidelines. Many advocates for the disabled or challenged feel that this statute will have the most impact on companies and organizations in this country since the Civil Rights Act of 1964, which prohibited discrimination based on race, color, gender, religion, or national origin. The ADA, coupled with the Architectural Barriers Act, which required that all facilities built with any percentage of federal monies must be accessible to the challenged, will help insure greater accessibility for the disabled in this country (Block, 1995).

CONCEPT #386: *The Americans with Disabilities Act of 1990 is viewed as the most significant civil rights legislation in the past 25 years.*

Reiner (1994) indicates that the intent of the Act is not to separate but to include, integrate, and mix those individuals without disabilities and those individuals who are challenged. The ultimate goal is to dispel stereotypes and prevent wholesale discrimination based solely on any person's disability.

Impact of the ADA

In the United States approximately 17 percent of the total population can be classified as having a disability. That means that 1 in 6 of our citizens are disabled. The result of the act is that some 43 million Americans will have adequate access to goods, programs, and services of all types (Nasser, 1993).

This far-reaching statute affects almost all companies (over 4 million) and organizations in this country, including schools (Hall, 1993). The only groups exempted from the ADA guidelines are religious organizations and entities controlled by religious organizations. Nevertheless, many such organizations have voluntarily agreed to abide by the ADA law (Block, 1995; Epstein, McGovern, & Moon, 1994; Munson & Comodeca, 1993).

There is a publication to guide individuals in the construction of new buildings and facilities as well as the rehabilitation and renovation of existing facilities (indoor and outdoor) (Petersen & Piletic, 2006). See the *ADA and ABA Accessibility Guidelines for Buildings and Facilities* (2004, July 23).

ADA as an Extension of Section 504 of the Rehabilitation Act of 1973

The ADA was indeed a significant and sweeping piece of civil rights legislation. The act extended Section 504 of the Rehabilitation Act of 1973 to the private sector. This law (Section 504) specifically states: "No otherwise qualified handicapped individual in the United States shall, solely by reason of his handicap, be excluded from the participation in, be denied the benefits of, or be subjected to discrimination *under any program or activity receiving federal financial assistance"* (emphasis added). In essence, discrimination based on physical or mental handicap is prohibited in all programs receiving any type of federal financial assistance.

Section 504 prohibited federal agencies and organizations that received federal funding from discriminating against people with disabilities. The private employer section of the act became law in July 26, of 1992. The ADA became effective in July 1993 requiring companies with at least 25 employees to accommodate workers with disabilities. For employers with 15-24 employees, the act became law in July of 1994. In 1994, the law was extended to employers with at least 15 workers (Lawlor, 1993).

The Scope of the ADA

The ADA prohibits discrimination on the basis of any disability. The impact of the law affects almost every organization in this country and many aspects of life in the United States, including where we work, what facilities we utilize, how we live, how we travel, what programs and activities are available to us both at work and at play. Its impact is significant and its scope is extensive. The ADA strictly prohibited discrimination on the basis of disability in terms of employment, public accommodations, and public services, including public transportation (ADA Compliance Guide 1992; Hall, 1993; Nasser, 1993; Block, 1995).

> **CONCEPT #387:   The ADA prohibits discrimination on the basis
> of any disability.**

Definitions

The ADA act uses the broadest meaning of *disability.* Specifically, a person with a disability is any individual with (1) a mental or physical impairment that impedes or hinders one of the major life functions; (2) who is regarded as having a disability or impairment; or (3) who has a history of disability or impairment. A disabled individual is someone with a physical or mental impairment that limits one or more "major life activities," or who has a record of such impairment. One cannot be discriminated against because of past problems or disabilities. The major life activities include walking, seeing, hearing, speaking, breathing, learning, or working. Thus, "the disabled" becomes an all-inclusive term covering a broad range of circumstances, including the wheelchair-bound, hearing impaired, visually impaired, and mentally impaired.

Individuals who are currently involved in drug rehabilitation programs are considered disabled under current ADA guidelines. Those who would not be considered disabled include kleptomaniacs, transsexuals, drug abusers, sex offenders, and those who practice voyeurism.

The Five Sections within the ADA

The ADA has five specific chapters or "titles" in the statute. *Title I* forbids discrimination in employment in the private and public sector against individuals with disabilities (Munson & Comodeca, 1993; Block, 1995). The Equal Employment Opportunity Commission (EEOC) enforces Title I of the ADA.

Hiring, firing, not rehiring, promotion, and all other employment practices fall under the jurisdiction of the ADA. Although companies do not have to hire the disabled, by the same token one cannot discriminate against the disabled candidate. That means one cannot fail to hire a person merely because that individual has a disability covered by the ADA legislation. Medical questions may not be asked of potential employees, nor can one ask about absenteeism, accident claims, or medical problems at previous workplaces.

Employers need to be sure to define the essential functions of any job vacancy so that a disabled person is not eliminated from consideration because of the disability when a reasonable accommodation would enable that person to handle the duties and responsibilities of the position. To determine whether a person is indeed qualified and competent to perform a specific job or assume a certain responsibility, the potential employer must identify, in advance, the "essential" and "nonessential" elements or functions of the job or position. Then there can be an honest and realistic determination as to whether the individual can or cannot perform the job. For those individuals who become disabled while in the employ of a company, that person shall be provided reasonable assistance so as to be able to continue such employment.

CONCEPT #388:   *Employers need to define the essential function of any job vacancy.*

There is a need for supervisors, administrators, and staff to update organizations' and companies' policies, procedures, and practices, to provide auxiliary aids, and to improve accessibility unless that would impose an undue (financial or otherwise) hardship on the organization or company. Policies need to be established whereby individuals can notify the organization of the person's disability and special needs. There should be a trained and interested compliance officer appointed, much like the Title IX compliance officer or the Section 504 compliance officer. Additional suggestions pertaining to the hiring process include:

1. There is a need for clear and explicit job description for each position within the organization

2. All job descriptions should have defined essential and nonessential functions

3. Be prepared, in advance, to be aware of the type of reasonable accommodations that could be provided for the position

4. All personnel policies should be reviewed in light of the ADA act

5. Safety procedures and accident procedures (including first aid, evaluation, transportation, etc.) should be established and/or renewed

6. All personnel should be trained in the intricacies of the ADA in an effort to keep all staff and administrators up-to-date with local, state, and federal rules and regulations

7. All legal and pertinent ADA rules and regulations should be prominently posted

8. There should be an oversight review by an impartial individual(s) of each search process for new vacancies

9. Search committees and administrators involved with each search for a vacancy should be "charged" with their mission by a trained and competent personnel staffer

10. Make sure that individuals who are disabled are made aware of the vacancy or vacancies

Title II became effective January 26, 1992. It applies to all state and local governments, their departments and agencies, and any other special purpose districts of state or local governments. This section prohibits discrimination by public services and on public transportation. In short, this section of the ADA prohibits governmental entities from preventing or discouraging individuals with disabilities from participation in state and local governmental activities, programs, services, or the use of transportation. This also covers public entities such as local governments sponsoring community youth sport programs and interscholastic sport programs (Reiner, 1994).

The reality of the Act necessitates that selected public sites must be accessible to the disabled. "This means that elevators, ramps and wheel-chair-height fare machines are made available" (Hall, 1993, p. 7-A). The consequences are that more and more organizations are going to have disabled individuals attending private and public facilities, programs, and activities because they will have access to transportation as never before.

Title III is that section that deals with the complete, full, and equal use by the disabled individual of goods, services, programs, activities, facilities, privileges, and advantages of any facility or site that is owned, leased, rented, or operated by a private entity and is available to the public. This involves almost every sporting entity in the country, including private entities, such as the YMCA and Little League of America, that are open to the public. *Public accommodation* is an umbrella term that includes stadiums, auditoriums, convention centers, gymnasiums, ballparks, recreation centers, and the like.

CONCEPT #389:   *The ADA requires sport entities to allow the disabled to participate in appropriate athletic and recreational programs.*

The legislation also requires sport organizations to allow participation by disabled persons in appropriate sport programs. It is unlawful to discriminate against disabled individuals and prohibit them from participation unless their involvement would result in the likelihood of dangers to themselves, others, participants and/or spectators. "In order to justify exclusion, the athletic program would have to show that the likelihood of injury is much greater than in the normal course of participating in a program" (Munson & Comodeca, 1993). In recent years there has been little reluctance on behalf of school-aged athletes and their parents to sue for the right to have exceptions to state eligibility requirements because of the young athlete's disability (Cohen, 1995).

In these cases reasonable accommodations must be made for the disabled individual that would not disrupt the program or significantly distort the activity. However, the interpretation of what constitutes "reasonable accommodations" can differ significantly. So too, how one defines what constitutes a significant disruption of the sport activity is open to varying interpretations. The law requires that the disabled must be accommodated in a fair, equal, and appropriate manner. When there are disagreements in terms of what is fair, equal, and appropriate in light of "reasonable accommodations" without "significant disruption" of the actual activity, the disagreement may very well find itself in a court of law. At the federal level, the Justice Department is assigned as the enforcement arm of the government for this particular section.

The ADA and Its Impact on Existing and Renovated Facilities

CONCEPT #390:   *The application of ADA regulations is different for new, existing, and renovated structures.*

In terms of facilities, all new construction and significant alterations of public accommodations must adhere to current ADA standards and guidelines. The regulations are different for (1) new structures, (2) existing structures, and (3) those which receive major overhauls or are otherwise significantly renovated.

> "For existing facilities, the law is less clear-but. . . The rule states that entities must remove all architectural and communication barriers to disabled access that are structural in nature; this applies only where removal is 'readily achievable,' which is defined as removal that is easy to accomplish and can be carried out with little difficulty or expense" (Munson & Comodeca, 1993, p. 16).

The bottom line is that barrier removal in existing facilities need not require a great deal of effort or expense. The rule is to use common sense.

CONCEPT #391:   *Use your "common sense" is the rule of thumb when renovating existing structures (in light of the ADA laws/regulations).*

It is interesting to note that not only owners of facilities but also tenants are held responsible for seeing to it that all areas within a facility where public accommodations and public services are provided are accessible for the disabled. There is no justification for failure to adhere to the ADA regulations.

Some of the areas that should be closely examined to see that accessibility is available and meets ADA standards include: parking lots, sidewalks, ramps leading to doors and the entrance to buildings, door sizes, interior mobility within the facility, front desks, restrooms (wider stalls and grab bars), concession areas and vending machines, accessibility to telephones, water fountains, signs, Braille dots, raised letters signage, removal of obstructing furniture and objects, elevators, seating availability, size of aisles, availability of wheelchair spaces, seats with removable aisle-side armrests, elevators, and rest rooms, among others *(The Voice, 1994)*.

"If possible, seating should be dispersed throughout the seating area, provide lines of sight, and choices of admission prices comparable to those for members of the general public, adjoin an accessible route of egress in case of emergency, and permit individuals to sit with family and other friends" (Munson and Comodeca, 1993, p. 16). The goal is to enable the disabled to gain access to the building or facility, have mobility within it, and be able to view and/or participate in the programs or to receive the goods and services available there. To accommodate the disabled, organizations may need to remove or alter any obstacles that would prevent the individual from having access to the stadiums, courts, fields, rest rooms, and locker rooms that are accessible to the general public (Munson and Comodeca, 1993).

> **CONCEPT #392:** *Changes in existing facilities need only be made if they are "readily achievable."*

Title IV deals with telecommunication services. Those with disabilities of hearing and sight are most affected by this section of the Act. It requires telephone relay services for persons who are deaf and telecommunications must be accessible to those who are hearing impaired. A quote from the Act itself states: "(a) A public entity shall take appropriate steps to ensure that communications with applicants, participants, and members of the public with disabilities are as effective as communications with others" (Wentzel, 1994, p. 16-A). Employees who develop a disability may ask for a reasonable accommodation.

The final chapter of *Title V* is a general category or section dealing with housekeeping tasks—for example, the determination of exceptions to the Act, the awarding of attorney fees, and the various responsibilities of Congress and how the Act itself may be amended (Munson & Comodeca, 1993).

Challenges to the ADA Act as Written

One of the perceived problems with the ADA act as it was written was its lack of specificity. ADA is deliberately broadly written. As a result it will be up to the courts to provide specifics of the law and to define the exact boundaries, the essence of the act. The fact that the ADA is subject to various interpretation is a land mine waiting to be stepped on. The courts will be needed to guide both organizations and the disabled to maneuver their way through this minefield.

One of the results of the lack of specificity for sport organizations and schools is the extensive litigation that schools and organizations are being subjected to. Cohen (1995, p. 34) complains that people are out in the communities "fighting because of an inarticulate law, passed by Congress, that wasn't explicit in its intent and coverage, and is costing us a lot of time and money and aggravation." The real-

**Moving Through the "Traffic"
for the Game Winning Score.**
*[courtesy of Rochester Raging Rhinos, New York,
James D. Lalthrop, photographer]*

ity of the situation is that the ADA is couched in vague terms, leaving to the Equal Employment Opportunity Commission (EEOC) and the courts the responsibility of defining them.

This can be seen in the tremendous number of complaints (11,550) implemented since July 26, 1992, the date that ADA became effective for the private employer section of the act and only 12 months later, in July 1993. However, then attorney general Janet Reno has gone on record as stating that "knowing its requirements is a key to compliance" (Dillon, 1993). Reno also indicated that one of the more significant results of the act will be to not only remove the physical barriers for our citizens of all ages but also to reduce and remove social barriers.

In an effort to help define specific sections of the Act relating to facilities and accessibility, Reiner (1994) cites the Architectural Transportation Barriers Compliance Board, more recently referred to as the Access Board, which worked on developing a clearer definition of how the ADA applies to public and private recreation facilities. The Access Board may be contacted for an updated ADA publication checklist by calling 800-USA-ABLE.

Reasonable Accommodations Required by the ADA

Facilities and activities must be available and readily accessible. However, in terms of employment, this does not mean that special accommodations are needed to make an unqualified person qualified. However, employers must be able to modify work equipment or to secure such items. They must adjust work schedules and make existing facilities accessible for the disabled. The act requires that reasonable accommodations be made depending on each individual's specific disability. As defined by the Equal Employment Opportunity Commission (EEOC) regulations, a "qualified individual with a disability is someone able to perform the 'essential functions' of a job, with 'reasonable accommodation.'"

Although the act does not specifically address how the facilities or programs are to be made accessible nor define what "reasonable" is, it does mention that there should not be an undue burden on the organization. An undue burden is defined in the law as "an unduly costly, extensive, substantial, disruptive, or, one that will fundamentally alter the nature of the program." Many experts have voiced the opinion that most commercial organizations can make their facilities accessible for less than $500.

Penalties for Violating ADA

There are civil and punitive damages that can be administered for violations of the Act. Fines of not more than $50,000 for an initial violation and $100,000 for subsequent infractions may be levied. In addition, individuals can seek temporary restraining orders or permanent injunctions through the court system. However, only those individuals whose civil rights are being violated can bring suit under the ADA. Others cannot do it on their behalf.

In terms of employment, violation of the ADA allows the injured party to receive back wages and reinstatement to the position the person previously held or had applied for. Then-President Bush signed a new civil rights act in November of 1991 that provides for punitive damages of up to $300,000 on the basis of "pain and suffering." Individuals bringing complaints under the ADA act may sue to insure that their rights are respected under Title II of the Act and are entitled to receive the same relief as provided under Section 504 of the Rehabilitation Act of 1973, including reasonable attorney's fees (Reiner, 1994).

The Attorney General of the United States may initiate, under Title III of the ADA, a civil action if it is determined that there has been a consistent pattern or practice of discrimination in equal employment opportunities or in accessibility to facilities, services, and programs on the basis of a disability.

Additional Information: ADA

Interested professionals and/or those with disabilities may secure additional information or submit a complaint by contacting the Office on the Americans with Disabilities Act, Civil Rights Division, U.S. Department of Justice (Hot Line: (202) 514-0301 or (800) 5140301) or the Equal Employment Opportunity Commission, (800) 669-4000.

OCCUPATIONAL SAFETY AND HEALTH ADMINISTRATION (OSHA, 29 *V.S.C.* SEC. 651)

The Occupational Safety and Health Administration (OSHA) was created in 1970. Its purpose is to protect the health and welfare of employees by insuring that safe and appropriate physical environments are provided in the workplace (Fisher, 1996). The goal is to provide a safe and wholesome workplace for individuals of all ages. OSHA is concerned with preventing accidents in the workplace, insuring that safe work environments are provided, that employees are adequately trained in areas of safety, and that appropriate accident and follow-up procedures and policies are in place. Toward this end, OSHA requires covered companies, businesses, and organizations to prepare written programs relating to safety and to establish policies, procedures, and practices regarding safety precautions and plans of action in the event of injury or accident.

> *CONCEPT #393:* **Sport leaders (and organizations) are held accountable for the safety and welfare of their employees as well as volunteers in the workplace.**

A wide range of areas within various businesses and companies (both profit and non-profit) are covered by the OSHA rules, regulations, and standards, which have been established to cover various types of work sites, including public and private schools (all levels), and the private business sector. Noncompliance can be especially costly to those businesses and organizations that are found guilty, with fines up to $70,000 levied against violators of the law (O'Leary, 1995).

> *CONCEPT #394:* **OSHA affects a wide range of areas within businesses and organizations.**

In the sport world, OSHA affects a wide range of areas within the organization, from equipment management (the handling of blood-soaked or bloodstained laundry) to operations of facilities, such as pools, spas, whirlpools, and concessions, among others. In terms of dealing with blood-soaked or stained laundry, sport managers need to be aware of and follow the stipulations and standards established by the Public Employees Risk Prevention Act, passed by Congress in July of 1994. This law requires employers to establish policies and procedures for their employees who may be exposed to blood or other potentially infectious materials on the job.

FEDERAL, STATE, COUNTY, AND MUNICIPAL LAWS AND REGULATIONS

> *CONCEPT #395:* **Sport programs and organizations must always be in compliance with all applicable laws, regulations, rules, ordinances, and statutes; to be otherwise is like shooting oneself in the foot.**

There are numerous laws, ordinances, rules, statutes, and regulations at the federal, state, county, and municipal levels that have both direct and indirect impact on any number of sport organizations and their respective activities. Some of these regulations have to do with securing permissions or permits to be allowed to do something. Some relate to insurance coverage, while others concern health matters. Still others are associated with tax laws.

The important thing for sport managers and leaders to remember is that all applicable laws must be adhered to—both in terms of the letter of the law and the intent of the regulation. It is imperative that organizers and administrators not attempt to shirk their responsibility by disregarding the existence of such rules, laws, and regulations. Failure to abide by existing and applicable rules, laws, and regulations can have disastrous results for the sport leaders, the sport organization itself, and for the public or patrons who are involved with the activity or program.

CONCEPT #396:   *There Is never an acceptable reason for failure to be in compliance with appropriate laws, rules, and regulations.*

There can be no justification for failing to be in compliance with applicable rules and regulations-period. If the sport administrator was not aware of such laws or regulations, the individual should have been aware, period. And, if a sport administrator was aware of such regulations, but nevertheless ignored them or failed to take appropriate positive action, that individual acted in a totally irresponsible fashion because of the person's failure to do what is right, what is required, what is necessary.

Tax Laws and Regulations

The tax codes for U.S. citizens are very complicated. For businesses, including sport businesses, the situation can sometimes be even more complicated and intimidating. There is a wide range of tax laws at the federal, state, county, and municipal levels that sport leaders must be cognizant of.

Additionally, many sport entities are faced with the question of whether or not to apply for official federal not-for-profit or nonprofit status with respect to the Internal Revenue Service (IRS) and their own state tax code. This decision is one that must be answered on an individual case-by-case situation, taking into account a multitude of facts and factors. Nevertheless, the decision must be made whether to apply for tax-exempt status if the sport organization is eligible for such a classification. In this respect, it is well to seek the advice of qualified counsel.

Fair Labor Standards Act (FLSA)

August 2004 saw the Fair Labor Standards Act become law which affects the whole world of overtime work for those who earn less than $23,600. For administrators in colleges and universities this act has significant implications in that coaches (earning less than the magical figure of $23,600 (or who are not otherwise exempted from the Act) must be paid overtime (time and a half) if they work more than 40 hours in any given week. This holds true even for volunteers. The underlying reason for this Act is to prevent individuals from being exploited, to see that fair compensation is paid to those who work long hours and are minimally paid.

CONCEPT #397:   *The Fair Labor Standards Act (since 1938) establishes minimum wage, overtime regulations, and record keeping methods for employees*

There are several notable exceptions or exemptions to this rule. For example, (1) one must earn more than the $23,600 or $455 per week, (2) be paid on a salary rather than hourly basis, and (3) have specific job responsibilities that are considered exempt. The FLSA "defines *a primary duty* as 'the principal, main, major, or most important duty that the employee performs.'" Interestingly, teachers are exempt from the Act and can be paid any amount of money. And, academic administrators (academic advisers, for example) need only be paid $23,600 to be considered exempt (Scholand, 2005).

Alcohol and Gambling Laws

As is the case with tax regulations and laws, there are statutes governing the sale and use of alcohol and gambling (games of chance) activities at various governmental levels. Sport leaders must be sure that the appropriate rules and regulations are strictly adhered to due to the very nature of alcohol and gambling, coupled with the potential for lawsuits arising from incidents related to the misuse of alcohol and inappropriate gambling activities.

Accounting Rules and Regulations

The area of business affairs/financial accounting is one that can involve many complicated issues for some sport entities, while others can be the very model of simplicity itself. The more complicated the sport operation is the greater the likelihood that professional accounting services will be needed. When in doubt always consult with an experienced and knowledgeable accountant or financial adviser.

Health Regulations and Rules

There are numerous health rules, regulations, and laws in addition to ADA and OSHA that can have a significant impact on sport organizations. Some of these regulations pertain to how concession stands are to be staffed and operated. Other rules relate to the physical environment of the various indoor and outdoor facilities in terms of fire and safety (including seating capacity, ingress and egress avenues, placement of fire exits, lighting standards, etc.).

Insurance Laws and Regulations

Every sport business or organization needs to be cognizant of insurance rules and regulations as they pertain to the sport entity. Insurance involves not only liability insurance for the organization and its employees, but may also include health insurance, vehicle insurance, and so on.

CONCEPT #398:   *Sport entities must be adequately insured.*

In a complicated society sport leaders and managers need to be knowledgeable and understand the term of various types of insurance policies relating to their organizations. They must recognize whether or not specific policies actually provide appropriate and suitable protection for the sport entity itself, the employees, the participants, and the patrons (customers and consumers).

Adequate insurance coverage is a must, an absolute must. Insurance, by its very nature, provides protection, financial protection for the organization and individuals as well as peace of mind. Financial protection can take the form of providing reimbursement for financial losses as well as protection against successful lawsuits based on accident, negligence, and oversight.

CONCEPT #399:   *Modern sport leaders are knowledgeable about insurance coverage for their organizations, programs, and activities.*

Managers and administrators must be constantly on the alert that their sport activities, programs, and facilities are adequately protected against financial damages and possible ruin in the event of negative occurrences dealing with people, things, and activities. In this respect, foresight is an integral part of the administrator's repertoire of skills and competencies.

SPORT LICENSING LAWS

More and more sport organizations, such as colleges and universities as well as recreation departments and even some high schools, have joined the ranks of the professional teams in terms of becoming involved in sport licensing efforts. The major reasons for this are simple: to increase the funding base of each organization and to increase name recognition associated with the sport organization.

> **CONCEPT #400:** *Increased income and an expansion of name recognition places greater importance on sport licensing laws.*

It is essential that today's sport organization create an identity, a link, between the general public, the fans and supporters, and the sport entity through the use of team mascots, logos, and colors. The individual logo, mascot, and/or symbol that is representative of the sport entity is an essential element in the overall marketing strategy of any organization.

The importance of such symbols cannot be overemphasized. However, just as the creation and use of such logos, mascots, and symbols are important, so too is the protection of the exclusive right to use them by the sport entity and those other organizations that have been given permission (through licensing agreements) to use them.

Sport Licensing Forms the Foundation of the Sport Organization's Marketing, Promotion, and Public Relations Efforts

> **CONCEPT #401:** *More and more sport entities are registering and obtaining trademark registration (protection) for their unique logos and/or mascots.*

Sport licensing is defined as authorizing, for a specific fee, another organization or company or individuals to become a licensed producer and/or seller of a wide variety of goods bearing a team's or school's trademark, which may consist of a special, unique logo or mascot. Almost anything can be licensed. The Federal Trademark Act of 1946 (known as the Lanham Act) authorized the licensing of characters, sayings, slogans, names, and symbols, as well as athletic logos and mascots. The Trademark Law Revision Act that was passed and signed into law in 1989 updated the Lanham Act.

> **CONCEPT #402:** *An increasing number of sport entities are licensing their registered trademarks for use on a variety of goods to be sold by various vendors and businesses.*

Sport licensing "enables the holder of the trademark to retain quality control of the merchandise bearing the trademark, to enjoy expanded market opportunities, and to realize significant potential royalties from the sale of merchandise bearing the protected trademark" (Stier, 1994, p. 187). *Indicia* refer to those trademarks, names, designs, and symbols that are associated with the holder (the sport organization, the company, or the school) of the trademark.

> **CONCEPT #403:** *The demand to purchase sport and sport-related products (identified with specific teams and/or individuals) by the general public has never been greater than today.*

"As the sports industry has grown, so has consumer demand for sports-related items, and so has trademark litigation. . . Under the Federal Trademark Act of 1946, the sale of goods involving trademarks is prohibited without a licensing agreement if the sale is 'likely to cause confusion in the mind of the consumer about who is sponsoring or producing the goods'" (Wong & Barr, 1991, page 18).

Abandonment of Sports Trademark

Securing the protection of the federal registered trademark protects the school or sport organization from unauthorized use (referred to as a trademark infringement) of the registered trademark, whether it is a logo, mascot, saying, character, symbol, or name.

> **CONCEPT #404:** *Holders of trademarks must vigorously defend their right to use such trademarks lest they be judged to have abandoned same.*

It is imperative that organizations protect their trademarks and not abandon them in the eyes of the law. "Abandonment is one means by which an entity can relinquish rights to a trademark. In the past, courts have decided that abandonment has occurred when a trademark has lost all significance as an indication of its origin" (Wong & Barr, 1991, p.

18). Additionally, abandonment can also result when the organization that holds the trademark fails to defend its right to hold the trademark aggressively against those who might infringe on that right. Failure to defend may lead to abandonment.

Problems with Logos, Mascots, and Trademarks

It has become increasingly important for sport entities to be politically correct. Nowhere is this more important than in terms of the use of nicknames, logos, and mascots. Some traditionally acceptable nicknames, logos, and mascots have now become not only questionable but also offensive.

> **CONCEPT #405:**   *Some sport logos, nicknames, and mascots that have been in use for many years are nevertheless offensive to some individuals and groups within our society.*

Beginning with the 1970 American Indian Movement, the sport world was made keenly aware of the politically sensitive situation surrounding the use of Indian names as mascots. As a result, several colleges and universities actually changed their logos and/or the names of their mascots. In the 1990s there has been great concern about the use of inappropriate and/or insensitive team names and mascots in the secondary, collegiate, and professional ranks. Today, any decision whether to utilize certain names, mascots, and logos needs to be made not only from a politically correct (public relations) perspective but also from a business and legal position (Cohen, 1993). By 2007 most college/universities had dropped Indian names as mascots.

> **CONCEPT #406:**   *Insensitive and inappropriate use of team logos, mascots, nicknames, and trademarks that are offensive, inconsiderate, and insulting to those individuals and groups should be discontinued.*

Professional teams are also subject to criticism in terms of their logos as well as other actions associated with their teams' names. Witness the Atlanta Braves and the Tomahawk Chop, which became famous (or infamous) during their World Series appearances in 1992 and 1993. Similarly, the Cleveland Indians (with their Chief Wahoo logo) as well as the Washington Redskins have also come under severe criticism for their registered trademark of a Native American.

There continues to be a concerted effort, initially started in the early 1970s, to have all sports teams stop the use of sports nicknames, logos, and mascots that would be offensive to any recognized racial or ethnic group within our society. This is especially so with the Native American population due to the fact that there are so many teams with Indian nicknames, mascots, and logos.

The issue of politically correct nicknames of athletic teams extends to those names that have the word *Lady* associated with the mascot itself. For example, as early as 1987 college women's basketball teams began to remove the word *Lady* from their nicknames. This was part of the gender equity movement that was sweeping the country (Politically correct nicknames, 1996). Some reasoned that because athletic programs did not identify male athletic teams as Gentlemen Eagles or Gentlemen Bears there were no reasons for women's teams to have nicknames such as Lady Eagles or Lady Bears.

> *CONCEPT #407:*   *Whether the term* **lady** *is retained in women's college athletic nicknames depends on the circumstances and situation associated with each institution.*

However, not all women's collegiate teams have rushed to remove all such references from their nicknames. In fact, of the 16 teams in the NCAA final Sweet 16 during the 1996 season, one-half still used *Lady* with their institution's nicknames. Supporters of retaining *Lady* in the school nicknames claim that the term provides their women players with an identity. These schools include Tennessee (Lady Vols), Louisiana Tech (Lady Techsters), Texas Tech (Lady Raiders), Penn State (Lady Lions), Stephen F. Austin (Lady jacks), Georgia (Lady Bulldogs), San Francisco (Lady Dons), and Old Dominion (Lady Monarchs). In fact, one institution, Texas Tech, actually went against the trend in political correctness by changing their nickname from Red Raiders to Lady Raiders in 1990 (Politically correct nicknames, 1996).

> *CONCEPT #408:*   *Sometimes what may be appropriate or politically correct for one sport organization may not be appropriate or suitable for a different sport organization—it depends on the circumstances surrounding each.*

The implications of having politically correct nicknames, mascots, or logos for women's teams necessitates that the choice of the sports team nickname, and the process of actually choosing such names, be viewed as appropriate for the team and the sponsoring organization. Similarly, the nickname must accurately and adequately reflect the nature of the team and the institution, and not be offensive to the athletes, the community as a whole, or any specific group of individuals within that community.

The author served as athletic director at the NCAA division III institution, Ohio Northern University, in 1982. There, women decided to retain the term *Lady* and to be referred to as the Lady Polar Bears. This reflected the desires of the athletes, the coaches, the alumni, the fans, and the local community. However, when the author later moved to the State University of New York-Brockport, the opposite action was taken. At SUNY Brockport, the women's teams were officially designated as the Golden Eagles and the word *Lady* was officially removed when referring to the women's teams. Again, the reason for this action was in response to the wishes of the athletes, the coaches, the alumni, the fans, and the community.

Sport managers must remain constantly vigilant of any action (conscious or unconscious, deliberate or accidental) that would offend any individual or group of individuals. The concern for managers in sport is threefold. First, there is always the possibility of negative consequences resulting from decisions in a court of law. Second, there can be severe financial consequences as a result of a loss of patronage at specific sporting events. Third, sport administrators must be concerned with doing or not doing things because "it is the right thing to do or the right thing not to do."

POLITICAL CORRECTNESS IN OTHER AREAS OF SPORT

> **CONCEPT #409:** *It is imperative to be politically correct in our society— not just because failure to do so can have severe consequences, but because it is the right thing to do.*

The words and terms we use as well as the actions we take or fail to take as members and citizens of our society are evidence of and reflective of the attitudes that we possess towards ourselves, others, and our communities. It is imperative that members of any profession, including the sport field, be aware of acceptable and unacceptable behavior.

Today, this encompasses the area of political correctness, a phrase that refers to the actions that are deemed socially acceptable in our society. There are a wide range of actions and spoken words and phrases that in the past might have been acceptable in polite society, but today, with increased knowledge, understanding, and perception of human needs, these same actions and words are deemed inappropriate and, in many cases, actually offensive.

CONCEPT #410:   *Political correctness involves an attitude as well as use of words and actions (or inactions).*

It is important for sport professionals to be cognizant of what actions and words are unacceptable in our society because of their offensive nature to some individuals, groups, or to the society as a whole. Failing to use common sense when speaking or in carrying out one's duties and responsibilities can have grave consequences. For example, Jimmy the Greek's insensitive response to a reporter's question as to why African American athletes excelled in sports cost him his lucrative television announcing-commentary contract. Management at the network could not survive the subsequent negative fallout as a result of television replays of his comments.

CONCEPT #411:   *Misuse or abuse of language can have severe consequences, personally as well as careerwise.*

Another example is Marge Schott, the former principal owner of the Cincinnati Reds. She was fined and then eventually suspended from day-to-day operations by major league baseball because of her insensitive remarks regarding Hitler and his infamous actions during World War II. Such situations can play havoc with public relations and the marketability of an organization.

Neither ignorance nor forgetfulness are excuses readily accepted by the community at large when it comes to outrageous and insensitive and hurtful remarks and/or actions. This has become increasingly so in recent years with the growing sensitivity on the part of more and more of our citizens regarding politically correct actions and communications.

CONCEPT #412:   *The choice of words can indeed hurt and harm.*

Communication is very important in our society, as well as in the world of sport management. Choosing one's words with care, with foresight, and with an understanding of how these words will affect others is essential.

Nonsexist Use of Language

It is very important that professional organizations, such as sport entities, utilize nonsexist language in all of their written publications as well as over the airways. "Because language plays a central role in the way human beings think and behave, we still need to promote language that opens rather than closes possibilities for women and men" (National Council, 1985, p. 1). The central issue is one of fairness and equality for both men and women.

CONCEPT #413:   *Nonsexist language is expected of professionals— both verbally and in written form.*

The goal in the adoption of nonsexist language is to attempt to offer alternatives to traditional usage of words, terms, and phrases that, today, are considered to be sexist and/ or detrimental to women in our society. The use of such alternatives is strongly encouraged, in both written and verbal communication.

Problems with the English language include the use of the psuedo-generic *man* as well as sex-role stereotyping. Common problems with the traditional use of *man* are identifying men and women in different ways. Instead, men and women should be identified in the same way; that is, diminutive or special forms to name women are usually unnecessary. Rather, use generic terms such as doctor or actor to include both males and females. Also, such terms as *stewardess, authoress, waitress, coed, lady lawyer,* and *male nurse* should be avoided and in their stead the following should be used: *author, food server, student, lawyer . . . she, nurse . . . he* (National Council, 1985, p. 2).

CONCEPT #414:   *Language that patronizes or trivializes women is totally unacceptable.*

It is also important that language does not patronize or trivialize women. Nor should language that reinforces stereotypical images of either men or women be used. For example, instead of using the statement that "team X has scheduled too many weak sisters," the following should be used: "team X has scheduled too many weak opponents." Another example is the use of "the president of the company hired a gal Friday." This should be changed to "the president of the company hired an assistant" (National Council, 1985, p. 3; Miller & Swift, 1980).

Negative Connotations of Some Words and Terms That Refer to Individuals with Disabilities.

The objective is for sport leaders, managers, and administers to create and promote environments that are positive for individuals with disabilities. The environments at work and at play must be conducive to enabling individuals to take advantage of the purposes for which the environment was created or provided in the first place. Frequently, such a positive environment can be greatly facilitated by the usage of correct or appropriate language. "Person first" language is the recommended method of speaking, which means that the individual is emphasized first while the disability (what it happens to be) is second. Thus, an individual who does not have a disability should be referred to as *nondisabled* rather than *normal* or *able-bodied.* Also, the term *handicapped* should not be used when referring to an individual, but it is appropriate when talking about a condition or a physical barrier. For example, the steps are a handicap for John, or Mary is handicapped by the lack of a suitable desk (Person first, 1992).

When dealing with individuals with disabilities, the word *handicapped* is no longer acceptable. In fact, the term *handicapped* originated in Great Britain shortly after the Crimean War, when veterans returned to England with severe injuries. The English Parliament made it legal for these injured veterans to beg on the streets. Hence, the word *handicapped* implies that people with disabilities are being made into beggars (Douglas, 1992).

CONCEPT #415: *Although sticks and stones" (words) may not break anyone's bones—carefully choose words and the context in which they are used lest individuals and groups be injured and/or offended.*

TABLE # 12.1: *Examples of Affirmative and Negative Phrases*

Affirmative Phrases	Negative Phrases
person who is blind	the blind
person who is deaf	suffers a hearing loss
person who has multiple sclerosis	afflicted by MS
person affected by cerebral palsy	CP victim
person who has muscular dystrophy	stricken by MD
person with mental retardation	retarded; mentally defective
person with epilepsy	epileptic
person who uses a wheelchair	confined or restricted to a wheelchair
person without disabilities	normal children
physically disabled	dumb; moot
seizure	fit
successful, productive	courageous (implies the person is a hero or martyr)

Frequently, political correctness simply means using different words and phrases; affirming positive rather than negative terms and phrases are the order of the day. When describing individuals with disabilities, it is important that the individual's worth and abilities, not the disabling condition, be the emphasis, be the focus of the words or terms. Examples of affirmative and negative phrases are provided in Table 12.1 (Douglas, 1992).

Problems with Political Correctness

Not all actions on behalf of political correctness are without controversy. Take the Spartanburg (South Carolina) Methodist's diversity plan in regard to the college's efforts to achieve what its leaders referred to as adequate diversity. The school, "claiming its athletic teams should reflect the racial composition of its I,OOO-member student body, wanted more white players on what has been an all-black men's basketball team" (White, 1996, p. 6-C). With a population of 73 percent white students, 24 percent African American, and 3 percent Hispanic and Asian, the school was committed to diversifying its athletic teams. As a result, the diversity policy regarding the athletic teams went into effect in January of 1996 and one of the consequences was the termination of the head men's basketball coach, Scott Rigot, when he refused to comply. The same thing happened to the women's tennis and soccer coach, Jim Rinker (White, 1996).

CONCEPT #416:   Not all efforts to be politically correct are without controversy.

The issue raised by this action by this small, two-year college in South Carolina is whether the recent Supreme Court decision outlawing preference according to race is being violated. When asked to comment on this specific controversy, Alex Johnson, a University of Virginia law professor, indicated that he is troubled by the situation. He was quoted in a *USA Today* article (White, 1996, p. 6-A) as saying: "Politically and legally, I think it would be difficult to defend a concept where you hold slots open for people of a certain race...It would be similar to a school setting aside a number of scholarships for blacks." Although the college is a private college, there are very few such institutions that receive absolutely no state or federal support money. And, if Spartanburg Methodist does receive such financial assistance, it runs the risk of violating established law should they actually establish quotas.

BEING COGNIZANT OF THE INTENT AND THE LETTER OF THE LAWS AND REGULATIONS AFFECTING SPORT PROGRAMS AND SPORT ORGANIZATIONS

> *CONCEPT #417:* *It is imperative that sport administrators and managers be conscientious in following all applicable laws and regulations; both the intent and the letter of such laws must be adequately addressed.*

Leaders in sport organizations have a very real responsibility when it comes to being knowledgeable of and following the letter and the intent of various laws and regulations. These leaders also share the responsibility of insuring that their staffs, both paid and volunteer, are also aware of and obey or adhere to such regulations, rules, and laws.

> *CONCEPT #418:* *Sport managers and administrators remain keenly aware of all laws and moral expectations if they are to be truly effective and efficient.*

There can be no excuse for not being aware of legal requirements or restrictions. Ignorance is no excuse. One of the major responsibilities of sport managers and administrators, those individuals entrusted with leadership roles within sport entities, is to insure that all aspects of the sport operation be conducted in appropriate ways, that is, in compliance with all requirements imposed by society and by the communities in which the sport entity operates.

> *CONCEPT #419:* *Sport leaders should do what is right, what is just— not because it is required but because it is right, it is just.*

This responsibility extends to areas in which there may not be specific laws or regulations governing some actions or inactions. For example, there may be occasions or situations in which something is legally permissible but morally (sensibly) one clearly understands that something should be done or that something should not be done. Sport administrators, sport leaders, should not hide behind the law, should not use the law (or the absence of a law or regulation) as a shield or an excuse for inappropriate behavior. The key concept is for the sport leaders and sport followers to do what is right, to do that is just—not because it is legally required but because it is right and it is just, period.

Conclusions

It is not only important for modem sport managers to be cognizant of the legal aspects of their organizations and their programs, but it is imperative that actions taken on behalf of the sport entities be in complete compliance with all applicable laws and regulations. Failure to operate within the legal restraints can have disastrous consequences for the sport organization, its programs, and its personnel. Not only can there be severe legal consequences but there can be tremendous negative public relations fallout as well when laws and regulations are not scrupulously adhered to by representatives of the sport entity. In terms of the legal aspects of sport management, it is best to be on the safe or conservative side rather than risk the dangers of being guilty of or being perceived to be acting contrary to the legal requirements.

References

Acosta, R.V. and Carpenter, L.J. (1992a). As the years go by-Coaching opportunities in the 1990s. *Journal of Physical Education. Recreation and Dance, 63*(3), 36-41.

Acosta, R.V. and Carpenter, L.J. (1992b). *Women in intercollegiate sport—A longitudinal study-Fifteen year update* 1977-1992. Unpublished manuscript, Brooklyn College.

ADA compliance guide. (1992). Washington, DC: Thompson Publishing Group.

ADA and ABA accessibility guidelines for buildings and facilities. (2004, July 23). *Federal Register,* 69(141). (Retrieved 2-21-06: http://www.access-board.gov/adaaba/final.htmk#pgfld-1007001)

Administration to suspend 'set-asides,' report says. (1996, March 8). *USA Today.* pp. 1-A, 4-A.

Altman, J., Jr. (2001, March 28). Affirmative action takes another hit. *Cincinnati Enquirer,* A-3.

Baize, S. (1995, October/November). Hiring for diversity. *Athletic Management. 7(5),*40-43.

Beck, J. (1997, April 15). Affirmative action: End, don't mend it. *Democrat and Chronicle.* p. 8-A.

Blauvelt, H. (1996, October 2). Women slowly crack athletic director ranks. *USA Today.* pp. I-C, 2-C.

Block, M.E. (1995). Americans with disabilities act: Its impact on youth sports. *Journal of Physical Education. Recreation and Dance, 66*(1), 28-32.

Clinton to put affirmative action programs on hold. (1996, March 8). *USA Today,* p. 1-A.

Cohen, A. (1993, October). Chief injustice. *Athletic Business, 17*(10), 16, 18.

Cohen, A. (1995, March). Running risks. *Athletic Business, 19*(3), 16, 18.

Dillon, T. (1993, July 26). Reno: Disability law will be enforced. *USA Today,* p. 9-A.

Discrimination because of sex under Title Vll of the Civil Rights Act of 1964. as amended; Adoption of final interpretive guidelines. Federal Register, November 10, 1980,74676-74677.

Douglas, R. (1992, October). Speech presented to senior executive service (by the executive director of the President's committee on employment of people with disabilities) and reprinted in Faculty Connection (Fall 1996), pp. 2, 3. State University of New York, Office of Student Affairs.

Dziech, B. and Weiner, L. (1984). *The lecherous professor-Sexual harassment on campus.* Boston: Beacon Press.

Epstein, R.S., McGovern, J. N., and Moon, M. S. (1994). The impact of federal legislation on recreation programs. In M. S. Moon (Ed.), *Making school and community recreation fun for everyone: Places and ways to integrate* (pp. 87-96). Baltimore: Paul H. Brookes.

Fisher, K. (1996, November). Slip up. *Athletic Business, 20*(11), *26.*

Gray, R.T. (1995, December) Shaky declarations of independence. *Nation's Business,* pp. 26-28.

Hall, M. (1993, July 22). More access due under landmark law. *USA Today,* p. 7-A.

Henry, T. (1996, October I). More kids sue school over peer sex harassment. *USA Today,* p. 1-D.

Hill, D. (2003, April/May). What's age got to do with it? *Athletic Management, XV*(3), 63-67.

Holland, G. (1996, October 24). Calif. seems poised to vote out affirmative action. *USA Today,* p. 4-A.

Johnson, K. (1995, January II). Affirmative action next target in California. *USA Today,* pp. 1-A, 2-A.

Jones, D. (1996, October I). 'Code words' cloud issue of discrimination at work. *USA Today,* pp. 1-B, 2-B.

Klein, J. (February 13, 1995). Time to pull the plug on affirmative action, *Readers Digest.* pp. 105-107.

Lackey, Donald. (1990). Sexual harassment in sports. *Physical Educator, 42*(2) 22-26.

Lawlor, J. (1993, May 10). Business owners feel weight of laws. *USA Today,* p. 2-E.

Leo, J. (1995, March 13). Endgame for affirmative action. *U.S. News & World Report,* p. 18.

Loyle, D. (1995, January). Sexual harassment: The employer minefield. *Club Industry,* pp. 18-20, 22, 23-25.

MacKinnon, C. (1979). *Sexual harassment of working women.* London: Yale University Press.

Marchell, T., Hofher, J., Parrot, A., and Cummings, N. (1992, November). Prevention by education. *Athletic Management, IV(6), 44-48.*

Marklein, M. B. (2001, March 28). Judge: Minority admissions policy is illegal. *USA Today,* p. 3-A.

Marklein, M.B. (2003, October 2). Colleges ponder the 'legal' way to achieve ethnic diversity. *USA Today,* p. 11-D.

Marklein, M.B. (2003, December 23). Admissions, tuition generate the heat. *USA Today,* p. 8-D.

Mauro, T. (1995, June 13). Court signals 'end for era' in civil rights. *USA Today,* pp. 1-A, 2-A.

McWhirter, D.A. (1993). *Your rights at work* (2nd ed.). New York: John Wiley & Sons, Inc.

Meyer, M., 'Berchtold, I., Oestreich, J., Collins, E, and Chaddock, P. (1981). *Sexual harassment.* New York: Petrocelli Books.

Miller, C. and Swift, K. (1980). *The handbook of nonsexist writing: For writers, editors and speakers.* New York: Harper and Row.

Moon, M.S. (Ed.). (1994). *Making school and community recreation fun for everyone: Places and ways to integrate.* Baltimore: Paul H. Brookes.

Munson, A. L. and Comodeca, J. A. (1993, July). The act of inclusion. *Athletic Management, V(14), 16-19.*

Nasser. H. E. (1993, December 29). Calif. firm sued under disabled rights act. *USA Today,* p. 3-A.

Nasser, H. E. (1998, March 5). Ruling puts workplace behavior under a harsher spotlight. *USA Today,* p. 2-A,

National Council of Teachers of English. (1985). *Guidelines for nonsexist use of language in NCTE publications* (Revised). Urbana, IL.

O'Leary. (1995, February-March). Evading exposure. *Athletic Management, VII(2), 55-57.*

Person first: A lexicon affirming those with disabilities. (1992, November). *Brockport Statements.* Brockport, NY: SUNY–Brockport, p. 2.

Perry, P. M. (2001, September). Independent study. *Athletic Business, 26(9),* 40.

Petersen, J.C., & Piletic, C. K. (2006). Facility accessibility. *Journal of Physical Education, Recreation and Dance, 77*(5), 38-44.

Pike, L. (1994, August). Harassed: Sexual harassment could prove costly to athletic departments. *Athletic Business, 18*(8), 12-13.

Politically correct nicknames. (1996, March 22). *USA Today,* p. 4-C.

Price, R. (1997, April 9). Preference ban upheld in California. *USA Today,* p. 1-A.

Prop. 209 still under fire. (November 9, 1996). *Democrat and Chronicle,* p. 11.

Reiner, L. (1994, August). The ADA challenge. *Athletic Business, 18*(8), 27-30, 32, 34.

Same-sex harassment illegal. (1998, March 5). *Democrat and Chronicle,* pp. 1-A, 7-A.

Sandler, B. and Associates. (1981). Sexual harassment: A hidden problem. *Educational Record, 20,* 52-57.

Scholand, G. (2005, April/May). Keeping score on overtime. *Athletic Management, XVII*(3), 43, 44, 46, 48-51.

Somers, A. (1982). Sexual harassment in academe: Legal issues and definitions. *Journal of Social Issues, 38*(4), 23-32.

Steele, S. (1994). *The content of our character.* Unpublished manuscript.

Stier, W.F, Jr. (1994). *Successful sport fund-raising.* Dubuque, IA: Wm. C. Brown & Benchmark.

Stier, W.F., Jr. (2005). An Overview of Sexual Harassment. *Strategies, 18*(4), 13-15.

The Voice. (1994, May). State University of New York, p. 2.

Wentzel, M. (1994, April 3). Getting ready for the ADA. *Democrat and Chronicle,* p. 16-A.

White, C. (1996, July 22). Spartanburg Methodist's diversity plan raises concern. *USA Today,* p. 6-C.

Wong, G.M. (Ed.). (1996, October). Contract law. *Athletic Business, 20*(10), 10, 14.

Wong, G.M. and Barr, C. A. (1991, June). Sports licensing gets a boost from Carolina case. *Athletic Business, 15*(6),18,21.

Wong, G.M. and Barr, C.A. (1994, October). Pay attention. *Athletic Business, 18*(10), 10,14.

Workplace: The cost of sexual harassment. (1992, May). *Inc.,* p. 145.

DISCUSSION TOPICS

1. List possible consequences for sport management personnel in situations where laws and regulations are not adequately followed.

2. Provide examples of sport businesses engaging both employees and independent contractors to perform tasks.

3. Define the essence of grievance procedures and policies within the sport entity for its personnel.

4. Outline the history of affirmative action in this country up to the present time, including the California Initiative (Proposition 209).

5. Cite examples of offensive behavior that might be considered to be sexual harassment of another person.

6. Explain the statement: *Knowledge of the Law Itself Is Not Sufficient for the Sport Manager* in terms of sport managers.

7. Indicate how, with specific examples, the ADA can affect most sport, recreation, and fitness programs.

8. How can OSHA affect the planning, management, and maintenance of sport programs? Provide a specific example in an area of sport, recreation, or fitness and wellness.

9. Why is it important for the sport organization to be concerned with political correctness in terms of decisions and the behavior of its employees and representatives?

10. Explain how grievance procedures work.

Chapter

13 School Sports and Title IX— Equality in Opportunities

Women Play a Major Role in Competitive and Recreational Sports Programs.
[photo courtesy of State University of New York, Brockport, James Dusen, photographer]

CHAPTER HIGHLIGHTS

This chapter will help the reader to:

- Explain the history of Title IX and the rationale for its passage;
- Indicate why there was a need for Title IX to be passed;
- Comprehend the reasons behind the lack of compliance by schools after the passage of Title IX;
- Specify the type of schools that are subject to Title IX today;
- Understand the sport opportunities available for women prior to Title IX;
- Comprehend how booster club generated funds are affected by Title IX;
- Indicate the consequences upon IX by the Civil Rights Restoration Act of 1987;
- Comprehend the results/implications of the long awaited 1992 Gender Equity Survey, issued by the NCAA;
- Explain one of the most important consequences of the passage of Title IX;
- Differentiate between the Brooklyn College, Brown University and West Chester University cases in terms of their activities relating to Title IX;

- Appreciate the importance of the case: *Franklin* v. *Gwinnet County Public Schools*, 117 L. Ed. 2d 208 [1992];
- Reveal the essence of the clarification in 2005 by the Department of Education;
- Describe the implications of Grove City versus Bell case;
- List the components of the three-pronged test created by the United States Office for Civil Rights;
- Cite the current challenges relating to gender equity;
- Appreciate the importance of the 1994 Elementary and Secondary Education Act upon Title IX.

TITLE IX AND GENDER EQUITY

With the enactment of Title IX of the Educational Amendments of 1972 (the Education Amendments to the Civil Rights Act of 1964), which was signed on June 23, 1972, the role of women in competitive sports was changed irrevocably. Specifically, Title IX forbade sex discrimination in educational institutions that received any type of federal funds. The law specifically states: "No person in the United States shall, on the basis of sex, be excluded from participation in, be denied the benefits of, or be subjected to discrimination under any program or activity receiving Federal financial assistance" (Title IX, 44 Fed. Reg. at 71413).

> **CONCEPT #420:**   *Title IX affects every school sports program where the school itself receives federal assistance.*

As initially interpreted, this law had a direct effect on the sport program in every junior high, senior high, and college or university in this country that received any type of federal assistance whatsoever. Today, some proponents of gender equity have taken the position that the definitive definition of gender equity is "when either the men's or women's sports program would be pleased to accept as its own the overall program of the other gender" (Herwig, 1993a; Herwig, 1993b).

COMPETITIVE SPORT OPPORTUNITIES FOR WOMEN PRIOR TO TITLE IX

To better grasp the tremendous impact that Title IX initially had on women's athletics, both in high schools and colleges during the past 30+ years, one must understand the status of women's sports prior to the passage of this federal mandate. To put it bluntly, prior to the mid-1970s opportunities for athletic competition for girls on the secondary level were far behind the opportunities available for boys in most schools in this country. At the collegiate level the situation was similarly dismal. Although there were some exceptions, for the most part girls and women were treated as second-class citizens in terms of sport participation opportunities.

Lack of Encouragement Coupled with Outright Discouragement

> **CONCEPT #421:** *It is hard to obtain an increase in sport participation when individuals are not encouraged to do so or are actually discouraged from such participation.*

For the most part, girls and women were neither encouraged to participate in competitive sports nor were they financially supported to the degree that the boys and men were at the high school and collegiate levels. Even when sport programs and activities were made available for girls and women, the amount of financial and other types of support provided fell far, far short of what was provided for boys and men in similar situations.

> **CONCEPT #422:** *There were many reasons in the past for the lack of competitive sport opportunities for girls and women.*

In many instances girls and women were actually discouraged from seeking additional competitive sport opportunities or from taking advantage of those programs and activities that were available. This was done for several reasons. First, because the belief that any increase in sport involvement by girls and women might impair or hinder the sport programs for boys and men. The view was that there were only so many sport dollars available and an increase in female sports might mean a corresponding decrease in the financial support of male sports. Second, in some quarters, females participating in competitive sports were viewed as being unfeminine, inappropriate, or even unhealthy. Third, females did not

Night Games Greatly Increases Exposure to Fans.
[courtesy of St. Lucie METS, Port St. Lucie, Florida, photo by Jimmy Fertitta]

truly have interests in becoming involved in competitive sports. And, fourth, there was no overriding reason, internal or external, to change the status quo.

As a result, opportunities for competitive athletic experience for girls and women were minimal at best, prior to the federal mandate referred to as Title IX. At the collegiate level participation was hampered because of the small number of high school graduates coming to college with prior competitive sport experience. Yes, schools offered intercollegiate sports for women but the number of sports were fewer than those provided for men, and the resources (financial and otherwise) supporting the women's sports were far, far inferior, for the most part, to what was available to men's sports.

In summary, girls in high school and women in college were not given their just due either in terms of opportunities for competitive sports or support, financial or otherwise, for adequate sports programs. The reasons were many and varied but the consequence was the same: Sexual discrimination was pervasive in our schools throughout the country insofar as sports were concerned.

Changes Brought about by Title IX

Title IX, passed in 1972, required that, by 1978, all educational institutions receiving federal aid practice nondiscrimination on the basis of sex (Title IX of the Education Amendments, 1972). One of the largest consequences was the expansion of sport opportunities for women, especially in the area of sport participation (Durrant, 1992). For example, in the state of Indiana the number of female participants involved in interscholastic sports recognized by that state's High School Athletic Association increased from 27,000 in 1972 to over 50,000 in 1992.

On the national level, similar gains have been experienced. In 1972 some 300,000 girls participated in organized competitive sports at the secondary level compared to over 1.8 million just 20 years later (Sawyer, 1992). By the 1994-1995 school year the number of girls participating in organized competitive sports at the secondary level was at an all-time high. In fact, 2,240,461 girls were participating during that year (Girls' participation, 1996).

CONCEPT #423:   *Title IX has changed school athletics in innumerable ways.*

Similar gains have been realized at the collegiate levels. For example, the average number of women's sports offered by colleges and universities increased from 5.61 per school in 1977 to 7.24 in 1990 (Berg, 1990). During the 1994-1995 academic year there were over 105,532 women participating in organized competitive sports at the collegiate level (Girls' participation, 1996). An interesting result of recent court rulings has been the inclusion of booster club funds in the Title IX equation. This means that the money generated from the efforts of a booster club must be shared or distributed equally and appropriately with both male and female teams, even if the booster club was organized around or for a single gender (Berry, 2001).

However, even the passage of Title IX did not result in total equality, then or today. In fact, the schools of this country were brought kicking and screaming into some resemblance of compliance as a result of Title IX, but certainly not total compliance (Acosta & Carpenter, 1990; Fox, 1992; Acosta & Carpenter, 1992).

The Challenges of Compliance and Title IX

However, there was still strong resistance to the changes suggested by Title IX. Some of this resistance was subtle. Other instances were not. The attitude held by many athletic administrators is best summarized by the response obtained by a survey of sport departments within small colleges and universities. One of the respondents, in answering a question of whether the respondent's institution was in compliance with all aspects of Title IX, replied: "We are in compliance until someone tells us we are not" (Stier, 1983).

Another challenge associated with Title IX is that an inordinate percentage of athletic administrators in both junior colleges and in smaller 4-year colleges and universities believed that not only were they currently in full compliance but that they had always been in conformity with the mandates of Title IX, even before it was enacted (Stier, 1982-1983; Stier, 1984a; Stier, 1984b). Of course, this was not the case for most schools, regardless of size or level. Nevertheless, some 85 percent of the respondents indicated that for their sports programs, this was indeed the case. Either athletic administrators had faulty memories or they did not understand the full implications and ramifications of the act.

Grove City versus Bell

The teeth were temporarily taken out of Title IX insofar as sports were concerned when the United States Supreme Court ruled on February 28, 1984 that specific programs, not an institution, must receive federal funds in order to fall under the auspices of Title IX. This suit (*Grove City College v. Bell*, 465 U.S. 555, 79 L. Ed. 516, 104 S. Ct. 1211 [1984]) was a result of Grove City College of Pennsylvania challenging the tenets of Title IX. Thus, because practically no athletic department was receiving federal funds directly, the athletic programs were not under the purview of Title IX legislation. Unfortunately, many of the lawsuits that had been filed under Title IX and were in the process of being litigated became moot with the *Grove City versus Bell* ruling.

CONCEPT #424: The Grove City case took the "teeth" out of Title IX.

Closing the Barn Door after the Horse Ran Out

However, this temporary setback to Title IX legislation for equality in sports for girls and women did not curtail the existing opportunities for sport participation for girls and women. It was like attempting to close the barn door after the horse ran out. The tremendous growth experienced by women's sports in the 1970s and early 1980s could not be reversed. In fact, opportunities continued to increase, albeit not at the same rate as prior to the Grove City case.

The Civil Rights Restoration Act

The teeth were put back into Title IX by the Civil Rights Restoration Act of 1987, which was passed by Congress on March 22, 1988 over then-President Reagan's veto. This law restored institution-wide coverage of Title IX, effectively nullifying the Grove City versus Bell ruling. Almost immediately after the passage of this act several law suits were filed or filed again under Title IX. For example, on June 13, 1988, Temple University settled a Title IX lawsuit just three weeks after going to trial. The lawsuit, originally filed in 1980, prior to the Grove City case, charged the school with systematic sex discrimination by its athletic department. As a result of the agreement, Temple University agreed to add two women's sports and to raise its women's athletic participation rate from 34 percent to 43 percent.

CONCEPT #425:   *The Civil Rights Restoration Act of 1987 put the "teeth" back into Title IX.*

Opening the Door to Punitive Damages under Title IX

The Supreme Court made a most important legal decision relating to Title IX on February 26, 1992. The decision *(Franklin* v. *Gwinnet County Public Schools*, 117 L. Ed. 2d 208 [1992]) resulted from a suit filed by a secondary school student in the state of Georgia who accused a teacher, who was also a coach, of sexual harassment. The Supreme Court ruled in the Gwinnet County case that individuals who file a lawsuit under Title IX are eligible for *monetary damages in addition to having their grievances redressed.* This decision of the court significantly raised the penalty for noncompliance with this law at schools and colleges that receive federal aid by making athletic departments liable for punitive damages if found to be in violation of Title IX (Mauro, 1992).

CONCEPT #426: *Now that monetary damages may be awarded, in addition to having grievances redressed, it is far more costly to be found in violation of Title IX.*

Previously, if schools were found guilt of noncompliance, they were, in effect, slapped on the wrist and told to get in compliance. There was not a great risk in failing to comply with the letter and the intent of the Title IX legislation prior to this latest decision by the Supreme Court (Supreme court rules, 1992). Subsequently, however, there was more motivation for adhering to the Title IX regulations, and that motivation was fear of monetary damages being awarded. The matter of monetary damages also served as a motivating factor on behalf of potential plaintiffs and attorneys. Now, lawyers would be able to secure potentially greater financial awards for their plaintiffs (and for themselves) as a result of favorable Title IX verdicts, than in the past.

On February 27, 1992, the United States Office of Civil Rights rendered a decision in which it found that Brooklyn College (a Division I NCAA institution) was in violation of 10 of the 13 areas that comprise Title IX compliance. This investigation resulted from a complaint filed some 14 months earlier (December 1990) by athletes and staff at that institution. As a result of this ruling, the school agreed to remedy the discrimination but, shortly after, elected to eliminate all collegiate competitive sports and disbanded the entire athletic department for the next year.

Cheerleaders are a Very Important Element in the World of Sports.
[courtesy of University of Montana, Todd Goodrich, photographer]

On March 11, 1992, the NCAA released its long-awaited Gender Equity Survey, revealing that after some 20 years of Title IX, college men still receive twice as many athletic scholarships as women at NCAA institutions. Additionally, while women make up 50 percent of the NCAA institutions in terms of full undergraduate population, they receive only 20 percent of athletic budgets and a measly 18 percent of the recruiting budget.

Determining Gender Equity: Three Criteria for Determining Compliance with Title IX

Today, there are three generally accepted criteria by which compliance may be determined in terms of competitive athletics. The three-pronged test emanated from the United States Office for Civil Rights and should be utilized to determine whether gender equity exists in competitive athletics in any given school or institution. Meeting any one of these criteria would be prima facie evidence of compliance with Title IX and meeting the benchmark for gender equity in the competitive sports arena (Frankel, 1992; Internet Surveys, 2005).

These benchmark tests or criteria include: (1) providing opportunities for competitive sport participation for women and for men that are substantially proportionate to their respective rates of enrollment within the school, (2) showing a history and continuing practice of expanding opportunities for the underrepresented sex, (3) actually proving that the organization has truly accommodated (fully and effectively) the interests and abilities of the underrepresented sex (Achieving gender equity, 1994; Lederman, 1995; Bickford, 2001). The proportionality concept is an important one in that "it means that the gender ratio of the student body should be a benchmark for participation opportunities for athletes" (Herwig, 1993a).

West Chester University (Pennsylvania) Found in Violation of IX (2004)

West Chester University tried to eliminate a women's team (gymnastics) in the spring of 2003. It was quickly slapped with a preliminary injunction in November of that same year by a Federal Judge. Edward Matejkovic, the school athletic director and the individual who elected to drop gymnastics (along with men's Lacrosse), was ordered by the Federal judge to not only reinstate the women's tennis team but ordered him to provide funding (a budget) equal to or greater than what the team had the previous year. In addition, the judged ordered that the coaching staff as well as facilities and equipment be equal to or greater than what the team had the previous year. "We knew the lawsuit was a perfect 10 when we filed it" said attorney Leslie Brueckner, "And we stuck the landing" (Judge orders return. 2003).

Promotional Activities Can Take Place Before, During or After Athletic Contests.
[courtesy of St. Lucie METS, Port St. Lucie, Florida, photo by Jimmy Fertitta]

The school tried to defend its action but attorney Brueckner said: "In essence, the judge said that any time a school is out of statistical proportionality and cuts a women's team, that's a Title IX violation" (Smith, 2004, p.44). The school was not able to justify its attempt to eliminate a women's sport under the second prong because the last time it added a women's team was 10 years previously and before that a women's team was last added in 1979.

THE USE OF INTERNET-BASED SURVEYS

In attempting to satisfy the third prong, the U.S. Department of Education (DOE) attempted to clarify its position as how schools might show that the institutions were indeed satisfying the interests and abilities of the underrepresented sex. This was done when the Department of Education issued a clarification relative to Title IX on March 17, 2005. The clarification introduced a set of guidelines on how schools might actually measure student interest *which included the use of internet-based (e-mail) surveys of the existing student body* (Internet surveys, 2005). This internet-based survey technique (mass e-mailing) has generated a great deal of controversy but at present the survey method still is an approved method of gauging interest and abilities of the underrepresented sex (Waldron, 2006).

> *CONCEPT #427:* **Compliance with Title IX depends on more than having the appropriate number of teams for both sexes.**

There were nine general areas or components in 1996 that should have been examined in the athletic arena in terms of determining whether a school or department is in compliance with Title IX: (1) effective accommodation of student interests and abilities, (2) provision of equipment and supplies, (3) scheduling of games and practice times, (4) travel and per diem allowances, (5) opportunity to receive coaching and adequate compensation of coaches, (6) provision of a locker room, practice, and competitive facilities, (7) provision of medical and training facilities and services, (8) publicity, and (9) provision of support services (Paling, 1996).

In 2003, Moore cited the following 11 components within the Office of Civil Rights' document *Athletics Investigator's Manual* as the elements of an athletic program that should be addressed, in addition to the three prongs previously cited in this chapter.

1. Equipment and supplies
2. Scheduling of games and practice
3. Travel and per diem allowance
4. Access to experienced and quality coaches
5. Sport facilities
6. Medical and training facilities
7. Publicity
8. Recruiting resources
9. Academic tutoring services
10. Support services
11. Housing and dining facilities

The Elementary and Secondary Education Act

Title IX gained even more teeth when, on October 5, 1994, Congress passed and President Clinton, on October 20, 1994, signed, the Elementary and Secondary Education Act (more commonly known as "Improving America's Schools Act"). This law included the "Equity in Athletics disclosure" amendment that now required colleges to disclose information on their intercollegiate athletics programs relating to gender equity, starting October 1, 1996.

"Similar to the Student Right-To-Know Act, which requires colleges to release information and publicize graduation rates of their students participating in their intercollegiate athletic programs, the Elementary and Secondary Education Act mandated institutions that take part in the federal student-aid programs and have intercollegiate athletics to provide an annual report containing specifics about opportunities and benefits provided to male and female student-athletes" (Gender equity, 1995, p. 7). The reports are to contain, among other data, the following information:

1. Number of students by sex
2. Number of participants by sex
3. Total operating expenses for intercollegiate athletes
4. Gender of all head and assistant coaches
5. Amount of money spent on athletically related student aid
6. Recruiting expenses
7. Coaches' salaries for all men's and women's teams (varsity and sub-varsity)

The result of this 1994 law has been greater scrutiny on the spending for both men's and women's athletic programs at the collegiate level. High school students seeking an appropriate collegiate setting to become involved as a student and as an athlete now have much more data on which to base the important decision as to where they should go to college.

Half-time Activities are an Important Element of the Afternoon Football Game.
[courtesy of University of Tennessee, Sports Information Office]

A long, drawn-out court fight over Title IX was waged between April 9, 1992 and April 21, 1997 by Brown University, which contested the charge that it was violating Title IX. The initial suit was brought against Brown University by members of the school's gymnastics and volleyball teams alleging gender discrimination because, in May of 1991, the university had eliminated funding for these two sports in addition to men's water polo and golf. The school cited financial problems and a need to reduce almost a $1.6 million athletic budget deficit as a rationale for the withdrawal of financial support of the four teams.

After a long series of events and legal decisions (injunctions, charges, decisions, appeals, and a partial settlement) the United States Supreme Court was asked by Brown University to hear the case. The result was that on April 21, 1997 the Supreme Court, without comment, let stand the lower court ruling that determined that Brown University (Rhode Island) had indeed discriminated against women in its varsity sports offerings (Mauro, 1997; Brady & Wieberg, 1997).

Brown University was accused of lacking gender parity in light of the fact that only 38 percent of its varsity sport participants were women although women comprised 51 percent of the total student body. It should be noted that the U.S. Supreme Court's action was not a ruling but an act that let a lower court's ruling stand. Similarly, this act affects Brown University and other educational institutions in those states covered by the appeals court in this case, including Maine, Massachusetts, Rhode Island, New Hampshire, and Puerto Rico.

However, every educational and sport leader had been watching this case with great attention because of its potential fallout. Perhaps the real significance of this ruling was expressed by NCAA official Janet Justus who observed, "This is a significant moment in the history of Title IX. With this decision, I think way more schools are going to come in compliance" (Mauro, 1997, p. I-A).

VIOLATIONS OF CIVIL RIGHTS: EQUAL OPPORTUNITIES IN SPORT

Equal opportunities in sport continue to be a controversial topic at all levels of competition. In 1994, 12 girls who played slow-pitch softball for high schools in the state of Kentucky sued that state's high school athletic association, arguing that the Kentucky High School Athletic Association and the Kentucky State Board of Elementary and Secondary Education denied girls equal athletic opportunities. The sixth U.S. Circuit Court of Appeals ordered a federal judge to reconsider the girls' claim that the state sanctioned fewer sports for girls than boys and improperly refused to sanction girls fast-pitch softball, preventing them from competing for college scholarships (Jurisprudence, 1994).

THE 14TH AMENDMENT TO THE UNITED STATES CONSTITUTION: EQUAL PROTECTION

The 14th Amendment to the United States Constitution provides equal protection to the citizenry. This equal protection in the courts in which individual athletes are concerned has tended to result in the courts finding for females whenever there has been only one team offered by a school and that team has been for males. In these cases, girls and women have generally been allowed to join the boys' or men's teams. However, the opposite has not usually been the case, generally because of what the courts have felt would be unfair advantages which would accrue to the male should this individual be allowed to join an otherwise all female team (Durrant, 1992).

CONCLUSIONS

Crowds Can Add an Essential Element of Excitement to the Athletic Arena.
[courtesy of University of Tennessee, Sports Information Office]

The role of women in sports, at all level of competition and participation, has changed dramatically since 1972 as a result of Title IX. Yet, in spite of some very real advancements, there are still many challenges facing women today. And, there is really no end in site in terms of meeting the intent and letter of the law. In spite of the passage of Title IX, and subsequent laws and rules issued by the Department of Education (DOE), the Office of Civil Rights (OCR) and numerous courts and judges, complete and adequate compliance with Title IX still has a long way to go. It behooves sport administrators at all schools to see that their sport programs are in compliance with Title IX, not only because it is the law of the land but because it is the right thing to do.

Failure to do so can have some very real consequences for both the institution and the personnel involved. For administrators it is a case of being recognized as a competent leader of an athletic program that is in compliance with Title IX or recognized as one who is an ineffective and inefficient leader, one who fails to abide by the law of the land either through ignorance or deliberate decision making.

> *CONCEPT #428: There is no excuse for an athletic director at a school to have an athletic program that is not in compliance with Title IX.*

Today, it is very simple, that is, it is just unacceptable to be out of compliance of such a well-known and publicized federal mandate. If an administrator claims ignorance that one's program is out of compliance, the response is that a competent administrator should have known. And, if the administrator knew the program was out of compliance and nothing was done to correct the unlawful situation, the response is that the person is incompetent.

REFERENCES

Achieving gender equity, a basic guide to Title IX for colleges and universities. (1994). Overland Park KS: NCAA, pp. 61.

Acosta, R.V. and Carpenter, L. J. (1990). *Women in intercollegiate sport: A longitudinal study—Thirteenyear update.* Unpublished manuscript, Brooklyn College.

Acosta, R.V. and Carpenter, L. J. (1992). Job status: *Reflections of immobility and resistance to job change among senior women athletic personnel.* Unpublished manuscript, Brooklyn College.

Berg, R. (Ed.). (1990, October). Women in sports-Reluctant role model. *Athletic Business. 14*(10), 15.

Berry, L. (2001). Balancing booster budgets. *Athletic Management, XIII*(2), 31-33, 35, 36.

Bickford, B. (2001). Ensuring equity. *Training & Conditioning, XI*(3), 23-27

Brady E. and Wieberg, S. (1997, April 22). Ex-Brown player hails Title IX court move. *USA Today.* p. 3-C.

Calif. proposition motivates foes of anti-bias plans. (1996, November 10). *Democrat and Chronicle*, p. 4-A.

Carpenter, L. (1989). Legal issues: Sexual harassment. *Journal of Physical Education. Recreation and Dance. 60*(4), 18-20.

Durrant, S.M. (1992). Title IX-Its power and its limitations. *Journal of Physical Education. Recreation and Dance. 63*(3), 60-64.

Fox, C. (1992) Title IX at twenty. *Journal of Physical Education. Recreation and Dance. 63*(3), 33, 34.

Frankel, E. (1992, November). Charging ahead. *Athletic Management.1V*(6), 14-19.

Gender equity disclosure act signed into law. (1995, December/January). *Athletic Management, Vll*(I), 7.

Girls' participation in sports at an all time high. (1996, Summer). *GWS News, 23*(4), 6.

Herwig, C. (1993a, May 19). True equity, gender ratio top report. *USA Today*, p. l-C.

Herwig, C. (1993b, May 19). Gender task force has more work to do. *USA Today*, p. 8-C.

Internet surveys okayed. (2005 June/July). *Athletic Management, XVII*(4), 4.

Judge orders return. (2003, November 13). *USA Today*, p. 1 5-C. s

Jurisprudence. (1994. December 23). *USA Today*, p. II-C.

Lederman, D. (1995. November 3). Murky clarification. *Chronicle of Higher Education, XLlI*(10), A-51, A-52.

Mauro, T. (1992, February 27). Sex bias law applied to schools. *USA Today,* p. I-A.

Mauro, T. (1997, April 22). Sex equity in sports backed-Court supports Title IX. *USA Today,* p. I-A.

Moore, B. (2003). Have a seat. *Athletic Management, XV*(3), 21

Paling, D. (1996, June-July). High school's Title IX story. *Athletic Management, VllI*(4), 22-24, 27.

Sawyer, T.H. (1992). Title IX: Some positive changes have occurred. *Journal of Physical Education, Recreation and Dance, 63*(3), 14.

Smith, L. (2004, April, May 2004). Year in review. *Athletic Management, XVI*(3), 43-49.

Stier, W.F, Jr. (1982-1983). Physical education faculty and programs in small colleges and universities. *The Physical Educator, 39*(4), 23.

Stier, W.F, Jr. (1983). Athletic policies, procedures, and practices in small colleges and universities. *Athletic Administration. 17*(4), 14.

Stier, W.F, Jr. (1984a, Spring). Physical education and athletic programs on the junior/community college campuses in the United States. *Research Consortium —Research Papers—Abstracts.* American Alliance for Health, Physical Education, Recreation and Dance.

Stier, W.F, Jr. (1984b, December). Survey determines present status of junior colleges. *Athletic Administration, 14*(2), 14.

Supreme court rules that victims of intentional sex bias can sue colleges for punitive damages under Title IX. (1992, March 4). *Chronicle of Higher Education, XXXVllI*(26), A39.

Waldron, J.J. (2006, April). Web-based surveys undermine Title IX. *Journal of Physical Education, Recreation and Dance, 77*(4), 4-6.

DISCUSSION TOPICS

1. What comprises the three-prong test used in meeting the requirements for Title IX?
2. What did the 1992 Gender Equity Survey released by the NCAA reveal?
3. How did Title IX come to "lose its teeth" and under what circumstances did the law once again become effective?
4. What were some of the reasons in the past for the lack of Competitive sport opportunities for girls and women prior to Title IX?
5. Today, how can schools determine whether they are meeting the needs (student interests) of women regarding Title IX?

6. What were the major differences between West Chester University's run-in with the Federal Judge regarding Title IX and Brown University's effort to confront this law?

7. What are the implications of the 1994 Elementary and Secondary Education Act, signed by then President Clinton?

8. Identify the school cited (with a preliminary injunction) by a federal judge as violating Title IX when the athletic director eliminated women's gymnastics and men's lacrosse, and cite the major ruling why.

9. List the 11 areas within the Office of Civil Rights' document, *Athletics Investigator's Manual,* which administrators should look at to insure that male and female teams and athletes are treated appropriately under Title IX?

10. How has the 14th Amendment to the United States Constitution affected athletes in our schools in terms of equal protection to our citizenry?

Chapter

14 Risk Management and Legal Liability in the World of Sport

Wise Sport Administrators Plan in Advance for the Worse Case Scenario.
[courtesy of Clemson University Sports Information, Bob Waldrop, photographer]

CHAPTER HIGHLIGHTS

This chapter will help the reader to:

• Illustrate instances where waivers can be successfully used against charges of ordinary negligence;

• Be cognizant of potential of litigation for activities sponsored or carried out by sport personnel;

• Understand tort liability insofar as sport organizations are concerned;

• Explain how sport, recreation and fitness programs should be active in terms of risk management activities and risk management audits;

- Know the role that CAPS play in the area of legal liability and risk management;
- Define the term negligence and cite its implications for sport entities and their personnel;
- Differentiate between civil law, criminal law and contract law;
- Explain the various forms of negligence—slander, libel and defamation of character;
- List the essentials for proving slander, libel and defamation of character;
- Illustrate the differences between contributory and comparative negligence;
- Cite common areas of concern for negligence in sport, recreation and fitness programs;
- List the Ten Commandments of Aquatic Risk Management;
- Explain the advantages and importance of using a risk statement document and release forms;
- Comprehend the concept of product liability.

CONCEPT #429:   *Sport managers must be constantly aware of the potential for litigation as a result of the activities they sponsor or provide.*

It is imperative that activities and programs of sport businesses be conducted in a safe and secure manner. This is especially true in what has become a truly litigious society in which we currently live and work. Today, liability is a very real concern for professionals at all levels who are involved in sports, recreation and fitness programs. "Litigation has become the nation's secular religion and it is practiced regularly against public and private park, recreation, sports, and leisure enterprises" (Kaiser, 1986, p. 1.)

Appenzeller (1993) traces the tremendous increase of sports-related injury litigation, in part, to a 1964 case *Miller v. Cloidt.* This case was one of the earliest lawsuits which a person sought damages because of a failure for a physical education teacher to properly supervise a student who was subsequently injured. The fact that the lawsuit resulted in the astronomical and unprecedented sum (at that time) of $1.2 million dollars in damages opened the flood gates for future litigation in the area of sport injuries.

It should be pointed out, however, that the *Miller v. Cloidt* decision was certainly not the first case involving a lack of supervision involving a youngster involved in a physical activity. As early as 1937 a lawsuit was initiated when a youngster in a physical education class received injuries while being supervised by a school janitor (Berg, 1993).

TORT LIABILITY

Tort liability has been the basis for most of the litigation which has been brought before the American courts by injured parties who have been hurt as a result of their involvement in and association with sport, recreation and fitness activities. "A tort is a private or civil wrong or injury, other than a breach of contract, suffered as a result of another person's conduct" (Wong, 1989, July, p. 16).

The fundamental objectives of sport managers involved in conducting and supervising various sport, recreation and fitness programs should be threefold. First, there is a matter of attempting to provide a safe and secure environment. The reason for this, obviously, is so that few, if any, personal injury accidents occur. It is imperative that the individual sport organization and its agents be able to prevent injuries and harm to individuals associated with the sport entity (Berg, 1996).

> **CONCEPT #430:** *Securing adequate insurance protection is a key element in the world of risk management.*

The second fundamental objective to protect the sport organization itself and its employees as well as volunteers from the potential threat and consequences of legal action brought about because of a charge of negligence (Cotten, 1993). The third objective is to provide financial protection for itself and its agents (employees as well as volunteers) against findings of negligence in a court of law through adequate liability protection. This third objective can typically be met by securing adequate insurance coverage or protection (Lubell, 1987; Conn, 1994, April/May).

CONSEQUENCES OF AN UNSAFE ENVIRONMENT

The negative consequences of failing to conduct a safe and secure environment for the sport organizations are many. First of all, there is the matter of the actual injury(ies) to the person(s) who sustained the damage as the result of the incident. Second, there is the not inconsequential matter of financial exposure in the event of a successful and substantial lawsuit. And in the climate we all live in today this financial risk is often significant. Third, there is the matter of negative public relations and adverse publicity that all too frequently accompanies an accident and injury.

> **CONCEPT #431:** *The negative fallout from serious accidents and harmful injuries can be significant and varied.*

Fourth, there can be an important loss of prestige and image for the sport organization as a whole as well as for specific personnel, distinct programs or activities sponsored by the organization. And finally, there can be very real negative consequences resulting from any negative publicity surrounding an accident and injury. For example, fallout from an accident can include reduced patronize and support (funding) by the general public, fans, patrons and constituencies.

All in all, the consequences of accidents and injuries associated with the sport operation can be significant for the organization, for its programs and activities, and for its personnel. The risks are great indeed if care is not taken to prevent those accidents and injuries that are preventable. Providing a safe environment for all associated with the sport entity is one of the top priorities of the sport leader and manager (Hart & Ritson, 1993, van der Smissen, 1990).

PROVIDING A SAFE AND HEALTHY ENVIRONMENT

> *CONCEPT #432:   Athletes, sport patrons, employees and volunteers deserve to have a safe and secure environment and experience in their involvement with the sport organization or business.*

No one wants to be responsible for an injury to another human being. Nor would anyone want to be sued for negligence. To prevent such scenarios it is essential that risk management be at the forefront of every sport manager. Obviously, sport fans, patrons, employees and volunteers deserve a safe and protected environment and a secure experience in their association and involvement with the sport entity. It is the responsibility of the sport managers to see that such an environment is created and maintained as part of the overall sport experience.

RISK MANAGEMENT

> *CONCEPT #433:   Risk management implies looking at the worse case scenario.*

Sport managers must be constantly vigilant in the area of *risk management*. Today, risk management is a popular buzz phrase in both in management and legal circles. Risk management implies the evaluation of risks associated with any activity or event and planning for the worse case scenario. Risk management involves the concept of planning, planning well in advance, in an effort to prevent situations in which accidents might occur and injuries result. It involves the management of acceptable risks with the goal of preventing those accidents and injuries that are preventable. It is always best to prevent accidents than to have to deal with such occurrences and the potential injuries that often result, both from the perspective of financial exposure and from the standpoint of negative public relations.

CONCEPT #434: *Risk management involves managing acceptable risks with an eye toward preventing those accidents and injuries that are preventable.*

An important element in risk management is education. A national organization called the Coalition of Americans to Protect Sports "CAPS" was established in December of 1987. Originally it was incorporated as PRODUCT LIABILITY—SPORTS but changed its name in 1988. A year later CAPS was authorized to transact business in the state of Florida (on May 3, 1989). CAPS is a not-for-profit service organization and program of the Sporting Goods Manufacturers Association (SGMA). CAPS exists in order to educate the American sports and recreation community on the dangers created by the ever present liability and litigation problems facing such programs (Lincoln, 1992).

Today, an important role of CAPS is to conduct risk management education programs (clinics, workshops and seminars) for a wide range of sport and recreation professionals. The objective of such educational efforts seek to make these various sport providers not only aware of possible risk management techniques, which might reduce the risk of injury to sports participants—but capable of taking proactive measures to prevent or minimize the number and type of situations which might result in injuries and subsequent lawsuits. The ultimate goal is to encourage healthy and safe sport and recreation activities thereby reducing "the threat of litigation while maximizing the health of both the athletes and the sports programs" (Dropkin, 1996). The organization provides manuals and video as well as a variety of brochures that are used by volunteer instructors in the educational programs which are provided throughout the country.

Cotten (1993, p. 58) has identified four specific components of risk management. These include (1) identifying or revealing real and potential risks, (2) evaluating these risks, (3) determining the acceptable and appropriate approaches in handling the dangerous situation(s); and, (4) attempting to prevent the risky situation(s) from either continuing or coming into existence by implementing and taking timely and effective action which will minimize the possibility of accidents and injuries.

A well thought out risk management plan can be an excellent means of protecting a sport, fitness or recreation entity from litigation and from being found negligent. No plan, regardless of how well thought out it may be, can eliminate all risks or injuries or lawsuits. Nevertheless, this fact does not diminish the wisdom and the necessity for creating and implementing a sound risk management plan of attack. The phrase "plan of attack" denotes a proactive rather than a reactive posture on behalf of the sport leader or manager (Siegenthaler, 1996; Peterson & Hronek, 1992).

CONCEPT #435:   *Sport managers and others in authority are held responsible for the actions and inactions of their agents, employees and volunteers.*

Within any organization, those individuals having responsibility and authority over different areas within the entity have responsibility for those individuals working (either as paid employees or as volunteers) for them within the organization. This assumes that the employees and/or volunteers are acting in their official responsibilities as assigned by the administration.

Thus, it is imperative that managers and supervisors carefully supervise those individuals who are delegated specific responsibilities and assigned defined duties. This is because the ultimate responsibility rests with the managerial staff responsible for delegating tasks, duties and responsibilities to others. Needless to say, the sport organization itself is responsible for the actions of all of its personnel, both paid and unpaid.

CONCEPT #436:   *Accidents happen and injuries occur—sometimes they are preventable, other times they are not.*

Accidents will happen and injuries will take place—sometimes in spite of all of the care taken and the planning accomplished by highly qualified and dedicated sport managers and sport leaders (Cohen, 1996). On the other hand, preventable accidents and predictable injuries will also take place, unfortunately. There are two major responsibilities facing sport managers in the area of risk management. The first is to attempt to avert those preventable accidents and injuries. And second, to react in an appropriate and in a timely fashion to those accidents and injuries which do occur—for whatever reason.

CONCEPT # 37:   *Risk management involves planning to prevent accidents as well as planning how to react and handle accidents should they occur.*

Risk management involves the establishment of written plans dealing with the prevention of situations which might lead to injuries and harm to individuals. It involves an assessment of those areas (physical facilities and programmatic domains) in which hazards exist and accidents are more likely to occur. And it involves plans for preventing such calamities from occurring and, should catastrophes actually take place, how to effectively and efficiently deal with such emergencies.

> **CONCEPT #438:** *All employees and volunteers of the sport organization should be actively involved with risk management.*

Every person involved in the sport organization, whether employee or volunteer, should be cognizant of the safety issues and factors related to their own areas of responsibility. No one within a sport business or organization is exempt from being actively assertive in the area of risk management. *It is everyone's concern.* It is everyone's duty and obligation commensurate with their assigned responsibilities to play a role in preventing dangerous situations from happening.

NEGLIGENCE

Within the realm of legal liability, the term negligence refers to the failure to act or perform one's duties and responsibilities to the standard (of care) that is expected of a prudent professional in similar circumstances. The standard of care or standard of performance to which sport professionals are held accountable in terms of legal liability or negligence center on what is generally accepted practice and behavior within the profession by one's peers (Gray, 1995).

> **CONCEPT #439:** *The determination of negligence is made in light of what is normally expected of professionals (peers) in similar situations and under similar circumstances.*

"Negligence is the failure to act as a *reasonable and prudent professional* would have acted in a similar situation, assuming the person possessed similar educational credentials, practical experiences, training and expertise" (Stier, 1994, 126). In reality, the question asked is: "what action or behavior would a similarly trained, educated and experienced professional have taken in a similar situation and under comparable circumstances?"

CIVIL LAW, CRIMINAL LAW AND CONTRACT LAW

**Being Able to Quickly and Adequately
Treat Injuries is Imperative**
[courtesy of Indiana University Sports Information]

Civil law involves an individual bringing charges against another person or entity based upon a violation of law. What is sought is to make the injured or damaged party or person "whole" again, to correct the injustice. Compensation can take the form of actual or compensatory damages as well as punitive damages. Compensatory damages seek to make whole, to correct, to compensate for damage, pain, suffering and loss. he objective of punitive damages is seek to punish the defendant rather than to merely compensate the injured person. Punitive damages are awarded when the defendant is found to have acted maliciously, fraudulently, or with a wanton or reckless disregard of the rights and feelings of the plaintiff.

A plaintiff who successfully sues may be entitled to be awarded past, current and future medical expenses. Additionally, lost of earnings may also be awarded the successful plaintiff as well as compensation for loss or impairment of the individual's future earnings. Judgments in favor of plaintiffs may be based on past, current and future physical and mental pain and suffering. Even injuries or disabilities based upon emotional distress can result in sizeable monetary awards to the injured (wronged) party.

Preponderance of Evidence in a Civil Lawsuit

> **CONCEPT #440:   *To prevail in a civil lawsuit requires a different degree
> of evidence than in a criminal case.***

To prevail in a civil lawsuit it is necessary that there be a preponderance of evidence. This means that the evidence is very convincing and most satisfying in light of the facts revealed. The proof necessary to sustain charges brought by the plaintiff against the defendant is far less in a civil case than is required under criminal law.

Criminal law involves a situation in which the "State" or an individual brings charges against the defendant for violation of the criminal code. The defendant is arrested on the basis of the charges, and must answer the charges in a court of law. To be found guilty of violating criminal law it just be shown beyond a shadow of doubt (beyond a reasonable doubt) that the person is guilty as charged. Sanctions against a convicted defendant can include incarceration. In American justice, the burden of proof is upon the prosecutor as the defendant is presumed innocent until proven guilty.

Contract law refers to violations relating to agreements between two parties, individuals as well as organizations. As such, employment contracts, gender equity and Title IX all fall within contract law. Lawsuits can be laid against sport entities, employers, and employees for alleged violations of laws applying to each of these areas, (Pittman, 2004). Thus, it is very important that sport managers fully comprehend the intent and letter of the laws as they pertain to contract provisions in the area of civil rights, such as gender equity and Title IX (Clement, 1993).

Governmental Immunity

The doctrine of governmental immunity is based on the English legal concept or principle that "the king (government) can do no wrong." Thus, some elements of governmental organizations, in some instances, are immune from lawsuits (Berg, 1995, March). "Governmental immunity means, generally speaking, that school districts, school boards, or authorities in charge of public schools are immune from tort liability in the absence of legislative enactment or judicial abrogation of the doctrine of governmental immunity (Baley and Matthews, 1989, p. 40). However, it is important to remember that the concept of immunity refers to the corporate entity and does not necessarily provide any protection for employees or volunteers associated with the organization, whether they be managers, supervisors or lower level personnel.

DETERMINING NEGLIGENCE FOR THE SPORT PROFESSIONAL

How does one become legally responsible or liable for being negligent in the performance of the person's job? Generally speaking, there are five criteria that must exist for an individual to be held legally liable in the area of negligence. First, the sport organization or professional (employee or volunteer) must owe a *duty or obligation* to provide a safe environment for the individual who becomes injured (Carpenter, 1994). Second, this duty or obligation must be breached. That is, there must have been a failure to perform the duty, either by omission of commission. For example, an employee or volunteer must have done something or must not have done something that breached this duty to another person.

Third, what took place or did not take place must have been the actual or proximate cause of the damage to the person who was actually injured. Fourth, the injury must have been avoidable. And, the injured party must not have been responsible for one's own injury or predicament. And, lastly, there must actually have been some type of injury or damage (physical, emotional or psychological) to someone (Stier, 1995, p. 416).

Other Forms of Negligence—Slander, Libel and Defamation of Character

Negligence, an intentional tort or wrong against another person or entity can also take the form of slander or libel. The distinction between the two is that slander involves verbal communication while libel is concerned with the written word. Defamation law protects against defamation of character. It also guards against an individual's reputation being impinged by untrue, damaging statements, within the public forum (Wong and Covel, 1995, August, p. 20.). The defense against a charge of libel, slander or defamation of character is the truth. If a person writes the truth or speaks the truth (and it can be shown to be true) charges of liable, slander and defamation of character will not be sustained. The key to protecting and defending oneself against such charges is to always document things, to keep detailed records and to speak and write honestly and truthfully.

CONCEPT #441: *Ignorance is usually no defense in determining responsibility or negligence.*

Within the realm of legal liability the claim of ignorance is usually no defense against a charge of negligence if one has responsibility for a given situation. This is because the sport professional, by the mere fact that the person has accepted a particular job or a specific responsibility, should not be ignorant in the performance of that job with the commensurate obligations and responsibilities. In short, the person with the responsibility or job should possess the knowledge, wisdom, judgment and skill to do that job. Ignorance is no excuse.

CONCEPT #442: *Negligence can result from acts of commission as well as acts of omission.*

Accidents and injuries (involving negligence) can result from either acts of commission as well as acts of omission. An act of commission is when an individual *does something that should not have been done* and the consequence is that an unsafe situation resulted and an accident took place. And, the ultimate consequence is that a person is injured. For example, if a concessionaire operation sold meat that was contaminated and the result was that customers became violently ill—the person(s) in charge of the concession operations might well be determined to have been negligent. Similarly, if defective merchandise is sold or premiums given away at an athletic contest with the result being that several youngsters who played with the items became injured—negligence might well be determined in a court of law.

On the other hand, the *failure to do something* (omission) can also result in a charge of negligence being determined in a court of law. For example, a liquid was accidentally spilled by a fan or patron on a concrete surface near a concession stand located at a sporting event. The end result is a slippery surface. If this slippery service is not cleaned up in a reasonable time (i.e., very, very quickly) and if someone slipped, fell and injured themselves as a result of the liquid—negligence might very well be present.

Another example of omission involves the failure to check, on a timely basis, the structural integrity of the stadium seats. If there is subsequently a structural failure and fans are injured when the bleachers collapse—there might well be negligence through omission.

DEFENSES AGAINST NEGLIGENCE

In defending oneself or one's organization against a charge of negligence in a court of law it is necessary to show that one or more of the five essential elements of negligence (listed above) did not exist in that particular situation or case. For example, proving that there was no duty or obligation for the injured person; or, if such a duty did exist, that the duty was not breached; that the act or failure to act did not cause the injury; that the injury was unavoidable, not foreseeable and not preventable; and/or, that the plaintiff did not receive any real or actual injury.

CONCEPT #443:   *There are numerous factors that may negate or mitigate charges of negligence in a court of law.*

An Act of God

Sometimes accidents just happen. They are truly just accidents, just dumb, freak chance happenings. They cannot be prevented. They are called *Acts of God*. This is true even when the consequence of the accident is horrific. The determining factor is that the incident or accident is unavoidable because of the forces of nature which would not normally have been anticipated, foreseen or prevented. These are true accidents, chance happenings, Acts of God.

Assumption of Risk

There are a number of other factors which might negate or mitigate the responsibility and exposure to a finding of negligence. One such factor is referred to as *assumption of risk* (Sharp, 1996). Assumption of risk comes into play when an injured party assumes certain risks when that person willingly becomes involved with or participated in a specific event or when the person freely enters a designated area or facility (Wolohan, 1995).

There are always some risks that one must assume when involved in specific activities. These are the normal and expected risks that one would normally expect when being involved in specific activities. There are common, customary and normal risks that come with the territory and individuals voluntarily expose themselves to such risks. However, it is important for sport personnel to remain cognizant that the concept of assumption of risk does not exempt them from liability resulting from actual negligent supervision. Berg (1995, March) pointed out that this concept was reinforced in two court cases, specifically, the 3rd District Court of Appeal's ruling in the case involving *Zalkin v. American Learning Systems*, 1994 and the 4th District Court of Appeal's ruling in the 1993 case *Nova University v Katz*.

Contributory Negligence

Contributory negligence is an applicable defense when it can be shown that the injured contributes to or was at fault in causing one's own injury. Contributory negligence is more difficult to use as a defense in those cases in which the injured party is very young. If the injured youngster is younger than eight years of age there is almost no chance of proving contributory negligence. Even if the injured youngster is between 9 and 13 years of age it is extremely difficult to use contributory negligence as a defense or mitigating factor since the burden of proof is usually placed on the defendant. However, if the individual is 14 or older contributory negligence can be more easily shown, especially so if the person injured is legally considered an adult.

Comparative Negligence

Comparative negligence is a term increasingly recognized in more and more states. When used, comparative negligence completely replaces the concept of contributory negligence explained above. The concept of comparative negligence is based upon a determination (or comparison) of negligence between the plaintiff and the defendant. A percentage of blame (responsibility) is assigned to both. Thus, the injured party may be found to be only partly responsible for an injury to another party (and assigned a percentage of guilt or responsibility). Similarly, the defendant is also held partly respon-

Big Crowds Can be Expected when Craft Shows are Organized.
[courtesy of ESMC Consultants]

sible (and assigned an appropriate percentage of guilt or responsibility). In this situation, there is an apportionment of guilt or fault (expressed in percentages) made between the plaintiff and the defendant. Again, the age of the plaintiff plays a significant role in whether the apportionment favors the defendant or the plaintiff.

THE MATTER OF FORESEEABILITY

> *CONCEPT #444:   Foreseeability is the key to preventing catastrophes in terms of accidents and legal liability.*

Foreseeability is the key to preventing accidents and injuries that might result in lawsuits and determination of negligence (Neal, 1995, August/September). Being able to anticipate possible negative consequences is a very important skill for sport managers. So too is the willingness and ability to do all that is humanly possible to actually prevent accidents (or diminish the consequences) from taking place. Some of the common areas of concern for negligence in sport include: (Promote Safer Sports for Youth, 1993; National youth sports, 1993; Stier, 1995).

1. Failure to warn others of possible perils and dangers associated with the activity, equipment, supplies and facilities, etc. (Turner, 1994, August).
2. Slow, insufficient or inadequate medical attention (Gray, 1993; Wong & Barr, 1993, July; Berg, 1994).
3. Inappropriate or unsafe reactions to accidents or injuries (Pike & Rello, 1994; Berg, 1995, September).
4. Unsuitable, faulty or dangerous facilities (Maloy, 1995; Maloy, 1993; American College of Sports Medicine, 1992).
5. Improper instruction or coaching (Wong & Barr, 1993, July).
6. Lack of proper supervision of participants (Rauschenbach, 1994; Borkowski, 1996; Borkowski, 2003).
7. Improper, defective or inappropriate equipment (Blauvelt, 1993; Brown, 1993; Wong G. M. and Corvell, 1995)
8. Use of defective supplies (Eye protection recommendations, 1981; Kroll, 1990).
9. Lack of safety equipment and warning signs (Turner, 1994, August).
10. Use of poorly or ill fitted uniforms and/or protective items such as helmets (Borkowski, 1993, May/June).
11. Lack of staff training and/or coaching education (Sharp, 1993).

12. Having an individual perform an activity which is not appropriate and/or safe for that particular person (for any number of reasons) (Lehr, 1993).

13. Grouping teams by age instead of size in youth sports (Borkowski, 1993, October/November; Lehr, 1993).

14. Inadequate pre-participation physical exams (Edwards, 1993).

15. Presence of attractive nuisances, that is, circumstances or situations that could be hazardous to certain individuals but yet are very inviting and attractive to these same persons (Berg, 1995, May).

16. Inadequate physical conditioning programs and training errors (Gaskin, 1993; Sharp, 1993).

17. Failure to do warm-ups, stretching and cool down exercises (Merriman, 1993).

18. Hazardous or unhealthy practice or playing conditions associated with grounds, playing fields as well as buildings and other facilities (Herbert, 1995).

19. Improper selection of activities (Adams, 1993).

20. Inappropriate or improper instruction or directions to individuals, including athletes (Gray, 1995).

21. Inappropriate or insufficient teaching, instruction or coaching decisions (Pine, 1991).

22. Lack of crowd control and protection for spectators, fans and patrons (Antee & Swinburn, 1990).

23. Having participants engage in inappropriate or unsafe activities (Conn & Tompkins, 1994, April/May).

24. Allowing athletes or sport persons to play or participate while injured (Girvin & Cirvan, 1993).

25. Travel injuries (Pittman, 1993; Neal, 1995, August/September).

CONCEPT #445:   *Be especially cautious when dealing with injured athletes lest their injuries be exacerbated and a charge of negligence be determined.*

Sport managers must be especially concerned whenever there is a situation in which an athlete has been injured. Once injured, the athlete must be provided quality medical care (Gray, 1993). This includes immediate first aid, evaluation and treatment of the injury, as well as rehabilitation of the injury. An injury to an athlete also requires a careful evaluation of when the injured party may be allowed to return to practice and to actual competition. Far too often the athlete (as well as the coach) are super anxious for the injured athlete to return to action. Sometimes the athlete returns too soon and the consequence is that the injury is further aggravated and exacerbated.

Informing Participants as to the Potential Risks Involved in any Activity

Those involved in the sport experience must be well acquainted with the potential risks and dangers involved in the activity. For competitive athletes, for members of a health or fitness club or for individuals partaking in a physical activity as part of a recreation program, this means that they must be adequately forewarned of what might happen to them even if they perform the activity in an acceptable fashion. This inherent danger or risk must thorough be explained to participants, and if these individuals are minors, to their parents or guardians.

> **CONCEPT #446:** *Fans, volunteers patrons, and participants deserve to be warned of the inherent dangers and risks associated with the activities in which they are to be involved.*

If the individuals involved in the sport experience are fans or spectators it is advisable that representatives of the sport organization adequately inform these individuals as to the inherent dangers or risks of their involvement. Such actions can have a significant impact upon the incidents of accidents and injuries. "With the abundance of lawsuits, court decisions and payoffs taking place, a facility's signs and their placement take on added significance" (Turner, 1994, August, p. 66).

This might mean placing appropriate signs and making timely announcements informing individuals of potential dangers. For example, those spectators arriving at a ice hockey game might be warned about the potential danger of being hit by a flying puck if their seats are located within a specific section of the arena. Similarly, baseball fans can be warned of possible foul balls being hit into certain sections of the stadium.

> **CONCEPT #447:** *It is the responsibility of the sport managers to provide warnings of risks to those involved in activities which involve significant risks.*

Failure to Warn Participants

The concept of "failure to warn" in sports-related injuries can be traced to the $6.4 million dollar judgment in 1982 against the Seattle school system (*Thompson vs. Seattle School District*) in Washington state. The case resulted from a catastrophic injury to a high school football athlete. In this particular situation, the parents sued on behalf of their son who was paralyzed (quadriplegic) as a result of an injury while playing competitive football for a school team. The injury did not result from the athlete doing anything wrong or from the athlete failing to properly execute a skill. Rather, the youngster "sustained a neck injury from lowering his head to ward off the tackler . . ." (Leigh, 1980; Girvan & Girvan, 1993, p. 26 citing Lubell, 1989). Nevertheless, the athlete was paralyzed in an accident involving an activity that was part of the game of football.

CONCEPT #448:   *Sponsors of strenuous or inherently dangerous physical activities or sports must adequately warn participants (and parents if the participants are minors) of the risks involved.*

The parents in the Seattle, Washington case claimed that they and their son had no idea that such a catastrophic and permanent injury would be possible as a consequence of normal performance of football skills and tactics in practice or competition. The parents claimed that they should have been adequately forewarned of the potential dangers of such catastrophic and horrific injuries that accompany the participation in such a violent and hazardous sport as football. The court, in finding in favor of the plaintiffs, indicated that the school representatives had failed to warn the athlete and the parents in explicit terms that one of the risks of playing the sport of football was becoming paralyzed, that is, being a quadriplegic.

As a result, it is strongly recommended that individuals involved in activities that inherently involve some very real aspect of risk and potential peril to their persons be adequately informed (in writing) of such risks and possible consequences. This has severe repercussions for school based athletic programs, recreation sport activities, as well as other organizations that sponsor vigorous physical activities or sports which can be considered inherently dangerous, i.e., ski resorts, sponsors of white water rafting, health and fitness clubs, etc.

Use of a Risk Statement

A sample Risk Statement that is currently in use at the university level to warn participants who are involved in potentially dangerous or risky physical activities in provided in box 14.1. A variation of this form was first utilized in 1989 at SUNY Brockport when the author, as Athletic Director, mandated its usage. The current version of this statement requires that the individual student sign the statement acknowledging that the individual has read and understood the warning statement regarding the risks involved and the possible severe consequences of injury and illness. It is especially important that sport managers plan for such warning statements to be given to those individuals involved in competitive athletics or in strenuous recreational physical activities and sports.

BOX 14.1:
Warning Notice or Risk Statement
for Participation in Strenuous Activities

Risk Statement

Department of Physical Education and Sport
State University of New York, College at Brockport
Brockport, New York

This Physical Education Performance course requires vigorous activity that may be hazardous to your health. Especially at risk are those individuals with cardiopulmonary disease and those who have not recently engaged in strenuous exercise. There is a possibility of musculoskeletal injury, which may include paralysis or death. Any costs as the result of injury or illness connected with participation in this course or activity are solely the responsibility of the student. If you have a disability that you believe requires accommodation, please notify the instructor prior to participation in class activities.

AUTHORIZATION: I, _____ HAVE READ THE ABOVE AND AM AWARE OF THE INHERENT RISKS INVOLVED. MY SIGNATURE ALSO INDICATES THAT I HAVE RECEIVED A COPY OF THIS RISK STATEMENT.

_____

SIGNATURE

_____

Print Name

_____

Date

Use of Waiver, Permission or Release Forms

CONCEPT #449:   *Use of a waiver slip can help protect the sport entity and personnel in selected instances.*

A charge of negligence can sometimes be successfully defended in a court of law by showing that the injured party (an adult) freely sighed a written document waiving that person's right to sue for injuries which result from their involvement in an activity or at a particular site (Berg, 1995, November). Such forms require the person signing the document to acknowledge that they understand and accept the normal risks associated with the sport, activity or program that they or their children are to be involved in.

Wolohan (2006) states that at least 45 of the 50 states in the US will recognize a properly worded/crafted waiver as protecting facility owners and recreation providers from liability resulting from what is commonly referred to as so-called ordinary negligence. However, a word of caution, operators and managers would be short-sighted indeed if they relied exclusively on such written/signed documents to protect them from successful lawsuits resulting from charges of negligence.

CONCEPT # 450: *Parents cannot waive the rights of their children to sue for negligence.*

It must be remembered that not all states and courts treat such waiver or release forms the same, especially in the case where parents sign the permission or waiver forms on behalf of their children. Some courts in some states have ruled the use of such forms invalid (Wong, 1988, October; Herbert, 1996). It is important to note that minors are not held accountable for signing such waivers since they cannot waive their rights to sue. And, neither may parents or guardians sign such a binding waiver on behalf of their minor children since parents/guardians cannot sign away the rights of minors to sue. In a Washington State case, *Scott v Pacific West Mountain Reso0rt (834 P.2d 6 [1992])* the court declared that it is the general rule that: ". . . in the absence of statutory or judicial authorization, a parent cannot waive . . . a minor child's cause of action merely because of the parental relationship" (Cotton, 1999, p. 28).

Use of a Permission Slip or Consent Form

The permission slip or consent form is a document created by the sport manager that is used to secure permission of the parents to allow their minor offspring to participate in a specific activity. This form simply provides the organization and its agents with documentation that the participant has permission to be involved in the stated activity or sport. Frequently, the permission slip is piggy-backed to the "warning statement" about the vigorous, strenuous or dangerous activity and specify the risks involved in said activity.

RESPONDING TO ACCIDENTS AND INJURIES

How one responds to or reacts to an accident or injuries is of the utmost importance. For example, there must be both appropriate and timely responses made in such situations in terms of providing immediate and temporary first aid until qualified medical help arrives. However, it is equally important that sound steps be taken in terms of record keeping during and following accidents involving personal injuries.

Hockey—a Sport that is Increasing Its Presence Outside of the North
[courtesy of Bemidji State University (BSU) Photography Services]

For example, an accident report should be completed as soon as possible following an accident. Names, addresses and phone numbers of all witnesses should be recorded as well as written statements regarding what each witness saw. Similarly, a written statement should be obtained from the injured party when deemed possible and appropriate.

CONCEPT #451: *Keeping accurate and detailed records will significantly aid in defending the sport organization and its personnel against a charge of negligence.*

Maintaining accurate records of all facts relating to personal injury situations simply cannot be overemphasized (Edwards, 1993). Keeping accurate and timely records of other pertinent factors throughout the calendar year is equally important. For example, being able to show that adequate warnings were given to parents and youngsters in a school setting can go a long way in defending the school district against charges of negligence (based on the "failure to warn" principle). Maintaining records indicating that a health and fitness club patron received personal instruction in terms of how to use each of the exercise machines in the club can be invaluable in showing that the patron, who was subsequently injured using one of the machines, was familiar with and knowledgeable in the use of the machines.

Similarly, having records of a physician's written statement giving the professional athlete the "all-clear" to participate in actual competition can put the team owners and coaches in good stead against a charge of negligence. And, finally, having records indicating that the class of beginning downhill skiers had been warned by their expert instructors to stay off of the advance slopes will also help protect the ski operators and owners (against a charge of negligence) if an adult student from the class was subsequently injured attempting to ski down the forbidden advance slope. The concept is simple, establish clear cut and intelligent policies, procedures and practices and document decisions made and actions taken, before and after accidents and injuries. One must keep appropriate, accurate, written records.

PRODUCT LIABILITY

Many times sport organizations need to be concerned with product liability. So too do sport manufacturers. Product liability is a cross between tort and contract law and involves warranties, express or implied, that the product in question is good, safe and appropriate when used for its stated purpose and under specific circumstances.

The phrase, *warranty of merchantability*, indicates that the burden of proof is upon the manufacturer that the goods or products are safe and appropriate. When sport entities create, produce, sell or give away items such as food, apparel or premiums to spectators the sport entities share responsibility with the manufacturers for the items sold and/or given away (The Crisis continues, 1988, August/September/October; Liability/sports, 1988). Product liability also is involved when items of equipment (football, baseball or ice hockey helmets; bats and balls; ski or exercise equipment, etc.) are sold to sport organizations as well as the general public. The manufacturer warrants that such equipment is safe to use under specified conditions and circumstances. It is imperative that sport managers pay particular attention to the quality of equipment and supplies used in the conduct of their programs and activities (Berg, 1995, May).

ESTABLISHING APPROPRIATE POLICIES GOVERNING THE SPORT ACTIVITY OR PROGRAM

One of the major challenges and responsibilities of sport managers today is to establish intelligent and appropriate policies, practices and procedures as they relate to the sport organization and the various activities associated with the entity. These operational policies, procedures and practices can relate both to internal operations as well as to external operations. They serve as a guide in terms of how the sport organization will be run and how its activities and programs are to be implemented and conducted. Some organizations have created a Risk Management Manual containing standard operating procedures (SOP) and operational activities which would be applicable at various levels of the operation and can be carried out by employees, including managers and supervisors (Conn, 1993).

> **CONCEPT #452:** *An organization's standard operating policies, procedures and practices should play a major role in preventing situations in which negligence results in personal injuries to others.*

Thus, there is a need to examine existing policies, procedures and practices to insure that they are effective and efficient in terms of facilitating, in a safe manner, the operations of the sport entity. Additionally, they should be reviewed so that they do not put individuals (fans, patrons, customers as well as the organization's own personnel) or the sport entity itself at unnecessary and unacceptable risk.

An Example of Policies Relating to Aquatics

The following list, titled "The Ten Commandments of Aquatic Risk Management" is an example of appropriate policies, procedures and practices that administrators would do well to follow in their efforts to provide a safe and sound environment for patrons to utilize (Griffiths, 2000, pp 132-136,139-140).

1. Thou shalt supervise your lifeguards often
2. Thou shalt not operate without a certified aquatic facility operator or certified pool operator
3. Thou shalt maintain a group-use policy
4. Thou shalt warn against head-first entry
5. Thou shalt warn against breath-holding and underwater swimming
6. Thou shalt vigilantly guard children of tender years
7. Thou shalt remind parents to watch their children
8. Thou shalt post and follow a fecal-accident policy
9. Thou shalt warn and protect against entrapments and entanglements
10. Thou shalt not eliminate numerous benefits by eliminating all risks

Professional sports teams as well as collegiate teams and recreation entities must make decisions relative to crowd control. For example, how many security personnel will be present at specific contests? What will be their role, their authority and responsibility? Will they be stationed inside and outside of the actual playing facility? How will they react to specific types of situations? Will the concession stands sell alcoholic beverages at the contests? Will alcohol be served after a specific length of time (after half-time or after the sixth inning, for example). What type of lighting will be available in the parking lots for the health and fitness club, for the athletic contest, or for the recreation event? Will fans or customers be allowed to carry bottles into the event? How will a restrictive policy be enforced? By whom?

RISK MANAGEMENT AUDITS

When a risk management audit is conducted every aspect of the organization's operation is examine. The goal is to prevent injuries to and minimize risks (financial, public relations and embarrassments) associated with the sport, recreation or fitness operation

There is Always the Potential for Injury in Sports.
[courtesy of St. Lucie METS, Port Lucie, Florida, photo by Jimmy Fertitta]

(Borkowski, 2006). This necessitates looking at facilities, transportation, equipment and supplies, various operations as well as all procedures, policies, practices relating to all aspects of the entity (Olson, 1985; Olson, 1986, January; Cotten, 1993).

Such an audit or an assessment plan is a vital aspect of an organization's operation, one that can have a significant impact upon the overall success or failure of the entity itself and its personnel (Edwards, 1993). Gray (1991, pp. 29-30) suggests that a quality risk management audit include identifying various risks associated with the activity or program or facility; making an assessment as to the probability and the significance of possible injuries; determining a method of negating or mitigating the risks involved; and, finally, instituting or implementing necessary and appropriate managerial practices, policies and procedures.

CONCEPT #453:   A risk management audit involves a close inspection of all standard operating policies, procedures, and practices as they relate to every aspect of the organization.

ASSUMING A PROACTIVE STANCE IN RISK MANAGEMENT

Failure to be concerned about and alert to the potential dangers of being negligent in any sport operation invites disaster. Failure to take a proactive stance in the area of negligence and legal liability is indeed foolhardy in this litigious society. Adhering to the Boy Scout Motto of "Being Prepared" is a good and wise policy to follow. To do otherwise is to simply invite disaster and court adversity. The five steps of risk management listed below are excellent guidelines to follow in assuming a proactive position relative to risk management (Meyers, 1999, p. 36).

1. Avoid risks whenever possible
2. Assume some of the risk—through contract clauses—when necessary
3. Transfer the risk—when appropriate—to another party through identification clauses
4. Minimize the risk through preventatives and post-incident control measures
5. Insure against the risks that cannot be avoided, assumed, or transferred

CONCLUSIONS

Sport managers who are active in conducting effective risk management programs are usually successful in diminishing their organization's potential for legal liability and exposure. Sport organizations and their personnel always face the risk of potential lawsuits based on negligence and other reasons from any number of sources, including their own employees, their customers and the general public. If negligence is to be significantly reduced, sport managers need to assume a proactive approach in all aspects of their sport operation. Without such concerted efforts the consequences can be severe in terms of lost time, effort and resources.

REFERENCES

Adams, S.H. (1993). Duty to properly instruct. *Journal of Physical Education, Recreation and Dance, 64*(2), 22-23.

American College of Sports Medicine. (1992). *ACSM's health/fitness facility standards and guidelines*. P.O. Box 14409, Indianapolis, Indiana.

Antee, A. & Swinburn, J. (1990). Crowd management: An issue of safety, security, and liability. *Public Management, 72*(1), 16-19.

Appenzeller, H. (1993). *Managing sports and risk management strategies*. Durham, N.C.: Carolina Academic Press.

Baley, J.A. and Matthews, D.L. (1989). *Law and liability*. Dubuque, Iowa: Wm. C. Brown Publishing.

Berg, R. (1993, December). The risk of not watching. *Athletic Business, 17*(12), 22.

Berg, R. (1994, July). How much injury care is enough? *Athletic Business, 18*(7), 20.

Berg, R. (1995, March). California's immunity system breaks down. *Athletic Business, 19*(3), 19, 22.

Berg, R. (1995, May). Soccer safety goal has not yet been met. *Athletic Business, 19*(5), 24.

Berg, R. (1995, September). Feeling mistreated, injured athletes sue. *Athletic Business, 19*(9), 24.

Berg, R. (1995, November). Grudging support for liability waivers in Florida. *Athletic Business, 19*(11), 24.

Berg, R. (1996, October). Advise and consent. *Athletic Business, 20*(10), 9.

Blauvelt, H. (5/18/93). Safety worries hit titanium bats. *USA Today*, p. 10-C.

Borkowski, R.P. (1993, May/June). Safety in football. *Scholastic Coach, 62*(10), 5, 6.

Borkowski, R.P. (1993, October/November). Avoiding the gavel. *Athletic Management, V*(6), 22, 24 - 26.

Borkowski, R.P. (1996, December/January). Safety through supervision. *Athletic Management, VIII*(1), 12.

Borkowski, R.P. (2006, April/May). Full court pressure. *Athletic Management, XVIII*(3). 25-27.

Borkowski, R.P. (2003, August/September). Hall of shame. *Athletic Management, XV*(5), 22-24.

Brown, S. C. (1993). Selecting safe equipment—What do we really know? *Journal of Physical Education, Recreation and Dance, 64*(2), 33-35, 65.

Carpenter, L. (1994, March-April). Perfect or perilous: When is a teacher negligent? *Strategies, 7*(6), 23-25.

Clement, A. (1993). Civil rights—The first, fourth and fourteenth amendments. *Journal of Physical Education Recreation and Dance, 64*(2). 16-17, 62.

Cohen, A. (1996, August). Save situations. *Athletic Business, 20*(8), 33-38.

Conn, J.H. (1993). The litigation connection—Perspectives of risk control for the 1990s. *Journal of Physical Education, Recreation and Dance, 64*(2), 60-61.

Conn, J.H. & Tompkins, R. N. (1994, April/May). In the shadows. *Athletic Management, IV*(2), 18-22.

Cotten, D.J. (1993). Risk management—A tool for reducing exposure to legal liability. *Journal of Physical Education, Recreation and Dance, 64*(2), 58-61.

Cotton, D.J. (1999, June). Waive of the future. *Athletic Business, 23*(6), 28-30.

The crisis continues . . . Another manufacturer forced to cease production. (1988, August/September/October). *Sports Liability News*, p. 2.

Dropkin, B. (1996, October 29). *CAPS: History & miscellaneous information.* Personal Letter.

Edwards, K. (1993, August). Risk-management program. *Scholastic Coach, 63*(1), 5-6.

Eye protection recommendations for racquet sports players. (1981). National Society to Prevent Blindness. New York: New York.

Gaskin, L.P. (1993). Establishing, communicating, and enforcing rules and regulations. *Journal of Physical Education, Recreation and Dance, 64*(2), 26-27, 63.

Girvan, G. & Girvan, J.T. (1993). Risk management practices in athletics—A content analysis. *Journal of Physical Education, Recreation and Dance, 64*(4), 26-28.

Gray, G.R. (1991). Risk management planning: Conducting a sport risk assessment to enhance program safety. *Journal of Physical Education, Recreation and Dance, 62*(6), 29-31, 78.

Gray, G.R. (1993). Providing adequate medical care to program participants. *Journal of Physical Education, Recreation and Dance, 64*(2), 56-57, 65-66.

Gray, G.R. (1995). Safety tips from the expert witness, *Journal of Physical Education, Recreation and Dance, 66*(1), 18-21.

Griffiths, T. (2000, December). The Ten Commandments of aquatic risk management. *Athletic Management, 24*(12), 132-136, 139-140.

Hart, J.E. & Ritson, R J. (1993). *Liability and safety in physical education and sport.* Reston, VA: AAHPERD.

Herbert, D.L. (1995, November). The liability of off-premise activity. *Fitness Management, 11*(12), 18.

Herbert, D.L. (1996, April). Another release fails to bar suit against club. *Fitness Management, 12*(5), 20.

Kaiser, R. (1986). *Law and liability in recreation, parks and sport.* Englewood Cliffs, New Jersey: Prentice-hall.

Kroll, B. (1990). Evaluating strength training equipment. *National Strength and Conditioning Association Journal, 12*(3), 56-65.

Lehr, C. (1993). Proper classification. *Journal of Physical Education, Recreation and Dance, 64*(2), 24-25, 63.

Leigh, P. (Ed.). (1988). A common sense of view of liability. *Parks & Recreation, 23*(9), 53-55.

Liability/sports—Rawlings: Helmets not worth the hassle. (1988, July). *Athletic Business, 12*(7), 16.

Lincoln, S. M. (1992). Sports injury risk management & the keys to safety—Coalition of Americans to protect sports (CAPS). *Journal of Physical Education, Recreation and Dance, 63*(7), 40-42, 63.

Lubell, A. (1987). Insurance, liability, and the American way of sport. *The Physician and Sports Medicine, 15*(9), 192-200.

Lubell, A. (1989). Questioning the athlete's right to sue. *The Physician and Sports Medicine, 17*(24), 242-244.

Maloy, B. P. (1995, January). Dangerous base paths. *Athletic Business, 19*(1), 59-62.

Maloy, B. P. (1993). Legal obligations related to facilities. *Journal of Physical Education, Recreation and Dance, 64*(2), 28-30, 64.

Merriman, J. (1993). Supervision in sport and physical activity. *Journal of Physical Education, Recreation and Dance, 64*(2), 20-21, 23.

Meyers, C. (1999, September). Planning for danger. *Successful Meetings*, pp. 36-38, 40, 41.

National youth sports—National youth sports injury-prevention month. (1993). National Youth Sports Foundation for the Prevention of Athletic Injuries, Inc., Needham: Massachusetts.

Neal, T. (1995, August/September). Anticipating away game injuries. *Athletic Management, VII*(5), 32-35.

Olson, J.R. (1985, November). Safety checklists: Making indoor areas hazard-free. *Athletic Business, 9*(11), 36-39, 42.

Olson, J.R. (1986, January). Are your gymnasts safe from injury? *Athletic Business, 10*(1), 38-39, 41.

Peterson, J.A. & Hronek, B.B. (1992). *Risk management for park, recreation, and leisure services* (2nd ed.). Champaign, IL: Sagamore.

Pine, D, (1991). Preventing sports related eye injuries. *The Physician and Sports Medicine, 19*(2), 129-130, 133-134.

Pike, L.L. & Rello, M. N. (1994, July). Training rules. *Athletic Business, 18*(7), 10, 13.

Pittman, A.T. (1993). Safe transportation—A driving concern. *Journal of Physical Education, Recreation and Dance, 64*(2), 53-55.

Pittman, A.T. (2004). Vicarious liability against university and coach. *Journal of Physical Education, Recreation and Dance, 75*(8), 9-10.

Promote Safer Sports for Youth. (1993). *Journal of Physical Education, Recreation and Dance, 64*(4), 12.

Rauschenback, J. (1994). Effective supervision practices. *Journal of Physical Education, Recreation and Dance, 65*(5), 66-68.

Sharp, L.A. (1993). Employment of qualified personnel. *Journal of Physical Education, Recreation and Dance, 64*(2), 18-19, 62-63.

Sharp, L.A. (1996, September). Fault lines. *Athletic Business, 20*(9), 10, 14.

Siegenthaler, K.L. (1996). Supervising activities for safety. *Journal of Physical Education, Recreation and Dance, 67*(2), 29-30, 36.

Stier, Jr., W.F. (1994). *Successful sport fund-raising.* Madison. Wisconsin: Wm. C. Brown & Benchmark.

Stier, W.F., Jr. (1995). *Successful coaching—Strategies and tactics.* Boston, Massachusetts: American Press.

Turner, E.T. (1994, August). Vital signs. *Athletic Business, 18*(18), 65-67.

van der Smissen, B. (1990). *Legal liability and risk management for public and private entities.* Cincinnati, Ohio: Anderson Publishing.

Wolohan, J.T. (1995, January). Assume nothing. *Athletic Business, 19*(1), 10-11.

Wolohan, J.T. (2006), September). Paper slip. *Athletic Business, 30*(9), 32, 34, 36.

Wong, G. M. (October, 1988). Washington court says release forms invalid. *Athletic Business, 12*(10), 14.

Wong, G.M. (1989, July). Athletes aren't fair game for cheap shots. *Athletic Business, 13*(7), 16.

Wong, G.M. & Barr C.A. (1993, July). Practice and malpractice. *Athletic Business, 17*(7), 16.

Wong, G.M. & Covell, D. (1995, March). Duty-bound. *Athletic Business, 19*(3). 13, 14.

Wong, G.M. & Covell, D. (1995, August). War of words. *Athletic Business, 19*(8), 10, 14, 20.

DISCUSSION TOPICS

1. List the components of a sound risk *management* plan for a hypothetical sport entity.

2. What are some areas of concern that managers should pay special attention to in sport organizations, recreation programs and in fitness and wellness entities?

3. Provide examples that illustrate the differences between criminal law, contract law and civil law for the sport manager and the sport organization.

4. Indicate how a sport manager might assume a proactive stance in terms of slander, libel and defamation of character.

5. Cite examples in the fitness industry and in professional sports of negligence taking place as a result of acts of commission as well acts of omission.

6. What are commonly used defenses against accusations of negligence?

7. Elaborate on the advantages and deficiencies of both Waiver or Release Forms and Permission Slips/Consent Forms in terms of participants in sport, recreational or fitness programs.

8. Explain why and how a sport organization and its personnel should be concerned with *product liability* in terms of the organization's and personnel's utilization of different products in the conduct of their day-to-day work?

9. Explain how the phrase *looking at the worse case scenario* is helpful in terms of risk management.

10. Explain the value and limitations of waivers in defending against charges of ordinary negligence.

15 Problem Solving in the World of Sport and Sport Management[1]

Professional Sports are Big Business
Requiring Competent "Problem Solvers" and "Problem Preventers"
[photo courtesy of Buffalo Bills]

CHAPTER HIGHLIGHTS

This chapter will help the reader to:
• Understand the importance of properly addressing problems;
• Outline the processes of problem solving;
• Identify sources of problems for sport and recreation managers:
• Understand use of problem solving principles in administering sport and recreation programs;

---

[1] Portions of this chapter were adapted from Stier, W.F., Jr., (2013). *Athletic Administration: Sound Decision Making, Problem Solving and Appropriate Risk Taking.* (2nd edition) Boston, MA: American Press.

- Conceptualize problem solving as a table with five legs;
- Differentiate between the "art" and "science" of problem solving;
- Articulate that successful problem solvers are made rather than born;
- Justify the need for attending professional conferences as sport and recreation managers;
- Be cognizant that problems will almost invariably happen within sport and recreation managers;
- Appreciate that problems can also be opportunities for sport and recreation managers;
- Be familiar with the risks associated with problem solving;
- Describe successful decision making strategies involved in problem solving;
- Provide examples of appropriate time management strategies;
- Realize the importance of credibility when solving administrative problems.

INTRODUCTION TO PROBLEM SOLVING FOR SPORT AND RECREATION MANAGERS

Sport managers are often expected to assume a variety of very different roles in the performance of their duties. They are frequently expected to become authority figures for coaches, staff members, athletes as well as a host of other individuals, both inside and outside of the sport or recreation setting. Additionally, they frequently become risk takers, decision makers, facilitators, leaders, delegators, motivators, disciplinarians, counselors, mentors, teachers, recruiters, as well as mediators and arbitrators.

One of the most important and all encompassing roles that any sport manager or administrator can assume, at any level, is that of problem solver (Stier, 1993). Without the ability and willingness to solve, on a timely basis and in an appropriate manner, the multitude of problems, difficulties, and challenges that inevitably arise in any sport organization or entity—sport personnel fall far short of the minimum level of competency that is expected of them. Staffo (2001, p. 37) recommends that " . . . nothing be left to chance or taken for granted. Often it's the seemingly obvious tasks that are overlooked, and problems can result."

TACKLING PROBLEMS AND OVERCOMING CHALLENGES

It is essential for those individuals who serve as administrators or managers within recreation or sport programs to develop insight and skills in recognizing and dealing appropriately and timely with potential as well as with actual problems. Problem solving involves dealing successfully with people, individually and in groups—both large and small.

> **CONCEPT #454:**   *The challenge of problem solving involves being able to deal successfully and consistently with all types of people, individually and in groups, both large and small.*

There are five distinct tasks that are associated with the process of dealing with problems. *First*, to anticipate possible problems before they arise, as much as is humanly possible. *Second*, to be able to prevent possible problems from occurring or at least to reduce the impact such problems might have upon the program and individuals. *Third*, to resolve difficulties and negative consequences within a reasonable amount of time and with a reasonable expenditure of resources before the so-called problem(s) becomes a significant nuisance or worse, a hindrance to one's sport program and/or recreational activities. *Fourth*, to implement damage control in terms of negating or mitigating the negative consequences emanating from the problem itself. And *lastly*, to preclude the reoccurrence of such (or similar) challenges or problems in the future.

It is possible to conceptualize the process of problem solving as a table with five legs, figure #15.1 (Stier, 2010a, p. 4). The tabletop itself represents the problem(s) or challenge(s) facing the sport organization or its programs and activities. Each of the five legs represents the five tasks involved in dealing with the problem. If any of the legs are inadequate in terms of supporting the tabletop or are missing—the table tilts, or falls. Thus, the difficulty or problem itself becomes exacerbated and the situation is worse than before because of the inability (within an appropriate time frame) to deal with and resolve the problem that has arisen.

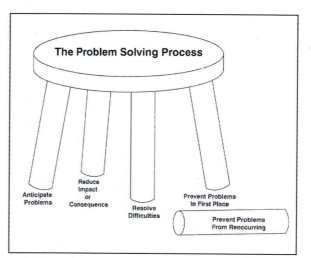

FIGURE 15.1. The concept of problem solving.

AN OVERVIEW OF PROBLEMS AND PROBLEM SOLVING

Webster's dictionary (1973, p. 917) defines a problem as "an intricate unsettled question, raised for inquiry, consideration or solution." Such questioning can often become a source of perplexity, distress, or vexation. A challenge can be thought of a dispute, a taking exception to the status quo or a calling into question that which is thought to be unjust, invalid, or outmoded. In the real world problems and challenges can frequently be viewed as threatening and intimidating as well as provocative, stimulating and inciting. Manager and administrators can experience all of the above in the performance of their duties.

THE PROCESS OF PROBLEM SOLVING—AN ART AND A SCIENCE

In today's world of recreation and sports programs, problem solving may be considered to be both an art and a science. It is an art because the strategies and tactics that any individual—male or female, superior or underling, experienced or inexperienced—seeks to employ in dealing with problems "can be affected and enhanced through the creative and innovative utilization and application of these principles and concepts" (Stier, 2010b, p. 59).

However, problem solving may also be considered to be a science. It is a science because there are generally accepted principles, concepts and a body of knowledge underlying and supporting the tasks and processes involved both in solving problems and addressing contentious issues in our society. These foundational principles and concepts hold true and are applicable regardless of the setting in which recreation or sport managers and sport managers find themselves.

BEING A COMPETENT PROBLEM SOLVER

The question is often asked: Are competent problem solvers made or born? Both antidotal information and scientific research suggest that problem solving can indeed be a learned skill. One way for sport managers to acquire the knowledge and to develop the necessary skills and competencies to be a successful sport problem solver is to combine both formal study with real-life experiences, on the so-called "firing line" of competitive sports (Stier, 1996).

CONCEPT #455: Competent and timely problem solvers are made, not born.

Problem solving is not easy. Rather, it takes concerted effort and concentrated work to become competent as a problem solver and to remain current with the times. An individual becomes more skilled in problem solving through experience, both successful and unsuccessful. Getting one's nose bloodied, if you will, by living through a problem or challenging situation can be a great learning and teaching experience. There is nothing more authentic than actually living through a confrontational situation—and surviving professionally.

> **CONCEPT #456:**   *To be a competent problem solver one learn from the mistakes of others as well as our own because we don't live long enough to learn <u>only</u> from one's own mistakes*

No individual can merely learn from one's own experience. This would be far too limiting. Rather, one must learn also from the experiences, both successes and failures, of others. None of us will live long enough to learn from only our own experiences. We must learn from the experiences (present and past) of others. One way to do this is to observe and learn how others have dealt with and are currently dealing with the challenges of problem solving, that is, how others attempt to prevent problems, resolve difficulties, reduce negative consequences and eliminate their reoccurrence.

> **CONCEPT #457:**   *One must remain current in one's professional reading and attend professional meetings if one is to be a competent problem solver.*

It is important, however, that one not assumes that practical experience is the only way to gain knowledge and develop competency in solving problems. Far from it. In addition to practical experience, it is also important for the would-be problem solver, for the sport or recreation manager, to develop a conceptual understanding of the problem solving process itself, regardless of the competitive level, the setting or the circumstances involved.

This conceptual understanding, this knowledge base, can be obtained from formal study involving (1) actual college course work at the undergraduate and graduate levels, (2) keeping current with one's professional reading (such as this book as well as any number of professional journals and popular magazines and newspapers), and (3) through attendance at appropriate professional conferences, conventions and meetings. The ultimate goal for the sport and recreation administrator is to become more enlightened about the whole problem solving (and prevention) process, that is, to develop an appropriate level of understanding, knowledge and skill necessary to be successful as a leader and problem solver within the sport/recreation world. For in the final analysis, the mark of a truly successful leader/administrator/manager is one who can adequately deal with and resolve, if not prevent, problems.

THERE IS A MULTITUDE OF CHALLENGES AND PROBLEMS WITHIN SPORT CIRCLES

> **CONCEPT #458:   *Problems occur—that is the very nature of the sport scene.***

Invariably, problems seem to be everywhere in today's complicated society. And the sports world is no exception. In reality, there is certainly no shortage of problems and challenges, both large and small; facing today's modern day sports organizations/ programs. There is certainly no lack of problems facing a wide variety of recreation and sport programs and the individuals who are associated with them. And there is no end in sight.

To the contrary, it seems that competitive and recreational sports, and those who are intimately associated with such activities and programs, will experience not only a greater number of problems but also more severe and complicated problems as time progresses. One of the consequences is that the process of preventing and solving problems and dealing with controversial and divisive issues within the sport matrix is going to be much more difficult, time consuming and taxing (Stier. 2003).

> **CONCEPT #459:   *Problems and challenges should also be viewed as actual professional opportunities.***

To some, the very existence of problems can be viewed as a great professional opportunity, an opportunity to demonstrate one's talents, skills and capabilities in reaction to and handling such problems, difficulties and challenges. The result, if one is successful in dealing with problems, can very well mean professional advancement of one's career.

The concept is simple. If there were not significant and numerous problems facing sports programs, facing schools, programs, athletes, parents, coaches and administrators, then there would be no need for skilled, highly trained sport and recreation managers. However, since there are many difficult challenges facing sports programs and the people associated with them, it is necessary that there be highly trained and experienced problem solvers in leadership positions on the administrative/managerial staff. Not every Tom, Dick and Harry or Mary, Jane and Sue can be successful as a problem solving administrator. It does take skill, it does take competency, it does take effort, and it does take experience to be a competent leader as a sport administrator.

Thus, the very existence of problems or controversial situations can result in the enhancement of one's career—if these problems and situations can indeed be successfully resolved and/or serious consequences averted. Being recognized as a competent administrator, both in terms of the technical aspects of managing the sport activity, program and/or the department and the ability to prevent and resolve difficulties can do wonders for one's prestige, reputation and career. Solving difficulties in a professional manner can also be personally satisfying and invigorating, which is not an insignificant factor in and of itself.

> **CONCEPT #460**   *One must never lose sight of the ultimate goal of administering the sport or recreation program when confronting problems.*

It is imperative that one not lose sight of the ultimate objective regardless of the extent of the problem(s) or the number of problems. Sometimes sport managers become so immersed in the process of solving a particular difficulty that they forget about the ongoing or ultimate objective or goal. Yes, solving the problem is important. But so too is the proper operation of the sport organization, its programs and activities. Don't become distracted by the presence of a problem or challenge or the consequences or aftermath to such an extent that one's normal efforts at managing a quality sport program suffer and the sport or recreation activities are hampered.

Problem Solving and the Element of Timeliness

One of the challenges in dealing with controversial issues and problems is that spot managers need to understand the process and risks involved in dealing with people, individually and as members of different groups, constituencies and the general public. An important aspect of successful interpersonal relationships is patience.

> **CONCEPT #461:**   *Truly effective problem solvers exhibit patience combined with resolve/persistence.*

Problems are not solved overnight. Nor are they solved easily, without effort, work and time. Far too often inexperienced managers or administrators act rashly in their attempt to solve problems. One must have patience. On the other hand, it is also necessary to be able to exhibit perseverance. This combination of patience and perseverance enables the sport administrator to work toward the established objectives while still paying attention to the details, the crossing of the "T"s and the dotting of the "I"s.

EFFICIENCY AND EFFECTIVENESS IN THE PROBLEM SOLVING PROCESS

Frequently, it is not enough merely to be *effective* as a problem solver. In many instances, one must also be *efficient* in the process of resolving or solving the problem and limiting negative consequences. Of course, resolving a problematic situation is very important. But it is equally important to remain cognizant that must one also be capable of efficiently accomplishing the task at hand, that is, solving the problem.

CONCEPT #462:   *Successful problem solvers are both effective and efficient.*

Effectiveness is doing the right job or the correct tasks—whatever the job or tasks might be—that are necessary for the successful resolution of the difficulty or challenge that one faces. Efficiency pertains to how the job or task is done, that is, doing the job right or correctly.

One must always ask oneself (because others invariably will ask): "can the problem solving process be carried out in an efficient manner in terms of time spent as well energy expended and resources utilized?" Managers/administrators must be both effective and efficient in their efforts to recognize, confront, prevent and/or solve the various problems and challenges that will invariably crop up in the course of their professional and personal activities.

PROBLEM SOLVING RISKS ASSOCIATED WITH SPORT AND RECREATION MANAGEMENT

No one ever said that directing a recreation program or managing a sports staff would be easy. And no one believes that the life of a sport manager is uncomplicated. Rather, assuming the role of problem solver—whether as a high level executive or of a lower lever staffer (underling)—involves a high degree of personal and professional risk. Not only can an administrator (at any level) quite literally put one's present job, or even one's career, in jeopardy by assuming the role of problem solver, but the individual often can exert a truly significant effect, either positive or negative, on the lives of others, both inside and outside of the sport entity.

CONCEPT #463: *When facing problems—risks are inherent both in terms of processes and outcomes.*

Problem solvers are, by definition, risk takers. Usually one cannot make real progress or achieve real success unless and until one is willing to stick one's neck out and take calculated risks. The danger of assuming risk(s) is often exacerbated by the fact that sport managers usually do not solve problems, address controversial issues or resolve difficulties in a vacuum. There are usually other individuals or even groups of individuals involved in the problematic situation. In addition, the process of problem solving is all too frequently undertaken in the public eye, for all to see. This is especially true in terms of the actual outcome or aftermath of the problem solving effort or process.

Risk of Failure

When acting as a problem solver, one always runs the risk of failure in that effort—either by not being able to do anything or by doing something that ends in failure. This is significant because many times such failure becomes a public failure, that is, the failure on behalf of the sport administrator is viewed by many other individuals, the general public as well as one peers and supervisors. One has to be both willing and able to "stand the heat or else get out of the kitchen" as former President Harry Truman was quoted as saying. In terms of problem solving, sport managers need to be able to withstand the public and professional scrutiny when faced with the prospect of dealing with problems and challenges—or else choose another profession.

Operating in the Open—For All to See

> **CONCEPT #464:   *All sport managers operate under a magnifying glass—in front of the public.***

Since the outcome or results emanating from the attempt to resolve a problem is often visible to the public, there is the potential for greater impact upon both the problem solver and others involved with the situation. This visibility aspect sometimes makes the process itself more difficult and cumbersome because of the additional challenge of operating under the proverbial magnifying glass, that is, in the public eye. Public scrutiny places more pressure on the problem solver and that individual's superiors. Anytime an individual operates within the full view of the public there is a great deal of exposure and risk, both in one's efforts to address the problem and in the actual outcome of one's decisions. For one thing, if one is successful or unsuccessful, others, including superiors, are all too often aware of that fact.

With Power Comes Responsibility

Another aspect of risk associated with an attempt to solve a problem or address a controversial situation is making a mistake, committing an error in judgment or an inappropriate decision—resulting in negative consequences for others. It is this very possibility of harming other individuals (or the program itself) that discourages some individuals from assuming the role of problem solver. It is indeed important for one to possess sufficiently broad shoulders to make the difficult decisions often associated with solving problems or resolving difficulties.

THE ULTIMATE POWER AND AWESOME RESPONSIBILITY OF SPORT MANAGERS

Sport managers, by the very nature of their positions, as chief operating officers, have great power and equally significant responsibilities. It is important that one remembers that decisions made in an effort to solve problems or resolve controversial issues have the potential for grave and far reaching consequences for a whole host of others (individuals and groups, adults and children/minors) as well as for oneself.

CONCEPT #465: *Sport managers possessing the power to solve problems wield great power over other people's lives— They need to use it judiciously.*

By dealing with problems and resolving controversial issues, sport administrators exercise a tremendous amount of power over activities and programs as well as individuals, especially young, impressionable athletes. Part of the role of any sport manger involves being able to handle and resolve problems—necessitating making decisions, decisions that can significantly affect the lives of others. However, there is a risk in assuming this power lest such authority and accompanying responsibility be misused or abused.

ASSUMPTION OF RISKS AND REACTIONS TO PROBLEMS AND CHALLENGES

Generally, there are several courses of action an individual can take when faced with problems. *First,* one can simply ignore the problem. This tactic sometimes takes the form of avoiding the problem by simply not addressing it. This is done with the expectation that others will accept or assume the responsibility for dealing with the problem. Or, that the problem will simply go away, vanish. *Second,* an individual can always make the conscious decision to leave, that is, to remove oneself from the problem situation.

This tactic can involve actually quitting one's position and moving on to another job, perhaps in another organization. Or, one can attempt to simply move to another area of responsibility within the same organization, where one would not be faced with such problematic situations. And, of course, a *third* course of action when faced with problems is to meet such challenges head-on, deliberately addressing each problem in an effort to honestly, fairly and expeditiously address the difficulties for the good of the organization or program and for the good of those individuals involved.

THE DIFFICULTY OF SOLVING PROBLEMS

> *CONCEPT #466:   If it was easy—anyone could do it.*

The fact is, problem solving is usually not an easy task—that is why it is referred to as *problem solving.* To the contrary, it is a difficult process. Not everyone can be an effective problem solver. If it was easy, if anyone could do the job of preventing and resolving problems within the recreation and sport arena, then there would be no need for highly trained, experienced and dedicated professionals serving as problem solvers (sport managers). This is true in the world of sport organizations and sports programs/activities as it is for any other organization or program.

> *CONCEPT #467:   Many people believe they know more than the sport manager and that they can do a better job in administering and managing the sports program and recreation activities.*

As a sport manager, it sometimes seems like everyone believes that they know more about how to run or manage a sport program than the person who holds the official title of sport manager or director. This in itself is not an insignificant problem. When the general public as well as many individuals closely associated with a sport or recreation program feel that they are as knowledgeable or more knowledgeable (competent or more competent) than the individual officially assigned to be the official leader and manager of the organization/program, the potential problems are innumerable and often frequent.

Thus, it is imperative that those who are sport managers clearly and consistently demonstrate an atmosphere of competency and proficiency as leaders, managers/administrators, decision makers and problem solvers. Failure to do so, failure to act as a knowledgeable and confident recreation administrator or sport manager only invites a multitude of problems instigated by others who sense a weakness or deficiency in the individual given the responsibility and authority of sport leader (recreation administrator).

Effort versus Results

> **CONCEPT #468:   *Results are what counts—not talk or mere effort.***

Since sport managers live in the real world it is important to recognize that effort alone is simply not enough. True, effort is important in everything a human being does in our society. However, even more important than effort are the actual results. As stated previously, the manager might have put great effort and spent a significant amount of time in doing something, either attempting to prevent a problem or attempting to resolve a problem. However, if the problem is not solved, the end result is still failure.

This is because although one tries very hard and spends a great deal of time on a task, such as problem solving or problem prevention, it all doesn't mean very much unless there are meaningful and tangible results. Good intentions, regardless of how noble or meritorious, are often simply not enough. What counts are actual results. The outcome is often perceived, especially by the general public, as being far more important than the process involved or effort expended. Thus, actual production (spelled *results)* in our society is viewed as paramount, with effort and time spent on task being relegated to secondary importance, especially in the world of competitive sports.

For problem solvers, especially sport managers, it is imperative that one does not rely on the crutch of merely attempting to do something (i.e., solve a problem) without being equally concerned with the results of one's efforts. Effort without results counts for naught.

The Importance of Wise Decision Making in Problem Solving

> **CONCEPT #469:   *Results are the consequences of good decision-making.***

Generally speaking, solving problems is significantly dependent upon one's decision-making ability. Usually, someone has to make an appropriate and well thought out decision, or series of decisions, in addressing a particular problem, challenge or difficulty.

For without timely and correct decisions, desired results are frequently neither feasible nor possible. However, before suitable decisions can be made, accurate facts and information must be obtained. But even with all available information, there is no guarantee of an easy or appropriate resolution of a problem. For the crux of solving any problem rests in the decision-making skill of the problem solver(s). Without quality (appropriate) decision making no problem can be adequately addressed.

PROBLEM SOLVING—A MATTER OF TIMELINESS

It is important to remember that decisions not only have to be made correctly and in a consistent manner but must be timely as well. The matter of timeliness is all-important. Decisions can be correct and the resulting actions can be efficient in terms of time spent and resources utilized, but if the decisions and the implementation of action plans are not timely, the results can be catastrophic.

> *CONCEPT #470:* **The matter of timeliness in addressing a problem is often critical to its final solution.**

There is a tightrope that must be walked by every problem solver in terms of being considered either (1) rash in one's decision-making and actions or (2) a procrastinator, a fence sitter. One must be capable of acting with due dispatch but not be viewed by other as rushing. One can just as easily be criticized for being too rash in one's decision-making and actions as for being too timid or hesitant. The old saying, "you are damned if you do and damned if you don't" is most appropriate while acting as a problem solver.

A mark of a competent problem solver is being able to successfully maneuver this proverbial tightrope. An individual who is unable or unwilling to take a definitive position, to make a decision or decisions, and thus act in a timely fashion, is going to meet resistance from a whole host of individuals, groups and organizations.

A highly prized skill for any spot manager is being able to make decisions within an acceptable time frame. An equally important skill is the ability to implement on a timely basis the plan resulting from the analysis of the problem situation (problem solving analysis). It is important to be cognizant that determining an acceptable time frame for any course of action in light of any problem is dependent upon the individual situation itself, the accompanying circumstances, and the individuals who are involved. This is where experience comes into play.

Efficient Problem Solving Required Effective Time Management

The use of time wisely is an important element of efficient problem solving. In many instances, time is of the essence (or it seems to be) when sport managers are confronted with problems or challenges. Many decisions must be made in a timely manner lest opportunities become lost or mistakes made or compounded. This is especially true when dealing with the feelings of others. The wise use of the time available is essential in the problem solving process.

One must use time wisely when faced with the problem or challenge and it is important that others are aware that the sport administrator is using time wisely and frugally. Perhaps nothing destroys the credibility of the problem solver as the perception of dragging one's feet, wasting valuable time and resources and/or being hesitant to address the problem itself. Proper time management implies that the individual is indeed addressing the problem itself in a timely and forthright fashion. It also implies that there will be a concerted effort to obtain the facts within a reasonable amount of time. And, lastly, proper time management implies that a just and appropriate decision (and course of action) will be initiated in a timely manner—as viewed by all parties involved.

Obviously not every final decision and/or action taken by a sport manager in response to a particular problem will be agreeable or acceptable to everyone involved. However, a significant number of interested or involved parties should be generally satisfied with the *process of dealing with the problem itself.* This is especially true in respect to the time element in which the problem was recognized, evaluated and eventually resolved.

One Example of an Inappropriate Response in Addressing a Potential Problem

In 1990 the McDonald Corporation (of hamburger fame) got international positive publicity and advertising when it announced that it was planning on frying all of the French fries in 100% vegetable oil. This promotional campaign was especially well received in India and in Muslim countries. However, fast forward to 2001 and the McDonald's corporation was threatened not only with a public relations disaster but a $1B lawsuit as to boot as a result of what commonly became known as the *French fry fiasco.*

It seems that Harish Bharti filed a class-action lawsuit against the hamburger giant contending misrepresentation as to the contents of its French fries being meatless. In reality, the fries contained "a trace of beef flavoring in the potatoes, added at the processing plant" (Horovitz, 2001, p. 2-B.) Even though the company attempted to apologize by including a statement initially only on its web site, the attorney was unimpressed with such an effort and claimed that such a meager effort was just part of the overall deception by the company.

Had the company reacted quicker to this significant problem that affected millions of Hindus throughout the world it would not have found itself facing a billion dollar lawsuit as well as a million-dollar public relations nightmare. Reacting quickly and in an appropriate manner is an absolute must in today's world of instant communication and global commerce. Failure to do so can create a PR nightmare for the organization and its managers as well as a potential financial catastrophe.

Another Example of Inappropriate Timing in Solving Problems

> **CONCEPT #471:** *Failure to tell the truth and to act expeditiously often results in disaster.*

One of the biggest snafus at the national level in recent memory involved the American Red Cross (ARC) following the infamous September 11, 2001 terrorists' attack on the World Trade Buildings. Shortly after this tragic attack on America, the ARC announced that it was establishing a separate fund [Liberty Fund] to accept donations and contributions to specifically benefit the victims of this attack. However, in reality, the American Red Cross was forced [as a result of national media exposure] to admit some weeks later *that it was not going to spend all of the money donated*—estimated to be $550 million at the time—*for those victims of the September 11th attack.*

Representatives of the American Red Cross were forced to admit that less than half of the money raised on behalf of the victims was to be spent for the victims—their families or rescue workers. It was acknowledged that the rest of the donated money was earmarked to be spent for an upgrade of its own organization as well as for other needy causes involving other disasters elsewhere in the country. This announcement outraged many, many people in this country as "donors expected their money to be helping now" (Tyrangiel, 2001, p. 77).

The consequence was a loud and consistent outcry and severe criticism from a wide range of constituencies, from individuals as well as the news media *throughout the country*. Those individuals who had donated money to this special fund only to find out that their donations were not being used for the purpose promised by the Red Cross were especially outraged and most vocal. Numerous radio shows roasted (criticized) the ARC because the organization had initially promised that all of the money in this special fund [Liberty Fund] would benefit the victims of September 11th while in reality the ARC simply lied about what was going to be done with the money. In reality the ARC decided to take a significant amount of the money donated for this purpose and chose to spend it for other purposes, some charitable (elsewhere, not for victims of the World Trade disaster) and some for a computer system upgrade for the organization itself.

> **CONCEPT #472:** *"Credibility is everything."*

The *Chicago Tribune* published a searing editorial that appeared on October 31, 2001 (Red Cross squanders goodwill) that included the following quote that succinctly summed up the controversy.

> "Besieged by the controversy, the Red Cross announced Tuesday that it had stopped seeking donations for the Liberty Fund and that the money in the fund will be directed to victims of the Sept. 11 and future victims of terrorism. This is what is known as damage control. The Red Cross has some real work to do to restore its reputation. It can start by establishing a very simple idea as rule number one: Don't mislead your donors. . . . The fiasco at the Red Cross carries a reminder for everyone involved in philanthropy. Credibility is everything" (p. 14).

Finally, the American Red Cross relented and changed it public position, but not without severe negative consequences that damaged the reputation of the ARC and its personnel. In point of fact, on November 13, 2001, over national television, the ARC made an announcement that it was doing an abrupt turnaround and that contrary to its earlier position, the ARC would indeed spend 100% of the money ($543 million) that had been donated for the victims (Liberty Fund) of the September 11th attack to the victims and their families (Nasser, 2001; Roy, 2001). But it was too late to curtail the severe damage to the organization, its programs, its fundraising capability and specific personnel. The eventual fallout even included the resignation of the president of the American Red Cross.

CONCEPT #473:   *Failure to tell the truth and to act expeditiously often results in disaster.*

As a result of the ARC fiasco, it became clearly evident that the negative consequences had escalated beyond anything the organization had ever anticipated. The public outcry was important but it was the power of the press (news media), the national exposure of the media, which brought down the ARC and forced the organization to back track and change its untenable position. In short, it was the national outcry by the public coupled with the repeated attacks, commentary and exposure in the media that literally forced the organization's change of heart (and policy). Unfortunately, it is too bad that it took a national outcry from the various publics and repeated criticism in the media to "force" such a decision.

CONCEPT #474:   *Never understate the power, the influence of the wrath of the general public and/or the news media.*

In the end, the new leaders of the ARC reached the right decision and an appropriate plan was subsequently and efficiently carried out. But, it was too late for optimal damage control. For the damage (to the reputation of the organization, its program, and selected personnel) had already taken place by the time the American Red Cross elected to do the right thing *and* do the thing right. And, all because of the outcry from general public and the media.

And, the two above examples are not unique it seems. A more recent controversy revolved around the distribution of funds donated to the families of the December 14, 2012 mass murder at the Sandy Hook Elementary school (Newtown, Connecticut). Specifically, of the approximately $15 million that had been raised (as of May 2013) for victims of the shooting tragedy in Newtown, **none of the contributions had been distributed to the victims or their families** after six months (as of June 17, 2013).

In fact, most of the money, nearly $11 million, had been raised by United Way of Western Connecticut, which subsequently created a foundation to distribute the funds to the victims. In point of fact, the *controversy grew in scope* when it was learned that not all of the money raised for the victims of this tragic shooting would indeed even be distributed to the actual victims—but that some funds would be held back and used for other charitable purposes in the Newtown area in the future (Liebelson, D. April 8, 2013; Victim Rights Attorney, 2013, June 18). As of the time of this writing the funds are still being held in abeyance waiting a decision and resolution into how the donated funds will actually be used, i.e., distributed to the victims and their families and/or to other charitable purposes in the area. Nevertheless, the members of the press are continuing to shine a light on this indecisiveness and failure to act in a prudent and timely manner. In reality, only time will tell whether the entities responsible for distributing the donations will do so in an appropriate manner and in a timely fashion.

The moral of these stories is two-fold. *First*, there is a real need to act in a timely fashion, while the iron is hot, when faced with any problem. *Second*, never underestimate the power, anger or doggedness of either the general public or representatives of the news media.

CONCLUSION

It is necessary to be able to do two things at once when confronted with a problem. *First*, one must deal with the actual problem at hand and all that that entails. And *second*, one must maintain at least a minimum level of effort, energy and initiative in conducting the actual sport program so that the program and activities don't suffer as a consequence of the problem. Being able to accomplish both tasks involves the proper determination of priorities and the appropriate allocation of resources. The concept is simple; one must remain focused on the normal sport operation as well as on solving the problem. Neither can be neglected, at least for very long.

REFERENCES

Horovitz, B. (2001, May 25). Attorney hopes for 1B in McDonald's french fry suit, *USA Today*, p. 2-B.

Liebelson, D. (2013, April. 8). What past mass shootings tell us about what might happen with Sandy Hook donations. http://www.motherjones.com/politics/2013/04/ where-does-money-donated-victims-mass-shootings-go

Nasser, H.E. (2001, November 15). Sept. 11 Victims will receive all of Liberty Fund, *USA Today*, p. 5-A.

Roy, Y. (2001, November 15). Red Cross now says all monies to go to victims of 9-11 attacks, *Democrat and Chronicle*, p. 6-A.

Red Cross squanders goodwill. (2001, October 31). *Chicago Tribune*, p. 14.

Staffo, D. (2001). A first down. *Athletic Management, XIII* (2), 37-41.

Stier, W.F., Jr. (1993, May). The ins and outs of evaluating coaches. *Athletic management, V* (3), 34-37, 39.

Stier, W.F., Jr. (1996, May). An overview of administering competitive sports programs through effective marketing, fundraising and promotion. *Applied Research in Coaching and Athletic Annual*, Volume 11, 116-128.

Stier, W.F., Jr. (2003). *Marketing, fundraising and promotions—For sport, recreation and fitness programs.* Boston: American Press.

Stier, W.F., Jr. (2010a). *Coaching: Becoming a successful athletic coach* (3rd ed). Boston: American Press.

Stier, W.F., Jr. (2010b). *Coaching: A problem solving approach* (2nd ed). Boston: American Press.

Webster's new collegiate dictionary. (1973). Springfield, MA: G. & C. Merriam Co.

Tyrangierl, J. (2001, November 5). The Charity Olympics. *Time*, pp. 75, 77.

Victim rights attorney wants donations paid to Sandy Hook families. (2013, June 18). http://www.wwlp.com/dpp/news/local/hampden/victim-rights-attorney-wants-donations-paid-to-sandy-hook-families

DISCUSSION TOPICS

1. Discuss why the process of problem solving is both an **art** and a **science**.
2. Why are competent problem solvers not born, but are made.
3. Under what circumstances can problems and challenges also be viewed as opportunities? Elaborate.

4. Provide an example of a sport manager who neglects the overall goal of the sport program when facing problems.

5. Explain what is meant when one says that recreation or sport administrators should be both efficient and effective in addressing problems facing the department and the programs.

6. Elaborate on the statement: "sport managers should not operate via the crisis mode."

7. If you are a competent problem solver you are "worth your weight in gold"— explain this statement.

8. What are two essential elements in effective decision-making? Why?

Appendix

A Sources of Information Pertaining to Facilities and Equipment

1. Amateur Softball Association of America—2801 Northeast 50th Street, Oklahoma City, OK 73111 (405) 424-5266

2. Field Hockey Association of America, Inc.—1750 East Boulder Street, Colorado Springs, CO 80909-5764 (719) 578-4567.

3. American Amateur Racquetball Association—815 North Weber, Suite 101, Colorado Springs, CO 80903 (719) 623-5396 or United States Handball Association, 930 North Benton, Tucson, AZ 85711 (602) 795-0434.

4. American Youth Soccer Organization—5403 West 138th Street, Hasthorne, CA 90250 (213) 643-8066.

5. The Association for Higher Education Facilities Officers (APPA)—1643 Prince Street, Alexandria, VA 22314-2818 (703) 684-1446.

6. The Association of Quality clubs (IRSA—a not-for-profit trade association representing over 1600 clubs worldwide)—253 Summer St., Boston 02222 (617) 951-0055 or 800-228-4772.

7. Athletic Equipment Managers Association (AEMA)—723 Keil Court, Bowling Green, Ohio 43402 (419) 352-1207 or Mr. Jeff Boss, Louisiana State University, P.O. Box 25095, Baton Rouge, LA 70894 (504) 388-1151.

8. National Collegiate Athletic Association (NCAA)—6201 College Blvd., Overland Park, Kansas 66211-2422 (913) 339-1906.

9. National Federation of State High School Associations—P.O. box 20626, Kansas City, MO. 64195 (816) 464-5400.

10. The National Health Club Association—P.O. Box 2378, Corona, CA 92718-2378 (714) 371-0606 or 12596 West Bayaud Avenue, 1st Floor, Denver, CO (303) 753-6422 or (716) 467-4653.

11. National Hockey League, Montreal Office—1155 Metcalfe Street, Suite 960, Montreal, Quebec H3B 2W2.

12. National Junior College Athletic Association (NJCAA)—P.O. Box 7305, Colorado Springs, CO 80933.

13. National Spa and Pool Institute—2111 Eisenhower Avenue, Alexandria, VA 22314-4678 (703) 838-0083.

14. Nautilus Spots/Medical Industries—(800) 628-8458.

15. NIRSA,—850 S. W. 15ᵗʰ St. Corvallis, OR 97333 (503)737-2088 or 737-2088.

16. Sporting Goods Manufacturing Association, 200 Castlewood Drive, North Palm Beach, Florida, 33408.

17. Sports Turf Managers Association [STMA] —1455 E. Tropicana, Suite 390, Las Vegas, NV 89119. 702-739-8052.

18. Sportsplex Operators & Developers Association, P.O. Box 24263, Westgate Station, Rochester, New York 14624-0263—(716) 426-2215.

19. StairMaster Sports/Medical Products, Inc., 12421 Willows Road, N.E., Suite 100, Kirkland, Washington 98034—(800) 635-2936.

20. United States Badminton Association—501 West Sixth Street, Papillion, NE 68046 (402) 592-7309.

21. United States Soccer Federation—1750 East Boulder Street, Colorado Springs, CO 80909 (719) 578-4678.

22. United States Squash Racquets Association, Inc.—211 Ford Road, Bala-Cynwyd, PA 19004 (215) 667-4006.

23. United States Swimming, Inc.—1750 East Boulder Street, Colorado Springs, CO 80909-5770 (719) 578-4578.

24. United States Team Handball Federation—1750 East Boulder Street, Colorado Springs, CO 80909 (719) 632-5551 ext. 4582.

25. The United States Tennis Court and Track Builders Association—3525 Ellicott Mills Drive, Suite N., Ellicott City, MD 21043 (410) 418-4875.

26. Universal Gym Equipment, Inc.—P.O. Box 120, Cedar Rapids, IA.

27. W.A. Schmidt Corporation (manufactures, designs and installs fitness facility mezzanines (800) 523-6719.

Index